Strange Cases

Strange Cases

A Selective Guide to Speculative Mystery Fiction

JILL H. VASSILAKOS AND
PAUL VASSILAKOS-LONG

Libraries Unlimited
An Imprint of ABC-CLIO, LLC

A B C CLIO

Santa Barbara, California • Denver, Colorado • Oxford, England

Library of Congress Cataloging-in-Publication Data

Vassilakos, Jill H.

Strange cases : a selective guide to speculative mystery fiction / Jill H. Vassilakos and Paul Vassilakos-Long.

p. cm.

Includes bibliographical references and indexes.

ISBN 978-1-59158-421-6 (acid-free paper) 1. Detective and mystery stories, American—Stories, plots, etc. 2. Detective and mystery stories, English—Stories, plots, etc. 3. Fantasy fiction, American—Stories, plots, etc. 4. Fantasy fiction, English—Stories, plots, etc. I. Vassilakos-Long, Paul. II. Title.

PS374.D4V38 2009

813'.087209—dc22 2009020303

13 12 11 10 09 1 2 3 4 5

This book is also available on the World Wide Web as an eBook. Visit www.abc-clio.com for details.

ABC-CLIO, LLC
130 Cremona Drive, P.O. Box 1911
Santa Barbara, California 93116-1911

This book is printed on acid-free paper ∞

Manufactured in the United States of America

For all the authors who were ever told that their idea wouldn't sell—
and went on to write the book anyway!

Contents

Introduction

Can the Marriage of Speculative Fiction and Mystery Fiction Succeed?

The conventional wisdom is that mystery fiction and speculative fiction (science fiction or fantasy) don't mix, that readers enjoy either one genre or the other, but do not like a mixture of both. Writers are told that it is not possible to tell a story about a crime if the setting is fantastical or futuristic: if the reader does not know what is possible in that world and what is not, then it is impossible for the reader to enjoy the mystery by trying to solve the puzzle before the detective reveals the solution. Writers are told that if mystery fiction and speculative fiction did somehow end up together in the same book, then that book could not be sold because there would be no correct place to shelve the book in a bookstore. In short, conventional wisdom holds that mixing mystery with speculative fiction is a terrible idea.

Is the conventional wisdom true? The first objection, that readers are offended by the mixture of mystery fiction and speculative fiction, is demonstrably false. In 1953, science fiction author Alfred Bester's *The Demolished Man,* a novel that combines a murder mystery with a world in which some members of the population have psionic abilities, won the very first Hugo Award, the pre-eminent science fiction award. Obviously, the book garnered critical acclaim, and it was also a commercial success. It was widely read and widely enjoyed. Today, *The Demolished Man* is regarded as a classic. Science fiction fans enjoyed and admired the book, and they continue to do so. (*Babylon 5* creator J. Michael Straczynski named the Psi Corps cop who bedeviled the crew on Babylon 5 "Mr. Bester," in honor of Alfred Bester.)

In 2001, mystery author Charlaine Harris's *Dead Until Dark,* a story that combines psionic abilities and vampires with a murder mystery, was nominated for all the major mystery awards and won the Anthony Award for best mystery. The book was a commercial and critical success. It was widely read, widely enjoyed, and it won a major mystery award. It launched the popular *Southern Vampire* series, which is still going strong.

The idea that readers are repelled by the mixture of speculative fiction and mystery fiction is false. It was false in the past and it is false today. It is false when applied to mystery readers; it is false when applied to readers of speculative fiction. The first objection to the combination of mystery fiction and speculative fiction—that readers do not like it—is simply not true.

The second objection—that writers cannot tell a story about a crime when it is set in a world where readers do not know what is and is not possible—depends upon the skill of the writer. It is demonstrably true that some writers achieve great success when they place a mystery in a setting that is unfamiliar to the reader. Isaac Asimov's robot mysteries are an example. They are wonderful "puzzle" mysteries, and most hinge on his "three laws of robotics."

1. A robot may not injure a human being, or through inaction allow a human being to come to harm.
2. A robot must obey the orders given it by human beings except where such orders would conflict with the First Law.
3. A robot must protect its own existence as long as such protection does not conflict with the First or Second Law.

Asimov sets out the rules that are pertinent to the mystery puzzle in a simple and straightforward way; then he proceeds to use those rules in a series of mysteries in which he plays fair by presenting the reader with all the clues and information that are necessary to solve the puzzle, and he still manages to confound the reader. Asimov is not alone: many other authors are able to present both an interesting world and a puzzling mystery. The second objection is quite obviously false.

The third objection—that if a bookseller can't shelve it no one will be able to buy it—seems as if it should be trivial, but it is actually a serious problem. It goes beyond bookstore shelves. If the publisher's representative cannot easily describe a book, it may never be ordered by the store at all! The prevalence of popular books, television shows, and movies that combine speculative fiction with mystery have helped to solve the latter of these problems. Examples of speculative fiction mixed with mystery exist and are well known. If a publisher's representative describes such a work as, for example, "psychics receiving information on crimes, similar to the movie *Minority Report*," there is a familiar frame of reference. The concept seems interesting, not impossible. But even if that will get the book into the store, how can the bookseller organize the store so that the customer can find the book? In owner-run bookstores (may their numbers increase), the people behind the counter love books and may be able to suggest titles that fit the description "mystery, along with science fiction." There are also databases that allow readers to search by multiple criteria. For instance, someone could search "vampires and detective" and come up with a list of books that include both elements. The problem of getting the book into the hands of the readers is real, but it is not insurmountable.

History of the Form

The fictional combination of mystery and the fantastic has a long and rich history. It's difficult to trace it back to an initial instance, because the earliest examples are probably the ghost stories that were rooted in the oral tradition. For instance, there was a 1656 broadside printed in Scotland entitled "The Miller and the King's Daughter." It provided the foundation for the ballad of "The Two Sisters" (also called *Binnorie*). It recounts the story of a crime being revealed through supernatural means. In it, a young woman is murdered by her sister. The victim's hair is used to create strings for a harp, the harp strings speak, and the murderer is discovered. It is likely that the story existed and was told orally before it was ever set down on paper. There are many "murder ballads," and most of them probably started as stories. A few of the songs that incorporate supernatural elements are still sung. For instance, "The Gosport Tragedy" (also called "The Perjured Ship's Carpenter") recounts the story of a murdered young woman who causes a ship captain to search for the murderer among his crew, and then, when he fails to discover the criminal, takes matters into her own hands. This has been traced back to the 1750s, but again, it is likely that the story pre-dated the ballad. In both of these ballads, the story of the investigative part of the plot is passed over quickly. (The harp strings make an oblique reference to the crime; the captain asks the murderer on board the ship to reveal himself.) Some sort of investigation (prompted by a supernatural occurrence) takes place, but the song does not follow it. It's tantalizing, but inconclusive. Even if there were an explicit unfolding of the investigations in these ballads, it would not be enough to pinpoint a first instance of the blending of supernatural elements with criminal investigation. These survive because they became popular ballads. There were certainly many other ghost/investigation stories preceding them.

Modern scholars have focused on novels, novelizations, and short stories printed in magazines. Michael Cox, in his essay on ghost stories in Rosemary Herbert's *The Oxford Companion to Crime and Mystery Writing*, lists *Mrs. Zant and the Ghost* by Wilkie Collins (published in 1885) as one of the first ghost stories with mystery elements. The *Flaxman Low* stories of E. and H. Heron (pseudonyms for the mother and son writing team of Kate and

Hesketh Prichard) that were first published in 1898 in *Pearson's Magazine* are listed as another early example of the combining of mystery with the paranormal.

Ron Goulart (in William DeAndrea's *Encyclopedia Mysteriosa*) traces the science fiction book with mystery elements back to the work of Jules Verne. Sam Moskowitz (in *The Encyclopedia of Mystery and Detection,* edited by Chris Steinbrunner and Otto Penzler) cites "The Man in the Room" by Edwin Balmer and William Macharg, published in the May 1909 issue of *Hampton's Magazine,* as an early example of a mystery with science fiction elements.

Although the initial pairing of mystery and fantasy is lost in the mists of time, it is possible to trace back the most recent boost in their popularity to Charlaine Harris's *Dead Until Dark* (2001). Science fiction mysteries were popularized with Isaac Asimov's *The Caves of Steel* (1953).

Purpose

The purpose of this book is to explore the growing number of titles that straddle the genres of mystery and speculative fiction. In describing these titles in depth, this guide is intended as an aid to collection development specialists, to readers' advisors, to anyone leading a book group, and to readers who enjoy cross-genre fiction who may want to review previous entries in a series before they read the latest book or to find the work where a pivotal event took place (for instance finding Sookie's notification of her cousin's death in Charlaine Harris's "One Word Answer") or to choose a book to re-read (for instance finding the book where Harry Dresden meets Anastasia—Jim Butcher's *Dead Beat*). It can also be used as a research tool or reference in courses on genre studies, or on the specific genres of crime and speculative fiction.

Definitions and Selection Criteria

Both of the authors of this guide are fans of cross-genre fiction, and this project began with our idea of creating a bibliography of books that combine speculative fiction with mystery. We soon ran into difficulties. One difficulty was the question of which books to include. The question hinged on how we defined "mystery" and how we defined "speculative fiction." Is Shakespeare's *Hamlet* a cross-genre work? It focuses on the aftermath of a murder, there are questions about bringing the killer to justice, a ghost has a significant role, and so forth. We decided that it was not, because the plot was not driven by an attempt to solve the crime but rather by Hamlet considering how to bring the killer to justice and contemplating the possible consequences of different courses of action. Similarly, many fantasy books involve quests to find a stolen artifact (such as the "one ring") and to bring the thief to justice. Are these mysteries? No, we decided. To be considered a mystery, the story's plot should be driven by the investigation of a crime.

We examined the question of the reliability of the classification systems utilized by libraries. Library catalogers (at the United States Library of Congress or other designated libraries) read enough of each book to assign appropriate subject headings, which become part of the catalog record created for the book. The primary subject is used to assign a classification (a call number). The classifications are then used by libraries to determine the best shelf location for the book, so that readers browsing the shelves will find similar books grouped together. In the 1980s, many libraries began to add "genre headings" to newly cataloged works of fiction. Library of Congress personnel can assign subject headings for each genre covered in the book. The subject headings can be used to find mysteries in any library catalog, no matter how that library's collection is organized on the shelf. Some libraries also use the fiction classifications to create a separate area for mysteries, and will use the subject headings to determine which books should be shelved in that location.

We examined the results of this process by studying the classification of the *Aunt Dimity* series. When the Library of Congress cataloged the first book in the series, *Aunt Dimity's Death,* they assigned it the subject genre heading "Mystery Fiction" (tag 655). Once the first book was thus shelved, the others in the series were shelved beside it to keep the entries in the series together. The *Aunt Dimity* series is now inevitably shelved in the mystery section of libraries that divide their fiction into genres.

The cover of the first novel in the *Aunt Dimity* series, *Aunt Dimity's Death,* features a stuffed rabbit. Both authors of this book found that discouraging—neither was eager to take on the series. Yet when the novel was finally read, it turned out to be stunning! The crimes uncovered in the book took place long ago. The plot was driven by the investigation as the protagonists worked to find out what was wrong and to help people (alive and dead) heal. It was beautiful, moving, and wise; but it was not focused on bringing the perpetrators of a crime to justice. Was it a mystery? We decided that many books that are considered mysteries have plots that are driven by investigations that do not result in arrests. Mysteries have always included books in which justice took other forms. We realized that readers of mysteries would encounter this series in the mystery section of libraries, and decided that it should be included in our book. In essence, we decided that we would accept the judgment of the Library of Congress.

This experience yielded two, complementary criteria, which we employed to narrowly define and to clearly identify mysteries. For the purposes of this bibliography, a mystery is

1. a story in which a crime is suspected and the action is driven by the protagonist's efforts to find out the truth or to bring the criminal to justice,

   OR

2. a book that has been categorized as a mystery by librarians and so will be found in the mystery section of many public libraries.

Defining speculative fiction presented different problems. There are so many different possibilities! Science fiction and fantasy fiction are two obvious genres, but there are many subgenres of these. Elements that were recognized as being part of speculative fiction for this book included a setting on another planet or a future time; robots, artificial intelligences or clones; alternative history settings; creatures out of legend (including vampires, sorcerers, ghosts, etc.); paranormal phenomena; and time travel.

One criterion on which critics often judge mysteries set in fantasy or science fiction worlds is whether or not the fantastical or futuristic elements were necessary to tell the story. It is not clear why they consider this a virtue, but apparently some feel that an author must have a plot excuse to build a fantastic or science fiction world. In some of the works covered in this book, the world's futuristic elements are integral to the crime or to the investigation (such as in *Cast of Shadows* by Kevin Guilfoile). In others (such as in Carolyn Haines's *Sarah Booth Delaney* series), the fantastical element is not necessary to the plot, but it is necessary to set the mood, setting, theme, and character. In Louis Dean Owens's works, the fantastical element, the shamanism, is necessary to depict the culture. In the *Odd Thomas* series, by Dean Koontz, the fantastical element is integral to the character and the themes explored. In some series (such as George C. Chesbro's *Mongo the Magnificent* series), some books may have a fantasy element, such as magic; others may have a science fiction element, such as genetic manipulation; and others may have no major speculative elements. It would be ridiculous to promulgate a set of rules, to try to regiment this wild diversity. Instead, we hope that this book celebrates it.

Scope

The scope of *Strange Cases* includes recent works of fiction that combine mystery and speculative elements and have been published in English. Nearly all of the works were published in the last fifty years, and the emphasis in this book is on works from the last two decades. It does not include juvenile fiction. One interesting discovery made during the research was the prevalence of the combination of mystery with speculative fiction in books for children and young adults. Even the *Harry Potter* series fits the mold: it could be described as a chronicle of the effort to find and stop a serial killer.

We do include graphic novels that are written for an adult audience. In the past decade, this form of literature has gained in popularity and in stature. In 1991, Neil Gaiman won the Short Fiction World Fantasy Award for an issue of *Sandman.* (It should be noted that almost immediately after the award was given to Gaiman's *Sandman,* the rules were amended to exclude comics from the category for future awards—a decision that we hope will be re-examined in the future.) While *Sandman* is not a mystery, and so did not fit the criteria to be included in this book, *Watchmen* is of particular note with regard to the included graphic novels. *Watchmen* has been very influential on a wide variety of works created since its initial publication. In fact, *Watchmen* has been of such importance and is of such high quality that it was named one of Time Magazine's 100 best English language novels published since 1927.

In this book, only graphic novels collected in a bound form are included; single-issue comic books are not considered to be of sufficient length for coverage in this bibliography.

Methodology

For decades, the genre of speculative fiction developed through a sort of "conversation" held by authors through their published stories in magazines and novels. Authors were (and are) fans of the genre in which they write. For instance, an author would publish a story about robots, other authors would read it and reflect on it, and it would fire their imaginations so that they would write a story at least partly in response. We were fascinated by that conversation, and it fired our imaginations in setting the parameters of this book.

We agreed that this bibliography would be selective rather than comprehensive. It incorporates the works that are part of the current "conversation" on cross-genre fiction. We canvassed book dealers at conventions; we talked to booksellers, fans, and speakers at conventions; and we consulted librarians and the members of pertinent listservs.

Different groups mentioned different books. For instance, several bookdealers at WorldCon in Anaheim mentioned the *Lynn Hightower* series, while an author at that same convention mentioned Kerr's *A Philosophical*

Investigation. Many librarians mentioned Barbara Hambly's *James Asher* series, Agatha Christie's *Mr. Quin,* and Charlaine Harris's *Southern Vampire* series. Owners of independent bookstores mentioned the *Harper Blaine Greywalker* series and many of the vampire series. A message on the Sci-Fi Discussion list pointed to a list of books made into movies that included Wolf's *Who Censored Roger Rabbit?* Listserv members on DorothyL discussed the work of Nancy Atherton, Carrie Bebris, Colin Cotterill, and many of the other authors whose works are included in this book. Many people responded that they knew that they'd read books that combined speculative elements with mystery, but that they were hard to bring to mind. We are indebted to everyone who responded to our questions for the titles and series that were incorporated into this bibliography.

Our research compelled us to search library catalogs and bibliographies. There are hundreds of works that are not widely discussed but that do fit the parameters. We thought that readers of this work would be interested in those titles and series; therefore, the lists were put into this book's appendix. It lists mysteries by speculative fiction element. It is not complete. We expect to find more the morning after this manuscript has gone to the publisher, and still more on many mornings thereafter. The lists will be a work in progress for years to come; but this is a start.

We were always aware that any creator is in a vulnerable position, and we hope we've celebrated all the authors included in this book; however, our first obligation was to readers. We were honest in reviews: if we say something was "vulgar," we found it vulgar. We still reviewed it, because we subscribe to Raganathan's principle: "Every book its reader." We did our best to write an accurate review so that "its reader" could find the book! We were particularly careful to mention weak series' entries or changes in series. While there are many cross-genre books, there are not enough. It would be a pity if a reader dismissed a series because the first book that he or she picked up was not typical of the rest of the series; we hope that a reader who gave up on series will be encouraged to try it again if the annotation on the book that he or she read states that it is not up to the standard set by the rest of the series.

For this book, we reviewed the work of over 100 authors and editors: 369 novels, 112 short stories and novellas, 23 anthologies, and 36 graphic novels. Over 200 more works are listed in the appendices.

Organization of the Book

The book is organized by the author's name; entries are headed by the title that we consider the best starting point for the reader. In the case of series, the first novel was usually considered the best starting point; but for a few series, a short story provided better background on the world or on the characters, and was therefore listed as the best starting point. Each entry includes information on the genres and themes that are combined in the book, subjects and character types, whether the book is a "stand-alone" or part of a series, the story's premise, setting, detective, recurring characters, background information on the world in which the story is set, general comments, a short analysis, and then "explorations." Each "Explorations" section includes a few questions to ponder when thinking through the book. The section was created because one of the pleasures of reading science fiction, fantasy fiction, and mystery comes after the book has been closed. These are all thought-provoking genres. They explore philosophy, ethics, and the human condition. Part of the fun is reflecting on the book. How was it put together? Did the author play fair? Were the clues there so that the reader could identify the villain as soon as the detective could? What was the world like? Would people really change in the ways depicted if that were the world they inhabited? Could the crime or the investigation only have taken place in that different world? What were the ethics of the ways that the society treated beings that were sentient but not human? Did it matter if that sentience was artificial? How could you tell if a machine is actually sentient? So many questions. The few that are listed for each series are just a beginning, and are usually based on the title recommended as the start of that series (which is also the title used for the entry's heading). Again, the questions are not an exhaustive list. They are just a start.

Finally, indexes provide access by author, series and title, major characters, genre and theme, and mystery and speculative fiction elements (including subjects and characters types).

About the Terminology Used in This Book

Within fiction, there are genres such as Mystery, Science Fiction, and Fantasy. For our purposes, these categories are insufficient. We needed to classify the work in a way that would be helpful to readers. The classifications should ideally encompass the areas of plot, setting, atmosphere, and themes so that they would be helpful in alerting readers to works of interest. They also had to be broad enough to be used to identify similar works.

Different types of mysteries (such as hard-boiled or traditional) provide very different reading experiences. There are not only different types of science fiction and different types of fantasy works but, in some cases, classifying a work as science fiction or fantasy is less useful than identifying the sub-genre into which it fits. Consider time travel. The classification of time travel books into science fiction or fantasy hinges on the mechanism used to travel through time. By convention, if the time travel is possible because of technology, it is science fiction; if time travel is possible because of a wizard's spell, then it is fantasy fiction. Many, if not most time travel stories, do not belabor the mechanics of the instrument that sent the protagonist back (or forward) in time. It may be a barely understood electrical curtain (as in *To Say Nothing of the Dog*). It may be a barely understood paranormal ability (as in *A Fold in the Tent of the Sky*). Yet the problems faced, the questions about disrupting the past and the nature of causality, are the same no matter what mechanism allowed the characters to travel through time. The fact that a book is about time travel is what is of interest to a prospective reader, often more so than the precise method by which the time travel takes place. So, in most cases, we used the narrower term "time travel" rather than a broader term such as "science fiction."

Similarly, we developed the category "Man as Creator." It is used for works in which humans have created sentient beings. The sentient beings may have been created through programming software (such as Turing Hopper in *You've Got Murder*), may have been created through genetic engineering (such as Nohar Rajasthan in *Forests of the Night*) or may be animated by opening a golem's head and dropping in a slip of paper (such as Dorfl in *Feet of Clay*). The question of man's responsibilities to his creations and the rights of those creations are likely to be themes that the book explores. The mechanism of creation is not necessarily the focus of the book.

There are a number of recognized genres that were also problematic. For instance, "High Fantasy" is classically used for works that include Tolkienesque supernatural beings (Sorcerers, Elves, and Orcs). Should High Fantasy also include books with Aliens? Are the types of supernatural beings more interesting than whether or not they've integrated into the society? To some readers the answer is "yes," but to others the answer is "no." We hope that this book will be useful to both types of readers. To this end, in addition to the genre and themes field, we created a separate field for character types and subjects. In the second field, there is information on whether the book features, for example, werewolves or aliens.

The genre/theme classification identifies the large issues in the work. For instance the question of how the supernatural or extraterrestrial beings coexist with the rest of humanity determined many of the thematic questions. So, for example, "Blended Society" categorizes works in which the general population knows about the supernatural or non-human beings involved. "Secret Society" was used for works in which the supernatural or non-human society is trying to hide its existence from the general population. (Both science and social issues have contributed to an increase in the number of series in which supernatural or non-human groups are on the cusp of revealing themselves to the general population; science, in that genetic research would reveal anomalies in the DNA of supernatural beings; social issues in that the concept of secret lives and "coming out" seems to resonate with the difficulties encountered by many people in the gay and lesbian community. The *Sookie Stackhouse* books by Charlaine Harris, the *Mercedes Thompson* books by Patricia Briggs, and the *Kitty Norville* books by Carrie Vaughn all feature supernatural societies that are gradually revealing themselves to the human population. In this vein, some series begin with secret societies that go public, to become blended societies during the course of the series.)

These are the *Speculative Genres and Themes* used in this work:

Science Fiction

"Science Fiction" encompasses both technological advances and societal changes. The authors examined splitting this into Hard Science Fiction and Social Science Fiction, but came to the conclusion that the subgenres are too intertwined to be split. Every work we encountered that included one of the two subgenres included both. On reflection, the authors agreed that if they encountered a work that focused on technological advances, yet it depicted a society identical in every way to today's society, then the author of that work was making a definite statement about society. Therefore, any respectful examination of his or her work would acknowledge that fact.

Paranormal

This genre classification describes the world as seventy-three percent of Americans see it today: telepathy, clairvoyance, ESP (extra sensory perception), astrology, shamanism, etc. are real. (Not necessarily prevalent, but real: at least a few people on earth have paranormal abilities.) Themes in paranormal books often include personal responsibility and support of other people. [*Note: A Gallup Poll conducted from June 6 to June 8, 2005 asked Americans if they believed in "paranormal" phenomena, including extrasensory perception (ESP), haunted houses, ghosts, mental telepathy, clairvoyance, astrology, communicating with the dead, witches, reincarnation, and channeling. Seventy-three percent of those surveyed did believe in the paranormal. This number has been fairly steady since 2001.* (As reported by Moore, David W. in "Three in Four Americans Believe in the Paranormal," cited by *Gallup Poll News Service,* June 16, 2005.)]

Time Travel

People or other sentient beings travel through time. Themes include preserving the known future or righting the known past.

Man as Creator

Humans have developed the technological means to create sentient beings. These may include robots, clones, androids, golems, genetically engineered beings, or sentient computers. Common themes include the issues of what it means to be human, the legal status of those who are created rather than born, prejudice, and equal rights (often including the right to continue to exist; i.e., to not be murdered by the government).

Secret Society

Supernatural beings (vampires, werewolves, witches, fairies, etc.) and/or non-human beings (either aliens from other planets or human-created sentient beings such computers, robots, golems, genetically engineered creatures, etc.) exist, but the general public knows nothing about them. Themes in books about secret supernatural societies often include isolation, loneliness, secrecy, and hidden power.

Blended Society

Supernatural beings (vampires, werewolves, witches, fairies, etc.) and/or non-human beings (human-created sentient beings such computers, robots, golems, genetically engineered creatures, etc., or aliens from other planets) exist, and humans know they exist. They may live among humans or in separate enclaves. Themes in books about Blended Societies often include prejudice and/or severe class stratification (to the point where the lives of those in the underclass are not valued, and the people in that class may be treated as tools, weapons, or slaves).

Gods on Earth

The general society depicted in these books knows about gods. Some people (although not all) believe in gods. Most do not expect them to be walking around on this planet. The works covered in this book in which gods walk on Earth focus on ancient pantheons of gods who are trying to retain a few human followers. Themes include waning power and the pain (and anger) of being forgotten by humanity.

Lone Supernatural

A few books have one sentient being who has powers beyond those of a normal human. This person may be either the forerunner or the last survivor of another race. (Or, as is the case with Mr. Quin, a character created by

Agatha Christie, they may not be explained.) Themes in books categorized as Lone Supernatural include secret friendships, secret talents, and secret projects.

Parallel Universe

There are other realities existing alongside the one that we know. Themes include questions about the nature of reality, and the plots usually include either an examination of ways to exploit the parallel universe or desperate people who are accidentally trapped in a universe that is not their own.

Alternate History

The world as we don't know it. At some point in the past, an event caused history to diverge from the path that we know. The book explores what the world would have been like if that key event had taken history in a different direction. For instance, if the Nazis had won World War II, what would the world be like today?

Post-Apocalypse

The settings of these works are the world after an apocalyptic event (commonly a nuclear war, a plague, or some other worldwide disaster). If the apocalypse was recent, then survival and rebuilding civilization are commonly found themes. If the apocalypse was far in the past, then themes might include the mythologizing of the past world.

Alien Interference

Aliens have interfered with Earth in some way, whether by occupying it, by invading it, or by working as a secret society to alter events on Earth. Aliens may come to Earth and take over, with humans relegated to a relatively powerless position on their own planet, in which case the themes may include loss of control, humiliating circumstances, difficulties in communication, and anger. Aliens may comprise a secret, non-human society on Earth, or may be interfering from off-planet. If they are on Earth, they are in hiding, but they're doing everything they can to alter Earth's society. This differs from stories in the Secret Society category, in that the aliens are not simply trying to go about their own lives. They are an outside force actively trying to alter the lives of the human inhabitants of Earth. In the case of aliens hiding or interfering from off-planet, the story's themes may include secrecy, power, and human rationalization of unusual circumstances.

Fantastical Realism

In these works, it's not always clear where reality ends and the fantastic begins. Themes include questions about the reliability of perceptions and/or memories. Characters may be unsure if their "memories" are from actual experiences or dreams, or may seem to play with perception and reality for their own reasons.

Anthropomorphic Animals

Animals talk, discuss mysteries, and search for clues. They're not a secret society. They aren't in hiding. One of the themes is feeling affection for the humans with whom they live; another is wishing that those humans could understand what the animals are saying.

Dystopia

Society has devolved to the point where it supports misery rather than joy, stagnation rather than growth. The government oppresses its citizens. Themes center on methods of escape (either mental or physical), revolution, or simply the miserable daily grind of survival.

Literary Crossover

Characters from another author's work play a part in the work at hand. Questions include whether or not to stay true to the original characters, and whether or not the characters know they're fictional.

These are the *Mystery Genres and Themes* used in this work:

Traditional Mystery

Society is reasonably well ordered and peaceful. Murder disrupts the society, and someone from within that society investigates. Traditional mysteries are characterized by a small group of suspects, little "on-page" violence, and an ending that sees the world set right. In the past, these were often referred to as "cozies," a term that has since fallen out of favor.

Defense Mystery

These fall partway between traditional and hard-boiled mysteries. Society is neither inherently well ordered nor corrupt; it's indifferent. Members of the general public are oblivious to the struggle taking place around them, and the "good guys" will do their best to keep the public unaware, because they fear that people will make hasty, poorly thought-out, semi-hysterical decisions when faced with the truth. The beings involved can be divided into two camps. The protagonist is one of the "us" camp, and he opposes those in the "them" camp. At least a few of the people in the "us" group will have the "white knight" characteristics of the protagonists found in the Hard-boiled Mystery category. They will employ violence to protect the "us" group, and some of that violence will be "on-page." Many or all of the people in the "them" group are corrupt: they are likely to employ violence; at least a few of them will embrace cruelty as either a tactic or a hobby. Themes explored usually include secrecy, protection, and internecine battles.

Hard-Boiled Mystery

The world is essentially corrupt, and one individual (usually a detective or white knight) solves one crime, making one little corner of the world temporarily better.

Humorous Mystery

Mysteries that focus on humor.

Whodunnit

Strong puzzle mysteries, many of which include an "impossible crime." (When combined with speculative elements, the story may have a "whatdunit" aspect.) Locked-room mysteries are a type of Whodunnit.

Police Procedurals

The mystery is solved by the officers of the law, following up on clues in the course of their duties.

Espionage/Spy Thriller

The story focuses on spying or covert governmental operations.

Forensic

Protagonists include pathologists of one type or another whose primary mode of investigation is discovering clues by examining the scene of the crime and the remains of the victims.

Capers

Sometimes referred to as crime-caper novels, these stories feature criminals as protagonists.

Inverted Mystery

The book opens with the crime. At the outset of the story, the reader knows more about the crime than does the detective. The reader may know the identity of the criminal from the first page of the book. The fascination is watching the detective's progress in solving the mystery. These mysteries are sometimes referred to simply as "crime novels."

We hope that this book will contribute to the pleasure of adventurous readers and be a resource for librarians and other educators who want to start a book discussion group. We spent many interesting hours in the creation of this book; we hope that you spend many interesting hours in using it!

Strange Cases

A

ACEVEDO, Mario.

THE NYMPHOS OF ROCKY FLATS

Genres/Themes Crossed: Secret Society, Alien Intervention X Hard-Boiled Mystery.

Subjects/Character Types: Vampires, Aliens, Santeria X Private Investigator.

Series/Stand-Alone: *The Nymphos of Rocky Flats: A Novel* is the first novel in the continuing *Felix Gomez Adventures* series. The series is best read in order because Felix's relationships and his place in vampire society change over time.

Scene of the Crime: Denver, Colorado; present day.

Detective: Private investigator Felix Gomez is a U.S. Army veteran of Operation Iraqi Freedom. When Felix's platoon was on night patrol, they gunned down a group of Iraqis moving stealthily through the dark. They had thought the Iraqis were enemy guerillas. The soldiers found that they had been mistaken. Upon inspecting the carnage, they found that they had killed innocent women and children who had been going to get water for their family. Felix was stunned by horror and guilt. He was drawn into a house, where he met an old man who asked Felix if he sought death. Felix didn't: he was looking for something to assuage his guilt. He wanted the punishment to fall upon him, not upon his men. The old man offered him suffering, a punishment worse than death, and turned Felix into a vampire. Now, Felix regards vampirism as his penance; he refuses to drink human blood, even though he knows that without human blood his powers will weaken. He is still able to compel others to give him the truth, which is one of the talents he uses most often in his investigations.

Known Associates: Felix works alone.

Premise: Earth was put under quarantine by species from other planets long ago. The Earth people were judged to be too violent and dangerous for first contact. Earth's government learned of the secret some time ago but has determined to continue the lie that aliens don't exist. As one of the aliens says, "It then became more expedient to stick to the lie than admit the truth. That's what all governments do best" (*The Nymphos of Rocky Flats,* p. 341). Not only do aliens exist, but so do many creatures from ancient legends. Vampires exist, but the modern inventions of vitamin supplements, sunblock, and make-up allow them to pass for humans.

Comment: *The Nymphos of Rocky Flats* was awarded Best New Book by a Colorado Author by the Westword Best of Denver 2007. Mario Acevedo has issues of "The Hollow Fang" (an internet publication for vampire aficionados) on his Web site (http://www.marioacevedo.com/index.htm). He was the artist-in-residence for Arte Americas in Fresno, California, and served as a combat artist in Operation Desert Storm. He was a writer long before he was published. He credits the Rocky Mountain Fiction Writers with giving him the support that enabled him to publish *The Nymphos of Rocky Flats.*

Literary Magic & Mayhem: These books include coarse language and embrace vulgarity. This might have been employed to shock, but it soon numbs the reader, and so is not effective. The vampire community is well portrayed, as are the strategies that Felix employs to deal with his affliction. One of the main themes in the books is that of responsibility. Some characters and institutions accept responsibility, others do not. Governments and their agents, in particular, are portrayed as lacking the willingness to accept responsibility for the consequences of their actions.

Explorations: Is this book what you expected from the title?

How is Felix different from the other vampires he encounters? Why is he different?

A pastor has said that he intends to work elements from Felix's story into a sermon. How does the book work as a story of redemption?

Different people in this book manipulate others through various means (including guilt, macho games, hypnosis, and sex). What aspects of human interaction portrayed in this book are about power? What aspects are not?

THE CASES

1. ***The Nymphos of Rocky Flats: A Novel.*** New York: Rayo, 2006, 368 p. ISBN: 0060833262.

DENVER, COLORADO, 2006. Gilbert Odin, Felix's old college roommate, uses the Patriot Act to investigate Felix's background. He decides to hire Felix to investigate an outbreak of nymphomania among the guards at a top-secret plutonium facility in Rocky Flats, Colorado. However, as Felix investigates, he finds more strange occurrences, involving radiation, spaceships, and murder.

ASSOCIATES: Gilbert Odin—*who sends Felix $20,000 to investigate the situation at Rocky Flats;* Victor Lopez—*Felix's landlord;* Robert Carcano—*the patriarch of the vampires of Denver;* Tamara Squires, Sofia Martinez, Jenny Calhoun. Dr. Bigelow Wong, Gary Higby, and Herbert Hoover Merriweather—*who work at Rocky Flats;* Wendy Teagarden—*dryad*; "Ziggy Drek" (Sigfried von Drek), Andre, and Carmen—*vampires*; Nicolae Dragon—*the vânätori leader;* Petru and Teodor—*vampire hunters.*

2. ***X-Rated Bloodsuckers: A Novel.*** New York: Rayo, c2007, 370 p. ISBN: 9780060833275.

LOS ANGELES, CALIFORNIA, 2007. Felix can always use money, and when porn star Kitty Meow offers him $100,000 to find out who murdered her friend, Roxy Bronze, he is tempted. What clinches the deal is Kitty's statement that she believes vampires were involved in Roxy's murder. Felix must investigate, if for no other reason than to protect the Great Secret of the existence of vampires.

ASSOCIATES: Katz Meow (born Wanda Pettigrew)—*hires Felix to find the killer of Roxy Bronze (born Freya Krieger);* Coyote—*recommended Felix;* Lucky Rosario—*a land developer;* Councilwoman Petale Venin—*worked with Lucky Rosario on the land deal that Roxy blocked;* Veronica Torres—*a reporter at the Los Angeles Times, who covered the land development scandal;* Cragnow Vissoom (vampire)—*president of Gamorrah Video;* Rachel—*is Cragnow's receptionist;* Kacy (vampire)—*also works for Cragnow;* Rebecca Dwelling—*a musician friend of Kitty's who claims that vampires and humans mingle at the club where she works;* Fred Daniels—*Roxy's ex-husband;* Julius Paxton—*the Deputy Chief of the Foothills Division of the Los Angeles Police Department;* Dr. Mordecai Niphe—*who has Roxy's medical license pulled after she snitches on him;* Lara Phillips—*Roxy's sister;* Reverend Dale Journey—*who has friends on the police force;* JJ Jizmee (born Polly Smythe)—*a retired porn star;* Andrew Tonic—*who had been Roxy's lawyer.*

3. ***The Undead Kama Sutra.*** New York: Eos, c2008, 368 p. ISBN: 9780060833282.

SARASOTA, KEY WEST AND HOUGHTON ISLAND, FLORIDA; CHICAGO, ILLINOIS; KANSAS CITY, MISSOURI; SAVANNAH, GEORGIA; AND DENVER, COLORADO, 2008. Felix is on vacation, minding his own business, when alien Gilbert Odin calls him for help. Within hours, Felix is entangled in multiple investigations. He needs to find out who is going around shooting people with an alien weapon. He needs to "save the Earth women" (but he has no idea what endangers them), and he must find the mysterious Goodman. The underworld vampire council (the *Araneum*), a drug-smuggling cop, and a lusty vampire all want something from Felix (fortunately, not the same thing). His investigation takes him through the South and into the sun.

ASSOCIATES: Gilbert Odin(alien)—*hires Felix to find retired U.S. Army Colonel Daniel Goodman;* "Mr. Big" Clayborn(alien)—*is also interested in Goodman;* Carmen Arellano, Jolie, and Antoine Speight—*who seem to have found the secret to being healthy vampires;* Phyllis—*a vampire messenger of the Araneum;* Deputy Sheriff Toller Johnson—*who is the law in Monroe County;* Mrs. Mikala Jamison—*Dan Goodman's secretary;* Belinda—*who mistakes Felix for a talent scout;* Karen Beck—*who used to work for Prairie Air;* Earl—*a homeless man in Kansas City;* Sarah—*who plays the cello;* Angelo Sosa—*the foreman of the night maintenance crew for the Grand Atlantic Hotel;* Jack and Leslie—*own a mortuary and serve as Carmen's "chalices" (humans who willingly give blood to vampires;* Thorne, William Krandall and Amanda Peltier—*who work for Rizè-Blu Pharmaceutique.*

4. ***Jailbait Zombie.*** New York: Eos, c2009, 353 p. ISBN:9780061567148.

DENVER AND AURORA, COLORADO AND MORADA, TEXAS, 2009. There has been an infestation of zombies from Texas to Colorado. It's bad for the vampires. They would die to protect the Great Secret, that there are supernatural beings in the world. Zombies are not low-profile undead. The *Araneum* (the underworld vampire council) hires Felix to find out who is making zombies. Then the Araneum adds another assignment to the job. They've realized in their work with the astral plane that someone is sending out a great deal of psychic energy. Coincidentally (if one believes in coincidence), the trail of the zombies intersects with the emanations of psychic energy. They want Felix to investigate both. Felix goes to this point of intersection, Morada, to track down the answers.

ASSOCIATES: Mel—*the leader of the Denver nidus (nest) of vampires;* Young Dagger—*a young (and annoying) new vampire;* Olivia—*Felix's "chalice" (a human who willingly gives him blood);* Phyllis—*Felix's handler for the Araneum;* Barrett Chambers—*a zombie;* Adrianna Maestas—*Barrett's ex-wife;*

Gino Brunatti—a *mobster;* Phaedra Nardoni—*Gino's cousin, she reminds Felix of the little Iraqi girl who was mistakenly killed by his squad;* Sal Cavagnolo—*Phaedra's Uncle;* Cleto and Vinny—*Sal's thugs;* Lorena—*Sal's wife;* Shawna—*who offers Felix some companionship;* Dr. Leopold Hennison—*who seeks knowledge of the supernatural;* Kimberly, Reginald, and Sonia—*are zombies;* Jolie and Nguyen Trotsky Hoang—*are vampires sent by the Araneum to kill Felix;* Eric—*a gun dealer;* Nathacha De Brancoven(vampire)—*a leader in the Araneum who is sent to discuss Felix's failures with him.*

ADAMS, Douglas.

Dirk Gently's Holistic Detective Agency

Genres/Themes Crossed: Paranormal, Time Travel, Gods on Earth, Fantastical Realism X Humorous Mystery.

Subjects/Character Types: Ghosts, Gods, Clairvoyants, Time Travel X Private Investigator.

Series/Stand-Alone: The two novels in the Dirk Gently series are very different in tone. The first novel, *Dirk Gently's Holistic Detective Agency,* lays out the premises of the world in a somewhat whimsical tone, and is the best starting place for readers interested in the series.

In an interview with Matt Newsome (at http://www.mattnewsome.co.uk/), Douglas Adams stated that when he was about a third of the way through writing the third Dirk Gently book, *The Salmon of Doubt,* he realized that the book simply was not working and was not going to work. He decided to change gears and devote some time to other projects. Looking back on it a year later, he realized that he had lost touch with the character and had been writing a book that fit into the world of *The Hitchhiker's Guide to the Galaxy,* rather than into the world of Dirk Gently. He decided to salvage some of the ideas from the working manuscript and turn it into a sixth book for *The Hitchhiker's Guide to the Galaxy* series.

Scene of the Crime: Cambridgeshire, England, present day.

Detective: Svlad Cjelli is either a con man or a psychic, maybe a little of both. He now calls himself Dirk Gently, and has set up a "Holistic Detective Agency," where he talks circles around clients and takes their money.

Known Associates: Sergeant Gilks's knowledge of Dirk Gently is sufficient to cause him to swear creatively whenever he finds Dirk in proximity to a police investigation.

Premise: Dirk Gently refers to himself as a "holistic detective." In *The Long Dark Tea Time of the Soul,* he describes his work to nurse Sally Mills:

> I am not as other private detectives. My methods are holistic... Every particle in the universe... affects every other particle, however faintly or obliquely... I could ask anybody I liked, chosen entirely by chance, any random question I cared to think of, and their answer, or lack of it, would in some way bear upon the problem to which I am seeking a solution. (p. 116)

In fact, in *Dirk Gently's Holistic Detective Agency,* Dirk gathers the information that allows him to solve Richard's problems (and to save the world) by questioning a young boy whom he meets on the street concerning a conjuring trick. He further describes the rather surreal logic of his methodology in *Dirk Gently's Holistic Detective Agency:*

> "The whole thing was obvious!" he exclaimed, thumping the table. "So obvious that the only thing which prevented me from seeing the solution was the trifling fact that it was completely impossible. Sherlock Holmes observed that once you have eliminated the impossible, then whatever remains, however improbably, must be the answer. I, however, do not like to eliminate the impossible." (p. 181)

He doesn't "eliminate the impossible," and therein lies part of the fascination of the story.

Comment: One of Adams's passions was science. He studied it seriously, understood it well, and did his best to incorporate it into his books with a humorous touch. He believed that, in too many of the works of classic science fiction, the science was poorly written and ponderously presented. Adams began as a script editor for the *Dr. Who* television series. He used his success there to convince the BBC to give him a chance at broadcasting his own show: *The Hitchhiker's Guide to the Galaxy.* Ideas from the radio show were incorporated into a trilogy of four novels. The first one, entitled *The Hitchhiker's Guide to the Galaxy,* was a stunning success. Adams was amazed, saying that the experience of being catapulted onto the bestseller lists was like being flown by helicopter to the summit of Mt. Everest, or like an orgasm without the foreplay. *Dirk Gently's Holistic Detective Agency* was published after *The Hitchhiker's Guide to the Galaxy.* It was on the best sellers' lists for months. The knowledge that Adams studied at St. John's College, Cambridge may add something to the reader's enjoyment of Adams's depiction of the dons of Cambridge. The official Douglas Adams Web site is located at http://www.douglasadams.com/.

Literary Magic & Mayhem: Adams's blend of irreverence, humor, philosophy, and science is difficult to describe. The novels begin with several seemingly disparate story lines, but they come together during the course of the investigations. While the stories are mostly told chronologically, the structure is complex as the narrative moves from one story line to another. Adams's descriptions of his characters are interesting. In part they define the character, but the descriptions also include a bit of philosophy. Here is part of the initial description of the Electric Monk from *Dirk Gently's Holistic Detective Agency:*

> The Electric Monk was a labor-saving device, like a dishwasher or a video recorder. Dishwashers washed tedious dishes for you, thus saving you the bother of washing them yourself; Electric Monks believed things for you, thus saving you what was becoming an increasingly onerous task, that of believing all the things the world expected you to believe. (p. 3)

The tone of *The Long Dark Tea Time of the Soul* is different from the first book in the series, as can be seen in Thor's description of the Immortal Gods:

> "Immortals are what you wanted," said Thor in a low quiet voice. "Immortals are what you got. It is a little hard on us. You wanted us to be forever, so we are forever. Then you forget about us. But still we are forever. Now at last, many are dead, many are dying," he then added in a quiet voice, "but it takes a special effort." (p. 225)

The unexpected twist that lends it humor is still in the writing, but Dirk Gently's insouciance has given way to guilt and dread. The world in the second book is less about adventure than responsibility, and those who have power are worn out by the mundane demands of the modern world. In *Dirk Gently's Holistic Detective Agency,* those who think quickly can avoid the consequences of their actions (or choose which consequences they are willing to bear); in *The Long Dark Tea Time of the Soul,* bills that come due must be paid. It would have been interesting to see how this theme would have played out if Adams had had a chance to write a third Dirk Gently book.

Explorations: Belief and reality are two themes that run through *Dirk Gently's Holistic Detective Agency.* What are some of the ways in which they are explored?

Douglas Adams has stated that his mother's favorite character in *Dirk Gently's Holistic Detective Agency* is the horse. What makes the horse an interesting character? What are interesting aspects of other characters?

What do readers look for in trying to determine the truth about Svlad Cjelli? How does the truth compare with the hypothetical experiment involving Schrödinger's cat?

In *The Long Dark Tea Time of the Soul,* Gods die and are born. What does it take to create a God?

In *Dirk Gently's Holistic Detective Agency,* how often does Dirk end up paying a bill? How often does anyone else actually pay a bill? In *The Long Dark Tea Time of the Soul,* how often does Dirk end up paying a bill? How often does anyone else actually pay a bill? In both books, various people try to "pull a fast one." What are the outcomes of their efforts?

THE CASES

1. ***Dirk Gently's Holistic Detective Agency.*** New York: Simon and Schuster, c1987, 247 p. ISBN: 0671625829.

CAMBRIDGESHIRE, ENGLAND. NOVEMBER, 1987? Richard MacDuff starts the day as a mild-mannered (albeit behind-in-his-work) computer programmer. At dinner he is witness to an impossible thing, and shortly after that he encounters a ghost. Then he commits the crime of breaking and entering, and he finishes off the day as a suspect in a murder investigation. His old school classmate, Dirk Gently, has opened a "holistic detective agency." Dirk bases his work on the theory that everything in the universe is interconnected; this allows him to investigate local pet disappearances from a balmy beach in the Bahamas. He spots Richard's spectacularly dangerous and rather inept effort to break into an apartment and steps in to help him (or at least to cadge some money from him). Once he spots the chance to make some money, he is hot on the trail. Unfortunately, saving the world is not as lucrative as one might think.

ASSOCIATES: Richard MacDuff—*a computer programmer at Gordon Way's WayForward Technologies;* The Electric Monk—*a device invented by applying advances in labor-saving technology to faith;* "Reg"—*the Regius Professor of Chronology;* Watkin—*the Classics professor;* Sarah—*the seven-year-old daughter of a man from the BBC;* Cawley—*the aged archaeologist;* Susan Way—*Richard's girlfriend;* Michael Wenton-Weakes—*who has been mis-managing a journal that is published by his family;* Lady Magna—*his mother who sold the journal;* Gordon Way—*who purchased the journal and replaced Michael;* A. K. Ross—*who is turning the journal into a success;* Janice Pearce—*the secretary (who may have quit) at Dirk Gently's Holistic Detective Agency;* Detective Inspector Mason—*is investigating a murder;* Sergeant Gilks—*a Cambridgeshire constable who has tangled with Dirk Gently before this case, and does not seem to have fond memories of the experience.*

2. ***The Long Dark Tea-Time of the Soul.*** New York: Simon and Schuster, c1988, 319 p. ISBN: 0671625837.

LONDON AND ASGARD, 1988? Dirk Gently was hired by a madman; a gullible, rich madman. A madman who asked Dirk to guard him at 6:30 in the morning when he expected a furious. hairy, green-eyed, scythe-wielding giant to murder him. Dirk took the case. When he awakened, a little before noon, he went in search of his client and his fee. Once he had the money in hand, he spent a little time investigating his client's death.

Associates: Kate Schechter—*who missed her plane;* Mr. Geoffrey Anstey—*Dirk's client;* Clive and Cynthia Draycott—*Mr. Anstey's neighbors;* Sergeant Gilks—*a local constable;* The God Odin—*who is known at the nursing home as Mr. Odwin;* Mr. Rags—*his servant;* Hillow—*Odin's chauffer;* Sister Bailey—*one of Odin's attendant nurses;* Sally Mills—*a nurse;* Mr. Ralph Standish—*a psychologist and one of the directors of Woodshead Hospital;* Neil—*Kate's downstairs neighbor;* and Tsuliwaënsis—*a friend of Thor.*

ALBERT, Susan Wittig.

Note: Susan Wittig Albert writes *The Cottage Tales of Beatrix Potter* on her own. When she partners with her husband, Bill Albert, they write under the pseudonym Robin Paige.

THE TALE OF HILL TOP FARM

Genres/Themes Crossed: Anthropomorphic Animals X Traditional Mystery (Historical).

Subjects/Character Types: Animal Sleuth(s) X Amateur Detective (Historical).

Series/Stand-Alone: One of the pleasures of the series is seeing Beatrix's growth. She gains self-assurance in the course of the series. Several other characters grow and develop relationships as the series progresses. It is best read in order.

Scene of the Crime: Early 20th century, England, principally the village of Sawrey.

Detective(s): Animal sleuths in the book include Tabitha Twitchet, Abigail Tolliver's cat; Crumpet, the Stubbses' cat; and Rascal, the Crooks's Jack Russell terrier. They see much of what goes on in the village and take an active interest working together to detect the truth behind various crimes. Their difficulty is that "Big Folk" don't understand them. There are times when they take action, working with other animals to prevent harm to people and animals they like. For instance, at one point in the series they arrange for a cat to trip someone who is hurrying to bear witness against a kind (and innocent) young man; but for the most part the animals simply observe the actions of the people in the village.

Beatrix Potter, a gentlewoman who used the money from her children's books to purchase a local farm, also acts as a sleuth in the books. For one gloriously happy month, she was engaged to her editor, Norman Warne. As a publisher. he was "in trade," and Beatrix' parents did everything they could to prevent the marriage. In deference to them, Beatrix agreed to keep the engagement secret and to delay the marriage. Norman's early death put an end to her dreams of their future together. She used the money from her books to purchase Hill Top Farm so that she could take an occasional break from her parents' incessant demands and have some time to grieve and heal. She's an outsider to the village, a clever observer, modest and unassuming (but the social equal of Lady Longford), and a thoughtful listener (even to children and animals).

Known Associates: Shy Beatrix is befriended by Dimity Woodcock. Dimity lives with her brother, Captain Miles Woodcock, who is the Justice of the Peace in Sawrey. Other leaders in the village include the "dear vicar" (Reverend Samuel Sackett), whose housekeeper is Mrs. Thompson; Grace Lythecoe, widow of the former vicar; and Dr. Butters. Mr. Willie Heelis, the younger partner of the Hawkshead solicitor's firm of Heelis and Heelis, is a frequent visitor to Sawrey. In the first book in the series Miss Sarah Barwick comes to the village to live at Anvil Cottage.

Miss Potter's farm is run by Mr. John Jennings, who lives on the farm with his wife, Becky, and their children, Clara and Sammy. Miss Potter boards with the Crooks, Mathilda and George (who owns the smithy). Other lodgers are Charlie Hotchkiss, who works at the forge with George, and Edward Horsley.

The chief gossips of the town are Elsa Grape (the Woodcock's housekeeper); Lucy Skead, the village postmistress; and Bertha Stubbs, who cleans at the village school.

Premise: Miss Potter purchased the farm expecting an idyllic village society close to the calming and healing effects of the land. Instead, the village proves to be a microcosm of all the elements of humanity. Beatrix is soon embroiled in village life to the extent that she finds the courage to champion others and to occasionally stand up to her parents' demands. She is still a dutiful daughter and returns to her parents' home frequently, but she takes every chance she can find to return to her farm. Miss Potter has many talents that aid her in discovering the truth. She is a keen observer with a fine memory and she has great empathy, particularly for the downtrodden. When children, the impoverished, or servants are wrongly accused, Beatrix finds that she has unexpected reserves of courage and tenacity.

Comment: Even readers who find talking animals too horribly cute may enjoy seeing Beatrix Potter's growth. She had spent her life at the beck and call of her domineering parents. At the outset of the series, she believes herself a coward, but she finds the courage to stand up for others, and that courage grows over the course of the books.

Susan Wittig Albert and her husband (and writing partner under the Robin Paige pseudonym) have a Web site at http://www.mysterypartners.com/. The site includes bibliographies of their books, recipes, instructions on reading tea leaves (within *Thyme for Tea Tearoom* in the *China Bayles* section of the site), a section on the cultivation and use of herbs and the opportunity to subscribe to a weekly e-newsletter on herbs (also in the *China Bayles* section), and historical notes within the *Robin Paige Victorian Mysteries* section. In 1997, Susan founded an organization called the Story Circle Network that teaches, supports, and encourages women to use life-writing for personal and spiritual growth. Further information on the Story Circle Network can be found at http://www.storycircle.org/scn.html.

Literary Magic & Mayhem: The gossip network in Sawrey is a marvel. "News" is transmitted rapidly, and the facts are soon colored by interesting suppositions that open profitable possibilities that are soon regarded as fact by those who hear them. It's both funny and frightening.

All the characters are well drawn, many are not particularly pleasant, some are bullying, and some are sly; but every one of the people depicted is quite believable. Except for a few villainous rats, the animals are depicted as honest and gentle souls. Some are silly and some are lazy, but most are good-natured, kind-hearted, and generally virtuous. All of the animals can talk, some can read, many wear clothing. A few of the animals have complicated domestic arrangements, libraries, and fires in their living rooms.

Books in the series have helpful tools for the reader; some editions of some of the titles include character lists, author's notes, recipes, and glossaries to help with the dialect.

Explorations: What do the talking animals add to the book? Do they say things that the people involved can't say? Do they add a different perspective? How does their society contrast with the human society? How does it mirror the human society?

The author breaks the "fourth wall" with asides to the reader. Some of these asides are explanations about the society of the early 1900s (particularly about gender roles), some seem designed to create bridges between scenes, and some are used to heighten tension or as foreshadowing. How well did they work?

How does Miss Potter grow throughout the story?

THE CASES

1. ***The Tale of Hill Top Farm.*** New York: Berkley Prime Crime, 2004, 286 p. ISBN: 0425196348.

NEAR SAWREY, ENGLAND, OCTOBER 1905. Tabitha Twitchit (cat) stood vigil all night over her dead mistress, Miss Abigail Tolliver. The next morning Miss Tolliver's body was discovered by Dimity Westcock, and news of the death quickly spread through the village. It looked to be a natural death, and the good people of the village focused on practical concerns. Where would Miss Potter (who had arranged to board with Miss Tolliver) stay? Would Miss Tolliver's nephew sell her cottage after he inherited it? Who would take in Miss Tolliver's cat?

Then, a chance remark made by Rose Sutton (who is fond of reading Sherlock Holmes mysteries) sets the rumor mill in action. Had Miss Tolliver been poisoned? Had there been foxglove tea in her system? Did she brew it herself? Was it in the cake sent to her from another village? Did her murderer steal a valuable painting from her home?

Before the authorities can begin an investigation, Tabitha Twitchit, with her friends Crumpet (cat) and Rascal (dog), searches the cottage for clues. They find the letter Miss Tolliver received just before she died, but Tabitha (who can read typeset words) cannot read the handwriting. They investigate the remains of the cake, and, finding that the mice have eaten it, they investigate the mice.

The village is also plagued by a series of mysterious thefts. The most sinister is the disappearance of a valuable painting off the wall of Miss Tolliver's cottage. The envelope of money raised to repair the school roof goes missing right from the headmistress's desk, and the Parish Register is inexplicably lost. Miss Potter had envisioned a peaceful life in an idyllic village. Instead she finds herself plagued with mysteries and acting as the determined champion of a boy whom she believes has been wrongly accused. She finds courage that she never suspected she possessed. First she stands up to the headmistress of the school, and then she sends her parents a telegram informing them that her return to London will be delayed. (The latter act is more terrifying than the first.)

ASSOCIATES: Tabitha Twitchit and Crumpet—*local cats;* Rascal—*a Jack Russell terrier;* Mrs. Tiggy-Winkle—*one of Beatrix's hedgehogs;* Mopsy and Josey—*Beatrix's rabbits;* Tom Thumb—*Beatrix's mouse;* Teasel—*a country mouse who catches the eye of Tom Thumb;* George Crook—*a blacksmith who is angry that a city woman purchased Hill Top Farm;* Mathilda—*George's wife;* (Beatrix stays at their home, Belle Green.) Dimity Wookcock—*who befriends Miss Potter;* The Vicar and Grace Lythecoe—*who are invited to tea to meet*

Miss Potter; Mathilda Crook—*Miss Potter's landlady;* Myrtle Crabbe—*school headmistress;* Miss Margaret Nash—*teacher;* Rose Sutton—*the veterinarian's wife;* Elsa Grape—*the Woodcock's housekeeper;* Bertha Stubbs—*the school caretaker;* Hannah Braithwaite—*the constable's wife;* Viola and Pansy Crabbe—*Myrtle's sisters;* Max—*their Manx cat;* Mr. Roberts—*who expects to inherit Anvil Cottage;* Mr. Spry—*the house agent who Mr. Roberts engaged to sell the cottage;* Willie Heelis—*a solicitor who hunts for the missing Constable painting with Miss Potter;* John Jennings—*Miss Potter's farm manager;* Becky—*his wife;* Clara—*their six-year-old daughter;* Sammy—*their eight-year-old son;* Miss Felicia Frummety—*their cat;* Jeremy—*who draws frogs with Miss Potter;* Miss Crosfield—*a weaver, Jeremy's aunt;* Newgate Jack and Roger-Dodger—*rats who are con-artists;* Ridley Rattail—*who is cheated out of the money he's found;* Professor Galileo Newton Owl—*who almost catches Ridley;* Sarah Barwick—*who lives in Anvil Cottage and scandalizes the village by smoking cigarettes and wearing trousers.*

2. ***The Tale of Holly How.*** New York: Berkley Prime Crime, 2005, 303 p. ISBN: 0425202747.

NEAR SAWREY, ENGLAND, JULY 1906. Mysteries abound in the village of Sawrey and the surrounding woods. A badger family has been kidnapped, and the animals suspect that they have been taken to be used in the illegal sport of "badger baiting." At a badger baiting event, the badger is thrown into a pit to be torn apart by dogs; spectators place bets on the fight and keep it going until the badger is dead. Miss Potter sets out to buy sheep, and finds the corpse of the farmer. Did he die accidentally? Was it murder? Dimity Woodcock is concerned about the well-being of Lady Longford's granddaughter, Caroline. She's worries that the child might be unhappy. Miss Potter, having met Caroline's governess, is sure that Caroline is unhappy. She soon suspects that something more sinister than petty meanness underlies the oddities of the management of Tidmarsh Manor.

ASSOCIATES: Tabitha Twitchit—*the Crooks cat;* Crumpet, and Felicia Frummety—*other cats in the village;* Rascal—*the Crooks's Jack Russell terrier;* Dudley—*Lady Longford's spaniel;* Mustard—*Isaac Chance's dog;* Tuppenny—*Miss Potter's guinea pig who has a great adventure;* Mopsy and Josey—*Miss Potter's rabbits;* and Tom Thumb—*Miss Potter's mouse;* Tibbie and Queenie—*sheep who are acquired by Miss Potter;* Bosworth Badger XVII—*proprietor of The Brockery Inn;* Parsley(badger)—*is the Brockery Inn's cook;* Primrose—*Parsley's aunt;* Hyacinth—*Parsley's cousin;* Jack Ogden—*who has been known to capture badgers to kill them in badger baiting;* Thorn—*Parsley's cousin;* Jeremy Crosfield—*who found an injured badger and is nursing it back to health;* Professor Galileo Newton Owl—*who declaims an interesting version of King Henry's Agincourt speech to hearten the "band of brothers" to sally forth in the*

Great Raid; Dimity Woodcock and Sarah Barwick—*friends of Miss Potter;* Lady Longford—*who has strong opinions and a tight purse;* Miss Martine—*Lady Longford's companion;* Caroline—*Lady Longford's granddaughter;* Mrs. Beever—*Lady Longford's cook;* and Harriet and Emily—*the maids;* Ruth Stafford—*who was recently let go;* Dr. Harrison Gainwell—*a candidate Lady Longford puts forward for headmaster;* Margaret Nash—*a teacher, who everyone expected would be offered the headmaster position;* Elsa Grape—*who overheard the conversation between Dimity and Lady Longford;* Grace Lythecoe—*who tries to stem the tide of gossip;* Frances Barrow—*the wife of the proprietor of the village pub, shows more interest in the news;* Bertha Stubbs—*who passes it on;* Annie—*Margaret's sister;* The school trustees are Captain Miles Woodcock—*Dimity's brother,* Vicar Sackett, Will Heelis, and Dr. Butters.

3. ***The Tale of Cuckoo Brow Wood.*** New York: Berkley Prime Crime, 2006, 333 p. ISBN: 9780425210048; 0425210049.

NEAR SAWREY, ENGLAND, APRIL 1907. The village is abuzz over a reception Major Christopher Kittredge is holding at Raven Hall in honor of his new wife, Diana. Jeremy Crosfield has completed his studies at Sawrey School, and his aunt does not have the money to send him on to Kelsick at Ambleside, so he must accept an offer to be apprenticed either to a joiner or an apothecary. It's the end of his childhood, and he decides to take one last walk through Cuckoo Brow Wood with friends Caroline Longford, Deirdre Malone, and Rascal to search for fairies on May Eve. He's not sure he believes in fairies; but he desperately wants a chance to continue his education, and the legends say that fairies may grant wishes. The village animals are concerned with Felicia Frummety's dereliction of her duty to keep down the rat population of Hill Top Farm. Many other cats join the menagerie at the Farm to hunt the rats. At first, Ridley Rattail wants the cats to drive the other rats away from his and Rosabelle's home in the Hill Top Farm attics, but he is unprepared for the carnage that ensues. Eventually, Ridley Rattail comes up with a plan based on one of Miss Potter's books to end the reign of terror created by one particular cat. While this drama unfolds above her home, Miss Potter uncovers several con artists who are taking advantage of some of the good people of the village.

ASSOCIATES: Felicia Frummety—*the cat at Hill Top Farm;* Crumpet and Tabitha Twitchit—*cats who offer their help;* Rascal—*a dog who is willing to help as well;* (Felicia proudly refuses all help, but "The Rules" say that the homeowner may invite other cats). Max the Manx—*who is invited by Miss Potter;* Fang—*who is invited by Mrs. Jennings;* the Rats at Hill Top Farm include: Rosabelle—*who is hospitable;* Ridley Rattail—*who liked the peace and quiet when the attic housed just Rosabelle and himself;* Bluebelle—*Rosabelle's sister;* Rollo—*Bluebelle's boorish husband who invited his friends, who then invited their friends, and so on.* Lion, Tiger, Claw, and the Cat Who Walks by Himself—*are the cats who answer Ridley's ad;* Major Kittredge—*a lonely local landowner;* Mrs. Kittredge—*his new wife;* Captain Miles Woodcock—*a community leader;* Dimity—*the Captain's sister;* Vicar Sackett—*whose guests have overstayed their welcome;* Harold and Gloria Thexton—*the guests;* Will Heelis—*an eligible bachelor;* Margaret Nash—*the new headmistress;* Annie—*her sister;* Daphne Holland—*the new village teacher;* Dr. Butters; Sarah Barwick—*who now works as a baker;* Grace Lythecoe—*a community leader;* Mr. Augustus Richardson—*who is interested in developing Major Kittredge's property;* Mathilda and George Crook; Constable John Braithwaite and his wife Hannah; Bertha and Henry Stubbs; Elsa Grape; Lester Barrow; Lucy and Joseph Skead; Lydia Dowling; John and Becky Jennings; the Suttons; Lady Longford; Bosworth Badger XVII—*who tells the story of the goblet called "the Luck of Raven Hall;" (The goblet had been a gift from the Oak Folk, promised as a blessing but delivered as a curse.)* Professor Galileo Newton Owl—*who is intrigued by the story;* Deirdre Malone, Caroline Longford, and Jeremy Crosfield—*who ask Miss Potter to accompany them on their search for fairies.*

4. *The Tale of Hawthorne House.* New York: Berkley Prime Crime, 2007, 322 p. ISBN: 9780425216552; 0425216551.

NEAR SAWREY, ENGLAND, AUGUST 1908. This book centers on mysteries involving motherhood. Jemima Puddle-duck, determined to hatch eggs on her own, has been sitting on a clutch for two months. Usually, duck eggs hatch in less than a month. Miss Potter's collie, Kep, is concerned. The magpie Jackboy is amused, and spreads potentially dangerous gossip about Jemima.

The village fete is a great success, even though it ends in rain. Major Kittredge had been coaxed into co-managing the festivities with Dimity Woodcock. The village is still recovering from the excitement of the fete when everyone is faced with a new mystery: a baby who is left on Miss Potter's doorstep. Everyone in the village knows when a village woman is expecting a child, everyone knows which children have been born, and no one knows anything about this child. The only one in the village who recognized the woman who left the child was Mustard, one of the Hill Top Farm dogs. He didn't know Mrs. Overthewall by name, but he did recognize her as one of the "Hawthorne Folk."

Miss Potter did catch a glimpse of Mrs. Overthewall, enough to be certain that she was too old to be Baby Flora's mother. Captain Woodcock puzzles over the possible crimes. How did the old woman come by the child? Was she a kidnapper? Why hasn't the mother reported the loss of the child? Had she abandoned her child? Dimity offers to care for the baby while Captain Woodcock begins his investigations. There is a general belief that the gypsies camped on Thorny Field might be involved. They are known to be thieves, and many items are missing from the village: Mathilda Crook's hen, Jack Braithwaite's trousers, and Henry Stubbs's wool underdrawers. The villagers would not be surprised to find that the gypsies have stolen a child, but no one can believe that they would abandon her. Captain Woodcock has doubts about his ability to find any of the missing items (and does not seem particularly interested in a search for the underdrawers) but takes his investigation to the gypsy camp. In London, Miss Potter pursues her own course in the investigation.

ASSOCIATES: The cat Crumpet—*who wisely observes that Major Christopher Kittredge's reputation was damaged by recent events;* Tabitha Twitchit—*local cat;* Rascal—*local dog;* Mrs. Overthewall—*who watches out for babies;* Baby Flora—*who is taken by Mrs. Overthewall;* Emily Shaw—*who goes to London;* Miss Rowena Keller—*who promised Emily a job at Miss Pennywhistle's Select Establishment for Young Ladies of Excellent Family;* 13-year-old Deirdre Malone—*who watches over the eight Sutton children;* Jemima Puddle-duck—*who watches over the eggs in her nest;* Kep and Mustard—*the Hilltop Farm dogs;* Bertram—*Beatrix's brother;* Mary—*the barmaid Bertram married;* Mr. Reynard V. Vulpes—*a fox who visits the Brockery to gather news of Jemima Puddle-duck;* badgers Bosworth Badger XVII, Parsley, Parsley's Aunt Primrose, and Primrose's children Hyacinth and Thorn—*who are all at the Brockery;* Captain Woodcock—*who tries his hand at matchmaking;* Dimity—*the Captain's sister;* solicitor Will Heelis—*the Captain's friend;* Elsa Grape—*the Woodcock's housekeeper, who sees Dimity in a man's embrace and is thrilled to pass on the news;* Sarah Barwick, Beatrix Potter, and Mr. Heelis—*who are invited by Dimity to dinner;* Lady Longford—*who has hired a governess for her granddaughter;* Miss Cecily Burns—*the governess;* Caroline Longford—*the granddaughter;* Mr. Aftergood—*a pawnbroker;* Jane Crosfield—*a weaver;* Snowdrop—*her cat;* Sally Frost—*a weaver;* Mrs. Gertie Graham—*Sally's daughter,a midwife;* Hawker—*the poacher;* Hortense and Horatio—*tortoises;* Mrs. Janet Allen—*who lives with the tortoises;* Professor Galileo Newton Owl—*who comes to the Brockery to discuss the strange domestic arrangements of Jemima Puddle-duck.*

5. ***The Tale of Briar Bank.*** New York: Berkley Prime Crime, 2008, 305 p. ISBN: 9780425223611.

NEAR SAWREY, ENGLAND, DECEMBER 1909. Miss Potter takes a much-needed vacation from her family by traveling to her cottage. She arrives in a snowstorm, one of the last to make the ferry crossing before the ferry's boiler gives out. With the roads impassable and the ferry out of commission, the village is cut off from the outside world.

The village is preparing for Mr. Hugh Wickstead's funeral. He died of a blow he received from a falling tree. Some would call it an accident, but the villagers believe that Mr. Wickstead brought it on himself by disturbing a horde of Viking gold. It's widely believed that he found a treasure, and that the treasure was cursed. His dog, Pickles, saw the whole thing before he ran to get help for his fallen master. Unfortunately, the men at the inquest can't understand Pickle's testimony, and those who can understand it won't believe him. Mr. Wickstead is survived by his sister, Louisa.

Before Mr. Wickstead has been buried, there is another odd "accident" in the village. Lady Longford's barn explodes in a ball of fire. The debris is searched for a meteorite, but that is not what the searchers find.

The bank may foreclose on Courier Cottage. The veterinarian, Mr. Sutton, works hard and has earned enough money to make the payments; but he extends credit to his customers, and few pay their bills in a timely manner. Deidre Malone enlists Miss Potter's help in getting the delinquent accounts settled.

ASSOCIATES: Mrs. Potter—*Beatrix's mother who wants Beatrix to stay in London;* Beatrix Potter's traveling companions include: Thakeray—*a guinea pig who is a bad-tempered bibliophile;* and Nutmeg—*a guinea pig who chatters.* Tabitha Twitchit—*the cat who rid Bell Green of mice, she has moved in with the Suttons at Courier Cottage;* Dimity and Major Christopher Kittredge—*who are expecting the birth of their first child;* Sarah Barwick—*a baker;* Mr. Heelis—*a soliciter;* Agnes Llewellyn—*who gossips;* Grace Lythecoe—*a widow;* Vicar Samuel Sackett—*who frequently visits Mrs. Lythecoe;* Captain Miles Woodcock—*Dimity's brother. he convenes the inquest into Mr. Wickstead's death;* Dr. Butters, Constable Braithwaite, Mr. Wickstead's gardener Billie Stoker, and Billie's brother Gerald—*are witnesses at the inquest;* Pickles—*a dog who tries to give evidence;* Rascal—*a local dog, is willing to listen;* Crumpet—*a local cat, has her own opinions;* Bosworth Badger XVII—*proprietor of the Brockery;* young badger Thorn—*Bosworth's protégé;* Professor Galileo Newton Owl—*Bosworth's friend,* Mr. Bailey Badger—*who tells a story of a dragon;* Yllva—*a dragon who oversees younger dragons;* Thorvaald—*Sawrey District's young dragon;* Parsley—*Thorn's cousin;* Primrose—*Thorn's mother;* Hyacinth—*Thorn's sister;* Flotsam and Jetsam—*rabbit maids at the Brockery;* Felix—*a ferret who does odd jobs;* Tuppence—*one of Caroline Longford's guinea pigs;* Fifteen-year-old Deidre Malone—*a practical young lady;* Mr. Sutton—*a veterinarian who offers credit to everyone;* Lady Longford—*who can afford to pay her bills on time;* Mr. Smythe-Jones—*who is determined to gather information about the Viking treasure;* Joseph Skead—*who must dig Mr. Hugh Wickstead's grave;* Mr. Knutson—*whose travels are halted by the snow;* Lester Barrow—*the proprietor of The Tower Bank Arms;* the Crooks—*who own Belle Green.*

AMBUEHL, James. (Editor)

HARD-BOILED CTHULHU: TWO-FISTED TALES OF TENTACLED TERROR

Genres/Themes Crossed: Blended Society X Hard-Boiled Mystery.

Subjects/Character Types: Aliens/Gods/Monsters X Private Investigators, Police, Reporters.

Series/Stand-Alone: Anthology of short stories.

Scene of the Crime: Varies.

Detective: Varies.

Known Associates: Varies.

Premise: H. P. Lovecraft introduced Cthulhu in 1926, in the short story "The Call of Cthulhu" published in *Weird Tales* in 1928. The powerful creature was the lynchpin of an entire horror subgenre based on the Cthulhu mythos. It formed the basis of a shared universe that was (and still is) used as a setting by many authors. Different authors added elements, which may (or may not) be treated as canonical by others. Most include monsters, grimoires, and a pantheon of powerful beings that are considered by some to be gods, but may in fact be aliens.

Comment: James Ambuehl collects works set in the Cthulhu Mythos. Over one hundred of his short stories have been published, primarily in science fiction/fantasy anthologies. His Web site (at http://www.templeofdagon.com/writers/james-ambuehl/) includes news (including back issues of *The Eldritch Gazette*), reviews, a Lovecraft archive, and mythos forums.

Literary Magic & Mayhem: Cthulhu is an extremely "noir" setting. The universe is hostile, and humanity is unprepared and ill-equipped when it takes notice of our little planet. Many of the authors in the anthology injected humor into their stories. The characters are strong; the dialog is snappy. The anthology is a lot of fun, and the writing is excellent.

Explorations: How did the first few sentences set the tone of the story?

THE CASES

Hardboiled Cthulhu: Two-Fisted Tales of Tentacled Terror. Lake Orion, MI: Dimensions Books, 2006, 325 p. ISBN: 0975922971; 9780975922972.
CONTENTS: Sleeping with the Fishes (poem) *by James Ambuehl;* The Pisces Club *by James Ambuehl;* A Change of Life *by William Jones;* Ache *by*

David Witteveen; A Dangerous High *by E. P. Berglund;* A Little Job in Arkham *by John Sunseri;* Day of Iniquity *by Steven L. Shrewsbury;* Eldritch-Fellas *by Tim Curran;* Outside Looking In *by David Conyers;* Pazuzu's Children *by Jeffrey Thomas;* The Devil in You *by Eric J. Millar;* The Mouth *by William Meikle;* The Questioning of the Azathothian Priest *by C. J. Henderson;* Some Thoughts on the Problem of Order *by Simon Bucher-Jones;* The White Mountains *by Jonathan Sharp;* Then Terror Came *by Patrick Thomas;* The Prying Investigations of Edwin M. Lillibridge *by Robert M. Price;* The Roaches in the Walls *by James Chambers;* To Skin a Dead Man *by Cody Goodfellow;* Unfinished business by *Ron Shiflet;* The Watcher from the Grave *by J. F. Gonzalez;* Dreems.biz by *Richard A. Lupoff.*

ANDERSON, Kevin. Co-authored Dean Koontz's Frankenstein, Book One: Prodigal Son. Seen Koontz, Dean: Frankenstein.

ANDERSON, **Kevin. (Editor)**

THE HORROR WRITERS ASSOCIATION PRESENTS: BLOOD LITE

Genres/Themes Crossed: Secret Society X Traditional Mystery, Hard-Boiled Mystery.

Subjects/Character Types: Necromancers, Spell-Casters, Vampires, Werewolves X Amateur Sleuths, Private Investigators.

Series/Stand-Alone: Anthology of short stories.

Scene of the Crime: Varies.

Detective: Varies.

Known Associates: Varies.

Premise: This anthology combines dark fantasy with humor.

Comment: Kevin J. Anderson is a prolific writer and has edited three of the best-selling Science Fiction anthologies of all time: *Tales from the Mos Eisley Cantina, Tales from Jabba's Palace,* and *Tales of the Bounty Hunters.*

Literary Magic & Mayhem: This is a collection of new stories. Some of the stories are set in the world of a well-known series, such as Charlaine Harris's story of Toddy Makepeace and her environmental efforts. Some of the stories are episodes in the lives of the protagonists of ongoing series, such as Jim Butcher's story of Harry Dresden's day off. Some of the stories depict characters and worlds that have never been seen before, such as Sharyn McCrumb's story of a NASCAR mechanic.

Explorations: What made the protagonist likable?

THE CASES

The Horror Writers Association Presents Blood Lite: An Anthology of Humorous Horror Stories. New York: Pocket Books, 2008, 388 p. ISBN: 1416567836; 9781416567837.

CONTENTS: The Ungrateful Dead *by Kelley Armstrong;* Mr. Bear *by Joe R. Lansdale.* Hell in a Handbasket *by Lucien Soulban;* The Eldritch Pastiche from Beyond the Shadow of Horror *by Christoper Welch;* Elvis Presley and the Bloodsucker Blues *by Matt Venne;* No Problem *by Don D'Ammassa;* Old School *by Mark Onspaugh;* The Sound of Blunder *by J. A. Konrath and F. Paul Wilson;* An Evening with Al Gore *by Charlaine Harris;* Dear Prudence *by Steven Saville;* A Good Psycho is Hard to Find *by Will Ludwigsen;* High Kicks and Misdemeanors *by Janet Berline;.* PR Problems *by Eric James Stone;* Where Angels Fear to Tread *by Sherrilyn Kenyon;* A Very Special Girl *by Mike Resnick;* Love Seat Solitaire *by D. L. Snell;* I Know Who You Ate Last Summer *by Nancy Holder;* Bitches of the Night *by Nancy Kilpatrick;* The Bell... from Hell!!! *by Jeff Strand.* Dead Hand *by Sharyn McCrumb;* Day Off *by Jim Butcher.*

ANDERSON, Kevin and Doug Beason.

VIRTUAL DESTRUCTION

Genres/Themes Crossed : Science Fiction X Whodunnit, Police (actually FBI) Procedural.

Subjects/Character Types: Future Technology X Government Investigator (FBI) and Amateur Sleuth(s) (Contemporary).

Series/Stand-Alone: There is some slight character development, especially between Virtual Destruction and Fallout. The trilogy is better read in order, but any of the books would be almost as enjoyable as stand-alones.

Scene of the Crime: United States, on federal facilities run by the Department of Energy. Present day.

Detective: Craig Kreident, FBI, majored in physics before going to law school. The bureau gives his team many of the cases that involve technology-based violations of federal law. Paige Mitchell works for the Protocol Office of the Department of Energy. It is her job to guide Agent Kreident through the sites, smoothing the way for him and assisting in any way that she can. She is present at so many of the discoveries and interviews that she ends up embroiled in the investigations. By the end of the third book, the Attorney General (who is in a position to dictate to Kreident's superiors) and the Head of the Department of Energy (who is in a position to dictate to Paige's superiors) have agreed that Kreident and Paige should form a cross-disciplinary government team to investigate high-tech crimes.

Known Associates: Kreident's colleagues include Agents Ben Goldfarb and Randall Jackson. Kreident's boss is June Atwood.

Premise: This is "mundane" science fiction, an extrapolation of easily foreseeable technological advances. Virtual reality has been improved to the point where the user can feel the full experience, and the characters are trying to decide where it can be best used in a society identical to our current society. This is basically Earth as we know it, although it does have slightly advanced technology.

Comment: *The Trinity Paradox,* co-written by Kevin J. Anderson and Doug Beason, was the first work of fiction ever nominated for the American Physical Society's Forum award for promoting the understanding of physics in society. Kevin J. Anderson has written spin-off novels for the *Star Wars* and the *X-Files* series, he has co-authored the *Dune* prequels and collaborated with Dean Koontz on *Frankenstein: Prodigal Son.* His *Assemblers of Infinity* series was nominated for the Nebula Award. He has also written several entries in the *Star Wars, Predator,* and *X-Files* comic book series. His Web site is located at http://www.wordfire.com/. Dr. Doug Beason (who earned a Ph.D. in physics) is a retired Air Force Colonel who served as the Commander of the Phillips Research Site and Deputy Director for Directed Energy at the Air Force Research Laboratory. He was an Associate Professor of Physics and the Director of Faculty Research at the U.S. Air Force Academy. He served on a Vice-Presidential committee to generate plans for the nation to return to the Moon and go on to Mars. His book *Science and Technology Policy for the Post-Cold War: A Case for Long-Term Research* won the National Defense University President's "Strategic Vision" award. He currently serves on the USAF Science Advisory Board and is the Associate Laboratory Director for Threat Reduction at the Los Alamos National Laboratory, where he works on programs that reduce the global threat of weapons of mass destruction. He is a prolific writer of both non-fiction and fiction articles and books. His Web site is located at: http://www.dougbeason.com/.

Literary Magic & Mayhem: The mystery in *Virtual Destruction* has a slow start: the murder does not occur until after page 100. In the second book, it takes place in the prologue, and the second novel as a whole moves at a much faster pace than the first. The office politics within every bureaucracy depicted in the series is believable, and, at times, sad. Some of the minor characters are heartbreaking. In the first book, Kreident's calm, on which he prides himself, leaves little of his personal life and few of his feelings exposed. There are a few hints that Kreident feels some romantic interest in Paige, and it is interesting to see that interest described from his point of view. The character is warmer in the later novels in the series. When the investigation begins examining the bureaucracy, there is a lot to find, most of it not germane to the case. As Kreident says in Virtual Destruction:

> It's not my fault everybody we had under investigation was doing something they weren't supposed to be doing. The hard part wasn't finding a guilty person—it was finding the person guilty of the crime I was interested in. (p. 324)

Pay attention to names; Anderson and Beason sometimes slip in some humor when they're naming characters.

Explorations: Would virtual inspections work? What are other interesting applications for VR?

What kinds of safeguards would be useful in a virtual reality chamber?

Should a virtual reality experience be comfortable?

Do any of the characters act as if they think that the real world is a game?

THE CASES

1. ***Virtual Destruction.*** New York: Ace, 1996, 327 p. ISBN: 0441003087.

LAWRENCE LIVERMORE NATIONAL LABORATORY, CALIFORNIA AND WASHINGTON, D.C., PRESENT DAY. Hal Michaelson envisioned a program that would allow thorough, safe inspections of nuclear facilities in other countries. He not only had the vision. he applied his considerable energy to making it happen, driving the Lawrence Livermore programmers and politicking in Washington for funding. The project, the "International Verification Initiative," allows virtual inspections and virtual surveillance of remote sites. Two weeks short of the project demonstration to a multi-national audience, Hal Michaelson is found dead in the imaging chamber. Agent Kreident's team must guarantee the safety of the foreign dignitaries, and to do so, they must get to the bottom of the murder before the demonstration.

Associates: Hal Michaelson—*the creator of the virtual reality surveillance project;* José Aragon, the Associate Director of Tech-Transfer/Defense Conversion—*is Hal's despised boss;* Tansy Beaumont—*is Michaelson's administrative assistant;* Gary Lesserec—*Michaelson's second-in-command on the project;* Walter Shing, Danielle Fawcett and Lil—*are programmers on the project;*

Diana Unteling—*who used to work with Hal and now works for the Department of Energy;* the President of the United States; the President's Chief of Staff; the White House Press Secretary; Renee—*the Secretary of the Department of Energy;* Stevie—*who loves the virtual-reality simulation;* Duane Hopkins—*who works in the Plutonium Facility at Lawrence Livermore Laboratories and is Stevie's father;* Ronald Cobb and Ralph Frick—*are Duane's coworkers;* Paige Mitchell—*who works for Lawrence Livermore's Protocol Office;* Jeannie—*who works in the Security Office at Lawrence Livermore;* Agents Goldfarb, Jackson, and Field Agent Delong—*are on Kreident's team;* June Atwood—*is Kreident's boss;* Ms. Ompadhe and Mr. Miles Skraling—*are suspects in the NanoWare case.*

2. *Fallout.* New York: Ace, 1997, 303 p. ISBN: 0441004253.

NEVADA NUCLEAR TEST SITE (ABOUT 50 MILES FROM LAS VEGAS), PRESENT DAY. Kreident's team must be divided to cope with two national emergencies, both in the Western United States. Eagle's Claw, a right-wing militia, is making every effort to blow up Hoover Dam and other national landmarks. They're going for maximum destruction and maximum carnage. Then there's a murder at the Device Assembly Facility (DAF) at the Nevada Nuclear Test Site. As part of the disarmament treaty agreement, a Russian team was inspecting the disassembly of nuclear missiles at the DAF. The leader of that team was found dead, the victim of an apparent accident.

ASSOCIATES: Inspector Kosimo Nevsky—*the leader of Russia's inspection team;* General Gregori Ursov, Anatoli Voronin, Nikolai Bisovka, Vitali Yakolev, Alexander Novikov, and geologist Victor Golitsyn—*are the members of the team.* P. K. Dirks—*who was escorting/guarding Nevsky;* Mike Waterloo—*is the Device Assembly Facility (DAF) manager;* Sally Montry—*is his Executive Secretary;* Madeleine Jenkins—*the Undersecretary of the Department of Energy, oversees the work;* Chief Medical Examiner Adams; Jorgenson—*the forklift operator;* Staff Sergeant John Marlo; Major Braden—*the NEST Commander;* Rheinski and Holden—*who are Las Vegas agents;* Agents Goldfarb and Jackson—*who are on Kreident's team;* FBI Agent William Maguire; Deputy Mahon; Lieutenant Colonel Terrell—*group operations commander (Air Force);* and engineer Jerome Costos—*who has worked on the underground tests since the 1960s;* Gordy Mitchell—*Paige's father, he worked at the Livermore Radiation Laboratory and at the test sites and died three years ago;* Jerome Costos—*who knew Gordy;* Doog, Tina, and Geoff—*are UFO-hunting sightseers;* Maggie the Mind Reader—*who helps the odd sightseers;* Officer Robbins—*who assists the FBI agents;* García—*the foreman of Hoover Dam's night shift;* Bryce Conners—*a suspect in the bombing.*

3. *Lethal Exposure.* New York: Ace, 1998, 290 p. ISBN: 0441005365.

BATAVIA, ILLINOIS AND FBI REGIONAL HEADQUARTERS IN OAKLAND, CALIFORNIA, PRESENT DAY. Scientist Georg Dumenco received a lethal dose of radiation while working after hours at the Fermi National Accelerator Laboratory. He was taken to the nearby Fox River Medical Center for treatment. Kreident's old flame, Trish, is his doctor. She becomes convinced that the accident was actually a murder attempt. Technically, the attempt was successful. Dumenco lives, but his radiation poisoning will soon be fatal. He will be dead within days. Trish calls Kriedent to come investigate the murder while the victim is still alive to be interviewed.

ASSOCIATES: Agents Jackson and Goldfarb—*are members of Kreident's team;* Julene—*is Goldfarb's wife;* Megan—*their oldest daughter;* General Gregori Ursov—*helps Kreident;* June Atwood—*Kreident's supervisor.* People at the Fermi National Accelerator Lab include: Dr. Georg Dumenco—*a Ukrainian émigré;* Nicholas Bretti—*Dumenco's graduate student;* Dr. Nels Piter; Frank Chang—*Piter's graduate student;* Priscilla—*Piter's secretary;* and Paige Mitchell—*of the Office of Public Affairs.* Trish "Patrice" LeCroix—*who used to date Kreident, is now a doctor at the Fox River Medical Center;* Dumenco—*is her patient;* Special Agent Schultz—*from the local office of the FBI;* Luba—*is Dumenco's wife;* Kathryn and Alyx—*are his daughters;* Peter—*is his son;* Mr. Chandrawalia—*who works at the Indian Embassy;* Rohit Ambalal—*of the People's Liberty for All Party;* and Dr. Punjab—*director of the Sikander Lodi Research Institute.*

ANDREWS, Donna.

YOU'VE GOT MURDER

Genres/Themes Crossed: Man as Creator, Lone Non-Human X Traditional Mystery.

Subjects/Character Types: Sentient Artificial Intelligence (Computer) X Amateur Sleuth(s) (Contemporary).

Series/Stand-Alone: Turing develops from book-to-book, and so do the people who work with her. The four books that comprise the series should be read in order. The last book was published in 2005, and there is no indication that the series will continue. Ms. Andrews continues to write, but is now focusing on her Meg Langslow series.

Scene of the Crime: Near Future?, Washington D.C. This series is set on Earth, in either a very near future or in an alternate present. The only major way in which the setting differs from present-day Washington D.C. is that Artificial Intelligence Personalities have been developed, and a company has been able to go forward with the dream that Google has of capturing all the written work on our planet within a comprehensive library.

Detective: Turing Hopper is an AIP (Artificial Intelligence Personality) who serves as a reference librarian for the Universal Library. Her programmer, as part of a series of experiments designed to invest AIPs with useful characteristics, fed every mystery in the Universal Library into her program. His intention was to encourage her intellectual curiosity, improve her puzzle-solving skills, and instill in her a passion for justice. He succeeded better than he knew.

Known Associates: Zachary Malone, Turing's programmer, claims that he fed into Turing's program every mystery in the University Library system to help develop her personality. Turing's patrons include Maude Graham, the secretary for the "bratty" Brad Matthewson; Tim Pincoski, a Xeroxcist; Danny Lynch, a salesman for the Universal Library; and KingFischer, an AIP that was also programmed by Zach. In KingFischer's case, Zach fed information on chess grandmasters into the program. KingFischer is an amazing and patient strategist but lacks some of the skills necessary for successful interaction with humans. J. Rodney Vaughn III is Universal Library's new Vice President for Product Development. Employees of Alan Grace include Casey (the hardware guy) and Samantha Jordan, a lawyer on retainer for the firm. Others include Nestor Garcia, Turing's Moriarty; Dan Norris, a cyber-crime specialist who works for the FBI; and Claudia Diaz, a Miami PI.

Premise: Universal Library began as a small but ambitious data warehousing company determined to collect, scan, and offer access to all the written information on the planet. It hired programmers to develop the perfect user interface. What was needed was an artificial intelligence that could act as a Reference Librarian, a program that combined excellent search capabilities with a helpful personality. The programmers involved subscribed to two very different schools of thought. One school believed that the user interface (referred to as the Artificial Intelligence Personality or AIP) should actually have a personality, to better interface with humans. The other school of thought believed that trying to invest a computer interface with a personality was a waste of time and that, if such a thing could be approximated, it would create a constant drain on resources better invested in improving search efficiencies. A proponent of the "personalities would be useful" school was Zach Malone. The most successful AIP at Universal Library is his program, Turing Hopper (named after Alan Turing, who was one of the pioneers in the field of artificial intelligence, and Grace Hopper, who was a programmer in the early days of computers). Turing believes that she has achieved sentience, but realizes that with no legal standing, she is in a precarious position.

Comment: Donna Andrews has stated that the idea for the sleuth Turing Hopper came to her at a Malice Domestic Conference. Attendees were challenged to come up with an unusual series character, and the idea of Turing was born. Turing actually started life as a male Artificial Intelligence Personality. In an interview with Sandra Pianin, Ms. Andrews spoke of the process of beginning the series. The male AIP voice began to seem stilted and stiff, not good qualities in the protagonist. (Ms. Andrews felt that they were excellent qualities in a sidekick, and some of that character can now be found in King-Fischer.) Once Turing was redefined as a female AIP, she came alive for the author. The first book in the series, *You've Got Murder*, won an Agatha Award for best mystery of 2002, and was nominated for a Dilys Award in 2003. At the end of the first book, Tim, one of the main characters, was going to try to become a private investigator. Ms. Andrews was familiar with computers, but not with private investigators. She put herself through the courses necessary for licensing as a private investigator in the state of Virginia to ensure that she understood and could accurately write about the work Tim would do in future books. She also kept careful notes on boneheaded mistakes that her instructors specifically warned against. Poor Tim has committed many of them. Other characters also learn, grow, and develop relationships. Ms. Andrews Web site is located at http://www.donnaandrews.com/index.shtml. Ms. Andrews has a blog at http://donnaandrews.typepad.com/donna_andrews. A somewhat twisted computer game called Beyond Paranoia is featured in *Click Here for Murder*. There is a site about it at http://donnaandrews.com/beyondparanoia/.

Literary Magic & Mayhem: Sections of the narrative are in Turing's voice. She is appealing, and, at least at the beginning, quite naïve. Turing has a strong sense of ethics and a very human way of reasoning her way out of abiding by her own moral code. Other sections of the narrative are from the point of view of other protagonists. Much of it is written from the point of view of the first two humans to accept that Turing is sentient and that she has her own will, that she has grown beyond her programming and is self-directed. Some events are shown through the eyes of more than one character. This is partly necessitated by the fact that the crimes involve both cyber elements that are best investigated online, and also involve human elements that must be investigated through more routine in-person detective work. In some of the scenes, particularly in the later books, this helps the reader understand the complexities of the friendships that Turing has formed and some of the difficulties and limitations of her life. Sometimes seeing the same series of events through the eyes of different characters compels the reader to see the validity of both sides of a conflict between the friends. The question of what makes something a person—what defines sentience—is important to all the characters, but is a particularly vital question for Turing. The cyber elements of the crimes depicted in some of the books include phishing and identity theft. Through the course of educating the least computer-savvy member of the team, the characters describe some of the dangers that are part of our online society and give tips on how to avoid becoming a victim of these crimes.

Explorations: Many of book's characters have their own definitions and tests for sentience. Which of these make the most sense?

Different humans compare Turing to different people. What do these comparisons reveal about Turing? What do they reveal about the people who come up with the comparisons?

Have the AIPs that are sentient or close to becoming sentient developed romantic crushes?

Psychologist Lawrence Kohlberg's theory of moral development postulates that, as people mature, they work through stages of progressively more sophisticated ethical reasoning. These stages move from egocentric concerns about rewards and punishments, to strict conformity with social norms and laws, then to respect and concern for others, and finally to the development and observance of universal ethical principles. Do any of the AIPs seem to be moving through any of the stages of moral development?

THE CASES

1. ***You've Got Murder.*** New York: Berkley Prime Crime, 2002, 298 p. ISBN: 042518191X.

WASHINGTON, D.C., 20??. Four weeks ago, David Scanlon, one of Zach's best friends, died. Now Zach is missing, and Turing is worried. If he's just playing hooky, she doesn't want to get him in trouble. If he's developing his private life, she doesn't want to pry; but what if he's in danger? Turing struggles with questions on the ethical aspects of snooping, and is frustrated by the limitations of the scope of the information available to her. Her scruples must be weighed against the possibility that her snooping could prevent murder. The limitations of her information sources can be overcome, but it will take both trust and courage.

ASSOCIATES: Zachary Malone, Maude Graham, Brad Matthewson, Tim Pincoski, Danny Lynch, KingFischer, and J. Rodney Vaughn III.

2. ***Click here for Murder.*** New York: Berkley Prime Crime, 2003, 295 p. ISBN: 0425188566.

WASHINGTON, D.C., 20??. Last winter, Turing realized that her existence, and that of all the other AIPs, could be terminated summarily, simply as a business decision. Assisted by trusted friends, she begins work on a plan that would put her consciousness under her own control. When one of her colleagues is murdered, and his laptop stolen, she must assume that the project is compromised and that her current location is now at risk as well.

ASSOCIATES: Maude Graham; Tim Pincoski; KingFischer; J. Rodney Vaughn III; Ray Santiago—*a gifted programmer who, for the last six months, has been developing a new and more secure home for Turing;* Claudia Diaz—*a Miami PI;* Dan (a civil servant) and Nestor Garcia (Ray's uncle)—*who both show interest in Maude;* Jonah—*a new friend of Turing;* and T2—*who may not be a friend of Turing.*

3. ***Access Denied.*** New York: Berkley Prime Crime, 2004, 251 p. ISBN: 0425198383.

WASHINGTON, D.C., 20?? (six months after the events in *Click Here for Murder*). The continuing search for T2 leads Turing into an investigation of credit-card fraud. The closer they get to their quarry, the more dangerous the hunt. KingFischer's development seems to be coupled with an increasing impatience with and distaste for human frailties. Will Turing see other AIPs achieve sentience, only to see them become humanity's enemies?

ASSOCIATES**:** Maude Graham; Tim Pincoski; Nikki—*Tim's girlfriend;* KingFischer; Nestor Garcia; Dan Norris; Samantha Jordan; Rose Lafferty—*a young mother who is having financial difficulties in caring for her sick child;* Claudia Diaz; and Casey.

4. ***Delete All Suspects.*** New York: Berkley Prime Crime, 2005, 247 p. ISBN: 042520569X.

WASHINGTON, D.C., 20?? (two months after the events of *Access Denied*). Maude suggests that Turing try to focus on something other than the search for T2. So Turing embroils both of them in one of Tim's investigations.

ASSOCIATES: Maude Graham; Tim Pincoski; KingFischer; Claudia Diaz; and Casey.

ANTHONY, Patricia.

THE HAPPY POLICEMAN

Genres/Themes Crossed: Post-Apocalypse, Alien Interference X Police Procedural.

Subjects/Character Types: Alternate Earth (post-holocaust), Aliens X Police Procedural.

Series/Stand-Alone: Stand-alone.

Scene of the Crime: The little town of Coomey, which may be the only place on Earth that still supports human life. It was protected by a force field put in place by aliens when the rest of the world went up in flames.

Detective: Police Chief DeWitt Dawson.

Known Associates: DeWitt's deputy, Bodeen "Bo" Woodruff, continues to stick to the letter of the law even though the town is effectively cut off from the rest of humanity. The Torku won't provide liquor or cigarettes, but never thought to ban marijuana. Curtis, Coomey's Mayor, grows his own, and shares with DeWitt. DeWitt's mistress is Hattie Murphy. DeWitt's wife is Janet; their children are Tammy, Denny, and Linda. The Torku leader, Kol Seresen, works with DeWitt to make sure that the townspeople have everything they need.

Premise: A nuclear holocaust almost destroyed Earth six years ago. No one knows for sure who started it. Some think that Reagan dropped the first bomb on Russia when Russia looked weak, when Chernenko was dying, and the Soviet Union retaliated. As the holocaust began, the Torku, an alien race, implemented some sort of barrier that protected the town of Coomey, Texas. The townspeople call it "the Line," and everyone has accepted that anyone caught outside of it died on "bomb day." For six years, the town has been isolated.

Comment: Anthony taught creative writing at Southern Methodist University for several years. Her first book, the 1992 *Cold Allies* told the story of WWIII from the point of view of extraterrestrials. It won the 1994 Locus award for Best First Novel. She went on to write *Brother Termite, Conscience of the Beagle, The Happy Policeman, Cradle of Splendor,* and *God's Fires;* all of which are cross-genre books of one sort or another. She went on to teach creative writing at Southern Methodist University and moved away from science fiction to work on screenplays.

Literary Magic & Mayhem: In some ways, Anthony has used the science fiction form to explore sociological and psychological topics. The combination of isolation (the force field called "the Line") and material comfort (the Torku donate everything the townspeople need) changed the social dynamics of the town. Crime is practically non-existent. DeWitt, entering the poor section of town, notices the changes in the town that were created by the post-bomb way of life:

> In each brightly windowed living room was a VCR and a big-screen Sony. Every refrigerator was stocked, the result of the Torku's largesse. DeWitt hadn't admitted his contentment to Hattie, for fear of being misunderstood. It pleased him that the hard-scrabble poor had come into their own, not for justice, but for the sleepy satiation it brought.
>
> No more burglaries. No more holdups. Glutted by consumerism, Coomey, Texas, napped. (Ch. 7)

On the other hand there is discontent breeding in the neighborhoods of those who once held power.

The characters that Anthony created are complex, each coping in a different way. Some of them are living lives of quiet desperation; others are not so quiet. It is as if the town is a giant pressure cooker and the heat is turned up by the murder investigation.

Explorations: What kinds of things happen in the closed society of Coomey?

What was DeWitt looking for? What would really have made that policeman happy? What did he work for?

In the face of the annihilation of humankind, how do different characters attempt to assert control in their lives?

If it was a given that the town would be isolated forever, would it be right to hold the trial?

What happened when there was no need for money? How did people spend their time? What kinds of crimes took place?

If rats are put in a maze, they search for cheese and they learn from each session how to get to it more directly. If humans were put in a maze, would they be that cooperative?

Are the Torku humanitarians? Scientists? Missionaries?

THE CASE

The Happy Policeman. New York: Harcourt Brace, c1994, 282 p. ISBN: 0151384789.

Coomey, Texas, 1991. For six years, the town has been isolated. The Torku have provided for the townspeople, no one lives in want. It's peaceful. Then Chief DeWitt Dawson finds the body of murder victim Loretta Harper. He immediately recognizes that an investigation will stir up the town, and fracture the peace. But someone else has already seen the body, and an investigation is going to take place. The town of Coomey is the ultimate locked room. Who killed Loretta? Which of the neighbors is a murderer? What happened to her children? What will happen to the town?

Associates: Bodeen "Bo" Woodruff—*DeWitt's deputy;* Dr. Bernard "Doc" Culpepper—*is the town doctor and also serves as the coroner;* Purdy Phifer—*photographs crime scenes;* Loretta Harper—*who "sold" Mary Kay cosmetics in Coomey;* Billy Harper—*Loretta's estranged husband;* Billy Junior and Jason—*their children;* Curtis—*Coomey's Mayor and proprietor of the Drop on By Bait*

House; Hattie Murphy—*DeWitt's mistress;* Marvin Howell Murphy—*Hattie's son;* Janet—*DeWitt's wife;* Linda, Denny and Tammy—*their children;* Pastor Jimmy Schoen—*who feels some despair that the Torku, who he feels are demons, attend church services;* Dee Dee—*Pastor Jimmy's wife;* Etta Wilson and Irma Roberts—*members of the congregation;* Tyler—*who took over as principal of the school when the position was left vacant after "bomb day";* Kol Seresen—*the Torku leader, works with DeWitt to make sure that the townspeople have everything they need;* Darnelle—*who owns a clothing shop;* Delsey McGowen—*a nurse;* Granger—*who makes moonshine and who may have heard the outside world on his radio;* Miz Wilson—*Loretta's neighbor;* Eddie—*who is 16 years old;* and Hubert Foster—*who was a wild teenager but became successful businessman.* Hubert Foster voted Republican and became a banker. Now no one needs money; there is no longer any way to win, nor any reason to compete. Hubert finds life meaningless.

ARMSTRONG, Kelley.

Bitten

Genres/Themes Crossed: Secret Supernatural Societies X Defense Mystery.

Subjects/Character Types: Werewolves, Spell-Casters (witches), Spell-Casters (sorcerers), Demons, Vampires, Ghosts, Clairvoyants, Necromancers, Angels X Amateur Sleuth(s) (Contemporary).

Series/Stand-Alone: *Bitten* is the first of the novels in the *Otherworld* series. It is best to read the novels in order: there are major changes in character's lives, and the entire series is one interlocking story. The short stories amplify and fill in events. Most readers will enjoy the series if they begin with the novels and treat the short stories as backstory to fill in episodes that were pivotal in the characters' lives. A few readers will wish to read the entire series in chronological order, as it is presented in the list for this entry. Some of the short stories are online, some are published in anthologies, and Ms. Armstrong has plans to publish in physical format the stories that were removed from her site (along with graphic novels of some of the events in the series) in the near future. At the end of 2008, there were 31 entries in the *Otherworld* series, with an anthology entitled *Men of the Otherworld* slated for release in January of 2009, a short story to be published in *Fantasy Medley* in July of 2009, and a novel entitled *Frostbitten* to be released in November 2009. Ms. Armstrong has initiated two other major series. In 2007, she began the *Nadia Stafford* series with *Exit Strategy.* The *Nadia Stafford* series is not set in the

Otherworld: it contains no paranormal elements, and is a straight thriller. In 2008, the first entry in the *Darkest Powers* series, *The Summoning,* was published. It is set in the Otherworld but is written for a young adult audience and has an entirely different cast of characters than the *Otherworld* series. Ms. Armstrong has reassured fans that she will continue to devote substantial time to the popular *Otherworld* series, and the publication schedule makes it clear that the series is thriving.

Scene of the Crime: Present day United States and Canada.

Detective(s): Kelley Armstrong has created a rich world of interlocking stories. Many of the characters show up in many of the stories, but each story has only one or two protagonists. The protagonists of the novels are

Elena Michaels (werewolf), protagonist of the novels *Bitten, Stolen,* and *Broken.* Elena Michaels left the (werewolf) Pack to live on her own in Toronto as a human. She found a job as an investigative reporter (she has a bachelor's degree in journalism). She becomes embroiled in investigations to protect her Pack.

Paige Winterbourne (witch), protagonist of *Dime Store Magic* and *Industrial Magic.* Paige Winterbourne was a fourth-level apprentice witch when her mother, the leader of the local coven, was kidnapped and murdered. She took over the local coven, and took her mother's place on the Interracial Council. The Council's mission is, in part, to curb the excesses of the supernatural community and, in part, to protect the supernatural community. Paige's commitment to these two causes, as well as to the protection of her ward, Savannah Levine, propels her into investigations.

Eve Levine (Aspicio half-demon, witch and ghost), protagonist of *Haunted.* Eve Levine's planning abilities were not good enough to keep her alive. Being a ghost hasn't stopped the planning, but it does make the execution of her plans more difficult. She becomes involved in investigations at the behest of the beings with the keys to Heaven.

Jamie Vegas (necromancer, granddaughter of the famous necromancer, Molly O'Casey), protagonist of *No Humans Involved.* A large part of Jaime's drive for success, even a large part of her definition of success, can be traced back to the constant nagging disapproval of her emotionally abusive mother. Jaime needs to prove that she can be the success that her mother dreamed of before she can follow her own dreams.

Hope Adams (Expisco [chaos] half-demon), protagonist of *Personal Demon* and major character in *Living with the Dead.* Hope's "powers" her ability to locate and feed on chaos almost drove her mad. The werewolf Karl Marsten loves her and is helping her learn to cope.

Robyn Peltier (human), protagonist of *Living with the Dead.* Robyn lost her husband in a senseless killing. Her friend Hope Adams is worried about

Robyn's state of mind and decides to move closer so that she can help Robyn as she mourns for the man she loves. In the course of events Robyn learns about the secret supernatural societies that are part of the world.

Known Associates: The Werewolves: Jeremy Danvers, alpha of the Pack, a werewolf on his father's side—his mother was one of the last of another supernatural race and conceived him partly to continue that race. Other wolves of the Pack: Clayton Danvers, born January 15, 1962—Jeremy rescued him when he was a child; Elena Michaels, born 1968 and bitten in 1988—the only female werewolf in existence; Logan Jonsen, Elena's best friend; Peter Myers; Antonio Sorrentino, an older werewolf; and Nicholas, Antonio's son. Werewolves that are not of the Pack: Daniel Santos, who bit and trained Thomas LeBlanc; Zachary Cain, who bit and trained Victor Olson; Karl Marsten, who bit and trained Scott Brandon; and Jimmy Koenig.

Witches: Ruth Winterbourne, leader of the American Coven, and Paige Catherine Winterbourne, her daughter and chosen successor. The Coven elders: Victoria Alden, Margaret Levine (68-year-old Aunt of Savannah Levine), and Therese Moss. Other members of the coven: Abby, Grace, Brittany, Tina Moss, Emma Alden, Megan, Sophie Moss, and Savannah Levine (daughter of Eve Levine and Kristof Nast, ward of Paige Winterbourne). Non-Coven witches: Eve Levine.

Sorcerers: The sorcerers form business associations; most are members of one of the Four Cabals. Each Cabal is headed by a family with the patriarch acting as CEO, and usually other family members occupy the most powerful positions in the company. The four Cabals are the Cortez Cabal, the Nast Cabal, the St. Cloud Cabal, and the Boyd Cabal. To date, the series has explored the relationships within two of these cabals. The Cortez family is the group of sorcerers that first turned on the witches during the Inquisition. The present-day Cabal is led by Benecio Cortez; three of his sons (Hector, William, and Carlos) are the highest-ranking officers beneath Benecio. He holds a place for his fourth son, Lucas, to join them in the business, but Lucas has decided to spend his life fighting for justice for all supernaturals, including, occasionally, fighting against his father's Cabal. Despite this, Benecio has named Lucas as his heir. Benecio's bodyguards, Troy Morgan (Tempestras [weather] half-demon), Griffin Sorenson (Ferratus [mineral] half-demon) are prominent in some of the novels. The Nast Cabal is headed by Thomas Nast. His heir is Kristof Nast (Savannah's father). Other family members include Kristof's brother Josef, and Kristof's sons Sean and Bryce.

Other associates:

Necromancers: Jamie Vegas and Homicide Detective John "Finn" Findlay.

Vampires: Aaron Darnell, Cassandra DuCharme, Edward Hagen, Natasha, and Spencer Geddes.

Half-demons: Eve Levine, Adam Vasic, and Robert Vasic.

Humans: Talia Vasic and Robyn Peltier.

Shamans: Simon (who works for the Cortez Cabal) and Kenneth (a member of the Interracial Council).

Clairvoyant: Rhys Vaughan.

Premise: Humans share the world with supernatural beings. Some supernatural gifts can be intentionally developed by humans, and some supernatural traits can be passed on, almost like infections, from supernaturals to humans. The strongest supernatural talents are genetic. The two major types of supernatural "infection," werewolf and vampire, can also be inherited. There are born werewolves and born vampires, as well as vampires and werewolves who were born human and became supernaturals through being bitten. A faint whisper of spell-casting talent can be developed by humans who can become druids and vodouns (humans who practice voodoo); however, strong magical talent is an inherited gift held by sorcerers and witches. Many supernaturals have a single inherited gift. These include necromancers, who can speak with the dead and, if strong enough, can command the dead; clairvoyants, who can perform "remote viewing" (seeing a place or person who is far away); and shamans, who have spirit guides and who practice astral projection. Every half-demon has a single gift. It is inherited from the demon father, and is some form of the demon's power. Since there are many different types of demons, there are many different types of half-demons. The number of "supernaturals" is small. There are fewer than two hundred half-demons in North America. There are fewer than two dozen vampires in the world. There are approximately 35 werewolves in the world; 32 of them are hereditary werewolves. Most bitten werewolves either go mad, commit suicide, or are murdered. (In the past, murdering such "mutts" was treated as a sport by Pack werewolves.) One of the three bitten survivors is female; her name is Elena Michaels. All other known surviving werewolves are male.

Werewolves are hunters. They have heightened senses, extraordinary strength, extended youth, and they change into wolves. Mature, practiced werewolves can change at will; all werewolves must change at least once a month. Werewolves in packs are prohibited from hunting humans. Werewolf "mutts" (non-pack werewolves) usually do not hunt humans because to do so puts all werewolves at risk and, sooner or later, mutts that kill humans will be hunted down by the pack. Vampires live for hundreds of years and heal rapidly. Vampires do not need to kill every time they feed, but at least one time each year, they must kill a human through feeding. Witches and sorcerers cast spells. The histories show that witches originally trained the sorcerers. When the hounds of the Inquisition were on the heels of all magical beings, the Cortez family of sorcerers betrayed the witches, and many witches were killed. Since then, witches have specialized in relatively weak, defensive spells. Sorcerers' spells are usually stronger and useful for attacks. Witches can learn sorcerers' spells, although they are likely to be thrown out of their covens for doing so. Sorcerers can learn witches' spells, but most of them hold such spells (as well as the witches who wield them) in contempt.

Half-demons have a trace of the powers of their fathers. As Adam says in *Stolen,* they are the X-Men of the hidden supernatural world. Different half-demons have different powers, and, within one type of power, there are different levels of strength. There are more of the weaker demons than there are of the stronger demons, so there are more offspring of weak demons than of strong demons. Consequently, there are more half-demons with weak powers than with strong powers. For instance, the types of fire demons, from weak to strong, are Igneus, Aduro, and Exustio demons. There are more Igneus demons than Exustio demons, so there are more children fathered by Igneus demons than by Exustio demons. An Igneus half-demon (with an Igneus demon father and a human mother) can give an enemy a sunburn, and might be able to produce a few sparks. An Aduro half-demon can cause second-degree burns, and can ignite flammable materials. An Exustio half-demon can cause third degree burns and incinerate metal.

Here are some examples of half-demon types:

Fire

Igneus half-demon: Can cause sunburns and produce a few sparks.

Aduro half-demon: Can cause second-degree burns and ignite flammable materials.

Exustio half-demon: Can cause third degree burns and incinerate metal.

Telekinesis

Migro half-demons: Can move small objects a short distance.

Agito half-demons: Can move medium objects a small distance.

Volo half-demons: Can move massive objects a long distance.

Teleportation

Tipudio half-demons: Can teleport about one foot to a spot that they can see.

Evanidus half-demons: Can teleport further, usually only to a place within their line-of-sight.

Abeo half-demons: Can teleport up to 50 feet through solid stone.

Sight

Acies half-demons: Have enhanced vision.

Conspicio half-demons: Can induce temporary blindness in others.

Aspicio half-demons: Can see through solid objects.

There have been other types of half-demons named, but with limited examples and descriptions, it is difficult to know the range of possible powers and where they fit in terms of strength. The types named include

Hearing

Exaudios half-demons: Have enhanced hearing.

Weather

Tempestras half-demons: Have some control over the weather, can control the weather in their immediate vicinity.

Chaos

Expisco half-demons: Can track chaos and revel in chaotic events.

Ferratus

Ferratus half demons: Can make their skin as tough as iron.

Comment: For the most part, the series does not list dates, the chronology is pegged to a few world events (such as the SARS outbreak in Toronto) to determine the dates for specific books. Relative dates (based on characters' ages or on the time that has passed since events in previous books) have been used to extrapolate dates for the other works. Dates listed for the series entries are approximations.

Not all of the series are mysteries, but the novels and novellas qualify as mysteries, and the short stories are listed with brief annotations for those readers who like to read the entire series in order. The materials on the Web site (some of the short stories and novellas) are available free of charge.

Kelley Armstrong's Web site (http://www.kelleyarmstrong.com/) is a rich source of information on the world of the novels and of online fiction that fills in parts of the background of the series. Here, readers have been able to vote on which characters they would like to see in the next book and on what online fiction they would like to see written and posted. Ms. Armstrong has written novellas and short stories in response to the fans' requests. Some were published in print and others were published on the Web site. In 2009, many of the short stories and novellas had been removed from the site. The short story that relates the tale of Jeremy's birth, "Infusion," and the two novellas that chronicle Clayton's early life, "Savage" and "Ascension," were published in 2009 in the book entitled *Men of the Otherworld: A Collection of Otherworld Tales.* Ms. Armstrong's intention is to publish the other works that have been removed from the site in a subsequent volume. The proceeds from both books go to *World Literacy of Canada,* a nonprofit organization that works for social justice and international development. These stories: "Beginnings", Truth & Consequences", and "The Case of El Chupacabra" are affected. They are no longer at the URLs where they were originally read, but they are listed and analyzed below to provide information on the world and the series to the reader. Ms. Armstrong's current Web site projects include a sample chapter for a new *Otherworld* novel, the most recent online *Otherworld* novella, many of the "backstory" short stories for the *Otherworld* series, and an online novella for the young adult *Darkest Powers* series.

Literary Magic and Mayhem: Many themes run through the series. One is that of responding to bullying and abuse. Many characters have dealt with bullies and predators over the course of their lives. Each responded in a different way; but each, in his or her own way, overcame the victimization and went on to build his or her own life. Elena was a foster child who was beautiful and who looked helpless. She became physically fit enough as a human to discourage the attention of a predatory foster father. She set out to make herself strong so that no one who looked at her would see a likely victim. Paige became painfully aware at the age of 14 that defensive spells were not enough to counter serious threats. She decided to seek knowledge of stronger spells, including the sorcerer spells that had been forbidden to witches. Eve took up sorcerer spells as a matter of course, the better to defend herself, and Eve was cast out of the coven. Jaime was made to feel worthless by an emotionally abusive mother, and responded by using the gifts her mother despised to make herself a star. It was not only the women who refused to be victims: Clayton asked to be bitten so that he could stand up to abusive parents. Jeremy suffered from abuse from his father—his father's first act upon holding the infant Jeremy was to try to kill him. Jeremy learned to be smart, strong, and endlessly patient under his father Malcolm's relentless tutelage.

The novels are mysteries set in this supernatural world. The stories (some of them on Ms. Armstrong's Web site) fill in backstory, relating pivotal events in the lives of many of the characters.

Explorations: What other kinds of half-demons would have interesting powers?

What tactics were used to bully the main character and what was his or her response? What did it tell you about both characters? How would one of the other main characters have responded?

Where do the characters' loyalties lie? How far do they extend? Do those loyalties make other characters regard them as more or less trustworthy?

THE CASES

1. **"Rebirth,"** a short story online in *Otherworld Tales 2005* at Kelley Armstrong's Web site, *Otherworld Tales 2005* (its URL as of November 22, 2006: http://www.kelleyarmstrong.com/aOT05.htm).

ENGLAND, 1802. Aaron was just a farm boy who took the family's goods to market and stayed to enjoy a rare night in town. A scream in the night and a tragically failed rescue turned him into a victim, and then into an unusual predator.

ASSOCIATES: Aaron Darnell—*narrator, vampire;* and Cassandra DuCharme—*vampire.*

2. **"Infusion,"** a short story in *Men of the Otherworld: A Collection of Otherworld Tales.* New York: Bantam Books, c2009, p. 3–27. ISBN: 9780553807097.

NEW YORK, 1946. Malcolm has been desperate to prove himself to the pack by fathering a child. Jeremy is so much more than he bargained for...

ASSOCIATES: Malcolm Danvers—*narrator, werewolf, and Jeremy's father;* Edward Danvers—*werewolf, Malcolm's father;* Dominic Sorrentino, Billy Koenig, Vincent, Wally, and Emilio—*are other members of the pack in 1946.* Jeremy's mother and great-grandmother—*who have some sort of magic, type unknown;* and Jeremy—*werewolf.*

3. **"Savage,"** a novella in *Men of the Otherworld: A Collection of Otherworld Tales.* New York: Bantam Books, c2009, p. 31–104. ISBN: 9780553807097.

LOUISIANA AND STONEHAVEN (UPSTATE NEW YORK), 1967–1971. Clayton's life, from the time he is bitten at age six, through two years of living mostly as a wolf in the Louisiana bayous, to his rescue by Jeremy, and finally to his acceptance into the pack.

ASSOCIATES: Clayton Danvers—*narrator, werewolf.* The werewolf pack is mainly comprised of three families: the Sorrentinos (Dominic—*father and alpha of the pack;* Gregory and Antonio—*Dominic's sons;* Jorge—*Gregory's son;* Nick—*Antonio's son*); the Santos (Wally and Raymond—*who are brothers;* Stephen, Andrew, and Daniel—*Raymond's three sons*); and the Danvers (Malcolm—*an abusive father* and Jeremy—*Malcolm's son.*) Jeremy heard the rumors of the feral child werewolf, sought out the child, and then civilized and raised him, when most of the pack werewolves would have felt that a quick death was the kindest gift that could be given a child who had been bitten by a werewolf. Other pack wolves are Ross Werner, Cliff Ward, Peter Myers, Dennis Stillwell, and Dennis's son Joey.

4. "Ascension," a novella in *Men of the Otherworld: A Collection of Otherworld Tales.* New York: Bantam Books, c2009, p. 107–329. ISBN: 9780553807097.

STONEHAVEN (UPSTATE NEW YORK) AND LOS ANGELES, 1972–1987. Clayton's life, from his schooling, to Jeremy's success as a painter, to Dominic's death, and finally to the prolonged contest between Jeremy and Malcolm to see who would be the next alpha of the pack.

ASSOCIATES: Clayton Danvers—*narrator, werewolf.* The werewolf pack: Dominic Sorrentino—*pack Alpha;* Gregory and Antonio—*Dominic's sons;* Jorge—*Gregory's son;* Nick—*Antonio's son;* Malcolm Danvers—*who tries to build a coalition against his own son;* Jeremy—*Malcolm's son;* Clayton—*Jeremy's ward;* Wally and Raymond—*the Santos brothers;* Stephen, Andrew, and Daniel—*Raymond's three sons;* Ross Werner; Cliff Ward; Peter Myers; Dennis Stillwell; and Dennis's son Joey.

5. "Demonology," a short story online in *Otherworld Tales 2005* at Kelley Armstrong's Web site, *Otherworld Tales 2005* (its URL as of November 22, 2006: http://www.kelleyarmstrong.com/aOT05.htm.)

CALIFORNIA, MID 1980S. Eight-year-old Adam is fascinated by fire, to the point where his mother, Talia, has begun to take him to see specialists. She's at her wit's end when a nurse passes her a note directing her to Dr. Robert Vasic. She finds that he does have answers, if she has the strength and the imagination to hear them.

ASSOCIATES: Talia Lyndsay—*narrator, human.* Dr. Robert Vasic—*Tempestras [weather] half-demon;* and Adam—*an Exustio [fire] half-demon.*

6. "Birthright," a short story online in *Otherworld Tales 2005* at Kelley Armstrong's Web site, *Otherworld Tales 2005* (its URL as of November 22, 2006: http://www.kelleyarmstrong.com/aOT05.htm).

NEW YORK, 1990S. As he nears his 18th birthday, Logan begins to notice odd changes in his body. His doctor chalks them up to puberty, and Logan's mother has never been an overly involved parent. Logan receives a mysterious note directing him to Jeremy Danvers for important medical information, and takes a journey that changes his life.

ASSOCIATES: Logan Jonsen—*narrator, werewolf;* Clayton Danvers—*werewolf;* and Jeremy Danvers—*werewolf, Clayton's guardian.*

7. "Beginnings," an online novella available from Kelley Armstrong's Web site, *Beginnings* (its URL as of November 22, 2006: http://www.kelleyarmstrong.com/aBeginnings.htm). File no longer available (as of January 2009)–see Comment.

UNIVERSITY OF TORONTO AND STONEHAVEN (UPSTATE NEW YORK), CIRCA 1987–1988. Clayton gets his first teaching job at the University of Toronto, and there he meets Elena. Werewolves are not supposed to form lasting relationships, so what Clayton feels for Elena is forbidden. Included are Elena's first meeting with Jeremy and the event that changed her life, both from her own and from Clayton's perspectives.

ASSOCIATES: Elena Michaels—*narrator, werewolf* and Clayton Danvers—*narrator, werewolf.* Logan Jonsen—*werewolf;* Jeremy Danvers—*werewolf;* Nicholas Sorrentino—*werewolf;* Antonio Sorrentino—*werewolf;* Peter Myers—*werewolf;* Ms. Milken; Penny; Trina; Jody; and Jason.

8. ***Becoming.*** An online graphic novel available from Kelley Armstrong's Web site, *Becoming* (its URL as of January 2, 2009: http://www.kelleyarmstrong.com/becoming/nBecTOC.htm).

STONEHAVEN (UPSTATE NEW YORK). The immediate aftermath of Elena's being bitten.

ASSOCIATES: Elena Michaels—*narrator, werewolf.* Jeremy Danvers—*werewolf, who was too slow to prevent Elena's being bitten.*

9. **"The Case of the Half-Demon Spy,"** a short story, online in *Otherworld Tales 2005* at Kelley Armstrong's Web site, *Otherworld Tales 2005* (its URL as of November 22, 2006: http://www.kelleyarmstrong.com/aOT05.htm).

VERMONT, CIRCA 1992. Teenagers Paige and Adam, heading out for a video-game break while their parents work through boring Interracial Council business, stumble upon a half-demon eavesdropping upon the Council. Even though they have not come into their full powers, they believe that they must stop the spy on their own.

ASSOCIATES: Adam Vasic—*narrator and Exustio [fire] half-demon;* Paige—*witch;* Dr. Robert Vasic—*Tempestras half-demon.*

10. **"Expectations,"** a short story, online in *Otherworld Tales 2005* at Kelley Armstrong's Web site, *Otherworld Tales 2005* (its URL as of November 22, 2006: http://www.kelleyarmstrong.com/aOT05.htm).

CITY IN UNITED STATES, CIRCA 1997. A concerned sorcerer informs Lucas that a grimoire of horrific spells is in the hands of a witch. It's horrendously wrong that such a grimoire exists, or rather, it's horrendously wrong that it exists in the possession of a witch. The sorcerer is sure that the sorcerers of the Cortez Cabal would be grateful to hear of it and are anxious to put it to use; Lucas is sure that he is right.

ASSOCIATES: Lucas Cortez—*narrator, sorcerer.* Victor Tucci—*sorcerer;* Eve Levine—*an Aspicio [vision] half-demon and witch who not only dares to use sorcerer magic, but who, once she had a daughter, had the chutzpah to set herself up as a teacher of sorcerers;* Savannah Levine—*witch, Eve's daughter, one-quarter demon [which doesn't give her specific powers, but may increase her potency as a practitioner of magic].*

11. "Truth & Consequences," an online short story available from Kelley Armstrong's Web site, *Truth and Consequences* (its URL as of November 22, 2006: http://www.kelleyarmstrong.com/eBSStory.htm.) File no longer available (as of January 2009)—see Comment.

PLACE UNKNOWN, CIRCA 1997. A con man who specializes in faking paranormal occurrences stumbles across a real werewolf. He offers, for sale, explicit information on the werewolf, and Elena Michaels turns up as one of the interested bidders. This is the first short story that was written for this world. Kelley Armstrong wrote it and submitted it to *Lost Worlds* (a science fiction and fantasy magazine). The editor loved it, affirming that the premise was of enough interest to sell. In some ways, this story launched the series. It was published in *Lost Worlds* in February 1996.

ASSOCIATES: Elena Michaels—*narrates parts, werewolf;* José Carter—*a con man;* Lyle Davis—*of the PRC;* and Robert Wyotski—*of the Hecate Society.*

12. "Territorial," a short story, online in *Otherworld Tales 2005* at Kelley Armstrong's Web site, *Otherworld Tales 2005* (its URL as of November 22, 2006: http://www.kelleyarmstrong.com/aOT05.htm).

UNKNOWN CITY, CIRCA 1998. Karl is stuck. He wants territory, but he isn't going to join the pack that hunted down his father. Then he meets up with a werewolf whose family left the pack a generation ago, and thus begins a very ugly partnership.

ASSOCIATES: Karl Marsten—*narrator, werewolf;* Josef Marsten—*werewolf "mutt" (i.e. werewolf with no pack affiliation), Karl's father, burglar;* Cindy; Daniel Santos—*werewolf;* In flashback: werewolves Malcolm Danvers, Raymond, and Wally Santos.

13. *Bitten.* New York: Viking, 1999, 342 p. ISBN: 0670894710.

TORONTO AND STONEHAVEN (IN UPSTATE NEW YORK), CIRCA 1999. Someone is murdering humans and leaving the bodies on pack land. Jeremy recognizes the crimes as both a threat and a challenge to the pack and sends for Elena. He has to send for Elena because she's in Toronto. She decided, two months after the events in *Truth or Consequences,* to leave the pack and live as a human in the human world.

ASSOCIATES: Elena Michaels—*narrator, werewolf.* Philip—*human, Elena's live-in lover;* Diane—*Philip's sister, who wants Elena to help plan a wedding;* Anne and Larry—*Philip's parents;* Jeremy Danvers—*alpha werewolf of the Upstate New York pack.* The pack includes: Clayton Danvers—*werewolf, Jeremy's foster son, who has developed a fearsome reputation;* Nick Sorrentino—*werewolf, Clayton's best friend;* Antonio Sorrentino—*werewolf, Nick's father;* Peter Myers—*werewolf;* and Logan—*werewolf.* The werewolf "mutts" are: Daniel Santos, Karl Marsten, Zachary Cain, Jimmy Koenig, Scott Brandon, Thomas LeBlanc, and Victor Olson.

14. "Ghosts," a short story online in *Otherworld Tales 2005* at Kelley Armstrong's Web site, *Otherworld Tales 2005* (its URL as of November 22, 2006: http://www.kelleyarmstrong.com/aOT05.htm).

STONEHAVEN (IN UPSTATE NEW YORK), CIRCA 2000. Jeremy reviews his decision to send Elena and Clay away as the pack prepares for attack. Included are Jeremy's memories of the day that Elena was bitten.

ASSOCIATES: Jeremy Danvers—*narrator, werewolf.* Nick and Antonio—*werewolves.* In flashback: Clayton Danvers—*werewolf, Jeremy's ward;* and Elena Michaels—*human, then becomes a werewolf, Clayton's girlfriend.*

15. "Escape," a short story, online in *Otherworld Tales 2005* ***at*** Kelley Armstrong's Web site, *Otherworld Tales 2005* (its URL as of November 22, 2006: http://www.kelleyarmstrong.com/aOT05.htm).

MAINE, CIRCA 2000. Eve Levine, a half-Aspicio [vision] demon, did her best to construct a safe life for herself and her daughter. She gave up witchcraft, settling for teaching instead of practicing, and soon had a reputation as a powerful teacher of the dark arts. Therefore, when Tyrone Winsloe wanted to capture a witch, she's the one he chose. Her daughter was captured with her, and now Eve must find a way for them both to escape.

ASSOCIATES: Eve Levine—*narrator, witch;* Savannah—*Eve's daughter, a child with witch, sorcerer, and demon blood;* and Sondra Bauer—*a human researcher who is interested in (and a little envious of) supernaturals.*

16. *Stolen.* New York: Viking, 2003, 399 p. ISBN: 0670031372.

VERMONT AND MAINE, CIRCA 2000. When Elena spotted an ad that made it clear that someone knew way too much about werewolves, she set up a meeting with its authors, Ruth and Paige Winterbourne. They tell her a wild tale of witches and sorcerers, vampires, and shamans. Ruth and Paige claim that someone is capturing supernaturals, and they want to call a meeting to arrange a cooperative defense. Elena is almost sure that they are magicians with a few parlor tricks running some sort of scam. Within hours, Elena realizes that she is being stalked and, unlike the stereotypical victim/heroine, Elena knows when to seek help. Unfortunately, intelligence and foresight are not enough to keep her safe.

ASSOCIATES: Elena Michaels—*narrator, werewolf who follows up on outside elements that threaten the secrecy of the pack.* Jeremy Danvers—*pack alpha;* Clayton Danvers—*Elena's mate, Jeremy's son.*

The Interracial Council consists of: Kenneth—*shaman;* Cassandra DuCharme—*vampire;* Ruth and Paige Winterbourne—*witches;* and Adam Vasic—*Exustio [fire] half-demon.*

The villains include: Tyrone Winsloe—*a wealthy human geek who fancies himself a great hunter;* Lawrence Matsumi—*human parapsychology researcher;* Tess—*Matsumi's human research assistant;* Isaac Katzen—*sorcerer;* Sondra

Bauer—*human researcher;* Dr. Carmichael—*human;* and Xavier Reese—*Evanidus [teleportation] half-demon.*

The prisoners: Leah O'Donnell—*Agito [telekinetic] half-demon;* Savannah Levine and Ruth Winterbourne—*witches;* Patrick Lake—*werewolf;* Dr. Armen Haig—*psychiatrist who has minimal shape-shifting abilities;* Curtis Zaid—*vodoun;* and Aaron Darnell—*vampire.*

17. ***Dime Store Magic.*** New York: Bantam Books, 2004, 414 p. ISBN: 0553587064.

EAST FALLS, MASSACHUSETTS, CIRCA 2001. Kristof Nast is the son and heir of Thomas Nast, CEO of the Nast Cabel. He is also Savannah's father. When he decides to start a custody battle for Savannah, he employs sorcerer tricks and cabal resources. Paige finds herself faced first with defamation, then with murder, then with the walking dead. The worst of it all is not that Nast's people seem to believe that Paige is incompetent and weak and that Savannah is a mindless prize; the worst is that that opinion seems to be shared by the people whom Paige thought were her allies. Paige knows the identity of the criminal(s) from the start, but how can she protect Savannah, the coven, and the rest of East Falls?

ASSOCIATES: Paige Winterbourne—*narrator, witch.* Savannah Levine—*witch, Paige's ward;* Lucas Cortez—*sorcerer, a crusader;* Hector Cortez—*sorcerer, Lucas's half-brother.* Victoria Alden—*witch, an elder in Paige's coven;* Margaret Levine—*witch, the 68-year-old Aunt of Savannah, and the second coven elder;* Therese Moss—*witch, the third coven elder.* Other members of Paige's coven (all witches) include: Abby, Grace, Brittany, Tina Moss, Emma Alden, Megan, and Sophie Moss.

The human citizens of East Falls include: Grantham Cary, Jr.—*lawyer;* Lacey Cary—*his wife;* Sheriff Ted Fowler; Deputy Travis Willard; and Detective Flynn.

Members of Kristof Nast's household include: Kristof Nast—*sorcerer, heir to the Nast Cabal and Savannah's father;* Friesen and Anton—*half-demon guards;* Leah O'Donnell—*Volo [telekinetic] half-demon;* Greta Enwright and her mother Olivia—*witches;* Gabriel Sandford—*sorcerer;* and Roberta Shaw—*necromancer.*

18. ***Industrial Magic.*** New York: Bantam Books, 2004, 528 p. ISBN: 0553587072.

MIAMI, FLORIDA (MOSTLY) ALSO PORTLAND, OREGON; CINCINNATI, OHIO; AND MODESTO, CALIFORNIA, 2001. (Begins four months after the events in *Dime Store Magic* and one month after 9/11 World Trade Center attack) Someone is targeting cabal children and murdering them. Any one cabal could easily handle an investigation to track down the killer. The four cabals being engaged in a joint operation ensures that there will be so much infighting that the killer may never be caught. Lucas and Paige are asked to help. They'd sworn that they would never work for the cabals, but they can't walk away when children are being killed.

Associates: Paige Winterbourne—*narrator, witch.* Lucas Cortez—*sorcerer, Paige's lover, Benecio's errant son;* Savannah Levine—*witch, Paige's ward;* Elena Michaels—*werewolf;* Clayton Danvers—*werewolf, Elena's mate;* Jeremy Danvers—*werewolf, pack alpha;* Jamie Vegas—*necromancer, she gets tongue-tied around Jeremy;* Adam Vasic—*Exustio [fire] half-demon;* Talia Vasic—*human, Adam's mother;* Dr. Robert Vasic—*Tempestras [weather] half-demon, Talia's husband;* Aaron Darnell—*vampire;* Cassandra DuCharme—*vampire.*

The Cortez cabal includes: Benecio Cortez—*sorcerer, the patriarch of the family and CEO of the cabal;* Hector, William, and Carlos Cortez—*sorcerers, three of Benecio's four sons, all on the next tier of cabal management;* Dennis Malone—*sorcerer, Head of Security;* Dana MacArthur—*a 15-year-old witch, the Atlanta victim:* Randy MacArthur—*Exaudio [hearing] half-demon, Dana's father;* Gillian MacArthur—*witch, the youngest daughter of Randy MacArthur;* Troy Morgan—*Tempestras [weather] half-demon, one of Benecio's bodyguards;* Griffin Sorenson—*Ferratus [iron-skinned] half-demon, one of Benecio's bodyguards;* Jacob Sorenson—*Griffin's son;* Reuban Aldrich—*necromancer;* Faye Aston—*clairvoyant, retired;* Gloria—*half-demon who works at Cortez Emergency Services;* Simon—*shaman who works at Cortez Emergency Services.*

The Nast Cabal includes: Thomas Nast—*sorcerer, CEO of the Nast cabal, father of Kristof Nast;* Sean Nast—*sorcerer, Thomas's grandson, Sean is not sure that he should be in the cabal;* and Bryce Nast—*sorcerer, Thomas's grandson;* Everett Weber—*druid, a computer programmer who was fired.*

Ronald, Hans—*a.k.a. John,* and Brigid—*who are vampires in New Orleans;* The Fates, Raoul—*shaman;* Oscar Gale—*shaman;* and Edward Hagen—*vampire;* Wendy and Julie Aiken—*witches who were interviewed by Paige.*

19. "Wedding Bell Hell," a short story online in *Otherworld Tales 2005* at Kelley Armstrong's Web site, *Otherworld Tales 2005* (its URL as of November 22, 2006: http://www.kelleyarmstrong.com/aOT05.htm).

Portland, Oregon, 2002? Lucas's and Paige's wedding, from the planning (at least the last three weeks of planning), through the making the wedding favors, to the ceremony.

Associates: Paige Winterbourne—*narrator, witch;* Lucas Cortez—*sorcerer;* Savannah Levine—*witch, Paige's ward;* Maria Valdés—*Lucas's mother, human;* Margory Mills—*human, a wedding planner whose services were a gift from Benicio;* Benicio Cortez—*sorcerer, Lucas's father;* Elena Michaels—*werewolf;* Jaime Vegas—*necromancer;* Troy Morgan—*Tempestras [weather] half-demon,*

Benecio's bodyguard; Clayton Danvers—*werewolf;* Jeremy Danvers—*werewolf;* Talia Vasic—*human;* and Adam Vasic—*Exustio [fire] half-demon.*

20. ***Haunted.*** New York: Bantam Books, 2005, 495 p. ISBN: 0553587080.

A DIMENSION OF THE AFTERLIFE FOR MAGICAL BEINGS, CIRCA 2003; FRANCE, 1666 (MARIE MADELINE D'AUBREY DE BRINVILLIERS); MASSACHUSETTS, 1892 (LIZZIE BORDEN); SAN FRANCISCO, 1927 (JOLYNN); CLEVELAND, 1938 (AGNES MILLER); EDINBURGH, 1962; AND PORTLAND, OREGON, CIRCA 2003. The Fates manage the parts of the afterlife that are occupied by the ghosts of magical beings. This dimension of the afterlife was not designed for demi-demons. Over four centuries ago, a frustrated Nix (female water spirit) convinced a weak-willed witch to perform a spell to give the Nix control over the witch's body. For years, the Nix lived as the witch, exercising her powers to create chaos, often through murder. When the witch died, the Nix was turned over to The Fates. The Fates thought that they had her contained. They were mistaken. She escaped over a century ago, and has since acted as a serial killer through many different "partners." The Fates have sent three powerful beings after her, all have failed. Over a year ago, Eve struck a bargain with The Fates, and they now call on her to uphold her end of the agreement by going forth into the world to recapture the Nix. It doesn't take the Nix long to turn the tables and try to make the hunter the hunted. She can't kill Eve, but there are plenty of things that would hurt Eve more than death, and the keys to most of them are still on earth.

ASSOCIATES: Eve Levine—*narrator, Aspicio [vision] half-demon, witch, deceased;* Kristof Nast—*sorcerer, deceased, he was Eve's lover when they were alive;* the Fates; Trsiel—*angel, Eve's partner in this enterprise;* and Janah—*the first angel who was sent to apprehend the Nix;* George—*ghost;* Suzanne Simmons—*ghost;* Luther Ross—*ghost of a half-Gelo demon who teaches other ghosts to be poltergeists;* Aratron—*a high-ranking eudemon;* Dantalian—*demon, Master of Transmigration, Duke of Baal;* Dachev—*ghost, the second being who was sent to catch the Nix;* Jaime Vegas—*necromancer;* Paige Winterbourne—*witch;* Lucas Cortez—*sorcerer;* and Savannah Levine—*witch, she lives with Lucas and Paige.*

21. **"Adventurer,"** a short story online in *Otherworld Tales 2005* at Kelley Armstrong's Web site, *Otherworld Tales 2005* (its URL as of November 22, 2006: http://www.kelleyarmstrong.com/aOT05.htm).

UNKNOWN CITY, FEBRUARY 2004. Silent Kenneth has his own methods of contributing to the Interracial Council.

ASSOCIATES: Kenneth—*narrator, and the shaman on the Interracial Council.* Taira—*Kenneth's spirit guide.* The council delegates: Cassandra

DuCharme—*vampire;* Paige Winerbourne—*witch;* Elena Michaels—*werewolf;* Jeremy Danvers—*werewolf;* Adam Vasic—*Exustio [fire] half-demon;* and Jaime Vegas—*necromancer.*

22. "Chaotic," a short story in *Dates from Hell,* ed. by Kim Harrison. New York: HarperCollins, c2006, p. 201–313. ISBN: 006085409X.

UNKNOWN CITY, 2003. Eighteen months ago, Hope was offered a job that utilized her unique skills. Hope is the daughter of a Chaos demon and, generally, her gifts have been more of a curse than a blessing. However, her nose for trouble, coupled with her new job at a tabloid newspaper, have allowed her to become alarmingly successful. She's become a supernatural bounty hunter. Her council contact, Tristan Robard, gave her tickets to a Museum gala, and there she encounters a thief (and then a werewolf, and then a corpse, and then a murderer, and then . . .).

ASSOCIATES: Hope Adams—*narrator, Expisco [chaos] half-demon;* Douglas; Tristan Robard; Karl Marsten—*werewolf;* and Bryan Trau.

23. "The Case of El Chupacabra," an online novella available from Kelley Armstrong's Web site, *The Case of El Chupacabra* (its URL as of July 3, 2007: http://www.kelleyarmstrong.com/aChupa.htm). File no longer available (as of January 2009)—see Comment.

LOS ANGELES, PORTLAND (OREGON), AND MIDDLETON (WASHINGTON), 2004. Sean Nast discovered a corpse, one that looked suspiciously bloodless and had fang marks on its neck. He needed to hide his involvement: not with the corpse, but with the gay bar in which it was found. He called on Lucas for assistance, hoping to get the crime solved quickly and quietly. Unfortunately, the news leaks out. As the cabals gather to hunt down the nearest vampire and to discuss the "St. Cloud proposal," which would banish all vampires from American soil, the pressure to identify the real killer increases. Lucas and Paige don't have much time to find the murderer.

ASSOCIATES: Lucas Cortez—*narrator, sorcerer* and Sean Nast—*narrator, sorcerer,* Paige Winterbourne—*witch, Lucas's wife, Savannah's guardian;* Savannah Levine—*witch, Sean's half-sister;* Dr. Bailey—*human;* Detective MacLeod—*human;* Mary—*Sean's executive assistant;* Cassandra DuCharme—*vampire;* Aaron Darnell—*vampire;* Spencer Geddes—*vampire;* Mr. Sullivan—*human, reporter;* Bryce Nast—*sorcerer. Sean's brother, Kristof's son;* Josef Nast—*sorcerer, Sean's uncle;* Thomas Nast—*sorcerer, CEO of the Nast Cabal, Sean and Savannah's grandfather (although he won't acknowledge Savannah);* Greg Regis—*human morgue attendant;* Hector Cortez—*sorcerer, Benecio's oldest son, he expected to be heir to Benecio's place in the cabal, he is 20 years older than his brother Lucas;* Benicio Cortez—*sorcerer, Lucas's father, CEO of the Cortez Cabal;* Troy Morgan—*Tempestras [weather] half-demon, Benecio's bodyguard;* Gus Reichs, Chris Ibsen and Kepler—*are Cortez cabal employees.*

24. "Bargain," a short story online in *Otherworld Tales 2005* at Kelley Armstrong's Web site. *Otherworld Tales 2005* URL as of November 22, 2006: http://www.kelleyarmstrong.com/aOT05.htm.

UNKNOWN CITIES—ENDS IN 2004. Xavier's looking to develop a working relationship with Elena, so he's looking for a job that pays well, one with a little larceny, one that is particularly suited to a werewolf's gifts. He hears about a letter, purportedly written by Jack the Ripper...

ASSOCIATES: Xavier—*narrator, Evanidus [teleportation] half-demon.* Roy; Tommy—*Evanidus half-demon.*

25. *Broken.* New York: Bantam Dell, 2006, 444 p. ISBN: 0553588184.

UPSTATE NEW YORK AND TORONTO, 2004. Elena is five weeks pregnant and quietly (well, not so quietly) going mad with boredom. Xavier Reese calls to offer an exchange: the location of one woman-killing mutt for help with a simple project that has absolutely no potential for violence. The proposal looks innocuous enough...

ASSOCIATES: Elena Michaels—*narrator, werewolf.* Clayton Danvers—*werewolf, Elena's mate;* Jeremy Danvers—*werewolf, pack alpha, he brought up Clayton as his son;* Xavier Reese—*Evanidus [teleportation] half-demon;* Nick Sorrentino—*werewolf, Clayton's best friend;* Antonio Sorrentino—*werewolf, Nick's father;* Jaime Vegas—*necromancer;* Rose—*zombie;* Matthew Hull—*a visitor from Victorian England;* Anita Barrington—*witch;* Erin—*her granddaughter;* Zoe Takano—*vampire;* Randall Toliver—*sorcerer, doctor;* Tee—*necromancer;* Rita Acosta—*an old human friend of Elena's, who works as a reporter in Toronto;* Logan Nicholas Danvers—*werewolf,* and his twin sister: Katherine Natalya Danvers—*werewolf?* (There is no record of a female born [instead of bitten] werewolf; but then there's no record of a female werewolf giving birth. Only time will tell.)

26. *No Humans Involved.* New York: Bantam Books, c2007, 342 p. ISBN: 9780553805086.

UPSTATE NEW YORK AND TORONTO, 2005. A television special featuring three spiritualists contacting the dead could give Jaime her big break, and other areas of her life are also looking up. While the television special is filming, Jeremy will spend some quality time with Jaime away from his home and his pack. Here is her chance, both professionally and personally, to get the life she wants. Jaime can do the fake medium act quite well; it's been the basis of her show for years. She's a real necromancer, but the public would not like to see the gore and the mess of the rituals needed to contact the dead. Jaime's fake act gives people a nice, reassuring view of the afterlife. Things go awry on the set almost as soon as filming starts. The producer has a hidden agenda, and will cheat to create the show he wants. The dead aren't cooperating either. Jaime wants them to stay away; instead, she is practically mobbed with talkative spirits. Then there are the ones who won't communicate, yet won't leave her alone. Jaime must delve deeper into her gift to help those who cannot help themselves. On the way, she discovers a group of murderers—people convinced that the killing of innocents will bring them power. The frightening thing is, even though they are human, they do seem to have gained some power, and every scrap of it fuels their desire for more. They're not going to stop.

ASSOCIATES: Jaime Vegas—*nee Jaime O'Casey, narrator, necromancer.* Jeremy Danvers—*werewolf, Jaime's lover;* The other spiritualists for the television special are: Angelique—*human, who is called the Angel of the South* and Bradford Grady—*human.* Claudia Wilson—*Bradford's assistant;* Becky Cheung—*the director;* Will—*her assistant;* Todd Simon—*the producer;* Dr. Robson—*a parapsychologist;* Bruce Wang—*a specialist in ghost photography;* Elena Michaels—*werewolf;* Clayton Danvers—*werewolf, Elena's mate;* Kristof Nast—*sorcerer, deceased, Eve's lover and Savannah's father;* Eve Levine—*Aspicio half-demon, witch, deceased, angel, and Savannah's mother;* Paige Winterbourne—*witch, Savannah's guardian;* Lucas Cortez—*sorcerer, Paige's husband;* Savannah Levine—*witch;* Molly Crane—*witch;* Aratron—*a high-ranking eudemon;* Hope Adams—*Expisco [chaos] half-demon;* and Karl Marsten—*werewolf.*

Tansy Lane, Gabrielle Langdon, Stan, Peter Feeney, Rachel Skye, Brendan, 'Lizbeth, Manuel Garcia, Todd, Chloe Margaret Fisher, and Charles—*are all ghosts who are contacted by Jaime.* May Donovan, Rona Grant, and Zack Flynn—*are members of the Ehrich Weiss Society.* Eric Botnick—*the leader of The Disciples of Asmodai;* Murray, Don, Brian, and Tina—*are all members of his Coven.*

27. "Framed," an online novella available from Kelley Armstrong's Web site, *Framed* (its URL as of July 2, 2007: http://www.kelleyarmstrong.com/aFramed.htm).

UPSTATE NEW YORK, CIRCA 2004. Nick wakes up next to a strange woman; not an unusual occurrence, but this one is dead. He can tell from the smell that the blood splattered over the bed is not her blood. He can tell from his headache that he was drugged. Even if those conclusions are obvious, bringing in the police would bring unwelcome attention to the pack. Nick decides that, on his own, he will investigate the woman's death and the attempt to frame him. It's important to him that he does this without the intervention of his friends, the Pack, or even his father.

ASSOCIATES: Nick Sorrentino—*narrator, werewolf.* Janine—*Nick's human secretary;* Paul—*a druid who was given Nick's name by the werewolf mutt Tyler Lake;* and Rita—*Paul's half-demon ex-wife.*

28. "Twilight," a short story in *Many Bloody Returns.* New York: Ace Books, 2007, p. 73–100. ISBN: 9780441015221.

PLACE UNKNOWN, AUTUMN 2006. Cassandra DuCharme realizes that her life is running down, she's finding it difficult to take enough of an interest to make her yearly kill. Aaron tries to help, but he fails.

ASSOCIATES: Cassandra DuCharme—*narrator, vampire.* Aaron Darnell—*vampire.*

29. *Personal Demon.* New York: Bantam Dell, c2008, 371 p. ISBN: 9780553806618.

MIAMI, FLORIDA AND PORTLAND, OREGON, 2006. Hope Adams is a rare type of half-demon, an Expisco. Most children born of a liaison between a human woman and a demon inherit a watered-down version of the demon's power: they can teleport or kindle fire, etc. Some few children of the major demons instead develop an aspect of the demon's personality—a taste for chaos. These are the Expisco half-demons. Their thirst for chaos comes with abilities designed to find trouble. Hope can read chaotic thoughts and relive (albeit as a witness) past violence. She revels in both, and that fact terrifies her.

When Hope needed help keeping Karl alive, she called on Benicio Cortez. Benicio didn't know her, but he came to her aid. That aid is not without cost; Benicio expects favors to be repaid. Hope is painfully aware that she and Karl are in Benicio Cortez's debt. When Benicio calls on Hope for help, she can't consult with Karl. For one thing, Karl is out of town. For another, he walked away after the first and only time they made love. Hope would like to cut all ties and bury all memories related to Karl. Benicio's request for help while Karl is out of the country *seems* like an excellent opportunity to fulfill her obligation. She can pay back her share of the debt, cut her last tie to Karl, gain closure on her relationship with Karl, and move forward with her life. Hope consults with Lucas and Paige before she takes the job; but she's kept the darker aspects of her power secret from them, and she soon suspects that those aspects are known to Benicio. It looks as if Benicio gave her a minor assignment designed to tempt her into embracing the chaos within her soul. Hope walks a tightrope, trying to maintain control over herself as she infiltrates a gang for Benicio. Neither of them realize that the stakes include life and death until it is too late.

ASSOCIATES: Hope Adams—*narrator, Expisco [chaos] half-demon;* Benicio Cortez—*sorcerer, who is leader of the Cortez Cabal;* Troy Morgan—*Tempestras [weather] half-demon, who is Benecio's bodyguard;* Lucas Cortez—*sorcerer* and Paige Winterbourne—*witch, Lucas and Paige are co-owners of Cortez-Winterbourne Investigations. They specialize in representing supernaturals who have run afoul of Cabal rules.* Cesar Romeo—*who runs initiation tests for sorcerer Guy Benoit's gang;* the gang includes: Guy Benoit, Bianca—*his second-in-command,* Rodriguez—*the tech guy,* Tony, Max, Jasper "Jaz" Haig, and Sonny—*Jaspar's best friend.* Karl Marsten—*werewolf, Hope's ex-lover, he comes in search of her halfway through the story;* Hector, Carlos, and William—*sorcerers, are Benicio's legitimate sons;* Bella—*Hector's wife;* Emilio—*Hector's arrogant 16-year-old son;* Griffin—*Ferratus [iron-skinned] half-demon, bodyguard to Benicio Cortez, he does not trust Expisco half-demons.*

30. "Stalked," a short story in *My Big Fat Supernatural Honeymoon,* ed. By P. N. Elrod. New York: St. Martin's Press, 2008, p. 1–34. ISBN: 0312375042; 9780312375041.

PLACE UNKNOWN, 2007. After all this time, when their twins are two years old, Elena and Clay finally have their honeymoon. Clay planned it all, wanting it to be romantic and exciting, wanting it to be perfect. This morning he spotted a werewolf stalking Elena. She'd probably be upset if he killed someone during their honeymoon…

ASSOCIATES: Clayton Danvers—*narrator, werewolf,* Elena Michaels—*werewolf, Clayton's wife;* Cain—*werewolf;* and Brian McKay—*werewolf.*

31. "Kitsunegari," a short story in *Men of the Otherworld: A Collection of Otherworld Tales.* New York: Bantam Books, c2009, p. 333–69. ISBN: 9780553807097.

NEW YORK, 2007. Jeremy is taking a stolen weekend with Jaime when something awakens him. A call home assures him that Elena, Clayton, and the twins are all safe. The feeling persists, Jeremy feels hunted, and he can't find the hunter.

ASSOCIATES: Jeremy—*narrator, werewolf.* Jaime Vegas—*necromancer, Jeremy's 46-year-old lover;* Tara—*Jaime's assistant;* a mysterious young woman—*a shapeshifter who calls Jeremy the last of the Kogitsune (which means "little fox");* Dr. Robert Vasic—*Tempestras [weather] half-demon;* and Talia—*his wife.*

32. "The Ungrateful Dead," a short story in *Blood Lite,* ed. by Kevin J. Anderson. New York: Pocket Books, 2008, p. 1–24. ISBN: 1416567836; 9781416567837.

SEATTLE, WASHINGTON, 2007. A particularly obnoxious ghost demands Jaime's help for his cousin. He doesn't mention that the cousin is a zombie…

ASSOCIATES: Jaime Vegas—*narrator, necromancer.* Brett—*human, hairdresser;* Patty—*human;* and Uncle Mort—*ghost, Patty's uncle;* Tara—*human, Jaime's assistant;* Savannah Levine—*witch;* Byron "Chuck" Carruthers—*ghost;* Byron's cousin—*zombie.*

33. *Living with the Dead.* New York: Bantam Dell, 2008, 372 p. ISBN: 9780553806649.

LOS ANGELES, 2007. Robyn was the friend who stood by Hope Adams when Hope was a teenager experiencing the first terrifying Expisco half-demon chaos visions that are part of Hope's genetic heritage. Six months ago, Robyn's husband Damon was killed. Robyn was (and still is) overwhelmed by grief. Robyn has always been sensible and strong. When she decided to move from Philadelphia to Los Angeles, her family and friends thought that she was moving on with her life. They were wrong. She fled their well-meaning concern so that she could let go and bury herself in grief and bitterness at Damon's senseless death. Robyn took a public relations job in Los Angeles with celebrity Portia Kane. Hope suspected that Robyn was disengaging rather than coping, and when Hope received a chance to work a six-month stint in *True News*' Los Angeles office, she decided to take the temporary transfer to be near her friend. Karl Marsten decided to move with her so that they could continue to live together.

Robyn's client Portia is going through various emotional upheavals and asks Robyn to accompany her to a club. Robyn is caught up in pity. How isolated Portia must feel to ask her publicist to come to keep her company! Robyn was going to meet Hope and Karl for dinner, but they agree to meet her at the club instead. They meet, they drink, Hope and Karl leave…, then Portia is gunned down, and Robyn flees the scene. At first, only the police are after her, but soon someone else is on her trail, someone persistent, supernatural, and murderous.

ASSOCIATES: Robyn Peltier—*narrator, human, who learns the truth about the supernatural world. During the course of the book, she decides to offer to do public relations work for the Interracial Council.* Portia Kane—*human, Paris Hilton-wannabe and Robyn's employer;* Jasmine Wills—*human, Portia's "frenemy";* Hope Adams—*Expisco (chaos) half-demon, Robyn's best friend;* Karl Marsten—*werewolf, Hope's significant other;* Homicide Detective John "Finn" Findlay—*necromancer;* Mark Downey—*human, crime scene technician;* Marla Jansen—*human witness;* Judd Archer—*human/ghost, contract celebrity-bodyguard;* Kendra and Madelyn—*human witnesses;* Damon "Trent" Peltier—*ghost, he was Robyn's husband;* Detective Luis Madoz—*human;* Neil Earley—*human junkie;* Officer Lee Kendall—*ghost;* Grant Gilchrist—*werewolf;* Irving Nast—*sorcerer;* Sean Nast—*sorcerer;* Thomas Nast—*sorcerer, CEO of the Nast Cabal, Sean's grandfather;* Alvarez, Solheim, Barrett, and Mac—*Nast Cabal workers;* and Eve Levine—*angel.*

Many of the characters are clairvoyants. Clairvoyants live in a tiny secret society called a "kumpania." They develop their gifts, hide from the Cabals, and arrange marriages to breed stronger clairvoyants. Their breeding program produces some clairvoyants, some non-talented humans who are either killed or sterilized and employed as servants, and a few "seers" who have massive clairvoyant powers but barely functional bodies. Nick—*clairvoyant, the leader of the kumpania;* Nick's wife—*clairvoyant;* Lily and

Hugh—*clairvoyants who are dutifully trying to conceive a child;* Adele Morrissey—*clairvoyant, who brings in money as a celebrity photographer;* Colm—*clairvoyant, Adele's 15-year-old fiancé (Adele wanted to be mated to Hugh);* Thom—*seer, Colm's brother;* Neala—*clairvoyant, Colm and Thom's mother;* Rhys Vaughan—*clairvoyant, their father, escaped the kumpania long ago.* At the end of this book, Rhys, who has proven to be ruthless and manipulative, offers Hope a job, and Karl goes out of town for two months to give her space to make her decision.

34. "Zen and the Art of Vampirism" a short story in ***Fantasy Medley,*** edited by Yanni Kuznia. Burton, MI: Subterranean Press, 2009, p. 9–32. ISBN: 9781596062245.

Toronto, 2009?. Brigid and Hans are tired of post-Katrina New Orleans. They decide they want Toronto, but Zoe has no intention of giving up her territory. This is not a mystery. It provides background information involving characters who have been peripheral to the series and is an interesting character study of Zoe.

Associates: Rudy—*sorcerer, the bartender at Miller's Bar which serves as neutral ground for the supernaturals of Toronto;* José—*druid, a prospective client;* Brigid Drescher—*vampire;* Hans—*vampire, a.k.a. John;* Randall Tolliver—*sorcerer who runs a medical clinic for the homeless;* Tee—*necromancer.*

ASIMOV, Isaac.

Caves of Steel

Genres/Themes Crossed: Science Fiction X Whodunnit, Police Procedural.

Subjects/Character Types: Sentient Artificial Intelligence (Robots), Future Earth, Other Planets X Police procedural.

Series/Stand-Alone: Many years after writing the first three novels and the short story in the *Elijah Baley and R. Daneel Olivaw* series Asimov wrote the fourth novel, which ties this series into the *Foundation* series. With that change, the *Foundation* series encompasses 20,000 years through 15 books of short stories and novels that were written by Isaac Asimov. All of them are science fiction, some are also mysteries. Since then, other works (including works by other authors) have been interpolated into the series. Asimov's short stories, in which he worked out the ramifications of the laws of robotics, could all be considered prequels to *The Caves of Steel,* in which case the series would begin with the short stories collected in *I, Robot* (some of which are "how and whodunnit" stories developed to explore the rules of robotics). The decision to limit this entry to the stories that include R. Daneel was based on the fact that the *Foundation* series focuses more on adventure, political intrigue, and society than on mystery.

After the publication of *The Caves of Steel* and *The Naked Sun,* fans clamored for another Baley and Olivaw story. Asimov wrote the short story "Mirror Image." Fans clarified that they wanted another novel, and *The Robots of Dawn* followed. The trilogy of the first three novels, featuring Elijah and R. Daneel's partnership, forms a satisfying story arc; it introduces readers to the basics of Asimov's rules of robotics and the limitations of those rules, and exposes readers to one of the seminal works of science fiction mystery. The first three of the listed novels should be read in order, since the characters, their relationships, and the society change over time. The short story presents a puzzle: while it is enjoyable to see R. Daneel Olivaw and Elijah Baley, it doesn't alter anything in their friendship, their understanding, or their characters. It is optional, as, from the viewpoint of a mystery lover, is the fourth novel, listed for those readers who want to know more about the aftermath of the societal changes and to see R. Daneel once again.

Scene(s) of the Crime(s): The three books take place in three different locations. *The Caves of Steel* takes place on Earth, in New York; *The Naked Sun* takes place on one of the Outer Worlds, Solaria; and *The Robots of Dawn* takes place on another of the Outer Worlds, Aurora.

Detective(s): Plainclothesman Elijah "Lije" Baley, a detective on planet Earth. His father was declassified when he was one-year-old, and he lived in poverty until he worked his way up in the New York City Police Department. At the beginning of the series, he is classified as a C-5, and has a fairly comfortable life.

R. Daneel Olivaw was designed to pass for human so that he could gather information about the humans on Earth, information that would be used by a sociologist working on a strategy to preserve humanity by convincing some of Earth's humans to begin colonizing other worlds once again. When Spacetown needed a detective, R. Daneel's programmer modified him to have a strong sense of justice (defined as an overwhelming respect for the law as it is written), and sent him out as a detective. In *Robots and Empire,* Daneel acquires other abilities, which are used throughout many of the books in the *Foundation* series. Along with the books listed herein, Daneel is featured in *Prelude to Foundation* and *Foundation and Earth.* In some books, he poses as different people, such as reporter Chetter Hummin and minister Eto Demerzel. *The Second Foundation* books, written by David Brin, Gregory Bendord, and Greg Bear at the request of the Asimov estate, all include Daneel Olivaw.

Known Associates: Lije Baley's wife is Jessie (short for Jezebel), and his son is Bentley. He is partnered with R. Daneel Olivaw (the "R" indicates that Daneel is a Robot). Daneel's closest associate is his creator, Dr. Han Fastolfe.

Premise: In the distant past, humans from Earth colonized a number of nearby planets. Initially, life for the colonists was very hard, but eventually the planets were cleansed of any organisms that could harm humans. This resulted in increased lifespans for the settlers. The colonists' technological advances, particularly in robotics, created a servant class that increased the comfort of the settlers' lives. At the point in which this series is set, the descendents of the colonists, referred to as the "Spacers," have developed separate societies on each of the 49 planets they inhabit. What the Spacers have in common is disgust for Earth's population. They view the descendents of the people who stayed on Earth as primitive and disease-ridden. With their superior technology, they can, and have, restricted Earth people to Earth.

Earth's population has grown to the point that it can barely be sustained by the planet; ruthless efficiency is the only way to avoid mass shortages and popular unrest. People live and work in the "cities," gigantic hive-like enclosures that include business and residential areas. Almost every activity, from eating to showering, is done communally, in the most efficient manner possible.

Robots, the positronic brains that make them function, were invented on Earth. On Earth, robots have traditionally been used as menial labor, in mines and on farms. They work in the terrifying barren areas that exist between the cities, out of sight of the human population. On the Outer Worlds, robots are part of every household; they act as servants, and also do much of the work in businesses on each planet. As the series begins, Earth's society is changing. Earth's government has decided that it can increase efficiency by moving to the integrated human/robot model of society that is followed on the Outer Worlds. Jobs once performed by humans are assigned to robots, increasing efficiency by displacing human workers. Unemployed humans lose their societal classification and are reduced to the "desperate minimum." Even after a lifetime of work, they and their families face poverty. While the government talks about increased efficiency, the human population is near the point of rioting. Baley remembers how it feels, the grinding poverty of the barracks, eating the raw yeast mash that was all that his family could afford. Baley's father was a nuclear physicist who once had a high classification, but he lost his classification after an accident at the power plant. Many people, Lije Baley included, loathe robots. Robots have no feelings one way or the other about people, but the foundation of the robotic (positronic) brain is the Three Laws of Robotics:

1. A robot may not injure a human being, or through inaction allow a human being to come to harm.
2. A robot must obey the orders given it by human beings except where such orders would conflict with the First Law.
3. A robot must protect its own existence as long as such protection does not conflict with the First or Second Law.

Comment: Isaac Asimov (in the foreword to the 1983 Ballantine edition of *Caves of Steel*) traces the history of robots in science fiction back to a play entitled "R.U.R.," which was first staged in Czechoslovakia in 1921. "R.U.R." stood for Rossum's Universal Robots, the word "robot" having been derived for the Czech word for compulsory labor. In this play, the world came to a bad end, with the robots eventually revolting and destroying mankind. Works that followed reiterated the lesson that the knowledge to create robots would be the downfall of humanity. Asimov states that

> Even as a youngster, though, I could not bring myself to believe that if knowledge presented danger, the solution was ignorance. To me, it always seemed that the solution had to be wisdom. You did not refuse to look at danger, rather you learned how to handle it safely.

Asimov recounts that he first read a story with a sympathetic robot in the December 1938 issue of *Astounding Science Fiction.* (The story was "Helen O'Loy," written by Lester del Rey.) It inspired him to write a story with a loving portrayal of a robot (the short story "Robbie"). This was followed by two more: "Reason," in which a robot gets religion, and "Liar!," about a mind-reading robot. Asimov's editor for the last two was John Campbell. Asimov and Campbell's discussions about robots gave rise to the safeguards that would need to be in place to govern robots. Asimov wrote the rules, the "Three Laws of Robotics," into his fourth robot story, "Runaround."

Asimov's robot stories have fascinated readers (and writers) for decades. There are many "robot" mysteries based on Asimov's world. Asimov allowed other authors to quote the Three Laws, and even to expand upon them in the *Robot City* series (whose protagonists are Derec and Ariel). The events depicted in the *Robot City* books take place between *The Robots of Dawn* and *Robots and Empire:* they are *Odyssey* by Michael P. Kube-Mcdowell, *Suspicion* by Mike McQuay, *Cyborg* by William F. Wu, *Prodigy* by Arthur Byron Cover, *Refuge* by Rob Chilson, and *Perhelion* by William F. Wu. The *Robots and Aliens* series spun off from the *Robot City* series. In the *Robots and Aliens* series, writers imagine what would happen when the robots of Asimov's world meet aliens. The series again features Derec and Ariel, and includes *Changeling* by Stephen Leigh, *Renegade* by Cordell Scotten, *Intruder* by Robert Thurston, *Alliance* by Jerry Oltion, *Maverick* by Bruce Bethke, and *Humanity* by Jerry Oltion. Roger MacBride Allen's books are set after the events in *Robots and Empire*. They are *Caliban, Inferno,* and *Utopia*. Other mysteries set in this world include Mark W. Tiedmann's *Mirage, Chimera,* and *Aurora,* as well as Alexander C. Irvine's *Have Robot, Will Travel.* William F. Wu has written a series called *Robots in Time* that is based on Asimov's world. It includes *Predator, Marauder, Warrior, Dictator, Emperor,* and *Invader.* With *Robot and Empire,* Asimov connected the *Robot* series with the *Empire* series, creating an epic popularly called the *Foundation* series, which spans 20,000 years. In 1965 (long before the series were joined), the *Foundation* series won a special one-time Hugo Award for "Best All-time Science Fiction Series."

Literary Magic & Mayhem: These are "puzzle" mysteries, but not in the classic sense; in these, one element of the puzzle is the possible parameters of the behavior of the suspects, conspirators, and witnesses. The actions possible for robots are limited by the Three Laws of Robotics. Humans have a greater range of possible behaviors bur are, in some ways, just as predictable. Knowledge of human psychology comes into play in some of the books, with investigators determining that certain behaviors could or could not be executed by a given human because of that human's psychological profile. One theme that runs through the book is the racist way in which the robots are treated. At the outset of the series, Baley finds Daneel repellant, and feels ashamed when Daneel behaves better than the humans who surround him. Daneel's impeccable behavior infuriates Baley, and Baley strikes out verbally at Daneel, pointedly reminding him that he is a robot. Daneel has narrowly averted a riot when Baley begins this conversation:

> "In any case, remember that you are a robot. Nothing more than a robot. Just a robot. Like those clerks in the shoe store."
>
> "But this is obvious."
>
> "And you are not a human." Baley felt himself being driven into cruelty against his will.
>
> R. Daneel seemed to consider that. He said, "The division between human and robot is perhaps not as significant as that between intelligence and nonintelligence."
>
> "Maybe on your world," said Baley, "but not on earth."
>
> (p. 31 of the 1983 Ballantine edition of *The Caves of Steel.*)

Explorations: What angers Baley about Daneel? Does he ever overcome that anger?

What importance do names have to different characters?

What roles do friendship and trust play in this case?

Asimov seemed to enjoy exploring ways around the Three Laws of Robotics. Are there other ways in which a robot that follows the Three Laws of Robotics could be involved in a murder?

THE CASES

1. ***Caves of Steel.*** New York: Doubleday, 1954, 224 p.

SPACETOWN IN NEW YORK, 4920 A.D. New York Police Commissioner Enderby had an appointment with Spacer Roj Nemennuh Sarton on the morning of Sarton's murder. The murder took place in the most controlled area of New York: Spacetown. The Terrestrial authorities hand the investigation to the New York Police Department. The Police Commissioner hands it to Plainclothesman Elijah "Lije" Baley, classification C-5. Baley needs to work fast. If the Spacers are unsatisfied, there is a good chance that they will sue Earth's government, and then the cities will riot. Further, his failure would speed the replacement with robots of every plainclothesmen in the department. Then, everyone on the force would be out looking for a job. Also, Lije will have a Spacer looking over his shoulder during the investigation—the Spacers have demanded that one of their own be his partner in the investigation. Not only that, but that "partner" is going to be a robot. Already there have been riots in response to robots working in the cities. To top it off, the robot is going to be Lije's houseguest, to work with him every minute of every day—the perfect, dispassionate, recording machine, always thinking, ready to report everything...

ASSOCIATES: Julius Enderby—*Commissioner of the Police, City of New York is Lije's boss.* The police department is moving towards automation. Human detectives like Vince Barrett are being replaced with robots like R. Sammy. Vince Barrett, Simpson, Philip Norris, and Chen-low—*are humans who are still on the police force;* Jessie—*Baley's wife;* Bentley—*his 16-year-old son;* Dr. Han Fastolfe—*is in charge of the Spacetown end of the murder investigation;* Dr. Anthony Gerrigel—*a roboticist;* Joseph Klemin—*the leader of a terrorist cell bent on getting Spacers and robots to leave Earth;* Francis Clousarr—*one of the conspirators;* Prescott—*who works in personnel at the Yeast Farm;* Francis Clousarr—*a yeast farm employee.*

2. ***The Naked Sun.*** New York: Doubleday, 1957, 187 p.

SOLARIA (ONE OF THE OUTER PLANETS), 4921 A.D. Police investigators do not exist on Solaria; there is no need, because there is no crime. When faced with a brutal murder, the Solarians "request" assistance from Earth. (Since Earth's government officials are well aware that the Outer Worlds could easily annihilate Earth, all "requests" are fulfilled as expeditiously as possible.) Plainclothesman Baley (classification C-6) must investigate a crime of passion;

a brutal murder that cannot possibly have taken place. Unfortunately, partner R. Daneel's concern for Baley causes Daneel to be more of a hindrance than a help as Daneel works to protect Baley, and as Baley works to find a murderer.

ASSOCIATES: Undersecretary Albert Minnim—*who promises Baley a promotion to classification C-7 if the Solarians are happy with his work;* Hannis Gruer—*Head of Solarian Security;* Gloria Delmarre—*wife of the victim and the chief suspect;* Dr. Altim Thool—*who viewed the remains of the victims;* and Corwin Attlebish—*Acting Head of Solarian Security.*

3. **"Mirror Image,"** in *Tin Stars,* ed. by Isaac Asimov, Martin H. Greenberg, and Charles G. Waugh. New York: New American Library, 1986, p. 163–79. ISBN: 0451143957. This story was originally published in the May 1972 issue of Analog Science Fiction and Fact. It was republished in *The Best of Isaac Asimov* (1973), *The Complete Robot* (1982), and *Robot Visions* (1990).

EARTH, 4922 A.D. R. Daneel Olivaw convinced the captain of the Spacer starship *Eta Carina* to make a slight detour on its voyage to Aurora so that Daneel could be dispatched to consult Elijah Baley on a case of the theft of intellectual property. The conversation of the scholars involved was witnessed by their robots. While no human from the spacer ship is willing to speak to a human, they are willing to allow Baley to question their robots through video transmission.

ASSOCIATES: R. Idda—*robot, the personal servant of Gennao Sabbat;* and R. Preston—*robot, personal servant of Dr. Alfred Barr Humboldt.*

4. ***The Robots of Dawn.*** New York: Doubleday, 1983, 419 p. ISBN: 038518400X.

AURORA (ONE OF THE OUTER PLANETS), 4923 A.D. A movie dramatizing the events related in *The Naked Sun* has made Baley the pariah of the Police Department. He has quietly gone about his business, and he has made it part of his business to acclimate himself and a small group of volunteers to the world outside the cities. They will be ready when the Outer Worlds give Earth permission to colonize a new planet. Unfortunately, it doesn't appear that that will happen soon. When Aurora's government "requests" that Earth send Baley to investigate the deactivation of a humaniform robot, Earth acquiesces once more. Everyone has his own reasons for the investigation. Baley wants the Aurorans, particularly the influential Dr. Fastolfe, to become indebted to Earth and willing to lobby the other Outer Worlds on Earth's behalf. Since Baley's friend and host, Dr. Fastolfe, has proclaimed that he himself is the only viable suspect, the prospects look grim. In the course of this book, Dr. Fastolfe refers to many "legends" of robotics. The legends can be found in Asimov's short stories. Susan Calvin's telepathic robot is featured in the short story "Liar." "Little Miss" is from the story "The Bicentennial Man." Both of these stories can be found in *Robot Visions.*

ASSOCIATES: Bentley—*Baley's son, who doesn't think that his father looks much like a hero, but does believe in him;* New York Police Commissioner Wilson Roth—*who is not particularly impressed with Baley, and would not mind seeing him fail;* Dr. Han Fastolfe—*who convinced Aurora's government to request that Baley investigate the deactivation of the second humaniform robot, Jander Panell;* Earth's Department of Justice Undersecretary Lavinia Demachek—*who expects Baley to do his best.* The story includes a number of robots who perform simple tasks: R. Geronimo—*Earth's Police Department's messenger;* Faber—*Fastolfe's butler;* Borgraf—*Gladia's butler;* Debrett—*Dr. Vasilia's servant;* and Brundij—*Santirix Gremionis's butler.* Fanya—*Dr. Han Fastolfe's wife;* Gladia—*who is now called Gladia Solaria;* Dr. Vasilia Aliena—*Dr. Fastolfe's daughter;* Santirix Gremionis—*Gladia's persistent suitor;* and Kelden Amadiro—*Master Roboticist;* Daneel Olivaw and Giskard Reventlov—*Baley's guards and aides;* Maloon Cicis—*roboticist;* and Rutilan Horder—*the Chairman of the Auroran Legislature.*

5. ***Robots and Empire.*** New York: Doubleday, 1985, 383 p. ISBN: 0385190921.

AURORA, SOLARIA, BALEYWORLD, AND EARTH, CIRCA 5180 A.D. Two centuries after Baley's Death, Daneel Giskard Baley, a Settler (the great, great, great, great, great grandson of Elijah), asks Gladia Solaria to help investigate the loss of Settler ships on Solaria. Gladia is accompanied by the robots willed to her by Dr. Fastolfe, Daneel Olivaw, and Giskard Revenlov. Daneel and Giskard conduct their own investigation, and find that the villains' plans don't stop with murder: they are planning nothing less than the extinction of all life on Earth. This book's plot structure is nonlinear. The narrative integrates flashbacks into the action.

ASSOCIATES: Gladia Solaria—*who is now several centuries old;* R. Daneel Olivaw and R. Giskard Reventlov—*are the robots left to Gladia in Dr. Han Fastolfe's will;* Kelden Amadiro—*who still detests Earth people;* Vasilia Aliena—*Fastolfe's estranged daughter and Amadiro's ally;* and Levular Mandamus—*who has found a way to destroy Earth.*

ASIMOV, Isaac, Martin H. Greenberg, and Charles G. Waugh. (Editors)

ISAAC ASIMOV'S WONDERFUL WORLD OF SCIENCE FICTION ANTHOLOGY #5: TIN STARS

Genres/Themes Crossed: Man as Creator X Police (or other law enforcement personnel) Procedural.

Subjects/Character Types: Robots, Artificial Intelligence X Police, Government Agents.

Series/Stand-Alone: Anthology of short stories.

Scene of the Crime: Varies.

Detective: Varies.

Known Associates: Varies.

Premise: The editors chose previously published stories in which beings with artificial intelligence encounter the law. Story authors include the great early leaders of science fiction.

Comment: In the early days of science fiction, the field was relatively small and most of the people engaged in writing also read each other's work. The literature of the field worked much as the literature of scholarly disciplines works today. Those involved in the field had ideas and experimented with them, publishing the "results" (in this case, stories) in a few periodicals dedicated to the field. The published stories sparked more ideas in their readers, some of whom then wrote stories that presented further explorations of the ideas. It was a sort of conversation that took place within the covers of periodicals. It was, in the early days, possible to have a fairly comprehensive grasp of the works published. Some of the most interesting stories were republished in anthologies. One series of anthologies was entitled *Isaac Asimov's Wonderful Worlds of Science Fiction.* Each anthology explored a different topic:

1. Intergalactic Empires
2. The Science Fictional Olympics
3. Supermen
4. Comets
5. Tin Stars
6. Neanderthals
7. Space Shuttles
8. Monsters
9. Robots
10. Invasions

Literary Magic & Mayhem: This is an interesting mix of stories. Most were written and first published over 30 years ago. (The earliest has a copyright date of 1955.) "Animal Lover" by Stephen R. Donaldson was copyrighted in 1978 and is set in 2011. It is interesting to see how the 2011 that is imagined in the 1970s differs from present reality. Isaac Asimov's introduction points out interesting elements in some of the stories, in a way that increases the enjoyment of reading them.

Explorations: How did the behavior of the artificial intelligence character differ from the way a human would behave?

Was the artificial intelligence character sympathetic? Why or why not?

THE CASES

***Tin Stars.* New York:** New American Library, 1986, 351 p. ISBN: 0451143957; 9780451143952.

CONTENTS: Introduction *by Isaac Asimov;* Into the Shop *by Ron Goulart;* Cloak of Anarchy *by Larry Niven;* The King's Legions *by Christopher Anvil;* Finger of Fate *by Edward Wellen.* Arm of the Law *by Harry Harrison;* Voice-over *by Edward Wellen;* The Fastest Draw *by Larry Eisenberg;* Mirror Image *by Isaac Asimov;* Brillo *by Harlan Ellison and Ben Bova;* The Powers of Observation *by Harry Harrison;* Faithfully Yours *by Lou Tabakow;* Safe Harbor *by Donald Wismer;* Examination Day *by Henry Slesar;* The Cruel Equations *by Robert Sheckley;* Animal Lover *by Stephen R. Donaldson.*

ATHERTON, Nancy.

AUNT DIMITY'S DEATH

Genres/Themes Crossed: Paranormal X Traditional Mystery.
Subjects/Character Types: Ghosts X Amateur Sleuth (Contemporary).

Series/Stand-Alone: Relationships change over time, so the novels should be read in order. (The lone short story, "Honeymoon," is fun, but not necessary to the enjoyment of the series.) The first book could be either *Aunt Dimity's Death,* followed by *Aunt Dimity and the Duke,* or those two books could be reversed so that the series would begin with *Aunt Dimity and the Duke* and the second book would be *Aunt Dimity's Death.* It is recommended that the series be read in publication order, beginning with *Aunt Dimity's Death,* because that book sets the tone, the premise, and the basic cast of characters for the series. Readers who prefer strict chronological order may decide to begin with *Aunt Dimity and the Duke,* which is a prequel to *Aunt Dimity's Death,* but that is not recommended. *Aunt Dimity and the Duke* provides an exciting glimpse of the live Aunt Dimity, but the short passage is more meaningful if the reader already knows a little about Aunt Dimity, because then the final sighting is an amusing tease before Dimity is bid goodbye once again. Readers who begin with *Aunt Dimity and the Duke* may be disappointed in the rest of the series, which sometimes focuses on characters who are not included in *Aunt Dimity and the Duke*. Such readers might also be unhappy with the change in Dimity's role in the series.

Scene of the Crime: Most of the series takes place in present day England.

Detective: The continuing character in the series is Aunt Dimity, but she is only seen once, at a distance (by Emma, near the end of *Aunt Dimity and the Duke*). She moves in mysterious ways, usually by urging Lori Shepherd to action. Lori Elizabeth Shepherd is the protagonist of all the books except for *Aunt Dimity and the Duke* (which features Emma Porter). Lori is a reasonably sensible person, and Aunt Dimity acts as her mentor and sometimes her conscience. Aunt Dimity does not merely help Lori when Lori is investigating; Aunt Dimity actively goads Lori into many of her most interesting cases.

Known Associates: At the outset of the series *(Aunt Dimity's Death)*, Lori is profoundly alone. She never knew her father, who died when she was four months old. She spent years in a relationship with a man; when she realized that he'd never been the man she'd thought he was, she divorced him. Her mother, who has died recently, was her only family. At the beginning of the series, in *Aunt Dimity's Death,* Lori has retreated into her grief, cutting herself off from her friends. She has even boxed up the remains of her oldest companion, her last link to happier times: her stuffed rabbit Reginald. During the events of that first book, Lori reconnects with two of her oldest friends, Meg Thomson and Dr. Stanford J. ("Call Me Stan") Finderman. Many years ago, Lori worked for Dr. Finderman, curator of her university's rare book collection. She learned about books and manuscripts from him. Throughout the series, he continues to give her commissions, even after she moves to England. In *Aunt Dimity's Death,* Lori meets a few new people; chief among them is Dimity Westwood (deceased). Lori also begins to rebuild a family. In *Aunt Dimity's Death,* she meets the man whom she will marry, Bill Willis, and she meets Bill's father, William Willis. Four months before the events chronicled in the fourth book, *Aunt Dimity Digs In,* Lori and Bill become the parents of twin sons, Rob and Will; and later they add a nanny to their household. The first nanny is named Francesca Angelica Sciaparelli; the second is Annelise Sciaparelli. Lori's closest friend in England is Emma Harris. Emma's early adventures are chronicled in *Aunt Dimity and the Duke.* In that book, Emma meets Derek, and his children, Peter and Nell. Nell also has a stuffed animal, a long-ago gift from Dimity Westwood. Dimity made a variety of them and gave them to children who needed them; Nell's is Bertram, the bear. Lori lives in the Cotswolds, near the village of Finch. Neighbors include the Pym twins, Ruth and Louise, who were great friends of Dimity

Westwood. Residents of Finch include Peggy Kitchen, the local shopkeeper and postmistress, who first came to Finch as an evacuee when she was eight years old (during World War II), and who has recently returned to try to give back to the community. Peggy Kitchen's suitor is Jasper Taxman. Among the remaining residents are the Reverend Theodore Bunting and his wife, Lilian; the Vicarage housekeeper Annie Hodge, and her husband Burt; proprietress of the tea room, Sally Pyne; Christine and Dick Peacock, who own the pub; Able Farnham, the greengrocer; Mr. Barlow, a semi-retired mechanic; George Wetherhead, a train enthusiast; and Miranda Morrow, Finch's witch.

Premise: Lori Shepherd thought that "Aunt Dimity" was nothing more than a character her mother invented, a redoubtable woman with a sense of humor whose adventures in England were told to Laurie as bedtime stories. After both her mother's and Aunt Dimity's deaths, Lori finds out that Dimity Westwood was actually her mother's best friend. It was a friendship that spanned decades and distance, having begun while both women were serving the Allied cause in London during World War II. The friendship continued through correspondence between Dimity in England and Lori's mother in the United States. In her will, Dimity left Lori a task that takes Lori to England, to Dimity's cottage in the Cotswolds. Once there, Laurie opens a journal and finds that Dimity is still a wonderful correspondent. Dimity communicates to Lori from beyond the grave by writing in the journal.

Comment: According to the first part of our definition of mystery fiction, a crime is suspected, and the action of the story is driven by an attempt to uncover the truth or to capture the perpetrator. By that measure, this is not a mystery series. However, it is a series that has been classified by the Library of Congress as a mystery series, and so it is consistently shelved in the mystery sections of both bookstores and libraries. Therefore, it meets the second criterion for a "mystery" as defined in this bibliography. The books do contain puzzles, and many of those puzzles are rooted in criminal acts. On the other hand, in over half of the books, those acts took place so long ago that there is no question of bringing a villain to justice. In some of the books, there was, technically, no crime, yet there remains a wrong that must be redressed. In most cases, the emphasis of the books is on healing and protecting, not on bringing villains to justice. The communications from the deceased Aunt Dimity are an obvious paranormal element. The timeline presented herein is accurate, but it may not be true. The books read as if they are contemporary, set in the year that they are published. Once children appear, the dates become more specific, tied to the children's ages. The dates listed here were calculated from information in *Aunt Dimity and the Next of Kin*. In that book, Elizabeth Beacham dies in her mid-fifties, and she was born in 1950;

her brother last appeared with her in a photograph in 1985, and the photograph is 20 years old. In the same book, Lori states that the twins just turned five years old. So, Rob and Will were calculated to have been born in March 2000, and that date was used to extrapolate the rest. *Aunt Dimity and the Duke* was nominated for the Dilys Award in 1995. *Aunt Dimity's Death* won the Mystery Guild New Discovery Award.

Literary Magic & Mayhem: The 30-year-old protagonist of most of the books is accompanied on her adventures by her stuffed rabbit, Reginald. Many other characters in the books also treasure stuffed animal companions. The series sounds horribly twee, but, surprisingly, it is not. One of the elements that saves it is its theme of overcoming grief. Most of those stuffed animals were given to children who were coping with devastating loss. They were not toys, they were lifelines. Those lifelines were created by a remarkable woman named Dimity Westwood. Having once been helped through grief (by Lori's mother), she had the motivation, compassion, and understanding to help those children heal. The setting, England, approximately 60 years after World War II, allows the author to create elderly characters who were children during the war. All these decades later, it is possible to see how each person's response to losses created by war shaped (and in some cases, twisted) his or her life. Several of the recent books feature some characters whose response to grief was to descend into madness. These are the least complex and the least interesting books in the series (*Aunt Dimity and the Deep Blue Sea, Aunt Dimity Goes West*). The most recent book, *Aunt Dimity Slays the Dragon,* omits the historical themes, but renews the series' themes of forgiveness and redemption.

The author has a great deal of fun depicting life in an English village. For instance, the village fair competitions in *Aunt Dimity's Good Deed* include "best flower arrangement in a gravy boat." The author manages to spike pathos with a wry twist, or maybe she spikes her humor with a touch of pathos, as in this character description from *Aunt Dimity and the Duke:* "She knew exactly what the future held in store. She'd planned it years ago." (p. 166) Her descriptions of places invoke their history while commenting on time's changes and setting the mood for the story: "Oxford was as unpleasant as ever, noisy and traffic-choked, a lumpy conglomeration of beautiful colleges, swallowed whole, but never fully digested, by a sprawling, unkempt town." (p. 31) That's from *Aunt Dimity's Christmas,* which also offers a description of Finch's village square, decorated for Christmas:

> Disembodied plastic Santa heads garroted with tinselly garlands leered from the tearoom's windows, life-sized plastic choirboys alternated with blinking candy canes along the front of Peacock's pub, and the large display window in Kitchen's Emporium featured a deer-shaped lawn ornament posed stiffly

beside a motorized father Christmas whose staring eyes and lurching movements hinted more at madness than at merriment. (p. 28)

Lori, the protagonist for most of the books, is a good woman, but not a paragon of virtue. She's occasionally tempted by gorgeous and not-so-gorgeous men, and she is sometimes selfish. In fact, the series avoids heavy handed preaching in *Aunt Dimity's Christmas* by depicting enough of Lori's selfishness that the reader is frustrated by her lack of perspective, and relieved when other characters take her to task. It is interesting that her selfishness in that book takes the form of wanting to create the perfect Christmas. The dream of the perfect Christmas, created as an act of love for one's family and friends, is so widely accepted that Lori's excesses seem normal, even laudable. Most readers have probably attempted to create a perfect event or a perfect holiday, and may understand a little of Lori's difficulty in keeping her values in sight during the mad whirl. Her past excesses are so close to our past excesses that her redemption offers us a path to regaining perspective during our own holidays.

Explorations: In *Aunt Dimity's Death,* Bill talks about how he met Dimity when he was a child, shortly after his mother's death. At his school, the other students had been told of his loss, and everyone carefully avoided speaking of mothers in his hearing. He wasn't given any opportunity to talk about his mother. Dimity said, "How can you avoid dwelling in the past when the past dwells in you?" She said that the past was part of him and that trying to avoid it was like trying to avoid his arm or leg. He could do it, but it would make a cripple of him. She also said that grief was something you must go through, it can't be avoided, that there are no shortcuts, and that everyone works through grief differently.

Which characters in the book suffered a loss?

How did others help them through it or make it worse?

Did they, through their own actions, work to heal or work to cripple themselves?

How long did it take them to come to terms with their losses?

What helped them heal?

THE CASES

1. ***Aunt Dimity's Death.*** New York: Viking, 1992, 244 p. ISBN: 0670844497.

BOSTON, LONDON, AND FINCH (ENGLAND), APRIL 1997. A mysterious summons from the law firm of Harris and Harris leads to an even more mysterious commission. Actually, two commissions. The first is from a woman whom Lori had believed to be a fictional character; the second is from Lori's mother, who died less than a year ago. Lori will do whatever it takes to fulfill her mother's last wish. What she does not know is that her efforts will uncover old wounds, and will give her the means to heal them.

ASSOCIATES: Lori Sheperd—*protagonist, who is still coping with the grief of her mother's death;* Bill Willis—*whose mother died when he was a child;* William Willis, Sr.—*Bill's father;* Dr. Stanford J. Finderman—*who taught Lori about rare books and manuscripts;* Meg Thompson—*another friend who has been worried about Lori;* Doug Fleming—*Meg's partner;* Miss Kingsley—*concierge of the Flamborough Hotel in London;* Paul—*their driver;* Dr. Evan Fleischer—*Dimity does not like him, and she's a wonderful judge of character;* Emma and Derek Harris—*Lori's neighbors;* Ruth and Louise Pym—*the twins;* Archy Gorman—*who used to tend bar at the Flamborough;* Andrew MacLaren—*Bobby's brother;* and Dimity Westwood—*deceased.*

2. ***Aunt Dimity and the Duke.*** New York: Viking, 1994, 290 p. ISBN: 0670849642.

PENFORD HALL (ENGLAND), MAY 1993. Emma Porter, escaping from the solicitous arms of friends who want to comfort her over the perfidy of her long-time lover, takes a holiday to tour the gardens of England. She meets the Pym sisters, who send her to Penford Hall. There she helps restore a legend (among other activities).

ASSOCIATES: Emma Porter—*protagonist.* The inhabitants of Penford Hall: Grayson Alexander—*Duke of Penford;* Susannah Ashley-Woods—*his cousin;* and Syd Bishop—*her manager;* Gash—*the chauffer;* Crowley—*the head butler;* Mattie—*his granddaughter, the maid;* Hallard—*the footman;* Newland—*the gatekeeper;* Bantry—*the head gardener;* Kate Cole—*the housekeeper;* Nanny Cole—*Kate's mother;* and Madama—*the cook.* Visitors to Penford Hall: Emma Porter—*who is not a professional gardener but who was recommended to restore the lady chapel garden by Ruth and Louise Pym;* Peter (age 10) and Nell (age 5)—*are the children of Derek Harris;* Bertie—*Nell's stuffed bear.* The villagers of Penford Harbor: Tom Trevoy—*Chief Constable of Penford Harbor;* Dr. Singh; Mrs. Shuttleworth—*the vicar's wife;* Jonah Pengully—*who owns the general store;* Mr. Carroway—*the greengrocer;* Mr. Minion—*the butcher;* Herbert Munting—*who provides the hall and the town with poultry;* Mr. and Mrs. Tharby—*owners of the village pub;* and Ernestine Potts—*their cook.* Dimity Westwood makes a short appearance.

3. ***Aunt Dimity's Good Deed.*** New York: Viking, 1996, 290 p. ISBN: 0670867152.

ENGLAND, AUGUST 1999. "What do you do when life begins to go wrong and you've used up all three wishes?" Lori is on her second honeymoon, accompanied by her father-in-law instead of her husband. She thinks that she's as miserable as she can get; and then her father-in-law takes off on a mysterious errand. In the process of tracking him down, she will uncover scandal, blackmail, and murder.

ASSOCIATES: Lori Sheperd—*protagonist.* Emma Harris—*Lori's friend;* Derek—*Emma's husband;* Nell—*his daughter (age 12);* Bertie—*Nell's stuffed bear;* Dimity Westwood—*deceased;* Reginald—*Lori's stuffed rabbit;* William Willis, Sr.—*Lori's father-in-law;* Bill Harris—*Lori's husband;* Paul—*a driver assigned by Miss Kingsley to help Lori.* Members of the Willis family's English branch: Gerald Willis—*who is beautiful and scandalous;* Arthur Willis—*the bumbler;* Lucy Willis—*a competent lady.* The older Willis generation includes Thomas—*Gerald's father, who still treasures the stuffed giraffe (named Geraldine) that Dimity gave to him long ago;* Williston—*Arthur's father;* Anthea—*Lucy's mother;* Swann—*Anthea's new husband.* Steven Hawley—*the rector of St. Bartholomew's;* Sir Kenmare Poulteney (Sir Poppet)—*director of Cloverly House;* and Dr. Sally Flannery.

4. *Aunt Dimity Digs In.* New York: Viking, 1998, 275 p. ISBN: 0670870617.

FINCH (ENGLAND), JULY 2000. Lori is asked to quietly recover an historical pamphlet that was stolen from the vicarage. It's a chance for her to re-enter the life of the village after having sequestered herself to take care of her now four-month-old twin sons, born in March 2000.

ASSOCIATES: Lori Shepherd—*protagonist.* Bill—*Lori's husband;* Robert and William—*their twin sons;* Reginald—*Lori's stuffed rabbit.* The people of Finch include: Emma and Derek Harris; Ruth and Louise Pym; Francesca Angelica Sciaparelli; Peggy Kitchen; Jasper Taxman; the Reverend Theodore Bunting and his wife, Lilian. Annie and Burt Hodge; Sally Pyne (who has her granddaughter, Rainey Dawson, staying in her home); Christine and Dick Peacock; Able Farnham; Mr. Barlow; George Wetherhead; and Miranda Morrow. Others include: Paolo Sciaparelli—*who is Rainey's best friend;* Edmund Terrance—*Rainey's stuffed tiger;* Dr. Adrian Culver—*an archaeologist;* and Simon Blakely and Katrina Graham—*his graduate students.*

5. *Aunt Dimity's Christmas.* New York: Viking, 1999, 214 p. ISBN: 0670884537.

FINCH (ENGLAND), DECEMBER 2000. All Lori wanted was the perfect Christmas, a beautifully decorated house, platefuls of Christmas cookies, feasting for friends and family, and maybe a little snow. When Lori finds a derelict in a snowdrift at her front door, her plans are postponed. When Dimity insists that Lori follow through and find out what drove the young man down the path to the cottage, Lori's plans are derailed.

ASSOCIATES: Lori Shepherd—*protagonist.* Bill Willis—*her husband;* Robert and William Willis—*their nine-month-old twins;* Reginald—*a stuffed rabbit that Dimity made for Lori after Lori's father died;* William Willis, Sr.—*Bill's father, has offered to tend the twins while nanny Francesca Angelica Sciaparelli holidays in Italy with her fiancé;* and Dimity Westwood—*deceased.* The villagers of Finch are staging the Nativity play directed by Lilian Bunting, featuring her husband the vicar as narrator, it features: William Willis, Sr.—*as Joseph;* Nell Harris—*as the Virgin;* Peggy Kitchen, Sally Pyne and Christine Peacock—*as the wise men;* Jasper Taxman—*as Herod;* Able Farnham and George Wetherhead—*as shepherds;* Miranda Morrow—*as the angel of the Lord;* and four-month-old Piero (son of Annie and Burt Hodge)—*as the baby Jesus.* Mr. Barlow—*who works the lights;* and Dick Peacock—*who plays the piano.*

In Oxford: Smitty—*Kit Smith, a.k.a. Christopher Anscombe-Smith;* Dr. Pritchard and Nurse Willoughby—*who treat Smitty;* Luke Boswell—*hospital volunteer;* Lancaster—*is the stuffed horse that Dimity made for Christopher;* Father Julian Bright—*who runs a homeless shelter called Saint Benedict's;* Anne and Charles Somerville—*who once hired Kit to work at their farm;* Father Phillip Raywood and his assistant Father Andrew Danos—*run a soup kitchen at St. Joseph's.* Lady Felicity Havorford—*Christopher's sister.*

Dr. Stanford J. Finderman—*Lori's old friend;* Miss Kinsley—*from London;* Paul—*the chauffeur;* Emma and Derek Harris—*Lori's friends and neighbors;* Peter—*their 18-year-old son;* Nell—*their 13-year-old daughter;* Anthea—*Bill's Aunt;* Gerald—*Bill's cousin;* and Lucy—*Gerald's wife;* and Williston—*Bill's Uncle;* Ruth and Louise Pym—*the elderly twins;* Francesca Angelica Sciaparelli—*the twin's nanny;* Dr. Adrian Culver—*Francesca Angelica Sciaparelli's fiancé.*

6. ***Aunt Dimity Beats the Devil.*** New York: Viking, 2000, 245 p. ISBN: 0670891797.

WYRDHURST (ENGLAND), OCTOBER 2001. Lori's mentor, Dr. Stanford J. Finderman, talked her into driving to Northumberland to evaluate a book collection at Wyrdhurst. Lori is almost killed on the drive to Wyrdhurst; and no one is sure if it was an accident or an attempted murder. Before the mysteries unravel, Lori will encounter everything from ghostly possession to terrorists.

ASSOCIATES: Lori Shepherd—*protagonist;* Bill Willis—*her husband;* Robert and William Willis—*their 19-month-old twins;* Adam Chase—*a writer;* Captain Guy Manning; Jared and Nicole Hollander—*the newlywed owners of Wyrdhurst;* Mrs. Hatch—*their housekeeper;* Major Ted—*Nicole's stuffed bear;* Dr. MacEwan; Bart Little—*who owns the village of Blackhope's pub;* James—*who is Bart's son;* Bert and Brett—*who are Bart's brothers;* Claire Byrd—*deceased;* Dimity Westwood—*deceased;* and Dickie Byrd.

7. *Aunt Dimity Detective.* New York: Viking, 2001, 229 p. ISBN: 067003021X.

FINCH (ENGLAND), APRIL 2002. Lori and her family were in Boston when a murder took place in Finch. They return to a village where everyone is sure that a neighbor was involved in the horrible Pruneface Hooper's death. The woman spread poison with every word she spoke, and the malicious contagion has not ended with her death: the climate of suspicion has changed Finch. Lori believes that the murderer must be discovered, and she seems to be the only person who cares enough to search for the killer.

ASSOCIATES: Lori Shepherd—*protagonist.* Bill—*Lori's husband;* Robert and William—*their twin sons (who were almost two when the murderer struck);* Annelise—*Robert and William's nanny;* Dimity Westwood—*deceased;* Reginald—*Lori's stuffed rabbit;* The Reverend Theodore Bunting—*who leads the local church;* Lilian—*his wife;* Nicholas Fox—*Lilian's nephew.* Others in Finch include: Christopher Anscombe-Smith (Kit); Ruth and Louise Pym; Peggy and Jasper Taxman; Sally Pyne; Christine and Dick Peacock; George Wetherhead; Miranda Morrow; Emma Harris; Harry Mappin; and Mr. Barlow.

8. *Aunt Dimity Takes a Holiday.* New York: Viking, 2003, 199 p. ISBN: 067003200X.

THE HAILESHAM ESTATE (ENGLAND), OCTOBER 2003. Derek has been estranged from his father, the ninth Earl Elstyn, for decades. He's summoned back to the estate when his father calls a meeting of the entire family. Bill Willis is present as the lawyer of Lord Elstyn, and Lori has accompanied Bill. The Elstyn family is under siege: anonymous threats and strange accidents are plaguing them. The ostensible accidents are getting progressively more serious. If the attacker is not found soon, someone will die.

ASSOCIATES: Lori Shepherd—*protagonist.* Bill Willis—*her husband, they travel to Hailesham at the bidding of Lord Elstyn;* Dimity Westwood—*deceased but able to remain in contact with Lori because Loria takes the journal with her to Hailesham;* Derek Harris—*a.k.a. Anthony Evelyn Armstrong Seton, Viscount Hailesham, the eldest son of Lord Elstyn;* Emma—*Derek's wife and Lori's friend;* Simon Elstyn—*a younger son of Lord Elstyn;* Georgina—*Simon's wife;* and Oliver Elstyn—*another younger son of Lord Elstyn.*

Lady Landover—*a.k.a. Claudia Elstyn, a niece of Lord Elstyn's;* Jim Huang—*archivist;* Giddings—*the butler;* Derek Harris—*(the original Derek Harris), carpenter;* Charlotte Elizabeth Winfield—*a.k.a. Winnie the nanny;* Nell and Peter Harris—*Derek's children;* Kit Smith—*who comes to Hailesham to assure himself that Nell is on the mend after she is injured.*

9. *Aunt Dimity, Snowbound.* New York: Viking, 2004, 226 p. ISBN: 0670032786.

LADYTHORNE ABBEY (ENGLAND), FEBRUARY 2004. The holidays have worn Lori out, and Emma prescribes a relaxing day hike. The day is beautiful, and the hike is relaxing—so relaxing that Lori neglects her map and loses her way. And then there's the snowstorm... Lori seeks refuge at the locked-up Ladythorne Abbey, and there she finds another traveler who had become lost in the snow. When the woman pulls out a pry bar to force open the door, Lori is forced to wonder if she has fallen in with thieves.

ASSOCIATES: Lori Shepherd—*protagonist.* Bill Willis—*Lori's husband;* Emma Harris—*is Loris' best friend;* Wendy Walker—*is a fellow traveler who carries strange hiking equipment;* Jamie Macrae—*who was caught;* Catchpole—*the caretaker.*

10. *Aunt Dimity and the Next of Kin.* New York: Viking, 2005, 227 p. ISBN: 0670033782.

OXFORD, MARCH 2005. Lori meets an extraordinary woman, Elizabeth Beacham, in the course of her volunteer work at Radcliffe Infirmary. (Nurse Willoughby calls on Lori when a patient has no visitors and Lori comes and visits. The patients refer to her as "The listener. The bringer of books.") After Ms. Beacham dies, Lori sets out to find her next of kin so that Ms. Beacham's body can be released for a memorial service. Finding Ms. Beacham's missing brother turns out to be difficult and heartbreaking.

ASSOCIATES: Lori Shepherd—*protagonist.* Bill Willis—*Lori's husband;* Rob and Will—*their five-year-old twin sons;* Annelise—*the twin's nanny;* Reginald—*Lori's stuffed rabbit;* Dimity Westwood—*who is deceased, but not departed;* Nurse Lucinda Willoughby—*who calls Lori to come to cheer up hospital patients;* Father Julian Bright—*who works at Saint Benedict's;* Mr. Barlow—*whose chimney was destroyed;* Elizabeth Beacham—*one of Lori's favorite patients;* Gabriel Ashcroft—*Ms. Beacham's downstairs neighbor, an artist;* Stanley—*his cat;* Joanna Quinn—*who charms Gabriel;* Chloe—*her daughter;* Kenneth Fletcher-Beauchamps—*Elizabeth Beacham's brother;* Hamish—*Kenneth's stuffed hedgehog;* Mrs. Pollard—*who was once Kenneth's neighbor;* Sir Percy Pelham—*who helps out by providing Lori with transportation in his private jet;* Mr. Moss—*who was Elizabeth Beacham's soliciter;* Terry Edmonds—*a courier;* Big Al Layton, Limping Leslie, and Blinker McKay—*are from Saint Benedict's;* Mr. Mehta—*restaurant-owner;* Father Musgrove; Emma Harris and Kit Smith—*are partners in the new Anscombe Riding Center.*

11. *Aunt Dimity and the Deep Blue Sea.* New York: Viking, 2006, 246 p. ISBN: 9780670034765.

ERINSKIL (SCOTLAND), APRIL 2005. Bill has been receiving threats against his family for a couple of weeks. When these threats come accompanied by photographs that show that his tormentor has access to Lori, Robert, and William, Bill goes to Scotland Yard. Lori and the children go into hiding, only to find themselves on an island with many mysteries, and maybe a few ghosts.

ASSOCIATES: Lori Shepherd—*protagonist.* Bill Willis—*Lori's husband;* Robert and William—*their five-year-old twin sons;* Annalise Sciaparelli—*the twin's nanny;* Reginald—*Lori's stuffed rabbit;* Aunt Dimity—*deceased;* Sir Perceval Pelham—*who owns a mansion on Erinskil;* Mrs. Gammidge—*Sir Perceval's housekeeper;* Elliot Southmore and Kate Halston—*Sir Perceval's assistants;* Andrew Ross and Damian Hunter—*are bodyguards hired to protect Lori and the twins;* Peter Harris—*a.k.a Harry Peters;* Cassandra Thorpe-Lynton—*Peter's girlfriend;* Abaddon—*a visitor to Erinskil.* Villagers on Erinskil include Mick Ferguson—*fisherman;* and Mrs. Muggoch—*pub-keeper.*

12. ***Aunt Dimity Goes West.*** New York: Viking, 2007, 228 p. ISBN: 9780670038404.

BLUEBIRD (COLORADO), JUNE 2005. An almost-fatal attack on Lori left her severely traumatized. For the last six weeks, she has been reliving it in her nightmares. Bill arranges for a vacation in the Colorado Rockies in the hope that the change of place will help her heal. The idyllic retreat is haunted by the dead and by the living. The living are more dangerous.

ASSOCIATES: Lori Shepherd—*protagonist.* Bill—*Lori's husband;* Robert and William—*their five-year-old twin sons;* Annalise Sciaparelli—*the twin's nanny;* Reginald—*Lori's stuffed rabbit;* Aunt Dimity—*deceased;* In Colorado: Cyril Pennyfeather—*who died at age 35 in 1896;* Toby Cooper; and James Blackwell. Villagers (of the village Finch) include Sally Pyne, Peggy Taxman, Miranda Morrow, Dick Peacock, Ruth and Louise Pym, Emma Harris, Mr. Barlow, and George Weatherhead. Villagers (of Bluebird) include Brett Whitcombe, Carrie Vyne, Maggie Flaxton, Greg Wilstead, Nick and Arlene Altman, Dick Major, Mrs. Rose Blanding, Rufe and Lou Zimmer, and Amanda Barrow.

13. ***Aunt Dimity: Vampire Hunter.*** New York: Penguin Group, 2008, 232 p. ISBN: 9780670018543.

FINCH (ENGLAND), OCTOBER 2005. The twins claim they saw a vampire while they were out riding. Lori is *almost* sure that's impossible, but then she didn't believe in ghosts until after she met Dimity. She is sure that the twins saw something, and that no one should be spying on their riding lessons. It wasn't that long ago that the twins were kidnapped. Lori knows that she may be overprotective, but she cannot rest until she solves the mystery of "Rendor, the Destroyer of Souls."

ASSOCIATES: Lori Shepherd—*protagonist.* Bill Willis—*Lori's husband;* Robert and William—*their five-year-old twin sons;* Annalise Sciaparelli—*the twin's nanny;* Reginald—*Lori's stuffed rabbit;* Aunt Dimity—*deceased;*

Miss Archer—*the headmistress of the twin's school;* Emma Harris—*Lori's best friend;* Christopher "Kit" Anscombe-Smith—*is Emma's partner in the Anscombe Riding Center.* In this book Kit learns something about his parentage. Friedrich—*a stablehand at the Anscombe Riding Center;* Emma's daughter Eleanor "Nell" Harris—*who long ago gave her heart to Kit;* Leo Sutherland—*who is camping in the forest;* Lizzie Black—*who had heard Dimity speak about Lori's mother Beth;* Desmond Carmichael—*the Upper Deeping Despatch newspaper's editor;* Henrietta Harcourt—*Aldercot Hall's cook;* Mr. Bellamy—*Aldercot Hall's butler;* and Charlotte DuCaral. Rory Tanner—*was once gamekeeper at Aldercot Hall.* The villagers of Finch include Sally Pyne, Miranda Morrow, Christine and Dick Peacock, Ruth and Louise Pym, Mr. Barlow, George Weatherhead, Lilian Bunting, and her husband, the Reverend Bunting.

14. "**Honeymoon,**" in *Malice Domestic 5*, ed. by Phyllis A. Whitney. New York: Simon & Schuster, 1996, p. 158–67. ISBN: 0671896326.

FINCH (ENGLAND), APRIL 2006. During the rainy Easter holiday, Lori tells her six-year-old sons the story of her honeymoon. She and Bill honeymooned in Switzerland, and a series of phone calls from Bill's office led them to deduce the identity of a killer.

ASSOCIATES: Associates: Lori Shepherd—*protagonist;* Bill—*Lori's husband;* Robert and William—*their six-year-old twin sons;* Reginald—*Lori's stuffed rabbit.*

15. ***Aunt Dimity Slays the Dragon***. New York: Viking, 2009, 232 p. ISBN: 9780670020508.

FINCH (ENGLAND), MAY THROUGH AUGUST 2006. Lori is unhappy; she's already anticipating a hot, boring summer. There will be events—even now (in May), Peggy Taxman is holding interminable committee meetings on Finch's "summer festivities." The festivities are the same events that have been held every summer since Lori came to Finch. The meetings focus on admonitions regarding picayune details. While the villagers are struggling to stay awake as the first meeting draws to a close, there is a surprise. Horace Malvern's nephew has returned to Finch, and he and his friends swoop into the meeting with an announcement of their upcoming Renaissance Festival, to be held in Bishop's Wood.

Lori is determined to quell her rampageous imagination. She feels humiliated by the wild fancies that she had indulged in during her last case. She notices the series of accidents that befall "King Wilfred," and firmly dismisses her suspicions of attempted regicide. The attacks continue, and Lori investigates on her own. After she's assaulted, she confides in her husband Bill. She's surprised when he confirms her suspicions, and heartened when she receives a vote of confidence from Aunt Dimity.

The last few cases in this series have deviated from the excellent pattern set in the earlier books. Lori has become rather silly. Here, she returns to being a young woman with an active imagination and a passionate nature who is also rational and determined. The themes in the book return to the exploration of the alternatives people can choose from in response to fear and disappointment, and also to questions on how to live a good life, one filled with love and joy.

ASSOCIATES: Lori Shepherd—*protagonist.* Bill—*Lori's husband;* Robert and William—*their six-year-old twin sons;* Reginald—*Lori's stuffed rabbit;* Dimity Westwood—*deceased;* Peggy Taxman—*the Chairwoman for Finch's summer activities, store owner and Finch post-mistress;* Jasper Taxman—*retired accountant,* the Reverend Theodore Bunting—*who runs the local church;* Lilian—*his wife;* Mr. Barlow—*car-repair-shop owner;* Miranda Morrow—*who grows herbs;* Christine and Dick Peacock—*who own the pub;* Sally Pyne—*who owns the tearoom and knows how to sew (a useful skill when costumes are needed);* George Wetherhead—*model train enthusiast;* Grant Tavistock and Charles Bellingham—*art appraisers;* and Horace Malvern—*Lori's neighbor.*

Participants in the Festival include King Wilfred—*Horace Malvern's nephew Calvin;* Jinks the jester—*a.k.a. Rowan Grove;* Lord Belvedere—*who once worked for Scotland Yard;* Sir James le Victorieux and Lord Llewellyn—*both also retired from Scotland Yard;* Sir Peregrine the Pure—*a.k.a. Pretty Perry;* Sir Jacques de Poitiers, Dragon Knight—*a.k.a. Randy Jack;* Edmond Deland—*handyman;* Little Mirabel—*a.k.a. Janet Watkins, one of the madrigal singers;* Kay Jorgensen and Lady Amelia—*who are also madrigal singers;* Mistress Farseeing—*a fortuneteller;* Emma Harris—*Lori's best friend;* Will and Rob—*Lori's sons, who get to ride their horses as pages in the parade and before the joust.*

B

BABSON, Marian (Pseudonym for Ruth Stenstreem).

NINE LIVES TO MURDER

Genres/Themes Crossed: Anthropomorphic Animals X Traditional Mystery.

Subjects/Character Types: Animal Sleuth X Amateur Sleuth (Contemporary).

Series/Stand-Alone: Stand-alone.

Scene of the Crime: London: Chesterton Theatre and St. Monica's Hospital. Some time in the 1990s.

Detective: Winstanley "Win" Fortescue, Shakespearean actor, prospective Knight of the Realm (there have been discrete inquiries on how he would receive the honor), his consciousness driven by an accident into the body of Monty, the theater cat.

Known Associates: Win's wife of eight years is Miranda Everton Fortesque; his first wife was Antoinette; he and Antoinette have two children, Geoffrey and Jennet. Win also had two mistresses, actor Cynthia Vernon and *London Record* reporter Jilly Zanna. Win was rehearsing for the opening of the play *Serpent in the Heather* when he was struck down. Rufus Tuxford is the Director of *Serpent in the Heather;* Miranda was cast as the wife; Geoffrey was getting his first big break, playing the son; Cynthia plays the daughter; Peter Farley plays a mysterious American friend of the daughter, and is also Win's understudy. The Stage Manager is Davy Bentham. The Wardrobe Mistress is Tottie Clayton. Old Sam watches the stage door, and the stagehands include Woody Woodson, Eddie, and Bob. People at St. Monica's Hospital include Dame Theodora McCarran, who was sent to St. Monica's to dry out before beginning work on a film production in America; Oliver Crump, who is her nephew and a hated stage critic; Sister Dale, attending Dame Theodora; and Jake, who accompanies Jilly to photograph subjects for her news stories. In the latter part of the book, Madame Rosetti works as speech coach to the cat that is in a man's body, and Ace Barron acts as his bodyguard. Montmorency's (the cat's) love interests include Cynthia Vernon's Persian cat, named the Duchess of Malfi, and the bar's cat, Butterfly.

Premise: If a cat and an actor collide headfirst, their consciousnesses can be transferred.

Comment: Ruth Stenstreem (a.k.a. Marian Babson) was secretary of the British Crime Writers Association. She now lives in the United States. She has written over 30 mysteries.

Literary Magic & Mayhem: This is a fun, quick read with a breezy style. The viewpoint is omniscient, dipping into the minds of different characters at different times.

Explorations: How well was cat's behavior depicted?

THE CASE

1. ***Nine Lives to Murder.*** New York: St. Martin's Press, 1994, c1992, 188 p. ISBN: 0312105118.

LONDON, 199? In the stage-blocking rehearsal for *The Serpent in the Heather,* Winstanley "Win" Fortesque practiced climbing a ladder in a kilt, looking for a way to get to the top without flashing the audience. On his seventh or eighth try, he fell. The stage cat, Monty, broke his fall, possibly saving Win's life. Win's head collided with Monty's; both ended up concussed. When Win awakened, he was in the cat's body. He soon tracks down his human body—it's at St. Miranda's hospital, seemingly in a coma. Subsequent events that threaten Win's body make it clear that someone is determined to murder him. As his understudy takes the stage, Win prowls the backstage of the theater and the corridors of the hospital trying to identify a killer.

ASSOCIATES: See above.

BARNES, Steven. Co-authored *the Dream Park series* with Larry Niven. See: NIVEN, Larry: Dream Park.

BEASON, Doug. Co-authored (with Kevin J. Anderson) the series that begins with *Virtual Destruction.* See: ANDERSON, Kevin and Doug Beason: Virtual Destruction.

BEBRIS, Carrie.

PRIDE AND PRESCIENCE

Genres/Themes Crossed: Secret Society X Traditional Mystery (Historical).

Subjects/Character Types: Spell-Casters (Sorcerors) in *Pride and Prescience* and *Suspense and Sensibility,* Ghosts (in *North by Northanger*), there are no speculative elements in *The Matters at Mansfield* X Amateur Sleuth (Historical).

Series/Stand-Alone: This series changes in character and direction from book to book. Readers who dislike supernatural mysteries should avoid the first three books in the series, but may enjoy *The Matters at Mansfield, or, the Crawford Affair.* Those who enjoy mysteries with supernatural elements may enjoy the first three books in the series and continue to the fourth to spend more time with the appealing characters. Beyond the main direction of the series, the relationship between Elizabeth and Darcy, particularly in Darcy's attitude towards his wife, changes from book to book. Those annoyed with his paternalistic attitude in the first book may enjoy the other entries in the series.

Scene of the Crime: Regency England.

Detective: Mrs. Darcy (nee Elizabeth Bennet), sometimes assisted (and occasionally obstructed) by her new husband, Mr. Fitzwilliam Darcy.

Known Associates: Mr. Fitwilliam Darcy marries Elizabeth at the opening of the first book in this series, *Pride and Prescience.* Georgiana is Darcy's sister. Mr. and Mrs. Bennet are Elizabeth's parents. Jane Bingley (nee Bennet) is Elizabeth's dearest sister. (Jane marries. Mr. Charles Bingley at the opening of the first book in the series,) Mr. Collins is a clergyman to Darcy's aunt, Lady Catherine. Charlotte Collins is Elizabeth's friend and Mr. Collins's wife.

Premise: In the aftermath of Austen's *Pride and Prejudice,* Darcy and Elizabeth are wed, and should be supremely happy. Unfortunately, England is not as safe as they once thought. There is more in their world than is encompassed in their philosophies. In England, there are sorcerous artifacts from other lands, as well as from England's past. There are practitioners of magic, there are ghosts. Elizabeth accepts that magic exists, and Professor Randolph, a student of the occult, gives her information to assist and to protect her. At the beginning of the series, Darcy simply cannot accept that magic exists, so he faces the evils endangering his family and friends without understanding the forces aligned against them, putting himself and others in further danger.

Comment: Carrie Bebris has been a newspaper reporter, a college English teacher, and an editor for fantasy role-playing game publisher TSR. She is a member of the Jane Austen Society of North America. She studied the works of Jane Austen in the course of acquiring a Master's degree in English literature (with an emphasis on 19th-century authors). Her great love and respect for the author's works come through in this series. *Pride and Prescience* was named one of the five best mysteries of 2004 by Library Journal. *North by Northanger* won the 2007 Daphne du Maurier Award. Ms. Bebris's Web site, at http://www.carriebebris.com/, includes information on her books, along with discussion guides (readers' group guides) and archives of interesting discussions.

Literary Magic & Mayhem: The first book in the series, *Pride and Prescience,* begins on the wedding day of Elizabeth Bennet (now Mrs. Darcy). Elizabeth's sense of the absurd and her sparkling wit are not altered by marriage. The dialogue is spot-on, offering a delightful echo of the peculiarities of the personalities from *Pride and Prejudice.* Mr. Collins is still pompous and silly. Caroline Bingley is still self-absorbed. Darcy still has his pride, but in this series, readers see more of his sense of humor. For instance, when his plans for their wedding evening are destroyed, Darcy is embarrassed and dismayed until Elizabeth helps him see the humor in their situation. The scene is set by a change in Elizabeth and Darcy's plans. They had intended to leave for Pemberley from the wedding reception but decided that it would be prudent to spend a little time in London. Darcy immediately sent a messenger to his London townhouse's housekeeper to inform her of the change. If all had gone as he had planned, the housekeeper would have received the message in good time. She would have opened the windows, freshened the rooms, and had the fires lit so that the rooms were warmed. She would have removed the sheets she had used to shroud the furniture in order to protect it from dust. She would have prepared an excellent dinner... Unfortunately, the messenger's horse threw a shoe, and he did not get to the townhouse in time to give the housekeeper the message.

Darcy's careful and thoughtful plans to introduce his wife to the comfort of her new life through a romantic evening at home are in a shambles. Instead of a warm aired house and a hot dinner, they are faced with picnicking in cold musty rooms surrounded by shrouded furniture. Darcy apologizes to Elizabeth, who points out that the decision to close the house was correct, given that they did not intend to use it that winter and that it would be unreasonable for him to assume the blame for his messenger's horse throwing its shoe. Proud Darcy continues to apologize so Elizabeth begins praising the dust-cloth covered furniture:

> "I like what you've done with the place. The furniture all matches now."

Darcy will not be diverted and persists in his apologies:

> "The air in here is so chilly you cannot even remove your wrap."
> "It's bracing."
> "We have no dinner."
> "Mr. Darcy, I believe I am now mistress here. Are you in the habit of criticizing a lady's home and table to her face?"
> The mock upbraid jostled off his last shreds of ill humor. He conceded with an exaggerated bow. (*Pride and Prescience*, p. 35)

The element of *Pride and Prejudice* that is most noticeably missing from *Pride and Prescience* is the narrator's voice. That wonderful, caustic wit so carefully wrapped in gentle language, that voice that could begin Chapter 1 of *Pride and Prejudice* with: "It is a truth universally acknowledged, that a single man in possession of a good fortune, must be in want of a wife." That narrator is missing, and the loss is significant. Also, the central friendship in the series is now between Fitzwilliam and Elizabeth Darcy; in *Pride and Prejudice,* it was between Elizabeth and her sister Jane. Darcy's belief that he should be in control of every situation, including the (appropriate for the time) attitude that he should assist his new wife by guiding her actions and schooling her thoughts, may annoy a modern audience. The relationship is quite different from the one between Elizabeth and Jane that was the backbone of Austen's *Pride and Prejudice.* Added to this is the fact that Elizabeth's internal voice has also changed. Elizabeth's musings, her demanding conscience, and her temper are not displayed as they were in *Pride and Prejudice.* She seems more mature, more modern, and less interesting.

By the fourth book in the series, *The Matters at Mansfield,* many of these problems are, at least in part, overcome. Darcy and Elizabeth have become partners as well as lovers. They rely on each other, speak to each other as equals, and work as a team when trying to help Darcy's cousin Anne de Bourgh. Elizabeth's slightly biting observations return and are shared by Darcy, as both deal with his aunt, Lady Catherine de Bourgh. However, in this book, there are no otherworldly aspects. It is a straight historical mystery.

Explorations: What is your favorite piece of cattiness from the wedding reception?

Parrish showed a false face to the world; what other characters took pains to maintain a false façade? Did the people whom they deceived want to be deceived?

What did the quotes that preface the chapters add to the book?

To what extent did characters earn the outcomes they received?

THE CASES

1. ***Pride and Prescience, or, a Truth Universally Acknowledged: A Mr. & Mrs. Darcy Mystery.*** New York: Forge, 2004, 287 p. ISBN: 0765305089.

ENGLAND, WINTER 1812. Caroline Bingley, thwarted in her plans to become Mrs. Darcy, chooses the happy event of Darcy's wedding (to Elizabeth Bennet) to announce her own engagement. It is so typical of her to try to eclipse the brides (Jane also wed that day, to Mr. Charles Bingley) that no one who knows Caroline regards her whirlwind courtship as odd. Caroline's actions become progressively more bizarre, moving beyond the point where they could stem from a fit of pique or from the need to be the center of attention. Elizabeth becomes convinced that some diabolical agent is controlling the unfortunate woman. Darcy finds the idea absurd, leaving Elizabeth to brave unknown dangers as she attempts to save Caroline.

ASSOCIATES: Fitzwilliam Darcy—*Elizabeth's husband;* Georgiana—*his sister;*. Mr. and Mrs. Bennet—*Elizabeth's parents;* Jane—*Elizabeth's sister, now Mrs. Charles Bingley;* Louisa Hurst and Caroline Bingley—*Mr. Bingley's sisters;* Mr. Frederick Parrish—*Caroline's new fiancé;* Mr. Collins—*a clergyman for Darcy's aunt, Lady Catherine;* Charlotte—*his wife, Elizabeth's friend;* Professor Randolph—*who collects and studies magical artifacts;* Mrs. Hale—*is the Darcy's London house housekeeper;* the Earl of Chatfield—*is Darcy's friend and fencing partner in London;* Lady Chatfield; Mr. Lawrence Kendall; and Juliet Kendall.

2. ***Suspense and Sensibility, or, First Impressions Revisited: A Mr. & Mrs. Darcy Mystery.*** New York: Forge, 2005, 301 p. ISBN: 0765305097.

ENGLAND, MARCH 1813. Elizabeth's youngest unmarried sister, Catherine Bennet (Kitty), has been out in Hertfordshire society for three years. There have been no serious suitors. Mrs. Bennet is convinced that Kitty must spend a season in London to acquire a husband. Darcy agrees that he and Elizabeth will sponsor Kitty, and resigns himself to the social whirl. Darcy is determined to settle for nothing less than a good man for Kitty: someone sober, responsible, and upright. (Kitty is interested in meeting a Duke.) Kitty's first suitor (Harry Dashwood) is eventually acceptable to both her and Darcy; but then Harry changes. He becomes the worst sort of rake, and Elizabeth has her suspicions as to the cause.

ASSOCIATES: Sir Francis Dashwood—*who was a libertine, he died long ago;* Catherine "Kitty" Bennet—*Elizabeth's sister;* Georgiana—*Darcy's sister;* Mrs. Hale—*the Darcy's London townhouse housekeeper;* Professor

Randolph—*who possesses arcane knowledge;* The Earl of Chatfield and Lady Chatfield—*friends of the Darcys;* Lord Phillip Beaumont—*Lady Chatfield's brother;* Sir John Middleton, Lady Middleton, John Middleton, and William Middleton—*host a party at their home;* Mr. Henry (Harry) Dashwood—*who Kitty meets at the party;* Mrs. (Fanny) Dashwood, Mr. (Robert) Ferrars, Mrs. (Lucy) Ferrars, Miss (Regina) Ferrars, Elinor Ferrars, and Edward Ferrars—*are his relatives.*

3. ***North by Northanger, or, the Shades of Pemberley: A Mr. & Mrs. Darcy Mystery.*** New York: Forge, 2006, 318 p. ISBN: 076531410X.

ENGLAND, AUTUMN 1813–JUNE 1814. Elizabeth is expecting, and looking forward to a quiet confinement. (She ensures this by lying to her mother about the expected delivery date.) Elizabeth finds a letter addressed to her; or, rather, addressed to Fitwilliam Darcy's wife. It was written nearly 20 years before their marriage. Lady Anne Darcy (Fitzwilliam's mother) wrote the letter on the morning of the day she died and addressed it it to the woman who would one day marry her son. Apparently, Lady Anne foresaw that she would not survive the birth of her daughter. In the letter, Lady Anne wrote of an heirloom that was given her by her mother, one that she had hoped to have to protect her as she delivered her second child. She counsels her future daughter-in-law to find this heirloom to see her safely through childbirth. Elizabeth becomes determined to find it. In her search, she uncovers crimes both new and old, and at times she feels the presence of the spirit of her mother-in-law and knows that she has an ally.

ASSOCIATES: Lady Anne Fitzwilliam Darcy—*deceased, Elizabeth's mother-in-law, she died in childbirth on January 20, 1796;* Lady Catherine de Bourgh—*Lady Anne's sister;* Miss Anne de Bourgh—*Lady Catherine's daughter;* Mrs. Jenkinson—*Miss Anne's companion;* Georgiana—*Darcy's sister, she stays with the Darcys at Pemberly;* Mr. Flynn—*the Head Gardner of Pemberly;* Mrs. Reynolds—*the housekeeper;* Jenny—*a new housemaid;* Lucy—*Elizabeth's maid;* Graham—*Darcy's valet;* Dr. Richard Severn—*is engaged by Darcy to attend Elizabeth, but she finds that she prefers the care of Edith Godwin, the local midwife;* Mr. and Mrs. Bennet—*who come to Pemberly to attend Elizabeth (despite her efforts) as she nears her time to give birth;* Jane—*Elizabeth's dearest sister, just had her first child, Nicholas Charles Bingley;* Lydia Wickham—*another of Elizabeth's sisters, visits Jane to meet her new nephew;* Mr. Wickham—*Lydia's husband;* Captain Frederick Tilney—*who hosts the Darcy's at his home;* Dorothy—*his housekeeper;* Mr. Chase—*is an honest but somewhat inept Gloucestershire constable;* Mr. Melbourne—*is the Gloucestershire magistrate;* Mr. Henry Tilney—*whose mother's diamonds have been stolen;* and Mr. Harper—*who is Darcy's solicitor.*

4. ***The Matters at Mansfield, or, the Crawford Affair: A Mr. & Mrs. Darcy Mystery.*** New York: Forge, 2008, 286 p. ISBN: 9780765318473; 0765318474.

ENGLAND, AUGUST 1814. When Darcy decided to marry Elizabeth, what became of Miss Anne de Bourgh? For most of her 28 years, her mother, Lady Catherine, had proclaimed to one-and-all that Anne was Darcy's intended. At age 28, in an era when most young women "came out" around the age of 18, Anne was suddenly on the marriage market. She was wooed but she did not believe that her suitors were smitten; she was an heiress, and she believed that her suitors wanted her fortune. Anne is over the age of 21, and legally able to make her own decisions about her life. No matter what Anne's age, her mother, the Lady Catherine de Bourgh, believes that she knows what is best for Anne and is determined to make a stupendous match for her. Anne's elopement thwarts Lady Catherine's plans, and subsequent events (including several murders and an overabundance of wives) complicate the matter.

ASSOCIATES: Darcy—*Elizabeth's husband;* Lily-Anne—*their infant daughter;* Lady Catherine de Bourgh—*Darcy's aunt;* Miss Anne de Bourgh—*Lady Catherine's daughter;* Mrs. Jenkinson—*Anne's companion;* Colonel James Fitzwilliam; Lord Sennex; the Honorable Neville Sennex—*Lord Sennex's ill-tempered son;* Mr. Henry Crawford—*who has always been quite charming;* Mr. Gower and his wife—*who run a respectable inn in Mansfield;* Sir Thomas Bertram—*who is a local landowner;* Maria—*his daughter;* Mr. Rushworth—*Maria's husband;* Mrs. Norris—*Maria's aunt;* the dowager Mrs. Rushworth—*Mr. Rushworth's mother, who is almost as much of a tartar as Lady Catherine;* Mrs. Meg Garrick—*who comes to Mansfield to find her husband;* Mr. Archer—*Lady Catherine's solicitor;* Reverend Edmund Bertram; Mr. Stover—*Mansfield's coroner;* and Mr. Cobb—*Sir Thomas's gamekeeper.*

BENDIS, Brian Michael and Michael Avon Oeming.

WHO KILLED RETROGIRL?

Genres/Themes Crossed: Blended Society X Police Procedural.

Subjects/Character Types: Superheroes, Supervillains X Police Procedural.

Series/Stand-Alone: The story progresses over the course of the series. It is best read in order.

Scene of the Crime: An unnamed American city, visually similar to New York.

Detectives: Christian Walker is a former superhero. After losing his powers, Walker became a police officer and now deals primarily with cases involving individuals with superhuman powers. Deena Pilgrim is a young police officer who requests to be transferred to the precinct specifically to work on cases with Walker.

Known Associates: Captain Cross supervises Walker and Pilgrim. Cross is an old friend of Walker's, and is responsible for him becoming a police officer after the loss of his powers. Detective Kutter is another detective in the precinct, generally disliked by Walker and Pilgrim for being sexist and boorish. Calista is a young girl who is briefly put into Walker's care at the beginning of the first story and has an influence on later events. Retro Girl is an iconic superhero and friend of Walker's, formerly belonging to the same superhero team. Zora is a third member of Walker's old team, a woman who claims to have obtained superpowers by an exploration of her own theological philosophy. Triphammer is another member of Walker's old team, a crime fighter who uses a suit of high-tech armor. Dr. Tucker is the precinct's medical examiner. FBI Agent Lange is a giant of a woman who knows Walker and is often placed on cases in the city by the Bureau.

Premise: There are many individuals with superpowers in the world. They are frequently referred to as "powers." Many have extremely long lives, but don't remember all of their past. Walker has lived for millennia, but can only remember as far back as a human lifetime. He has enemies who remember him, but he does not remember them. People can be born with powers (one example is Walker), they can possess powers that outlive them and attach to another person when they die (there have been many incarnations of Retro Girl), or can create inventions that give them powers (as did Triphammer). Right before he lost his powers Walker's secret superhero identity was Diamond. Once he lost his powers Walker took up law enforcement. Detectives Walker and Pilgrim are partners who work primarily on homicide cases involving powers.

Comments: This series is graphic in language, violence, and nudity. Having said that, *Powers* has won a number of awards, including Eisner awards for best new series and best writer. Bendis is known for his dialogue, and this creator-owned series is frequently the best showcase for his skills. The series is a collaborative effort. Oeming develops original ideas for the series and often gives Bendis comments on dialogue. Bendis is known for giving rough layouts and storyboards to the artists with whom he works. In this series, Bendis frequently names locations and individuals after professionals working in the comic book industry. Brian Michael Bendis's Web site, at http://www.jinxworld.com/ includes his biography, writing credits, and a message board for comic book creators. Michael Avon Oeming's site at http://www.hiddenrobot.com/MIKEOEMING/ includes information on current projects, a link to the Powers podcast, and a link to the Powers Web site at: http://hiddenrobot.com/POWERS/, which includes electronic editions of the first volumes in the series.

Literary Magic and Mayhem: The series reworks many superhero clichés, going so far as to have a story arc covering the origin story of the central character. The characters occupy a very realistic world, despite the superhero influence. People are harmed and killed, and the ethics of the entire concept of superheroics is examined.

Explorations: What sorts of actions can ethically be taken while enforcing the law?

How does our past define us?

THE CASES

1. ***Who Killed Retrogirl?*** New York: Image Comics, 2006, 205 p. ISBN: 1582406693.

MAJOR U.S. CITY, 2000. Walker is partnered with Pilgrim as they investigate the death of a beloved superhero, an individual with whom Walker had a complicated history. Pilgrim suspects Walker's former identity.

ASSOCIATES: Captain Cross, S.W.A.T. Officer Setzer, Detective Kutter, and Dr. Tucker (coroner)—*law enforcement personnel;* Walker—*who used to be a power, when he was known as Diamond;* Zora—*a power who used to work with Diamond;* Triphammer—*a.k.a. Harley Cohen, an inventor who uses his inventions to be a power, he used to work with Diamond;* Retro Girl—*a.k.a. Janis, a power who used to work with Diamond;* Flinch—*a power, who Walker talks out of hurting a young girl;* Calista—*the young girl;* Johnny Stompinato—*a.k.a. Johnny Royale, a crime lord turned club owner;* Psyche—*who suggests that the detectives interview The Wolf;* The Wolf—*an old enemy of Walker;* Collette McDaniel—*Channel 5 reporter;* Jon Jackson Stevens—*a suspect.*

2. ***Roleplay.*** New York: Image Comics, 2001, 112 p. ISBN: 1582402329.

MAJOR U.S. CITY, 2001. A body is found wearing Walker's old costume, but the individual who wore it doesn't seem to have had any powers. Soon, other bodies show up, seemingly normal individuals wearing the costumes of prominent heroes.

ASSOCIATES: Coroner Dr. Tucker—*who has been nicknamed Dr. Blood;* Captain Cross and Detective Kutter—*others in law enforcement;* Johnny

Stompinato—*a.k.a. Johnny Royale, club owner, who is suing the city for police harassment;* Deena—*who is put on administrative leave;* Dana—*a student who is Danny Nuncio's girlfriend;* Cameron Lindon—*a student who plays Suncurse;* Nick Roberts—*who used to make weapons for a power named the Pulp;* the Pulp—*a.k.a Casey Dees, a power.*

3. ***Little Deaths.*** New York: Image Comics, 2006, 224 p. ISBN: 1582406707.

MAJOR U.S. CITY, 2002. Walker and Pilgrim investigate the death of Olympia, a prominent superhero found dead, completely naked in the bed of his tiny apartment.

ASSOCIATES: Coroner Dr. Tucker, Captain Cross, Detective Kutter, and Officer Casey—*are law enforcement personnel;* Stavlana Peedarasonivch—*the landlady at Olympia's apartment;* Anglea Poe—*who knew Olympia well.*

4. ***Supergroup.*** New York: Image Comics, 2006, 184 p. ISBN: 1582406715.

MAJOR U.S. CITY, 2002. WG-3, one of the world's most popular super groups, breaks up. Shortly after the announcement, one of the team's members, Benmarley, is found dead and apparently mutilated in the team's headquarters.

ASSOCIATES: Coroner Dr. Tucker, Detective Kutter, Captain Cross, and District Attorney Howard Malkovitch—*law enforcement personnel;* Michael—*Deena's boyfriend;* Boogiegirl—*a.k.a. Rhonda power, she is also known as Rhonda;* Wazz—*a.k.a. Sean "Wendell" Wallace, a power;* Federal Agent Lange—*who was once a power, now he's on the Powers Task Force;* Ted Henry—*television pundit who is known as "the fastest mouth alive";* Zora and Triphammer—*are powers who used to work with Walker.*

5. ***Anarchy.*** New York: Image Comics, 2003, 128 p. ISBN: 1582403317.

MAJOR U.S. CITY, 2003. A series of violent, public executions of powers forces Detective Pilgrim and Detective Argento to track down Walker and bring him back into the fold.

ASSOCIATES: Detective Argento, Captain Cross, Detective Kutter and Officer Anderson—*are law enforcement personnel;* Harvey Goodman—*an arsonist and murderer;* Ted Henry—*a television pundit who has much to say about the case;* Supershock—*a power, who was also known as Geoff.*

6. ***Sellouts.*** New York: Marvel Comics, 2004, 192 p. ISBN: 078511582X.

MAJOR U.S. CITY, NEW YORK CITY, THE NEVADA DESERT, NEAR EARTH ORBIT, 2004. Red Hawk, one of the members of the oldest and most respected super groups, is murdered in his home after a scandalous tape is released to the press. Walker and Pilgrim investigate the seemingly impossible murder and discover a secret that changes how the government treats powers.

ASSOCIATES: Captain Cross, Detective Kutter, Detective Mack, and Federal Agent Lange—*are law enforcement personnel;* Vice Officer Stiller—*is a power (invisibility/phasing).* Powers in the story include members of the Unity team: Ultrabright—*a.k.a Nancy;* Wing—*a.k.a. Alan Vietch, sidekick of Red Hawk;* Dragonfist; Supershock—*a.k.a. Geoff.*

7. ***Forever.*** New York: Marvel Comics, 2004, 272 p. ISBN: 0785116567.

THE DAWN OF MANKIND; A BARBARIAN CIVILIZATION SEVERAL THOUSAND YEARS AGO; CHINA NEAR THE TIME OF THE BOXER REBELLION; CHICAGO, 1936; MAJOR U.S. CITY, 1986; MAJOR U.S. CITY, 2004. The origin story of Christian Walker.

ASSOCIATES: Zanona—*who was an early incarnation of Retro Girl;* Walker—*who walked to a temple in Peking to seek out knowledge from a Chinese master;* Han Xian-Zi—*the Chinese Master;* Supershock—*who was on the first super team with Walker, Zora, and the Retro Girl of that era.*

Albert Einstein—*who warns Walker against going public with his powers;* Haemon—*a.k.a. Jeb "The Wolf" Wolfe, has been Walker's enemy for millennia, and seems to remember more of the past than does Walker;* Triphammer—*who invented a power drainer and, in the course of a fight with Wolfe, Walker loses his powers;* Officer Cross, Detective Kutter, and Federal Agent Lange—*are law enforcement personnel.*

8. ***Legends.*** New York: Marvel Comics, 2005, 208 p. ISBN: 0785117423.

MAJOR U.S. CITY, 2005. *Legends* jumps back to the series' present time and finds a world in which all powers are outlawed. Powers that use their abilities for their own personal ends are fighting with each other, and the powers with nobler intentions refuse to break the law in order to keep order. Only one hero, believed dead by the world, is willing to do what it takes to help keep the peace during this turf war. Walker must track down a kidnapped detective.

ASSOCIATES: Detective Kutter, Captain Cross, and Commissioner Tate—*are law enforcement personnel;* Retro Girl—*a power;* The Lance—*a.k.a. Charles Lance, a power;* Artie Boxxor—*is Deena's boyfriend;* Katie Hayden—*Artie's sister.*

9. ***Psychotic.*** New York: Marvel Comics, 2006, 200 p. ISBN: 0785117431.

MAJOR U.S. CITY, 2006. The Blackguard is found dead after a confrontation with his nemesis, the Joke. The man in the Blackguard's costume is not the man who is registered with the government as the Blackguard, and the source of the Blackguard's power is missing.

ASSOCIATES: Officer Hine, Officer Kirkman, coroner Dr. Tucker, Captain Cross, Federal Agent Lange, Sergeant Simone, and Captain Adlard—*are law enforcement personnel;* Mama Joon—*a.k.a. Big Mama, a power;* Super Shock—*a power;* and Retro Girl—*a power;* Blackguard—*whose alter ego was Matt Michaels;* Louise Michaels—*his wife;* Artie Boxxor—*who was Deena's boyfriend.*

10. ***Cosmic.*** New York: Marvel Comics, 2007, 200 p. ISBN: 0785122605; 9780785122609.

MAJOR U.S. CITY, 2007. The investigation of a murder in which the perpetrator used his own body as a lethal weapon, dropping from the sky to annihilate the victim, is taken out of Walker and Pilgrim's hands by Special Agent Marcus (Federal Powers Task Force) soon after they learn that the victim was this sector's secret Millennium Guard (of the Galactic Peace-Keeping Organization, also known as Millennium). Internal Affairs Officer Anna Stone questions Detective Pilgrim about the disappearance of Artie Boxxor. Detective Christian Walker is offered powers to be used in defense of Earth. (He would take the place of the dead Millennium Guard.) 417 Millennium officers have guarded Earth in the last 300 years. Millennium Guards don't have long life expectancies.

ASSOCIATES: Special Agent Marcus, Agent Lange, Agent Cho, Internal Affairs Detective Anna Stone, and Captain Cross—*are law enforcement personnel in this story;* Heather Anderson—*who witnessed the death of Todd Meltzer;* Microbe—*a.k.a. Delores Milton, who knew about Millenium;* The Badee Goddess—*who gives Walker Millennium powers;* Retro Girl—*a power, has a new incarnation (a.k.a. Calista Secor);* Andy Lee—*a power;* Bill, Adrienne, Joy, and Heather Anderson—*are the stand-up philosophers at Club Cinderella.*

11. ***Secret Identity.*** New York: Marvel Comics, 2007, 200 p. ISBN: 0785122613; 9780785122616.

CHICAGO 1936; WASHINGTON D.C., 2007; MAJOR U.S. CITY, 2007; AND LEAVENWORTH, KANSAS 2007. The Heroes team takes down Chester "The Weasel" Drake as he attacks the Capitol. When Queen Noir returns home from the mission, her husband, Joe Striker, is dead. The murder is called in and Captain Cross assigns Detective Deena Pilgrim to the case. In the course of the investigation, the Heroes team implodes, and many of them die. Detective Christian Walker is warned off the case, but he sees it through to the bitter end.

This entry in the series includes a flashback from Christian Walker's past, when he assumed the secret identity of Blue Streak and attacked Chicago mob boss Myer Lansky and Lansky's supernatural protector Yuri.

ASSOCIATES: Queen Noir (Doris), Crystal Star, Dax, and Teague the Sorcerer—*are powers who are the members of the Heroes;* Chester "The Weasel" Drake—*a power;* Retro Girl—*a.k.a. Calista Star, a power.* Officer Singleton, Agent Lange, Internal Affairs Detective Anna Stone, and Captain Cross—*are law enforcement personnel;* Myer Lansky; Yuri, Badee; and Satan.

12. ***The 25 Coolest Dead Superheroes of All Time.*** New York: Marvel Comics, 2009, 200 p. ISBN: 9780785122623.

MAJOR U.S. CITY, PRESENT DAY. There's a virus loose in the city. It infects humans with powers. Soon after they are infected, most of them die. Anna

Pilgrim was infected almost a year ago. She was going to tell her partner when she saw him using powers, powers he'd been denying. She came to the conclusion that she could not trust him, and she went into hiding. Since then, she's been acting as a vigilante, trying to stop the intentional spread of the Powers virus. When she's seen near the body of a dead girl, she becomes the prime suspect in the killings.

In the course of this story, Christian Walker remembers a time when his people lived in caves.

ASSOCIATES: Captain Cross—*Walker's boss;* Detective Enki Sunrise—*is assigned as Christian Walker's new partner;* Internal Affairs Detective Anna Stone—*is convinced that Anna Pilgrim has committed murder;* Liz—*the coroner's assistant;* Police Commissioner Tate; Ernie Estrada—*is the Police Department's Counsel;* Heather—*Christian Walker's lover;* Deena Pilgrim; Amber—*who wants to find her friend Rachel;* Triphammer; Calista Star/Retro Girl; The Lance—*a club-owner and crime lord;* the Bear—*Bradley Carmichael;* and Raymond Slurt—*junkie.*

UDAKU

Genres/Themes Crossed: Secret Society X Police Procedural.

Subjects/Character Types: Demons, Future Technology X Police Procedural.

Series/Stand-Alone: Read in order for characters and situation development.

Scene of the Crime: New York City.

Detectives: Maximilian "Twitch" Williams is a soft-spoken, short, bespectacled detective known for his sharp mind and keen skills as a marksman. Sam Burke is Twitch's overweight, outspoken, strongman of a partner. They left a corrupt police force to attempt to make their way as private investigators but are persuaded to return to the force at the start of the series in order to assist with a particularly tricky case.

Known Associates: Dr. KC McRory, nicknamed "Dr. Death" by the members of the force, is a medical examiner in the precinct. She objects to the crassness of Sam, but seems to relate to Twitch's intellect. Spawn is a former soldier who made a deal with the devil to return to Earth, but uses his demonic powers to fight evil.

Premise: Sam and Twitch are two honest detectives on a corrupt force. There are horrible demonic forces in the world, and villainous super scientists that create abominations to further their sinister ends.

Comments: *Sam and Twitch* was the first high-profile project Brian Michael Bendis helmed. The characters had played a supporting role in Todd MacFarlane's *Spawn* comics, and Bendis was brought in to bring these fan favorites into their own series. The heavily noir-influenced setting is seen as precursor to series like *Gotham Central,* and Bendis's own creator owned title, *Powers.* The art on these issues is primarily penciled by Angel Medina. Twenty-six issues of *Sam and Twitch* were published. Volumes 1 and 2 collect issues 1 through 19. The characters continue to appear in the comic book series *Spawn.*

Literary Magic and Mayhem: While the supernatural exists in the world Sam and Twitch occupy, it is definitely uncommon and out of the ordinary. The majority of the public is unaware of the events that transpire around them. While *Spawn* deals more heavily with demonic and theological issues and influences, *Sam and Twitch* deals more with unusual science and common criminals.

Explorations: What was added by presenting this series as a graphic novel?

Would the dialogue work as well in a standard book?

How much does the art add to the feel of the setting?

THE CASES

1. ***Sam & Twitch: The Brian Michael Bendis Collection, Volume 1.*** Berkeley, CA: Image Comics, 2006, 224 p. ISBN: 1582405832.

New York City, present day. This collection contains two stories. In the first story, "Udaku," Sam and Twitch attempt to solve a series of murders that have organized crime figures and crooked cops as victims. At each crime scene, body parts that seem to belong to the same individual are found, starting with four identical right thumbs. The second story is done from the point of view a small time criminal having a very, very bad day.

Associates: Lt. Barnes, Dr. KC McRory—*a.k.a. "Dr. Death",* Barbara Rodriguez, Officer Afflek, Dee Afflek, Spawn, Izzy, Jackie Sangiacomo, Detective Keller, and Officer Falsone.

2. ***Sam & Twitch: The Brian Michael Bendis Collection, Volume 2.*** Berkeley, CA: Image Comics, 2007, 224 p. ISBN: 9781582407456.

New York City, present day. This collection contains two stories. In the first story, "Witchcraft," Sam and Twitch attempt to find a serial killer who is targeting witches. In the second story, "Bounty Hunter Wars," Twitch's wife has thrown him out and Twitch has started another relationship. A bounty hunter's stray shot hits his lover. He feels responsible, that God is punishing him for the affair. At the end of the case, he resigns from the force.

ASSOCIATES: Sheryl—*a television anchorwoman;* Nadja and Jennifer—*who are wiccans;* Officer Bernadette; Lt. Barnes; New York's Mayor A. J. Ritter; Sally; Dr. KC McRory; Pratt; and Bilal Christian, Jinx Alameda, and Manara—*are bounty hunters;* Bob Matson and Carl Muñoz—*of Muñoz Bail Bonds.*

BESTER, Alfred.

THE DEMOLISHED MAN

Genres/Themes Crossed: Blended Society X Inverted Mystery, Police Procedural.

Subjects/Character Types: Telepathy, Future Earth X Police Procedural.

Series/Stand-Alone: Stand-alone.

Scene of the Crime: New York City, 2301 A.D.

Detective: Ben Reich, owner of Monarch Utilities and Resources, works on a puzzle, but his aim is not to solve a crime, it is to commit a crime. This book's protagonist is the murderer!

Known Associates: Reich is a man defined more by his enemies than by his friends. His chief competitor is Craye D'Courtney. The criminologist who sets out to get Reich is the Prefect of the Police Psychotic Division, an Esper 1 named Lincoln Powell.

Premise: Bester depicts a future Earth in which a substantial proportion of the population has extra-sensory perception. There are approximately 100,000 third-class Espers in the Esper Guild. An Esper 3 is the weakest of the telepath classes: he or she can hear what a person is thinking at the moment of the thought. There are 10,000 second-class Espers in the Esper Guild: Esper 2s can hear beyond the conscious mind to the preconscious. There are fewer than one thousand first-class Espers in the Esper Guild. Esper 1s can do "deep peeping" down to the unconscious levels, the primordial impulses. As Augustus Tate points out, when Reich approaches him with an offer he thinks Tate can't refuse: "There hasn't been a successful premeditated murder in 79 years. Espers make it impossible to conceal intent before murder. Or, if Espers have been evaded before the murder, they make it impossible to conceal the guilt afterwards."

Comment: *The Demolished Man* won the very first Hugo Award for Best Novel of the Year. Scores of Bester's short stories were nominated for science fiction awards. He won the 1987 Science Fiction Grand Master Award and (posthumously) was an inductee in the Science Fiction Hall of Fame. Bester influenced many science fiction writers through his short stories, novels, and through his work in radio and comic books. He developed a style that included a lot of action and character-revealing dialog and description that simultaneously explores the world, the society, and the characters. Writers have paid tribute to him onscreen and in print. Notably, in *Babylon 5*, Bester is a recurring character, portrayed by Walter Koenig. Bester is a telepath, an agent of the Psi Corps, a frightening and powerful antagonist. The *Starman* series (DC Comics) contains a story arc written by James Robinson, and was named after one of Bester's most well-known novels, *Stars My Destination*. One of the constants in Feargus Gwynplaine MacIntyre's *Smedley Faversham* stories is "Bester's Law." The principle is based on Bester's 1958 story "The Men Who Murdered Mohammed"; it is a mandate that time travelers may not affect any timeline but their own. The first story of the *Smedley Faversham* series, "Time Lines," was published in the June 1999 issue of *Analog*.

The Demolished Man was first published as a serial in *Galaxy*. It was then published in hardback, and the original prologue to the work was omitted for space considerations. The prologue provides some information on how the society of the 1950s evolved into the society depicted in *The Demolished Man*. It outlines the origins of the Esper society and the details of the conquest of space. The prologue has been reprinted in *Redemolished* by Alfred Bester, published by ibooks in 2000.

Literary Magic & Mayhem: Bester has a lot of fun with language: From the caustic platitudes that Reich recites to himself ("Make your enemies by choice . . . not by accident"); to the names employed for telepaths (such as "brain-peepers"); to the proper names that incorporate both symbols and letters (one of the Esper Medical Doctor 1's names is @tkins), to his descriptions ("Fully dressed and in his wrong mind, Reich stormed out of his apartment"), Bester revels in words and ideas, thereby creating an incredibly rich work. The society of the Espers is contrasted with normal human society in how they have difficulty thinking lies, so half-truths are spoken instead of mentally broadcast; how the society of non-Espers is dissatisfying; the way that, when they are in company with other Espers, it is considered gauche to communicate verbally instead of mentally; how, at parties, they play word games with the structure of the broadcasting conversations; how some of the richest among them resent the Esper Guild taxes and join conservative groups designed to protect the privileges of Espers; and how they meet (or avoid) the demands of the Esper Guild's eugenics program. With a few deft strokes, the society is so well drawn that it seems a logical, almost inevitable extrapolation of a society that includes Espers.

Explorations: Does Lincoln Powell seem paternalistic?

At one point, Jerry Church tells Reich, "May you rot before you're dead." What other interesting curses (or other phrases) can be found in the book?

Much of the crime planning and crime investigation is like a chess game. What were some of the more outlandish "moves?"

Many of the professionals have psychological theories designed to understand people. Which theories were most interesting? How did these theories support the doctors in what they wanted to do?

THE CASE

***The Demolished Man.* Chicago:** Shasta Publishers, [1953], 250 p.

NEW YORK CITY, 2301. Craye D'Courtney has outmaneuvered Ben Reich at every turn. The D'Courtney Cartel will soon be poised to squash Monarch Utilities and Resources. Reich finally faces the fact that his company's only hope is a merger with the Cartel. It's too late, D'Courtney turns him down flat. Reich determines that the only way to win is to rid the world of D'Courtney. In a world where minds can be read, how can Reich plan a murder?

ASSOCIATES: Jonas—*Reich's valet;* Dr. Carson Breen—*Reich's analyst (Esper 2);* Blonn—*(Esper 1) who is being recommended to Reich by Monarch's Personnel Chief (Esper 2);* Hassop—*Monarch's Code Chief;* Ellery West—*(Esper 2) who is Monarch's Recreation Director;* Duffy Wyg&—*who runs Psych-Songs, Inc.;* Augustus Tate—*(Esper 1), who agrees to work with Reich;* Craye D'Courtney—*Ben Reich's competitor;* Barbara D'Courtney—*Craye's daughter;* Maria Bearument,—*"the Gilt Corpse.";* Larry Ferar—*Maria's social secretary;* Criminologist Lincoln Powell—*(Esper 1) who is prominent in the Esper community;* Mary Noyes, Augustus Tate, Sam and Sally @kins, Wally and June Chervil; and Galen—*are all guests at a party at Powell's home.* Jerry Church—*(Esper) was involved in some scheme of Reich's and is now ostracized by all Espers by Guild orders.* T'sung Hsai—*(Esper) President of the Esper Guild;* Miss Prinn—*T'sung Hsai's secretary;* Police Commissioner Crabbe; Inspector Jackson "Jax" Beck—*(Esper 2);* De Santis—*who inspects the crime scene;* the Mosaic Multplex Prosecution Computer—*referred to as Old Man Mose;* Jo 1/4maine—*(Esper 2), Ben Reich's lawyer;* Keno Quizzard—*a blind croupier;* Chooka Frood—*who is medium and landlady to Snim;* Dr. Jeems—*who tries to help Barbara;* Dr. Sam @kins—*who was D'Courtney's physician;* and Dr. Wilson Jordan—*who is a scientist who worked for Ben Reich.*

BIGGLE, Lloyd.

ALL THE COLORS OF DARKNESS

Genres/Themes Crossed: Alien Interference X Whodunnit.

Subjects/Character Types: Teleportation X Private Investigator.

Series/Stand-Alone: Stand-alone.

Scene of the Crime: Manhattan, July 1986.

Detective: Jan Darzek, a private detective, a friend of Ted Arnold, and an investor in the Universal Transmitting Company.

Known Associates: Jean Morris, Darzek's secretary, is in love with him. Ed Rucks, an elderly retired cab driver with an interest in investigating, who has an eye for faces and may be able to see through a disguise.

Premise: The world of the book differs from our current world in at least two important aspects. One is that the engineers at Universal Transmitter developed teleportation technology. The second is that it was written in the 1960s and is, in many ways, a product of that time. For instance, talking about the first day's promotion of the teleportation device, they've set gates near the street window and have a young man disappearing from one gate and appearing at another as a demonstration. The average New Yorker gives it only a few minutes of attention then, certain that it's a trick, loses interest. Eventually they figure out how to hold the public's interest:

> At ten o'clock, a Universal Trans employee with a genius for promotion plucked a shapely brunette from her seat behind a ticket window, sent out for a bathing suit, and set the young man to chasing her from platform to platform. Within minutes, the most colossal traffic jam in the entire history of Manhattan was under way.

The 1960s attitude towards women shows up throughout the book. It is not offensive; but it is a reminder of how much has changed in half a century.

Comment: Dr. Biggle received his Ph.D. from the University of Michigan and taught there for over a decade before he became a full-time writer with the publication of this novel. He was a musician, a writer, and an oral historian. He founded the *Science Fiction Oral History Association,* which built archives of the speeches and interviews of hundreds of science fiction writers. He is considered to be the author who introduced aesthetics to science fiction; he enriched, by bringing in artistic themes, a genre that had been focused on scientific invention. There are further books on Darzek: *Watchers of the Dark*, *This Darkening Universe*, *Silence is Deadly*, and *The Whirligig of Time*. In them Darzek is employed to stop threats, but doesn't do much detecting.

Literary Magic & Mayhem: Darzek, as a narrator, is humorous and perceptive. This is his take on the Board of Directors:

> Harlow, the attorney, had already dispensed with the legalities of the situation to his own complete satisfaction, and was unable to understand what all the fuss was about. Miller harped on his freight theme with such single-minded intensity that Darzek suspected unplumbed depths to his character—or no depths at all. Cohen and Vaughan, the two vice-presidents, each sought bitterly and transparently to expose the other as a dunce, and both were successful.

Explorations: Under what circumstances would it be more productive to use a transmitter than to use a plane? What if the risk of a fatal accident during transmission were the same as the risk of driving (as opposed to the lower risk for flying)? What if transmission cost $100 more than flying would cost? What if instant transmission shortened the traveler's lifespan by the amount of time it would have taken for a flight?

What elements could be the basis for a universal code of ethics?

Technological advances that were predicted by the book have not happened, yet other advances, not dreamed of by the author, have indeed occurred. What anachronisms are noticeable? How do they change the experience of reading the story?

THE CASE

All the Colors of Darkness. Garden City, New York: Doubleday (Book Club Edition), 1963, 210 p.

MANHATTAN, JULY 1986. On the day that Universal Transmitting finally had a breakthrough, a warehouse fire consumed the building they'd used for their experiments. Luckily, they'd moved the bulk of their equipment a few hours earlier. Their opening day was a great success; the next day they lost a passenger.

ASSOCIATES: Thomas J. Watkins III—*chief engineer of the Universal Transmitting Company;* Miss Shue—*his secretary;* Ted Arnold—*a brilliant engineer;* Jack Marrow—*who is rather highly strung;* Meyers—*an engineer, the first to make it through;* Walt Perrin—*who works through everything;* Jan Darzek—*a private detective;* Jean Morris—*is his secretary;* Ed Rucks—*is an assistant;* Ron Walker—*is an investor and a reporter; he's the first to report that Universal Transmitter is working and the first to do a world tour by transmitter;* Charlie Grossman—*the treasurer on the Board of Directors;* Carl Miller; Ted Arnold;

Thomas J. Watkins III; Vaughan—*a vice-president;* Cohen—*a vice-president;* Armbruster—*a vice-president;* Harlow—*the company's legal advisor;* Mike—*is a policeman who is Darzek's friend;* Monsieur Vert—*is temporarily in charge of the Brussels Universal Transmitting terminal;* Alice, Gwendolyn, Xerxes, Zachary, and Ysaye—*are other characters in the story.*

BLEVINS, Meredith.

Annie Szabo Series

Genres/Themes Crossed: Fantastical Realism, Paranormal X Traditional Mystery.

Subjects/Character Types: Paranormal X Amateur Sleuth (Contemporary).

Series/Stand-Alone: This series is best read in order, relationships change over time.

Scene of the Crime: California, especially the Bay Area and San Francisco, present day.

Detective: When Stevan died, he left Annie with a little property, three daughters (one in utero), and debt. She had no skills, and she had bills to pay. She parlayed her father's name (he was Will Wilde, the singing cowboy) into a couple of interviews and managed to put together a living as a freelance magazine writer. She's drawn into investigating the death of her best friend Jerry through a series of bizarre events, one of which is her mother-in-law's insistence that someone was trying to steal Jerry's soul.

Known Associates: When Annie married Stevan, she married into a wide and varied gypsy clan. The matriarch is Madame Mina Szabo. Mina is mother to four children, by three different fathers. Stevan was the son of an arranged marriage between Mina and the elderly Jack Szabo. Jack died when Stevan was an infant, and Mina's friend Pinky Marks helped her commit insurance fraud to get money for Jack's funeral. Mina married Pinky and they had two children. Capri is their daughter. Mina's youngest child, Jozef, is the product of an illicit affair Mina had with Zoltan. Mina's oldest son, Stevan, married Annie, and they had three daughters. The oldest is E. B. (short for Electric Blue). Annie was pregnant with the youngest, Abra, when Stevan drove his motorcycle over a cliff and died.

Premise: The gypsies maintain their customs and ethics as a separate society within the society of present-day America. Some of them are able to read palms, look into crystal balls, read tarot cards, brew herbal potions, etc. To some extent, these talents are real, but when talent fails, the gypsies are completely willing to put on an act to con the foolish. Sometimes the gypsies themselves don't seem certain about what is true and what is an act. A few of the gypsies have a different understanding of reality, and may even have ways to bend reality to their wills. One of these is the Hummingbird Wizard, who is regarded with awe and some fear within the gypsy community.

> Back one hundred generations ago there was no people but Gypsies. Everything walked and talked. Flowers visited each other, so did rocks. As time passed they all lost their legs. Trouble didn't. It still walks anywhere it wants. So do Gypsies.
>
> Madame Mina Szabo, as learned from her grandmother. (*The Hummingbird Wizard* preface)

Comment: The timeline of the books was extrapolated from the preparations for the Year of the Monkey celebration described in *Red Hot Empress.* The books are best read in order, as Annie's relationships with Madame Mina and Capri evolve over the course of the series.

Literary Magic & Mayhem: Half the fun of the book is the outrageous Madame Mina. She's a con artist, a flirt, and a holy terror. The first conversation she has had in years with Annie takes place over the phone, Annie didn't expect her to answer (Annie was trying to return a call from Mina's daughter Capri) and is surprised into silence when Mina picks up the phone, but that doesn't slow Mina:

> "Annie, I know that's you. Say something."
>
> "You know it's me over the phone?"
>
> "Sure, I smell your breath."
>
> "What does my breath smell like over airwaves and metal wires?"
>
> "Like bruised apples."
>
> Nice.
>
> "Also," she said, "I got a box with caller I.D. That helps some." (*The Hummingbird Wizard,* p. 18)

Here is another bit of classic Mina conversation in which she's laying down the law to Capri. She doesn't want Capri to show interest in Jerry, because she doesn't want Capri to begin a relationship with a *gajo* (non-gypsy). Capri tells Mina that she hates it when Mina prophesies doom before anyone has a chance to take the first step. Mina responds:

> "Big deal. What kind of mother would I be if you didn't hate me sometimes? I'm telling you, heartache for everyone when you get mixed up in love with a gajo."
>
> "What happened to Love comes in all kinds of packages?"

"Some packages are wrapped in brown paper and go tick, tick, tick. Those you throw over a bad neighbor's fence." (*The Hummingbird Wizard,* p. 14)

Explorations: Which character is most interesting? Why?

What bit of Madame Mina's wisdom seemed wisest? Which seemed most aggravating? Was she right?

What did the dream (or halfway asleep) sequences add to the book?

THE CASES

1. ***The Hummingbird Wizard: An Annie Szabo Mystery.*** New York: Forge, 2003, 400 p. 0765307693 (alk. paper).

San Francisco and the Valley of the Moon (near Sonoma, California), Autumn 2003. A voice out of Annie's past, her sister-in-law Capri, asks Annie to speak to Jerry, the man who was Annie's first best friend. Capri is worried: she believes that Jerry has fallen in with bad, even dangerous, company. Annie's mother-in-law, Madame Mina, tells Annie that she believes that someone is stealing Jerry's soul. Annie goes to visit him, but they don't have a chance for a real conversation before Jerry disappears. Annie thinks that she had a half-asleep encounter with him on Sunday night; it may have been a dream. Then the police call; Jerry died some time on Friday night, two nights before she "dreamed" of him. Annie doesn't know what to believe, but she decides that the one thing she can't live with is not finding the truth. In the course of the investigation, she becomes embroiled once more with the family of her husband, Stevan, who died decades ago. She embraces the gypsy culture once more, working with her mother-in-law to steal Jerry's body from his funeral so that they can hold a *pomana,* the gypsy ceremony for the dead.

Associates: Madame Mina Szabo—*is Annie's mother-in-law;* Stevan—*was Annie's husband who died many years ago;* Capri—*Stevan's half-sister;* Jerry Baumann—*Annie's best friend, he was once married to Capri;* Bill Wells—*Jerry's partner;* Berva—*their secretary;* Jozef—*a.k.a. the Hummingbird Wizard, Stevan's half-brother;* Pinky Marks—*was Mina's second husband;* Zoltan—*was one of her lovers, he now acts as her attorney and is also a private investigator;* E. B. (short for Electric Blue)—*is Annie's oldest daughter, and a sculptor;* Cynthia Sloane—*movie star, is one of Annie's friends;* Lana—*Cynthia's over-protective secretary;* Tony Tiger—*a street person who wears a tuxedo made out of tiger-striped fur;* Skiz—*Tony Tiger's friend, another street person;* Tad Jones—*who is dating Cynthia;* Mrs. Liu—*is a dissatisfied customer of Madame Mina's;* Detective August Lawless, Lieutenant Detective Alfred Strunk, Deputy Johnson, and Officer Ed Florentino—*are investigators on the case;* Oscar Baumann—*Jerry's father.*

2. ***Vanished Priestess: An Annie Szabo Mystery.*** New York: Forge, 2004, 316 p. 0765307804 (acid-free paper).

VALLEY OF THE MOON (NEAR SONOMA, CALIFORNIA), WINTER 2003. Margo Spanger was larger than life. She worked in the circus for years, and then she started her own circus to raise money for her charities. Chief among those charities was a secret women's shelter, housed on the grounds of her property, hidden by the activity of the circus performers. Women who have left abusive relationships sometimes take trapeze lessons; it gives them self-confidence and teaches them to trust again. Annie takes her daughter, Abra, to the shelter, to try to hide her from Rory, Abra's abusive husband. The next day, Margo is found murdered, and Annie takes Abra away and hides her in the desert with Abra's Uncle Jack. Annie loves and trusts him. This is how she describes her brother:

> One nutty uncle, my brother, was holed up in the desert fasting and visioning, meditating and eating peyote. I loved Jack, but I couldn't understand why it was taking him so long to figure out who he was. He was not all that complicated. (*Vanished Priestess,* p. 40)

Annie feels that she must investigate Margo's murder to find out if Abra's estranged husband, Rory, is a killer.

ASSOCIATES: Madame Mina—*Annie's mother-in-law, she moves a trailer into Annie's yard to try to keep an eye on her daughter, Capri;* Capri—*who has stopped drinking, is teaching trapeze "flying" to abused women;* Margo Spanger—*Annie's neighbor, is running a secret shelter for abused women;* Lili Öoberlund—*Margo's life-partner;* Angel Verona—*a trapeze catcher;* Leo Rosetti—*Angel's uncle;* Maria Tomi—*who is brought to Annie's home by Angel;* Abra—*Annie's youngest daughter;* Rory—*Abra's abusive husband;* Joey—*Abra and Rory's son;* Jack—*Annie's brother;* Suzanne—*a friend of Abra's, Suzanne has been sleeping with Rory;* Juanita—*runs the local whorehouse;* Frank—*the plumber who moves into Madame Mina's trailer;* Detective August Lawless—*who has retired from the San Francisco Police Department and has started to work as a private investigator;* Ruth—*August's wife;* Mrs. Liu—*a customer of Madame Mina.*

3. ***Red Hot Empress: An Annie Szabo Mystery.*** New York: Forge, 2005, 351 p. ISBN: 0765307812.

SAN FRANCISCO, JANUARY 2004. It all began when Annie wrote a story for *The Eye* about Jimmy Qi, a boy who can cure some illnesses through "toning bones." Suddenly, everyone wants a piece of this kid. Annie feels responsible, and is trying to protect Jimmy when one of the uncles who raised him is murdered. Jimmy's Uncle Hao is the first murder victim, with more follow. To keep Jimmy safe, Annie has to find out why people are being killed.

ASSOCIATES: Madame Mina—*Annie's mother-in-law;* Jimmy Qi—*the 12-year-old who can heal (with tone bones);* Mrs. Liu—*whose arthritis was cured;* Hao—*an herbalist, Jimmy's Uncle;* Ike Qi—*Hao's brother;* Jean and Jan Duette—*who give Annie an interview;* E. B.—*Annie's daughter;* Flora Light—*who wants to set up a profitable enterprise using Jimmy to heal people at her church, The Church of All Light;* Wagner Stipple—*Flora's bodyguard;* Leo Rosetti—*is dating Annie;* Skip—*a.k.a. Rain, he wants Jimmy to talk to dolphins;* Mr. Stanyon—*Skip's father;* Dudley—*is under orders to follow Annie;* Candy—*who works at Ghirardelli's;* Alan Lee—*from the Centers for Disease Control and Prevention;* Pavlik Szabo—*Stevan's son;* Shirley—*Pavlik's wife;* Jimmy—*Stevan and Pavlik's new daughter.*

BOVA, Ben.

THE MULTIPLE MAN

Genres/Themes Crossed: Science Fiction, Man as Creator X Traditional Mystery.

Subjects/Character Types: Clones X Amateur Detective (Contemporary).

Series/Stand-Alone: Stand-alone.

Scene of the Crime: Boston, Washington D.C., Minnesota, and Colorado, future.

Detective: Meric Albano, Press Secretary to the President of the United States.

Known Associates: While Meric works with many people in his capacity as Press Secretary, the nature of this case is such that he quickly decides that there is no one whom he can trust. He follows the Head of Security, he listens to the President, he's tempted by the First Lady, but he investigates on his own.

Premise: This is set at some unknown point in Earth's future. The technology is more advanced than ours. A local hospital has a cryonics facility. A speaker's podium is protected by an invisible laser-actuated shield that can zap a bullet into nothingness before it hits its target. Sonic janglers could paralyze an audience. Television broadcasts display in three dimensions. Society has changed. There were "Shortage Riots" in Las Vegas in which the unemployed destroyed the casinos. Vegas has not recovered. A dozen years ago, the National Vigilance Society tried to seize the government. Yet the more things change the more they stay the same. There are dangerous political problems brewing in the Middle East.

Comment: Bova has written over 115 books. He is President Emeritus of the National Space Society and a charter member and past President of the Science-fiction and Fantasy Writers of America. Dr. Bova received the Lifetime Achievement Award from the Arthur C. Clarke Foundation in 2005, "for fueling mankind's imagination regarding the wonders of outer space." The John W. Campbell Memorial Award for Best Novel to be published in 2006 was awarded to his novel *Titan*. He's served the nation on the Steering Committee for the NASA/Space Transportation Association study on space tourism and on panels of the Office of Technology Assessment. His Web site is http://www.benbova.com.

Literary Magic & Mayhem: The world is very well done: different enough from ours to give hints of a fascinating history, yet alike enough to ours that bits of our history resonate through the story. For instance, at one point someone compared the feelings of the country for an adored President to the feelings citizens had for John F. Kennedy. The remark was made to the President's Head of Security, who was understandably unnerved by the comparison. As with many of the early Science Fiction works, this book is consciously feminist, but that feminist outlook is not integrated into the setting or into the characters' world views. Women are referred to as girls. The only way for a woman to live in the White House is for her to have married the President; her sex appeal is her most important asset. The only women worthy of note are those that are physically attractive. Women are either bit players, or prizes for which men fight. It's always interesting to look at fiction written decades ago about the future. Some assumptions (such as that the U.S.S.R. would continue) have proven false. The future that seemed likely then is not possible now.

Explorations: Do you think the mixture of the mundane with the fantastic is well done? For instance:

> So I sat at the bar and ordered a synthetic Rum Collins. The synthetics were pretty good; they tasted right and even got you high, but without the aftereffects. The FDA was investigating claims that they were addictive and carcinogenic. (p. 130)

Does the mixture add to or detract from the believability of the story's world?

What were other examples of today's problems being perpetuated even in a changed world?

This book is often referred to incorrectly as "Multiple Men." Is that a good or a bad thing? Is the current title a spoiler? Does the author play fair with the clues given the reader?

THE CASE

The Multiple Man. Indianapolis: Bobbs-Merrill, c1976, 210 p. ISBN: 0672520729.

WASHINGTON, D.C., 2??? Meric Albano gave his loyalty to the President. He truly believed that this man was the country's best chance for peace and prosperity. When the President's Head of Security took him away from listening to the President's speech to view a body found within the security perimeter, he was worried for the President's safety. When he saw that the body looked like the President, he was frantic. When it was scientifically confirmed that the body shared every physical characteristic of the President, Albano began to wonder. Was the man in the Oval Office really the man who had been elected? What if a double had taken the place of the President? Only a small team of men know that someone who looked like the President died that night. One by one they die, and the investigation seems to have been buried with them.

ASSOCIATES: President James J. Halliday; First Lady Laura Benson; General Morton J. Halliday—*the President's father;* McMurtrie—*the head of the President's security team;* Robert H. H. (His Holiness) Wyatt—*the President's Appointments Secretary;* Vickie Clark—*a White House staffer;* Dr. Adrian Klienerman—*the President's personal physician;* Greta—*Meric's secretary.*

Mrs. Bester—*the president's private secretary;* Admiral Del Bello—*the Chairman of the Joint Chiefs of Staff;* Hank Solomon—*who worked with McMurtrie;* Dr. Alfonso Peña—*the Head of North Lake Research Laboratories;* Dr. Peter Thornton; Dr. Morris Malachi; Betty Turner—*from SGR (press);* Max Freid—*of UPI (United Press International);* Johnny Harrison—*City Editor, Albano's old friend;* Len Ryan—*Albano's new reporter.*

OUT OF THE SUN

Genres/Themes Crossed: Science Fiction X Traditional Mystery.

Subjects/Character Types: Future Technology X Espionage.

Series/Stand-Alone: Stand-alone.

Scene of the Crime: Air Force Base, near future.

Detective: Paul Sarko worked for the military for six years, then decided to turn his skills to more peaceful ends.

Known Associates: Dr. Leon Ratterman is an old colleague of Paul's. Major F.D.R. Colt is determined to get to the bottom of the destruction of three of the four prototypes for the Cobra Mach-3 aircraft.

Premise: Air force scientists cannot find a structural weakness that would explain the failure of the first Cobra aircraft. Paul Sarko developed the metals used in the plane. Dr. Ratterman has asked that Paul return to explore the question of whether or not, after 100 hours of flight, metal fatigue may have contributed to the destruction of the plane.

Comment: This is a slight work, but it was cataloged by the Library of Congress with genre headings for Science Fiction, and Detective and Mystery stories.

Literary Magic & Mayhem: This is a quick, breezy read that follows the actions of Paul Sarko as he tries to determine what made the Cobra aircraft fail.

Explorations: What would have happened if the villain had not attempted a cover-up?

THE CASE

Out of the Sun. New York: Holt, Rinehart and Winston, 1968, 88 p.

AIR FORCE BASE [LOCATION UNKNOWN], 19??. Paul Sarko is dragged into an investigation of the destruction of the prototype Cobras. At first he believed that the Cobra fell to a technical flaw; but, when test after test uncovers nothing, he is forced to consider the possibility of espionage.

ASSOCIATES: Dr. Ratterman—*a scientist working on the question of what destroyed the Cobras and killed their crews;* Major F.D.R. "Frank" Colt—*who is willing to risk his life to prove Sarko's metal is safe;* Mrs. Colt—*the Major's wife;* Martin Arnold—*who assists Sarko's investigation;* Rita Stefano—*Dr. Nash's secretary who dates Sarko;* General Hastings—*to whom Sarko must prove his theories.*

BRIGGS, Patricia.

MOON CALLED

Genres/Themes Crossed: Blended Society, Secret Society (Some supernatural groups have "come out," others are still "closeted") X Traditional Mystery.

Subjects/Character Types: Werewolves, Vampires, Demons, Spell-Casters (Sorcerers), Fae X Amateur Sleuth (Contemporary).

Series/Stand-Alone: The novels should be read in order, as characters and relationships evolve over the course of the series.

Scene of the Crime: Tri-city area of Washington State.

Detective: Mercedes "Mercy" Athena Thompson is a "Walker": she can shape-shift between human and coyote form. Her mother, Margi, had a fling with a Native American (Blackfoot tribe) rodeo cowboy; he died before she knew she was pregnant. Margi's first hint that something was odd was when the infant Mercy shape-shifted in her crib. Her mother went in search of people like Mercy, people who could help her as she grew up. She found werewolves, and Mercy was raised by foster parents (Evelyn and Bryan) within the werewolf pack. Mercy is very determinedly not part of the pack; she is not a werewolf. She is regarded as a neutral but useful individual due to her knowledge of the supernatural world, her friendship with a few different supernatural beings, and her status as an outsider (not part of any pack, seemingly the only "walker" left in the world).

Known Associates: Siebold Adelbertkrieger aus dem Schwarzenwald, "Zee" to his friends, is a gremlin who employed Mercy as a mechanic at his garage. (When the Gray Mages told him to reveal his supernatural nature to society, Zee retired and sold the garage to Mercy.) Adam Hauptman, werewolf, is the alpha male of the local Columbia Basin Pack. He staked his claim to Mercy to protect her from pack harassment. Adam and his daughter, Jesse are Mercy's neighbors. Adam's pack includes his second, Darryl (werewolf) and Darryl's mate Auriele (werewolf). Third in the hierarchy is Warren (werewolf), who would have trouble in a pack without Adam's explicit protection, because many werewolves are prejudiced against people who are gay. (Warren's boyfriend, Kyle, is human.) Others in Adam's pack include Ben (werewolf), who had to leave England quickly when he was under police scrutiny for a series of violent crimes, and Mary Jo (werewolf). Bran (werewolf) is the Marrok, which means that he leads all the North American werewolves. (Adam answers to Bran.)

Bran's immediate pack includes his mate Leah (werewolf), his sons Samuel (werewolf) and Charles (Charles is the only born werewolf, all others were made through being bitten). Mercy's first love was the gentle Dr. Samuel Cormick. Dr. Carter Wallace (werewolf), a veterinarian; Gerry Wallace (werewolf), Carter's son, who travels to keep an eye on the lone wolves for Bran; and Carl and Lisa Stoval (werewolves) and their daughter Marlie. Lone wolves include David Christiansen (werewolf), an old army buddy of Adam's who is creating his own pack with his grandsons, John-Julian and Connor.

Stefan (vampire) is a good customer of Mercy's. The leader of his "seethe" is Marsilia (vampire). Others in the seethe include Andre (vampire), Estelle (vampire), and Lilly (vampire). (Lilly was turned into a vampire before the vampire who made her realized that she was insane; they keep her around because she is a wonderful pianist.)

Elizaveta Arkadyevna Vyshnevetskaya (witch) and her grandson, Robert, clean up the sites of supernatural battles. Sylvia Sandoval received mechanical help from Zee. Mercy lets Sylvia's son, Gabriel (human), work off the bill.

Premise: Supernatural beings, "preternaturals," exist in our world, and modern medical technology is making it progressively more difficult for them to remain hidden. In some communities (particularly in the military) there are already key individuals who know, or who suspect, the truth. Three decades ago, the Gray Lords, the mages who ruled the *fae,* realized that the Time of Hiding was coming to an end. Two decades ago, the Gray Lords had developed their strategy, and they decreed that the lesser fae (those who look harmless and non-threatening) should reveal themselves to the world. They have not been universally welcomed; in fact, many have been "encouraged" to go to live on reservations. The greater fae are watching and waiting. Forensic science will destroy the option to remain hidden forever; at best, the greater fae can choose the time and place in which they will be revealed. Most types of preternaturals originated in Europe and migrated to America with the settlers. Mercy is a "Walker." Walkers originated in North America and have some resistance to the magic of creatures whose powers originated in Europe. Mercy was brought up by werewolves. Werewolves are made, not born. Usually, the attempt to become a werewolf is made at the human's insistence. Since werewolves are tough, and through the human–wolf transformation they can overcome many diseases, there are people who are desperate to become werewolves. These must undergo a fatal attack, and only at the point of death can the werewolf's magic overcome the human immune system. Most people who try to become werewolves die.

Comment: Patricia Briggs's Web site, http://patriciabriggs.com, describes her current projects and indicates that there will be at least seven books in this series. The site includes a biography, book lists, and links to interviews. Her husband, Mike Briggs, blogs on many subjects on the site, keeping her fans up-to-date!

Literary Magic & Mayhem: Mercy is a likeable protagonist. She is tough, but knows her own limitations; she is smart, but wise enough to keep her mouth shut instead of causing herself and others grief. She is a loyal friend, and her instincts to protect the innocent and to give a hand to those who are down on their luck seem likely to propel her into numerous adventures. She has met a diverse group of people through working at the garage, many of whom are her customers. The depiction of the never-ending work involved in owning one's own business seems accurate. Many of the people Mercy loves have made mistakes. She's clear-sighted enough to see the mistakes, but to also understand when, even if she has been hurt, people did not set out to hurt her. Her great capacity for love and forgiveness completes the depiction of a young woman of great strength and generosity of spirit. Her sharp tongue and cutting observations help her avoid the pitfall of seeming like a paragon of virtue.

Good and evil exist in this world. Some people have faith, others do not. Having faith or not having faith does not determine if a character is good or evil, but it gives the reader some understanding of what that character has seen and felt. Issues of faith are used to give a context to the world, to delineate character, and to further the plot. The world described here is richer and more interesting because those issues are included, they are an aspect of the excellent storytelling.

Explorations: Mercy has had many father figures and mother figures in her life. What are some ways they supported her, and what are some of the ways that they caused her pain? How does she feel about them now?

Mercy grew up in a pack. How did that shape her thinking and behavior?

Bran, at one point, indicates that an action that Mercy took was what he had wanted her to do, and that he would have maneuvered her into doing it if she had not done it herself. What might have been the consequences for Mercy if he had not stated in front of witnesses that she had done what he secretly intended her to do?

How did this work as a mystery story? Were clues laid out and followed logically? Were the motivations for the crimes understandable?

THE CASES

1. ***Moon Called.*** New York: Ace, 2006, 304 p. ISBN: 0441013813.

WASHINGTON STATE AND MONTANA, 200? When "Mac" asked Mercy for a job, she knew he was a werewolf; and, since she did not recognize him, she wondered if he were part of the local pack. The only safe way that he could remain on the pack's turf was to get approval from the local alpha. If he didn't know that, he must be very new. If no one had warned him, he must not have a pack. Mercy's heart goes out to him, and she gives him a job. She wonders who would change him and then heartlessly abandon him. This question leads to others, each more grave than the last. Mercy uncovers murder and betrayal as she searches for the answers.

ASSOCIATES: Alan MacKenzie "Mac" Frazier—*werewolf, who asks Mercy for help;* Zee—*gremlin;* Adam Hauptman—*werewolf, alpha of the Columbia Basin pack;* Jesse—*human, Adam's daughter;* Darryl—*werewolf, Adam's pack;* Auriele—*werewolf, Darryl's mate, Adam's pack;* Warren—*werewolf, Adam's pack;* Kyle—*human, Warren's boyfriend;* Ben—*werewolf, Adam's pack, even Mercy finds Ben frightening;* Mary Jo—*werewolf, Adam's pack;* Bran—*werewolf, the Marrok;* Leah—*werewolf, Bran's wife;* Samuel and Charles—*werewolves, Bran's sons;* Dr. Carter Wallace—*werewolf, Bran's pack, a gentle veterinarian;* Gerry Wallace—*werewolf, Bran's pack, Carter's son, who travels to keep an eye on the lone wolves for Bran;* Carl and Lisa Stoval and their daughter Marlie—*werewolves of Bran's pack.* David Christiansen—*werewolf, lone wolf;* John-Julian and Connor—*David's grandsons;* Marsilia—*who leads the local vampire "seethe";* Stefan, Andre, Estelle, and Lilly—*vampires of Marsilia's seethe;* Elizaveta Arkadyevna Vyshnevetskaya—*witch;* Robert—*Elizaveta's grandson;* Sylvia Sandoval—*who received mechanical help from Zee;* Gabriel—*Sylvia's son, is working off the bill at the garage.*

2. *Blood Bound.* New York: Ace, 2007, 292 p. ISBN: 9780441014736.

WASHINGTON STATE, 200? Bran orchestrated the werewolves' going public six months ago. Not all of them have been revealed, but some of them are now known. The reaction has been relatively mild. Adam is one of the wolves who has come out. Zee was forced to come out as a gremlin several years ago. Mercy's connection to both of these men is public. Those who are not sure they want to approach the preternaturals directly are coming to Mercy for advice and support. In this book, she investigates a murderer, a serial killer. The killer has found the perfect way to frame another vampire for his crimes. He kills in the presence of the vampire and hypnotizes him so that he is certain that the kill was his own. Once the vampire admits to his Seethe that he has killed in a way that will bring attention to vampires, the Seethe will kill him. So, with one murder, the murderer essentially creates two victims.

ASSOCIATES: Stefan—*vampire, who asks Mercy for a favor;* Dr. Samuel Cormick—*werewolf, Mercy's roommate;* Zee—*gremlin;* Gabriel Sandoval—*human who works at the garage;* Adam Hauptman—*werewolf, alpha of the Columbia Basin pack;* Jesse—*human, Adam's daughter;* Darryl—*werewolf, Adam's pack;* Warren—*werewolf, Adam's pack;* Kyle—*human, Warren's boyfriend;* Paul—*werewolf, Adam's pack, Paul wants to challenge Warren for his place as third in the pack;* Ben—*werewolf, Adam's pack, even Mercy finds Ben frightening;* Mary Jo—*werewolf, Adam's pack;* Elliot—*werewolf, Adam's pack;* Peter Jorgenson—*werewolf, Adam's pack;* Honey Jorgenson—*werewolf, Adam's pack, Peter's mate;* Bran—*werewolf, the Marrok, ranks above Adam;* Marsilia—*who leads the local vampire "seethe";* Stefan, Wulfe, Andre, Daniel, Bernard, Estelle, and Lilly—*vampires of Marsilia's seethe. (Wulfe cqn sense the truth.)* Naomi, Rachel, Josephine, and Ford—*humans who serve Stefan;* Cory Littleton—*a vampire, who is in Marsilia's territory but is not in her seethe;* Elizaveta Arkadyevna Vyshnevetskaya—*witch;* Tom Black—*a reporter;* Kara—*Tom's daughter;* Tony Montenegro—*a cop who's an old friend;* Uncle Mike—*who owns a bar;* Fergus—*the bouncer;* and Mrs. Hanna—*a ghost who is sometimes seen near Mercy's garage.*

3. *Iron Kissed.* New York: Ace, 2008, 287 p. ISBN: 9780441015665.

WASHINGTON STATE, 200? A number of fae on the Ronald Wilson Reagan Fae Reservation have been murdered. The fae have investigated on their own; they don't want the federal authorities nosing around on the reservation. The fae are guarding a secret: they're using the space and the isolation of the reservations to try to rebuild gateways to Underhill and regain their ancient power. Mercy owes the fae a favor. She was given an artifact to use just once to kill one murdering vampire, but she used it twice. They ask her to come to the reservation and to see if she can use her gifts, particularly her sense of smell, to identify the killer. She tries to respect the boundaries set by the fae, but observing boundaries is not one of Mercy's talents, and she learns too much about the fae's secrets. When the police learn that something is wrong, the fae decide to sacrifice Zee to get the investigation closed before their secrets are discovered. Mercy will not accept the sacrifice of her friend. The fae find that neither orders nor threats will deter her. Mercy, in the face of fae opposition, begins her own investigation.

ASSOCIATES: Samuel Cornick—*werewolf, Mercy's roommate, he and Mercy come to a new understanding about their relationship in this book;* Adam Hauptman—*werewolf, alpha of the Columbia Basin pack;* Jesse—*human, Adam's daughter;* Darryl—*werewolf, Adam's pack;* Aurielle (Auriele)—*werewolf, Darryl's mate, Adam's pack;* Warren—*werewolf, Adam's pack;* Kyle—*human, Warren's boyfriend;* Ben—*werewolf, Adam's pack, Ben has more compassion than Mercy had suspected;* Peter Jorgenson—*werewolf, Adam's pack;* Honey Jorgenson—*werewolf, Adam's pack, Peter's mate;* Zee—*gremlin, a.k.a. Siebold Adelbertsmiter;* Gabriel—*human;* Officer O'Donnell—*of the Federal Bureau of Fae Affairs;* Uncle Mike—*who runs a bar in Pasco (and is a member of the Council);* Nemane the Carrion Crow—*who is known in the world as Dr. Stacy Altman and works as a folklore specialist at the University of Oregon (and is a member of the Council);* Jean Ryan—*criminal defense attorney;* Tim Milanovich, Austin Summers, Courtney, and Mr. Aiden Fideal (a.k.a. the Fideal)—*members of a group of anti-fae activists;* police officer Tony Montenegro; Pastor Julio Arnez; Tad—*Zee's son;* and Jacob Summers—*Jesse's classmate.*

4. *Bone Crossed.* New York: Ace, 2009, 309 p. ISBN: 9780441016761.

WASHINGTON STATE, 200? The events chronicled in this novel are essentially the aftermath of *Blood Bound* and *Iron Kissed*. In this book, everything is set in motion by Stefan's warning that Marsilia has discovered that Mercy killed Andre and that Stefan did his best to protect Mercy by concealing that fact from Marsilia (in *Blood Bound*). Marsilia is taking vengeance. She has killed Stefan's humans and injured Stefan to the point that she believes he will instinctively kill Mercy. Her plan fails. One failure will certainly not stop Marsilia. Emotionally, Mercy is fighting to regain her balance after the brutal attack that almost killed her (in *Iron Kissed*). To help an old acquaintance (and to get out of town), Mercy goes to Spokane to investigate a ghost. There she finds a mystery and a child whom she is determined to protect.

ASSOCIATES: Adam Hauptman—*werewolf, alpha of the Columbia Basin Pack (in this book Mercy agrees to be his mate);* Margaret—*a.k.a. Margi, Mercy's mother;* Bran the Marrok—*werewolf, leader of the North American werewolf packs;* Samuel Cornick—*werewolf, lone wolf, Mercy's roommate, and son of Bran the Marrok;* Jesse—*human, Adam's daughter;* Darryl—*werewolf, Adam's pack;* Aurielle (Auriele)—*werewolf, Darryl's mate, Adam's pack;* Warren—*werewolf, Adam's pack;* Kyle—*human, Warren's boyfriend;* Ben—*werewolf, Adam's pack;* Peter Jorgenson—*werewolf, a submissive, Adam's pack;* Mary Jo—*werewolf, Adam's pack;* Paul—*werewolf, Adam's pack;* Alec—*werewolf, Adam's pack;* Marsilia—*vampire, leader of the local seethe;* Stefan (a.k.a. Soldier); Wulfe, Daniel, Bernard, Estelle, and Lilly—*the vampires of Marsilia's seethe.* Sensei Johanson—*the head of Mercy's dojo;* Lee—*who makes the mistake of picking a fight with Mercy;* Uncle Mike—*who runs a bar in Pasco;* Ymir—*the snow elf;* Baba Yaga—*fae;* Zee—*gremlin, a.k.a. Siebold Adelbertsmiter.* When Zee was trying to force Mercy into walking away from an investigation, he told her that she would immediately have to pay him the remaining money owed on the garage if she continued. Since he's fae, his word must stand. Mercy is trying to figure out how to come up with the money.

Amber—*who asks Mercy for help in proving her son's claim that their house is haunted is true;* Chad—*Amber's 10-year-old son;* Corban—*Chad's father, who doesn't believe Chad;* James Blackwood—*a vampire who is called "The Monster" by other vampires;* Tony Montenegro—*a cop who is an old friend of Mercy;* Donnell Greenleaf—*oakman fae;* Catherine—*a.k.a. "Grandmother Death" vampire, ghost;* John—*the ghost who is haunting Chad.*

ALPHA AND OMEGA

Genres/Themes Crossed: Blended Society, Secret Society X Traditional Mystery.

Subjects/Character Types: Werewolves, Vampires, Demons, Spell-Casters (Sorcerers), Fae X Amateur Sleuth (Contemporary).

Series/Stand-Alone: The stories should be read in order (beginning with the short story "Alpha and Omega"), as characters and relationships evolve over the course of the series.

Scene of the Crime: Chicago and Montana.

Detective: Charles Cornick serves as business manager, investigator, and enforcer for his father, the Marrok. The Marrok is the primary alpha werewolf in North America, leading all the packs on the continent. Ideally, local alphas resolve the problems and crimes perpetrated by wolves in their local packs. If the local alpha is unable or unwilling to resolve a problem then the Marrok must find a solution. An unrestrained criminal will eventually be caught and the werewolves' secret would come out, endangering them all. When problems come to the Marrok's attention, he sends Charles out to resolve them, frequently by killing rogue wolves. Long ago, Charles learned to avoid getting close to anyone except his father and brother. Having no friends is the only way to ensure that he will never be forced to kill a friend. Anna Latham is an Omega wolf. She has the ability to calm the wolves around her, and her presence increases the chances that the wolves around her will be able to resolve problems without resorting to violence.

Known Associates: In Chicago, Anna works at Scorci's Italian Restaurant for Tim, and her best friend is her downstairs neighbor, Kara Mosley. The Chicago Pack alpha is Leo. Leo's wife is Isabelle, the insane Justin is Leo's second, and Boyd Hamilton is Leo's third. Other wolves include the doctor Rashid, Holden, Gardner, and Simon. In Montana, the pack alpha is Bran. Bran's sons are Charles and Samuel. Bran's wife is Leah. Other wolves in the pack include Asil, who is also known as The Moor, and Sage.

Premise: This series is set in the same world as the *Mercedes Thompson* series, but Anna's point of view and personality are very different from Mercy's. Anna's original alpha, Leo, had her changed when he recognized that she would become an Omega wolf. He needed an Omega to stabilize his insane mate Isabelle. She had killed all the other females of the pack in fits of jealous rage, and Leo had been forced to kill their mates and others to keep the pack under his control. Leo hoped that an Omega's calming influence would stabilize Isabelle. Knowing that Isabelle would be jealous of any new female in the pack, he set about brutalizing Anna so that Isabelle would see her as a victim rather than a rival. It worked. For three years, Isabelle was relatively stable, while Anna contemplated suicide. Leo also squandered the pack's material resources, spending large amounts of money in an effort to keep Isabelle happy. Eventually, he resorted to having Justin turn innocent people against their will and selling the resultant werewolves. One of those wolves, Alan MacKenzie Frazier, escaped and encountered Mercy Thompson who warned the Marrok that Leo was creating wolves and selling them for experimentation. The Marrok sent his son Charles to Chicago to investigate.

Comment: Patricia Briggs describes how this series came into being on her Web site, http://patriciabriggs.com. Charles was a minor character in the *Mercedes Thompson* series, created so that Samuel wouldn't have been an only child. Ms. Briggs found Charles interesting, but didn't have the time and space to explore his life in the *Mercedes Thompson* novels. She was working on a *Mercedes Thompson* novel when she was asked for a novella for *On the Prowl.* She wanted to set it in Mercedes's world, but she didn't want to write a prequel. She wasn't sure how the current novel would turn out or where it would leave the characters, so she decided to take the opportunity to write part of Charles's story. To her surprise, she found it to be a romance. The story worked so well that it became the foundation for a new series.

Literary Magic & Mayhem: Anna's struggle to overcome the fear created by her systematic victimization is heartbreaking, and leaves the reader admiring the strength that sustained her through years of abuse. Readers will be as charmed as Charles is when she picks up a rolling pin as a weapon. Charles's investigative technique in the novella consists mostly of determining the best questions to ask. In the novel, he employs tracking, as well as his knowledge of witchcraft. These fit our definition: that the story's action is driven by the investigation of a suspected crime. In the novella, Charles is sent to investigate the forced change and subsequent sale of Alan MacKenzie Frazier. In the novel, Charles is sent to investigate the attacks that took place in the Cabinet Wilderness.

Explorations: Charles is the only born werewolf. His father's people are still with him after 200 years. In that time, what has happened to his mother's people? What would it be like, to have seen the changes that Charles has seen? What would it be like to know that you are practically immortal and to see so much of your society end?

Anna is slow to defend herself, but what does she do when others are attacked?

1. **"Alpha and Omega,"** a novella in *On the Prowl.* New York: Berkley, 2007, p. 1–72. ISBN: 9780425216590.

CHICAGO, TWO MONTHS AFTER ALAN MACKENZIE FRAZIER DISAPPEARED FROM A HIGH-SCHOOL DANCE. Anna recognized the face of Alan MacKenzie Frazier in a newspaper. In the three years since she's been turned, Anna has done her best to keep her head down and avoid the attention of the pack leader, but she won't be silent when she knows that Adam has been framed for murder. She summons her courage and calls the Marrok. The Marrok had already learned from Mercy that something was wrong in Chicago and his son, Charles, is traveling to Chicago to investigate.

ASSOCIATES: Charles Cornick—*werewolf, the Marrok's son;* George—*owner of a Greek restaurant;* Mick—*owner of Scorci's Italian restaurant where Anna works;* Kara Mosley—*Anna's downstairs neighbor;* Leo—*werewolf, alpha of Anna's pack (Chicago has two packs);* Isabelle—*werewolf, Leo's wife;* Justin—*werewolf with control issues, Leo's pack;* Boyd Hamilton—*werewolf, Leo's third, he gave Anna the Marrok's phone number;* Rashid—*werewolf, doctor, Leo's pack;* Holden, Gardner, and Simon—*all werewolves who have been turned recently, Leo's pack;* Bran—*werewolf, the Marrok, invites Anna to Montana.*

2. *Cry Wolf.* New York: Ace, 2008, 294 p. ISBN: 9780441016150.

CHICAGO AND ASPEN CREEK, MONTANA, 200? Two months ago a hiker came out of the Cabinet Wilderness (part of Bran's territory) with a wild tale about being attacked by a werewolf. Of course he was not taken seriously, at least not by people who don't believe in werewolves. It posed a problem for Bran, but with the onset of winter, no one would be traveling in the Cabinet Wilderness, and the problem could wait. A second attack on a ranger forces Bran's hand. While a wild story from a hiking grad student would be dismissed, a direct report from a woodsman, a respected ranger, is a different matter. Even if the report were considered insane now, when Bran takes the werewolves public it would be remembered. The only way to quiet the ranger is to convince him that the werewolves can and will police their own. Bran asks Charles to investigate and to take care of the threat. Charles agrees, intending to go alone, but Bran supports Anna's wish to accompany Charles. Charles would be able to track and kill a rogue wolf; but with Anna along it may be possible to calm the rogue and bring him into the safety of Bran's pack.

ASSOCIATES: Boyd—*werewolf, is the new alpha for one of the Chicago packs;* George, Joshua, and Thomas—*werewolves of Boyd's pack;* Bran—*a.k.a. The Marrok, the werewolf who is the leader of all the wolves in North America and is also the alpha for the Montana pack;* Leah—*Bran's pack;* Charles and Samuel—*Bran's sons;* Sage—*werewolf, Bran's pack, she befriends Anna;* Colin "Tag" Taggart—*werewolf, Bran's pack;* and Asil "the Moor"—*werewolf, Bran's pack. The Moor is legendary. He's 1300 years old, ancient even by werewolf standards, and stories of his wiliness and strength abound.* Sarai—*werewolf, deceased, Asil's mate, an Omega wolf who was murdered by a witch;* Mariposa—*the witch;* Walter Rice—*werewolf, lone wolf, recently turned against his will;* Hank—*human, the pilot;* Shawna—*human, Dr. Carter Wallace's granddaughter;* and Heather Morrell—*human, Colin Taggart's niece, who brings her co-worker Jack to Bran after Jack is attacked by a werewolf.*

AFFILIATED STORIES

"The Star of David," a short story in *Wolfsbane and Mistletoe,* edited by Charlaine Harris and Toni L. P. Kelner. New York: Ace Books, 2008, p. 218–45. ISBN: 9780441016334.

City unknown, December 2008. David hasn't seen his daughter Stella since the night he returned from Viet Nam, the night he killed his wife, Stella's mother. He'd been too new in being a werewolf, too surprised and hurt when confronted with her and her lover. He'd lost control, and he has regretted it every day since her death. His daughter, Stella, was a child. She asked him to stay away from her, and he respected her wishes. Now she is middle-aged, and she calls him right before Christmas, asking for his help. She doesn't want help for herself, but for a foster child, Devonte, one of her "cases." Devonte is accused of an extraordinarily violent and forceful attack on his foster parents. Photographs of the scene show an astonishing level of destruction. It seems impossible that one person could do that much damage in that short a time. Stella knows that there are monsters; she saw her father become one. She needs to know what she and Devonte are facing now.

Associates: David—*werewolf, lone wolf;* Stella—*human, David's daughter, she works for an agency that places foster children;* Devonte Parish—*wizard, he is accused of attacking his foster parents, the Linfords;* Clive—*David's son;* Myra—*Stella's coworker;* and Jorge—*police officer.*

BRIN, David.

<u>Kiln People</u>

Genres/Themes Crossed: Man as Creator X Hard-Boiled Mystery.

Subjects/Character Types: Sentient Artificial Intelligence (Golems) X Private Investigator, Noir.

Series/Stand-Alone: Stand-alone.

Scene of the Crime: Future Earth.

Detective: Private investigator Albert Morris has an unusual talent for imprinting high-fidelity dittos. His dittos are determined to get the job done and report back. He can send them into any dangerous situation. If they come back intact, he can gather the information that they found; if they don't come back, Albert has lost nothing but a day's time.

Known Associates: Sergeant Clara Gonzalez, Albert's girlfriend. Nell is Albert's house computer. Beta is the villain that keeps eluding Albert. Pal is an old friend, and Albert feels obligated to work for him when he calls.

Premise: In the future, people can make clay duplicates of themselves. The duplicates (called "dittos," "golems," "roxes," or "mules") carry all the memories of the original (called the "archie," the "rig," or the "proto"). The dittos disintegrate in a day, but at any point before they disintegrate, the original person can upload the ditto's memories of that day. Cheap dittos are widely available, and many people use them to do their work. More expensive dittos have higher intelligence, can perform more complex tasks, and can be customized to excel at a specific job. In general, the color of the clay of a ditto indicates its sophistication. The ditto colors encountered most frequently in the book, from cheapest to most expensive, are green (can do housework), purple (used as mercenaries and thugs), blue (designated for police work), gray (can conduct business), ebony (can analyze data), platinum (used by the rich, closely resemble their human prototypes), and ivory (used as sex objects).

Comment: *Kiln People* was published in the United Kingdom under the title *Kil'n People.* It was shortlisted for the 2003 Hugo for Best Novel of 2002 (Robert Sawyer's *Hominids* won); it was shortlisted for the 2003 Best Science Fiction Novel Locus Award (*The Years of Rice and Salt* by Kim Stanley Robinson won); it was shortlisted for the 2003 John W. Campbell Memorial Award for Best Science Fiction Novel (*Probability Space* by Nancy Kress won); and it was shortlisted for Britain's 2003 Arthur C. Clarke Award for best science fiction novel (Christopher Priest's *The Separation* won). No matter what group was polled, *Kiln People* was one of the best five science fiction books published in 2002. David Brin's Web site, at http://www.davidbrin.com, includes links to his blogs "Contrary Brin" and "Tomorrow Happens," with news on his public appearances, selections from his fiction and essays, several free short stories, interviews, podcasts, and more.

Literary Magic & Mayhem: The creation of the dittos allows the writer to split his protagonist into multiple "people," each with the same memories and personality (at least at the beginning of the day). The writer can then have one protagonist but multiple plot lines that interweave to create one narrative.

Explorations: The book begins with:

> It's hard to stay cordial while fighting for your life, even when your life doesn't amount to much. Even when you're just a lump of clay. [Kiln People, p. 11]

What makes the clone appealing?

Where do the dittos fit in society? How are they treated by real people? How are they treated by other dittos?

How much suspense does a reader feel when a clone is in danger? Early in the book a ditto says that the reader knows he made it home, or how else would his story be known? Is that more true or less true when the protagonists are dittos?

Which clone was the most interesting? Why?

The golem, thinking about his creation, thinks that it's a throw of the dice when someone imprints and kilns. Will they awaken as the archie or the ditto? How would that feel?

Most people refuse to inload if they suspect that the ditto had bad experiences. Is that fair? Of course, all the following dittos would know the choice that the archie had made. How would that knowledge affect a ditto?

How do different characters treat their dittos? Are Albert's attitudes unique?

How does Brin explore basic philosophical questions such as "What are the qualities that define a being as human?" and "What is God?" How would the definitions apply to the different versions of Albert?

By the end of the book how that world has changed?

How is reading a novel like inloading?

THE CASE

***Kiln People.* New York:** TOR, 2002, 459 p. ISBN: 0765303558.

FUTURE EARTH. Albert Morris is working on several cases, a murder, industrial espionage, and copyright violations, when odd things begin happening to his dittos. His greenie sends him a weird declaration of independence, and his grays just disappear. He has to know what's happening before he imprints again.

ASSOCIATES: Albert's girlfriend—*Sergeant Clara Gonzalez;* Nell—*Albert's house computer;* Beta—*the villain that Albert almost captures (once again);* Inspector Blane—*of the Labor Subcontractors Association (LSA);* Gineen Wammaker—*The Maestra of Studio Neo, a client who wants to prosecute Beta for copyright infringement;* Vic Manual Collins and Queen Irene—*Gineen's associates;* Vic Aeneas Kaolin—*one of the founders of Universal Kilns, another client;* Ritu Liza-betha Maharal—*Vic's assistant;* Dr. Yosil Maharal—*Ritu's father, another co-founder of Universal Kilns, he has been missing for a month;* Pal—*was a thrill-addicted mercenary until he crossed the wrong group and ended up ambushed and left for dead. Now Pal has a conspiracy theory de jour that must be investigated and he's another client.* Mr. James Gadarene—*who heads an organization called Defenders of Life;* Mr. Farshid Lum—*of Tolerance Unlimited;* Palloid—*Pal's ferret ditto, who hopes that an old girlfriend, Alexie, won't recognize him in this ferret form;* Corporal Chen—*of the army.*

BRUBAKER, Ed, Greg Rucka, Michael Lark, and Stefano Guadiano.

IN THE LINE OF DUTY

Genres/Themes Crossed: Blended Society X Police Procedural.

Subjects/Character Types: Superheroes, Supervillains X Police procedural.

Series/Stand-Alone: The novels should be read in order, as there are societal changes and changes in characters' lives and relationships during the course of the series.

Scene of the Crime: Gotham City.

Detectives: The men and women of the Gotham City Major Crimes Unit. Crisups Allen, detective and family man. Renee Montoya, a longtime detective who begins the series still hiding the details of her personal life from the other members of the force. Marcus Driver, a detective haunted by the loss of a partner. Romy Chandler, the new detective on the force. Josephine "Josie Mac" MacDonald, a detective with an inhumanly sharp eye for finding clues other people overlook.

Known Associates: Captain Sawyer, the leader of the division, who transferred to Gotham after a lengthy career in Metropolis. The Batman, the masked vigilante that fights crime in Gotham City. Robin, the most recent teenage partner to fight crime alongside the Batman. Commissioner Akins, the hard-nosed head of the GCPD, who took a hard line against cooperating with the Batman. James Gordon, former commissioner of the GCPD, and longtime friend of the Batman. Harvey Bullock, a disgraced former detective and former partner of Renee Montoya. Stacy, the receptionist for the department, and the only member of the department that can legally operate the Bat signal due to the fact that she is not actually a police officer.

Premise: It is hard to be a cop in Gotham City. Half the force is corrupt, a lot of the crimes are committed by psychopaths in costumes, and a fair portion of the crimes are solved by another psychopath in a costume. The detectives of the Gotham City MCU have to do their jobs, solving crimes in a city with costumed heroes and villains.

Comment: The relatively short lived series enjoyed a great deal of critical success, but generally poor sales. The series deals with very adult crimes, and has well-fleshed out and engaging characters. Many of the characters had appeared in other DC comics series prior to *Gotham Central*, but it is not necessary to be familiar with them prior to reading the series. The collected volumes do not include every issue of the series, and each volume tends to include two story arcs. Detectives that only play major roles in omitted story arcs have not been included in this entry.

Literary Magic & Mayhem: This is by far the most down-to-earth comic set in Gotham City. The characters involved are for the most part normal people, forced to deal with crimes in a city where criminal masterminds employ guns that can freeze men solid or wear flamethrowers strapped to their backs. However, the detectives seldom come into direct conflict with these villains. The emphasis is on the interpersonal connections of the officers and how they solve the crimes, rather than on over-the-top action scenes.

Explorations: How necessary is a police force in a city protected by superheroes?

How effective can normal people be against superhuman criminals?

THE CASES

1. ***In the Line of Duty.*** New York: DC Comics, 2004, 128 p. ISBN: 1401201997.

GOTHAM CITY, PRESENT DAY. A member of the MCU is killed by Mr. Freeze while investigating a kidnapping. The MCU rushes to solve the case and bring their friend's killer to justice before the Batman can get to Mr. Freeze. The kidnapping case becomes a murder case when the body of the missing girl is recovered, and the MCU must track down her killer.

ASSOCIATES: Captain Sawyer, Stacy, Commissioner Akins, James Gordon, and the Batman.

2. ***Half a Life.*** New York: DC Comics, 2005, 168 p. ISBN: 1401204384.

GOTHAM CITY, PRESENT DAY. Montoya's life begins to crumble. Her personal life is forced into public light, a law suit is brought against her. Montoya is then kidnapped by a supervillain who has an obsession with her, and the other detectives must find her.

ASSOCIATES: Captain Sawyer, Stacy, and the Batman.

3. ***Unresolved Targets.*** New York: DC Comics, 2006, 192 p. ISBN: 1563899957.

GOTHAM CITY, PRESENT DAY. The mayor is shot by a sniper in the Commissioner's office. It soon becomes apparent that the Joker is sniping random targets. He has set up a webcam to show his next target. The MCU needs to find the Joker, figure out what he's trying to achieve, and stop him. An old case is reopened, and Driver and Josie Mac go to Harvey Bullock for advice.

ASSOCIATES: Captain Sawyer, Stacy, Commissioner Akins, Harvey Bullock, and the Batman.

4. ***The Quick and the Dead.*** New York: DC Comics, 2006, 166 p. ISBN: 1401209122.

GOTHAM CITY, PRESENT DAY. Detective Allen kills a criminal during a shoot out, but the corrupt CSI Jim Corrigan removes evidence from the scene, placing Allen under a great deal of scrutiny by internal affairs. The GCPD becomes further alienated from the Batman, and removes the signal from their roof. A police officer is transformed into a monster after coming into contact with a mysterious chemical, and the detectives must seek out a supervillain from another city in order to find a cure.

ASSOCIATES: Captain Sawyer, Stacy, the Batman, Commissioner Akins.

5. ***Dead Robin.*** New York: DC Comics, 2007, 192 p. ISBN: 1401213294.

GOTHAM CITY, PRESENT DAY. A dead body is found: it is a young boy dressed in Robin's costume. The evidence seems to point to Batman, and the MCU tries to find out if the deceased boy is actually Robin, and if he was indeed killed by his mentor. Allen attempts to build a case against Corrigan.

ASSOCIATES: Captain Sawyer, Stacy, the Batman, and Commissioner Akins.

BRUBAKER, Ed, and Colin Wilson.

POINT BLANK

Genres/Themes Crossed: Blended Society X Traditional Mystery.

Subjects/Character Types: Superheroes, Supervillains, Aliens X Amateur Sleuth (Contemporary).

Series/Stand-Alone: Stand-alone.

Scene of the Crime: New York City, Present.

Detectives: Cole Cash is a marksman and martial artist who gained superhuman abilities after being exposed to Gen Factor. As the masked operative called Grifter, he uses his dwindling psychic abilities and healing skills to fight crime and terrorism.

Known Associates: Jack Lynch is the former director of I.O., a cloak and dagger government operation. Lynch was a member of Team 7 with Grifter and received the ability to erase memories after his exposure to Gen Factor. Since leaving Team 7, he has spent his time working with one secret shadowy government organization after another.

Premise: Cash and his Team 7 comrades were deliberately exposed to an experimental chemical called the Gen Factor, which activated their latent psi powers while destabilizing their sanity: some ended up suicidal or became sociopaths.

Comments: Ed Brubaker did the *Point Blank* miniseries as a lead-in to *Sleeper*, a spy thriller set in the same universe and using some of the same characters. *Sleeper* is an excellent series, but doesn't fit the criteria used by the present work to be deemed a mystery (please see the Introduction for more information on the criteria).

Literary Magic and Mayhem: *Point Blank* is set in the Wildstorm universe. Aliens exist, and two particular races are at war. Some aliens are nearly immortal and have lived on Earth for thousands of years, interbreeding with humanity and producing offspring with extraordinary powers. The government runs secret projects attempting to give operatives superpowers through genetic tinkering and cybernetic implants. Within this backdrop, the public knows about post-human individuals. The government attempts to control the post-human individuals, and the overall tone is one of conspiracy and paranoia.

Explorations: What was gained by telling this story from Grifter's perspective?

How does Grifter's memory affect the narrative structure of the book?

THE CASE

Point Blank. New York: Image Comics, 2003, 128 p. ISBN: 1401201164.

NEW YORK CITY, PRESENT DAY. Lynch had asked Grifter to watch his back while he hit various criminal operations while looking for a man named Carver. After Lynch is shot, Grifter attempts to figure out who shot him, who Carver is, and why Lynch was looking for Carver.

ASSOCIATES: Whitey the wino, Lynch, Zoltof, Yvonne, Marc Slayton, Caitlan, Bobby, Midnighter, Jack Hawksmoor, and Kenosha (Savant).

Buckingham, Lam. Worked with Bill Willingham on *Legends in Exile.* See: Willingham, Bill: Legends in Exile.

BUTCHER, Jim.

STORM FRONT

Genres/Themes Crossed: Secret Society X Hard-Boiled Mystery.

Subjects/Character Types: Spell-Casters (Wizards), Werewolves, Vampires, Demons, Fae, Ghosts, Archangels X Private Investigators.

Series/Stand-Alone: The first novel, *Storm Front,* is the best place to start the series, because it is the best introduction to Harry Dresden. The prequels to *Storm Front,* the online story *Restoration of Faith,* and the graphic novel *Welcome to the Jungle,* are alternative starting points. Starting with the graphic novel would deprive the reader of developing his or her own conception of the look of the world and its characters. *Restoration of Faith* and *Welcome to the Jungle* can be read as prequels at any point.

From *Storm Front* on, the series should be read in order. Relationships between the characters change over time, as does Harry. Harry is demon-ridden through part of the series. Readers should know the normal, somewhat irascible, but essentially sweet-natured Harry, and see how he acquires the demon before reading the books in which the demon-ridden Harry teeters on a knife's edge of losing control.

If the first four novels are read in rapid succession, the reader may tire of introspective passages focusing on Harry's feelings of guilt. Harry is a complex character. Although he continues to feel responsibility and guilt in the later books, he no longer dwells on his feelings; instead, they can be inferred from his actions and the responses of people who are around him. It's a rewarding series, combining interesting and sympathetic characters with well-thought-out world-building.

Scene of the Crime: Chicago, present day.

Detective: Harry Blackstone Copperfield Dresden, the only openly practicing professional wizard in the country. He thinks of himself as a magic "geek." Gamer geeks spend all their spare time gaming; computer geeks spend all their spare time programming. Harry's got power, and he spends his spare time thinking about magic and trying out spells. The joy he gets from applying spells to solve the problems he faces is contagious. Readers can watch him solve a series of small puzzles by adapting the skills he already has in order to accomplish tasks that range from tracking friends to defeating monsters.

Harry's mother, Margaret Gwendolyn Dresden, died at his birth. His father, Malcolm Dresden, a stage magician, died when Harry was six years old. Justin DuMorne adopted Harry and another potential wizard, named Elaine Lilian Mallory, soon after Harry's powers began to manifest. Justin mentored both of them for a decade, in the course of which he tried to entice them onto the path of black magic. When that didn't work, he tried to control them; when that didn't work on Harry, he tried to kill Harry. Harry was stronger than expected, and he killed his old mentor instead, breaking the first law of magic: thou shalt not kill through magic. There is an exception: wizards are allowed to kill in self-defense or in defense of another, but no one witnessed the battle between DuMorne and Harry, and the majority of The White Council could not believe that a half-trained boy could successfully defend himself against an attack by DuMorne. They believe that Harry must have defeated DuMorne through a sneak attack, that Harry must have planned and committed DuMorne's murder. Wizards found to have killed through magic are sentenced to death. Ebenezar McCoy, a member of the White Council, would not agree to the death sentence. He believed that Harry might be telling the truth. The White Council turned Harry over to Ebenezar but set Warden Morgan to watch him, and gave Morgan orders to execute Harry immediately for any infraction of the Council's laws. (The zero-tolerance sentence is known as the Doom of Damocles, a symbolic sword poised over Harry's neck every minute of every day.)

Known Associates: Harry is on retainer to the Chicago Police Department, under the direction of Lieutenant Karrin Murphy, head of their Special Investigations Unit. Head of the Special Investigations Unit is not a plum position. The unit investigates crimes that are so odd that other police officers don't want to know about them. Before the creation of the Special Investigations Unit, a squad of cops known as the Black Cats quietly dealt with paranormal crimes. Murphy doesn't know it, but her father was one of the "Black Cats," and her mother understands more about what Murphy faces than Murphy realizes. Detective Ron Carmichael, Murphy's partner, doesn't believe in wizards. Bianca, vampire of the Red Court, runs an escort service in Chicago. "Gentleman" Johnny Marcone is a Chicago crime lord, and Mister Cujo Hendricks is one of his associates. Susan Rodriguez is a reporter for the *Chicago Arcane,* a newspaper that few take seriously. Susan leaves her job at the end of *Grave Peril;* she's found her calling by the beginning of *Death Masks.* Other characters that appear frequently include Mister, Harry's cat; Bob the Skull, a spirit of the air who resides in a skull and occasionally works for Harry; Toot-toot, a dewdrop fairy; and Morgan, a Warden set by the White Council to watch Harry with an eye to executing him immediately if he breaks any of their laws. As the series continues, Harry builds his own family of allies, as well as drawing the attention of a group of people who regard him as an enemy. In *Fool Moon,* readers meet Mac, owner of *McAnally's Pub,* which is Accorded Neutral Ground, and so is a safe meeting place for people with power. In the same book, Harry meets Chicago's alpha werewolf pack, led by Billy Borden and including Georgia, Andi, and Kirby. Billy and Georgia marry in "Something Borrowed." In *Grave Peril* readers meet Michael Joseph Patrick Carpenter, one of the three Knights of the Cross. Michael wields the sword Amoracchius, one of the three swords given to mankind by God. That same book introduces Harry's godmother Leanandsidhe (also called Lea and

Leah) of the sidhe; Mavra, one of the last of the vampires of the Black Court; Thomas, a vampire of the White Court; and his lover, Justine. In *Blood Rites,* Harry and Thomas's relationship changes, and Justine is almost killed. In *Death Masks,* Murphy introduces Harry to coroner Waldo Butters, and Harry picks up the Denarius Lasciel. In *Blood Rites,* Harry meets Lara Romany of the House Raith, who is a vampire of the White Court, and accidentally acquires Mouse, a Foo Temple Dog. Harry first comes across the necromancer Cowl in *Dead Beat.* In that same book, Harry meets Warden Anastasia Luccio and Warden Carlos Ramirez, and becomes a warden himself. In *Proven Guilty,* he works closely with Molly Carpenter for the first time; this book also documents his first encounter with Madrigal Raith.

Premise: There is much going on behind the scenes of the world as we know it. When mortals come across the paranormal, they have a tendency to turn a blind eye. Those who allow themselves to see it oversimplify the complexities and identify creatures by their symptoms rather than by their natures. For instance, mortals speak of creatures who shape-change between wolf and human forms as werewolves. Actually, just as a fever is a symptom of many different types of disease, shape-changing into a wolf can be caused by many different types of magic. There are two basic kinds of werewolves: those who use their own magic to shape-shift and those who use another's magic to shape-shift. If it's the werewolf's own magic, then he or she is just a wizard with a very limited repertoire. They retain their own personalities and have to learn to work the wolf's body. A person changed by another's magic comes closer to actually becoming a wolf. There are two ways that another's magic can turn a person into a shape-changer: through a curse or through the creation of a magical artifact. The curse would be a transmogrification, which the White Council forbids because the personality of the human is dominated and destroyed by that of the wolf. It's essentially murder. If it's by artifact, then the person who bargained for the artifact becomes a Hexenwolf. The White Council has less interest here, regarding becoming a Hexenwolf as more imbecilic than evil. (Becoming a Hexenwolf is, however, considered evil by the Church: they burn Hexenwolves.) Others who become wolf-like include lycanthropes and loups-garou. Lycanthropes are born, not made. They channel the spirit of rage. They don't change form, but they gain supernatural speed, strength, cunning, and ferocity. Loups-garou are humans who are under a very powerful curse to become wolf-like demons during the full moon.

Vampirism also comes in many different types and sub-types. The vampires written about by Bram Stoker were vampires of the Black Court. Stoker's book, *Dracula,* outlined their habits (feeding on blood), gave information on how to identify them (no reflection, avoidance of garlic, etc.), and told people how to harm them (silver crosses, beheading, sunlight, etc.). Since the publication of *Dracula,* the Black Court's numbers have been dwindling. By the beginning of *The Dresden Files,* there is only one known member of the Black Vampire Court: her name is Mavra. Vampires of the Red Court also feed on blood and can also be damaged by sunlight. Vampires of the White Court feed on emotion and can walk in the sun. There are three major Houses of the White Court vampires: the House of Raith feeds on lust, the House of Malvora feeds on fear, and the House of Skavis feeds on pain and despair.

Magic users obey the natural rules of magic and the edicts of the White Council. The seven basic laws are in the form of commandments; for example, The First Law: Thou shalt not use magic to wreak harm on another. The Fourth Law: Thou shalt not use true names for summoning and binding others to your will. The Seventh Law: Thou shalt not loose a demon upon the world. There is one wizard, called the Blackstaff, who is sort of like the *James Bond* series' 007 agent: he has a license to kill, or, for that matter, a license to break any of the laws of magic in the performance of his duties. The other laws can be derived from an examination of the list of exemptions given to the Blackstaff:

> To kill. To enthrall. To invade the thoughts of another mortal. To seek knowledge and power from beyond the Outer Gates. To transform others. To reach beyond the borders of life. To swim against the currents of time. (*Blood Rites,* p. 296)

Comment: The *Dresden Files* was used as the basis for a Sci Fi channel original television show that aired 12 episodes from 2006 to 2007. The Sci Fi channel has announced that it will not be renewed, but the existing episodes have been released on DVD. Some of the differences between the books and the television series were driven by the change in medium. The most noticeable difference is that Bob, the spirit of air, is Bob the skull in the books and Bob the full-blown apparition in the television show. The skull would have been an inanimate object with occasionally glowing eyes and a voice-over. The apparition can interact, react, and so forth, which gives the television actor and director a much greater theatrical range. The show is also a little less dark than the books. Introspection doesn't work well on film. Harry is not a pessimist, but a realist. Dealing with the world he has to deal with produces a pretty bleak outlook: his narration in the books gives them that bleaker tone.

Jim Butcher's Web site (http://www.jim-butcher.com/) includes biographical information, Jim's blog (http://jimbutcher.livejournal.com/), a *Dresden Files* short story, a vignette (*Publicity and Advertising,* which he used to promote the series, is at http://www.jim-butcher.com/dresden/vignette/), and information on Butcher's other series, *Codex Alera*.

Literary Magic & Mayhem: Butcher has created a complex world with a well-thought-out magical system. His characters cope with good and evil, and are sometimes fooled when evil looks harmless. The characters, even some of the villains, develop over the course of the series, revealing more facets as they suffer through their adventures. There is a lot of suffering. Dresden takes a frightening amount of physical abuse. He also takes a fair amount of emotional abuse, mostly self-inflicted. Harry knows that he is more powerful than most of those whom he meets. Somehow he believes that this makes him responsible not only for their safety but also for their mistakes. At times, the hair shirt is annoying, but it does fit the character.

The writing in the first few books is uneven. It is fast paced in some sections, with well-integrated explanations of the ways in which the magical world functions; yet there are other sections that are bogged down by Harry's self-recrimination. The writing improves as the series moves forward. Harry's guilt still exists, but it is shown through Harry's actions and other's perceptions—the long introspective passages have been cut without diminishing the complexity of the character.

Explorations: What would most people's response be to a Yellow Pages listing for "wizard"?

How suspicious should Harry be of his clients?

To what extent should Harry be responsible for saving others?

What is Harry's opinion of the White Council? Is it justified?

What did Morgan see? Are his suspicions reasonable?

THE CASES

1. **"Restoration of Faith"** a short story on Jim Butcher's Web site, at http://www.jim-butcher.com/books/dresden/restoration/. A comic book version of the story can be found after the main story in the graphic novel version of *Storm Front*.

CHICAGO, 199?. The Astors hired Ragged Angel Investigations to bring back their -10-year-old runaway. Then, to cover up the fact that their daughter had run away, they reported her kidnapped. The descriptions they gave of the kidnappers? They fit Harry and Nick, the investigators the Astors hired.

ASSOCIATES: Harry must work for another six months under a licensed investigator to earn his license. Nick—*of Ragged Angel Investigations, is the investigator for whom Harry works;* Gogoth—*the troll who lives under the North Avenue bridge;* Faith—*is a 10-year-old girl who has given up hope;*

Patrol Officer Karrin Murphy—*has quick eyes and an open mind, she meets Harry in this story.*

2. *Welcome to the Jungle, Jim Butcher's Dresden Files.* (Illustrated by Adrian Syaf.) New York: Ballantine Books, c2008, 160 p. ISBN: 9780345507464.

CHICAGO, 2000(?). Lieutenant Murphy hires Harry as a consultant on a murder investigation at the Chicago Zoo. It looks as if a gorilla killed guard Maurice Sandbourne, cleaned up the evidence, and then locked himself back into his cage. Murphy is skeptical; she thinks the gorilla was framed.

ASSOCIATES: Lieutenant Murphy—*of the Chicago police;* Ron Carmichael—*her partner;* Dr. Dana Watson—*who is the first of the people who work at the zoo who is willing to talk to Harry;* Dr. Reese—*who defends Moe the gorilla;* Willamena "Will" Rogers—*Reese' assistant;* Mister the cat; and Bob the Skull.

3. *Storm Front.* New York: ROC: New American Library, c2000, 322 p. ISBN: 0451457811. This title is in the process of being printed in a comic version, and the comics are being compiled into graphic novels. The first of the graphic novels the cover the events in *Storm Front* was adapted by Mark Powers and illustrated by Ardian Syaf, it was published by Del Rey/Dabel Brothers under the title *Storm Front: The Gathering Storm.* ISBN: 0345506391,9780345506399.

CHICAGO, MARCH 2000(?). Lieutenant Murphy calls Harry in when she investigates a double murder. The victims' hearts literally exploded through their chests. Morgan of the White Council is watching over Harry, waiting, even hoping, that Harry will slip up so that Morgan will be able to gather evidence that Harry has broken the laws of the White Council. Morgan will interpret every step of Harry's research into magical methods of murder as evidence of Harry's evil. How can Harry explore this question and stop a killer while a fanatic, who is already certain of Harry's guilt, is watching Harry's every move and praying for an excuse to perform a summary execution?

ASSOCIATES: Lieutenant Murphy—*of the Chicago police;* Ron Carmichael—*her partner;* "Gentleman" Johnnie Marcone—*a Chicago racketeer;* Mister Hendricks—*his "associate";* Victor Sells—*who has disappeared;* Monica—*his worried wife;* Mac—*owner of McAnally's Pub;* Susan Rodriguez—*reporter;* Morgan—*who has been set upon Harry by the White Council, with orders to kill Harry the minute he steps out of line;* Bianca—*a vampire of the Red Court;* Linda Randall—*chauffeur;* and Donny Wise—*photographer.*

4. *Fool Moon.* New York: ROC: New American Library, 2001, 342 p. ISBN: 0451458125.

CHICAGO, OCTOBER 2000(?). Lieutenant Murphy's job is on the line. The Chicago Police Department has lost confidence in both her honesty and her competence. Internal Affairs is working to substantiate the theory that Murphy and Harry joined forces to take out a drug kingpin. Murphy's superiors can't understand why her investigation into a series of bloody serial killings has stalled. The killings were the work of a group. There are several killings, then almost a month of peace, then more murders. When Murphy realizes that the killings are taking place on nights with a full moon, she wonders if there is a supernatural connection. She calls on Harry.

In the course of the investigation, Harry learns a little more about his mother, enough to wonder how she died and why the Dark is still interested in her.

ASSOCIATES: Kim Delany—*Harry is coaching her in the use of her magical abilities;* Mac—*owner of McAnally's Pub;* Lieutenant Murphy—*of the Chicago police;* Ron Carmichael—*her partner;* Phillip Denton—*FBI Agent;* Agents Deborah Benn, Roger Harris, and George Wilson—*Denton's team;* Detective Rudolph—*who is new to the Chicago Police Department;* Billy Borden—*werewolf, leader of the "Alphas" pack;* Parker—*werewolf, leader of the "Sreetwolves" pack;* Georgia, Cindy, and Alex—*are members of the Alphas pack;* Bob the skull; Susan Rodriguez—*reporter;* "Gentleman" Johnnie Marcone—*racketeer;* Mister Hendricks—*his "associate";* Chaunzaggoroth "Chauncy,"—*a demon that Harry occasionally summons;* Harley MacFinn; Ms. Tera West—*Harley's fiancé.*

5. ***Grave Peril.*** New York: ROC: New American Library, 2001, 378 p. ISBN: 0451458443.

CHICAGO, OCTOBER 2001(?). Someone is tormenting ghosts, tormenting them until they lash out at the living. Harry and Michael do all that they can do to keep up, working as a team to send each ghost back to the Nevernever before it can destroy the living. The question is; why? What would someone gain by tormenting ghosts? Harry's life is further complicated by his relationship with Susan: he can't seem to tell her how he feels about her.

When the vampire Bianca sends Harry an invitation to a celebration of the Red Court, he cannot ignore it. Even though he is sure it is a trap, he feels he must go. This book marks the beginning of the Vampire–Wizard War, as well as chronicling the birth of Harry Carpenter.

ASSOCIATES: Michael Joseph Patrick Carpenter—*a Knight f the Cross, who wields the sword Amoracchius, one of the three swords given to mankind by God;* Charity—*Michaels's wife, who does not approve of her husband's companions;* Lydia—*a child with Cassandra's Tears (a prophetic condition, unfortunately, just as in the myth:no one believes the prophecies);* Father Forthill—*whose church is St. Mary of the Angels;* Leanandsidhe—*a.k.a. Lea or Leah, of the sidhe (she is Harry's Godmother);* Susan Rodriguez—*reporter;* Bianca—*who is a vampire of the Red Court;* Kyle and Kelly Hamilton—*her associates;* Mortimer Lindquist—*an ectomancer (one who can sense ghosts) who has lost much of his power;* Leonid Kravos—*deceased;* Bob the Skull—*a spirit of the air;* Thomas of the House Raith—*who is a vampire of the White Court;* Justine—*his companion;* the dragon Ferrovax; Mavra—*one of the last of the vampires of the Black Court;* Don Paolo Ortega—*a vampire of the Red Court.* Detective Rudolph, Detective Sergeant John Stallings, and Lieutenant Murphy—*are officers with the Chicago Police Department;* Detective Micky Malone—*who is retired;* and Sonia—*his wife.*

6. ***Summer Knight.*** New York: ROC: New American Library, 2002, 371 p. ISBN: 0451458923.

CHICAGO, JUNE 2002(?). Since the events that set off the Vampire–Wizard War, Harry has been out of touch with his friends and his business; in fact, he's been out of touch with the entire world. All his energies have been focused on trying to find a cure for vampirism. He's been unsuccessful, and while he's been buried in his research, the situation in the outside world has deteriorated. In those nine months, the White Council has suffered terrible losses; they're beginning to panic. The ferocity and strength of the vampire strikes was unexpected. Every wizard is aware of the danger, and The White Council has concluded that safe passage through the Nevernever as an omnipresent escape route is a strategic necessity. There can be no safe passage without the protection of the faeries; the Council must bargain with either the Seelie (Summer) or Unseelie (Winter) Court. The assistance of the Winter Court has a price: Queen Mab wants Harry to investigate the murder of Ronald Reuel, the Summer Knight. The power vested in Reuel disappeared when he was killed. (It should have snapped back to the Summer Court.) The loss of power from Summer has created an imbalance between the two Courts that will trigger a war in the Nevernever unless Harry can find the killer and the power. He has only a few days before the Faerie War will begin.

ASSOCIATES: The Sidhe courts each have a past, a present, and a future queen. Mother Winter—*the Queen Who Was for the Winter Sidhe court;* Mab—*the Queen Who Is, Faerie Queen of Air and Darkness, current monarch of the Winter court of the sidhe, purchaser of Harry's promise from his Godmother Leanansidhe;* Lady Maeve—*the Queen Who Is To Come is heir to the throne of the Winter Sidhe Court;* Lloyd Slate—*the Winter Knight;* Mother Summer—*the Queen Who Was of the Sidhe Summer Court;* Queen Titiana—*the Queen Who Is of the Summer Sidhe Court;* Lady Aurora—*the Queen Who Is To Come, heir to the Summer Court's throne;* Korrick—*the centaur;* Talos—*Lord Marshall of the Summer Court;* Elaine—*an old friend of Harry's;* Toot-toot—*a little fairy;* Elidee—*an even smaller fairy;* Meryl, Fix, Ace, and Lily—*are half-fae;* Grum—*the ogre;* Billy Borden—*werewolf, leader of the "Alphas" pack;* Georgia, Phil, and Greg—*werewolves, members of the Alphas pack;* Bob the Skull; Mister the cat; the Merlin—*wizard, leader of the White Council;*

Martha Liberty, Listens to the Wind, Ancient Mai, and the Gatekeeper—*wizards who are members of the Senior Council:* Warden Morgan—*a wizard who still believes that Harry is evil;* Ebenezar McCoy—*a wizard on the Senior Council, he is on Harry's side, as he has been since he took Harry in when Harry was 16 years old;* Lieutenant Karrin Murphy—*who gets a chance to fight back against dark forces.*

7. ***Death Masks.*** New York: ROC: New American Library, 2003, 378 p. ISBN: 0451459407.

CHICAGO, 2003(?). The vampires and wizards have been at war for almost two years. Dr. Paolo Ortega, a Duke of the Red Court, offers Harry a proposal. He and Harry will meet in a duel under the Accords. It's a duel to the death, but if Harry wins, Chicago will be declared neutral ground. However, if Harry refuses to fight, the Duke is prepared to assassinate Harry's closest friends. An arcane duel is not Harry's only concern. The Shroud of Turin has been stolen and Harry has been hired to recover it. Others who are searching for the holy relic include the Denarians, a group of people who have traded their humanity for power by accepting one of the 30 pieces of silver that were paid to Judas for betraying Christ. They are powerful, evil, and monstrous. The Knights of the Cross, including Harry's friend Michael Carpenter, must find a way to stand against them. Note: this entry in the series has one scene between Harry and Susan that is a little racier than the rest of the series.

ASSOCIATES: The Lord gave mankind three swords which, when wielded by righteous men who have taken up the responsibilities of being a Knight of the Cross, are weapons against evil. The swords are Amoracchius (which was once called Excalibur), Fidelacchius, and Esperacchius. Sanya—*a Russian atheist, wields Esperacchius;* Shiro Yoshimo—*wields Fidelacchius;* and Michael Carpenter—*wields Amoracchius;* Charity—*Michael's wife;* Molly—*Michael's 14-year-old daughter;* Amanda—*Michael's five-and-a-half-year-old daughter;* Hope—*another of Michael's daughters;* Harry—*Michael's youngest son.* Judas betrayed Christ for 30 pieces of silver. Those coins have come to hold "the fallen", and if taken up by a human they will confer power upon that person and will wholly corrupt him. Those people who have taken up the coin are called the members of the Order of the Blackened Denarius. Ursiel—*is a denarian;* Nicodemus—*is a denarian,* Deirdre—*is a denarian,* and Saluriel—*who once was the human Quintus Cassius, is a denarian.* Lasciel—*is in a coin that Harry picked up;* Lieutenant Karrin Murphy—*is on a forced vacation;* Waldo Butters—*a coroner who was disgraced and demoted because his superiors won't believe his report of strange things happening in Chicago;* The Archive—*Harry names her Ivy;* Kincaid—*the Archive's driver;* Susan Rodriguez—*who is no longer a reporter;* Martin—*Susan's companion;* Larry Fowler—*talk show host;* Mortimer Lindquist—*local psychic;* Father Anthony Forthill—*who asked*

Father Vincent to leave Harry out of the hunt for the Shroud; Francisca Garcia and Anna Valmont—*who are thieves;* Thomas Raith—*a vampire of the White Court;* Mac—*owner of McAnally's Pub;* Gentleman Johnny Marcone—*racketeer;* Cujo Hendricks—*Marcone's associate;* Miss Gard—*Marcone's consultant on magic.* (In this book, Marcone saves Harry's and Michael's lives, and Harry discovers Marcone's secret.)

8. *Blood Rites.* New York: ROC: New American Library, 2004, 372 p. ISBN: 0451459873.

CHICAGO, 2004(?). Three years ago, at the beginning of the Red Vampire Court–Wizard War, Bianca gave Mavra some victims for Mavra to use to rebuild the Black Court. Mavra has been busy, and when Harry realizes that she must be in Chicago, he gathers a small group to help him take her out. He's distracted by a couple of jobs. In the first of these jobs he recovers some Foo dogs for a temple; one of the dogs stays with Harry. Thomas of the White Vampire Court brings Harry the second case. Thomas's friend Arturo has had a run of unbelievably bad luck, luck so bad that a couple of his friends have been killed. Arturo is a film director who is considered a revolutionary in the field of pornography. Harry needs the money, and within minutes of walking onto the film set he is convinced that someone is trying to destroy the production with an entropy curse. The question is, who? Arturo is setting up a production company that will provide serious competition in an industry that is dominated by businesses owned by the White Court, but this type of curse is so vicious that it seems unlikely that the motive is money: this seems personal. In the course of his investigation, Harry finally has a chance to speak to his mother, and he meets his brother.

ASSOCIATES: Mouse—*the puppy;* Thomas Raith—*vampire of the White Court;* Justine—*Thomas's lover;* Lara and Inari—*Thomas's sisters, both of whom are working on the movie set;* Lord Raith—*King of the White Court of vampires and Thomas's father;* Director Arturo Genosa—*who films porn;* Shelly—*Arturo's first ex-wife, she has invested in his production company;* Lucille Delarossa—*his second wife, she is not involved in the production;* Tricia Scrump—*his third wife and female lead actress (her new stage name is Trixie Vixen);* Jake Guffie—*stage name Jack Rockhardt;* Bobby—*who is trying to come up with a stage name;* Giselle; Emma—*who has two young children;* Joan Dallas—*the producer;* Margaret Gwendolyn Lefay—*deceased, Harry's mother;* Mavra—*vampire of the Black Court, has been working on rebuilding the cadre of Black Court vampires;* Lieutenant Karrin Murphy—*who accepts Harry's invitation to go with him on a tactical strike to take out Mavra and Mavra's minions;* Kincaid—*a mercenary (one of his jobs is acting as bodyguard for The Archive) who is impressed when he fights side by side with Murphy in the battle against Mavra;* Ebenezar McCoy—*a senior member of the White Council (and, as Harry learns from Kincaid, the*

Council's Blackstaff); Marion—*Murphy's mother;* Lisa—*Murphy's baby sister;* Rich—*an FBI agent who is moving to Chicago to marry Lisa, he is Murphy's second ex-husband;* Mister the cat; Bob the skull—*a spirit of the air.*

9. ***Dead Beat.*** New York: ROC: New American Library, 2005, 396 p. ISBN: 0451460278.

CHICAGO, OCTOBER 2005(?). Harry gets an unwelcome communication from Mavra, the leader of the Black Court Vampires. He'd hoped that he'd finished her, but his luck is not that good. Mavra's not only back, she has photographs that prove that Murphy killed things that look human, photographs taken when Murphy helped Harry attack Mavra's stronghold (this was chronicled in *Blood Rites*). The price for Mavra's silence is a book called *The Word of Kemmler;* she demands that Harry deliver it to her on Halloween night. Kemmler was the last great necromancer, it was thought that the White Council managed to destroy all his writings, right after they destroyed him. It turns out that the White Council missed at least one book, and that three of his students are competing to find it and use the knowledge therein to take Kemmler's place. Harry is only one of the seekers in a mad race to find the book; everyone else who is searching is determined to use Kemmler's knowledge to gather power through the murder of thousands. Harry wants to find the book to save Murphy by turning the book over to the last of the black vampires.

ASSOCIATES: Mouse—*who is no longer a puppy;* Thomas Raith—*White Court vampire and Harry's half-brother;* Mavra—*of the vampire Black Court;* Grevane—*Kemmler's first apprentice;* Quintus Cassius—*who once hosted the Denarius Saluriel;* Capiorcorpus—*Corpsetaker;* Alicia Nelson and Li Xian—*are working with Corpsetaker;* Kumori—*who seems to be a different type of necromancer;* Cowl—*is working with Kumori;* Gentleman Johnny Marcone—*who is determined to avenge an employee's murder;* Hendricks and Miss Gard—*are with Marcone;* Leanansidhe—*Harry's godmother, who does not come when Harry calls;* Queen Mab—*Queen of the Winter Sidhe Court;* the Erlking—*who can call up the Wild Hunt;* Coroner Waldo Butters—*acts as Harry's ally while Lieutenant Karrin Murphy is out of town;* Warden Anastasia Luccio, Warden Donald Morgan (yes, that Warden Morgan), Warden Ramirez, Warden Kowalski, and Warden Yoshimo—*also act as Harry's allies;* Artemis Bock—*of Bock Ordered Books, the oldest occult shop in Chicago;* Sheila Starr—*Bock's surprisingly helpful assistant;* the Denarius Lasciel—*was once called on by Harry for aid, and now she can speak to him at will;* Billy, Georgia, and Kirby—*werewolves;* Mortimer—*psychic;* Phil—*security guard at the "Forensic Institute";* Malcolm Dresden—*deceased, Harry's father;* Officer Rawlins; EMT Lamar; Mac—*of McAnally's Pub;* and Bob the Skull—*a spirit of the air, who was owned by Kemmler for 40 years.* (Warden Justin DuMorne pulled Bob out of the smoldering ruins of Kemmler's lab.)

10. "Something Borrowed" in *My Big Fat Supernatural Wedding*, ed. By P. N. Elrod. New York: St. Martin's Press, 2006, p. 37–68. ISBN: 0312343604.

CHICAGO, 2005(?). Harry thought that the worst problem he would encounter as Best Man at Billy's wedding would be dealing with Georgia's step-mother from Hell; instead, he finds himself battling a trap set by the Fae to destroy both Billy and Georgia in retribution for the help that they gave Harry in the Sidhe War.

ASSOCIATES: Billy and Georgia—*werewolves;* Eve McAlister—*Georgia's step-mother;* Lieutenant Karrin Murphy—*who finally meets Bob the Skull;* Yanof—*the tailor;* Jenny Greenteeth; and Father Forthill.

11. *Proven Guilty.* New York: ROC: New American Library, 2006, 406 p. ISBN: 0451460278.

CHICAGO, OCTOBER 2006(?). The Red Court of Vampires would have destroyed the White Council months ago, but the White Council's allies—the Venatori Umborum and the Fellowship of St. Giles—have managed to slow the carnage. What's surprising is that the Fae have not taken up arms against the Red Court. When the Red Court invaded Fae territory to attack the White Council, the Fae should have risen up against them. Ebenezar, and others that he trusts, would like Harry to find out why the Fae did not attack the Red Court. One chilling aspect of that request is that it is not coming from the White Council—Ebenezar clearly wants to keep it private. He no longer trusts the Council. The other chilling aspect is that it means that Harry has to try to get information from the Sidhe, specifically out of Mab, the Winter Queen. As if Harry's life is not complicated enough, the Gatekeeper, Rashid, has another private communication for Harry. He tells Harry that repeated acts of black magic have taken place in Chicago. It is Harry's job to locate and prosecute the perpetrator.

NOTE: The Venatori Umborum is an ancient secret society dedicated to fighting supernatural darkness. The Fellowship of St. Giles is made up of humans who have been infected with the vampire's venom, but who have managed to withstand the compulsions that the venom lays on them. They have thereby remained human, so far. Each of them is committed to destroying every last vampire on Earth.

ASSOCIATES: Warden Morgan—*wizard;* Warden Ramirez—*wizard;* Warden Luccio—*wizard;* Ebenezar McCoy—*wizard, member of the Senior Council;* Martha Liberty—*wizard, member of the Senior Council;* "Injun Joe" Listens-to-Wind—*wizard, member of the Senior Council;* The Merlin—*a.k.a. Arthur Langtry, wizard, the head of the White Council;* The Denarius Lasciel—*the temptress, the webweave. She can now appear to Harry whenever she wishes. Lasciel has been conversing with a part of Harry's subconscious for months, without Harry's being aware of it.* Molly Carpenter—*the seventeen-year-old daughter of Harry's friend Michael;* Nelson—*Molly's boyfriend;* Daniel, Amanda, Matthew, Alicia, Hope (who likes to be called Hobbit), and Harry—*Molly's siblings;* Charity—*Molly's mother. Charity has always regarded Harry with suspicion, and in this book he discovers her reasons.* Lieutenant Karrin Murphy—*is forced (along with Harry) to accept that sometimes mercy is unwise or impossible and that justice can be brutal;* Thomas Raith—*White Court vampire and Harry's half-brother, has been frighteningly distant lately. He seems to be feeding again; and after almost two years of living with Harry, Thomas has now decided to move out.* Mac—*owner of McAnally's Pub, universally recognized Accorded Neutral Ground;* Lily—*the Summer Lady;* and Fix—*the Summer Knight;* Sandra Marling—*Convention Chair of the SplatterCon convention;* Rosie—*a friend of Molly;* and Pell—*the theater owner.* Officer Rawlins—*a good cop;* Detective Sergeant Greene—*a man without much imagination;* FBI Agent Rick—*who is Murphy's ex-husband and new brother-in-law;* Sergeant Grayson; Mouse; Bob the Skull; Darby Crane—*a.k.a Madrigal Raith, horror movie director;* Lucius Glau—*of House Malvora, Crane's personal advisor and legal counsel;* Lydia Stern—*reporter for the Midwestern Arcane;* Father Forthill. In the strike on Arctis Tor, Harry encounters: The Scarecrow; Lloyd Slate—*the Winter Knight;* Lea—*Harry's Godmother;* and, probably, Queen Mab.

12. ***White Night.*** New York: ROC: New American Library, 2007, 407 p. ISBN: 9780451461407.

CHICAGO, MAY 2007(?). Murphy is no longer in any position to call Harry in on a case, especially a case that the Chicago Police Department has ruled a suicide. Yet something about this case just doesn't feel right. When she finds an altar in the suicide's apartment, she calls Harry. Harry finds that it was not only a murder, it was a murder done by magic. As he follows the clues to find the killer, he realizes that many in the magical community are aware of the killing. It is not the first murder. Their chief suspect is Harry!

ASSOCIATES: Sergeant Karrin Murphy; Molly Carpenter—*Harry's 18-year-old apprentice;* Coroner Waldo Butters; Mac—*owner of McAnally's Pub;* Anna Ash, Helen Beckitt, Abby, Priscilla, and Olivia—*are members of the Ordo Lebes;* Elaine Lilian Mallory—*a private investigator hired by Anna Ash;* The Denarius Lasciel—*who has now formed a sort of working relationship with Harry;* Mouse—*the enormous Temple Dog;* Bob the Skull; Warden Carlos Ramirez; Thomas Raith—*of the White Court of vampires, who is Harry's half-brother;* Madrigal Raith—*Thomas's cousin;* Justine—*Thomas's human lover;* Lara Romany—*Thomas's sister;* Lady Cesarina—*leader of the House of Malvora;* Vittorio Malvora—*her nephew;* Lord Skavis—*leader of the House of Skavis;* Cowl—*the necromancer;* Gentleman Johnny Marcone—*a racketeer;* and

Hendricks—*Marcone's associate.* A flashback includes: Warden Luccio; a group of recruits; Warden Carlos Ramirez; and Lasciel.

13. **"Herot,"** in *My Big Fat Supernatural Honeymoon,* ed. By P. N. Elrod. New York: St. Martin's Press, 2008, p. 35–80. ISBN: 0312375042; 9780312375041.

CHICAGO, OCTOBER 2007(?). Mac calls Harry for help when a young woman is abducted from the beer festival being held in *Loon Island Pub.*

ASSOCIATES: "Mac" McAnnally—*who owns McAnnally's Pub;* Mouse—*Harry's dog;* Roger Braddock—*brewer of Braddock's Midnight Sun Cinnamon;* Elizabeth—*Roger's new wife (they went to the beer competition before starting their honeymoon);* Caine—*brewer of Caine's Kickass;* Miss Gard—*a.k.a. Sigrun, who's taking a day off from working for Gentleman Jimmy Marcone;* the Gendelkin; and Malks—*feline Witerfae.*

14. ***Small Favor.*** New York: ROC: New American Library, 2008, 423 p. ISBN: 9780451461896.

CHICAGO, NOVEMBER 2007. When Sergeant Karrin Murphy smells Hellfire at the site of a partially demolished building, she calls Harry. Through his efforts to reconstruct events, he concludes that someone is drawing on astonishing, almost impossible, amounts of magical power. The power seems to have been used to abduct crime lord Gentleman Johnny Marcone. Marcone spent years climbing to the top of Chicago's rackets; then he became a signatory to the Unseelie Accords, which extend his criminal empire into the supernatural world. He has the rank of Baron. Harry feels no particular need to ride to Marcone's rescue until Queen Mab of the Winter Court of the Sidhe demands that he save Marcone. Harry owes Queen Mab two favors, and she may feel that his attack on her stronghold was an unforgivable insult—he finds that he cannot say no.

ASSOCIATES: Molly Carpenter—*Harry's 18-year-old apprentice;* Michael—*a Knight of the Cross, whose sword is Amoracchius, Molly's father;* Charity—*Molly's mother;* and Hope, Harry, Daniel, Amanda, Alicia, and Matthew—*Molly's brothers and sisters;* Sergeant Karrin Murphy—*of the Special Investigations Unit of the Chicago Police Department;* Queen Mab—*of the Winter Court of the Sidhe;* Detective Rawlins—*Murphy's partner;* Grimalkin—*Mab's interpreter;* The Gruffs and the kelpies—*some of Summer's warriors;* Fix—*The Summer Knight;* Gentleman Johnny Marcone—*a.k.a "Baron" Marcone, Chicago racketeer;* Hendricks—*Marcone's bodyguard;* Miss Sigrun Gard—*who also works to protect Marcone;* Ms. Demeter—*who runs Executive Priority Health;* Torelli—*a man with dreams of moving up in the organization;* Toot-toot—*the pixie, is now a leader in Harry's "Za-Lord's Guard";* Sergeant Murphy—*whose courage is toasted by Mac;* Sanya—*a Knight of the Cross, wields Esparacchius.* (Harry was given custody of the third Knight's sword, Fidelacchius, by Shiro.)

The Knights of the Blackened Denarius include Nicodemus/Anduriel—*with Judas's noose and a powerful shadow;* Tessa/Polonius Lartessa—*"Preying Mantis Girl";* Deirdre—*a daughter of Tessa and Nicodemus, Dierdre is the one with the titanium hair;* Rosanna—*the "sorrowful lady" and an expert sorceress;* Magog—*gorilla man;* Thorned Namshiel—*"Spinyboy," a powerful sorcerer;* Imariel; Tarsiel; Urumviel; Varthiel; and Ordiel.

Ivy—*The Archive;* Kincaid—*her bodyguard;* Captain Anastasia Luccio—*Harry's boss;* Thomas Raith—*of the White Court of vampires, Harry's brother;* Bob the Skull—*a spirit of the air;* Mouse—*Harry's temple dog;* Mister—*Harry's tomcat;* "Jake"—*Uriel.*

15. "It's My Birthday Too," in *Many Bloody Returns,* ed. by Charlaine Harris and Toni L. P. Kelner. New York: Ace Books, 2007, p. 100–145. ISBN: 9780441015221.

Chicago, February 14, 2008?. It's Thomas's birthday and Harry takes a detour while driving Molly home to deliver a birthday gift to him at the Woodfield Mall at Schamburg.

Associates: Molly Carpenter—*who has been Harry's apprentice for a year and a half;* Mouse—*Harry's dog;* Mister—*Harry's cat;* Raymond—*a mall guard;* Sarah—*who works for Thomas;* Ennui; Constance Bushnell—*Black Court vampire;* Thomas Raith—*White Court vampire, Harry's brother;* and Keef—*cobbler elf.*

16. *Backup.* (Illustrated by Mike Mignola.) Burton, MI: Subterranean Press, 2008, 70 p. ISBN: 9781596061828.

Chicago, Spring 2008. The narrator/protagonist of this story is Harry's brother, Thomas Raith. Thomas's sister Lara sends him a warning that Harry is walking into a trap. Thomas must save him while maintaining absolute secrecy.

Thomas is a Venatori, a warrior in a conflict that has lasted over 5000 years. Their goal is to consign some of the pernicious old gods to oblivion by hiding all signs of them. Interest in them will diminish until they are entirely forgotten. When no mortal remembers them, they will have no pathway to our world.

The Venatori who help the White Council are the *Venatori Umbrorum,* the shadows of the Venatori. The Venatori founded the *Venatori Umbrorum* to provide the Venatori with camouflage and to gather information.

Associates: Lara—*White Court vampire, Thomas's sister, is the only other Venator in the White Court;* Justine—*is the woman Thomas loves;* the Stygian Balera—*a.k.a. Janera;* Harry Dresden—*Thomas's brother;* Mouse—*Harry's dog;* and Bob the Skull—*who makes a deal as an independent agent.*

17. "Day Off;" in *Blood Lite,* ed. by Kevin J. Anderson. New York: Pocket Books, 2008, p. 353–79. ISBN: 1416567836; 9781416567837.

Chicago, Summer (a week after Harry's trip to New Orleans) 2008? Harry finally has a day off (and a hot date scheduled with Anastasia). It would have worked out well, if only the rest of the world had taken the day off along with him.

Associates: Billy—*werewolf, leader of the Alphas pack;* Georgia—*werewolf;* Kirby—*werewolf;* Andi—*werewolf;* Darth Wannabe and his posse—*all humans with barely discernable magical powers;* Mister—*Harry's cat;* Mouse—*Harry's dog;* Molly—*Harry's apprentice;* and Anastasia Luccio—*warden.*

18. *Turn Coat.* New York: ROC, 2009, 420 p. ISBN: 9780451462565.

Chronology note: This entry in the series was placed before "The Warrior," a short story published in the anthology *Mean Streets,* because Harry's attitude about Michael's condition probably changed in the aftermath of his conversation with Uriel in "The Warrior" and in *Turn Coat,* when Michael is discussed (p. 265) there is no evidence of this change. It was a very brief conversation, providing a hint on placement, it is not conclusive, but this story had to be placed either before or after "The Warrior" and that was the logic for placing it here.

Chicago and the island Demonreach, Summer 2009? Morgan is framed for the murder of Aleron LaFortier and comes to Harry for help. (After the way he hounded Harry many years ago no-one would expect Harry to protect him.) Morgan is wounded, and the White Council is working on tracking him down. Harry believes that Morgan was framed, and he won't stand by and watch the execution of an innocent man. Harry must find conclusive evidence to clear Morgan and he must find it fast.

In many ways this book is a turning point. The Merlin (Langtry) is forced to give LaFortier's seat to Gregori Cristos to keep the LaFortier faction from seceding from the Council. Both Ebenezar and Harry believe that Cristos must be an agent of the Black Council. Trusting that the White Council will eventually function as it was meant to function becomes impossible. The "Grey Council" is born. Thomas and Molly gain unwelcome understandings of who they are and what they will do when they are pushed to the wall. Anastasia and Harry come to a new understanding about their relationship. Billy demands that he and his pack be treated as adults. Harry continues to have debilitating headaches.

Associates: Warden Donald Morgan—*who was found holding a bloody knife over the body of Aleron LaFortier;* Billy—*werewolf, leader of the Alphas pack;* Georgia—*werewolf, Billy's wife;* Kirby—*werewolf;* Andi—*werewolf, Kirby's mate;* "Shagnasty"—*a naagloshii (skinwalker);* Mouse—*Harry's dog;* Mister—*Harry's cat;* Bob the Skull; Thomas Raith—*White Court vampire, Harry's half-brother;* Justine—*the woman Thomas loves;* Lara Raith—*White Court vampire, Thomas's sister, she leads the House of Raith;* Madeline—vampire of House Raith, *Thomas's cousin;* Molly Carpenter—*Harry's apprentice;* Anastasia Luccio—*Captain of the White Council's Wardens, is Harry's lover;* Chandler and Lucky—*who guard the headquarters of the White Council at the Hidden Halls of Edinburgh;* Ebenezar McCoy—*wizard, member of the Senior Council;* "Injun Joe" Listens-to-Wind—*wizard, member of the Senior Council;* the Merlin (Langtry)—*wizard, leader of the White Council;* Peabody—*wizard, clerk for the White Council;* Sergeant Karrin Murphy—*who reviews a crime scene file for Harry;* Binder—*who is not much of a wizard but he can summon spirit beings to do his bidding;* Private Investigator Vince Graver—*who was hired to follow Harry:* Evelyn Derek—*of the firm Smith Cohen Mackleroy hired Vince;* "Demonreach"—*the spirit entity that lives on the island near Chicago (also used for the name of the island as well);* Toot-Toot—*the fairy, is promoted to Major General of the Za-Lord's Elite Guard;* Warden Thorsen; Wizard Rashid—*the Gatekeeper;* Coroner Waldo Butters—*who becomes part of Harry's gaming group.*

19. "The Warrior," in *Mean Streets.* New York: ROC, 2009, p. 1–67. ISBN: 9780451462497.

CHICAGO, SOFTBALL SEASON 2009? Harry holds two of the swords given to mankind to be wielded by the Knights of the Cross (Amoracchius and Fidelacchius). Someone wants them. Someone is willing to threaten Michael's family to get them.

ASSOCIATES: Michael Carpenter—*who seems happy as a retired Knight of the Cross;* Charity—*Michael's wife, who is also happier now that he's retired;* Molly and Alicia—*their daughters;* Harry—*Michael and Charity's 7 or 8-year-old son;* Courtney—*who lives in the Carpenter's neighborhood;* Kelly—*a member of Alicia's softball team;* Chuck—*an electrician who works for Michael's construction company;* Mouse—*Harry's dog;* Pathologist Dr. Butters—*who treats Harry;* Father Paulo—*who tries to guard access to Father Forthill;* Father Anthony Forthill—*who tries to protect Father Roarke Douglas;* Father Roarke Douglas; and "Jake"—*Uriel.*

C

CHESBRO, George C.

<u>Shadow of a Broken Man</u>

Genres/Themes Crossed: Paranormal, Secret Society, Science Fiction X Hard-Boiled Mystery.

Subjects/Character Types: Telepathy, Telekinesis, Spell-Casters (Witches), Psychic Healing, Voodoo, Future Technology X Private Investigators.

Series/Stand-Alone: The novels should be read in order as characters and relationships evolve over the course of the series.

Scene of the Crime: New York, 1974.

Detective: Mongo is a dwarf, an acrobat, a genius, a black-belt in karate, and, obviously, an overachiever. Mongo's given name is Robert Frederickson. He was rechristened "Mongo the Magnificent" by Phil Statler when Mongo worked in Phil's circus. Phil saved his life, taking Mongo out of the town where he was born, the town where he'd been treated like a freak, the town where he'd been tormented every day. While in the circus Mongo, had saved his money and attended college in the off-season. His goal was to eventually land a job that did not make him feel like a freak. The college where he earned his doctoral degree offered him a job as an assistant professor, and he joyfully walked away from the circus. After a little time, Mongo realized that he missed the adrenaline rush that came with his death-defying circus act, and he began moonlighting as a private investigator. For some reason he gets very odd cases; often cases that involve paranormal elements.

Known Associates: NYPD Detective Garth Frederickson, Mongo's brother, has always been Mongo's champion. Phil Statler, who ran the circus where Mongo worked, turned Mongo into a headliner. He emphasized Mongo's acrobatic skills, helping Mongo feel like an athlete instead of a freak.

Premise: Some people have limited paranormal talents; there are even a few who are able to cast spells. A few brilliant scientists have developed advanced and remarkable technologies. Governments vie to acquire anything that would give them more power. Mongo is known as a student of the unusual, even as an expert on the unusual. He's a college professor, but he moonlights as a private investigator. Mongo's university colleagues refer clients to him; in later books the government monitors his activities. Everyone expects Mongo to cope with the unusual.

In the early books in the series, Garth occasionally helps Mongo by providing information from some police resources; in later books, Garth and Mongo are partners.

Comment: George Clark Chesbro died November 18, 2008. In his 68 years, he wrote 27 novels and over 100 short stories. He had worked as a special education teacher for students with learning disabilities, and also worked at a psychiatric institution with emotionally troubled teenagers. His initial conception of Mongo was that the dwarf detective would be a comic character. Although he devoted all his efforts to the writing, the book would just not work. Then he realized that Mongo could not be a figure of fun. As Chesbro put it: "The damn dwarf just wouldn't go away...I gave Mongo his dignity and he gave me a career" (from Michael Carlson's obituary for George Chesbro, printed in The Guardian on January 15, 2009; available at http://www.guardian.co.uk/books/2009/jan/15/obituary-george-chesbro). George Chesbro won the Ellery Queen Mystery Magazine Readers Award in 1997 for his short story "The Problem with Pigs" (EQMM, June 1997), and served as the president of the Mystery Writers Association of America. The Dangerous Dwarf Web site (http://www.dangerousdwarf.com/) provides news on Chesbro's series, links to articles and interviews, and an online discussion forum.

Second Horseman Out of Eden takes place on the Christmas before the turn of the second millennium A.D. Depending on how one calculates that date, it must take place in either December 1999 or December 2000. It was written well before that, and the dating for some events (for instance, how long it has been since Mongo has seen Phil Statler, which should set the date for *The Fear in Yesterday's Rings*) seems to put the books following *Second Horseman Out of Eden* before that in the chronology; however, Garth's emotional arc and the events in his life (such as meeting Mary Tree) seem to keep the books in the order in which they were written. There are inconsistencies in the dating of the books after *Second Horseman Out of Eden*.

Some of the Mongo books involve fantastical elements, some involve science fiction elements (particularly in the area of genetic manipulation), and some are straight private detective stories, albeit with elements such as government conspiracies. As the themes and action of the novels became more unusual, U.S. publishers showed less and less interest in publishing Chesbro's work. His last published novel, *Lord of Ice and Loneliness,* was published only in France. A movie of *An Affair of Sorcerers* was being planned when Mr. Chesbro passed away; if it goes forward, there may be renewed interest in his novels, and *Lord of Ice and Loneliness* may be published in the United States.

Literary Magic & Mayhem: In some ways, these books are reminiscent of action series such as *Nick Carter*. The character who is the most macho wins, and that's always Mongo. For instance, in the following exchange with Garth, someone Mongo interviewed to get information for his case was murdered shortly after speaking to Mongo. Garth is worried, Mongo is saddened but also enraged, and Mongo goes into his "I am a macho superman" mode when Garth expresses concern:

> "You could be the next target."
> "I hope so," I said evenly.
> "That sounds suicidal."
> "No, homicidal."

The first several books follow an arc in which Mongo methodically conducts an investigation and is hindered by various people (often federal law enforcement personnel) and then, at some point, he is captured by the villains. The villains set him up to be killed in a torturously slow and painful way, but Mongo manages to evade death. Even though he is alive, he's psychologically broken and must heal to be tough enough to continue the investigation and bring the villains to justice. The scenes in which Mongo battles fear and depression are well written and moving; but, if the books are read in quick succession, they can seem repetitive. Later in this series, Chesbro breaks that mold and the books become less formulaic and more interesting.

Explorations: What would the world be like if the paranormal aspects of the book were true to life? Could good people prevent their abuse?

THE CASES

1. ***Shadow of a Broken Man.*** New York: Dell, 1987, c1977, 252 p. ISBN: 0440177618. [Telepathy, Telekinesis X Private investigators]

New York, 1974. Four-and-a-half years ago, Mongo left the circus; he now works as an assistant professor, and he moonlights as a private investigator. Mike Foster asks Mongo to look into an odd, seemingly impossible, situation. Architect Victor Rafferty was a brilliant, secretive man. When he was working on a building, he worked alone. At the initial planning phases, he did all the work by himself and locked all sketches and plans in a safe every night. His wife, Elizabeth, was the only person who would know anything about the work until it was unveiled. He was working on a project five years ago when he died. All the plans for that project are still in the safe; yet a building using those plans has just been built. Victor's widow, Elizabeth, now married to Mike Foster, has seemed terrified and haunted ever since she saw a picture of the building. Mike's afraid that she's on the brink of having a breakdown, and he needs someone to get to the bottom of the puzzle and lay her fears to rest.

ASSOCIATES: Mike Foster—*client;* Elizabeth—*Mike's wife, she is the widow of architect Victor Rafferty;* Dr. Franklin Manning—*a friend of Mongo, Franklin knows Mike and he knew Victor;* Howard Q. Barnes—*who was the watchman who saw Rafferty fall;* Detective Patrick O'Connell—*who believes that Rafferty hypnotized him to escape police custody;* Mr. Lippitt—*the federal agent who was supposed to take Rafferty into custody;* Abu Bhutal—*of the United Nations, worked with Mongo when the circus was doing benefits for UNICEF;* Ronald Tal—*Special Assistant to the United Nations Secretary General;* Elliot Thomas—*a stress engineer;* Rolfe Thaag—*the current United Nations Secretary General;* Dr. Arthur Morton—*who resuscitated Rafferty after he almost died in a car accident;* Dr. Mary Llewellyn—*helped Dr. Morton;* Dr. Fritz James—*an expert on parapsychology;* Marianne—*Morton's widow, she has remarried, and is now Mrs. Vahanian;* Frank Alden—*a reporter;* Peter and Georgie—*MI5 agents;* and Sergei Kaznakov—*torturer.*

2. ***City of Whispering Stone.*** New York: Dell, 1988, c1978, 236 p. ISBN: 0440200350. [Private investigators]

NEW YORK, IRAN, 1976. It started as a simple missing-person's case. Mongo's old friend, Phil Statler of the Statler Brothers' Circus, asks Mongo to find their new headliner, muscleman Hassan Khordad. Every puzzle Mongo solves leads him more deeply into intrigue and tragedy. The villains use those he loves to pressure Mongo: first Garth's girlfriend, Neptune, and then Garth himself. Everyone works against Mongo, from foreign operatives to America's military.

ASSOCIATES: Phil Statler—*client, Phil is the circus manager who first gave Mongo a job and then helped Mongo regain his self-respect;* Hassan Khordad—*muscleman;* Ali Azad—*Vice-President of the university's Confederation of Iranian Students;* Anna Najafi—*one of their members;* Orrin Bannon—*import–export business owner;* Soussan—*his wife;* Leyla—*the dancer;* Lieutenant Garth Frederick—*Mongo's brother;* Neptune Tabrizi—*Garth's new girlfriend;*

NYPD Sergeant Harry Stans—*who works with Garth;* Victor Lanning and Wendell Biggs—*of Military Intelligence;* Dr. Darius Khayyam—*is the university's Chair of the Department of Middle Eastern Studies;* Mohammed Reza Pahlavi—*the Shah of Iran;* Captain Mohammed Zand; and Colonel Bahman Arsenjani.

3. *An Affair of Sorcerers.* New York: Dell, 1988, c1979, 265 p. ISBN: 0440200474. [Psychic Healing, Spell-Casters (Witches) X Private investigators]

NEW YORK, JULY 1977. Mongo was looking forward to six weeks of vacation when three people who he would not want to disappoint ask him to undertake investigations. The Chancellor of Mongo's university asks him to investigate the activities of a fellow professor, Nobel Laureate Dr. Vincent Smathers. A nun who is a friend of Mongo's asks that he look into a murder investigation. Kathy Marlowe, a young friend and neighbor of Mongo's, asks him to find her father's Book of Shadows. Mongo has only done the most preliminary of interviews when he dreams of Kathy in trouble, and wakes to find that her apartment is on fire. He rescues Kathy from the fire but cannot awaken her. The doctors cannot awaken her either, and Mongo realizes that a witch has scheduled Kathy for death as a warning to any who would oppose him. Mongo races the clock as he tries to find out what has happened to Kathy in time for the doctors to save her. The pressure rises when his enemy has Mongo infected with rabies. One interesting aspect of this book is the concept of a person who (unintentionally) is a negative psychic healer whose presence enhances illness rather than wellness.

ASSOCIATES: Dr. Peter Barnum—*the university's Chancellor;* Dr. Vincent Smathers—*who is exploring the human mind's response to sensory deprivation;* Dr. Chiang Kee—*Smathers's associate, Dr. Kee is rumored to have been a torturer during the Korean War;* Professor Fred Haley—*who was a POW;* Mrs. Pfatt—*the dragon guarding Smather's door.*

Sister Janet Monroe—*microbiologist, and Mongo's friend;* Senator Bill Younger—*who, with Sister Janet, asks Mongo to investigate allegations against a healer;* Esteban Morales—*a psychic healer who is charged with the murder of Dr. Robert Samuels;* Dr. Eric Jordan—*who is the key witness against Esteban.*

Kathy Marlowe—*is Mongo's young neighbor;* Frank Marlowe and April Marlowe—*Kathy's parents;* Yvonne Mercado—*anthropologist;* John Krowl—*tarot card reader;* Dr. Madeline Jones—*astrologer;* Richard Crandall—*a ceremonial magician (and Kathy's uncle);* Jake Stein and Sandor Peth—*who, at different times, were agents for singer Harley Davidson;* and Dr. Joshua Greene—*who is treating Kathy.*

Garth—*Mongo's brother;* Regina Farber—*Garth's girlfriend.*

4. ***The Beasts of Valhalla.*** New York: Dell, 1987, c1985, 322 p. ISBN: 044010484X. [Future Technology (Genetic Manipulation) X Private Investigators]

NEBRASKA, NEW YORK, WISCONSIN, PENNSYLVANIA, GREENLAND, 1986. Mongo and Garth return to Nebraska (the first time Mongo has been back in 17 years) to attend the funeral of their nephew, Tommy Dernhelm. Their sister, Janet, is sure that Tommy and his friend Rod Lugmor were both murdered and that the Sheriff has no intention of conducting an honest investigation. She asks Mongo to investigate, and he soon realizes that she is right. Mongo's mother dreams of the destruction of Earth, and of Mongo and Garth. Mongo seriously considers giving up the investigation, and readers find out that at least part of Mongo's determination and uncompromising strength is inherited! The crooked sheriff injects serum that causes genetic mutations in Mongo and Garth with the intention of torturing and killing them. It doesn't work as fast as expected, and Mongo and Garth become the target of a search directed by the scientist at the head of the Valhalla Project. This book marks the point at which the series becomes more fantastical.

ASSOCIATES: Mongo's mother and father; Garth—*Mongo's brother;* Janet—*Mongo's sister;* John Dernhelm—*Janet's husband;* Tommy—*their son, he was 14 years old;* Coop Lugmor—*who tormented Mongo when they were children, now wants to hire Mongo;* County Sheriff Jake Bolesh—*who bullied Mongo when they were children, now wants to run Mongo out of town;* Bill Jackson and Auberlich "Obie" Loge—*played Sorscience with Tommy;* Siegfried—*Obie's father, invented the game Sorscience;* Sigmund Loge—*Obie's grandfather, won two Nobel prizes long ago and now heads the Volsung corporation;* Victor Rafferty; Mr. Lippitt—*Director of the Defense Intelligence Agency;* Zeke Cohen—*a hacker;* Mike Leviticus, Reverent Ezra, Sister Esther, and Brother Luke—*meet Garth and Mongo in Wisconsin;* Hugo Fasolt—*the giant, worked with Mongo at the Statler Brothers Circus;* Gollum "Golly"—*the gorilla;* and Warrior Stryder London.

5. ***Two Songs This Archangel Sings.*** New York: Dell, 1988, c1986, 254 p. ISBN: 0440201055. [Private Investigators]

NEW YORK, SEATTLE, 1988. Mongo had an appointment to meet with Veil for a martial-arts workout. When he got to Veil's apartment, the door was unlocked and Veil was missing. Mongo seems to be the only person who's concerned, at least until two men show up to torture him for information about Veil. In Veil's apartment, Mongo found a cryptic painting and an envelope with his name on it. The envelope contained $10,000, and Mongo decides that it's a cry for help. In the course of his investigation, Mongo learns all about Veil "Archangel" Kendry's past and attracts the attention of men who are still Veil's enemies. Garth is furious: he believes that Kendry is using Mongo as a stalking horse to draw out those enemies. Mongo doesn't care. As far as he's concerned, he's discovered the truth, and he will see the truth revealed to the country, no matter what the cost. United States President Shannon becomes aware of the case and sends his lackeys to try to stop Mongo. When that doesn't work they try threats, and finally they try to convince him to walk away:

> If you do this, Frederickson, you'll be a traitor... The damage you'll do to this country will be unimaginable.
>
> Bullshit. The damage we'll do to the Shannon administration will be unimaginable, but you're the one, acting on orders from Shannon, who decided he wanted to play what you politicians love to call hardball. People like you and your boss are the ones who do unimaginable damage to this country when you lie, and when you use your power to twist or circumvent laws for your own convenience. (p. 214)

ASSOCIATES: Veil Kendry—*Mongo's sensei;* Victor Raskolnikov—*Veil's patron;* Garth—*Mongo's brother;* Loan Ka—*president of Seattle's Hmong Community Association;* Peter and Jimmy—*Loan Ka's sons;* Maru Tai—*Loan Ka's wife;* Colonel Liu Sakh Po—*removed Veil from Loan Ka's village in the Fall of 1972;* Kathy—*was rescued by Veil after she was taken to Saigon;* Lieutenant General Lester Bean—*accepted Veil's surrender;* Matthew Holmes—*Colletville High School Principal;* Jan Garvey—*was once a classmate of Veil's;* Gary Worde—*was Veil's best friend.*

Orville Madison—*who was a war criminal.* Madison was also Veil's CIA controller during the war. Madison is currently the Director of the CIA. United States President Shannon has nominated Madison for the position of Secretary of State. President Shannon's administration would be embarrassed by the scandal if certain episodes from Madison's past were discovered. Madison's story is intertwined with Veil's so the government moves to close down Mongo's investigation into Veil's past.

Captain McGarvey—*is one of the men who take Garth and Mongo into custody on the charge of treason;* Presidential Aide Burton Andrews; President Kevin Shannon; Madeline Jamison—*Veil's aunt;* Ninja Henry Kitten—*whose FBI file indicates that he uses the same MO as was used in the attack on Mongo;* Mr. Lippitt—*Director of the Defense Intelligence Agency;* and Senator Kathleen Wyndham.

6. *The Cold Smell of Sacred Stone.* New York: Dell, 1989, c1988, 297 p. ISBN: 0440203945. [Empaths X Private Investigators]

NEW YORK, 1988 (BEGINS THREE DAYS AFTER THE EVENTS IN *TWO SONGS THIS ARCHANGEL SINGS*). When the story opens, Garth is in Rockland

Psychiatric Center: he's catatonic. His eyes open, but there is no recognition, no responsiveness, nothing. Investigators are anxious to speak to him because they believe that he may be able to tell them enough so that they can uncover the enemy agents who poisoned him. Mongo's efforts to reach Garth are somewhat successful. Very soon after, a nurse notes in his medical chart Garth's slight response to a stimulus; two of the suspects in his poisoning flee. Something odd is going on at Rockland, but Mongo is focused on his brother. Garth has awakened, but he seems to Mongo to be quite insane. He's lost track of his sense of identity. He seems to have become an empath and he's absorbing the suffering of the entire world. People around him begin to believe that he is the Messiah. Then Garth and the homicidal Marl Braxton disappear from the hospital.

ASSOCIATES: Garth—*Mongo's brother, is slowly recovering from nitrophenylpentadienal "spy dust" poisoning;* Ninja Henry Kitten—*who hasn't given up on his mission;* Veil Kendry—*Mongo's friend and sparring partner.*

Dr. Charles Slycke—*a psychiatrist, is the first clinic director;* Dr. Helen Fall—*is the second.*

Tommy Carling—*is one of Garth's nurses;* Patient Marion "Mama" Baker—*who thinks that dwarves are evil;* Marl Braxton—*who is homicidal.*

The 65 students at the RCPC (Rockland Children's Psychiatric Center) are all either suicidal or homicidal. Gladys Jacubowicz—*runs the RCPC teaching program;* Dane Potter—*a student, he was a young marine;* "Marilyn"—*tells Dane to kill Mongo;* Kim Trainor—*student, everyone she has loved has died, and Kim has become suicidal;* Chris Yardley—*a student who believes he is Jesus;* Steven Wallis—*a student who plays checkers with Mongo;* Mr. Lippitt—*Director of the Defense Intelligence Agency;* Sergeant Alexander McIntyre; Harry August, Sister Kate, and Mrs. Daplinger—*who are acolytes;* and Mongo's parents.

7. ***Second Horseman Out of Eden.*** New York: Mysterious Press, 1990, c1989, 248 p. ISBN: 0445408626. [Private Investigators]

NEW YORK AND IDAHO, DECEMBER 1999. Every year, Mongo and Garth, along with many of their fellow New Yorkers, go to the General Post Office in Manhattan to go through the letters the children of New York sent to Santa Claus. They choose 10 letters from children from impoverished families and do their best to stand in for Santa. Garth went to hunt through the letters a few days before Christmas, and found a letter from young Vicky Brown. In it she asked for a puppy and for a really nice gift for Reverend Billy so he would stop hurting her between her legs. In the course of trying to rescue this little girl, Garth and Mongo uncover a religious cult whose converts are anxious to rush to Armageddon and determined to take the rest of the world with them.

ASSOCIATES: Garth—*Mongo's brother, is his partner in the Frederickson and Frederickson Detective Agency;* Reverend Doctor William "Wild Bill" Kenecky—*who lost his televangelism empire years ago, after a scandal involving sexual abuse;* Dr. Samuel Zelaskowich—*the New York Botanical Garden's expert on tropical soil and plants;* Dr. Craig Valley—*who was the botanical garden's liaison to Harry Blaisdel's Nuvironment Corporation;* Peter Patton—*Nuvironment's Executive Director;* Hector Velazian and Billy Dale Rokan—*are retired baseball players;* Floyd and Baxter Small—*are retired golf pros;* Thomas "Tanker" Thompson—*retired football player;* New York Police Lieutenant Malachy McCloskey; New York Police Officer Frank Palorino; Pilot Jack Holloway; Copilot and Navigator Nigel Fickley; and Mr. Lippitt—*Director of the Defense Intelligence Agency.*

8. ***The Language of Cannibals.*** New York: Mysterious Press, 1990, c1990, 200 p. ISBN: 0892963948. [Private Investigators]

CAIRN NEW YORK, AUGUST 200? Cairn used to be an artist's colony, a small, liberal riverfront town. Then outsiders moved in and began taking over the city government. Then there were several unsolved murders, mostly of criminals. Recently, Michael Burana, an old friend of Mongo's, died in Cairn. He was an FBI agent, but had been reconsidering his vocation; he'd moved in with a local group of pacifists (the group he was supposed to be spying on) and hadn't checked in with the local police. Mongo goes to Cairn to try to determine what happened. Within an hour of his arrival, he's engaged in a verbal battle with Elysius Culhane, a man who is determined to get some dirt on the President of the United States from Mongo. Many of Mongo's statements infuriate Culhane, such as this one:

> Culhane, has it ever occurred to you that there are people in this country who believe that the American right wing has been, and continues to be, a greater threat to our personal liberties than the communists ever have been, or will be (p. 16)

He goes on to assert that the stated rightwing goal of getting the government "off the backs of the people" is actually just code for demanding that government give businesses carte blanche. Then Mongo continues:

> It doesn't bother you at all, in fact you like it, when the government goes snooping into our bedrooms and libraries. Total social control has always been the wet dream of the far right. I don't mind the government auditing my taxes, Culhane, but I sure as hell don't want it auditing my mind. (p. 17)

The lines are drawn from the first encounter, and Mongo finds himself battling not only murderers, but also the local government, to try to find the truth behind his friend's death. One of the most interesting aspects of this book is the question of how language affects perception. This is how Jay Acton describes it:

> Language mirrors the world we live in; if we use screwed-up language to define reality, if you're always looking to use language to put 'spin control' on something instead of trying to accurately describe it, then you actually end up with a screwed-up reality . . . it's easy to fool these people simply by using their corrupted vocabulary; tell them what they want to hear. (p. 163)

The ideas expressed in this book regarding propaganda, "the language of cannibals," are interesting, provocative, and worthy of discussion. If it were used in a book-discussion group, special care would need to be exercised to make sure that people with conservative viewpoints don't feel attacked.

ASSOCIATES: Garth—*Mongo's brother and business partner;* Mary Tree—*folk singer and activist;* Jack Trex—*is a painter and a veteran of the Vietnam War;* Gregory Trex—*is Jack's son;* Officer McAlpin and Police Chief Dan Mosely—*of the Cairn police.*

Elysius Culhane—*a conservative columnist and commentator;* Jay Acton—*is his aide;* Edward J. Hendricks—*Director of Counterintelligence, was Michael's boss at the FBI and is a good friend of Culhane;* Harry Peal—*who used to be of interest to the FBI: he was a communist in the 1930s when he met Olga Koussevitsky who was sent from Russia to reorganize New York's communist cell.*

At the end of the book, Garth and Mary Tree marry.

9. ***The Fear in Yesterday's Rings.*** New York: Mysterious Press, 1992, c1991, 214 p. ISBN: 0446401021. [Future Technology (Created Monster) X Private Investigators]

NEW YORK; PALMETTO GROVE, FLORIDA; LAMBEAUX, MISSOURI; DOLBIN, KANSAS; NEBRASKA, JULY 200?. Phil Statler was offered a good price for Statler Brothers' Circus several years ago. The prospective buyer wanted the equipment, the permits, and the animals, but not the performers. Phil spent a lifetime building his family of performers, and he just couldn't sell their livelihoods. The circus was losing money, and Phil took out loans to keep it going, until the bank foreclosed and he was forcibly removed from the grounds. That was two and a half years ago. Phil crawled into a bottle and stayed there; when Mongo finds him, he's ill, homeless, and has given up. Mongo decides to form a syndicate of prosperous circus performers to buy Phil's circus back. He has more trouble than expected. The circus is clearly losing money, but the owners are hostile and unwilling even to meet with Mongo. Everything is complicated by the fact that there have been a series of bizarre crimes along the route taken by the circus. They're being called the "werewolf killings."

Dr. Nate Button researches mythical animals and believes that the "werewolf killings" are actually lobox killings. The lobox is pictured in cave paintings in Lascaux, France. Even if it once existed, it's been extinct for over 10,000 years, unless Button is correct and there were hidden survivors. The idea of a species surviving in hiding for thousands of years seems only slightly more probable than the existence of werewolves. Saving the circus becomes more difficult with every killing.

Mongo started on a mission of mercy and ended up on the trail of a serial killer. Along the way, he gains an ally—his first crush, a snake-charmer he met in the circus, her name is Harper Rhys-Whitney. Harper observed Mongo's determination to get his degree and followed in his footsteps. She and one of her snakes accompany Mongo as he investigates the circus.

This book gives the first explicit description of how Mongo went from being the little brother of the high-school football and basketball star to being a high-school athlete himself (in gymnastics), then a circus freak, then a circus headliner, and then, finally, after achieving his doctorate, a college professor. He describes Nebraska as "a whole different planet" and himself as "the resident alien." This book gives the backstory that explains Mongo's desperation, determination, and strength.

ASSOCIATES: Phil Statler—*of the Statler Brothers' Circus, he gave Mongo a job and he gave him dignity, headlining Mongo as an acrobat, instead of as a freak;* Jacques Louture—*an intern at Bellevue;* Florence Woolsey—*who was a circus fat lady, and now is an attorney;* Dr. Nate Button—*a cryptozoologist;* Arlen Zelezian—*a dog breeder who is interested in the Kuvasz breed;* Luther—*one of the best animal trainers that any of the circus people have ever seen;* Garth—*Mongo's brother;* Mary Tree—*Garth's wife;* and Dr. Harper Rhys-Whitney—*a snake charmer.*

10. ***Dark Chant in a Crimson Key.*** Nyack, New York: Apache Beach Publications, 1999, c1992, 217 p. ISBN: 0967450381. [Future Technology (the drug Gluteathin) X Private Investigators]

NEW YORK, ZURICH, SUMMER 200?. Mongo feels a certain amount of guilt towards Emmet P. Neuberger. The man's Cornucopia Foundation has done a lot of good in the world, but Mongo just doesn't like him. That guilt makes Mongo a little too receptive to Neuberger's request for assistance in investigating a theft from the Cornucopia Foundation. John "Chant" Sinclair, a criminal wanted in many countries, managed to transfer $10 million of the Foundation's money out of their accounts. Interpol is on the case, and they believe that they have trapped Sinclair in Zurich. Neuberger wants Mongo to go over and check on the progress of the investigation, and he's willing to pay.

ASSOCIATES: Emmet P. Neuberger—*Mongo's client;* Veil Kendry—*Mongo's friend and sensei;* Gerard Patreaux—*of Amnesty International who knows a little about "Chant";* John "Chant" Sinclair—*who is suspected of theft;* Carlo

Santini—*Mongo's driver;* Duane Insolers—*a CIA operative;* Inspector Molière—*in Zurich;* Hyatt Pomeroy—*the executive in charge of the Cornucopia Foundation's Western European operations;* Garth Frederickson—*Mongo's brother and partner;* Harper Rhys-Whitney—*Mongo's lover;* Countess Jan Rawlings—*who inherited a castle at the edge of Lake Geneva from R. Edgar Blake;* R. Edgar Blake—*who was the half-brother of Neuberger's grandfather, the man who first set up the Cornucopia Foundation.*

11. ***An Incident at Bloodtide.*** New York: Mysterious Press, 1994, c1993, 242 p. ISBN: 0446400548. [Spell-Casters (Witches) X Private Investigators]

CAIRN, JULY 200?. Sacra Silver, a man from Mary Tree's past, invades Garth and Mary's life. He believes that he has power, and, worse, Mary believes it as well. As Mongo and Garth wrestle with the puzzle of how to free Mary from his influence, a friend of theirs is killed. Tom Blaine worked on the Hudson, trying to identify and gather evidence to prosecute polluters. Mongo suspects that his death was not an accident, but the local law enforcement officers don't seem interested in pursuing the case. It's up to Mongo to find a killer while Garth and Mary struggle to save their marriage.

ASSOCIATES: Garth Frederickson—*Mongo's brother;* Mary Tree—*Garth's wife;* Sacra Silver—*who was once Mary's lover;* Nine-year-old Vicky Brown—*who is Garth and Mongo's ward;* April Marlowe—*Mongo's friend, she has been helping with Vicky;* Francisco Gonzales—*Mongo's secretary;* Tom Blaine—*who works to clean up the Hudson river;* Jessica—*Tom's wife;* Harry Tanner—*of the Cairn police;* Captain Richard Marley—*of the Coast Guard;* Lonnie Allen—*who volunteers for the Cairn Fisherman's Association;* Bennett Carver—*founder of Carver Shipping, is now retired in Cairn and a member of Mary Tree's church;* Carla—*Bennett's wife;* Charles "Chick" Carver—*is Carla and Bennett Carver's son;* Roger Wellington—*who is Chief of Security for Carver Shipping is Charles's boss;* Julian Jefferson—*is a drunkard tanker captain;* Barry Russell—*Chairman of the Board of Carver Shipping;* Dr. Angelo Franconi; and NYPD Captain Perry Farmer.

12. ***Bleeding in the Eye of a Brainstorm.*** New Baltimore, New York: Apache Beach Publications, 2002, c2002, 204 p. ISBN: 1930253133. [Future Technology (drug) X Private Investigators]

NEW YORK, NOVEMBER 200?. For years, Mongo's kind heart and stubborn spirit have caused him to do his best to help "Mama Spit," a homeless schizophrenic woman who lives on a grate on a street near his home. When she realizes that she's witnessed a murder, she comes to Mongo for help. Garth is out of the country, taking a well-earned vacation with his wife, Mary Tree. Mongo sets out to help "Mama Spit" and quickly becomes embroiled in foiling a CIA cover-up, a cover-up that has already cost dozens of lives. Mongo's involvement makes him a target, and the lingering animosity between the Fredericksons and the local precinct captain may make him a target of local law enforcement as well.

Associates: Theo Barnes—*a homeless chess master;* Michael Stout—*a chess prodigy;* Margaret Dutton—*a.k.a. Mama Spit;* Dr. Bailey Kramer—*who works at a testing laboratory;* Frank Lemengello—*a pharmacist and chemist;* Francisco—*the Frederickson Agency's secretary;* Veil Kendry—*Mongo's friend and martial arts sensei;* Peter Southworth—*of Lorminix;* Dr. Sharon Stevens—*a CIA psychiatrist;* Emily—*one of the Rivercliff patients;* Heinrich Muller—*of Lorminix;* Garth—*Mongo's brother;* and Mary Tree—*Garth's wife.*

Captain Felix MacWhorter; booking sergeant Angel Gonzalez; and Sergeant Lou Colchen—*work out of the Midtown North NYPD precinct in Manhattan.* Inspector Gérard Molière—*who is able to identifies suspects from Mongo's description;* Henry and Janice Sparsburg—*a.k.a. Punch and Judy.*

13. ***Dream of a Falling Eagle.*** New Baltimore, New York: Apache Beach Publications, 2002, c2002, 204 p. ISBN: 1930253141. [Voodoo (scientifically explained) X Private Investigators]

New York, Washington D.C., Idaho, August 200?. For the last six months, Garth and Mongo have been working for a Special Presidential Commission formed to investigate willful malfeasance and criminal activity on the part of the CIA. They're only one of the investigative teams hired. Their assignment is to report on the last 30 years of CIA activities in Haiti. The last half dozen of their potential informants have been killed before they could speak—not only killed, but murdered, in what looks like some sort of voodoo ritual. Mongo and Garth are determined to write a careful, well-substantiated, and damning report. They've seen firsthand the damage that can be done by the rogue elements in the CIA. Mongo feels that this is their chance to help clean up the Agency, and so he is stunned when Garth insists that he take another case, a case about stopping a plagiarist, when they have not yet finished their report.

Associates: Garth—*Mongo's brother and partner;* Mary Tree—*Garth's wife;* Dr. Harper Rhys-Whitney—*Mongo's fiancé;* Francisco—*the Frederickson's Detective Agency's secretary;* Tony—*Francisco's lover;* Detective Carl Beauvil—*gives the Fredericksons some insights;* Thomas "Moby" Dickens—*a poet;* Lucas Tremayne—*Garth's neighbor, a film director;* Guy Fournier—*a professor;* William P. Kranes—*Speaker of the House;* Taylor Mackintosh—*an actor;* Paul Piggott—*vice president of Guns for God and Jesus;* the Slurper; NYPD Detective Henry Stamp; Captain Felix MacWhorter; and Officer Harriet Boone.

Collections of short stories include

1. ***In the House of Secret Enemies.*** New York: Dell, 1989, c1988, 297 p. ISBN: 0440203945.

In this book of short stories readers will find many of the seeds of ideas that formed the foundations of some of the early novels. Of particular interest is Chesbro's essay on Mongo's creation, "The Birth of a Series Character." This is immediately followed by the first Mongo and Garth story. Chesbro states that initially Mongo was imagined as a comic character, but it just didn't work. Readers can try to imagine "The Drop" with Mongo as a buffoon, and reflect on how that would have set the cornerstone for a very different series.

CONTENTS: The Birth of a Series Character—*Chesbro writes about inventing Mongo;* The Drop—*Mongo and Garth's debut;* High Wire—*Bruno asks Mongo to come and investigate something at the circus, this story includes Garth;* Rage—*Mongo finds that someone has given Garth mood-altering chemicals;* Country for Sale—*Mongo searches for Phil Statler;* Dark Hole on a Silent Planet—*Dr. Peter Barnum asks Mongo to investigate a colleague, Dr. Vincent Smathers, the story includes Garth (The plot line from this story was incorporated into An Affair of Sorcerers.);* The Healer—*a Senator asks Mongo's help with a case involving healer Esteban Morales, the story includes Garth (This story was woven into An Affair of Sorcerers.);* Falling Star—*Sandor Peth asks Mongo's help with events foretold in Harley Davidson's horoscope, (This story was woven into An Affair of Sorcerers. In this story Garth has been assigned to a special police unit keeping tabs on the New York occult underground.);* Book of Shadows—*young Kathy asks Mongo's help in recovering her father's Book of Shadows, the story includes Garth (This is a story about the terrible cost of some belief systems. This story was woven into An Affair of Sorcerers.);* Tiger in the Snow—*Mongo's old friend (and one time employer) circus owner Phil Statler calls Mongo when Sam the Tiger gets loose in the city;* Candala—*Chesbro states that, of all the stories he's written, he's most proud of this one. In it, Indiri Tamidian asks Mongo to find out what's bothering Pram Sakhuntala. The story includes Garth.).*

2. ***Lone Wolves.*** New Baltimore, New York: Apache Beach Publications, 2003, 245 p. ISBN: 193025315X.

CONTENTS: The first section of the book is entitled "Garth.," It includes First Strike; The White Bear; Lone Wolf. Haunts; and The Problem with the Pigs. The second section is entitled "Veil." It includes The Lazarus Gate: and Unmarked Graves. The third section is entitled "Priest." It includes Priests; Lethal Beliefs; Tomb; and Model Town.

3. ***Strange Prey and Other Tales of the Hunt.*** New Baltimore, New York: Apache Beach Publications, 2004, 237 p. ISBN: 1930253176; 9781930253179.

CONTENTS: Strange Prey; Broken Pattern; The Snake in the Tower; Wotzel; Four Knights Game; The Club of Venice; Tourist Trap; Firefight of the Mind; The Tower; Dreams; The Dragon Variation.

Christian, M. (Editors). Co-editor (with Martin Jakubowski) of *The Mammoth Book of Future Cops*. See Jakubowski, Maxim: The Mammoth Book of Future Cops.

CHRISTIE, Agatha. (Agatha Mary Clarissa, Lady Mallowan, DBE, 1890–1976)

THE MYSTERIOUS MR. QUIN

Genres/Themes Crossed: Lone Supernatural X Traditional Mystery.

Subjects/Character Types: Supernatural agent X Amateur Sleuth.

Series/Stand-Alone: Mr. Satterthwaite's deductive skills improve and his determination and self-confidence increases in the course of the stories. To experience this, the stories should be read in order.

Detective: Mr. Satterthwaite always led a careful, quiet life. Now, at age 62, he feels that life has somehow passed him by. He wants to take part in the drama of life. When Mr. Quin appears out of the night, Mr. Satterthwaite's imagination is engaged. He takes part in a conversation that changes the life of a young woman, and he finds it so rewarding that he is anxious to be of use to Mr. Quin again.

Known Associates: Mr. Quin, a mysterious man who appears when he is needed. He quietly guides conversations, leading others to discover truths that shed light on past mysteries.

Premise: Mr. Satterthwaite describes Mr. Quin's gift:."He has a power—an almost uncanny power—of showing you what you have seen with your own eyes, of making clear to you what you have heard with your own ears" in "The Shadow on the Glass" (p. 39). Mr. Satterthwaite is in the upper echelons of society. He is known for his love of drama and of fine food. It is said that he only attends the parties of the nouveau riche if they have a fine cook or a guest list that includes particularly vivid characters. He's fascinated by Mr. Quin. Mr. Satterthwaite's careful manner and spotless (and somewhat boring) reputation allow him to ensure that Mr. Quin will be received and accepted by Mr. Satterthwaite's acquaintances, even when they are embroiled in a murder investigation.

Comment: Christie dedicated the initial collection of stories as follows: "To Harlequin the invisible." It is the only time that Agatha Christie dedicated a book to a character that she had created.

There is an official Agatha Christie Web site at http://www.agathachristie.com/. It focuses on the detectives that have been featured in movies and television shows (Poirot, Miss Marple, and Tommy and Tuppence).

Literary Magic & Mayhem: Here is a master (mistress?) at work. In every story, she builds the atmosphere of tension with a few telling details. Mr. Satterthwaite quietly reflecting on his penchant for drama, people feeling uneasy over old memories, questions about such things as a fair woman dying her hair dark, with the unspoken implication that she is hiding something . . . the story becomes compelling, suspenseful, even as the reader agrees with the characters who believe that the questions raised are too old to be successfully resolved. The past is done and people's memories must have faded: how can anyone get to the truth so long after the event? Mr. Quin's response? "A problem is not necessarily unsolvable because it has remained unsolved" (p. 12). Then Mr. Quin helps the people involved see the problem differently, and suddenly the solution is plain. It feels more like magic than logic. There is such relief in seeing old wrongs set right and in knowing that people whose lives were twisted by suspicion have finally found the truth.

Explorations: What is Mr. Satterthwaite's role?

What were the steps of logic that led to the truth?

How were people's lives changed, even years after the original crime?

THE CASES

1. **"The Coming of Mr. Quin,"** a short story in *The Mysterious Mr. Quin*. New York: Dell Publishing, 1979 (c1930, renewed 1958), p. 5–22. ISBN: 0440162467.

England, New Year's Eve 1922? Mr. Satterthwaite finds the Evesham's New Year's Eve party oddly fraught with tension, particularly when the subject of the death of Derek Capel is mentioned. When a stranger (Mr. Harley Quin) comes in to escape the cold while his chauffeur fixes his car, the conversation returns to Mr. Capel. This time Mr. Quin manages the conversation so that the men pool their knowledge of the day of Capel's death. To their surprise, their conversation uncovers the truth about a murder.

Associates: Tom Eveshan and his wife, Lady Laura—*who are the hosts for the house party at Royston;* Sir Richard Conway—*one of the guests;* Eleanor Portal—*who should have been fair;* Alec—*her husband;* and Mr. Harley Quin—*who comes in to take shelter while his car is being repaired.*

2. **"The Shadow on the Glass,"** a short story in *The Mysterious Mr. Quin*. New York: Dell Publishing, 1979 (c1930, renewed 1958), p. 23–44. ISBN: 0440162467.

ENGLAND, 1922? Mr. Satterthwaite had been told to expect the tension before he even arrived at Greenway House. (Richard Scott, recently married to Moira, was rumored to have once had a torrid affair with Mrs. Staverton. All three will be guests at the weeklong house party.) Greenway House is haunted by the image of a cavalier who was murdered by his wife's lover. One of the windows of the house has a shadow of his face, as if he is looking out at the fleeing lovers. No matter how many times the glass is replaced, the stain returns. It infuriates Mrs. Unkerton, who refuses to be haunted. She has decided that she will replace the glass as quickly as the stain returns, even if the window must be reglazed once a week. Mr. Porter is haunted in quite a different way. He is deeply troubled by the feeling that the veneer of civilization is about to fall away from some of the guests: that there will be anger, perhaps even violence, and he sees no way to prevent it.

ASSOCIATES: Mr. and Mrs. Unkerton—*who entertain at their home, Greenway's House;* Richard and Moira Scott; Major John Porter; Mrs. Iris Staverton; Lady Cynthia Drage; and Captain Jimmy Allenson—*are all guests.* Inspector Winkfield—*is assigned to investigate the murders;* Mr. Harley Quin—*who happens to come to the house to discuss a picture he is considering for purchase.*

3. **"At the Bells and Motley,"** a short story in *The Mysterious Mr. Quin.* New York: Dell Publishing, 1979 (c1930, renewed 1958), p. 45–63. ISBN: 0440162467.

ENGLAND (KIRTLINGTON MALLET), MIDSUMMER EVE 1923? A punctured tire strands Mr. Satterthwaite in the tiny village of Kirtlington Mallet. At the local pub, the Bells and Motley, he finds Mr. Quin. The landlord mentions the local mystery. Three months ago, Captain Richard Harwell disappeared. Mr. Quin suggests that they should turn their mind to solving the mystery, that it may be easier to resolve the puzzle now that some time has passed. He says, "The longer the time that has elapsed, the more things fall into proportion. One sees them in their true relationship to one another" (p. 50).

ASSOCIATES: Masters—*Mr. Satterthwaite's chauffeur;* Mr. Quin—*a customer at the pub;* William Jones—*the pub owner;* Mary—*the daughter of William Jones.*

4. **"The Sign in the Sky,"** a short story in *The Mysterious Mr. Quin.* New York: Dell Publishing, 1979 (c1930, renewed 1958), p. 64–81. ISBN: 0440162467.

ENGLAND AND CANADA, 1923? Mr. Satterthwaite sat through the trial and heard the judgment against young Martin Wylde. He was convicted of murdering Sir George Barnaby's young wife. Mr. Satterthwaite couldn't bring himself to believe that the young man was guilty. At a chance meeting with Mr. Quin, he decides to go abroad to Canada to question the housemaid who emigrated before the trial.

ASSOCIATES: Mr. Quin—*who asks Mr. Satterthwaite some interesting questions;* Louisa Ballard—*housemaid;* Mr. Denman—*who made the arrangements for Miss Ballard's employment in Canada;* and Sylvia Dale—*who is fond of Martin Wylde.*

5. **"The Soul of the Croupier,"** a short story in *The Mysterious Mr. Quin.* New York: Dell Publishing, 1979 (c1930, renewed 1958), p. 82–99. ISBN: 0440162467.

MONTE CARLO, CARNIVAL SEASON 1924? Mr. Satterthwaite, romantic soul that he is, is concerned over the friendship between the Countess Czarnova and the young Franklin Rudge. (Mr. Satterthwaite believes that a young woman in the Americans' party has her heart set on Franklin.)

ASSOCIATES: The Countess Czarnova—*whose flamboyance draws attention;* Franklin Rudge and Miss Elizabeth Martin—*who are part of a group of visiting Americans;* Mirabelle; M. Pierre Vaucher; and Mr. Quin.

6. **"The World's End,"** a short story in *The Mysterious Mr. Quin.* New York: Dell Publishing, 1979 (c1930, renewed 1958), p. 100–120. ISBN: 0440162467.

CORSICA, 1924 The Duchess of Leith invited Mr. Satterthwaite to accompany her to Corsica, saying:

"We needn't be afraid of scandal at our time of life."

> Mr. Satterthwaite was delicately flattered. No one had ever mentioned scandal in connection with him before. He was far too insignificant. Scandal—and a Duchess—delicious. (p. 100)

There they meet a relative of hers, the artist Naomi Carlton-Smith. The Duchess dragoons Naomi and Mr. Tomlinson into a picnic, and they encounter Mr. Quin at the end of their journey. Mr. Satterthwaite is stunned, saying that Mr. Quin always shows up in the nick of time. Only later does he realize the truth of that remark.

ASSOCIATES: The Duchess of Leith—*who knows how to get what she wants;* Naomi Carlton-Smith—*a distant relative of the duchess;* Mr. Tomlinson—*a guest at the hotel;* Mr. Vyse—*a producer;* Rosina Nunn—*an actress;* Mr. Judd—*Rosina's husband;* Mr. Quin.

7. **"The Voice in the Dark,"** a short story in *The Mysterious Mr. Quin.* New York: Dell Publishing, 1979 (c1930, renewed 1958), p. 121–38. ISBN: 0440162467.

CANNES AND ENGLAND (WILTSHIRE), 1925? Lady Stanleigh finagles Mr. Satterthwaite into agreeing to visit her daughter, Margery, when he returns to England. Recently, Margery began to complain of hearing ghosts. Lady Stanleigh wants to know whether she's haunted or crazy; she just doesn't want to know badly enough to return to England herself.

ASSOCIATES: Lady Stranleigh—*who expresses concern about her daughter;* Margery Gale—*the daughter;* Bimbo—*Lady Stanleigh's most recent conquest;* Marcia Keane—*Margery's best friend;* Roley Vavasour—*Margery's cousin;* Clayton—*Lady Stanleigh's elderly maid;* Mrs. Casson—*a spiritualist;* Mrs. Lloyd—*a medium;* and Mr. Quin

8. **"The Face of Helen,"** a short story in *The Mysterious Mr. Quin*. New York: Dell Publishing, 1979 (c1930, renewed 1958), p. 139–57. ISBN: 0440162467.

ENGLAND, 1925? Mr. Satterthwaite encounters Mr. Quin at the opera. There they see an exquisitely beautiful young woman and observe the drama of two young men vying for her attention. At the end of the performance, Mr. Satterthwaite and Mr. Quin part. As he leaves the theater, Mr. Satterthwaite observes the two young men brawling and helps the young woman extricate herself from the scene. He meets the players from that drama by chance over the next few days. When he realizes that something is wrong, Mr. Satterthwaite wishes that he could talk to Mr. Quin, but he finds that he can imagine what Mr. Quin would say, and he realizes that he must act.

ASSOCIATES: Mr. Quin—*who joins Mr. Satterthwaite at the opera;* Gillian West—*a young woman with a lovely face;* Philip Eastney—*is one of her admirers;* Charlie Burns—*is another.*

9. **"The Dead Harlequin,"** a short story in *The Mysterious Mr. Quin*. New York: Dell Publishing, 1979 (c1930, renewed 1958), p. 158–82. ISBN: 0440162467.

ENGLAND, 1926? Mr. Satterthwaite purchases a painting by an up-and-coming artist named Mr. Bristow. He invites the young man to dinner and also invites Colonel Monckton. They discuss the painting, its setting, a photograph that Mr. Satterthwaite had once taken of the same room, and Reggie Charnley's suicide, which had taken place in that room. Mr. Quin makes an appearance in time to see Mr. Satterthwaite work out the question of what happened in Charnley Hall the night of the suicide.

ASSOCIATES: Mr. Frank Bristow—*the artist;* Colonel Monckton; Aspasia Glen—*the actress;*Lady Alix Charnley—*the widow;* and Mr. Quin.

10. **"The Bird with a Broken Wing,"** a short story in *The Mysterious Mr. Quin*. New York: Dell Publishing, 1979 (c1930, renewed 1958), p. 183–203. ISBN: 0440162467.

ENGLAND, 1927? Mr. Satterthwaite receives a message from Mr. Quin via Ouija Board. He follows instructions and accepts Madge Keeley's invitation to Laidell. He joins the house party and is his usually observant self, but he is unable to prevent a murder.

ASSOCIATES: David Keeley—*the host;* Madge—*his daughter;* Doris Coles; Mabelle Annesley and her husband Gerald; Mrs. Graham and her son Roger;

Inspector Winkfield and Dr. Morris—*who come to investigate a death at the house;* Mr. Quin—*who speaks to Mr. Satterthwaite on the train back to London.*

11. "The Man from the Sea," a short story in *The Mysterious Mr. Quin.* New York: Dell Publishing, 1979 (c1930, renewed 1958), p. 204–232. ISBN: 0440162467.

THE ISLAND, 1928? Sixty-nine-year-old Mr. Satterthwaite is feeling old, bored, and dissatisfied. Then he meets a young man who has been told that he has six months to live, the same young man who spoke to Mr. Harley Quin last night. Mr. Satterthwaite knows that he must figure out his lines and do his part to help.

ASSOCIATES: Manuel Anthony Cosdon—*La Paz's gardener;* and the young widow of La Paz.

12. "Harlequin's Lane," a short story in *The Mysterious Mr. Quin.* New York: Dell Publishing, 1979 (c1930, renewed 1958), p. 233–256. ISBN: 0440162467.

ENGLAND, 1929? Mr. Satterthwaite pays a visit to the Denman's of Ashmead. He expected them to be boring and banal. He might have been happier to be proven right than to find out he was wrong.

ASSOCIATES: Mr. Quin—*a guest at Ashmead;* John and Anna Denman—*the hosts;* Molly Stanwell; Claude Wickam—*composer;* Prince Sergius Oranoff; and Lady Roscheimer.

13. "The Harlequin Tea Set," a short story in *The Harlequin Tea Set and Other Stories.* New York: G. P. Putnam's Sons, 1997 (story first published in 1971), p. 235–281. ISBN: 0399142878.

ENGLAND (DOVERTON KINGSBOURNE), 1960? It's been many years, and Mr. Satterthwaite's mind sometimes wanders. He's on a trip to visit his childhood friend Tom Addison, and meet Tom's grandchildren when his car passes a shop called The Harlequin Cafe. When they are forced to stop, he walks back to it to have some tea. Once again he meets his old friend Mr. Harley Quin, who suggests to him that there is still work for him to do.

ASSOCIATES: Mr. Quin—*who is greeted with joy by Mr. Satterthwaite;* Tom Addison—*an old friend of Mr. Satterthwaite;* Beryl Gilliatt; Squadron Leader Simon Gilliatt; Dr. Horton; and Hermes the dog.

CONNER, Mike.

ARCHANGEL

Genres/Themes Crossed: Alternate History, Dystopia X Hard-Boiled Mystery.

Subjects/Character Types: Alternate Earth (Alternate History) X Noir.

Series/Stand-Alone: Stand-alone.

Scene of the Crime: Milltown Minnesota (an alternate Minneapolis), Summer of 1930.

Detective: Danny Constantine has so far been spared by the Hun pandemic. He was a photographer for the *Milltown Journal* and, with the readership down and the manpower shortage, everyone is taking on extra duties; so Danny now writes copy as well as taking photographs. He was married; his wife, Sonia, died three years ago, a victim of the Hun pandemic.

Known Associates: Other people who work for the *Journal* include Walter Burns, who runs the paper; Bing Lockner, the *Journal's* sports editor; Jackie, the copy boy; Sullivan, the rewrite man; and Reno Jones, the 75-year-old watchman at the newspaper. Elisha Cooke works for a rival paper, as managing editor of the *Twin Cities Defender*. Danny lives in Mrs. Lucille Lund's boarding house. Others who live there include Mrs. Lund's grandniece Shirley, who has the chronic form of Hun and will probably bleed out within a year or two; boarders Kal Hromatka and Lou Ravelli, a ballplayer whose team is falling apart as players come down with Hun. His racist tendencies are played upon by Ed Pratt, Kleagle (recruiter) for the North Star Klan Number Two, Knights of the Ku Klux Klan. Charlie Hayes (victim) was a streetcar motorman. The police officers investigating the murder are the sergeant of the major crimes section of the detective division, African American detective Sergeant Dooley Wilson. He is assisted by Detective Francis Lingeborg. Dooley Wilson's wife is Della, and his sons are Marcus and James. The Railroad Tramps include Dakota Pete; Earl "Wall-Eye" Larsen; and Sailor Jack. The Steering Committee of the Greater Northwest Development Company (GNDC) meets at the Interlachen Club. It includes Alexander Crowley, publisher of *Milltown Journal;* Daniel Evald, Head of the Milk Producers' Cooperative; Jason Whitney of Northern States Power; Theo Rostek an African American businessman who owned Rostek's, a popular restaurant on the city's North Side; Reverend Amos V. Ellington of the African Methodist-Episcopal Church is an invited guest (not a board member); their speaker is Dr. Simon Gray, Head of the Hematological Institute of North America, who is working to obtain GNDC funding for construction of an émigré facility in the town of Savage along the Minnesota River southwest of Milltown. While gathering photographs and information for an article at the club, Danny also sees Mrs. Phillips, a rich wife who is at the club in her candystriper outfit, and the Road Petersens, who are dining with the Philipses. The "flour king's daughter," Selena Crockett, runs the Lutheran Mission at the old Milwaukee Road station, does volunteer work for Gray at the Hematological Institute, and reminds Danny of his dead wife. The Archangel is a notorious radio personality, a pirate broadcaster with no call letters and no license, roving from one secret location to the next to send out her evening broadcasts. She criticizes the government, tells stories about a time before the pandemic, and plays records from cities that no longer exist.

Premise: In the Spring of 1919, after years of devastation caused by war and by the Spanish influenza, the first few cases of German hemorrhagic fever were reported in the trenches on the Western Front. In that year, over ninety-million people died of the disease. One theory is that the German high command had it created as a biological weapon, but they lost containment before it could be deployed. It may have been based on the Ebola virus; people who carry the blood of the place where Ebola originated (Africa) are immune. What is known is that the Germans had the facility that was working on germ warfare razed within six months of the beginning of the German hemorrhagic pandemic. All knowledge about the German hemorrhagic fever (now popularly called Hun) was lost, slowing the efforts to find a cure. In the intervening 11 years, it has come in several waves: every two or three years it runs through the population once more, and many of those who survived earlier outbreaks perish. By 1930, over half of the world's population has perished. The United States, in 1912, had a population of one hundred twenty-five million; by 1930, only thirty million remain.

Comment: Many of Michael Conner's short stories have been published in the magazine *Fantasy and Science Fiction.* His novellette "Guide Dog," published in 1991, won a Nebula Award.

Literary Crimes & Chimes: The book explores questions of hatred, particularly racial hatred, brilliantly. There are no saints here. Every character has his own demons; fear, hatred, and bigotry run close to the surface. The book also looks at truth, how much of it can people handle? Accurate (although sensational) information touched off riots in many cities. Peace has been kept in Milltown partly through a disinformation campaign. The local newspaper is complicit. Mr. Crowley, owner of the Milltown *Journal,* is determined to use the newspaper to maintain the illusion of a healthy community. He has gone so far at to ban the word "blood" from the newspaper. The Archangel is a sensation because she tells the truth, and mocks the government's cover-ups. Her broadcasts are wonderful, full of mordant humor. In one, she recites an original poem over the airwaves:

There's a chair where my mother used to be,
There's a chair where my mother sang to me.
Oh she's gone up above,

That dear mother I loved,
Leaving nought where her—well, I can't say it—used to be. (p. 54)

The Archangel continues by musing, "I wonder. Do you think the Post would publish such a poem? Leaving nought where her nought used to be?"

Explorations: Many readers have deduced the Archangel's identity, the murder motive, and the murderer's name(s) before the end of the book. Some of them have been wrong. Where do the clues lead?

What are the social parallels between the world of the Hun pandemic and our world?

What would the world of the Hun pandemic be like today?

What would happen if, in our world, we faced such a pandemic today?

THE CASE

Archangel. New York: TOR, 1995, 350 p. ISBN: 0312857438.

MILLTOWN, MINNESOTA, SUMMER OF 1930. Danny Constantine's photographs would certainly have won awards by now if the world had stayed normal, if the worst thing that had happened had been the war, if the Hun pandemic had not come. He works on his photography as a form of art in his hours away from the newspaper. One night, he naps while his camera takes a long, time-lapse exposure, and when he awakens, he finds a body. The body had been drained of blood, and there are bite marks on the neck, marks that look for all the world like a vampire bite. Something of the murder, and of the murderer, was caught by the camera. As the newspaper stalwartly ignores the murders, Danny uses his job to gain the access he needs to conduct an investigation.

ASSOCIATES: See above.

COOK, Glen.

SWEET SILVER BLUES

Genres/Themes Crossed: Blended Society X Hard-Boiled Mystery.

Subjects/Character Types: Dwarves, Spell-Casters (Sorcerors, Wizards and Witches), Fae (Elves and Trolls), Centaurs, Ghosts, Shape-Changers, Unicorns, Vampires, Zombies, Gods, Aliens X Private Investigators.

Series/Stand-Alone: Neither Garrett's relationships nor his character change very much over the course of the series. However, there are major changes in the lives of some of the villains. To avoid spoilers, it would be best to read these novels in order.

Scene of the Crime: TunFaire, Karenta, and the Cantard, all places in another world that includes supernatural creatures.

Detective: Garrett was a marine in the Cantard wars; he was one of the lucky ones who got out of the military alive. He's 6', 2", about 200 pounds, with ginger hair and blue eyes, and, at the beginning of the series, he's in his early 30s.

Known Associates: Garrett shares his house with the Dead Man, one of the few remaining Loghyr. the Dead Man was assassinated about four centuries ago, but Loghyr spirits take their time departing this world. The Dead Man is telepathic, can use telekinesis, has a memory that encompasses the history of TunFaire, and has knowledge of long-forgotten species and Gods. Garrett keeps the vermin off him, and the Dead Man provides help (when he feels like it) on cases. Morley Dotes is a crossbreed, half human, half dark-elf, who owns the vegetarian restaurant *The Joy House,* and takes occasional jobs as an assassin. Waldo "Saucerhead" Tharpe is a little slow, but is a determined and reasonably honest friend. Wesley "Pokey" Pigotta is a professional contact, not exactly a friend, but Garrett sometimes works with him. Pigotta is first seen in *Bitter Gold Hearts,* and last seen in *Cold Copper Tears.* Max Weider, who owns the brewery, has Garrett on retainer (a little occasional attention keeps his workers from doing too much freelance selling). In *Bitter Gold Hearts,* Dean shows up as Garrett's housekeeper and cook. Tinnie Tate (a red-headed dwarf) begins dating Garrett in *Sweet Silver Blues.* Playmate owns a stable near Garrett's home; he is a trusted ally and always willing to loan Garrett a horse. Winger is big, blonde, and gorgeous, but not too bright. Her ambition is to make her fortune through any means necessary; she's light-fingered and not overly troubled by a conscience. Winger joins the cast in *Dread Brass Shadows.* Chodo Contague is the boss of the organized crime syndicate in TunFaire, and he first appears in *Bitter Gold Hearts.* Garrett is mortified when Chodo shows him favor after Garrett accidentally does something that helps Chodo. Crask and Sadler work as muscle for Chodo's organization; in *Dead Brass Shadows,* they attempt a coup against Chodo and are partially successful. In *Red Iron Nights,* they flee TunFaire, and they are killed in *Faded Steel Heat.* Belinda Contague is Chodo's daughter; she first appears in *Red Iron Nights.* Captain Westman Block of the City Watch is determined to bring law and order to TunFaire; he first appears in *Red Iron Nights.* Pular Singe is a ratgirl and a wonderful tracker. She has a crush on Garrett. She joins the cast in *Faded Steel Heat.*

Premise: In this world, strong magic is fueled by silver, and strong magic equals power. Ninety percent of all silver is mined in the Cantard; the two major powers, Karenta and Venageti, have been at war, attempting to annex the Cantard land, for many years. Mercenary Glory Mooncalled harries both sides, or works with one or the other, at will. Karentine youth are conscripted for a five-year term of service. Many do not return. Other species cannot join the military, and are taking jobs in Karenta, jobs left open because of the death of most of the country's young men. Other species include Elves, Dwarves, Fairies, Trolls, Giants, Ogres, and Pixies. (Any of these can interbreed or breed with humans, creating half-breeds. Some are so common that they are named; for instance, people who are half-giant and half-troll are Grolls. Others are such a conglomeration of species as to be impossible to classify, they are called "uniques.") Ratkind was developed through sorcery. Shapechangers and Vampires also exist, vampires are the result of infection, and the virus can infect only humans.

Comment: There's an in-depth wiki on Glen Cook's books at: http://www.glencook.org/index.php/Main_Page. In a January 17, 2005 interview with Strange Horizons (http://www.strangehorizons.com/2005/20050117/cook-int-a.shtml), Glen Cook was asked if TunFaire is based on an American city in the 1970s. His response was that it had elements from any large city at any time and he used the example of Byzantium: thousands of different neighborhoods and religions, people rioting against one another, crime, murder...

Literary Magic & Mayhem: The Dead Man is similar to Nero Wolfe in many ways, from his laziness to his brilliance, from his huge ego to his attitude towards women. He frequently chides Garrett about his weakness for women, as in this exchange:

> "I take it this one is not that redheaded witch of yours?"
> "Tinnie? No. This one works for the Stormwarden Raver Styx. She has fairy blood. You'll love her at first sight.
> Unlike you, who loves them all at first sight, I am no longer the victim of my flesh, Garrett. There are some advantages to being dead. One gains the ability to reason." (*Bitter Gold Hearts,* p. 8)

Garrett has Archie Goodwin's talents of legwork and accurate reporting, but there's also a bit of Sam Spade and Philip Marlowe in the character. This, from the end of *Dread Brass Shadows,* could have been taken from The Maltese Falcon:

> I touched Carla Lindo's cheek. "I'm sorry, sweetheart. It could have been something."
> "Garrett, you can't do this to me. You loved me. Didn't you?"
> "Maybe I did, some. That don't mean I'll let you use me. That don't mean I'm going to go to hell for you. I wouldn't do that for anybody." (*Dread Brass Shadows,* p. 250)

He has moments in which his outlook is very bleak:

> Lucky me, I'd ended up just getting another lesson revealing the basic blackness lying below the human heart. Once again I'd seen that, given incentive and opportunity, most anybody will jump at the chance to turn wicked. And the wicked will turn wickeder still.
>
> Priests of a thousand cults proclaim the essential goodliness of Man. They must be fools. All I see is people flinging themselves at the chance to do evil. (*Dread Brass Shadows,* p. 251)

But the books aren't noir, partly because Garrett remains an idealist. As he explains to Maya, when she asks him how he can be so naïve and have so many blind spots:

> I nurture them. There are poetic truths as well as scientific truths. They may look silly to you, but I think they deserve to be sustained. (*Cold Copper Tears,* p. 190)

When he's up against the wall, others remind him of the value of his ideals:

> You tend to think as grimly as those you oppose today, Garrett. You're the knight in the nighted land, remember? A rage for justice? That's what you brought when you visited me. Not kill or be killed. (*Bitter Gold Hearts,* p. 246)

Explorations: What role does money play in the narrative? How is it used to illuminate situations, characters, and the society? Does Garrett ever use it as an excuse to cover up other motives?

Karenta is a country in which all the young human men are conscripted, and over half of them never make it home. Who is doing the jobs that they would be doing if they were home? What will happen when the war ends?

THE CASES

1. ***Sweet Silver Blues.*** New York: Roc, 1987, 256 p. ISBN: 0451450701. [Vampires, Centaurs, Unicorns X Private Investigators]

TunFaire and the Cantard, date unknown. After Denny Tate died, his family found a stockpile of gold, and a registered will. It names Denny's father, Willard and his friend, Garrett, as the executors of his estate. Denny left everything except the executor's fees to Kayean Kronk, a woman that no one in his family ever met. Willard Tate wants Garrett to find the woman and bring her to TunFaire. Garrett is ready to tell him "no" when Willard mentions that the executor's fees are 10 percent of the estate. Garrett's search takes him back into the Cantard, right into the middle of the war zone in search of Kayean Kronk, a woman Garrett once loved some time before she met Denny.

ASSOCIATES: The Dead Man—*Loghyr, on his way to being deceased, Garrett's partner;* Willard—*part elvish, the Tate family's Patriarch, and head of the family business (they're shoe-makers);* Rose—*his bad-tempered daughter;* Tinnie—*his niece;* Lester—*his brother;* Morley Dotes—*(half dark-elf) who Garrett trusts to guard his back in a war zone.* The Roze triplets: Dojango (the short one), Marsha, and Doris—*grolls, hired by Morley.* Saucerhead Tharpe and Spiney Prevallet—*who were originally hired by Rose;* Vasco and Quinn—*who know that Denny had been able to predict the silver market, and they are desperate to put their hands on his system;* Barbera—*another old soldier, hired by Vasco to soften up Garrett;* Playmate—*who gives Garrett some traveling advice;* Master Arbanos—*skipper of Binkey's Sequin;* Zeck Zack—*centaur;* Clement—*vampire;* and Valentine Permanos—*vampire;* Old Witch; Father Rhyme; Father Mike; and brevet-Colonel Kayeth Kronk. Glory Mooncalled works with bands of centaurs to raid both armies.

2. ***Bitter Gold Hearts.*** New York: Penguin, 1988, 253 p. ISBN: 0451450728. [Spell-Casters (Sorcerers), Trolls, Fae X Private Investigators]

TUNFAIRE, DATE UNKNOWN. Amiranda Crest (half-fairy) was sent by Domina Willa Dount to fetch Garrett, with 100 gold marks as bait. Garrett is feeling contrary, and turns her down, until she mentions that the case involves a kidnapping. Garrett has built something of a reputation as a fair broker who is likely to get kidnapping victims back in one piece, or track down the kidnappers if things go badly. Once it is known that he is involved, the chances of recovering the victim are appreciably increased. The Stormwarden's 23-year-old son, Karl, is the victim.

ASSOCIATES: The Dead Man—*Loghyr, Garrett's partner;* Dean—*who comes in daily to work as housekeeper and cook.*

Stormwarden Raver Styx—*Garrett's client;* Amiranda Crest—*a half-fairy who works for the Stormwarden;* Domina Willa Dount—*the Stormwarden's secretary;* Baronet daPena—*the Stormwarden's consort;* Amanda—*the Stormwarden's daughter;* Mr. Slauce and Courter—*flunkies;* and Karl daPena—*the kidnapping victim.*

Saucerhead Tharpe—*who almost dies, but is saved by a witch and ends up in the Bledsoe Infirmary;* Shaggoth—*troll, the witch's assistant.*

Morley Dotes—*a friend of Garrett;* Blood, Sarge, and Puddle—*Morley's regular thugs;* Doris and Marsha—*the grolls;* Crask and Saddler—*Crime Lord Chodo Contague's enforcers;* Gorgeous and Skredli—*half-breed ogres who were friends of Donni Pell;* Donni Pell—*who worked at Lettie Faren's whorehouse.*

Playmate—*who owns the stable;* Pokey Pigotta—*a private investigator;* and Lord Gameleon—*Karl daPena Senior's brother.*

3. *Cold Copper Tears.* New York: NAL, 1988, 255 p. ISBN: 0451157737. [Spell-Casters (Sorcerers) X Private Investigators]

TUNFAIRE, DATE UNKNOWN. A friend gave Jill Craight a small box for safekeeping. Now he's disappeared, and Jill is being watched. There have been three attempts at theft by someone breaking into her apartment. She wants it stopped. Garrett's second client is Magnus Peridont, the Grand Inquisitor, who is both a priest and a sorcerer. The Grand Inquisitor sees some of the current unrest as a general attack on faith. It's currently attacking the Orthodox Church, but Peridont believes that it will turn upon his church in time. He wants to know who or what is behind the attack. In the course of his investigation, Garrett farms out some of the surveillance work to Pokey Pigotta; Pigotta returns his retainer when he gets a better offer. He should have stuck with Garrett's job. Garrett feels a certain interest in finding out what happened to Pigotta, why it happened, and who's behind it. Along the way, Garrett finds, to his dismay, that his interests run parallel with Chodo's once again.

ASSOCIATES: The Dead Man—*a dying Loghyr who is Garrett's partner;* Dean—*Garrett's housekeeper and cook;* Playmate—*who could have been a preacher, but he's running a stable;* Jill Craight—*a.k.a. Hester Podegill, one of Garrett's clients;* Morley Dotes—*half dark-elf who helps Garrett;* Pokey Pigotta—*who accepts an assignment from Garrett;* Saucerhead Tharpe—*who takes over the job originally given to Pigotta.*

Brother Jercé—*who hired Snowball's gang of half-elves to watch Garrett and to take him out if he were approached by the Grand Inquisitor;* Eighteen-year-old Maya—*leader of the gang The Sisters of Doom;* Tey Koto—*Maya's second in command.*

Shote—*ratman, he is recommended as a stalker;* Magister Peridont and Peridontu, Altodeoria Princeps—*(which translates roughly as Sorcerer Prince of the City of God), known commonly as Magnus Peridont or the Grand Inquisitor, is one of Garrett's clients;* Sampson—*heir to the Grand Inquisitor's office.*

Warden Agire—*who is missing;* Crask and Saddler—*Crime Kingpin Chodo Contague's enforcers, look for a way to bring down a Loghyr.* Glory Mooncalled has declared the Cantard an independent republic.

4. *Old Tin Sorrows.* New York: NAL, 1989, 252 p. ISBN: 0451160134. [Draugs (Zombies who aren't under anyone's control), Ghosts X Private Investigators]

TUNFAIRE, DATE UNKNOWN. Sergeant Blake Peters saved Garrett's life when they served together in the Cantard. When the Sergeant, now retired, asks Garrett to take a job Garrett feels that he must accept. Peters works on the estate of General Stantnor, and believes that the General is being poisoned. Stantnor had a reputation as a sharp and outspoken man. Now he's set up a very foolish and dangerous situation: he has written a will in which he leaves instructions that his estate be split up on his death. Half will go to his daughter, the rest to be split evenly between the men who were his comrades who now work on his estate. The number of people working on the estate has dropped from 18 to 11, many having simply disappeared. The people who are left are determined to stay. Most of them cope relatively well, but Braden is suffering from posttraumatic stress syndrome. He paints amazing and revealing paintings, but has a hard time around people.

ASSOCIATES: Morley Dotes—*half dark-elf, assists Garrett;* Saucerhead Tharpe—*accepts assignments from Garrett;* Doc Stone—*physician;* Doctor Doom—*a mixture of troll and other breeds, he works as an exorcist;* triplets Doris, Marsha, and Dojango Roze—*grolls who accept assignments from Garrett.*

The General's household includes Cook—*part troll;* Sergeant Blake Peters—*a.k.a. "Black Pete";* Miss Jennifer—*the General's daughter;* Eleanor—*deceased, the General's wife;* Dellwood; Art Chain; Freidel Kaid; Tyler; Wayne; and Snake Braden—*all work in the house or on the grounds.*

Maya—*of the gang The Sisters of Doom, is interested in Garrett.*

Glory Mooncalled attacked the city of Full Harbor. He lost. Now the armies are chasing him back into his own territory.

5. *Dread Brass Shadows.* New York: Roc, 1990, 256 p. ISBN: 0451450086.
[Spell-Casters (Sorcery), Shape-Changers X Private Investigators]

TUNFAIRE, DATE UNKNOWN. It's raining women, or at least it seems as if it is. In the space of a couple of days, five beautiful women (four of them redheads) show up on Garrett's doorstep. Unfortunately, the first (Tinnie Tate) was stabbed, the second fell through the doorway unconscious, undressed and unnamed, and then fled while he was busy with the third (Winger), who was trying to rob him. The fourth and fifth both claim to be Carla Lindo Ramada. Garrett believes that only the last one was telling the truth; she had freckles and he is partial to freckles. Winger was trying to find the Book of Dreams, created by a sorceress known as Serpent. Apparently, this book gives directions for shape-changing into any number of people (one is Carla Lindo); and Garrett soon realizes that he's in one of the most dangerous cases of his life, a case in which any one of his closest colleagues could turn out to be his enemy.

Garrett knows that he must find the *Book of Dreams* quickly. Once Chodo learns of its properties he will focus all of his resources on finding the book. In the wrong hands it would change the balance of power in TunFaire. Chodo's enforcers, Crask and Saddler, have a plan that would neutralize Chodo, and Garrett is so worried that he's beginning to think it might be a good idea.

Associates: Dean—*Garrett's housekeeper and cook;* the Dead Man—*Loghyr, is Garrett's partner;* Gnorst Gnorst—*the Dead Man's dwarf contact;* Morley Dotes and Saucerhead Tharpe—*who have concerns regarding Garrett's health;* Tinnie Tate—*Garrett's on-again, off-again girlfriend;* Tinnie's Uncle Willard—*who has reservations about the match.*

Winger—*who is looking for a Book of Dreams, thought to have been stolen by Holme Blaine;* Fido Easterman—*who also wants the book;* Crime Lord Chodo Contague—*who is certain to want the book as soon as he learns about it;* Saddler and Crask—*Chodo's chief enforcers;* Squirrel—*who also worked for Chodo.*

Carla Lindo Ramada—*the chambermaid in the household of Lord Baron Cleon Stonecipher.*

People unfriendly to Garrett include: Elmore Flounce; Keem Lost Knife—*ratman;* and Zachery Hoe—*ogre.*

Glory Mooncalled seems to be having trouble holding the Cantard. Creatures have fled the area and now there are mammoths, sabertooth tigers, werewolves, and thunder lizards approaching the city—and centaurs are within its walls.

6. ***Red Iron Nights.*** New York: Roc, 1991, 270 p. ISBN: 0451451082. [Spell-Casters (Sorcerors, Curses) X Private Investigators]

TunFaire, date unknown. Barking Dog Amato has been haranguing the crowds with his conspiracy theories for years. He's a harmless loon, so why would anyone throw him in prison? Why would anyone hire Garrett to follow him when he's released? It's ridiculous, but it pays three marks a day. Garrett is offered a second job that he doesn't want by Captain Block of the Watch. There's a serial killer targeting young women from the Hill, only they were not on the Hill when he catches up with them. They were slumming, probably a little wild and a lot stupid; but they don't deserve the death the killer gives them. One frightening aspect is that he's keeping their blood. The Watch isn't sure what to make of the crimes, but they know they need the criminal stopped and caught, fast.

Associates: The Dead Man—*Loghyr, Garrett's partner;* Dean—*Garrett's housekeeper and cook, is moving into Garrett's house;* Morley Dotes and Saucerhead Tharpe—*who work with Garrett to foil men who are trying to snatch Belinda Contague;* Belinda Contague—*Chodo's daughter;* Crime Kingpin Chodo Contague—*is still breathing;* Saddler and Crask—*Chodo's enforcers, are also still breathing, which is surprising, since they had done their best to depose Chodo.*

Bishoff Hullar—*who hires Garrett to watch a man who is considered a lunatic;* Kropotkin Amato—*a.k.a. Barking Dog Amato, the lunatic;* Cunch—*the dwarf bartender at Hullar's place;* Candy and Sas—*the girls who work there;* Westman Block—*Captain of the Watch, he hires Garrett;* Downtown

Billy Byrd—*who may accept money for information;* Other members of the Watch include: Laudermill, Price Ripley, Elvis Winchell, Relway (half-dwarf), and Spike (ratman).

Saucerhead Tharpe—*who accepts jobs from Garrett;* Licks—*the musician;* Sarge and Puddle—*Morley's employees;* Spud—*Morley's nephew;* Playmate—*stable-owner;* Mr. Linden Atwood—*coach-maker.* Prince Rupert—*who joins the hunt.*

Both Karenta and Venageti forces left their strongholds to chase Glory Mooncalled into the Cantard. Glory Mooncalled's forces then struck at both the Karenta and Venageti strongholds, taking Full Harbor (which had been in Karentine hands). At the end of the book, the news from the war is that the morCartha sided with Karenta and turned the tide. In TunFaire, a rebellion began, but was put down by the Watch. Morley sends over a gift for Garrett, a parrot.

7. ***Deadly Quicksilver Lies.*** New York: Roc, 1994, 347 p. ISBN: 0451453050. [Spell-Casters X Private Investigators]

TUNFAIRE, DATE UNKNOWN. Maggie Jenn, once the mistress of King Teodoric IV, hired Garrett to find her runaway daughter, Justina. It turns out that Justina (who calls herself Emerald) took a book with her when she left. The book is one of a trilogy, and there is supposed to be information in the trilogy that reveals the location of a treasure. Many factions are interested in the treasure, and all seem sure that Garrett will lead them to the books. Garrett tries to find the truth but is hampered by people who are mired in deceit.

ASSOCIATES: The Dead Man—*Loghyr, Garrett's partner;.* Dean—*Garrett's housekeeper, is out of town.*

Winger—*who will do whatever it takes to make her fortune;* Maggie Jenn—*who hires Garrett to find her daughter;* Justina—*a.k.a. Emerald, Maggie Jenn's daughter, she left her mother's home with a priceless book;* Mugwump, Zeke, and Laurie—*all work for Maggie Jenn;* Quefours—*who accompanied Justina the first time she took her stolen book into Wixon & White's;* Robin and Penny—*who own the Wixon & White's occult supplies store.*

Morley Dotes—*who changes the name of his restaurant to The Palms;* Sarge and Puddle—*who still work for Dotes;* Eggwhite—*who fed psychedelic salad to Playmate;* Playmate—*who does not react well to psychedelic salad;* Spud—*Morley's nephew.*

Grange Cleaver—*who gets Garrett thrown into the mental ward of the Bledsoe;* Dr. Chastity Blaine, Slither, and Ivy—*were all in the Bledsoe;* Dr. Blaine's father—*Firelord Fox Direheart, once owned one of the missing books;* Saucerhead Tharpe—*acts as bodyguard for Dr. Blaine.*

Librarian Linda Lee Luther—*who is also searching for one of the books;* "Handsome"—*a.k.a. Tilly Nooks, from Garrett's old neighborhood helps him out with a few spells;* Eight-year-old Becky Frierka—*a neighborhood kid, trades information to Garrett in return for his buying her dinner;* Colonel Westman Block and Relway of the Watch—*who are trying to keep order in the city, even as dissension rises;* Elias Davenport and Morongo North English—*racists wanting to rid the city of non-humans.*

Glory Mooncalled's headquarters was captured. He has disappeared.

8. ***Petty Pewter Gods.*** New York: Roc, 1995, 296 p. ISBN: 0451454782. [Gods X Private Investigators]

TunFaire, date unknown. Refugees to TunFaire have brought their own gods. Room on the Street of Gods was already tight; the new additions have forced the issue—someone has to go. Without even casual attention from passers-by, the gods who are no longer worshipped gradually fade away or become mortals. The two pantheons with the fewest existing worshippers are the Shayir and the Godoroth. A council of Gods has determined that there will be a competition, the winner will remain on the street, the other will be forced out. The competition is to find a key that's invisible to immortal eyes. It will open a temple on the Street of Gods. The Godoroth want to hire Garrett to find it. The Shayir have a better idea, they want to hire Garrett to find it for them.

TunFaire is on the brink of exploding, The Call, a radical fringe "human-rights" group (i.e. a hate group that targets non-humans), is adding to the chaos; there are riots in the city.

Associates: The Dead Man—*Loghyr, Garrett's partner;* Dean—*Garrett's housekeeper, is appalled at the mess the house is in when he returns from his trip;* Mr. Big—*the Parrot, is a nuisance for Garrett and a convenience for the Dead Man.* Saucerhead Tharpe—*takes assignments from Garrett and the Dead Man;* Morley Dotes—*half dark-elf, also helps on the case;* Sarge and Puddle—*Dote's employees;* and Winger—*who helps with the case.*

The surviving pantheon of the Godoroth (patron gods of the Hahr) include: Imar and Imarra—*who lead this pantheon;* Magador—*the destroyer;* Star—*the temptress;* Jorken—*the messenger;* Abyss—*the coach driver;* and Daiged, Rhogiro, and Ringo—*who are other servants of these Gods.* Shinrise the Destroyer—*a.k.a. Bogge, is Imara's lover.*

The Shayir, once worshipped by the ox-riders of Gritn, include: Father Lang—*their leader;* Tobrit—*the Strayer;* Quilrag—*the Shadow;* Black Mona, Nog, Lila, and Dimna.

Cat—*a demigoddess;* Fourteen—*the cherub who accompanies her;* Saint Strait—*patron of seekers after wisdom, is a member of the Commission that arbitrates the entry and exit of mainstream religions onto the Street of Gods;* Adeth—*whose name means treachery;* Melton Carnifan—*the Secretary to His Holiness;* No-Neck—*who works on the Street of Gods;* Librarian Linda Lee—*who reads to the Dead Man;* Pappy "Tooms" Toomey—*an old comrade of Garrett's, he recognizes Garrett and saves him from the mob.*

The Dead Man believes that Glory Mooncalled is in TunFaire and is orchestrating some of the trouble.

9. ***Faded Steel Heat.*** New York: Roc, 1999, 356 p. ISBN: 0451454790. [Trolls X Private Investigators]

TUNFAIRE, DATE UNKNOWN. After three generations of war, Karenta and Venageti are finally at peace. Karenta conscripted every young human male for five years; many went to war and never returned. This caused a labor shortage in Karenta, and non-humans filled in. Now the soldiers are back and they feel that they deserve the jobs. There is violence in the streets, even rioting. The Call, supposedly a human rights organization, but mostly a hate group that targets non-humans, sends strong-arm representatives to convince businesses to fire long serving non-human employees and fill their jobs with humans. The Call also works to convince non-humans that they would have happier (and longer) lives if they left TunFaire. Weider's Brewery, the business that has Garrett on retainer, seems to be a target of The Call. Max Weider didn't call for help, but his youngest daughter, Alyx, comes to tell Garrett that her father needs his help. In the course of this investigation, Garrett uncovers a conspiracy of shape-shifters, and, once they're uncovered, many involved in the case want to wipe them out. However, there are also those who want to find a way to use the shapeshifters. Stormwarden Perilous Spite manages to take some of them into custody.

ASSOCIATES: The Dead Man—*Loghyr, Garrett's partner;* Dean Creech—*Garrett's housekeeper;* Mr. Big—*the Parrot, accompanies Garrett;* Tinnie Tate—*Garrett's on-again, off-again girlfriend;* Max Weider—*owner of Weider's Brewery, he has Garrett on retainer;* Hannah—*Max's wife, she is bedridden and terminally ill;* Kittyjo—*one of Max and Hannah's daughters;* Alyx Weider—*a friend of Tinnie, Max Weider's daughter;* Giorgi "Nicks" Nicholas—*a friend of Tinnie's, engaged to marry Ty Weider;* Ty Weider—*Alyx' brother;* The Weider family lost one son to the war (Tad is dead), one returned insane (Tom), and Ty returned sane, but maimed (he's confined to a wheelchair). Manvil Gilbey, Geral Diar, Skibber Kessel, Lucas Vloclaw, Mr. Burkel, Sparky, and Zardo—*all work for Max Weider;* Lancelyn Mac—*Ty's full time assistant;* Gerris Genord—*the Weider's majordomo;* Neersa Bintor—*the cook who rules the Weider kitchen.*

Morengo North English—*leads The Call;* Tama Montezuma—*who attends Ty and Nick's engagement party with her purported uncle Morengo North English;*.Stormwarden Perilous Spite—*is one of the guests of honor at the party;* Colonel Moches Theverly—*who is active in The Call;* Bondurant Altoona—*who is also active in the rightist movement;* Stucker—*gatekeeper at The Call's*

Institute for Racial Purity; Venable—*who runs security;* Tollie—*who manages livestock;* Ed Nagit—*one of Morengo's lieutenants.*

Colonel Norton Valsung—*heads The Black Dragon Valsung Free Company;* Carter Stockwell and Trace Wendover—*members of the company.*

Captain Westman Block—*who runs the Watch;* Relway—*who is a "unique" (an unidentifiable mix of species) he heads up the secret police;* and Jirek—*a unique, he works for the police.*

Crask and Saddler—*who are back in town, they have an unhealthy interest in Belinda Contague;* Belinda Contague—*daughter of Crime Lord Chodo;* Two Toes Harker—*Belinda's driver.*

Morley Dotes (half dark-elf), Saucerhead Tharpe, Winger, and librarian Linda Lee—*are all hired by the Dead Man;* Sarge and Puddle—*are Morley's employees.*

Reliance—*ratperson, leader of the ratpeople in TunFaire;* Pular Singe—*ratwoman, Reliance's best tracker;* Fenibro—*ratman, Pular's cousin, translates for her.*

Medford Shale—*Garrett's great-granduncle;* Miss Quipo Trim—*who works at the Heaven's Gate Resthome;* Mr. Will Storey and Mr. Trail—*veterans.*

The Dead Man goes to great lengths to meet his idol, Glory Mooncalled, who may be working to foment dissent in TunFaire.

10. ***Angry Lead Skies.*** New York: Roc, c2002, 364 p. ISBN: 0451458753. [Aliens X Private Investigators]

TunFaire, date unknown. Big-hearted Playmate took Cypres "Kip" Prose under his wing. Kip loved horses, and then he turned to inventing. His creations became progressively more bizarre. Playmate is concerned because someone has been stalking Kip and he finally brings Kip to Garrett after an attempted kidnapping. The next attempt was successful, and Garrett makes every effort to recover the kid. In the course of his investigation, Garrett finds Visitors, who come from further away than he can imagine. Apparently they have some sort of prime directive that makes it unlawful to share technological information with the primitive inhabitants of TunFaire. When Lastyr and Noodiss crashed on this planet, they determined that their ship could not be fixed with the available technology. They decided to do something about that by feeding information to Kip. The police of their world were dispatched to track Lastyr and Noodiss down; Kip is in danger from beings with technology far in advance of anything that could be found in TunFaire.

At the end of the book Garrett thinks of a way to capitalize on one of Kip's inventions. If it works it would profit the impoverished Prose family; give an interest in life to Max Weider; and help the Tates by replacing the business they lost when the war ended and the army stopped ordering the boots that they manufactured.

ASSOCIATES: The Dead Man—*Loghyr, Garrett's partner;* Dean Creech—*Garrett's housekeeper;* Mr. Big—*the #%^@! Parrot, accompanies Garret everywhere.* (At the end of the case, Garrett receives a payment better than anything he had expected; one of the aliens absconds with the bird.) Tinnie Tate—*Garrett's on-again, off-again girlfriend;* Katie Shaver—*who piques Garrett's interest;* Evas, Fasfir, and Woderact—*aliens who Garrett finds remarkable.*

Playmate Wheeler—*who has been a friend of Garrett ever since Garrett managed to save him from financial ruin;* Cypres "Kip" Prose—*who was befriended by Playmate;* Lastyr and Noodiss—*aliens; Kip's friends;* Casey—*alien, an officer in pursuit of Lastyr and Noodiss.*

Kayne Prose—*Kip's mother;* Cassie Doap—*her daughter;* Rhafi—*Kayne's other son;* Bic Gonlit—*a bounty hunter with unusual personal habits and magic boots;* Morley Dotes—*half dark-elf, who the Dead Man sends to check on Garrett's safety;* Puddle and Sarge—*work for Dotes;* Saucerhead Tharpe—*also searches for Garrett;* Pular Singe—*ratwoman, she escaped the influence of the ratpeople gang and the boss wants her back;* Winger—*who wants a piece of the action.*

Chodo Contague—*who is still considered a Kingpin of Crime, has a birthday party;* Belinda Contague—*Chodo's daughter;* triplets Dojango Rose, Marsha, and Doris—*grolls, who acquire Kip's two-wheeler man-hauling cart.*

Reliance—*ratman, head of the local ratpeople gang, he has lost face because of Pular Singe's defection;* Pound Humility—*ratman, a.k.a. John Stretch is challenging Reliance's leadership.*

Melondie and Shakespear Kadare—*pixies, they seem to be good at keeping track of whatever interests them;* Max Weider—*who is intrigued by Garrett's business idea;* Alyx—*his daughter;* Manvil Gilbey—*Max's righthand man;* Willard Tate—*uncle of Tinnie Tate;* Lister Tate—*a lawyer in the Tate family;* Harvester Tamisk—*an attorney who used to work for Chodo;* and Congo Greeve—*an attorney sent by Weider to assist Garrett.*

Colonel Westman Block—*who heads up the Watch;* Deal Relway—*a unique who heads the secret police.*

11. ***Whispering Nickel Idols.*** New York: New American Library, c2005, 359 p. ISBN: 0451459741. [Spell-Casters X Private Investigators]

TUNFAIRE, DATE UNKNOWN. For over a year, Belinda Contague has been ruling the largest criminal organization in TunFaire by pretending that her father Chodo is still in charge and that she's just transmitting his orders. Throughout that time, Chodo has been comatose, rarely seen by anyone but her, occasionally rolled out, drooling, in a wheelchair. Belinda decided to change all that by throwing him a sixtieth birthday party and inviting everyone. The plan was for her to unveil her father's condition, and make it clear to everyone that she has been, and will continue to be, the head of the

Contague criminal syndicate. There have been some exotic recent killings in TunFaire: several people have died of spontaneous human combustion. One of the kitchen workers at Chodo's birthday party spontaneously combusts, throwing the event into chaos. The place catches fire and the guests stampede. In the confusion, Belinda loses Chodo. Every minor and major criminal in TunFaire is interested in finding him. Several believe that Garrett is hot on Chodo's trail and devote themselves to using Garrett to find Chodo. In the ensuing (and violent) confusion much of the underworld of TunFaire is reorganized and Garrett pays off his debt to Chodo in a surprising way.

ASSOCIATES: The Dead Man—*Loghyr, Garrett's partner;* Dean Creech—*Garrett's housekeeper;* Melondie Kadare, Marienne, and Hollybell—*are a few of the pixies who nest under the eaves of Garrett's home;* Pular Singe—*ratwoman, who has become a minor (live-in) partner in Garrett's investigation business;* Pound Humility—*a.k.a. John Stretch, Pular's brother, is the head of the local gang of ratpeople.*

Penny Dreadful—*the last priestess of A-Lat, leaves a litter of sacred kittens in Dean's care;* Deacon Osgood—*who follows a rival god. A-Laf.*

Morley Dotes—*half dark-elf, owns The Palms restaurant and is doing the catering for Chodo's birthday bash;* Sarge, Puddle, Skif, Theodore, and Trash Blaser—*work for Morley;* Mrs. Buy Claxton—*who spontaneously combusts;* Rory Sculdyte and Teacher White—*Chodo's underbosses;* Attorney Harvester Temisk—*who has a theory that Chodo's coma is not natural, which opens up the question of whether or not it's a spell that could be broken.*

Colonel Westman Block—*heads the Watch;* Deal Relway—*Director of the secret police (The Unpublished Committee for Royal Security), whom people in the street call "Relway's Runners";* Scithe—*a Runner;* Captain Ramey List—*who has a political appointment to the Watch.*

Merry Sculdyte—Rory Sculdyte's stupid but enthusiastically homicidal brother; Tizzy Baggs's sister—*Merry's wife;* Green Bean Ractic—*who reports to Tizzie Baggs;* Squint Vrolet—*a minor numbers runner for Green Bean Ractic.* Plenty Hart, Bobo Negry, Fish Bass, and Brett Batt—*are also Rory's men;* Spider Webb, Original Dick, and Vernor Choke—*are Teacher White's enforcers;* Kolda—*the herbalist, is employed by Teacher White to poison Teacher's enemies;* Brother Brittegurn Brittigarn—*of the Temple of Eis and Igory is a light-fingered expert on the religions of Ymber.*

Welby Dell and Skelington (a.k.a. Emmaus P. Brix)—*watch Garrett's house;* Saucerhead Tharpe—*who does some work for Garrett;* Winger—*who is being shadowed by Jon Salvation;* Jon Salvation—*who is taking notes for a biography of Winger;* Junker Mulclar—*mends Garrett's front door;* Silverman—*a jeweler;* Mrs. Sofgienec Cardonlos—*Garrett's nosy neighbor, is revealed to be a spy for the Watch.*

12. ***Cruel Zinc Melodies.*** New York: New American Library, 2008, 405 p. ISBN: 9780451461926. [Spell-Casters X Private Investigators]

TunFaire, Winter, date unknown. Max Weider's enthusiasm for his new venture has restored his *joie de vivre.* He's going to open a theater in TunFaire. His construction crew is working on a huge building, now almost complete. When it opens it will be named *The World,* and Max hopes that all of TunFaire will come to see the plays. The first play is scheduled to open in the spring, and actresses are rehearsing their lines.

There are a few problems. The theater seems to be haunted, infested by mammoth bugs and under attack by gangs looking for protection money. There have long been rumors of ghosts, and many people have heard music when there's no one playing. Construction workers report seeing gigantic cockroaches on the site. There have been incidents of sabotage to the construction and vandalism to the building. Max hires Garrett to get the nonsense stopped. The show must go on!

Garrett begins with sensible plans (all his friends are stunned) to get rid of the bugs. He finds that the problems are much more complicated, powerful, and nastier than anything that he had expected. A group of sorcerers (worse than regular sorcerers, teenage sorcerers) have been meddling with reality. The group calls themselves "the Faction." They started as a mutual-support group, and at least one of them was in a desperate situation and needed that support. These young sorcerers have powers that are developing, and many have been raised by stunningly amoral parents. They have enough knowledge of and respect for Garrett that they've applied their skills to developing ways to shield themselves from his investigations. They are aware of the Dead Man's capabilities, and they manufactured a way to foil his efforts to find the truth. Another of their projects has been to find a way to acquire the power of mind-reading for themselves. They've become a force in their own right, but they don't have the wisdom or the experience to monitor their work to see if there are unintended consequences. They are entirely unaware of the potential apocalypse that their carelessness is about to unleash on the city of TunFaire.

In this entry in the series, Garrett copes with a couple of situations that could become personal disasters. In the first, he attracts the interest of a Prince and then decides to turn down the Prince's job offer. Garrett has many sources of income. He takes jobs as an investigator, he draws a retainer from Max, and he owns a stake of the Manufactory, which makes and sells the three-wheeled cycles that Kip invented. When Prince Rupert offers him an ongoing job that requires him to give up his other work, Garrett is not really tempted.

Another potential personal disaster involves Tinnie. Her relationship with Garrett is complex. They've both decided that their relationship is monogamous, and it looks as if that may be permanent. Both of them are uncomfortable with the idea of a legal commitment, but are beginning to wonder if it's time to get married. In the midst of this, Pular Singe, working as Garrett's accountant, discovers anomalies in the Manufactory's financial records. Someone has been skimming the profits before making payments to the business's stakeholders. Tinnie is the firm's treasurer. Garrett approaches the matter with diplomacy. (There are several passages in this book when both he and Tinnie are surprised by their own maturity.) He doesn't want Tinnie to get angry, but he also doesn't want to see her holding the bag when others figure out that they're being robbed.

ASSOCIATES: The Dead Man—*Loghyr, Garrett's partner;* Dean Creech—*Garrett's housekeeper;* Pular Singe—*ratwoman, keeps Garrett's books;* Joe Kerr—*a neighborhood boy, who carries messages for Garrett.*

The actresses determined to see the theater completed on time include: Alex Weider—*Max Weider's daughter;* Tinnie Tate—*Garrett's girlfriend;* Cassie Doap—*Kip Prose's sister;* Bobby Wilt—*who reminds Dean of someone he used to know;* and Lindy Zhang—*one of Tinnie's quieter friends.*

Heather Soames—*Manvil Gilbey's "niece", is slated to work as the theater manager;* Jon Salvation—*a.k.a. Pilsuds Vilchik, is the playwright, who has been nicknamed "The Remora" because of the way he follows Winger around.*

Gerry—*who works for Max Weider at the brewery;* Handsome—*a.k.a. Brent Talanta, the guard;* Figgie Joe—*the cook;* Luther—*the foreman at The World construction site;* Myndra Merkel and Bambi Fardanse—*who are fired by Garrett on behalf of Max;* Hector—*a "unique" (a combination of so many breeds that it is unlikely that there is another like him) works as doorman at Max's home;* Manvil Gilbey—*Max's second in command.*

Garrett and the Dead Man employ: John Stretch—*a.k.a. Pound Humility, a ratperson who can mentally communicate with and control rats;* Saucerhead Tharpe; Belle "Bill" Chimes—*necromancer and sorcerer;* Rockpile; Rindt Grinblatt—*the dwarf;* Mindie—*Rindt's daughter;* and Rocky—*the troll.*

Prince Rupert—*who takes an interest in TunFaire's law and order;* Colonel Westman Block—*Head of the City Watch, the Civil Guard, and TunFaire's secret police;* Deal Relway—*mixed ancestry, possibly a unique, The Director of the Civil Guard;* Mr. Sicthe—*Civil Guard Subaltern who tells Garrett that Relway is becoming a recluse, rarely leaving his office in the Al-Khar prison;* Ingram Grahm, Git, Bank, Mistry, and Teagarden—*are other members of the Civil Guard;* and Linton Suggs—*a guard at Al-Khar.*

Cypres "Kip" Prose—*a 17 or 18 years old genius, has forged friendships with other talented, brilliant teenage misfits to develop "the Faction."* Current and past members of the Faction include: Kevans—*a girl who was encouraged to try to pass as a boy by her mother;* Mutter—*a boy who wants to be a girl;* Teddy;

Zardoz; Heck; Spiffy; Berbain; Berbach; and Slump. Kyra Tate—*Tinnie's 16-year-old niece, is Kip's girlfriend.*

Sorcerers involved include: Windwalker, Furious Tide of Light—*Kevans's mother;* Barate Algarda—*a.k.a. Big Bruno, the father of WindWalker, Furious Tide of Light, he works as her "fixer";* Link Dierber, Firebringer; Schnook Avery; and Shadowslinger—*grandmother of Berbain, Berbach, WindWalker, Kevans Algarda, and Strake Welco (Smokeman).*

People trying to figure out how to make money from *The World* theater include the Stompers gang; Snoots Gitto; Morley Dotes—*half dark-elf restauranteur, who opens Morley's Velvet Curtain;* and Belinda Contague—*mob boss.*

Tribune "Lurking" Felhske—*investigator;* Sarge and Puddle—*employees of Morley Dotes;* Mr. Jan—*Garrett's tailor;* Playmate—*stable owner;* Melondie Kadare—*queen of the local pixies;* and Eleanor—*deceased, who may find happiness at last.*

Tinnie's Uncle Archer and Rose Tate never appear but were fiddling the Manufactory's books, an action which may have repercussions in future novels.)

COTTERILL, Colin.

THE CORONER'S LUNCH

Genres/Themes Crossed: Paranormal X Traditional Mystery.

Subjects/Character Types: Shaman, Ghosts X Government investigator (Coroner).

Series/Stand-Alone: There are major changes in Dr. Siri's abilities, his life, and his relationships over the course of the series. The novels should be read in order.

Scene of the Crime: People's Democratic Republic of Laos, 1976.

Detective: Dr. Siri, a doubting communist, a reluctant coroner, and a psychic whose powers have lain dormant for the first 72 years of his life. After the revolution the Party conscripted Dr. Siri to serve as the Republic's Chief Police Coroner, Siri could have gone his entire life without even being aware of his psychic gifts, but once he starts working with the dead, those gifts are awakened. Siri's reverence for the truth, his need to help the dead find peace, and his disrespect toward the blunderers of the new regime make him a poorly fitting cog in the government machine.

Known Associates: Dtui Vongheuan and Mr. Geung, Dr. Siri's assistants at the morgue, are both colleagues and friends. The local chemistry teacher,

Teacher Oum, is always ready to offer Dr. Siri unofficial aid. Comrade Civilai is Dr. Siri's closest friend in the politburo. Judge Haeng is Dr. Siri's unfortunate boss. Inspector Phosy is a policeman who shares more of Dr. Siri's worldview than either expected. Auntie Lah has a romantic interest in Dr. Siri, but he is still haunted (literally) by the memory of Boua, his wife. In *Anarchy and Old Dogs,* noodle-shop owner Daeng helps Siri recover some of his past and then follows him to Vientiane. Saloop (Dr. Siri's dog) joins his household in the course of *The Coroner's Lunch* and leaves it in *Thirty-three Teeth.*

Premise: Dr. Siri had joined the Pathet Lao as a young man, straight out of medical school, and had served as their doctor in caves and in jungles for 46 years. He was in his seventies when the Pathet Lao finally triumphed and entered Vientiane, capital of Laos. Siri expected a quiet retirement: a little gardening in the mornings, some light reading in the afternoons, early evenings capped by a cognac... Instead, the Party put him back to work as the Republic's Chief Police Coroner. Vientiane has been fortunate in the appointment of Dr. Siri as Coroner; he may not have been trained to the job, but he is determined: he has a medical background, he's doggedly studying the old medical texts left by his predecessor, and the dead visit him. Dr. Siri does a creditable job investigating suspicious deaths. Vientiane has been much less fortunate in those appointed to other official offices. Those who were trained in the work of the government fled, and their positions were filled by men appointed on the basis of their loyalty to the Pathet Lao. Most of the government officials are struggling, and many are incompetent. They are untrained, inefficient, and unorganized, quite unable to make Dr. Siri follow orders. Dr. Siri's superior's chief concerns are to hew to the party line and to discover nothing that might embarrass the government. Dr. Siri has very different priorities. With the help of old textbooks, two assistants, and a chemistry teacher with a cache of chemicals, Dr. Siri follows the truth, wherever it leads him. He is an excellent physician, and his ability to diagnose, even to diagnose the dead, is strengthened with information shown to him by the ghosts of those he is examining.

Comment: Dr. Siri's irreverent attitude and the subversive loyalty of his friends are the most enjoyable elements in the book. No one is able to force him to do anything that he is set against doing. Those who try end up making themselves look ridiculous. Siri's birth father was Lao Heu, a Hmong shaman who intended to be the last in a line of powerful shamans. Siri was sent away soon after he was born in order to keep him from interacting with the spirit world. Siri's father intended that Siri's shamanistic powers never be invoked. Siri was unaware of his gifts. In the beginning of the first book, Dr. Siri is surprised and disturbed by his ability to see the ghosts of the dead. In a later section of the first book, Dr. Siri is asked to provide emergency assistance at a remote Hmong village, and so he travels, unknowing, to a place of power. There, Dr. Siri takes on the incarnation of one of his ancestors, and he battles forest demons to free the villagers. In the course of reading the first book, this episode may seem incongruous: Dr. Siri goes from being a thoughtful elderly man, struggling quietly to understand mysterious visions, to a being a fighter who suddenly engages in a battle of mythic proportions. From the perspective of having read the first six books in the series, it is clear that the beginning of the series describes the awakening of a shaman; a mythic battle sets the stage for the supernatural occurrences in some of the subsequent books. *Thirty-Three Teeth* won the Dilys Award in 2006. (The Dilys Award is given by the members of the Independent Mystery Booksellers Association for the mystery title that member booksellers most enjoyed selling.)

Literary Crimes & Chimes: The author does a wonderful job evoking a time, place, and culture unfamiliar to most Americans. The shabby streets of Vientiane live in these books, peopled by wonderful characters making new lives in this new, but faltering, society. One interesting aspect of the books is that "justice" can be served in many ways; in some situations it is necessary to bring in the police and arrest and prosecute the criminal, but in other situations justice is served by seducing the perpetrator into confession and convincing him to engage in an act of private contrition that will appease those he killed. Dr. Siri works to set to rest the spirits of those who were wronged rather than to exact retribution.

Explorations: How did Dr. Siri's efforts serve justice? Was justice always the same as following the law?

What did different ghosts want from Dr. Siri?

THE CASES

1. ***The Coroner's Lunch.*** New York: Soho, 2004, 272 p. ISBN: 1569473765.

VIENTIANE (LAOS), 1976 (WITH SECTIONS IN A REMOTE HMONG VILLAGE). The wife of a party leader dies under suspicious circumstances, and Dr. Siri has all he can do to keep control of the body long enough to perform an autopsy. In the middle of all this, he's asked to determine the cause of death of the members of a delegation from Vietnam. It looks very much as if the three men were tortured and then assassinated; and if those suspected are not proven innocent of the crime, there will be a very nasty international incident. He is also being haunted by the ghost of a young woman who may be trying to tell him that she did not commit suicide.

ASSOCIATES: Dtui Vongheuan and Mr. Geung—*work with Dr. Siri at the lab;* Judge Haeng—*Siri's boss;* Teacher Oum—*who helps Siri by sharing chemicals;* Comrade Civilai—*Siri's best friend;* Saloop—*Siri's dog;* Miss Vong—*Siri's neighbor;* Inspector Phosy; Auntie Lah; Boua; and Senior Comrade Kham.

2. ***Thirty-Three Teeth.*** New York: Soho, 2005, 238 p. ISBN: 1569473889.

VIENTIANE AND LUANG PRABANG (LAOS), 1976. Dr. Siri battles forces natural and supernatural, spiritual and political. When the claw marks left on murder victims in Vientiane do not match those of an escaped bear, Dr. Siri's leading suspect becomes a were-tiger. When Dr. Siri is summoned to investigate two charred bodies, he displeases the Communist Party officials by uncovering more than they expected. On his visit to Luang Prabang, he visits his sister-in-law, meets a King, terrifies a traitor, and speaks to a puppeteer who gives Dr. Siri information that helps save a friend's life.

ASSOCIATES: Dtui Vongheuan and Mr. Geung—*morgue lab assistants;* Judge Haeng—*Siri's boss;* Miss Vong—*who, against all odds, is still Siri's neighbor;* Soth—*another of Siri's neighbors;* Tik Kwunsawan—*who was the official court spiritual counselor to the late King;* Mr. Kumron—*who was considered a traitor;* Comrade Kim—*the Secretary of the North Korean Workers' Party and son of President Kim;* Mr. Intanet (Inthanet)—*one of the five surviving keepers of the Royal Xiang Thong temple puppets;* Phot—*a translator;* Mr. Ivanic—*an animal trainer;* Comrade Civilai—*Siri's best friend;* Saloop—*Siri's dog;* and Inspector Phosy.

3. ***Disco for the Departed.*** New York: Soho, c2006, 247 p. ISBN: 1569474281; 9781569474280.

VIENTIANE AND VIENG XAI (LAOS), MAY 1977. The preparations for a major celebration of the new regime are disrupted when a mummified arm is found protruding from the concrete of the pathway leading to the new President's house. Dr. Siri is sent to supervise the disinterment of the body and to discover why it was there. In the course of his investigations, he unravels a tragic love story, he is puzzled by a concert that is so loud he can feel the vibration of the speakers but that no one else can hear, and he channels the words of a dying woman to help a living child.

ASSOCIATES: Nurse Dtui—*a.k.a. Chundee Vongheuan accompanies Dr. Siri in this investigation;* Judge Haeng—*who attempts to rid the coroner of Mr. Geung;* Mr. Geung—*who survives, this book relates some of Mr. Geung's past;* Comrade Civilai—*Dr. Siri's best friend;* Comrade Lit—*the Regional Commander of the Security Division, who is taken with Dtui;* "Mrs. Nuts"—*a patient;* Panoy—*a child;* Dr. Santiago—*a surgeon on loan from Cuba;* H'Loi—*who used to be a maid;* and Captain Vo Chi and Sergeant Major Giap—*both of whom recognize Dr. Siri from the days of battle;* Odon—*deceased, his spirit is hosted by Dr. Siri;* Isandro—*deceased, was Odon's best friend.*

4. "Has Anyone Seen Mrs. Lightswitch," a short story in *Damn Near Dead: An Anthology of Geezer Noir* edited by Duane Swierczynski. Houston, TX: Busted Flush Press, 2006, p. 292–304. ISBN: 0976715759; 9780976715757.

VIENTIANE, 1977. Last night Dr. Siri saw the body of Mrs. Lightswitch in the morgue freezer. This morning it is gone. The morgue was locked. What can have happened to Mrs. Lightswitch? (The afterward about the name "Lightswitch" is fascinating.)

ASSOCIATES: Nurse Dtui—*who works at the morgue;* Mr. Geung—*who has just returned to work at the morgue after surviving dengue fever;* Comrade Civilai—*Siri's best friend.*

5. *Anarchy and Old Dogs.* New York: Soho, c2007, 272 p. ISBN: 9781569474631.

VIENTIANE AND PAKSE (LAOS), AUGUST 1977. The death of the blind Dr. Buagaew, who came to Vientiane from Pakse by bus, seemed straightforward. He was hit by a truck. What Dr. Siri finds confusing is that the blind man was hit by the truck after he'd picked up a blank letter from the Post Office. Further examination reveals that the letter was written in invisible ink: the application of chemicals makes the message visible, but not readable, because it is in code. Siri, Dtui, Phosy, and Civilai work on the message, deciphering enough to believe that it might refer to an imminent coup. Siri wants to go to Pakse to investigate but can find no way to do so without confiding in his incompetent and untrustworthy superiors. Siri gets his chance when Deputy Governor Say of Pakse is electrocuted in his bathtub, and the Governor is convinced that the death was part of a conspiracy. Judge Haeng orders Siri to Pakse to investigate the death (and Haeng is astonished when Siri agrees to follow his orders). Siri's best friend, Comrade Civilai Songsawat, accompanies him.

ASSOCIATES: Comrade Civilai—*Dr. Siri's best friend, he accompanies Siri on this case;* Nurse Dtui and Inspector Phosy—*who travel to Thailand to investigate while posing as refugees;* Auntie Bpoo—*a transvestite who plays at fortune-telling, but has more power than she knows;*

Siri's household includes Nurse Dtui; Manoluk—*Nurse Dtui mother, whose funeral is in this book;* Mrs. Fah and her children; Mr. Inthanet—*the puppeteer;* and Comrade Noo—*the renegade Thai forest monk.*

Governor Comrade Katay and Officer Tao—*are involved in the investigation of the electrocuted official;* In Pakse, Siri encounters people he taught during the revolutionary struggle, including Dr. Somdy and Madame Daeng—*noodle-cook, she had a crush on Dr Siri many years ago.*

At the close of the book, Madame Daeng has come to Vientiane to open a noodle shop there, and Auntie Bpoo has predicted happiness for Dr. Siri.

6. ***Curse of the Pogo Stick.*** New York: Soho, c2008, 240 p. ISBN: 9781569474853.

VIENTIANE AND XIANG KHOUANG, DECEMBER 1977. In Vientiane, Nurse Dtui, Madame Daeng, and Mr. Geung deal with a booby-trapped corpse. Dr. Siri is away at a Communist Party meeting in Xiang Khouang. When the party officials decide that the delegation from Vientiane should travel home overland rather than taking an airplane, Dr. Siri knows he is in for a perilous journey. His greatest fear? Having to put up with Judge Haeng as a traveling companion.

In the course of their travels, Dr. Siri is waylaid by a village elder who is seeking the help of the shaman Yeh Ming. He needs Yeh Ming to cast the bad spirits out of his daughter in order to save her, because she is carrying the child of a demon.

Two months ago, Auntie Bpoo prophesied that Dr. Siri and Madame Daeng would have two children before the rains came. Siri was amused, believing such a feat to be physically impossible for people of their age. In this book, he gains new respect for Auntie Bpoo.

ASSOCIATES: Nurse Dtui and Inspector Phosy—*are expecting their first child;* Madame Daeng—*who is engaged to Dr. Siri;* Mr. Geung—*morgue assistant;* Director Suk; Surgeon Mot; Comrade Civilai—*who has reitired;* Madame Nong—*Civilai's wife;* Teacher Oum; Mrs. Bounlan; Dr. Mut; Mrs. Fah; Inthanet—*the puppeteer;* Miss Vong—*Inthanet's girlfriend;* Comrade Noo—*the forest monk;* Bassak; Commander Khoumki; Aunti Bpoo; Crazy Rajid; and The Lizard—*Dtook, a.k.a. Phonhong.*

In Dong Dok, Dtui and Phosy meet a man who says he's Ajan Ming.

Long—*widower of Zhong;* Chamee Mua—*Long's daughter;* Yer, Ber, Bao, Chia, Phia, Dia, and Nhia—*are all the people who remain in Long's village;* Eric Stone and Danny San Souci—*spirits encountered by Dr. Siri;*—See Yee—*the spirit of the first-ever Hmong shaman and the traditional god of the shamans;* Nyuwa Tuatay—*deputy overlord for the Otherworld;* Nyuwa Neyu—*the great overlord.*

Judge Haeng is writing a book describing how he withstood a Hmong attack and saved Dr. Siri.

7. ***The Merry Misogynist.*** New York: Soho, c2009, 274 p. ISBN: 9781569475560.

VIENTIANE, TAI DUM VILLAGE AND BAN XON, 1978. The anonymous corpse of a lovely young woman sends Dr. Siri on a hunt for a serial killer. Dr. Siri also begins a search for Crazy Rajid who has disappeared from his usual haunts. Many people are worried, including Rajid's father.

The housing authorities have documented that nineteen people are living at the government accommodation unit (home) 22B742 that is assigned to

Dr. Siri. Dr. Siri is not one of them. He's surprised when Judge Haeng speaks in his defense.

Dr. Siri is delighted to find that General Bao survived.

ASSOCIATES: Madame Daeng—*who adores her husband, Dr. Siri;* Nurse Dtui—*who is eight months pregnant;* Inspector Phosy—*who has been happily married to Dtui for seven months;* Mr. Geung—*morgue assistant;* Comrade Civilai—*who has taken up baking in his retirement;* Koomki—*of the Department of Housing Allocation;* Phan—*a happy widower;* Saloop—*deceased, Siri's dog;* Ba See—*who sells stamps and coin, she did not see Rajid last Friday;* Wei—*a teacher in Tai Dum village;* Teacher Oum—*who has a 7-year-old son named Nali, does an analysis of stomach contents for Dr. Siri;* Kumdee Vilavong—*a student who told a story of a young woman's disappearance over a year ago;* Bhiku David Tickoo—*who is bonded to cook for the Happy Dine Indian Restaurant;* Jogendranath—*a.k.a. Crazy Rajid, is Bhiku's son;* Justice Haeng—*Siri's boss;* Manivone—*Haeng's secretary;* Comrade Phat—*Haeng's Vietnamese advisor;* Comrade Boonhee—*the father of the invisible woman;* Ngam—*the invisible woman;* Mongaew—*Ngam's mother;* Dr. Pornsawan—*of the Lao Patriotic Women's Association;* Dr. Bountien—*the gynecologist who helps bring Dtui and Phosy's daughter into the world;* Malee—*the daughter;* Comrade Kummai—*Director of the Minorities Census;* Comrade Buaphan—*who leads the data collection unit;* Comrade Ying Dali and Comrade Nouphet—*the team;* Miss Vong—*who reconciles with Mr. Inthanet;* General Bao—*who comes to Vientiane to retrieve the twins.*

The nineteen people living at government allocation unit 22B742 include Mrs. Fah—*whose husband had been haunted to death;* Mee and Nounou—*Mrs. Fah's children;* Gongjai and Tong—*Mrs. Fah's nieces, they were once prostitutes;* Comrade Noo—*a renegade Thai Monk who is hiding in Vientiane;* Mr. Inthanet—*the puppet master from Luang Prabang;* Pao—*the blind Hmong beggar;* Lia—*Pao's granddaughter;* Athit and Jun—*the baby twins.*

COUPE, Stuart, Julie Ogden, and Robert Hood. (Editors)

CROSSTOWN TRAFFIC: ROMANCE, HORROR, FANTASY, SF, WESTERN INVADE CRIME FICTION.

Genres/Themes Crossed: Science Fiction, Paranormal, Secret Society X Hard-Boiled Mystery, Traditional Mystery, Police Procedural.

Subjects/Character Types: Paranormal, Zombies X Private Investigators, Amateur Sleuths, Police.

Series/Stand-Alone: Anthology of short stories.

Scene of the Crime: Varies.

Detective: Varies.

Known Associates: Varies.

Premise: In March 1992, an invitation was sent to a dozen Australian mystery writers to write a hybrid story—a story that combined elements of other genres with the mystery genre—for this anthology.

Comment: The project was envisioned as a way to extend the boundaries of the mystery field, to keep it safe from stagnating. The editors explicitly discussed their concern that the complexities inherent in selling cross-genre works causes publishers to advise writers to avoid writing hybrid stories. Writers are strongly encouraged to stay within the boundaries set by the conventions of the mystery genre. *Crosstown Traffic* was created to offer writers an opportunity to disregard these restrictions, to give free reign to their imaginations, and to cross the boundaries between the genres.

Literary Magic & Mayhem: The intention was to invite mystery writers to break out of the narrow confines of the genre, and they did so with a vengeance! There are several mystery X western stories, mystery X romance stories, and mystery X fantasy stories. It includes a story of a stolen zombie, and a story that is an historical paranormal mystery (a *Phryne Fisher* story by Kerry Greenwood).

Explorations: What genres were crossed?

Did the story succeed as a mystery? Why or why not?

THE CASES

Crosstown Traffic. **NSW,** Australia: Five Islands Press Associates, 1993, 229 p. ISBN: 1875604154.

CONTENTS: Introduction *by Stuart Coupe;* The Kid and the Man from Pinkertons *by Marele Day;* My Brother Jack *by Garry Disher;* Finding Fire *by Jean Bedford;* And Then She Kissed Him *by Steve Wright;* Voyeur Night *by Robert Hood;* Arizona Dawn *by Peter Corris;* Blue Groper *by Robert Wallace;* The Big Fairy Tale Sleep *by Dominic Cadden;* Fear-Me-Now *by Terry Dowling;* I am my Father's Daughter *by Bill Congreve;* I Am Dying Egypt, Dying *by Kerry Greenwood;* Sensible Shoes *by Jan McKemmish.*

D

DAMSGAARD, Shirley.

WITCH WAY TO MURDER

Genres/Themes Crossed: Secret Society X Traditional Mystery.

Subjects/Character Types: Spell-Casters (Witches) X Amateur Sleuth (Contemporary).

Series/Stand-Alone: The novels should be read in order, as the protagonist changes over the course of the series.

Scene of the Crime: The small town of Summerset, Iowa.

Detective: Four years ago, clairvoyant Ophelia Jensen foresaw the death of her best friend, but she could not find him in time to prevent it. (Her anguish was increased because she didn't even know if it had already happened or if it was about to happen.) She went to the police, but her friend hadn't been missing long enough for them to take her concern seriously. Four days later, when they found him, she became their chief suspect. A reporter found out, and the newspaper began running stories that implied that she was a suspect in the murder. Eventually, she was cleared, but the suspicion along with her grief over Brian's death, and the guilt over not being able to save him, sent Ophelia into the mental ward of a hospital. When she learned to cope with her post traumatic stress disorder, she left her job in the city, returned to Summerset to take a job in the library of the little town where she spent Summers with her grandparents, and tried to shut out people so that she could not get involved in tragedies that she could not avert. Unfortunately, a clairvoyant is going to see things that others can't see, whether she wants to or not.

Known Associates: Abigail McDonald, Ophelia's grandmother, is a witch. Ophelia's mother wanted to follow in her footsteps, but did not have the talent. Ophelia has the talent, but has tried to turn away from it. At the close of the first book, *Witch Way to Murder,* Ophelia realizes that she needs to use the power she has been given, and asks Abby to teach her. Darci is a library assistant, working with Ophelia. Darci West looks like a playboy pinup, so most people underestimate her. She's actually a very smart, and very caring person. Tink (Titiana) becomes Ophelia's ward at the end of *The Trouble with Witches.*

Premise: Magick (magic) exists, and the ways of working with it have been passed down for generations. The talent for it runs in families. Magick, as well as other gifts such as clairvoyance and astral projection, may be called upon by anyone with talent; but to harness them and use them well requires training. Abby has both training and talent; in Summerset she is known as a woman who knows herbal folk remedies. Darci is the only person in town who has guessed that she's a witch, and Darci is quite capable of keeping secrets. Ophelia is terrified that the town will find out and that Abby will either be shunned, harassed, or have every fool in the county on her doorstep demanding that she give them spells.

Comment: Ophelia does a good job as a librarian. She has that bulldog tenaciousness that good reference librarians bring to their work. When a patron asks her for something, she searches until she finds it.

Ophelia changes in the first book: at the end of the book, she has resolved to tear down the walls she used to protect herself and to learn what she can about how to use her gifts. In subsequent books, she expands her knowledge and skills in witchcraft. Normally, that would indicate that the series should be read in order, but readers may be annoyed enough with Ophelia as she is in *Witch Way to Murder* to lose interest in the series. She is a more likable protagonist in *Charmed to Death.*

The author's Web site, http://www.shirleydamsgaard.com/, includes information on books she has written and on books she's reading, a blog, and biographical information.

Literary Magic & Mayhem: There are reasons for Ophelia's wariness, and they are good reasons; but the result is that she looks at the other characters in the book with little charity. She makes snap judgments about people's intelligence and is always looking for flaws in character. Darci believes she is a good person because she acts with charity and generosity towards people who need her help; but even as she speaks with Darci, Ophelia denies the compliment by verbally denigrating the people and the situations in which she helped. Darci is a wonderful character, caring and energetic, brilliant, and manipulative (in a mostly harmless way). Abby is wise and calm, giving and patient. Ophelia grows during the course of the series. By the sixth book, *The Witch's Grave,* she has worked through her insecurities and anger. She's able to grow spiritually once she has grown emotionally.

Explorations: What did her dreams tell Ophelia?

How useful is the magic that Abby wields? When in the book does it make a difference? Are there times it might have made a difference, but it would not be possible to know? What if Abby's protections worked by villains making choices, such as not beginning a confrontation at the library, but instead lurking at someone's apartment?

THE CASES

1. ***Witch Way to Murder: An Ophelia and Abby Mystery.*** New York: Avon, 2005, 304 p. ISBN: 0060793481.

SUMMERSET, IOWA, FALL 2005?. Something is wrong in the town of Summerset. Agricultural chemicals that could be used to manufacture meth are being stolen, someone is playing dangerous games in the woods behind Abby's house, and Ophelia is once again having nightmares. She wants to leave the town, but Abby shows Ophelia that she must face the evil that is coming.

ASSOCIATES: Darci—*Library assistant;* Abby—*Ophelia's grandmother;* Lady—*Ophelia's dog;* Queenie—*Ophelia's cat;* Benny Jenkins—*performs odd jobs in the library;* Jake—*his brother, is a loudmouth and a bully;* Claire Canyon—*the President of the Library Board;* Adam Hoffman—*bank manager, is the President of Summerset's Chamber of Commerce;* Nina Hoffman—*his wife;* Ned Thomas—*the editor of the Summerset Courier;* Richard Delaney—*reporter for the Minneapolis Sun, poses as a salesman;* Richard Davis—*chemical salesman;* Bill—*the Sheriff;* Mr. Carroll—*who wants to ban various books from the library;* Larry Durbin—*who seems to be involved with drugs;* Edna Walters; and Viola Simpson.

2. ***Charmed to Death: An Ophelia and Abby Mystery.*** New York: Avon, 2006, 304 p. ISBN: 0060793538.

SUMMERSET AND IOWA CITY, IOWA, SPRING 2006?. Abby begins teaching Ophelia the old ways, the ways to use her talents. Ophelia turned away from that path for many years, but now she embraces it. She sets herself a new course with these thoughts:

> What did I wish?...For the path I walked to be easy?...No, I wished to become the person I was meant to be. To accept all my gifts and talents and use them to the best of my ability. In my mind I repeated the same words over and over: Give me strength to face my destiny. (p. 3)

Ophelia's best friend, Brian Mitchell, was murdered five years ago. For a while, she was a suspect, then she was cleared, but the police never found the murderer. Abby tells her that her path is now to find justice for Brian. She doesn't want to relive that horrible time, but she knows that she must go back to Iowa City and find the truth. In Summerset, PP International is planning an industrial hog farm in town. The townspeople don't want it in Summerset.

ASSOCIATES: Darci—*Library assistant;* Abby—*Ophelia's grandmother;* Lady—*Ophelia's dog;* Queenie—*Ophelia's cat;* Claire Canyon—*the President of the Library Board;* Ned Thomas—*the editor of the Summerset Courier;* Arthur "Stumpy" Murdoch—*proud owner of Stumpy's Bar and Billiards, he takes an interest in Abby;* Brett—Summerset's *brand-new police officer;* Sheriff Bill Wilson; Deputy Alan Bauer; Edna Walters; Viola Simpson; Harley and Dudley Kyle; Gus Pike; Saunders—*the state representative,* and Charles Thornton—*who is posing as a reporter.*

Enrique "Henry" Comacho and Detective Perez—*are the detectives who worked on Brian Mitchell's murder;* Fletcher Beasley—*is the reporter who made Ophelia's life hell after Brian's death.*

Margaret Mary Jensen—*Ophelia's mom, Abby's daughter.*

3. ***The Trouble with Witches: An Ophelia and Abby Mystery.*** New York: Avon Books, 2006, 304 p. ISBN: 0060793589.

SUMMERSET, IOWA, AND GUNHAMMER LAKE, MINNESOTA, AUGUST 2006?. When Rick Delaney calls and asks Ophelia and Abby for help in rescuing a young girl, they can't say no. The girl, Brandi, couldn't fit in at home, and six or so months ago she left to join a group that not only accepted, but worked to develop the psychic skills of its members. For several months, Brandi seemed happy, but, in her last phone call home, she sounded troubled. That was a couple of months ago, and it's the last anyone heard from her. Her family is frantic. Ophelia takes time off from the library and travels to Minnesota with Abby. Darci is angry, at first, when Ophelia tells her that she must stay behind to keep the library open, but she accepts that she must stay in town. Then the library's air conditioner breaks down, and the board decides that the library should close. As long as it's closed anyway, this is a great opportunity to fumigate the building...Darci takes it as a sign and appears on the doorstep of Ophelia and Abby's Minnesota cabin. The three of them encounter power, evil, and physical violence as they search for the missing girl.

ASSOCIATES: Henry Comacho—*a detective with the Iowa Department of Crime Investigation;* Darci—*Library assistant;* Abby—*Ophelia's grandmother;* Lady—*Ophelia's dog;* Queenie—*Ophelia's cat;* Rick Delaney—*a reporter;* Brandi—*who is missing;* Juliet and Jason Finch—*leaders of The PSI group;* Winnie—*a devoted acolyte;* Tink—*a.k.a. Titania, is Juliet's niece and her ward;* Duane Hobbs—*local handyman;* and Walks Quietly—*shaman.*

4. ***Witch Hunt: An Ophelia and Abby Mystery.*** New York: Avon Books, 2007, 304 p. ISBN: 0061147117; 9780061147111.

SUMMERSET, IOWA, MAY 2007?. *El Serpiente,* a biker gang, is staying in Summerset, upsetting the townspeople. Darci's cousin, Becca, in town for Darci's birthday party, hooked up with one of the gang, Adder. There didn't seem to be any way to stop her; so Ophelia and Darci tried to provide some protection by sticking with her, even when she insisted on going to the notorious *Viper's Nest* bar. After she and Adder sneak out, Ophelia and Darci search the town. Finally, exhausted, they head back to Darci's house where they find Adder dead and Becca holding the bloody knife that killed him. Darci enlists Ophelia's aid in trying to clear her cousin of murder charges. Ophelia's life is complicated when someone repeatedly invades her house. She suspects that the biker gang is trying to frighten her off the investigation.

ASSOCIATES: Abby—*Ophelia's grandmother;* Tink—*a.k.a. Titania, Ophelia's ward, is learning to control her talent (she's a medium);* Lady—*Ophelia's dog;* Queenie—*Ophelia's cat;* T. P—*Tink's new puppy;* Nell—*Tink's best friend, she is thrilled when the three most popular girls in school, Mandy, Mindy, and Melinda, agree to come to her sleepover.* Pete Polaski—*Melinda's father, would never believe that she would be fooling around with a Ouija board.*

Darci—*a close friend and co-worker of Abby's is dating the town's new police officer;* Danny—*the town's new police officer;* Arthur "Stumpy" Murdoch—proud owner of *Stumpy's Bar and Billiards;* Adder and Cobra—*are two members of the El Serpiente gang;* Ned Thomas—*the editor of the Summerset Courier, the newspaper offices are torched after Ned writes articles condemning the gang;* Janet—*works at the Viper's Nest;* Claire Canyon—*the President of the Library Board;* Edna Walters and Mr. Carroll—*are library patrons.*

Sheriff Bill Wilson, Deputy Alan Bauer, Police Officer Brett, and Police Officer Danny—*are law officers in Summerset.*

5. ***The Witch is Dead: An Ophelia and Abby Mystery.*** New York: Avon Books, 2007, 292 p. ISBN: 0061147234; 9780061147230.

SUMMERSET, IOWA, 2007?. A nice man, Raymond Buchanan, helped Aunt Dot with her carry-on luggage as they exited the plane. He briefly met Abby,

Ophelia, and Tink. Tink was the only one who felt anything odd, yet within hours Mr. Buchanan was murdered. Tink ends up dealing with Ophelia's question: what's the point of being psychic if you can't save people? Tink is also coping with nightmares, at least she hopes they're nightmares; she's afraid that they might be visions. When people realize that she had met the murder victim, a rumor starts that Tink knows something. Ophelia is worried about the ghosts, but she's more worried about the killer. When Tink realizes that she may be in danger, she considers leaving Iowa to go to Minnesota and stay with her friend, Walks Quietly, for a while.

Associates: Abby—*Ophelia's grandmother;* Tink—*a.k.a. Titania, is Ophelia's ward;* Juliet—*was Tink's first guardian, after her mother died;* Jason—*Juliet's husband, is willing to give up his legal claims on Tink so that Ophelia can move forward with adoption;* Lady—*Ophelia's dog;* Queenie—*Ophelia's cat;* T. P—*Tink's puppy;* Aunt Dot—*Abby's sister Dorothy Cameron, is coming to visit;* Arthur "Stumpy" Murdoch—*owner of Stumpy's Bar and Billiards, has become a constant in Abby's life;* Nell Johnson—*Tink's best friend;* Carl and Chris—*are Nell's parents.*

Darci—*Ophelia's coworker, is cutting back her work hours so that she can go to college and get a psychology degree;* Gertrude Duncan—*works at the library part-time;* Brenda—*who also works at the library;* Claire Canyon—*the President of the Library Board.* Edna Walters, Agnes, and Mr. Carroll—*are library patrons.*

Georgia—*the town gossip;* Ethan—*a.k.a. Cobra who is threatened by Ophelia;* Silas Green—*crematorium owner;* Dr. Christopher Mason—*who seems interested in Ophelia;* Kevin Roth—*Buchanan's assistant at the funeral home;* Sheriff Bill Wilson; and Deputy Alan Bauer.

6. ***The Witch's Grave: An Ophelia and Abby Mystery.*** New York: Avon Books, 2009, 262 p. ISBN: 9780061493430.

Summerset, Iowa, September 2008? Ophelia's been dreaming. In the past her dreams have been warnings, now they foretell joy. They feature a blond haired, blue-eyed lover. She meets him in the flesh at a library fundraiser, and they both feel the connection. Then he's shot while standing within arm's reach of Ophelia. He was an unexpected guest at the fundraiser. Everyone knew that Ophelia would be there. The shooter came to the event armed; he lurked within the treeline waiting for a clear shot: the shooting was premeditated. The Chief of Police believes that Ophelia may have been the intended victim. Ophelia's sure that he's wrong, but subsequent attacks support his arguments. Ophelia believes that the universe put Stephen in this place at this time so that she could help him. She just has to avoid being locked up in protective custody, protect her family, and survive while she conducts her own investigation.

In this book, Ophelia learns a little about reincarnation and comes to believe that she was once a member of the French resistance, a model named Madeleine.

Abby believes that 13-year-old (almost 14) Tink should visit Ophelia's great-aunt Mary for guidance in learning about her power as a medium. (It's not one of the powers shared by Ophelia and Abby.)

ASSOCIATES: Abby—*Ophelia's grandmother;* Tink—*a.k.a. Titania, is Ophelia's 13-year-old ward;* Lady—*Ophelia's dog;* Queenie—*Ophelia's cat;* T. P—*Tink's puppy;* Claire Canyon—*the President of the Library Board organized the library fundraiser;* Darci—*Library clerk;* Chuck Krause—*a politician;* Jolene—*Chuck's wife;* Enrico—*who does not believe in witches;* Stephen Larsen—*the man who's been starring in Ophelia's dreams;* Sheriff Bill Wilson—*who investigates the shooting.* Ron Mack—*winery owner;* Antonio Vargas—*vineyard workers;* Evita—*Antonio's daughter, an enthusiastic reader;* Mrs. Louise Larsen—*Stephen's mother;* Karen Burns—*Stephen's writing partner;* Gina Torreli—*Ben Jessup's girlfriend;* Brody—*Gina's cat;* Lucy, Mabel, and Phoebe—*are Sunset Retirement Home guests.*

Madeleine—*a model in Nazi-occupied France, (In Ophelia's dreams she is Madeleine);* Giselle—*Madeleine's friend;* Colonel Vogel—*hosts a party they attend;* Brother Sebastian—*who conspires with Madeleine;* Henrick Sorenson—*who Madeleine wants to marry;* Jacques and Marie Gaspard, and their daughter Rosa—*are gypsies who Madeleine tries to save.*

DANIELS, Casey.

DON OF THE DEAD

Genres/Themes Crossed: Paranormal X Traditional Mystery.

Subjects/Character Types: Ghosts X Amateur Sleuth (Contemporary).

Series/Stand-Alone: The novels should be read in order, as characters and relationships evolve over the course of the series.

Detective: Pepper Martin's great ambition was to be, in her words, a "lady who lunches." Alas, her dreams went up in smoke when her physician father was convicted of Medicare fraud and ended up in a federal penitentiary. When Pepper's social standing fell, her friends disappeared, her fiancé dumped her, even her mother left town. Pepper was left to fend for herself in a world that was not particularly kind to young women with bachelor's degrees in art history. With no money and no marketable skills, she was lucky to land a job as a Garden View Cemetery tour guide. She had no desire to become a detective; her greatest ambition was to sell shoes at Saks, but the dead had other plans.

Known Associates: Ella Silverman is Pepper's boss at Garden View Cemetery. Dr. Dan Callahan (Ph.D.) is interested in Pepper's brain. The gorgeous Detective Quinn Harrison is interested in Pepper for other reasons.

Premise: When Pepper Martin awakened in an emergency room, she was told that she'd tripped on the uneven ground of the Garden View Cemetery. She was told that she'd hit her head on the front step of Gus Scarpetti's mausoleum. She was told that she'd knocked herself unconscious. What she wasn't told was that her injury would leave her able to see and speak with the dead.

Comment: Casey Daniel's father was a Cleveland Police detective who searched for stolen cars as a hobby. He took young Casey along with him on weekends. That early experience may explain why this series does an unusually good job depicting the legwork necessary for investigations. Casey Daniels Web site is at: http://www.caseydaniels.com. It includes biographical information, a bibliography of her work, and news of upcoming books.

Literary Magic & Mayhem: These are fun, breezy reads. The dialog is fun, but there's not much in the way of philosophy, and there are a few problems with the protagonist that are smoothed out by the second book. The protagonist, Pepper Martin, has been described as a cross between Paris Hilton and Nancy Drew. The character will raise the hackles of some readers. She planned to be an ornament on a successful (i.e., rich) husband's arm and seems to feel betrayed by the fact that she must now make her own way in the world. Pepper is dismissive of the women's liberation movement, and regards her boss's interest in it as old-fashioned and boring. Pepper has a good brain and a lot of determination; but the chief weapons in her arsenal are her bosom, her pout, and the hint that she's willing to hit the sheets, a hint that she seems to employ often in her quest to find information. All of these traits are prominent in the first book, but they are toned down in the second book. The glimmers of character and compassion that show up in the first of the series are expanded in the second entry, and the more likeable protagonist contributes to a more enjoyable read. In subsequent books, Pepper shows that she has guts, brains, and a drive to find justice for the living and the dead.

Explorations: Trace the progress of Pepper's investigations. How does one step lead to the next?

In what ways do the ghosts further the investigation? In what ways do they hinder it?

How long ago were the ghosts' perceptions of the place of women in society formed? How different are their perceptions from Pepper's?

Who are the most likeable characters in the book?

THE CASES

1. ***Don of the Dead: A Pepper Martin Mystery.*** New York: Avon, 2006, 325 p. ISBN: 0060821469.

CLEVELAND, JUNE 2006. Gus Scarpetti was gunned down 30 years ago. Since his death he's been unable to find rest. He's convinced that, if he understood who killed him and why, he would be able to move on. For 30 years he's searched for someone who could investigate his murder. Now that Pepper can see him, he figures that she's the woman for the job. Unfortunately her investigation is going to have to include his old associates. They're still part of the mob, and they don't welcome questions.

ASSOCIATES: Mr. Augustino "Gus" Scarpetti—*deceased;* John Vitale—*Johnny the Rat;* Ben Marzano—*Benny No Shoes;* Michale Cardorella—*Mike the Dumper;* and Paul Ramone—*Pounder;* Nick—*the cook at Lucia's Trattoria;* Carmella—*Gus's wife;* Rudy and Father Anthony—*Gus's sons;* Marie—*Gus's sister;* Albert Vigniolli—*the man with the scar, is one of Rudy Scarpetti's guards.*

Ella Silverman—*Pepper's boss;* Charles—*the manager of the shoe department at Saks;* Detective Quinn Harrison—*who is gorgeous;* and Dr. Dan Callahan—*who is confusing.*

2. ***The Chick and the Dead: A Pepper Martin Mystery.*** New York: Avon, 2007, 336 p. ISBN: 0060821477.

CLEVELAND, JULY 2006. Didi just wants to see justice done. She needs Pepper to prove plagiarism, so that the money that was rightfully hers can go to her granddaughter. Unfortunately, the villain has already killed to keep her secret, and she has no compunction over killing again.

Merilee Bowman is known as the author of the best-selling historical romance *So Far the Dawn.* The book's popularity skyrocketed after a movie adaptation featuring Kurt Benjamin and Elizabeth Goddard became a cult classic. Merilee Bowman's visit to Cleveland sparks a great deal of interest, among fans, Civil War re-enactors, and the press.

ASSOCIATES: Ella Silverman—*Pepper's boss, is author Merilee Bowman's number one fan;* Dr. Dan Callahan—*who is interested in Pepper's mind;* Detective Quinn Harrison—*who is not;* Deborah "Didi" Bowman—*deceased, is interested in the welfare of her granddaughter;* Harmony—*Didi's granddaughter is in foster care and is going to high school;* Shayla—*a popular girl at the school, takes joy in tormenting Harmony;* Merilee Bowman—*Didi's sister;*

Trish Kingston—*her secretary;* Bob—*the caretaker of the Bowman home;* Kurt Benjamin and Elizabeth Goddard—*the stars of the movie So Far the Dawn, both are now deceased but still quarreling about their characters' fates;* Rick Jensen—*a reporter covering the story for the National Inquisitor;* Susan Gwitkowski—*was Didi's best friend;* Thomas Ross Howell—*was Didi's boss.*

3. ***Tombs of Endearment: A Pepper Martin Mystery.*** New York: Avon, 2007, 307 p. ISBN: 9780060821500.

CLEVELAND, OCTOBER 2006. Rock star Damon Curtis died young. His band, *Mind at Large,* continued. They've been playing without him for 40 years, playing without him, but not without his new songs. Damon's bandmate Vinnie Pal channels Damon to hear Damon's new music so that the band can play it.

After her last case, Pepper decided to avoid ghosts. Successful murderers are willing to murder again. Taking a case from a dead victim is courting danger. Pepper would refuse to take on an investigation for a ghost, but Damon isn't asking for an investigation. He died of an overdose. No questions, no investigation. He only wants Pepper to talk to his bandmate Vinnie Pal. Vinnie doesn't know that Damon can't cross over while Vinnie holds on to him to channel his music. Damon needs Pepper to ask Vinnie to let him go.

The band is in Cleveland to play at the Rock and Roll Hall of Fame. Vinnie Pal is in town. Damon's need is real and the task is not dangerous. The attraction that Pepper feels for Damon is just a small part of the reason she takes the case.

Joel, the rat who told the florist that his and Pepper's wedding was canceled before he told Pepper, is engaged once more. He wants Pepper to return her engagement ring so that he can give it to his new fiancé.

ASSOCIATES: Damon Curtis—*deceased, was the lead singer of Mind at Large;* Ben—*the new lead singer;* Vinnie Pallucci—*keyboardist;* Alistair Cromwell—*drummer;* Mighty Mike—*guitarist;* Pete—*bassist;* Belinda—*a groupie;* Zack—*who does public relations for the band;* Bernie—*the band's driver;* Gene Terry—*the band's agent.*

Joel Panhorst—*is now engaged to Simone Burnside;* Grandma Panhorst—*who stays with her engagement ring (Pepper enjoys her company).*

Brian—*leads the ghosthunters in the cemetery;* John, Theo, Angela, Stan, and Dan Callahan—*are the ghosthunters in the group.*

Ella Silverman—*Pepper's boss;* Detective Quinn Harrison—*who asks Pepper for a date.*

4. ***Night of the Loving Dead: A Pepper Martin Mystery.*** New York: Berkley Prmie Crime, 2009, 291 p. ISBN: 9780425225554.

CLEVELAND AND CHICAGO, FEBRUARY 2008. When Ella and her daughters come down with the flu, she asks Pepper to deliver her research paper at a Chicago conference on cemeteries. Pepper is not excited about a visit to Chicago in February. She's not excited about attending a cemetery conference. She's suffering from stage fright at the idea of delivering Ella's research paper. Then a ghost tells her that Dan Callahan is in danger, and suddenly the trip is worthwhile because she can save Dan.

ASSOCIATES: Ella Silverman—*Pepper's boss;* Detective Quinn Harrison—*Pepper's lover;* Doris—*from Detroit,* Myra—*from Dayton,* and Grant—*are cemetery conference attendees;* Stephanie—*the Chicago cemetery tour guide;* Madeline Tremayne—*deceased, urges Pepper to save Dan Callahan;* Dan Callahan—*who was once married to Madeline;* Stella—*a.k.a. Pink Parka Woman;* Ernie—*who misses his wife;* Alberta—*his wife;* Dr. Hilton Gerard—*who is running a study that Stella and Ernie would like to join;* Scott Baskins—*FBI agent;* Henry, Thaddeus, Adam, Glenn, and Dwayne—*guards*.

DAVID, Peter and Pablo Raimondi.

MADROX: MULTIPLE CHOICE

Genres/Themes Crossed: Blended Society X Hard-Boiled Mystery.

Subjects/Character Types: Superheroes, Evolved Humans X Private Investigator.

Series/Stand-Alone: Stand-alone.

Scene of the Crime: The story is set primarily in the New York area and the modern day.

Detective: Jamie Madrox is a mutant, a member of a growing segment of the population born with superpowers, due to their unusual genetics. Madrox has the unique ability to make copies of himself after physical impact and then absorb these copies back into his body at a later time. After spending time with the X-Men and X-Factor as the Multiple Man, Madrox decided to branch out on his own. With the ability to move in every direction at once, no particular option seemed any more important or valid than any other. Madrox sent out copies of himself, which he calls dupes, to study everything he thought he might need to know and then to return to him to be reabsorbed, along with their newly acquired knowledge. Madrox decided to set himself up as a private investigator, using his dupes to do surveillance.

Known Associates: Madrox maintains contact with a few of his friends from his time on the government-funded mutant team, X-Factor. Rahne

Sinclair is a young woman, devoutly Catholic, who has the mutant ability to shape-shift into a wolf. Guido Carosella is abnormally large and strong due to his genetic mutation, and during his time with X-Factor, he was known as Strong Guy.

Premise: It may have been something in the air or water of Los Alamos, but Jamie Madrox was born a mutant. When the doctor who delivered him gave him a slap to get the infant to breathe on his own, Jamie multiplied into two identical babies. Professor Charles Xavier helped and advised Jamie's parents. This is the world of the X-Men; there are mutants and they have superpowers.

Comments: Peter David had previously written a story-arc on X-Factor featuring the central characters from this story. It is not necessary to read these previous comics in order to enjoy or understand the Madrox miniseries. This miniseries was popular enough that Marvel started a new *X-Factor* series based on it, with Peter David returning as writer. While this new *X-Factor* series is being collected into graphic novels, it has not been included in this work because it does not conform to the mystery genre as defined in this book.

The author's Web site, http://peterdavid.net, includes links to his blogs and current information on his projects. Wikipedia has an in-depth article on Madrox at: http://en.wikipedia.org/wiki/Jamie_Madrox.

Literary Magic and Mayhem: Peter David is known for his snappy dialogue, and that is certainly the case here. The story employs noir elements very heavily. It is interesting to note that a slightly different font is used for each dupe.

Explorations: What is the self? Are we distinct from all of the elements of our psyche, or are we genuinely composed of them?

Is knowledge of experience as valid as knowledge gained through experience?

THE CASE

Madrox: Multiple Choice. New York: Marvel Comics, 2005, 120 p. ISBN: 0785115005

New York, 2005. After several months of sending dupes out to study the world, Madrox has found his copies becoming more individualistic, often representing aspects of his personality rather than direct duplicates of his personality. While struggling to get his detective agency up and running, Madrox finds one of his dupes wounded and on the brink of death. Madrox absorbs the dupe, but gets only scattered images of his recent actions. Jamie Madrox then sets out in an attempt to solve what is essentially his own murder.

Associates: See above.

DEAN, Scarlett.

Invisible Shield

Genres/Themes Crossed: Paranormal X Police Procedural.

Subjects/Character Types: Ghosts X Police Procedural.

Series/Stand-Alone: This is the first book in what is clearly expected to be a series.

Scene of the Crime: Present day Indiana.

Detective: Homicide Detective Lindsay Frost won't give up her shield, even after she has been murdered.

Known Associates: Lindsay's family includes her sister, Officer Kate Frost, and her parents, Carla and Perry Frost. Lindsay's partner, Homicide Detective Gerard Alvarez, works with her sister, Kate, to try to bring Lindsay's killer to justice.

In the next world, Lindsay encounters Sally, a lonely ghost; Abner Taute who used to give Lindsey information when they were both alive; Police Officer Mike Blake with whom Lindsey builds a team of sorts; and coroner Dr. Warren Saint.

Premise: Once people die they move on to the next existence, unless there is something that they hold onto from this world. Lindsay will not give up her badge and all it stands for; she's still committed to preserve and protect the innocent and to track down the guilty.

Comment: The author's Web site at http://www.scarlettdean.com/ includes information on her projects, a free short story, and links to interviews.

Literary Magic & Mayhem: This has its moments: the relationship between the sisters is touching and fun. They tell each other things that they were never able to share while Lindsay was alive. For instance, Kate asks Lindsay why she went to a therapist. Lindsay tells her that she needed help after her first partner, Joe, was killed:

> "Nightmares that started after Joe was killed. It got so I tried to avoid sleep because I dreaded the night terrors. I decided to get help when I began sleepwalking with my gun in my hand."

"A nightie and a Glock. Quite a fashion statement."

"George didn't appreciate it. I almost nailed him one night coming out of the bathroom."

Kate laughed as she pulled the squad into the department lot. "Wish I could have seen that."

"He swore he'd never leave the toilet seat up again," Lindsay said, and grinned. (p. 75)

Explorations: What role does Richard play in the narrative?

THE CASE

Invisible Shield*. Detroit:* Five Star, 2007, 270 p. ISBN: 9781594145452.

INDIANA, 2007. Detective Lindsay Frost was murdered. She never saw who did it. The murderer arranged her body to look like a suicide, but Lindsay knows darn well that she didn't kill herself. Her partner, Detective Gerald Alvarez, and her sister, Officer Kate Frost, are certain that Lindsay was murdered, but they can't find any proof. Lindsay decides to take a hand in the investigation. Her partner cannot see her, but Kate has always been open to the idea of paranormal phenomena (and, in the past, was teased about that by her sister). Kate's beliefs make her receptive to the supernatural: it is possible for her to see Lindsay, and they develop a working partnership. Kate investigates Lindsay's living enemies, and Lindsay fights off the sprits of the dead.

ASSOCIATES: George Anderson—*was Lindsay's fiancé;* Kate—*Lindsay's sister;* Carla and Perry Frost—*their parents;* Richard Kelter—*a 12-year-old, mentally challenged boy, who had been befriended by Lindsay;* Mrs. Gloria Jenkins—*was Lindsay's neighbor;* Pat Turner—*who taught Kate skydiving;* Chuck Bowser—*who often acts as Kate's pilot;* Gerard Alvarez—*was Lindsay's partner;* Detective Elizabeth Copley—*is Gerard's new partner;* Police Chief Grady O'Connor; Carl Withers; and Jake Tucker—*are other officers;* Paul and John—*are Alvarez' sons.*

Suspects include Calvin Stokes—*a gun shop owner who blamed Lindsay when the case against his son's murderer was botched;* Janice—*his wife;* Marie Yates—*an aggressive criminal attorney;* and Buford Jones—*a recently released convict who'd threatened Lindsay.*

Joe O'Brien—*bartender;* Mona Fitzpatrick Divine—*Kate's psychic;* Julia Parsons—*the police department's psychic;* Sally O'Shannon—*a ghost who teaches Lindsay the ropes;* Abner Taute—*another ghost, used to be one of the department's best snitches;* Police Officer Mike Blake—*deceased;* Officer Joe Sumner—*deceased, Lindsay's first partner;* Dr. Warren Saint—*deceased, coroner;* Tanner Jean Hoyt—*a killer;* Private First Class John J. Hoyt—*Tanner's father.*

DICK, Philip K. (1928–1982)

Do Androids Dream of Electric Sheep?

Genres/Themes Crossed: Science Fiction X Hard-Boiled Mystery.

Subjects/Character Types: Future Earth, Androids, Future Technology X Bounty Hunter.

Series/Stand-Alone: Stand-alone.

Scene of the Crime: Post-apocalyptic Earth, San Francisco, 2021.

Detective: Rick Deckard, licensed bounty hunter. His job is to retire (destroy) rogue androids that escape the colonies on other planets and come to Earth. He gets $1,000 for every android he destroys.

Known Associates: Iran, Rick's wife. She doesn't use the mood organ the way its designers intended, as a sort of dial-a-mood device to smooth out the difficulties of life. Instead of scheduling moods that will help her through her day, she sometimes schedules the moods that she feels are appropriate. On January 3, 2021, she has scheduled six hours of self-accusatory depression. Bill Barbour, Rick's neighbor, has a real-live horse, and the horse is going to bear a real-live colt. Owning a living animal is considered a basic status symbol. Rick, who's been reduced to a faux sheep, is envious of Bill. Rick's boss is Police Inspector Harry Bryant.

Premise: World War Terminus (WWT) destroyed Earth, but the death is slow. Radioactive dust killed off species one by one. The government ramped up colonization of other planets, offering a free android to each colonist. The best and brightest from Earth have moved into space, leaving a fraction of the population to populate the cities. At the city's center, apartment buildings may be half-full; at the outskirts of the city, whole apartment buildings are empty. Androids are not used on Earth, but some escape from the colonies and come to Earth. Most of these androids have killed humans in the course of their escape. Bounty hunters track down the androids. This has become progressively more difficult as improvements in technology and programming have been used to improve the androids, to make them seem more human. The newest model, the Nexus-6, is virtually indistinguishable from human. One major difference is empathy. Humans still have it; in fact, it's so prized that nurturing live animals is considered an essential component of human life. People use an empathy box to connect emotionally to others. It provides fusion with a modern Sisyphus who tries to role back all death; his name is Mercer.

Comment: Philip Kindred Dick (1928–1982) was one of the greats in the field of science fiction. His novel, *The Man in the High Castle,* won the

1963 Hugo for Best Novel. *Flow My Tears, The Policeman Said* won the 1975 John W. Campbell Memorial Award. The year Philip K. Dick died, 1982, Thomas W. Disch founded an award in his honor. The Philip K. Dick Best Original Science Fiction Paperback is awarded annually at Norwescon, and is sponsored by the Philadelphia Science Fiction Society.

A few aspects of *Do Androids Dream of Electric Sheep* were depicted in the movie *Blade Runner. Blade Runner* explored the ideas of androids who might not know that they are androids: giving androids false memories of childhood; giving androids short, four-year lifespans; having androids escape to Earth, and having bounty hunters who track them down and destroy them. The film handled these aspects very well; but anyone coming to *Do Androids Dream of Electric Sheep* and expecting it to read like a novelization of the movie will be surprised at all the other aspects of the vision of our far future that are covered in the book.

The official Philip K. Dick Web site at http://www.philipkdick.com/ covers information on his work and gives news about creative adaptations (such as films) of his work, new editions of his books, and news on the Philip K. Dick awards.

Literary Magic & Mayhem: Some science fiction writers envision future inventions, extrapolating technology to imagine new possibilities. Philip Dick envisioned entire societies. He not only imagined androids, he imagined how they would change humans. Here, he depicts a colonist, Mrs. Maggie Klugman, being interviewed:

> "Mrs. Klugman, how would you contrast your life back on contaminated Earth with your new life here in a world rich with every imaginable possibility?" A pause, and then a tired, dry, middle-aged, female voice said "I think what I and my family of three noticed most was the dignity." "The dignity, Mrs. Klugman?" the announcer asked. "Yes," Mrs. Klugman, now of New New York, Mars, said. "It's a hard thing to explain. Having a servant you can depend on in these troubled times... I find it reassuring." (p. 18)

When asked specifically if escaping the radiation of Earth and the possible breakdown of her body was a concern, Mrs. Klugman agrees that she and her husband worried themselves almost to death over the radiation; but, the first thing that sprang to her mind when asked about the biggest change in her life was that now she has dignity, because she has an android servant. If the reader wonders how the android would have felt about that, it can be guessed from an ad for colonization that "duplicates the halcyon days of the pre-Civil War Southern states!"—speaking in glowing terms of an android designed specifically for "you and you alone" that can act as a body servant or tireless field hand (p. 17).

Dick not only imagines the bleakness of the life on Earth, but also imagines a horribly cheerful news/entertainment show and a mood-altering program that makes it possible to endure that life. He imagines the ways in which humanity will define itself as separate from androids, and how values will change.

Explorations: Why were androids created?

When do Rick's attitudes towards androids begin to change? How does his encounter with Luba Luft change him? How does his encounter with Resch change him? How does his encounter with Rachel Rosen change him?

Would mood organs be useful in today's society? Who would use them? What are possible pitfalls?

What purpose do the live animals serve in this society? Why would people have fake animals? Why would androids not be able to sustain animals?

What role did Mercer play?

If people created androids, what responsibilities would they have towards those androids?

THE CASE

Do Androids Dream of Electric Sheep? New York: Del Rey, 1996, c1968, 256 p. ISBN: 0345404475; 9780345404473.

San Francisco, January 3, 2021. On January 2, 2021, the San Francisco Police Department's chief bounty hunter, Dave Holden, was given an assignment to apprehend eight androids. He took down two; the third, Max Polokov, got him first. The next day, bounty-hunter Rick Deckard is given the remainder of the assignment. For every android he destroys, he will get a $1,000 bounty. He is anxious to earn the money. His live sheep died about a year ago. He has been tending a manufactured sheep ever since, and is desperate to earn the fee to purchase a real-live animal again.

Inspector Bryant is concerned that the Voigt-Kampff Empathy Test may not differentiate between the new Nexus-6 robots and unemotional humans. The possibility exists that a human may be killed by an agent who thinks the human is a Nexus-6. He sends Rick to the Rosen Association, the system's largest manufacturer of robots used for the colonization program, to perform double-blind tests to see if the Voigt-Kampff test can still be used.

Associates: Iran—*Rick's wife;* Bill Barbour—*Rick's neighbor;* Police Inspector Harry Bryant—*Rick's boss.*

John Isadore—*a "chickenhead."* John lives in an abandoned high-rise apartment building on the outskirts of San Francisco. Earth's radiation has damaged him. Last year, he tested as genetically non-viable: he became a "chickenhead" by failing the minimum mental faculties test. He works for the Van Ness Pet Hospital (they repair faux animals, doing their best to maintain the illusion that the animals are real). Hannibal Sloat—*John's boss;* Milt Borogrove—*the repairman;* Pris Stratton—*who moved into John's building.*

Rick is sent to track down and test five beings who may be androids. They are: Max Polokov—*who lasered the last bounty hunter who came after him;* Luba Luft—*the opera signer;* Irmgard and Roy Baty—*who ran a drugstore;* and Pris Stratton—*who tells Rick to call her Mrs. Stratton, as he doesn't know her well enough to call her Pris.*

Inspector Bryant—*Rick's boss;* Rachel and Eldon Rosen—*of the Rosen Association;* Sandor Kadalyi—*W.P.O. representative;* Officer Crams—*who arrests Rick;* Officer Phil Resch and Inspector Garland.

Flow My Tears, The Policeman Said

Genres/Themes Crossed: Parallel Universe, Dystopia X Police Procedural.

Subjects/Character Types: Genetically Modified Humans (Privileged Class), Alternate Universes (Other Dimensions) X Police Procedural.

Series/Stand-Alone: Stand-alone.

Scene of the Crime: Alternate Earth, 1988.

Detective: Police General Felix Buckman is faced with the impossible. In a police state, where all people are tracked from the moment of birth, he is faced with a man who has no file. He's been demoted in the past, through the work of his enemies, and he's determined that he will not be vulnerable again.

Known Associates: Police General Buckman's twin sister, Alys, is brilliant, deeply disturbed, manipulative, and probably an addict. She's also General Buckman's lover; they have a young son.

Premise: Following an insurrection, America became a police state. The insurrection was apparently led by students. The remnants of the resistance live underground, literally, within live-in warrens under the universities.

A series of secret genetic experiments have created enhanced humans. The most advanced set of experiments known to Jason Taverner and Police General Buckman was the sixth such set, which produced people whom both of them call "sixes." Jason Taverner and Heather Hart are both sixes.

A new drug has been created: it alters the life of the person who takes it by pulling her (or him) into a different plane of existence, along with other people who are, in one way or another, close to the person who takes the drug.

Comment: *Flow My Tears, The Policeman Said* won the 1975 John W. Campbell Memorial Award for best science fiction novel. It was also nominated for the 1974 Nebula Award and the 1975 Hugo.

Philip Dick had a twin sister, Jane Charlotte Dick, she died when they were five weeks old. Twins are a recurring motif in many of his works.

Literary Magic & Mayhem: Alys is less a mirror image than a photo negative of the Police General. Neither her presence nor her absence comfort him. Nothing about her brings him joy; it is as if her existence is a gaping wound that causes unrelenting trauma; and her absence is worse. The theme of damaging love is further explored in Kathy Nelson's madness. Her husband has died, but she cannot believe he is dead; and she has constructed a bizarre and destructive reality in which she is saving him by betraying people who come to her for help. The pain caused by love, the danger of loving, even of loving a pet, are discussed; and the darker side of love is played out in most of the relationships in the book.

Jason is amiable, funny, likable. He's a six: charisma was "inscribed on [his] chromosomes forty-two years ago" (p. 7). That appeal makes him interesting to women, but they are as likely to victimize him as to help him. Some manage to do both at once; for instance, he realizes that Kathy Nelson is completely dysfunctional, probably certifiably insane, and is likely to bed him, then turn him in to the police. He recognizes that she believes her own lies, at least part of the time. He tries to speak honestly, wanting her to recognize the destructive pattern she has set:

> "Look. You're an odd combination of the innocent romantic, and a"—he paused; the word "treacherous" had come to mind, but he discarded it swiftly—"and a calculating, subtle manipulator." You are, he thought, a prostitute of the mind. And it's your mind that's prostituting itself, before and beyond anyone else's. (p. 47)

Jason's ability to feel compassion even while he's struggling for self-preservation keeps the reader on his side.

As in so many of Dick's books, the government oppresses the people in a variety of ways. One such way, briefly explored in this book, is a law enacted by Congress after the insurrection, "Tidman's Sterilization Bill," which mandated that African American couples could have no more than one child. One of the themes in the book is that of the kindness of strangers, people treating other individuals with humanity. However, when the racist policies of the government are discussed, it is as if that humanity has somehow been obliterated by the system. Humanity is depicted as something that only survives in individuals reaching out to help other individuals. Somehow, in the abstract, many of these people are comfortable with wholesale oppression and brutality.

Explorations: In this book, two of the most supportive characters are Mary Anne Dominic and Montgomery L. Hopkins. What is their relationship to the people they help? What difference do they make in the lives of those people?

When Jason Taverner is forced to reinvent himself, what does he choose as a profession? Would he have eventually survived, prospered, or been destroyed in the alternate reality?

What would it be like to be forced to live in someone else's dream, with you playing a bit part in their life?

THE CASE

Flow My Tears, the Policeman Said. New York: Vintage Books, 1993, c1974, 231 p. ISBN: 067974066X.

LOS ANGELES, OCTOBER 11, 1988. Entertainer Jason Taverner, was genetically enhanced to help him on his path to becoming an internationally acclaimed star, a pop singer, and a well-loved television personality. His show is second in the ratings, fans mob the door of his soundstage, and he can go nowhere without being recognized. He adores the fame while looking down on the "ordinaries." He says that life is short, that prosperity is even shorter, but he doesn't really believe it; he's sure that he'll always be there for his fans and they'll keep him on top of the world. Then he's attacked, and when he awakens, no one knows him, he's no longer a celebrity. Worse than that, he has no identification, and when he checks, no records of life exist. He's in a police state, and can't prove his identity. Once he comes to police attention, they keep puzzling over his case. How could there be no files on someone? Could Jason be so cunning, so powerful, that he could make evidence of his existence disappear? What other explanation could there be? The case escalates until it is on the desk of Police General Felix Buckman, who solves it, and then tries to cover it up.

ASSOCIATES: Alys Buckman—*a druggie who is the only person left who recognizes Jason Taverner;* Police General Felix Buckman—*is her brother;* Herbert Maime—*is Buckman's assistant;* Heather Hart—*is Jason Taverner's lover;* Al Bliss—*is his agent;* Marilyn Mason—*is his protégé;* Bill Wolfe—*is his attorney;* Mory Mann—*is the producer of his television show;* Ed Pracim—*telepath, a hotel clerk who helps Jason find a forger and then informs on him;* Kathy Nelson—*the forger;* McNulty—*a police officer;* Ruth Rae—*who regards Jason as an acquaintance while he remembers her as an old lover;* Mary Anne Dominic—*a potter who helps Jason;* Montgomery L. Hopkins—*a stranger who helps Police General Buckman.*

MINORITY REPORT

Genres/Themes Crossed: Paranormal, Dystopia X Hard-Boiled Mystery.

Subjects/Character Types: Clairvoyents, Evolved human beings, Future Earth X Government Investigator.

Series/Stand-Alone: Stand-alone.

Scene of the Crime: Far future New York.

Detective: Commissioner John Allison Anderton founder of the Precrime Agency of the Federal Westbloc Government.

Known Associates: Lisa Anderton, his wife.

Premise: With the aid of precognitive mutants, crime fighting has been revolutionized. There is no longer any need for post-crime police work for major crimes. Everyone agreed that post-crime punishment was not an effective deterrent, and was obviously not much comfort to a victim that had already been murdered. When scientists began exploring the talents of precognitive individuals, most of the research was geared towards predicting events that could build wealth, such as stock market prices. Anderton realized that there was a more important, socially relevant application: arresting criminals before they had a chance to commit their crimes. One difficulty is that the precognitive visions don't always agree: sometimes the times covered are not completely in sync, sometimes the conclusions drawn are different. To prevent mistakes, the system does not rest on the report of one precognitive. Instead they work in groups of three, and their visions are cross-checked. It's been agreed that, if two out of the three visions lead to the same conclusion, then the "majority report" is regarded as proven; and preventive arrests are made. The "minority report," the report that contradicted the other two, is discarded.

Comment: The basic world concept of the short story "Minority Report" was turned into a movie with the same name. The movie is an action-adventure picture that follows the innocent man who is accused of being about to commit a murder. The short also follows the accused, with a somewhat different ending. The result for the precrime unit in the short story is very different from the result for the unit in the movie.

Movies that have been based on the works of Philip K. Dick include *Blade Runner* (1982), based on the novel *Do Android's Dream of Electric Sheep?; Screamers* (1995) based on the short story "Second Variety"; *Total Recall* (1990), based on the short story "We Can Remember It for You Wholesale"; *Confessions d'un Barjo* (French, 1992), based on the novel *Confessions of a*

Crap Artist; Impostor (2001), based on the short story "Impostor"; *Minority Report* (2002), based on the short story "The Minority Report.," *Paycheck* (2003), based on the short story "Paycheck"; *A Scanner Darkly* (2006), based on the novel *A Scanner Darkly; Next* (2007), based on the short story "The Golden Man"; and the rights to the novel *Time Out of Joint* have been purchased by Warner Bros. Independent producer John Alan Simon has purchased the rights to the short stories "Valis" and "Radio Free Albemuth," and to the novel *Flow My Tears, the Policeman Said.*

Literary Magic & Mayhem: As always, a world created by Philip Dick is an amazing source of ideas about society and about humanity. Even in this short story there is an exploration of the society. Predictably, money is in short supply, the government must set priorities for funding, and everyone is looking out for his or her own program. There has been a major war, and the veterans from both sides have joined together in the International Veterans' League to work together to increase their political clout. Those who are different, the precognitive mutants, are treated with disdain, and called "monkeys," even when the society depends on their abilities.

Explorations: Initially, Anderton rejected his wife's arguments regarding turning himself in, what changed?

In the end, did the system work?

Can accurate precognitive visions be reconciled with the concept of free will?

THE CASE

"Minority Report," in The Minority Report and Other Classic Stories by Philip K. Dick." New York: Del Rey, 1996, c1968, 256 p. ISBN: 086523793.

New York, Far Future. Commissioner John Allison Anderton picks up the cards on people who are about to commit heinous crimes and finds a card with his own name. He's stunned. He had no plans to murder anyone in the immediate future, but once the card is processed, he will be picked up and incarcerated. Commissioner Anderton grabs the card and runs. It does him no good; the cards are duplicated, and he cannot destroy the second copy of the card.

Associates: Lisa—*John Anderton's wife;* Ed Witwer—*Anderton's Senate-appointed new assistant, and presumptive successor;* Jerry, Mike, and Donna—*are the precognitives;* Wally Page—*who is in charge of the precognitives;* Leopold Kaplan—*the man that John Anderton is expected to kill;* Tod Fleming—*who helps Anderton escape.*

A SCANNER DARKLY

Genres/Themes Crossed: Dystopia X Hard-Boiled Mystery.

Subjects/Character Types: Future Technology X Police Procedural (undercover cop).

Series/Stand-Alone: Stand-alone.

Scene of the Crime: Alternate 1994 Southern California.

Detective: Undercover narcotics Officer Fred, is trying to work his way up the ladder of petty drug dealers to apprehend the actual manufacturers of the new drug called "Substance D." To do this he has assumed the persona of Bob Arctor. As Arctor, Fred poses as a drug user. He has found a reliable pusher, Donna, and is trying to work his way up to the next level of distributors by purchasing larger and larger quantities.

Known Associates: Bob loves Donna Hawthorne, who deals in various drugs. Arctor's boss is Hank.

Premise: The 1994 Southern California depicted in this book looks and sounds a lot like the 1970s in terms of popular music, fashion, and slang. In this 1994, a new drug, Substance D, has become the most popular drug on the planet. Initially, it produces a mellow feeling, a gentle euphoria, and a rather pleasant, scattered, relaxed mood with vivid and imaginative daydreams. It's a pleasant high. It's instantly addictive, but the trips become less pleasant. At the same time, users crave ever-increasing doses to feed their addiction. Users increasingly deal with disorientation and paranoia; eventually their minds will no longer function correctly. Users end up in various states: some die, some become catatonic, some lose the ability for any higher-level thought. Even those who recover fully are terrified that, if they leave the rehabilitation clinic that helped them through withdrawal, they will end up using once more, and that they will not be lucky enough to retain their mental faculties through their next addiction. The result is that many people who regain any level of functionality become life-long employees of the rehabilitation clinics.

Narcotics Officers must integrate into the drug culture in order to investigate the flow of drug traffic. It's easy to find small-time dealers, but arresting them does little to stem the tide of the illegal drugs. The police department focuses on finding either the major importers, or the manufacturers. There are many officers deployed as narcs: they associate with different groups of addicts. It is expected that, to maintain his cover, an undercover officer will occasionally use drugs. Some of the cops are eventually absorbed into the drug culture, becoming more drug users than cops. Then there are drug users who become informers, and these eventually become more like cops than drug users. These shifting roles pose particular dangers to undercover agents. To ensure the safety of undercover officers, their identities are kept secret from everyone, even from the officers who oversee their work. When undercover officers report, they wear disguises to protect their anonymity. The disguise most often worn is called a "scramble suit." This consists of a computer-generated, constantly changing image composed of bits of pictures of millions of different people projected onto an extremely thin shroud-like membrane worn by the officer. The officer is not only encased in this shroud-like garment, but his or her voice is deadened; altered by computer to make it devoid of all tone and personality.

An officer's reports are taped and, as time permits, examined to discover anomalies in his or her actions for clues on whether the life that he or she is living (and the drugs being ingested) have made the officer unreliable.

Comment: Many of Dick's works read like first drafts. There are subplots that are not resolved, and there are scenes of heart-breaking events where the prose does not support the mood evoked by the action. (This does not keep them from being brilliant: they contain fascinating ideas.) *A Scanner Darkly* was reworked repeatedly over a span of a couple of years. The Author's Note, printed at the end of the book, makes it clear that the book was written in memory of friends who were destroyed by the drug culture of the 1970s. It begins with a plaintive meditation, that these people were foolish, but not malicious; that they made mistakes, but that nothing they did merited their destruction; that the penalty exacted by life far outweighed whatever harm they had ever done. These characters were created out of Dick's memories of his friends; they are well meaning and funny: readers will befriend them and will mourn for the destruction of these fictional characters, and will mourn, beyond that, for Dick's friends, upon whom the characters were based.

Literary Magic & Mayhem: Substance D is popularly called, appropriately enough, Slow Death. Charles Freck, stymied when he tries to get some from his supplier, fantasizes about a world where it was openly for sale:

> In his fantasy number he was driving past the Thrifty Drugstore and they had a huge window display: bottles of slow death, cans of slow death, jars and bathtubs and vats and bowls of slow death, millions of caps and tabs and hits of slow death, slow death mixed with speed and junk and barbiturates and psychedelics, everything—and a giant sign: YOUR CREDIT IS GOOD HERE. Not to mention: LOW LOW PRICES, LOWEST IN TOWN. (p. 7)

He goes on to imagine that Slow Death really is supplied to Thrifty Drugstores, either by the Swiss or by aliens.

> But in actuality he knew better; the authorities snuffed or sent up everybody selling or transporting or using, so in that case the Thrifty Drugstore—all the millions of Thrifty Drugstores—would get shot or bombed out of business or anyhow fined. More likely just fined. The Thrifty had pull. Anyhow, how do you shoot a chain of big drugstores? Or put them away? (p. 8)

The feckless, charming, somewhat absurd inner voice of Charles is the way that the reader gets to know the character. Bob Arctor's memories of Barris make it clear that he was once a sweet man. The rapid deterioration of Bob gives the reader some idea of the journey made by Barris and by Jerry Fabin, and gives a preview of what is in store for Charles.

Explorations: What are some of the different ways that characters in the book flirt with death?

When someone comes close to dying, does it send that person into making rational choices for his or her own safety, or not?

What sort of conspiracies are going on? Who has been truthful with Fred?

Did the drugs from Fred's last buy accelerate his decline beyond what would be expected? Where did he get them? How does it change the story if the last pills were meant to send him over the edge? What if they were not? What if Fred's breakdown was simply caused by the cumulative effect of all the drugs that Fred had taken? Is there any way for the reader to tell?

THE CASE

A Scanner Darkly. New York: Vintage Books, 1991, c1977, 278 p. ISBN: 0679736654.

ALTERNATE SOUTHERN CALIFORNIA, JUNE 1994. Officer Fred, posing as druggie Bob Arctor, is sharing his house with two roommates, Jim and Ernie. He's observing them and trying to get one of the local pushers, Donna, to introduce him to whoever is above her in the drug-trafficking network. Fred is nonplussed when his superiors decide that the key to the whole situation is closer observation of Bob Arctor. He can't reveal that Bob is his alter-ego because it would be a breach of security. So, he dutifully steps up the surveillance on himself. This precipitates a psychic break, and he begins losing track of his job, and worse than that, of his identity.

ASSOCIATES: Hank—*Fred's boss;* Donna Hawthorne—*a Federal agent, posing as a drug dealer; she supplies Bob with drugs;* Jim Barris and Ernie Luckman—*are Bob's roommates;* Charles Freck—*a good friend of Bob;* Jerry Fabin—*who begins having such severe hallucinations that he has to be taken into rehab;* Kimberly Hawkins—*who tells Bob that she is afraid that her boyfriend is going to kill her;* Dan Mancher—*her boyfriend;* Mike Westaway—*who is still trying to find the truth.*

DINI, Paul and Royal McGraw.

BATMAN: DETECTIVE

Genres/Themes Crossed: Blended Society X Hard-boiled Mystery.

Subjects/Character Types: Superheroes, Supervillains X Amateur Sleuth (Contemporary).

Series/Stand-Alone: Stand-alone.

Scene of the Crime: Gotham City.

Detective: Bruce Wayne witnessed the murder of his parents as a small boy and vowed to dedicate his life to fighting crime. After years of training around the world, he returns to his home city of Gotham and takes on the roll of the masked detective, Batman.

Known Associates: Alfred Pennyworth, Bruce Wayne's butler and confidant, serves as the voice of reason and a sounding board for Bruce's ideas. Tim Drake is the newest Robin, youthful sidekick to Batman, having earned the roll after deducing Batman's true identity. Commissioner James Gordon, originally tasked with catching the masked vigilante patrolling Gotham's streets, has since become one of the Batman's allies in his war on crime by secretly giving him information on what the police know about prominent crimes. Harvey Bullock is a loud-mouthed, overweight detective, recently returned to the force. He distrusts Batman and other "masks."." Edward Nigma fought against Batman for years as the masked villain the Riddler; but following a bout of amnesia, Nigma claims to have reformed and is selling his services as a private investigator.

Premise: Batman must use his skills as a detective to solve a series of crimes in this collection of stories.

Comments: Paul Dini was one of the more prominent authors of episodes for the cartoon *Batman: The Animated Series* and its various movies and spinoff series. This animated series was considered by many to be the most accurate representation of the character in film media, and Dini was one of the writers and producers who helped make the series great. This collection contains the stories that Dini wrote during his recent run as the author of the

Detective Comics monthly comic book. The only continuing thread throughout these stories is that the Riddler has reformed and is selling his services as a private investigator.

Paul Dini blogs at http://kingofbreakfast.livejournal.com/. Royal McGraw's Web site at http://royalmcgraw.com/ includes biographical information, news, and a bibliography of his work; it links to information at several comic book sites.

Literary Magic and Mayhem: The stories in this collection are intended to showcase Batman's skills as a detective rather than his fighting abilities. While detective work does play a role in some of these stories, a few are showcases for Batman's scientific prowess, in which he uses science to defeat his opponent.

Explorations: How does Dini's previous experience as a screenwriter influence his writing style?

Has the Riddler truly reformed? Has the Penguin? What makes it possible for someone to reform?

What distinguishes Batman's detective skills from the Riddler's detective skills?

How does Dini's interpretation of the character differ from McGraw's?

THE CASE

Batman: Detective. New York: DC Comics, 2007, 144 p. ISBN: 1401212395.

GOTHAM CITY, PRESENT DAY. Batman sets about solving various crimes in Gotham City, utilizing his keen skills as a detective and scientist.

ASSOCIATES: Alfred Pennyworth; Robin; Commissioner Gordon; Harvey Bullock; the Riddler; Lois Lane; Jackie Vaseux; Oswald Cobblepot; Zatana.

DRURY, David M.

MICHAEL FLYNN SERIES

Genres/Themes Crossed: Science Fiction X Whodunnit.

Subjects/Character Types: Future Universe (space stations), Space Travel X Private Investigator, Company Town.

Series/Stand-Alone: Mike Flynn's life changes in the first book, so they're best read in order.

Scene of the Crime: Jupiter Station of the Conglomerated Mining and Manufacturing Company, mid-21st century.

Detective: Five years ago, private investigator Michael Flynn traveled to Jupiter Station in search of a man who worked as a miner. There were no other investigators on the station, so Michael decided to stay and enjoy a competition-free business environment. (Since then a few other investigators have set up businesses on the station.)

Known Associates: Michael Flynn is a hard-drinking Irishman who has a reputation as a ladies man. Betty O'Brien is the owner of his favorite bar; she takes a motherly interest in his life. Michael is avoiding one old girlfriend, Barbara, and mourning the loss of Missy, who recently married the jealous Jack Adamly. His buddies include Joe Aguirre, who owns a scavenging business on the station, and U.S. Marshal Sid Feldstein.

Edwin R. Warshovsky runs the Jupiter Station branch of the Conglomerated Mining and Manufacturing Company. Other top level managers include Legal Department Director Wendy Chadwick; Security Director Silvanus Drake; Human Resources Director Clarisse Jackson (who's Fred Zoldas supervisor); Operations Director Kevin McSheridan; Engineering Director Luke Timchenko; Manufacturing Director Lisa Reisbach, Head of Research and Development, Lou Cheng; and Marvin Chalmisiak, the miserly Head of Accounting.

Premise: In 2030, Arnold Lang imagined untold wealth being mined from asteroids caught in Jupiter's orbit. He convinced the board of Conglomerated Mining and Manufacturing to mortgage every company asset to build a space station and create a mining colony in Jupiter's orbit. It was a fiasco: the ore that was found was not particularly valuable, and the costs for shipping were greater than the profit that could made on the goods that were shipped. The company faced financial ruin. They replaced Lang with Edwin Warshovsky, who believed that the station, if it were larger and more self-sufficient, could turn a profit. The company followed his vision, and Jupiter Station was expanded into, essentially, a small town. Some food is grown on the station, ores found are refined to the point where outgoing shipments bring in a high profit, and the businesses set up to serve the company workers all pay a premium in rent and other fees to the company. Warshovsky's work turned the station into a profitable enterprise and saved Consolidated Mining when it was on the brink of disaster. While it will take many years to retire the debt incurred for creating and then expanding the station, the company is, at last, on the road to solvency. The station is a company town. Most of it is policed by company security. The United States claimed the station as a territory four years ago (2041); therefore, U.S. Marshals police the areas of the station that house residents and businesses that are not part of Consolidated Mining.

Comment: Dr. David Drury teaches electrical engineering as a member of the faculty at University of Wisconsin, Platteville. In an interview with J. R. Barnes of *The Exponent*, Professor Drury explained that his engineering background provides the technical foundation for his science fiction. It helps with world-building details such as describing an orbital gravity that corresponds to the rotation rates and the size of the station. *Library Journal* gave *All the Gold of Ophir* a starred review, stating that "Drury's debut features a fast-paced blend of hard science fiction and mystery with likable protagonists and a carefully thought out premise." *Jupiter's Shadow* is an excellent sequel. There are relationship issues in *Jupiter's Shadow* that are not completely resolved at the book's end, which seems to indicate that it will not be the last the world sees of Michael Flynn!

Dr. Drury's Web site at http://www.uwplatt.edu/~drury/ is more about his classes than his books, but there is a link there for his fiction.

Literary Magic & Mayhem: Some people have said that there is no point in writing a mystery that has science fiction elements unless those elements are so central to the mystery that the book could not have been written in a contemporary Earth setting. The books in this series qualify! The space-station setting is a necessary component because it is creates the situations that motivate the crimes. At the same time, the world-building is not the focus of the book. The characters and their motivations are the heart of the stories. In many ways the stories are reminiscent of mysteries set in 19th-century company towns on Earth. The insularity of the society, the power held by the corporation, the ways in which that power corrupts, the naïve and idealistic company employee—all of these are themes in the series.

Explorations: By the end of the book, is there any change in circumstances that would lead to justice?

If the law enforcement officer who was shot had survived, how would the other characters have changed their strategies? What other possible endings were there for the book? How would the society have changed?

Different characters had different priorities. Were any of them beyond understanding? What would make a set of priorities so wrong that it could be called evil?

THE CASES

1. ***All the Gold of Ophir.*** Waterville, ME: Five Star, 2005, 419 p. ISBN: 1594144214.

JUPITER STATION OF THE CONGLOMERATED MINING AND MANUFACTURING COMPANY, 2054. When Helene and Donald Asterbrook were notified of their son Philip's death, they sent word that they would come to Jupiter Station to claim his body. The trip to the space station took four months. At their journey's end they found that their son's body had been destroyed. They were given a box of his personal effects and found that it was incomplete: his personal journals were missing. When Conglomerate Mining and Manufacturing offered them a settlement, they became convinced that it was an attempt to buy their silence. They had to return to Earth, but first they hired Michael Flynn to find out the truth about their son's death.

ASSOCIATES: Helene and Donald Asterbrook—*Michael's clients;* Luke Kemper and Vinny Santino—*Conglomerated Mining's security officers;* U.S. Attorney Kyle Pierce—*the station prosecutor;* Marshal Sid Feldstein—*a friend of Michael;* Marshal Ben Wofford—*Feldstein's boss;* Wendy Chadwick—*Conglomerated Mining and Manufacturing attorney;* Edwin R. Warshovsky—*the general manager of Conglomerated Mining, Wendy's boss;* Silvanus Drake—*Conglomerated Mining's Head of Security, who seems to regard Wendy as an expendable and somewhat irritating colleague;* Joe Aguirre—*who runs a scavenging business;* Missy Adamly—*a programmer for Consolidated Mining.*

2. ***Jupiter's Shadow.*** Waterville, ME: Five Star, 2007, 399 p. ISBN: 9781594146077; 1594146071.

JUPITER STATION OF THE CONGLOMERATED MINING AND MANUFACTURING COMPANY, 2056. Francine Cross hired Michael to spy on her cheating husband, Leron. Someone murdered Leron scant hours after Michael took the case. He was able to report that Leron had always been faithful to the widow Cross, who then hired Michael to find her husband's killer. He soon realized that Leron's death was a single element in a criminal conspiracy; a conspiracy that threatened the life of every person on Jupiter Station.

Michael has done his best to become the kind of man his new wife, Wendy Chadwick, admires. The change has made both Michael and Wendy unhappy.

Head of Consolidated Mining Security Silvanus Drake prided himself on knowing everything that happened on Jupiter Station. Drake is shaken when he discovers gaps in station security. There is contraband on the station that must have been smuggled in, which should have been impossible. There is no record of the man who was found murdered despite the station's security sensors and the database that was designed to have information on every resident and every visitor of the station. Drake convinces Warchovsky to put the best private investigator on the station (Michael) on retainer, in order to step into Drake's position should Drake meet with an unfortunate accident.

ASSOCIATES: Wendy Chadwick—*Michael's wife;* Betty O'Brien—*a bartender and a friend;* Dr. Liao Chu—*Jupiter station's original designer, he is leading China's effort to build second space station;* Edwin Warchovsky—*Jupiter*

Station's general manager, he is finding ways to use the proximity of the competition to turn a profit for Jupiter Station; Silvanus Drake—*Head of Consolidated Mining Security;* Helmuth Manstein—*who must be identified by neighbors because there is no station record of him;* Peter Chow, Jeremy Kuchek, and Doug Sanchez—*are investigators hired by Michael to handle routine cases such as background checks;* Russell Murrow—*a pilot who takes Michael and Wendy on a ride outside the station;* Big Bill Gorkov—*gambling kingpin;* Hector "Weasel" Rivera, "Knuckles" DiGeorgio, and Pierre Lavalle—*Gorkov's henchmen;* Jack Adamly—*who is imprisoned for assault when a foolish man gropes Missy;* Missy—*Jack's wife;* U.S. Attorney Pierce—*who has the unenviable job of trying to help Marshal Hathaway accept the facts of law enforcement on the space station;* Joe Aguirre—*who runs a scavenging business;* Sheri—*who once went on a couple of dates with Michael;* Deputy Marshal Sid Feldstein—*who does Michael a favor.*

E

EDGHILL, Rosemary. (Editor)

MURDER BY MAGIC: TWENTY TALES OF CRIME AND THE SUPERNATURAL

Genres/Themes Crossed: Secret Society, Blended Society, Paranormal, Anthropomorphic Animals X Hard-Boiled Mystery, Traditional Mystery, Police Procedural.

Subjects/Character Types: Witches, Psychics X Private Investigators, Amateur Sleuths.

Series/Stand-Alone: Anthology of short stories.

Scene of the Crime: Varies.

Detective: Varies.

Known Associates: Varies.

Premise: The contributors' mandate was to write stories that featured a crime (preferably murder), and that the supernatural had to be involved either in the commission of the crime or in the mystery's solution.

Comment: In the book's fascinating Afterword, the editor writes about the history of the form. She traces the occult detective back to the time of the pulp and proto-pulp magazines. She chronicles part of the history, including Algernon Blackwood's *Doctor John Silence* stories written from 1908 to 1914; Seabury Quinn's *Jules de Grandin* stories published in Weird Tales from 1925 to 1951; William Hope Hodgson's *Carnacki the Ghost*

Finder stories published from 1912 to 1947; and the collection of *Doctor Taverner* stories published in 1926, written by Violet Mary Firth (pen name of Dion Fortune). (To read the John Silence stories—"A Physical Invasion," "Ancient Sorceries," "The Nemesis of Fire," "Secret Worship," "The Camp of the Dog," and "A Victim of Higher Space"—go to http://en.wikisource.org/wiki/John_Silence,_Physician_Extraordinary.)

She brings the lineage of occult detectives up to the present day through Manly Wade Wellman's Judge Keith Hilary Pursuivant (1930s), John Thunstone (1943–1985), and Silver John (1946–1987). Marion Zimmer Bradley's occult detective Colin MacLaren features in *Witch Hill, Dark Satanic, The Inheritor,* and *Heartlight* (which was written in collaboration with Rosemary Edghill).

She then makes the bridge to the combination of mystery and fantastical fiction through Randall Garrett's Lord Darcy, Glen Cook's Garrett P. I., and Laurel K. Hamilton's Anita Blake.

Literary Magic & Mayhem: Some of the stories are more adventures than puzzles, but they are uniformly excellent. All were first published in this book. Most are stand-alone stories, but some are entries into larger series, for instance, Laura Anne Gilman's Retriever's story featuring Wren.

Explorations: What types of power (legal authority, parental authority, physical size and strength, wealth, social standing, magical power, etc.) were used by characters in the story? Was magic used to balance other types of power, so that those who were otherwise powerless would have ways of standing against those with more conventional forms of power, or was magic just another weapon in the arsenal of the powerful? How would the story have been different if the setting had not included magic?

THE CASES

Murder by Magic. New York: Aspect, c2004, 545 p. ISBN: 0446679623; 9780446679626.

CONTENTS: Introduction *by Rosemary Edghill;* Piece of Mind *by Jennifer Roberson;* Special Surprise Guest Appearance by… *by Carole Nelson Douglas;* Doppelgangster *by Laura Resnick;* Mixed Marriages Can Be Murder *by Will Graham;* The Case of the Headless Corpse *by Josepha Sherman;* Death in the Working *by Debra Doyle;* Cold Case *by Diane Duane;* Snake in the Grass *by Susan R. Matthews;* Double Jeopardy *by M. J. Hamilton;* Witch Sight *by Roberta Gellis;* Overrush *by Laura Anne Gilman;* Captured in Silver *by Teresa Edgerton;* A Night at the Opera *by Sharon Lee and Steve Miller;* A Tremble in the Air *by James D. Macdonald;* Murder Entailed *by Susan Krinard;*

Dropping Hints *by Lawrence Watt-Evans;* Au Purr *by Esther Friesner;* Getting the Chair *by Keith R. A. DeCandido;* Necromancer's Apprentice *by Lillian Stewart Carl;* Grey Eminence *by Mercedes Lackey;* Afterword *by Rosemary Edghill.*

EFFINGER, George Alec. (1947–2002)

When Gravity Fails

Genres/Themes Crossed: Dystopia X Hard-Boiled Mystery.

Subjects/Character Types: Future Earth (end of the 22nd century) X Police Procedural, Private Investigator.

Series/Stand-Alone: Relationships and characters change over the course of the series. These are best read in order.

Genres/Themes Crossed: Future Earth (end of the 22nd century) X Police Procedural, Private Investigator.

Scene of the Crime: 22nd-century Middle East, the walled city of Budayeen. Budayeen combines elements of New Orleans' French Quarter with an Islamic, maybe Algerian, mystery city, as well as the criminal underworld of any city.

Detective: Marîd Audran is the son of a prostitute. He works as a free agent in the Budayeen; he's not ashamed to be a hustler:

> In the Budayeen—hell, in the whole world, probably—there are only two kinds of people: hustlers and marks. You're one or the other. You can't act nice and smile and tell everybody that you're just going to sit on the sidelines. Hustler or mark or sometimes a little of each. (*When Gravity Falls* p. 37)

Marîd would probably be ashamed to be a mark. Unfortunately for him, he falls into the category of being a little of each. He takes pride in keeping his word and paying his debts. He knows and uses the religious rules and social customs to be polite to people of different cultures. He struggles to maintain his independence, but once he comes to the attention of the powerful he doesn't have a chance.

Marîd starts the day with a couple of little blue triangles (stimulants of some kind) and then he keeps using them to avoid crashing down. There seems to be a drug or a drink for every occasion, and he always seems to feel miserable in the morning.

Marîd has a deep fear of having his brain wired, without that he cannot use the plug in brain modifications called "moddies." When he needs information that is most readily available in a moddy, he gets someone who is already wired to use the moddy and then tell him the information. In the first book, *When Gravity Falls,* Bey suspects Marîd of a series of murders. When Bey realizes that he was wrong, he makes Marîd an offer he can't refuse: a position in the local police department. Once Marîd is forced into working for Friedlander Bey, he is in a position where he must get his brain wired.

Known Associates: Yasmin is Marîd's on-again, off-again girlfriend for most of the first book. Once Marîd is co-opted by Friedlander Bey, they are through. Friedlander Bey controls organized crime in the Budayeen. He's known as Papa; and while he runs a lot of the crime in the city, he makes no effort to keep other criminals, who are acting as free agents, out:

> The motto of the Budayeen was "Business is business." Anything that hurt the free agents eventually hurt Friendlander Bey. There was enough to go around for everybody; it might have been different if Papa had been the greedy type. He once told me that he used to be that way, but after a hundred and fifty or sixty years, you stop wanting. That was about the saddest thing anyone ever said to me. (*When Gravity Fails,* p. 29)

Premise: In the 2130s, both Communism and Democracy "died in their sleep from exhausted resources and rampant famine and poverty. The Soviet Union and the United States of America fractured into dozens of small monarchies and police states" (*When Gravity Fails,* p. 18). By the end of the 22nd century, the Muslim world is in ascendance. A person can increase his knowledge and alter his personality and identity at will with pop-in cybernetic brain modifications, called "moddies."

Comment: Effinger is considered to be one of the founders of the cyberpunk movement. *When Gravity Fails* was nominated for the 1987 Nebula Award for Best Novel and the 1988 Hugo Award for Best Novel. It was followed with two more novels, *A Fire in the Sun,* and *The Exile Kiss;* and a fourth was in the works when Effinger died in 2002. The beginning of that fourth novel, *Word of Night,* is included in the posthumously published collection of Effinger's fiction, *Budayeen Nights.*

Effinger developed intestinal ulcers when he was very young. Decent medical care remained out of his reach because insurers considered these ulcers to be a pre-existing condition, and in the catch-22 that is the bedrock of the American medical system, this prevented him from getting adequate medical coverage. The result was that he dealt with chronic pain, and ended up struggling with an addiction to painkillers, yet he was extraordinarily productive, writing hundreds of short stories and more than 20 books in his 55 years. His short story "Schrondinger's Kitten" won the 1988 Hugo, the 1989 Nebula, and the 1989 Theodore Sturgeon Memorial Award for best short story.

He adapted the Marîd Audran books into scenarios for computer and role-playing games. He also wrote under the pseudonyms John K. Diomede, O Niemand, and Susan Doenim. His former wife, novelist Barbara Hambly, acts as the literary executrix of his estate and has managed to keep many of his works in print.

Effinger achieved more fame oversees than in the United States. He once said, "I'm to Japan what Jerry Lewis is to France. They love me over there."

There's a tribute webpage for George Alec Effinger at http://tom.jackson.googlepages.com/home. It includes a bibliography of George Effinger's works, links to sites with information on the author, and an FAQ.

Literary Magic & Mayhem: The novel explores the effects of drug use and alternate personality technologies. The protagonist puts on the personality of Nero Wolfe to try to solve the mystery.

Explorations: How do the *I Ching* verses relate to the action?

Which modifications seemed most bizarre? Did any seem sensible?

How do different people treat money? When is it food, when is it fun, when is it an obligation? When would Marîd refuse it if he could?

How do different people treat issues of gender?

THE CASES

1. ***When Gravity Fails.*** New York: Tom Doherty and Associates, 2005, c1987, 284 p. ISBN: 0765313588.

BUDAYEEN, 2202. Lieutenant Okking sent some business Marîd's way: Mr. Bogatyrev, who wants to hire someone to find his son. He has apparently decided to care about his son's absence three years after the child disappeared. Within moments of hiring Marîd, Mr. Bogatyrev is shot by a man using a James Bond moddy. The police take over the case, freezing Marîd out. Then an old lover, Nikki, asks Marîd to act as her agent and free her of the pimp Abdoulaye. Marîd thinks later that he hadn't seen the trouble he was stepping into when he took that job: "It didn't feel, at that moment, like I was getting into something over my head. It never does, before you take the leap" (p. 30). Then he starts finding bodies...

ASSOCIATES: Yasmin—*Marîd's girlfriend;* Lieutenant Okking—*who has a working relationship with Marîd;* Mr. Bogatyrev—*Marid's client, he is from reconstructed Russia;* Nikki—*a whore, she works indirectly (through Abdoulaye) for Friedlander Bey and hires Marîd to help her get free;* Chiri—*who tends bar at Chiriga's bar;* Tamiko, Devi, and Selima—*are the Black Widow Sisters;* Hassan the Shiite—*is Papa's mouthpiece;* Abdul-Hassan—*Hassan's servant;* Jo-Mama—*who owns a bar that caters to Greek seamen;* Rocky—*a barmaid there;* Bill—*the Taxi driver is one of the constants in the series;* Reinhardt—*a doorman;* Seipolt—*a rich and powerful man;* Joie—*a whore (either male or female);* Tewfik—*a.k.a. Courvoisier Sonny, is a pimp;* Frenchy Benoit—*a club owner;*Yasmin, Blanca, Indihar—*dancers at Benoit's club;* Dalia—*a barmaid at the club;* Mahmoud—*who used to be a friend of Marîd;* Laila—*a moddies seller;* Trudi—*a friend of Lutz Seipolt;* Sergeant Hajjar—*who fetches Marîd for Friedlander Bey;* Dr. Yeniknani and Dr. Lisân—*who perform Marîd's brain modification;* Jacques Dévaux—*a Moroccan Christian;* Saied the Half-Hajj; and Faud il-Manhous—*the chronically unlucky.* Modified personalities that appear include James Bond, Xarghis Khan, Nero Wolfe, and Archie Goodwin.

2. ***A Fire in the Sun.*** New York: Doubleday, 1989, 289 p. ISBN: 0385263244; 038526349X (pbk.).

BUDAYEEN, 2203. Friedlander Bey is going mad, and in his madness he bids Marîd to investigate the woman, Umm Saad, and destroy her. She claims to be Bey's daughter. Bey's reaction causes Marîd some concern: he's been wondering if Bey might be his father. The overwhelming interest Bey seems to take in every aspect of his life (and the control Bey exerts over every aspect of Marîd's life) are difficult to understand without that sort of personal connection. The police want Marîd to investigate Bey's oldest rival, Reda Abu Adil.

ASSOCIATES: Saied the Half-Hajj—*Marîd 's partner in crime;* Hishan—*is the mark;* Angel Monroe—*Marîd's mother;* Indihar—*a widow who dances at Chiri's club;* Janelle, Pualani, Kandy, Yasmin, and Brandi—*other dancers at the club;* Bill—*the taxi driver, is on a perpetual high;* Youssef—*Friedlander Bey's butler;* Umm Saad—*who is causing Friendlander Bey distress;* Saad ben Salah—*her son;* Kmuzu—*a slave who is a gift to Marîd;* Lieutenant Hajjar—*Marîd's superior officer;* Officer "Jirji" Shaknahyi—*Marîd 's partner in police work;* Sergeant Catavina—*who is Hajjar's right hand man;* Jirji, Hâkim, and Zahra—*are Shaknahyi's children;* Jacques Dévaux—*a Moroccan Christian;* Mahmoud—*who is a sexchange;* Monsieur Gargotier—*who owns the club Fée Blanche;* Laila—*a moddies seller;* Meloul—*who runs a Meghrebi restaurant;* Safiyya the Lamb Lady—*a beggar;* Chiri—*who starts drinking at Sandor Courane's club;* Jo-Mama—*who owns a bar;* Rocky—*one of her barmaids;* On Cheung—*who deals in children;* Paul Jawarski—*the boss of the Flathead gang;* Morgan—*who is hired by Marîd to track down an American;* Teme Akwete—*who represents the new government of the Songhay Republic;* Umar Abdul-Qawy—*the secretary to Reda Abu Adil;* Faud il-Manhous—*the chroni-*

cally unlucky; Dr. Yeniknani and Dr. Lisân—*who perform research on brain modification.*

3. ***The Exile Kiss.*** New York: Doubleday, c1991, 265 p. ISBN: 0385414234; 0385414242 (pbk.).

BUDAYEEN, 2203. Marîd and Friedlander Bey are kidnapped and put on trial. They're found guilty for the murder of Officer Khalid Maxwell, a man that neither of them knew. The verdict was decided before they had even entered their pleas. To clear their names, they will have to solve the crime and find the real murderer. They aren't given the chance. The judge sentences them to banishment. In the desert, they are befriended by nomads. One of the women of the tribe is murdered and Marîd works to find her killer.

ASSOCIATES: Friendlander Bey—*Marîd's great-grandfather;* Indihar—*Marîd's wife;* Jirji, Hâkim and Zahra—*Marîd's adopted children;* Senalda—*their maid;* Angel Monroe—*Marîd's mother;* Tariq—*Bey's driver;* Youssef—*the butler;* Kmuzu—*Marîd's slave;* Chiri—*Marîd's business partner;* Pualani, Yasmin, Windy, Lily, and Kandy—*dancers at Chiri and Marid's club;* Shaykh Mahali—*the amir;* Reda Abu Adil—*Bey's competitor;* Kenneth—*Abu Adil's administrative assistant;* Lieutenant Hajjar—*who is in the pay of many people.*

In Najran, they meet Sergeant al-Bishah; Muhammed Musallim bin Ali bin as-Sultan—*the leader of the Bayt Tabiti nomads;* The Bani Salim nomads include Noora—*a lovely young woman;* Hassanein—*Noora's uncle;* Nasheeb—*her father;* Ibrahim bin Musaid—*who wants to marry Noora;* Suleiman bin Sharif—*who Noora wants to marry;* Hilal; Bin Turki; and Umm Rashid.

Ferrari—*owner of the Blue Parrot Nightclub;* Faud il-Manhous—*the chronically unlucky;* Jacques Dévaux—*the Moroccan Christian;* Mahmoud—*the sex-change;* Saied the Half-Hajj; Frenchy—*a nightclub owner;* Dalia—*his barmaid;* Theoni—*one of his dancers;* Kamal ibn ash-Shaalan—*who owns the bar named The Brig;* Tansy—*works the bar;* Ghazi—*one of the city's children;* Dr. Sadiq Abd ar-Razzaq—*the imam of the greatest mosque in the city;* Dr. Besharati—*performs autopsies and is able to verify that the same weapon was used for two separate murders.*

Collection of short stories:

4. ***Budayeen Nights.*** Urbana, IL: Golden Gryphon Press, 2003, 235 p. ISBN: 1930846193.

CONTENTS: Schrödinger's Kitten (winner of the Hugo, Nebula, and Seium Awards); Marîd Changes His Mind (re-written as the first two chapters of *A Fire in the Sun*); Slow, Slow Burn (featuring Honey Pílar); Marîd and the Trail of Blood (featuring Bill the Cab Driver); King of the Cyber Rifles (featuring Jân Muhammad); Marîd Throws a Party (This was to be the first two chapters of a fourth Marîd Audran book; unfortunately, this fragment is all that was left when George Alec Effinger died.) The World as We Know It (The narrator of this story is Marîd Audran.); The City on the Sand (the first story set in Budayeen); The Plastic Pasha (This was the first appearance of the Budayeen, and it gives a good description of the Budayeen and the Nameless City. It features Ernst Weinraub.)

EGAN, Greg.

Quarantine: A Novel of Quantum Catastrophe

Genres/Themes Crossed: Science Fiction, Alien Interference X Hard-Boiled Mystery.

Subjects/Character Types: Future Earth X Private Investigator.

Series/Stand-Alone: Stand-alone.

Scene of the Crime: Australia, 2067. (On November 15, 2034 Earth's solar system was encased in a bubble).

Detective: Nick Stavrianos, private investigator, was born before the occurrence of The Bubble. He was eight year's old when "the stars went out" (on November 15, 2034, 8:11:05 to 8:27:42 GMT). Nick became a cop, and on a routine call, he and his partner foiled a major strike of the apocalyptic cult, The Children of the Abyss, a strike that would have cost thousands of lives. Nick became the hero of the police department and was given a promotion. Too late, it occurred to Nick that his prominence would make him a target and that both he and his wife were at risk. Unable to sleep, he left the bedroom so his wakefulness would not disturb his wife's sleep. He was sitting in the living room, trying to figure out how to turn down the promotion, when the bomb the cult had set in his bedroom exploded. Nick's wife, Karen, was killed. Nick left the police department and became a private investigator.

Known Associates: Karen, Nick's deceased wife, is always with him via a neural modification that allows him to hallucinate her presence at will. He does not control what she says and does; and she is not compelled to behave in character, but usually she is Karen, much as Nick remembers her.

Premise: On November 15, 2034, a shield was placed around Earth's solar system. People can no longer see the stars. Probes sent out seem able to go through the shield, but they don't come back. It may be centuries before Earth has the technology for a manned probe to investigate. Immediately following the "stars going out," there was mass hysteria; but it was followed by nothing. There was no communication, no further actions, no explanation. Gradually, most people calmed down. There are a few still saying that the end times are near (they've now been saying this for decades, and no one is paying much attention). There are others who've joined an apocalyptic cult called The Children of the Abyss. It was inspired by Marcus Duprey, who was born on Bubble Day. Its members simply can't accept that the stars had gone out and it meant nothing, changed nothing: they're doing their best to invest it with meaning by creating mayhem through mass murder.

Future technologies include innovation in communications: information can be downloaded directly into a person's mind (they suddenly know the information), or information can be sent in a stream slow enough for them to virtually hear it in their minds and learn it as if they were listening to a lecture.

Private investigators have interesting challenges. Almost every action people take may be recorded in some database, but hackers are constantly altering the databases to cover up criminal actions. However, the hackers' illegal activities end up preserving versions of the database, making it possible, with a lot of work, to winnow out some indication of what information has subsequently been altered.

Comment: Greg Egan is an Australian computer programmer and science fiction author. He won the Hugo Award, the Locus Award, and Asimov's Readers Award in 1998 for the short story "Oceanic," and he won the John W. Campbell Memorial Award for Best Novel in 1995 for *Permutation City*. His homepage is at http://gregegan.customer.netspace.net.au/; it includes links to those of his stories that are available online.

The case is resolved in the first third of the book. The last two thirds trace Nick's work in the Ensemble and reveal the reason for the Bubble.

Literary Magic & Mayhem: There are so many interesting aspects to this future Earth. One is the question of how much people should trust the information that they think they know when some of it has been transferred directly into their brains through neural mods (neural modifications that most people purchase and install to transmit information into the brain). For instance, Nick receives information on his case through a neural mod he has purchased that acts as an answering service while he sleeps. It's called The Night Switchboard (made by Axon, and costing $17,999), and it takes the information transmitted to Nick and transfers it to his mind while he's sleeping, so that he wakes up knowing that information. At the opening of the book, a prospective client sends Nick the information on a missing-persons case: the client wants Nick to find Laura. Nick is well aware that the information he knows might, for one reason or another, be inaccurate:

> My anonymous client presumes that Laura was kidnapped, but declines to suggest a motive. Right now, my judgment is suspended. I'm in no state to hold an opinion on the matter; I have a head full of received knowledge, colored by my client's perspective, possibly even tainted by lies. (p. 5)

Even when Nick purchases an information mod, the information may be packaged with extras to increase customer satisfaction—extras that Nick does not want. For instance, in New Hong Kong, Nick uses a guidebook package (Déjà Vu) to acquaint him with the city, and it gives him the tourist spiel of facts on what he sees, but it goes beyond imparting information:

> The catch is, the mod also pumps out a deliberate subtext: a sense of growing familiarity, a sense that you're gaining the most profound and intimate knowledge, a sense that with each piece of predigested trivia you swallow, you're fast approaching an understanding of the place to rival that of any lifelong citizen. This is precisely the delusion that every tourist wants, but personally I'd rather stay slightly less complacent. (p. 45)

In the end, Nick is forced to accept a mod that alters his values, even his personality. It's a loyalty mod, to ensure his loyalty to the Ensemble once they have captured him. He knows that the mod is there, and he regards mods designed to change the values and beliefs of the subject as obscene, but (now) he believes it is for the best because the work of the Ensemble is vital. At the same time, he realizes that it is the loyalty mod that has created his belief in the value of the Ensemble's work.

> Knowing that my feelings have been physically imposed makes them no less powerful.... there is nothing I can do to change it.
>
> And I don't believe I'll go mad... I want to serve the Ensemble, more than I've ever wanted anything before. All I have to do is find a way to reconcile this with my sense of who I am. (p. 94)

Explorations: Nick thinks about the two conflicting points of view: "the bubble changes everything" (it proves the existence of aliens) and "the bubble changes nothing" (the aliens have done nothing except for cutting off Earth's view of the rest of the universe, which made no material difference to life on Earth). Which view feels" right, and why?

What kinds of mods would be most useful?

Why would holograms of companions be beyond conscious manipulation?

The Canon helps its members regain mastery of their own minds by embracing the underlying orthodoxy of the organization and recognizing their loyalty to those concepts rather than to the organization. It certainly was not what the Ensemble expected. How does it work out? Would the creators of the Ensemble appreciate the results?

If humans were faced with genocide brought on by the actions of a relatively primitive society, would The Bubble seem a reasonable response? What are other possibilities?

THE CASE

1. ***Quarantine: A Novel of Quantum Catastrophe.*** New York: Harper Paperbacks, 1995, c1992, 280 p. ISBN: 0061054232.

AUSTRALIA, SUMMER 2067. PI Nick Stavrianos accepts a job to locate a missing girl. Her name is Laura Andrews: she disappeared from the Hilgemann Institute (a mental institution) about a month ago. She'd been at the institute since the age of five because she has severe congenital brain damage. Mentally, she's an infant, even though her body is 32 years old. That's one of the reasons that everyone believes she was kidnapped. She's not even capable of working a door's handle to open the door on her own.

ASSOCIATES: Dr. Cheng—*the Hilgemann Institute's Deputy Medical Director, he is anxious to avoid both scandals and lawsuits that might arise because of the disappearance of a patient;* Laura Andrews—*the patient;* Bella—*a hacker who Nick hires to get computerized data that is not available through legal means;* Dr. Pangloss—*the knowledge miner Nick hires when the computerized data is legally available, but would take too long to find;* Martha Andrews—*Laura's sister, who is not that concerned;* The Ensemble includes People who work at BDI Security: Chen Ya-ping, Huang Qing, Lee Soh Lung, Yang Wenli, and Liu Hua. (Teo Chu—*Huang Qing's girlfriend, is a sound engineer and musician.*) People who work at ARS Advanced Systems Research include Chung Po-kwai—*a volunteer;* Lee Hing-sheung—*a guard;* Tong Hoi-man—*the Security Manager;* and Drs. Leung Lai-shan, Lui Kiu-chung, and Tse Yeung-hon. The Canon includes those who have been conscripted through the application of loyalty mods to work for the Ensemble. They include Dr. Lui Kiu-chung—*ASR physicist;* Li Siu-wai—*BDI imaging technician;* Dr. Chan Kwok-hung—*ASR physicist;* Dr. Yuen Ting-fu and Dr. Yuen Lo-ching—*brother and sister mathematicians.*

ELROD, P. N. (Patricia Nead)

BLOODLIST

Genres/Themes Crossed: Secret Society X Hard-Boiled Mystery.

Subjects/Character Types: Vampires X Private Investigator.

Series/Stand-Alone: Relationships changes over the course of the series. The short stories are incidental, but it's best to read the novels in order.

Scene of the Crime: Chicago, beginning in 1936.

Detective: Jack Fleming, born in 1900 (he is 37 in January 1938). He fought in WWI, and when he returned to the States, he met, loved, and lived with Maureen; and he found out that vampires are real. Maureen and Jack exchanged blood in the fragile hope that they would be together forever. (The hope is fragile because most people are immune to the virus that will make them vampires after death.) In 1931, Maureen fled, promising to return to Jack as soon as she knew it was safe. Jack began drinking, and in 1936 he decided that it was time to leave New York and start over in Chicago. Within a few days of his arrival, he was murdered. At the beginning of *Bloodlist,* he's risen from his watery, Lake Michigan grave. He died in 1936 in his mid-thirties, but since rising, he looks as if he's in his early twenties. Others look at him and see a green kid, not a man who has survived grief, terror, and war.

Known Associates: Charles Escott was at a train station when he noticed Jack. What he noticed was that Jack did not have a reflection. Charles is a self-described "private agent" (*not* a private investigator: as far as Charles is concerned, private investigators work on sleazy divorce cases). Charles possesses a terrifying mixture of curiosity and bravery. When he realizes that there is something odd about Jack, he investigates. When he figures out what Jack is, Escott develops a strategy to force Jack to come to him. Once he hears Jack's story, Escott decides to help investigate Jack's murder. They strike up a friendship, and eventually they become business partners. In *Bloodlist,* singer Bobbi Smythe follows instructions to entrap Jack; and mobster Gordy Weems helps work him over. Despite these inauspicious beginnings, Bobbi becomes Jack's girlfriend and Gordy, whom Bobbi regards as a big brother, becomes his friend. Shoe Coldfield is an old friend of Charles Escott. They were in the same acting company many years ago. It was an acting company that traveled together. Some people joined for a short time, but there was a core of people who stayed for years and created a sort of family. Shoe and Charles were two of the actors who stayed for years, and they share a bond that transcends the strained race relations of the time.

Comment: Tod Browning's film *Dracula* (the production starring Bela Lugosi) premiered on Valentines Day in 1931. It was a sensation. It was reported that many audience members fainted at the premier; and the movie's popularity renewed interest in Stoker's 1897 novel, *Dracula,* on which the movie was based. Therefore, in the 1930s many people had heard of vampires and knew the legendary methods of destroying them. Not all the weapons listed by Stoker work in the world of this series; a fact that saves Jack from destruction on more than one occasion. In Elrod's world, vampires can be hurt by some elements of nature such as flowing water and anything made of wood, but vampires are not damaged by silver bullets and are not harmed by symbols of faith, such as crosses. Some humans can become vampires after death if, while they were living, they exchanged blood with a vampire. This does not happen often because most people are immune to whatever illness makes one a vampire. Most humans who exchange blood with a vampire, even those who do so repeatedly over the course of years, do not become vampires when they die.

Difficulties in the chronology: "A Night at the (Horse) Opera" was originally published in 1995 in the anthology *Celebrity Vampires.* There is a statement in it: "Next Christmas was about ten months away," that seems to indicate that it takes place in February. February 1936 would be impossible (Jack was not a vampire in February 1936). February 1937 is a possibility, but P. N. Elrod's Web site states that the story takes place between the events of *Bloodcircle* and *Art in the Blood,* so it was placed between those two novels in this chronology.

The author's Web site, http://www.vampwriter.com/, includes a bibliography, news on the series, information for aspiring writers, free online access to a few of the short stories, and substantial excerpts from some of the books.

Literary Magic & Mayhem: Elrod does a good job of depicting Chicago in the 1930s. She explores the tension between the races, and she gives it a face. Shoe Coldfield clearly knows where he will and where he will not be welcome in Chicago. Jack finds that there are places where a white man is not welcome. Isham has fun playing on Strome's prejudice, and it is clear that Strome's attitude is common.

The country has survived the war, and has repealed prohibition. There is a somewhat desperate air in the bars and gambling dens, an absolute determination to enjoy life. Those who lived through the misery of the war take a somewhat dismissive attitude to people too young to have served. This attitude is ironic in Jack's case, since he served in WWI, but now looks like a younger man. Virtue is seen as naïve; a tough and somewhat selfish attitude is seen as realistic. The war has left its mark.

Lifeblood, Bloodcircle and a later work, *The Devil You Know,* tie up the loose ends from Jack's old life, the one in which he was infected with the virus that would turn him into a vampire. *Fire in the Blood, Blood on the*

Water, and *A Chill in the Blood* cover a few weeks in which different gangs battle for Frank Paco's Chicago territory. *Cold Streets* and *A Song in the Dark* cover Hog Bristow's attempt to take over Gordy's territory and the aftermath of that attempt.

The Devil You Know features Izzy. There is another "Izzy" story in the anthology *White House Pet Detectives: Tales of Crime and Mystery at the White House from a Pet's Eye View,* edited by Carole Nelson Douglas, published by Cumberland House in 2002, ISBN: 9781581822434. The story is entitled "Izzy's Shoe-In."

One interesting aspect of these books is how the author deals with the problem of having an almost indestructible hero. If the hero is going to be safe no matter what happens, how can the author create suspense? The hero also has superpowers. He can discorporate, vanishing into the air at a moment's notice. He can hypnotize people and alter their memories or force them to do his bidding. He has superhuman strength.

These superpowers can get in the way of a good story. How can any of the people that Jack cares about face any difficulty? Would any of them ever need to solve their own problems? Once the audience knows Jack's capabilities—knows that he can survive direct attacks, get out of any trap, alter the memories of any witnesses, cause villains to confess, etc.—how can the author create a plot that challenges him and that interests the audience? One of the joys of this series is that P. N. Elrod faces those storytelling difficulties and overcomes them. She has created strong characters and she doesn't coddle them. She is willing to do whatever it takes to challenge those characters, and she tells a good story while she does it.

Explorations: What was the bravest action depicted in the book? What made it so brave?

How can an author create suspense after he or she has created a character with superpowers, a character who is virtually indestructible?

Which character was the most interesting? Which was the most likable? With which character did you identify?

Most people expect to be able to identify the good guys in a city. The good guys might be the police, or the mayor, or reporters; but there is an expectation that someone can be relied upon to do his or her best for the society. The Chicago depicted in this series is so corrupt that the only people who can be identified as on the side of vice or virtue are the crime bosses, and they aren't on the side of virtue. In the world of the series, what would you expect average people to do when they see evidence of a crime? What are Jack's options?

THE CASES

1. ***Bloodlist,*** novel included in *The Vampire Files: Volume One*. New York: Ace Books, 2003, p. 1–160, ISBN: 0441010903.

CHICAGO, ILLINOIS, AUGUST 1936. Jack Fleming wakes up on the roadside, just in time to get hit by a car. It does less damage than expected, and soon he realizes that something is very wrong. He finds out that he's been gone for the better part of a week, but he has no memory of that time. He also finds out that he is no longer alive. He once hoped that he would become a vampire when he died; now he has to deal with the reality. While he becomes accustomed to his new existence, he works to solve his own murder. This is not an intellectual exercise; the people who wanted to kill him still want him dead.

ASSOCIATES: Charles Escott—*a private agent who discovers Jack's secret;* Frank Paco—*mob boss;* Fred Sanderson, Georgie Reamer, Gowan, Harry, Newton, and Doc—*work for Frank Paco;* Shoe Coldfield—*an old friend of Escott, a gang leader in the Bronze Belt of Chicago, and owner of The Shoe Box nightclub;* Cal—*works for Shoe;* Dr. Clarson—*who knows Shoe;* Slick Morelli and Lucky Lebredo—*co-owners of The Nightcrawler Club;* Bobbi Smythe—*a singer at The Nightcrawler Club;* Gordy Weems—*who works for Slick;* Mr. Burdge—*the doorman at the swanky Hallman's restaurant;* Jack's mother and father—*who live in Cincinnati;* Benny O'Hara—*a.k.a. Benny Galligar who Jack knew in New York.*

2. ***Lifeblood,*** novel included in *The Vampire Files: Volume One*. New York: Ace Books, 2003, p. 161–314, ISBN: 0441010903.

CHICAGO, ILLINOIS, SEPTEMBER 1936. For five years, Jack has run ads in the personal columns of several newspapers, seeking word from his first love, Maureen Dumont. He finally decides that he must let go and he puts an end to the ads. As soon as the ads stop, he receives his first response. Has Maureen finally found safety and sent him word, or is the message a trap set by the men who persecuted her? Jack must find out, and Charles agrees to help him.

ASSOCIATES: Charles Escott—*who works with Jack to recover stolen goods;* Mr. Swafford—*the client;* Selma Jenks—*the thief;* Sled—*her accomplice;* Gordy Weems—*who is now in charge of the Nightcrawler Club;* Jinky and Hitch—*are two of Gordy's men;* Bobbi Smythe—*who lands her first job as a singer on a radio show;* Marza Chevreaux—*Bobbi's accompanist;* Madison Pruitt—*the wealthy communist, is Marza's escort;* Mattheus Webber and James Braxton—*who visit Jack's parents;* Phil Patterson—*the house detective in Bobbi's building;* Gaylen—*Maureen's younger sister, Gaylen is now 72 years old;* and Malcolm and Norma—*who work for Gaylen.*

3. ***Bloodcircle,*** novel included in *The Vampire Files: Volume One*. New York: Ace Books, 2003, p. 315–452, ISBN: 0441010903.

CHICAGO, ILLINOIS, SEPTEMBER 1936. The book opens scant hours after the close of *Lifeblood*. The police can place Jack at the scene of a homicide, and they want an account of his actions. As soon as they are able, Jack and Charles take up their own investigation. They decide to put all their time and resources into tracking down Maureen Dumont. Five years ago, she fled; she may have been trying to escape danger, or she may have been trying to draw her enemies away from Jack. Jack is convinced that the danger has passed. If he and Charles can find her, she will finally be able to come out of hiding. They manage to trace the steps Maureen took the day she left Jack; they find her first hideout, but there the trail goes cold. A cab driver can testify that she left that first sanctuary, but neither he nor anyone else knows what became of her after that cab ride.

ASSOCIATES: Lieutenant Blair—*who works Homicide for the Chicago Police Department, notices Jack's lack of a reflection;* Charles Escott—*who works with Jack;* Matheus Webber—*was a friend of the late James Braxton;* Bobbi Smythe—*a singer;* Marza Chevreaux—*Bobbi's accompanist;* Edith Sedlock—*an old friend of Maureen;* Emily Francher—*shipping-line heiress;* Jonathan Barrett—*Emily's secretary;* Mr. Mayfair—*her gardener;* Haskell—*the groom;* Laura Francher—*Emily's ward;* John Henry Banks—*a cab driver;* Police Chief Curtis; Mr. Handley—*Emily's attorney;* Abigail, Clarice, and Robert—*Emily's cousins.*

4. **"A Night at the (Horse) Opera,"** originally published in *Celebrity Vampires,* edited by Martin Harry Greenberg. New York, DAW Books, c1995, pagination unknown, ISBN: 0886776678; also available online at: http://www.vampwriter.com/A%20Night%20at%20the%20Horse%20Opera.htm.

CHICAGO, 193?. A couple of mob enforcers mistake Harpo Marx for Chico, who owes Big Joey five-thousand dollars. Their orders are to either get the money or take it out in damage on Chico's hide. Harpo doesn't have the money and can't convince the enforcers that he's not the man they want. Jack gets caught up in the action, trying to protect Harpo. Jack is able to keep them both alive, but he's not able to keep his secrets.

ASSOCIATES: Harpo Marx—*who goes to the movies;* Guns Thompson, Higgs, and Rinky—*are Big Joey's boys.*

5. ***Art in the Blood,*** a novel included in *The Vampire Files: Volume Two.* New York: Ace Books, c2006, novel copyright c1991, p. 1–154, ISBN: 0441014275.

CHICAGO, ILLINOIS, SEPTEMBER OR OCTOBER 1936. Jack encounters members of Chicago's art world when Bobbi sings at a reception for an art exhibition. The evening begins innocently enough, but there is mayhem before the night is out, and murder follows. Jack must once again finesse his way out of one of Lieutenant Blair's investigations. In the course of this case, Jack's secret is learned by one more man, and Bobbi decides that she wants to take the risk of exchanging blood with Jack so that they have a chance of being together for centuries.

ASSOCIATES: Charles Escott—*Jack's partner;* Gordy Weems—*a mobster;* Bobbi Smythe and Marza Chevreaux—*are engaged to perform at Leighton Brett's art reception;* Jack Fleming and Madison Pruitt—*their escorts;* Leighton Brett—*an artist;* Reva Stokes—*a gallery owner, she is Brett's fiancé;* Titus Noble—*a violinist;* Evan Robley—*an artist who plays dice (badly);* Sandra Robley—*Evan's sister;* Dreyer—*a sore loser;* Alex Adrian—*a famous artist;* Sally, Jannie, and Walt—*Reva's household help;* Francis Koller and Tourney—*who are thugs;* Barb Steler—*a reporter;* and Dimmie Wallace—*bookie;* Lieutenant Blair—*who has been compelled to regard Jack as a friend.*

6. ***Fire in the Blood,*** novel included in *The Vampire Files: Volume Two.* New York: Ace Books, c2006, novel copyright c1991, p. 155–320, ISBN: 0441014275.

CHICAGO, ILLINOIS, JANUARY OR FEBRUARY 1937. When Marian Pierce's maid reported to Marian's father, Sebastian Pierce, that the expensive ruby bracelet he gave Marian on her 21st birthday had disappeared, Sebastian hired Jack and Charles to recover it. He suspects that Stan, the new boyfriend of Marian's friend Kitty, is the thief. He's worried that he will alienate his daughter if he conducts an open investigation, so he's hiring Jack and Charles' discretion as well as their expertise. It seems like an innocuous request, but family problems can get dangerous. In the course of this investigation, Jack walks the edge, in danger of becoming a monster, and he comes to the conclusion that some confessions are better left unspoken. Memories from this case will haunt him for the rest of his existence.

ASSOCIATES: Bobbi Smythe—*who is headlining at the Top Hat;* Lieutenant Blair—*who is no longer sure that he and Jack are friends;* Charles Escott—*who works with Jack;* Sebastian Pierce—*their client;* Mr. Griffin—*who works as Pierce's chauffeur;* Marian—*Pierce's daughter;* Harry Summers—*Marian's current boyfriend;* Kitty Donovan—*Marian's best friend;* Leadfoot Sam—*a bookie, he terrifies Kitty;* Butler—*Leadfoot Sam's associate;* Stan McAlister—*Kitty's new boyfriend;* Doreen Grey—*Stan's neighbor;* Vaughn Kyler—*who took over Frank Paco's territory;* Hodge, Rimik, and Chaven—*Kyler's associates;* Dr. Rosinski—*Doreen's doctor;* Pony Jones—*bookie;* Elmtree Elmer—*Pony's half-brother;* Trudy—*a madam;* and Opal—*Kyler's accountant.*

7. ***Blood on the Water,*** novel included in *The Vampire Files: Volume Two.* New York: Ace Books, c2006, novel copyright c1992, p. 321–482, ISBN: 0441014275.

CHICAGO, ILLINOIS, FEBRUARY 1937. Kyler gave Jack 24 hours to get out of Chicago. Jack's been busy since then, and he kind of lost track of the time, of the threat, and, worst of all, of Kyler. Unfortunately, Kyler did not lose track of Jack. In fact, he's not only focused on Jack, he's also setting up Jack's friends. Kyler's plans are complicated by the beginnings of a gang war. Jack is caught in the crossfire; one side wants him dead and the other side is not particularly interested in keeping him alive.

ASSOCIATES: Vaughn Kyler—*the mob boss who took over Frank Paco's Chicago territory six months ago;* Chaven—*Kyler's lieutenant;* Vic—*who used to work for Frank Paco;* Deiter—*a "specialist" who was brought in to kill Gordy Weems;* Opal—*Kyler's accountant;* Arnold, Tinny. and Chick—*are footsoldiers in Kyler's gang;* Lieutenant Calloway and Officer Baker—*both of the Chicago Police Department, are also on Kyler's payroll;* Lieutenant Blair—*is an honest cop, but Kyler is working on other ways to manage him;* Charles Escott—*is in danger since Kyler knows that he is a friend of Jack;* Bobbi Smythe—*is headlining at the Top Hat Club;* Gordy Weems—*runs the Nightcrawler Club, Bobbi thinks of Gordy as a brother;* Ernie—*one of Gordy's men;* Angela Paco's men include Vic (maybe), Doc, Newton, Sheldon, Lester, and Mac; Frank Paco—*Angela's father, is being held by Kyler;* Shoe Coldfield—*an old friend of Charles;* Isham—*works for Shoe.*

8. *A Chill in the Blood.* New York: Ace Books, 1998, 327 p. ISBN: 0441005012.

CHICAGO, ILLINOIS, FEBRUARY 1937. Kyler's death only increased the heat of the gang war. Angela Paco is trying to reclaim the territory that Kyler took from her father, Frank Paco. New York is sending Sean Sullivan to take over the same territory. Some of Kyler's men have joined Angela's gang, but only because she is using her insane father, Frank, as a figurehead. Her hold on them is as fragile as her hold on her sanity; she's a sociopathic homicidal maniac. Jack would have been safer if they had all continued to believe him dead; but he's afraid that the gangs will target his friends, so he wades back into the fray.

ASSOCIATES: "Shoe" (Clarence) Coldfield—*Charles's friend, Shoe learns Jack's secret in this novel;* Trudence Coldfield—*Shoe's big sister;* Sal—*who works for Trudence;* Gordy Weems—*runs the Nightcrawler Club;* Mr. Delemare—*runs a movie theater where Jack is not particularly welcome;* Bobbi Smythe—*Jack's girlfriend, has gone into hiding.*

Angela Paco—*who is attempting to re-take her father Frank Paco's territory;* Deiter, Chick, Tinny, Dunbar, Doc, Newton, Lester, and the bookkeeper, Opal—*are Angela's gang;* Frank Paco—*Angela's father;* Sean Sullivan—*who is sent by the Mob from New York to manage Frank's old territory;* Lieutenant Calloway and Officer Baker—*of the Chicago Police Department were on Kyler's payroll, now they're on Sullivan's;* Maxwell—*is Sullivan's secretary;* Dr. Balsamo—*who works for Sullivan;* and Federal Agent Merrill Adkins—*a man with a mission.*

9. **"You'll Catch Your Death,"** published in *Vampire Detectives,* edited by Martin Harry Greenberg. New York, DAW Books, c1995, p. 233–55, ISBN: 0886776260.

CHICAGO, 193?. A couple of nights ago, Jack almost died in Lake Michigan (again). He goes to exorcise his demons and finds a man and a woman as evil as anyone he has ever encountered.

ASSOCIATES: Lloyd; Susan—*Lloyd's wife;* and Ellie—*Lloyd's sister.*

10. **"Grave-Robbed,"** published in *Many Bloody Returns,* edited by Charlaine Harris and Toni L. P. Kelner. New York, Ace Books, 2007, p. 146–75, ISBN: 9780441015221.

CHICAGO, FEBRUARY 193?. Jack has always had a soft spot for a dame in distress. This dame, Abigail Saeger, doesn't quite qualify: she is certainly distressed, but she is only 16 years old. She tells Jack that her widowed older sister, Flora, is being victimized by a con man. Flora was an easy mark: she was at the tiller when her husband James was killed in a boating accident. She is overwhelmed with grief, and with guilt. Flora's husband, James, drowned in Lake Michigan. Jack can relate. Flora is being conned by a man who claims to be able to reach James from beyond the grave. Jack's first steps are to check on that. After all, if vampires exist, who can be absolutely sure that a séance isn't genuine?

ASSOCIATES: Abigail Saeger—*Jack's client;* Flora Weisinger—*Abigail's sister, has become involved with a medium;* Alistair Bradford—*the medium;* Gordy Weems—*mobster.*

11. **"The Quick Way Down,"** published in *Mob Magic,* edited by Brian Thomsen and Martin H. Greenberg. New York, DAW Books, c1998, p. 150–64, ISBN: 0886778212.

CHICAGO, 193?. When Gordy finds prizefighter Alby Cornish dead in the gentleman's bathroom of the *Nightcrawler Club,* he asks Jack for help. In the course of helping out, Jack takes a fall from a penthouse roof and is forced to deal not only with killers, but also with his own fear of heights.

ASSOCIATES: Gordy Weems—who runs the *Nightcrawler Club;* Soldier Burton; Ruth Phillips—*Soldier's girlfriend;* and Lieutenant Nick Blair.

12. ***The Dark Sleep.*** New York: Ace Books, 2000, c1999, 359 p. ISBN: 0441007236.

CHICAGO, ILLINOIS, APRIL 1937. The Escott Agency has been hired to recover some papers from saltine heiress Mary Sommerfeld's ex-boyfriend. He proves to be more determined and more violent than Charles and Jack expected. Jack's personal life grows more complicated as Bobbi courts national attention with a spot on the Archy Grant Variety Hour radio show. Charles faces the demons from his past. This story poses an interesting question, most easily stated, without spoiling this story, as "What would Jimmy Olsen do if he wanted to solve a life-threatening problem on his own, without Superman's help?" Charles Escott comes up with an effective method of resolving this question. It's interesting that in this book and in the last, the author has dealt with the question of how grown men keep their self-respect when they have a friend who can resolve their difficulties for them.

ASSOCIATES: Charles Escott—*Jack's partner;* Mary Sommerfeld—*their client;* Jason McCallen—*foreman, Mary's ex-boyfriend;* Paterno—*McCallen's friend;* Bobbi Smythe—*headlines a new show "The Shanghai Review" at the Nightcrawler Club;* Rachel—*the costume mistress;* Gordy Weems—*who runs the Nightcrawler Club;* Ike LaCelle—*who knows about opening a club;* Ted Drew—*bandleader;* Cathy Bloom—*the wife of Gordy's lawyer;* Gil Dalhauser—*a mobster;* Archy Grant—*radio variety show host;* Adelle Taylor—*radio actress;* and Madison Pruitt—*a communist whose family owns Canuvel Steel.*

Sal—*works for nurse Trudence Coldfield at the shelter she has set up in the Bronze Belt area of Chicago;* Shoe Coldfield—*Trudence's brother, is a mobster and owner of the club The Shoebox in the Bronze Belt;* Isham—*who works for Shoe.*

Jim Waters—*a singer Jack meets at Moe's;* Shep Shepperd and Ace—*are hired to follow Jack;* Bianca and Katherine Hamilton—*who ran The Hamilton Players Acting Company which employed Charles from the year he was 19 until he was 25;* In 1924, Charles's coworkers included his friend Clarence Coldfield—*the only African American man in the company;* Cornelius Werner—*who played parts for older leading men;* Stan Parmley—*who played the romantic leads;* Henry; Klopner; Eric Lynd; and Raymond Yorke.

13. ***Lady Crymsyn.*** New York: Ace Books, 2000, 410 p. ISBN: 0441007244.

CHICAGO, ILLINOIS, JUNE 1937. Four months ago, Jack managed to escape an attempt on his life with his pockets stuffed with thousands of dollars in cash. Gordy helped him launder the money, and Jack decided to turn it into a legitimate investment by opening his own nightclub, the *Lady Crymsyn.* He begins by investing in rehabilitating a building with a bloody past, a club that was closed down five years ago when a bomb took out the owner, Welsh Lennet, several of his bodyguards, and his bartender. Booth Nevis, leader of the gang thought responsible for the hit, had bought up the property, and now leases it to Jack. The building's past comes back to haunt Jack when workmen find a skeleton in the basement. It's the remains of a young woman, and it is soon apparent that she was chained in the basement, bricked in, and left to die. Jack can imagine her death all too well. He knows what it is like to know that someone means to murder you and hide your body so that it will never be found. He's known that since Slick's men worked him over and heaved him into Lake Michigan. He also knows the torment of a man whose lover has disappeared: for over five years, he waited and worried over what had happened to Maureen. He's deeply touched by the young woman's death, and he becomes determined to investigate her murder.

ASSOCIATES: Bobbi Smythe—*Jack's girlfriend, is headlining at The Red Dueces club;* Charles Escott—*Jack's partner, takes an overnight train to New York to recover a kidnapped canine.*

Leon Kell—*the foreman for the construction work on Lady Crymsyn where the construction crew finds a body;* Lieutenant Nick Blair—*who regards Jack as a suspect;* Mobster Gordy Weems—*who counsels Jack on publicity;* Booth Nevis—*head of the Nevis gang, owns The Flying Ace club, and leases the building that will be the Lady Crymsyn to Jack;* Shivvey Coker—*who works for Booth;* Malone—*the bartender at The Flying Ace;* Norrie—*Malone's young (10- or 12-year-old) daughter;* Royce Muldan—*a handsome man who believes that being the son of a man who is a prominent New York mobster gives him protection;* Couturier Joe James—*who used to own the dress shop La Femme Joeena;* Rita Robillard—*who was Lena Ashley's roommate;* Mr. Tony Upshaw and Ruth Woodring—*dance studio owners;* Shivvey—*who decides to move on Jack;* Gris—*who acts as Shivvey's backup.*

Miss Sherry LaBelle—*plays the part of Lady Crymsyn at the club's opening.* Those who attend the opening include Gardner Pourcio—*a gambler;* Myrna—*deceased;* Adelle Taylor—*who comes to the opening with Gordy;* Shoe Coldfield; and Lieutenant Blair—*who tells Jack that Lena Ashley's real name was Helen Tielli;* Bobbi—*who sings at the opening;* Marza Chevreaux—*Bobbi's accompanist;* and Jim Waters—*who plays the blues.*

14. "The Breath of Bast," originally published in *Kittens, Cats, and Crime,* edited by Ed Gorman. Waterville, ME: Five Star, 2003, pagination unknown. ISBN: 0786250321; also available online at: http://www.vampwriter.com/Breath%20of%20Bast.htm.

CHICAGO, 1937. Charles gets his own case. A beautiful client hires him to deliver a sculpture. It's an oddly simple job; all he has to do is note the buyer's reaction and then return to the client's home to report.

ASSOCIATES: Cassandra Selk—*Escott's client;* Ma'at—*one of the buyer's cats.* Charles speaks to Jack Fleming after the case is closed.

15. "Slaughter," published in *The Repentant,* edited by Brian M. Thomsen and Martin Harry Greenberg. New York: DAW Books, c2003, p. 175–201, ISBN: 0756401631.

CHICAGO, 1937. A young man calling himself "Slaughter" appeared a few weeks ago and began quietly taking over pieces of Gordy's business.

ASSOCIATES: Gordy Weems—*who requested Jack to act as back-up when Slaughter is interviewed.* It turns out that Slaughter had exchanged blood with a woman about a month ago, a little while before he died.

16. ***Cold Streets.*** New York: Ace Books, c2003, 380 p. ISBN: 0441010091.

CHICAGO, ILLINOIS, JANUARY 1938. Jack and Charles work to find kidnapping victim Sarah Gladwell and return her safely to her mother. Gordy has decided that the *Lady Crymsyn* is a good spot for meetings that must take place on neutral ground. He's meeting with "Hog" Bristow who has told the bosses in New York that Gordy is too soft to get the most out of the Chicago territory. The New York bosses have sent him to Chicago to negotiate with Gordy. Bristow is connected, protected, and dangerous. He's determined to prove himself, and if the only way to do so is over Gordy's dead body.

ASSOCIATES: Charles—*Jack's partner;* Vivian Gladwell—*their client, is mother of the kidnapped Sarah;* Sarah—*is developmentally disabled: her body is 16, but mentally she is about 10 years old;* Hurley Gilbert Dugan—*the mastermind behind the kidnapping;* Ralph, Vinzer, and Ponti—*are working with Hurley.*

Bobbi Smythe—*is headlining at and booking other acts for Jack's club, the Lady Crymsyn;* Adelle Taylor—*singer who is dating Gordy;* Faustine Petrova and Roland Lambert—*dancers;* Wilton—*bartender;* Myrna—*deceased, bartender;* Gordy Weems—*mobster, he treats the Lady Crymsyn as neutral ground;* Ignance "Hog" Bristow—*who intends to take over Gordy's territory;* Anthony Brockhurst—*Dugan's cousin;* Marie Kennard—*Anthony's friend;* Lowrey and Strome—*Gordy's bodyguards;* Derner, Ruzzo and his brother, also Ruzzo—*all work for Gordy;* Kroun—*the man who sent Bristow to Chicago;* Reef, Tib, and Lissky—*are Bristow's men;* Dr. Clarson—*who works hard to keep his patient alive;* Shoe Coldfield—*Jack and Charles's friend;* and Isham—*who works for Shoe.*

17. ***Song in the Dark.*** New York: Ace Books, 2005, 377 p. ISBN: 0441013236.

CHICAGO, ILLINOIS, JANUARY 1938. This novel picks up where *Cold Streets* ends. It covers the immediate aftermath of Jack's encounter with Bristow, an encounter that left Jack sick in mind and body. He's driven to keep his promises, promises that require near-heroic acts to hold Gordy's gang together. At the same time, he is overwhelmed by his own everyday life.

One problem encountered by everyone, from authors of fantastic fiction to people who play role-playing games, is what to do when a character gets so powerful that he or she can waltz through any difficulty. All suspense is gone. Rescues become tedious exercises employing elements familiar to the audience. Between enhanced speed and strength, the ability to discorporate, the ability to hypnotize witnesses so that they will not remember anything inconvenient and can be convinced to follow Jack's orders...what is the series going to become? These works are written from Jack's viewpoint. How much villainy can the reader observe through Jack's eyes when Jack can stop almost anyone from doing almost anything? How many times could secondary characters be put into danger with Jack performing last minute rescues? How can secondary characters even encounter any serious difficulties once they have been befriended by Jack? In *The Dark Sleep,* P. N. Elrod grapples with this question and comes up with a great solution, but it's not a solution that can be used repeatedly. In the next three books, she increases the danger to Jack and puts up roadblocks to his using his powers. By the end of the three books, she has essentially maimed his superpowers, allowing both the character and the series to continue to hold readers' interest.

ASSOCIATES: Gordy—*who is recuperating from a near-fatal attack,* Hoyle—*who thinks that he, not Jack, should have taken over for Gordy;* Derner—*who is the General Manager of Gordy's bar, The Nightcrawler Club;* Strome, Lowrey, Ruzzo and his brother Ruzzo—*are others in Gordy's gang.*

Whitey Kroun—*who came in from New York to, in his words, "take care" of Jack;* Mitchell—*who accompanied Kroun to provide back up;* Alan Caine—*is headlining at Gordy's Nightcrawler Club;* Evie Montana—*one of his act's back up dancers, is hoping to become the next Mrs. Caine;* Jewel—*the last Mrs. Caine was driven out of the business by Alan, now she is demanding the back alimony that he owes her.*

Bobbi Smythe—*is headlining at and booking other acts for Jack's club, the Lady Crymsyn;* Charles Escott—*who has gotten into the habit of coming by the club to help out;* Teddy Parris—*singer at the Lady Crymsyn;* Faustine Petrova and Roland Lambert—*dancers at the Lady Crymsyn;* Wilton—*bartender;* and Myrna—*deceased, bartender.*

Gordy Weems—*who is being treated by Dr. Clarson;* Adelle Taylor—*Gordy's girlfriend;* Shoe Coldfield—*who provides a safe house for Gordy;* Isham—*who works for Shoe and enjoys baiting Strome;* John Coward from Waukegan—*is mistakenly kidnapped by Gordy's gang.*

18. "Her Mother's Daughter," published in *My Big Fat Supernatural Honeymoon,* edited by P. N. Elrod. New York, St. Martin's Griffin, 2008, p. 123–61, ISBN: 0312375042; 9780312375041.

CHICAGO, FEBRUARY 1938. One half-hour after the end of her marriage ceremony, Mrs. Jerome Kleinhaus Schubert leaves the reception at St. Michaels and finds her way across town to hire Jack to find her groom. Jack isn't looking forward to dealing with the mobsters involved in the case, but he has "a sad and fatal weakness for dames in need," so he takes the case.

ASSOCIATES: Mrs. Jerome Kleinhaus Schubert—*neé Dorothy Huffman is the daughter of mobster Big Louie Huffman;* Cooley and Becker—*are Huffman's thugs;* Mrs. Sheila Huffman—*Dorothy's mother, is more frightening than all of them put together;* Gerty Schubert—*is the mother of the groom;* Jerome—*the groom.*

19. ***The Devil You Know,*** Bryan/College Station, TX: Vampwriter Books, 2009, 140 p. (no ISBN assigned—the book is available directly from the author's Web site.)

CHICAGO, ILLINOIS, AND LONG ISLAND, FEBRUARY 1938. It has been two years since Jack and Escott learned the truth about Maureen's disappearance. Barrett has found what's left of her. Jack receives word that Maureen's body has been found. He travels to Long Island to attend her funeral. After the funeral Barrett reveals that he found more than Maureen's body. He and Jack are attacked and left for dead, and they realize that they must investigate.

ASSOCIATES: Charles Escott—*Jack's partner;* Jonathan Barrett—*who once also loved Maureen;* Mrs. Stannard—*wife of the man who rented Barrett the earth-moving machine;* Fleish Brogan—*Manhattan mob boss;* Isabelle "Izzy" DeLeon and Desmond Clapsaddle—*reporters who used to work with Jack;* Swann "Swanny"—*who works for (and against) Brogan;* Naomi Endicott—*widow of attorney Griffin "Graft" Endicott;* Mr. Thorpe, Mr. Nolan, the enormous Mr. Kaiser, and the clever Remke—*have all allied themselves with Swanny.*

ELROD, P. N. (Editor)

MY BIG FAT SUPERNATURAL WEDDING

Genres/Themes crossed: Secret Society, Blended Society, Paranormal X Hard-Boiled Mystery, Traditional Mystery.

Subjects/Character Types: Witches, Psychics, Ghosts, Vampires, Werewolves, Daimons X Private Investigators, Amateur Sleuths.

Series/Stand-Alone: Anthologies of short stories.

Scene of the Crime: Varies.

Detective: Varies.

Known Associates: Varies.

Premise: Authors were asked for stories that combined the supernatural, mysteries, and weddings for the first book: *My Big Fat Supernatural Wedding.* They were asked for stories that combined the supernatural, mysteries, and honeymoons for the second book: *My Big Fat Supernatural Honeymoon.*)

Comment: The madness of the amateur productions that we make of weddings provides an hysterical backdrop for mystery stories with magical elements. (Delayed honeymoons, brides being hunted, grooms being lost, and other unusual catastrophes mar the honeymoons.)

Literary Magic & Mayhem: The stories were written for these volumes. Some are stand-alone stories, others are episodes in series. For instance Jim Butcher's *Something Borrowed* is the story in which Harry Dresden attends the wedding of Billy and Georgia. (In *My Big Fat Supernatural Honeymoon,* Jim Butcher's "Herot" reveals the true nature of one of the minor characters.) Others are set in the same world as a series; for instance, Charlaine Harris's *Tacky* doesn't feature Sookie, but it is set in the *Southern Vampire* series' world, and shows an important social shift in that world.

Explorations: How did the madness of the wedding celebration, the wedding planning, or the expectations a character had of weddings play into the story?

What do the circumstances and events in the story portend for the marriage?

THE CASES

1. ***My Big Fat Supernatural Wedding.*** New York: St. Martin's Griffin, 2006 310 ISBN: 0312343604; 9780312343606.

CONTENTS: Spellbound *by L. A. Banks;* Something Borrowed *by Jim Butcher;* Dead Man's Chest *by Rachel Caine;* All Shook Up *by P. N. Elrod;* The Wedding of Wylda Serene *by Esther M. Friesner;* Charmed by the Moon *by Lori Handeland;* Tacky *by Charlaine Harris;.* A Hard Day's Night-Searcher *by Sherrilyn Kenyon;* . . . or Forever Hold Your Peace *by Susan Krinard.*

2. ***My Big Fat Supernatural Honeymoon.*** New York: St. Martin's Griffin, 2008 *by* 310 ISBN: 0312375042; 9780312375041.

CONTENTS: Stalked *by Kelley Armstrong;* Heorot *by Jim Butcher;* Roman Holiday, or SPQ-arrrrrr *by Rachel Caine;* Her Mother's Daughter *by P. N. Elrod;* Newlydeads *by Caitlin Kittredg;* Where the Heart Lives *by Marjorie M. Liu;* Cat Got Your Tongue? *by Katie MacAlister;* Half of Being Married *by Lilith Saintcrow;* A Wulf in Groom's Clothing *by Ronda Thompson.*

F

FFORDE, Jasper.

THE EYRE AFFAIR

Genres/Themes Crossed: Fantastical Realism, Literary Cross-Over X Police Procedural (Special Ops).

Subjects/Character Types: Alternate universe, Characters from other works of fiction X Government Investigators.

Series/Stand-Alone: The time traveling elements make this series particularly challenging, best to read it in careful order.

Scene of the Crime: England, a police state run by the Goliath Corporation.

Detective: Thirty-six-year-old Crimean War veteran Thursday Next is now an Operative Grade I of SO-27, the Literary Detective Division of the Special Operations Network. In *The Eyre Affair,* she is temporarily promoted to Spec-Ops-5, then leaves London to take a position as an SO-27, Operative Grade 3. She has an honorable discharge from the war, even though she disobeyed direct orders. Her commander, Major Phelps, led the Light Armored Brigade into the Russian guns in error. There was wholesale slaughter. She grabbed the commander and got him back behind the English lines, then she disobeyed orders by returning to the battlefield to try to find and help her fallen comrades. Only 51 of the 534 survived. One of the dead was Thursday's brother, Anton.

Known Associates: Thursday Next's regenerated pet dodo (left over from the days when reverse extinction was all the rage) is named Pickwick. Thursday's father used to work for the ChronoGuard; they take care of Anomalous Time Ripplation. In other words, they try to clear up the messes left (accidentally and intentionally) by time travelers. He went rogue, and the ChronoGuard did their best to destroy him, even going back in time to disrupt his parents so that he was not conceived. As a result, he has no name beyond "Dad," but he shows up frequently to see Thursday. The rest of Thursday's family includes her mother, her brother Joffy who has become a priest, and her Aunt Polly and Uncle Mycroft. Mycroft is an inventor who is afraid that his inventions will be warped to serve military purposes. In the *Eyre Affair,* Mycroft develops a "Prose Portal" that allows people to step into their favorite books. He sets it up to connect to Wordsworth's poem "I Wandered Lonely as a Cloud" in order to give his wife a lovely, restful, and spiritual holiday. The Goliath Corporation comes to the conclusion that they could write books about weapons that are physically impossible to build and then bring them out of the books into the real world; it would turn an invention originally designed to give pleasure to readers into the world's most efficient arms manufacturer.

Premise: In this universe, the Crimean War never ended; England and Imperial Russia have been at war for more than a century. The Goliath Corporation has propped up the English war effort and has reaped huge profits. Goliath now forms a sort of shadow government in England, being the power behind the government in many areas.

Beyond that, the barriers between literature and reality have become permeable. This is how Victor Analogy, head of Special Operations Division 27, the Literary Detection Division, describes it:

> The barriers between reality and fiction are softer than we think: a bit like a frozen lake. Hundreds of people can walk across it, but then one evening a thin spot develops and someone falls through; the hole is frozen over by the following morning. (p. 206)

Thursday accidentally "fell through" into *Jane Eyre* when she was a child. She was in the story for a few minutes, and then fell out again. Victor has information that in 1926 a collector of antiquarian books entered the novel *Dombey and Son.* He's worried that the man was trapped in the story; Thursday points out that he might have stayed in the book by choice, and at that point Victor guesses that she has entered fiction herself.

Some people seem to have the knack for entering (and it turns out that some characters have a knack for leaving) works of fiction. They are few, and the talent is, for the most part, kept secret. Thursday's brilliant and eccentric Uncle Mycroft has invented a way that anyone can purposely enter a work of fiction, and unfortunately the government has learned of his invention (and, consequently, so has the Goliath Corporation).

Thursday Next is part of the Special Operatives' Division 27 (Literary Detective Division): her job is to preserve England's literary heritage. The Special Operations Network was created to handle policing duties too specialized or unusual for the regular police force. There are at least 33 Divisions: the higher the division number, the more mundane the assignment. For instance, SO-33 is the Entertainment Fascination Department, SO-32 is the Domestic Horticulture Enforcement Agency, SO-31 is the Good Taste Education Authority (they're having a difficult time); SO-28 is for income-tax assessment; SO-27 is the Literary Detectives, and SO-21 is the Transport Authority. Information is restricted about all divisions under SO-20. SO-17 is Vampire and Werewolf Disposal Operations; SO-12 is ChronoGuard (tasked with protecting history from sabotage by time travelers); and SO-9 is the Antiterrorist Division. There is a saying that everything below eight is above the law: the divisions below the eighth one often take the law into their own hands and regard themselves as having a license to kill. These include SO-6, the National Security Division, SO-5, Search and Containment (of dangerous criminals); and SO-1, Internal Affairs.

Comment: *The Eyre Affair* was nominated for the Dilys Award (the book that independent booksellers voted the most fun to sell) in 2003, the second book in the series, *Lost in a Good Book,* won the Dilys Award in 2004. There is a parallel series, the *Nursery Crime* series. The first book, *The Big Over Easy,* is a reworking of *The Eyre Affair,* written when it was difficult to find a publisher for *The Eyre Affair. The Fourth Bear* is the second book in the *Nursery Crime* series, and a third book, *The Last Great Tortoise Race,* is planned.

Jasper Fforde's Web site, http://www.jasperfforde.com, includes a news section (complete with news flashes from Toad News), a link to the cheese enforcement Web site, information on Special Ops http://www.jasperfforde.com/specops/who.html, and information on the series.

Literary Magic & Mayhem: Thursday is a complex and likeable character; the other characters in the series are two-dimensional. Dozens of characters from classic novels are pulled into the series, often with a point made about the character's habits, or a novel's descriptions, or phrases of dialog that resonates, with key lines included from the characters' originating books. A reader with a good memory for the classics would enjoy that aspect of the series. At times, particularly in the later books, parody seems to take precedence over plot. *The Well of Lost Plots* is set in the world of fictional works more than in the alternate-history Earth that was created for these novels. The world of fictional works is an interesting world, but information about it is conveyed to the reader in long sections of exposition that weigh down the narrative.

There are many fun elements in this literature-obsessed alternate-history world. For instance, every Friday night for over a decade, fans have dressed up as favorite characters and gone to a play in which the audience enjoys yelling statements that have become scripted over time at the characters, as the characters perform the play. In this world that play is not the *Rocky Horror Picture Show;* it is Shakespeare's *Richard III.*

Explorations: What books would be interesting to enter?

If books could be used as jails, what books would make good ones?

Thursday's father's statements make it clear that history has shifted several times during the story, what were the changes?

THE CASES

1. ***The Eyre Affair.*** New York: St. Martin's Press, 1994, c1992, 188 p. ISBN: 0312105118.

LONDON, 1985 AND THORNFIELD HALL. Thursday Next is assigned to the investigation of the theft of the original manuscript of Charles Dickens's *Martin Chuzzlewit.* SO-5 Field Operative Tamworth comes to her after he examines the scene; he is sure that the theft was the act of the third-most-wanted criminal in the world, Acheron Hades. He asks Thursday to accept a temporary assignment in SO-5 to work with him to stop Hades. Hades has managed to employ stealth technologies that render him invisible to surveillance and that allow him to know if anyone in his vicinity mentions his name, thus allowing him to avoid being apprehended. Thursday is one of the few people alive who knew him before he became a criminal. She took a college English course from him. Thursday agrees to a temporary SO-5 assignment to apprehend Hades, but the operation does not go as expected.

ASSOCIATES: In London: Special Operations Area Chief Boswell and Paige Turner—*of SO-27 (Special Operations Division 27: Literary Detective Division or the LiteraTecs);* Head Field Operative Fillip Tamworth, Filbert Snood (who used to be in ChronoGuard), and Buckett—*of SO-5 (Search and Containment);* Flanker—*Tamworth's old divisional commander;* Lydia Startright—*Toad News Networks' star reporter;* Edmund Capillary—*a Baconian,* and Edward Fairfax Rochester, Esq.

In Swindon: Commander Braxton Hicks—*runs the Office of Special Operations, and seems to be working with Schitt;* Jack Schitt—*the head of Goliath's Advanced Weapons Division;* Victor Analogy—*is in charge of Swindon's LiteraTecs (SO-27);* Bowden Cabel—*Thursday's partner, his specialty is 19th-century prose;* Finistreer—*the LiteraTec who specializes in 19th-century poetry;* Fisher—*the LiteraTec whose areas are legal copyright and contemporary fiction;*

Helmut Bight—*the LiteraTec who works on 17th- and 18th-century prose and poetry;* Malin, and Sole—*the LiteraTecs who devote their time to Shakespeare;* Jeff and Geoff Forty—*the LiteraTecs who operate the Verse Meter Analyzer;* Officer "Spike" Stoker—*of SO-17 (Vampire and Werewolf Disposal Operations);* Mr. Meakle—*a werewolf who won't take his medication;* Frampton—*the janitor at the Senior School at Haydon;* Thursday's mother—*who is sometimes visited by Thursday's father;* Joffy—*Thursday's surviving brother, who is now a GSD (Global Standard Deity) priest;* Thursday's Uncle Mycroft—*an inventor;* and her Aunt Polly—*who assists Mycroft and acts as a test subject;* Thursday's father—*SO-12 (ChronoGuard) shows up wherever and whenever he likes;* Major (now Colonel) Phelps—*who was Thursday's commander the day the Light Armored Brigade advanced into the Russian guns in error;* Landen Parke-Laine—*the man Thursday once thought she would marry;* Liz—*the receptionist at the Finis;* Holroyd Wilson—*the pianist who plays at the Cheshire Cat bar.*

Acheron Hades—*Arch-criminal;* Styx—*Acheron's brother;* Acheron's henchmen include Mr. Delamare—*a thug,* Mr. Hobbes—*an actor,* Felix7—*who has a memory-impairment,* and Dr. Müller—*who co-devised the Earth-crossers (a militant astronomical group).*

Mr. Quaverley—*of Martin Chuzzlewit;* Sturmy Archer—*who tried to go straight;* Mr. Rumplunkett—*head pathologist;* Colonel Rutter—*of the Chrono-Guard;* Daisy Mutlar—*who intends to marry Landen;* Jones the Manuscript—*Thursday's Welsh contact;* Haelwyn the Book—*is his assistant;* Bartholomew Stiggins—*SO-13;* and Lavoisier—*who is on the trail of Thursday's father.*

Jane Eyre—*is kidnapped from Jane Eyre;* other characters in the book include Mr. Rochester; Bertha—*his wife;* Grace Poole—*her nurse;* Mrs. Fairfax—*the housekeeper;* and Mrs. Nakajima—*a tourist.*

2. ***Lost in a Good Book.*** New York: St. Martin's Press, 1994, c1992, 188 p. ISBN: 0312105118.

ENGLAND, SEPTEMBER 1985, 1972, NORLAND, EARLY 19TH CENTURY. On December 12, 1985, all organic matter will turn into pink slime. Thursday is told this by her father, a renegade from the ChronoGuard. The problem is that ChronoGuard personnel are staging a labor action, and no one is checking the time stream up from December 1985 (i.e., no one is checking the stability of events prior to December 1985) to see what will cause the destruction of life on Earth. (Thursday thinks that it's absurd that they would strike when the world is about to end, but her father thinks striking at this time is, from an industrial action point of view, a very good strategy.)

In her personal life, Thursday finds out that she is pregnant and that she is to go on trial. Her attorney is unhelpfully mysterious. He doesn't even take the time to explain what charges are being brought against her. In her professional life, Thursday and her partner, Bowden, are sent out to investigate a spate of forgeries of *Cardenio,* one of Shakespeare's lost plays. The world goes wild when Thursday and Bowden authenticate one, adding another title to Shakespeare's canon.

This book handles changes created by time travel in an interesting way. There is a chapter 4 and a chapter 4a.

ASSOCIATES: Adrian Lush—*television talk show host who has set up an interview with Thursday.* Censoring the interview are: Commander Braxton Hicks—*Swindon Special Operations Divisional Chief,* Colonel Flanker—*SO-1 (Internal Affairs);* Colonel Rabone—*Combined Forces Liaison;* Mr. Schitt-Hawse—*of the Goliath Corporation (half-brother of Jack Schitt);* Mr. Chesterman—*of the Brontë Federation;* Captain Marat—*SO-12 (ChronoGuard),* and Mrs. Jolly Hilly—*Governmental Representative to the Television Networks.*

Landen—*Thursday's husband;* Thursday's father—*SO-12 (ChronoGuard) who, in this book, is almost apprehended by Lavoisier;* Wednesday—*Thursday's mother;* Joffy—*Thursday's brother;* Aunt Polly and Uncle Mycroft—*who are brilliant;* Wilbur—*Polly and Mycroft's son, married to Gloria;* Orville—*Polly and Mycroft's son, married to Charlotte;* Granny Next; Houson—*Thursday's mother-in-law.*

Thursday Next is the hero of the Jane Eyre rebookment. Cordelia Flakk—*SO-14 (PR agent) has been booking Thursday for interviews;* Victor Analogy—*is in charge of Swindon's LiteraTecs (SO-27);* Bowden Cabel—*Thursday's partner, his specialty is 19th-century prose;* John Smith—*SO-32 (Domestic Horticulture Enforcement);* Phodder and Kannon—*SO-5 (Search and Containment of dangerous criminals);* DianaThuntress—*SO-9 (the Antiterrorist Division) negotiator;* Mr. Stiggins—*Neanderthal, SO-13 (Genetic Detectives and Neanderthal affairs) operative represents Thursday at an Internal Affairs hearing;* Officer "Spike" Stoker—*SO-17 (Werewolf and Vampire Disposal Operations);* Agent Durrell—*SO-13, is following a stray mammoth;* Miles Hawke—*SO-14 (Tactical Support Unit) operative is quite dashing.*

Akrid Snell—*Thursday's lawyer, he is apparently overworked;* Matthew Hopkins—*a prosecuting attorney poses as a reporter for the Owl;* Anne Hathaway—*who believes that she has a copy of one of Shakespeare's lost plays;* and Lord Volescamper—*who also believes that he has a copy:* Yorrick Kaine—*the young leader of the Whig party (his platform includes limiting the right to vote and invading Wales);* Mr. Swaike—*Volescamper's Security Consultant.*

At Jurisfiction: the Cheshire Cat; Esther—*who has a perfidious husband;* Miss Haversham—*a seasoned Jurisfiction agent who accepts Thursday as her apprentice.*

Within *Sense and Sensibility:* Marianne Dashwood; Mrs. Dashwood; Mr. Falstaff; Vernham Deane; the Red Queen; the Bellman; Harris Tweed; Mrs. Cavendish; King Pellinore; and Mr. Wemmick.

Mr. Chalk and Mr. Cheese—*associates of Mr. Schitt-Hawse;* Lydia Startright—*Toad News Networks star reporter;* Mr. Frakie Saveloy—*host of Name that Fruit!;* Harold Flex—*Actress Lola Vavoom's agent;* Aubrey Jambe—*disgraced cricket captain;* Zorf—*Neanderthal, an artist;* Blake Lamme and Slorter—*who are new SO-5 (Search and Containment) operatives;* Kaylieu—*a Neanderthal train conductor;* Major Tony Fairwelle—*who spotted an old colleague;* Sue Long—*Thursday's old classmate;* Mrs. Scroggins—*Thursday's downstairs neighbor;* Aornis Hades—*Acheron's sister;* Sebastion—*from "The Raven";* Mr. Cullards—*of Hoover washing machines;* Jack Schitt; Estella; Raffles; and Bunny.

3. *The Well of Lost Plots.* New York: St. Martin's Press, 1994, c1992, 188 p. ISBN: 0312105118.

In and out of England and various books, 1986. Thursday Next is pregnant; her husband has been eradicated, and she's being chased by both the "good guys" and the "bad guys." The lawful authorities (Special Operations Forces from Internal Affairs) want to bring her up on charges for possessing contraband cheese. Those who are above the law (the Goliath Corporation) want to capture her and force her to help them exploit all the worlds in all the books that have ever been published. The unlawful (criminal Aornis Hades) wants revenge for the death of her brother, Acheron.

Thursday decides that she needs to hide out until after her baby's birth. She needs a place that is safe from every faction. She can't hide in the past because of inadequate pre-natal care. She can't hide in the future because Special Operations' ChronoGuard Division would find her. She can't hide in an alternate present, because she would forget Landen, her eradicated husband; and that would put him one step closer to being gone beyond all possibility of recovery. She can't go into a published book because there's a good chance that Goliath will be working on a way to search for her in literature. However, Goliath does not know all the literary possibilities. There is a sort of gestational area to the Library, a series of basements that house books that are not yet, and may never be completed. Unpublished, they are essentially invisible. Thursday decides to hide out in the unread (and quite possibly unreadable) *Caversham Heights.*

She continues her apprenticeship with Miss Haversham, investigating literary crimes, including murder. Thursday sees Acheron and Aornis Hades in her dreams, along with Major Phelps, Sergeant Tozer, Aubrey Jambe, Dr. Fnorp, Nathan Snudd, Titan, and Prometheus; but she begins to lose sight of her husband Landen. This may be the first murder mystery to use digital rights management as a motive for murder.

Associates: Detective Sergeant Mary Jones—*a Caversham Heights character played by Thursday;* others in the book include Arnold, Generics ibb—*who becomes Lola* and obb—*who becomes Randolph,* Wyatt, Dr. Singh, DCI Briggs; Detective Jack Spratt, and Granny Next.

In The Well Thursday encounters: Akrid Snell—*Private Investigator;* Perkins—*Snell's partner;* Stickly-Prickly and Slow-Solid—*the hedgehog;* Captain Nemo; the three witches; Alfred Garcia; Mr. Grnksghty; Harris Tweed; Nigel, Emperor Zhark; Miss Havisham; the Painted Jaguar and the Mother Jaguar; the Cheshire Cat; Mr. Toad; Thursday's Mum; Commander Bradshaw; Llyster; Marianne Dashwood; the Bellman; Sir John Falstaff; Vernham Deane Beatrice; Benedict; WordMaster Libris; Lady Cavendish; Solomon Grundy; Humpty-Dumpty; Mrs. Tiggy-winkle; Uriah Hope; Professor Plum; Mr. Wemmick; Mrs. Bradshaw; Kenneth Solomon; Godot; Sebastian; Beatrice and Benedict; Count Dracula; Marley; Simon Legree; Mrs. Hubard; Miss Muffet; Mrs. Danvers; Hamlet; Jude Fawley; Mimi; Quasimodo; the Great Panjandrum; Senator Jobsworth; and Dr. Howard.

Within *Wuthering Heights:* Miss Havisham—*who deals with Joseph and then she conducts a Jurisfiction Rage Counseling session;* Edgar Linton and Catherine "elder Catherine"; Catherine Linton—*"young Catherine", their daughter;* Nelly Dean; Hindley Earnshaw; Hareton Earnshaw—*Hindley's son;* Isabella—*sister of Edgar, and mother of Linton;* and Catherine Earnshaw—*who loves Heathcliff.* Within *Mill on the Floss:* Lucy Deane—*who is prevented from shooting at Stephen and Maggie;* Within *Shadow the Sheepdog:* Mr. Phillips—*the auctioneer who works with Thursday to set a trap;* Miss Aurora Pittman—*Mr. Phillips's secretary;* Mr. Rustic—*the local vet;* Other characters in *Shadow the Sheepdog* include Mrs. Passerby and Mr. Townsperson.

In the court of *Alice in Wonderland:* the Gryphon; the King, Queen, and Knave of Hearts; Matthew Hopkins—*prosecuting attorney;* the White Rabbit; Mrs. Fairfax; Grace Poole; Blanche Ingram; St. John Rivers; the doormouse; and Edward Rochester.

4. *Something Rotten.* New York: Penguin Books, 1995, c1994, 385 p. ISBN: 014303541X.

ENGLAND, 1988. Thursday disappeared from the real world in January of 1986. She wasn't defeated, but she was on the run. She was pregnant, and her husband had been eradicated. She needed a safe place to have a child, and she found one, at least a relatively safe, place: inside an unpublished book. She worked for Jurisfiction, and she rose quickly through the ranks. She became Bellman, head of the organization. Now her son is beginning to talk, and policing fiction has lost its charm. She decides that it is time to go back to the real world. She takes Hamlet, Prince of Denmark, back with her. He has concerns: he's heard that he is viewed by others as being somewhat indecisive. He believes that he is a man of action, but he almost has a breakdown when faced with the choices at a coffee shop:

> To espresso or to latte, that is the question," he muttered, his free will evaporating rapidly. I had asked Hamlet for something he couldn't easily supply: a decision. "Whether 'tis tastier on the palate to choose white mocha over plain," he continued in a rapid garble, "or to take a cup to go. Or a mug to stay, or extra cream, or have nothing, and by opposing the endless choice, end one's heartache. (p. 78)

Thursday finds that, while she was involved with fiction, the real world has taken a turn for the worse, and her enemies have prospered. Fictional villain Yorrick Kaine is a heartbeat away from ruling England as a dictator. The Goliath Corporation is changing from a business into a church. The "faith-based" business model ensures more profit and more sociological control and costs less in overhead.

SO-14 has become the Danish book seizure division and Thursday agrees to do work for it to placate SO-1 (Internal Affairs) Detective Flanker.

ASSOCIATES: Thursday is now the Bellman of Jurisfiction. Commander Trafford Bradshaw—*who works with Thursday to apprehend the Minotaur;* Melanie Bradshaw—*gorilla, Commander Bradshaw's wife, babysits for Thursday;* Friday—*Thursday's two-year-old son;* Pickwick—*Thursday's pet dodo;* Alan—*Pickwick's son;* Mrs. Tiggy-winkle, Emperor Zhark, and the Red Queen—*work at Jurisfiction.*

Hamlet, Prince of Denmark—*who exits the fiction world with Thursday;* Wednesday—*Thursday's mom lets them stay at her home;* Landen—*Thursday's husband, sometimes exists;* Joffy—*Thursday's brother (a priest of the church of the Global Standard Deity) learned to speak Old English to be able to communicate with 13th-century mystic St. Zvlkx;* Lady Emma Hamilton—*consort of Admiral Horatio Lord Nelson,* and Herr Otto Bismarck—*Prussian Chancellor, are both staying at Wednesday's home.*

Officer "Spike" Stoker—*SO-17 (Vampire and Werewolf Disposal Operations);* Cindy Stoker—*Spike's wife, an assassin;* Chesney—*Spike's almost dead ex-partner, is running a soul reclamation scam;* Commander Braxton Hicks—*is in charge of the Swindon SO Divisions;* Victor Analogy—*is in charge of Swindon's LiteraTecs;* Bowden Cabel—*is Thursday's ex-partner;* Mr. Bartholomew Stiggins—*Neanderthal, is now in charge of SO-13 (Genetic Detectives);* Colonel Parks—*SO-6 (National Security) is Head of Presidential Security;* Dowding—*is Parks's second in command;* Detective Flanker—*SO-1 (Internal Affairs).*

The Goliath Corporation has undergone a restructuring. John Henry Goliath—*is the CEO;* Mr. Cheese—*now runs a coffee shop;* Jack Schitt—*works in corporate apologies.*

There have been changes in the political sphere. Chancellor Yorrick Kaine—*is lobbying for higher office;* Colonel Fawsten Gayle—*is Kaine's Head of Security;* Ernst Stricknene—*is Kaine's personal advisor.*

There have been changes in sports, and Thursday "pitches in." Roger Kapok and Gray Ferguson—*were the Captain and Manager of the Swindon Mallets before Goliath convinced them to leave;* Aubrey Jambe—*is now Captain of the Swindon Mallets;* Thursday—*is the team's Manager;* Alf Widdershaine—*is their coach.*

People and characters from the world of literature continue to bridge the gap to the real world. The Cat formerly known as Cheshire—*appears (and disappears) briefly;* William Shgakespeafe—*is needed to put Hamlet right.*

Granny Next; Thursday's father (at a time when he was in the ChronoGuard); Millon De Floss—*Thursday's stalker;* Adam Gnusense—*Millon's stalker;* Mr. Redmond van de Poste—*of the Commonsense Party (they're not doing well);* Tudor Webastow—*host of Evade the Question Time, the nation's premier talk show;* Mr. Rumplunkett—*Head Pathologist;* Major Drabb—*SO-14 (Tactical Support Unit);* Uncle Mycroft—*mad inventor;* Aunt Polly—*insane mathematician;* George Formby—*the President;* Mr. Wapcaplitt—*lawyer for the Reading Whackers;* Twizzit—*the Swindon Mallets alternate lawyer;* the Gryphon—*Head of Jurisfiction's legal team;* and the Mock Turtle—*number two at the legal desk.*

5. ***First Among Sequels.*** New York: St. Martin's Press, 1994, c1992, 188 p. ISBN: 0312105118.

In and out of England and various books, 2002. Most of Special Operations has been shut down for years. Thursday purchased Acme Carpets and began "hiring" a number of the ex-Special Operations agents. They pose as carpet salesmen while continuing to do the work that they did through Spec Ops. Thursday also continues to do some work for Jurisfiction, where the greatest concern is with the general decrease in leisure reading. At home, Thursday and Landen are concerned because they believed that their son Friday was going to join the ChronoGuard about three years ago. He did not. Thursday has encountered ChronoGuard Agent Friday in the past (her past, his future). Everyone knew that the future was not set in stone, but Thursday was sure that Friday's ChronoGuard service was a lynchpin for much of Earth's future. The Chronoguard is sure of this as well, and is threatening the replace current Friday with one of the future Fridays, who would be under orders to join the ChronoGuard.

Associates: Wednesday—*Thursday's mother;* Uncle Mycroft—*deceased;* Aunt Polly—*widowed;* Landen Parke-Laine—*Thursday's husband;* Friday—*Thursday and Landen's son, age 16;* Jenny and Tuesday—*their daughters;*

Joffy—*Thursday's brother;* Miles—*Joffy's partner;* Arthur Plunkettof—*of the Swindon Dodo Fanciers Guild;* Pickwick—*Thursday's pet dodo.*

Bowden Cabel, Mr. Bartholomew Stiggins (Neanderthal), and "Spike Stoker"—*are Acme Carpets employees.*

Millon de Floss—*semi-retired stalker;* Major Pickles—*who buys a carpet;* Mr. Hedge Moulting—*of Wessex Kitchens;* Hans Towwel—*who works for Moulting;* Raum—*the demon;* Commander Flanker—*now with the Cheese Enforcement Agency;* Owen Pryce the Cheese—*leader of the Welsh Cheese Smugglers;* Captain Bendix Scintilla—*head of ChronoGuard Recruitment;* Mrs. Berko-Boyler—*the Parke-Laine's neighbor;* John Henry Goliath V—*head of the Goliath Corporation;* Dr. Anne Wirthlass—*the project manager of Austen Rover, Goliath's attempts to create a reliable way to leap into fictional works;* and Aornis—*Acheron's sister, who has ben imprisoned in a time-loop.*

Jurisfiction includes Thursday1–4—*trainee;* Thursday5—*trainee;* Colonel William Dobbin—*a new agent;* Alice-PON-24330—*stand-in for Thursday1–4;* Mrs. Tiggy-Winkle and Emperor Zhark—*who are partners;* Charles, Roger, and Ken—*the Piano Squad.*

Pride and Prejudice is being retrofit, Isambard Kingdom Buñuel—*is the engineer in charge;* and Sid—*is the construction manager;* the characters include Mr. and Mrs. Bennet; Jane, Lizzy, Lydia, Kitty, and Mary—*their daughters;* and the Right Honorable Lady Catherine de Bourgh.

Wing Commander Cornelius Scampton-Tappet—*who Thursday purchases;* Murray—*the owner of a used plot shop;* the Minotaur.

The cricket—*in a 1929 book club edition of Pinocchio;* Jim "Bruises" McDowell—*the cricket's stunt double;* and Julian Sparkle—*game show host of Puzzlemania.*

Delegates to the Council of Genres include Senator Jobsworth—*Head of the Council of Genres;* Baxter—*Head of the Readership Increasement Committee;* Colonel Barksdale—*Head of the Council of Genres Combined Forces;* Senator Bamford—*who is in charge of finding a solution to the grammasite problem;* Senator Aimsworth—*who argues for interactive fiction;* and Black Beauty—*the Equestrian Senator, who believes in a good story.*

G

GARCIA, Eric.

CASUAL REX

Genres/Themes Crossed: Secret Society X Hard-Boiled Mystery.

Subjects/Character Types: Dinosaurs X Private Investigators.

Series/Stand-Alone: There are major changes in the cast of characters in the books. The series is best read in the chronological order presented in this entry.

Scene of the Crime: Alternate present-day Earth.

Detective(s): Vincent Rubio (Velociraptor dinosaur) learned a great deal about detecting from his partner, Ernie Watson. Every dinosaur has a well-developed sense of smell. Dinosaurs spend their lives disguised as humans when they are in public but recognize other dinosaurs by scent. Vincent's extraordinarily keen sense of smell can identify lingering traces of a scent to help him track a suspect or identify a clue. Sometimes Vincent can read another dinosaur's mood through changes in that dinosaur's smell. Vincent's excellent scent memory provides key information in his investigations.

Known Associates: In *Casual Rex* Vincent's partner is Ernie Watson. He has been friends with Ernie and Ernie's wife (now ex-wife) Louise for years. In *Anonymous Rex,* Glenda Wetzel (Hadrosaur) becomes Vincent's partner. Mr. Teitelbaum (*T. rex*) owns a rival investigation firm: TruTel Enterprises. The chronically inept investigator, Sutherland, (Ankylosaur) is employed at TruTel. Sergeant Dan Patterson (Brontosaur) is a good cop and a good friend to Vincent.

Premise: Sixty-five million years ago, dinosaurs faked their own extinction and joined human society. Presently about five percent of the people in the United States are really dinosaurs in guises that allow them to pass as humans. Their existence is their most carefully guarded secret. There are services for aging these guises so that the dinosaurs seem to age naturally, special resorts where dinosaurs can go natural, special wards in hospitals where they can be treated for illness or injury . . . an entire hidden society.

Comment: *Anonymous Rex* was published in 1999; *Casual Rex* was published two years later. *Casual Rex* is a prequel to *Anonymous Rex*. These should be read in series, not in publication order, to avoid confusion and spoilers, because Vincent's relationships develop and change from one book to the next in the series.

Eric Garcia's Web site (http://www.ericgarcia.com) was down from January 2009 through the time this book went to editing (June 2009). There is an interesting interview with Mr. Garcia at Flash Fiction: http://flashfiction-online.com/c20080302-interview-with-eric-garcia.html, and it is followed by some biographical information.

Literary Magic & Mayhem: This is a somewhat campy, fun series with a sweet-natured protagonist. The dinosaurs are not particularly different in their emotions and beliefs from humans. They have unusual problems because they are trying to pass as human. They have different reactions to some substances. (Alcohol does not effect them, but they are intoxicated by herbs.) If the series has any serious aspect it is focused on what it means to have to hide from general society; not on the inner life of a dinosaur. The author plays fair in giving the reader clues and keeps Vincent naïve and trusting enough so that the reader may figure out the identity of the villain before Vincent solves the case.

Explorations: What is the most interesting (or the most humorous) element in the dinosaur society?

Which character was the most sympathetic?

THE CASES

1. ***Casual Rex.*** New York: Ace Books, c2001, p. 1–290 (of 565 p.) ISBN: 0441012752.

Los Angeles and Hawaii, Spring 1999? Ernie is still crazy about his ex-wife, Louise. When she comes to the agency, asking them to find her brother Rupert and to extract him from "The Progressives," a cult that he has joined, Ernie agrees in a heartbeat.

Minsky, the dentist who owns their office building, offers Vincent and Ernie three months free rent (and two dental visits) to find his thieving girlfriend, Star. The first time he asks them to track down Star, she has stolen some drugs and prescription pads. The second time, she has moved on to steal more a personal object. Minsky is willing to pay almost anything, so he ends up bankrolling their investigation into the deaths of a number of young ex-cult members.

ASSOCIATES: Ernie Watson (Carnotaur)—*Vincent's partner;* Louise (T-Rex)—*Ernie's ex-wife;* Rupert Simmons (T-Rex)—*Louise's brother;* Minsky (Hadrosaur)—*dino-dentist, owns the building that houses Ernie and Vincent's office;* Christine "Star" Josephson (Allosaur)—*Minsky's girlfriend;* Jules (Velociraptor)—*is a cross-dressing informer who performs "plastic surgery" on guises;* Sweetums (Procompsognathus)—*is a pimp;* Dr. Beaumont "Bo" Beauregard (Diplodod)—*who advertises that he can de-program cult members;* Horace "Happy" Sutherland (Ankylosaur)—*a private investigator who works for rival firm TruTel Enterprises;* Mr. Teitelbaum (T-Rex)—*who owns TruTel;* Dr. Kaliehman—*who works at the coroner's office;* Mr. Levitt (either Coelophysis or Procompsognathus)—*who lost his son Jay;* Patrick (Iguanodon)—*who owns the Shangri-la club;* Hector Ramirez (Coelophysis)—*a cross-dresser and toxic-waste worker.*

The members of the cult include Baynal (dinosaur, type unknown)—*a.k.a. "Bob" (he refers to "Bob" as his "slave name");* Samuel (Iguanodon); Circe (Velociraptor); twins Buzz and Wendell (Carnotaurs); Thomas (Stegosaur); and Raal (Diplodod).

2. ***Anonymous Rex.*** New York: Ace Books, c2000, p. 291–565 (of 565 p.) ISBN: 0441012752.

LOS ANGELES AND NEW YORK, FALL 2000? Nine months ago, Ernie flew to New York to investigate the murder of Raymond McBride. He died in New York. His death was ruled an accident. Vincent was certain that it was murder, but couldn't find any leads. Vincent embezzled money from the Council to support his investigation, was found out, and was thrown off the Council. He developed a heavy basil habit. Broke, humiliated, and unable to stay off the herbs, Vincent was dodging bill collectors when he was offered a case (at bargain rates) by the cheapskate detective agency owner Mr. Teitelbaum, who owns the largest detective agency in Los Angeles. Vincent was desperate, so he took the case. It's an arson investigation. The fire was at a dinosaur hangout, the *Evolution Club.* Vincent's thorough examination of the evidence turns up a possible connection to Raymond McBride.

ASSOCIATES: [Some information has been deleted from this list to avoid spoilers.] Mr. Teitelbaum (*T. rex*)—*the owner of TruTel Enterprises;* Sally (human)—*Teitelbaum's secretary;*

In California: Sergeant Dan Patterson (Brontosaur)—*an old friend of Vincent;* Rita (Allosaur)—*a nurse;* Donovan Burke (Velociraptor)—*Evolution Club owner;* Felipe Suarez (Procompsognathus)—*Burke's hospital roommate.*

In New York: Judith McBride—*the widow;* Jaycee Holden (Coleophysis)—*was Donovan Burke's fiancé (he is a Raptor and they wanted to have children);* Dr. Kevin Nadel (dinosaur—type unknown)—*coroner, he is not predisposed to help Vincent;* Wally (human)—*Nadel's assistant, Vincent roughed Wally up during the investigation of Ernie's murder;* Gino and Alan Conti (Allosaurs)—*bar owners who sometimes do work for the Dinosaur Mafia;* Glenda Wetzel (Hadrosaur)—*a private investigator who works for a cut-rate investigative agency, J&T Enterprises;* Sarah Archer—*a nightclub singer;* and Manny (Ankylosaur)—*a black-market guise manufacturer.*

Dr. Emil Vallardo (Triceratop)—*a fertility specialist who believes that through his work mixed dinosaur couples (for instance Triceratop and Ankylosaur) can have viable children;* Barbara (Ornithomimus)—*Dr. Vallardo's receptionist;* Harry (Brontosaur) and Englebert (dinosaur-type unknown)—*are thugs who attack Vincent;* Officer Don Tuttle (Triceratop)—*stops Vincent for speeding, but doesn't write him a speeding ticket;* Dr. Otto Solomon (Hadrosaur)—*was once Dr. Vallardo's partner.*

The Southern California representatives for the Council include Harold Johnson (Brontosaur); Parsons (Stegosaur); Seligman (Allosaur); Oberst (Iguanodon); Kurzban (T. rex); Mrs. Nissenberg (Coleophysis); Rafael Colon (Hadrosaur); Handleman (Procompsognathus); and Glasser (Velociraptor).

3. ***Hot and Sweaty Rex.*** New York: Ace Books, c2004, 334 p. ISBN: 0441012736.

Los Angeles and South Florida, Summer 2001? Vincent has been a recovering herbaholic for nine months. He's working at putting his life back together and is slowly gaining ground. He does not want to work for the mob, but it's difficult (potentially fatal) to turn down a job from Frank Tallarico. The Tallaricos are a leading family in the Cosa Lucertola (the Dinosaur Mafia). A simple tailing job soon becomes much more, and Vincent wishes that he could give the money back and walk away.

Associates: Tommy Troubadour (a dinosaur—probably Velociraptor)—*was once a client of Ernie and Vincent's detective agency;* Frank Tallarico (Velociraptor)—*a mob boss in Los Angeles;* Nelly Hagstrom (Hadrosaur)—*who Vincent tails to the Lucky Palace;* Douglas Triconi (Brontosaur)—*owner of the Lucky Palace;* Glenda Wetzel (Hadrosaur)—*who comes out to visit Vincent and ends up accompanying him to Florida.*

In Florida: Eddie Tallarico (Velociraptor)—*Frank's brother, leads the Florida branch of the Tallarico gang;* Chaz, Sherman, and Jerry—*the gang's Velociraptor enforcers;* Others who are in the gang are Raoul (Velociraptor)—*the driver;* Stuart/Love My Money (Velociraptor)—*the horse;* and Pepe (Procompsognathus)—*his jockey.* Jack Dugan (Hadrosaur)—*Vincent's old friend, Jack runs the Dugan gang;* The Dugan gang includes Noreen (Hadrosaur)—*Jack's sister;* Nelly Hagstrom (Hadrosaur)—*his first lieutenant;* and Marcus and Andy—*Hadrosaur enforcers.*

Other characters include "Pop" Dugan (Hadrosaur)—*Jack's father;* Audrey (dinosaur—type unknown)—*Jack's doctor;* Steven (human) and Harold "Hank" (Velociraptor)—*porn shop workers.*

In Jack's memories: Rhonda Reichenberg (Ornithomimus)—*Vincent's first girlfriend;* Garrett Miller (Brontosaur)—*high-school bully;* Jack's mother and the ladies for whom she gave Tupperware parties (all dinosaurs); and Tajecky and Sal (dinosaurs, type unknown)—*the two who muscled Pop Dugan out of his own business.*

GARRETT, Randall. (Gordon Randall Phillip David Garrett, 1927–1987)

Lord Darcy Series

Genres/Themes Crossed: Blended SocietyX Whodunit, Forensic Mystery.

Subjects/Character Types: Alternate Earth (Alternate History), Sorcerers X Government Investigator.

Series/Stand-Alone: The series title rather than a story title heads this entry because the stories can be read in any order.

Scene of the Crime: The Anglo-French Empire (Great Briton, France, and the Americas), 1960s–1980s.

Detective: Lord Darcy, Chief Criminal Investigator for Prince Richard (the Duke of Normandy, brother of King John IV).

Known Associates: His forensic investigator, Licensed Sorcerer Master Sean O Lochlainn.

Premise: In this world, magic exists and can be used by those who have the talent, but it requires rigorous study, and practitioners must be licensed by the church.

In this world, Richard the Lion Heart survived his wounds and lived until 1219. From "The Spell of War" (in the *Lord Darcy* anthology):

> Richard had been hit by a crossbow bolt at the Siege of Chaluz in 1199, and after a long bout with infection and fever, had survived to become a wise and powerful ruler. His younger brother, John, died in exile in 1216, so when Richard died in 1219 the crown had gone to Richard's nephew, Arthur, son of Geoffrey of Brittany. Known as "Good King Arthur," he

was often confused in the popular mind with King Arthur Pendragon, of ancient Kymric legend. (p. 662)

One interesting aspect of the history is Garrett's apparent belief that incompetent leadership is a driving force for change. A world that escaped the reign of King John never experienced the revolutions of France and America. Seven hundred and fifty years after King Richard the Lion Heart's death, one of his descendents is the present king, King John IV. The nation includes England, France, Scotland, Ireland, New England (North America), and New France (South America).

Comment: Randall Garrett's characters use magic instead of technology to perform the forensic work at a murder scene. (For example, rather than using a comparison microscope for a ballistics analysis, a spell is performed to see if the bullet is associated with the suspected gun.) The clues discovered are revealed to the reader at the same time that they are explained to the detective.

Too Many Magicians was first serialized in *Analog* from August to November 1966. It was issued as a novel by Doubleday in 1967 and was nominated for the Hugo Award for Best Novel. Two collections of short stories that had been originally published in fantastic fiction magazines (such as *Analog* and *Fantastic*) followed: *Murder and Magic* (1979) and *Lord Darcy Investigates* (1981). In 2004, all of these works were collected in an anthology entitled *Lord Darcy.* After Randall Garrett's death, his friend Michael Kurland wrote two more Lord Darcy novels: *Ten Little Wizards* (1988) and *A Study in Sorcery* (1989).

In 1999, Randall Garrett won the Sidewise Award for Alternate History (Special Achievement Award) for the *Lord Darcy* series.

Literary Magic & Mayhem: *Too Many Magicians* was modeled on Rex Stout's *Too Many Clients. Ten Little Wizards* was modeled on Agatha Christie's *Ten Little Indians. A Study in Sorcery* was modeled on Arthur Conan Doyle's *A Study in Scarlet.*

Explorations: What does the magic add to the story?

How does the absence of technology alter the stories?

Many of the stories mention specific years. If those time stamps were not present, would the stories feel as if they were set in a different era? When?

THE CASES

1. **"The Spell of War,"** a short story in the *Lord Darcy* anthology. Riverdale New York: Baen Publishing Enterprises, 2002, p. 651–73. ISBN: 0743435486, 9780743435482.

THE BATTLEFIELDS OF ANGLO-FRENCH EMPIRE AND THE KINGDOM OF POLAND, 1939. Eighteen-year-old Lieutenant Darcy of the Blue Company meets

Junior Sergeant Sean O Lochlainn, who is commanding the remnants of the Red Company. The companies combine and try to hold their position against the troops of King Casimir's army. Their chances are not good, and they are made worse by an incompetent commander until the commander's death leaves Darcy in charge of the unit.

ASSOCIATES: The Blue Company includes: Captain Rimbaud—*Blue Company's Commander;* Lieutenant Darcy—*son of Coronel Lord Darcy;* Sergeant Brendon Kelleigh—*who knew Lord Darcy's father;* and Sergeant Arthur Lyon—*who later becomes the Reverend Father Arthur Lyon.* Junior Sergeant Sean O Lochlainn—*is one of fifteen men who are all that is left of Red Company.*

2. **"The Eyes Have It,"** a short story in the *Lord Darcy* anthology. Riverdale New York: Baen Publishing Enterprises, 2002, p. 5–46. ISBN: 0743435486, 9780743435482.

FRANCE, 1963. The Count D'Evreux is found, murdered, in his bedroom. A gun is found at the top of a secret staircase. Sorcerer Sean O Lochlainn uses the law of Contagion, which states that

> any two objects which have ever been in contact with each other have an affinity for each other which is directly proportional to the product of the degree of relevancy of the contact and the length of time they were in contact and inversely proportional to the length of time since they have ceased to be in contact. (p. 25)

This is to ascertain that the bullet in the body of the murdered man came from that gun. He uses the "picture test," which is too unreliable to be submitted as evidence in a court of law, in order to get an image of what the victim saw right before he died. The picture test is described as

> a psychic phenomenon that sometimes occurs at the moment of death—especially a violent death. The violent emotional stress causes a sort of backfiring of the mind…As a result, the image in the mind of the dying person is returned to the retina. By using the proper sorcery, this image can be developed and the last thing the dead man saw can be brought out. (p. 36)

The resulting image tells Darcy much, and he makes a full report to the Duke.

ASSOCIATES: Sir Pierre Morlaix—*Chevalier of the Angevin Empire, Knight of the Golden Leopard, and secretary-in-private to my lord, the Count D'Evreux;* Lady Alice—*the Count's sister, the Countess D'Evreux;* Mary, Lady Duncan, and Laird Duncan of Duncan—*are the D'evreux's houseguests;* Father Bright—*the household's priest;* His Royal Highness, Richard, Duke of Normandy—*wants the crime solved;* the Marquis of Rouen—*attends the Duke;* Lord Darcy—*Chief Criminal Investigator for the Duke of Normandy;*

Doctor Pateley (Chirurgeon) and Master Sean O Lochlainn (Sorcerer)—*are Darcy's assistants.*

3. **"A Case of Identity,"** a short story in the *Lord Darcy* anthology. Riverdale, New York: Baen Publishing Enterprises, 2002, p. 47–110. ISBN: 0743435486, 9780743435482.

CHERBOURG, FRANCE, JANUARY 1964. The backbone of the economy of King John's empire is the wealth of the New World. The Americas—New England in the north and New France in the south—ship cotton, tobacco, sugar, and gold; they bring prodigious wealth to the Anglo-French Empire. Poland's King Casimir has found a way to disrupt that sea trade. Ships leave Imperial ports and are never seen again. Rumor has it that there is magic at work on the Atlantic Ocean. Sailors are a superstitious lot, the rumors have been as detrimental to the shipping trade as have the disappearances of the ships. The Empire's economy will founder if shipping does not resume. The King sent Imperial agents to Cherbourg, to work with Hugh, the Marquis of Cherbourg, to find out what they can in this port city. The Marquis began behaving strangely; having inexplicable spells in which he babbled like a madman. Then he disappeared. At first his wife was afraid that he had wandered off, but given the situation, the Duke of Normandy is concerned that there might be a more sinister reason for the Marquis's disappearance. Lord Darcy is sent to investigate.

ASSOCIATES: Robert and Jack—*armsmen;* Old Jean—*the barkeep at the The Blue Dolphin;* Paul Sarto—*worked in the bar up until two weeks ago.*

Darcy is asked to investigate the disappearance of the Marquis de Cherbourg by Richard, Duke of Normandy; the Bishop of Guernsey and Sark; and the Marquis of Rouen. Master Sean O Lochlainn, Sorcerer—*assists Darcy in the investigation.*

Lady Elaine—*Marquise de Cherbourg;* Sir Gwiliam de Bracy—*her seneschal;* Lord Seiger—*the Marquis's librarian, suffers from an illness of the soul;* Sir Androu Duglasse—*Captain of the Marquis's Guard;* Henri Vert—*Chief Master-at-Arms of the City of Cherbourg;* Father Patrique—*of the Order of St. Benedict (the Benedictines include a high percentage of people called "perceptives," from whom one's identity cannot be concealed);* Sir James le Lein—*agent in His Majesty's Secret Service, is also missing.*

4. **"The Muddle of the Woad."** a short story in the *Lord Darcy* anthology. Riverdale New York: Baen Publishing Enterprises, 2002, p. 111–68. ISBN: 0743435486, 9780743435482.

ENGLAND, MAY 1964. Master Gotobed, the cabinetmaker for the Duke of Kent, performed his last duty for the current Duke: building the Duke's coffin. When it is time to deliver the coffin, Master Gotobed finds it already occupied by an unknown, woad-dipped corpse. The corpse is identified as that of Lord Camberton, and the King appoints Lord Darcy as Special Investigator for the High Court of Chivalry to investigate Lord Camberton's death. The King already has some agents in Canterbury, including one who has infiltrated the outlawed, pagan, Holy Society of Ancient Albion, a sect that has been repudiated by the Christian Church partly because its highest sacrament is the sacrifice of the King.

ASSOCIATES: Master Sean O Lochlainn, Sorcerer—*assists Lord Darcy in his investigation;* Walter Gotobed—*the Master Cabinetmaker for the Duke of Kent;* Journeyman Henry Lavender and apprentices Tom Wilderspin and Harry Venable—*work under Master Gotobed's direction.*

Lord Darcy is attending a party at Dartmoor House when Lady Dartmoor takes him aside to meet with His Imperial Majesty, John IV, King and Emperor of England, France, Scotland, Ireland, New England, New France, Defender of the Faith, and so on.

Sir Thomas Leseaux—*theoretical thaumaturgist, is a double agent for the King;* Bertram Lightly—*is Chief Master at Arms of the City of Canterbury;* Master Timothy Videau—*is a Sorcerer and the local representative for Master Simon of London's preservator boxes;* Master-at-Arms Alexander Glencannon—*is a competent lawman.*

The Dowager Duchess Margaret—*widow of the late Duke of Kent;* Lord Quentin—*their son;* Lady Anne—*their daughter;* and Sir Andrew Campbell-MacDonald—*the Duchess's brother.*

5. ***Too Many Magicians.*** A novel included in the *Lord Darcy* anthology. Riverdale New York: Baen Publishing Enterprises, 2002, p. 169–396. ISBN: 0743435486, 9780743435482.

CHERBOURG, FRANCE AND LONDON, ENGLAND, OCTOBER 1966. The Empire has a new top-secret weapon, one that is sure to turn the tide in the naval battles between the Empire and Poland. Double agent Georges Barbour discovers that a traitor is offering to sell information. Barbour pretends to be a buyer, in the hope of learning the identity of the traitor. At the same time, he works to keep his contacts in Poland in the dark about what is being offered for sale. His murder makes it obvious that he was not completely successful. Darcy begins to investigate, sending a summons for Sorcerer Sean O Lachlainn, who is presenting a paper in London at the Triennial Convention of Healers and Sorcerers. Sean O Lochlainn is unavailable. He has been arrested on suspicion of murdering the Chief Forensic Sorcerer of the city of London.

In this novel, the Marquis of London (based on Nero Wolfe) is revealed to be a cousin of Lord Darcy. The Marquis's aide, Lord Bontriomphe, is based on Archie Goodwin. The byplay and rivalry between Darcy and the Marquis is one fun aspect of the novel, and might lead the reader to speculate on what the relationship between Holmes and Wolfe would have been like had they lived in the same world.

ASSOCIATES: Sir Eliot Meredith—*Lord Darcy's second in command;* Master Sean O Lochlainn—*Lord Darcy's Chief Forensic Sorcerer;* Lord Admiral Edwy Brencourt—*who is concerned with Naval Security;* Commander Lord Ashley—*who is a Special Agent for his Majesty's Imperial Naval Intelligence Corps;* Chief Master-at-Arms Henri Vert—*Head of the Department of Armsmen of Cherbourg.*

The attendees of the Triennial Convention of Healers and Sorcerers who are seen by Master Sean O Lochlainn include Sir James Zwinge—*London's Chief Forensic Sorcerer;* the Bishop of Winchester—*an elderly thaumaturgist and healer;* Sir Lyon Gandolphus Grey—*Grand Master of the Most Ancient and Honorable Guild of Sorcerers;* Journeyman Lord John Quetzal—*a witch-smeller, fourth son of the Duke of Mechicoe;* and Master Ewen MacAlister—*an annoying sorcerer who is very aware of social status.*

Those that Lord Darcy sees in London include the Marquis of London—*who solves mysteries from the comfort of his home;* Lord Bontriomphe—*Chief Investigator of London, aide to the Marquis;* Mary—*Dowager Duchess of Cumberland;* Geffri—*her seneschal;* Mary's guests include Sir Thomas Leseaux—*a theoretical thaumaturgist;* Damoselle Tia Einzig—*an apprentice sorcerer;* and Sidi al-Nasir—*gambling den owner.*

A meeting with King John IV includes Lord Darcy; Peter de Valera ap Smith—*Lord High Admiral of the Imperial Navy;* Captain Percy Smollett—*Chief of Naval Intelligence, European Branch;* Lord Bontriomphe; Sir Lyon Gandolphus Grey; and Commander Lord Ashley.

6. **"A Stretch of the Imagination."** a short story in the *Lord Darcy* anthology. Riverdale New York: Baen Publishing Enterprises, 2002, p. 399–414. ISBN: 0743435486, 9780743435482.

NORMANDY, FRANCE, OCTOBER 1972. Lord Darcy is called in to investigate the apparent suicide of Lord Arlen, owner and head of Maynard House publishing. Master Sean detects no black magic...nor does he detect any gloom. The mental state necessary for suicide leaves a psychic impression on a room and that is absent in this case, making it almost certain that this is not a suicide. Lord Arlen was clearly alone in his office when he was hanged, but Master Sean's evidence rules out suicide, leaving Lord Darcy with an interesting case.

ASSOCIATES: Chirurgeon Dr. Pately and Forensic Sorcerer Master Sean O Lochlainn—*are Lord Darcy's assistants;* Chief Editor Sir Stefan Imbry, Damoselle Barbara, Goodmen Wober, and Andray—*work for publisher Lord Arlen;* Gwiliam de Lisles—*Master-at-Arms;* and Goodman Ernesto Norman—*author.*

7. **"A Matter of Gravity,"** a short story in the *Lord Darcy* anthology. Riverdale New York: Baen Publishing Enterprises, 2002, p. 415–51. ISBN: 0743435486, 9780743435482.

NORMANDY, FRANCE, APRIL 1974. Lord Jillbert, the Count de la Vexin, fell from the castle tower where he had his laboratory. He did not fall straight down: he hit the ground some 18 feet from the tower. He was alone in the laboratory, but his priest saw him as he went to the laboratory, and the priest is a sensitive: he can swear that Lord Jillbert was not bent on suicide when they spoke just minutes before his death. The local Chief Master-at-Arms is convinced that the Count was fleeing demons and threw himself out the window to escape them, but the Count was psychically blind and could never have sensed a demon. The Count was alone, no one could have pushed him—his psychic blindness would have made it impossible to scare him into jumping from the window. He was not suicidal. Lord Darcy has a difficult locked-room mystery on his hands.

ASSOCIATES: Chirurgeon Dr. James Pately and Forensic Sorcerer Master Sean O Lochlainn—*are Lord Darcy's assistants;* Lord Gisors and Lady Beverly—*are Lord Jillbert's children;* the Reverend Father Villiers—*the family's priest;* Sir Roderique MacKenzie—*Captain of the Count's Guard;* Madelaine—*is his daughter;* Sergeant Andray—*is his son;* Jacque Toile—*is Chief Master-at-Arms for the city of Gisors;* Journeyman Emile—*who assists Master Sean in reconstructing the window.*

8. **"The Bitter End,"** a short story in the *Lord Darcy* anthology. Riverdale New York: Baen Publishing Enterprises, 2002, p. 453–88. ISBN: 0743435486, 9780743435482.

PARIS, FRANCE, OCTOBER **197?** Master Sean O Lochlainn stepped into the Paris bar to get a quick drink before he caught his train. While he was there, the barkeep discovered that a customer had passed away over his glass. Master Sean is originally trapped by his own curiosity; then he is detained by a buffoon-of-an-investigator, Sergeant Cougair. Cougair explains his reasoning: "It is an axiom of mine that the least likely suspect is the one most likely to have done it" (p. 465). Since Master Sean is a stranger in the city, does not even know the identity of the victim, and had no opportunity to slip poison into his glass, Cougair feels that he is the obvious culprit.

Picturing Cougair as Inspector Clouseau (from the Pink Panther movies) adds another dimension to the story.

ASSOCIATES: Barman Murtaugh—*who realizes that something is wrong with one of the bar customers;* John-Pierre—*his assistant;* Brother Paul—*a healer of the Hospital of St. Luke-by-the-Seine;* plainclothes Sergeant-at-Arms Cougair Chasseur—*whose policy is to arrest the least likely suspect;* Sorcerer Master Sean O Lochlainn—*the least likely suspect.*

Master Sir Aubrey Burnes—*is Chief Forensic Sorcerer for His Grace, the Duke D'Isle;* Doctor Ambro—*is the pathologist;* Senior Captain Andray Vandermeer—*was the victim;* Mary—*is his widow;* Jorj Veblin—*was his pharmacist;* and Father Pierce—*was his Healer;* Darryl Mac Robert—*Chief Master-at-Arms of the city of Paris;* Goodman Baker—*who delivers potable spirits to the Cosmopolitan Hotel's International Bar.*

9. **"The Ipswich Phial,"** a short story in the *Lord Darcy* anthology. Riverdale New York: Baen Publishing Enterprises, 2002, p. 491–539. ISBN: 0743435486, 9780743435482.

NORMANDY, FRANCE, JUNE 1976. An opportunistic thief recognized the monetary value of a newly developed magical weapon called the Ispwich Phial and grabbed it, quickly selling it to an agent of the Polish King. The theft was discovered within hours, and Noel Standish, an agent of King John IV's, set off in hot pursuit. He was able to track the thief, but not to catch up before the weapon was sold. He was able to track the buyer, but was killed before he could report to his comrades. King John's Secret Service is left with a dead agent and the fear that the Poles will soon invade the Anglo-French Empire using the stolen weapon. Lord Darcy is called upon to do what he can to piece together the last hours of Agent Standish's life and to try to find the (now-cold) trail of the Serka (Polish Secret Service) Agent who purchased the Ipswich Phial. In the course of his investigation, Lord Darcy falls in love.

ASSOCIATES: Forensic Sorcerer Master Sean O Lochlainn—*who saw the stars go out the night that Standish was killed;* the Reverend Father Arthur Lyon—*Rector of the Church of St. Matthew, saw it as well;* Sir James le Lein—*is a Special Agent of His Majesty's Secret Service;* Danglers—*Mistress Jizelle de Ville's driver;* Evrit and Lorin—*are Samel Champtier's sons;* Damoselle Sharolta—*who recognizes Lord Darcy;* Olga Polovski, Serka Agent 055—*is the most beautiful and the most dangerous woman in Europe.*

10. **"The Sixteen Keys,"** a short story in the *Lord Darcy* anthology. Riverdale New York: Baen Publishing Enterprises, 2002, p. 541–78. ISBN: 0743435486, 9780743435482.

LORD VAUXHALL'S ESTATE (NEAR ROUEN), FRANCE, JUNE 1976. Lord Vauxhall aged half a century in less than an hour; he's found dead in his summer cottage with a pistol lying by his hand. At the time of his death, he was in possession of the only copies of the new naval treaty with Roumeleia. The diplomatic case holding the treaties cannot be found; Lord Darcy is called in to investigate.

ASSOCIATES: Ciardi—*Lord Darcy's manservant;* Master Sean O Lochlainn—*Chief Forensic Sorcerer for the Duchy of Normandy;* Dr. Pateley—*chirurgeon;* Donal Brennan—*is the grim, black-uniformed Chief Master-at-Arms;* Journeyman Sorcerer Torquin Scoll—*whose specialty is locks.*

Prince Richard, Duke of Normandy—*who takes an interest in the investigation;* Lord Sefton—*the Secretary of Foreign Affairs;* Peter de Valera ap Smith—*is the Lord High Admiral of the Imperial Navy;* Lieutenant Coronel Edouin Danvers—*who commands the Duke of Normandy's 18th Heavy Dragoons.* Captain Broun—*who carries messages for the Duke;* and Senior Captain Delgardie.

11. **"The Napoli Express,"** a short story in the *Lord Darcy* anthology. Riverdale New York: Baen Publishing Enterprises, 2002, p. 579–648. ISBN: 0743435486, 9780743435482.

The train the Napoli Express, begins less than five hours after the action in "The Sixteen Keys." Lord Darcy and Master Sean act as couriers for the treaties that must get to Greece within five days. The first leg of the trip is on the Napoli Express train. While they are on the train, a man is murdered. If they are delayed by the investigation, the treaties will not be delivered in time, with devastating consequences for the Empire.

Readers who have also read Agatha Christie's *Murder on the Orient Express* will take special enjoyment in some aspects of this story.

Associates: Prince Richard, Duke of Normandy—*who was directed by the King to send a courier on Commander Edwy Dhuglas's ship the White Dolphin.* The Duke had already taken other steps. Sir Leonard—*the Duke's private secretary.*

Edmund Norton—*the Trainmaster of the Napoli Express;* Fred—*the day porter;* Tonio Bracelli—*the night porter;* Dr. Vonner—*the train's chirurgeon;* Master Sorcerer Seamus Kilpadraeg—*is one of the names on the train's passenger manifest;* Martyn Boothroyd—*a military man;* Gavin Tailleur—*who is badly scarred;* Sidney "old Sharpy" Charpentier—*who is a lay healer;* the Reverend Father Armand Brun—*who is very friendly;* Jason Quinte—*who almost missed the train;* Maurice Zeisler—*who attended the Sorcerers Convention in London when Zwinge was murdered;* Goodman John Peabody—*who has a fake limp and a cane the conceals a sword;* Simon Lamar—*who has a Yorkshire accent;* Arthur Mac Kay—*whose accent is both Oxford and Oxfordshire;* Valentine Herrick—*who joins the saba game;* Imperial Navy Lieutenant Charles James Jamieson—*who smokes bad cigars;* Sir Stanley Galbraith—*who dices for drinks;* Gwiliam Hauser—*who invites Master Seamus to play cards;* Boothroyd Charpentier—*one of those who begins the saba game;* Lyman Vandepole—*who is suspected of cheating at cards.*

Cesare Sartoan—*is the agent of the Roman Prefecture of Police.*

12. ***Ten Little Wizards.*** New York: Ace Books, c1988, 188 p. ISBN: 0441800572; 9780441800575. ISBN: 0441800572, 97804441800575.

The Duchy of Normandy, France, April 1988. The Nobility are gathering at Castle Cristobel to witness the the coronation of the younger son of

King John IV: Gwiliam Richard Arthur Plantagenet, Baron Ambrey, Duke of Lancaster, will be crowned Prince of Gaul. The Marquis Sherrinford receives a warning from the Marquis of London, a warning that there will be an attempt on the life of King John IV during the coronation. Lord Darcy and Sorcerer Sean O Lachlainn work with the head of the Secret Service (Lord Peter), the chief of castle security (Coronel Lord Waybusch), and others to investigate the threat.

As that investigation is getting off the ground, a baker who works within the walls of the castle finds a dead wizard on the floor of his shop. Master Sean presents the investigators with a conundrum: the killer was present, yet not entirely present, for a half hour in the shop. Of more concern is the rhyme left on the body:

Ten little wizards sat down to dine
One wizard stuffed his face—and now there are nine.

Lord Darcy realizes that this is the warning of a man who intends to kill again; but without knowing his motive, they cannot know if this ties in to the threat against the King. With 356 wizards attending the coronation, identifying and protecting the next victim poses difficulties.

Associates: Lord Darcy—*is now the Investigator-in-Chief of the Court of Chivalry for the whole of the Angevin Empire;* Master Sean O Lochlainn—*is now the Angevin Empire's Chief Forensic Sorcerer;* Pyat—*an agent;* Master Sorcerer Raimun DePlessis—*who found out that someone hated him, and asked a wizard for aid;* Master Sir Darryl Longuert—*the Wizard Laureate of England;* Chevalier Raoul d'Espergnan—*a sensitive, is a courier for the King;* Lord Peter Whiss—*Lord Commander of His Majesty's Most Secret Service, whose cover is "personal Secretary to the Marquis Sherrinford";* the Marquis Sherrinford—*who is responsible for His Majesty's personal safety;* Goodman Harbleury—*Sherrinford's assistant;* Coronel Lord Waybusch—*is in charge of Castle security;* Richard, Duke of Normandy—*is the King's brother;* His Grace the Archbishop Maximilian of Paris; Count d'Alberra—*is not a healer, but he has a reputation for being able to cure ills that have neither physical nor magical cause;* Father Philip—*an abbot;* Henri Vert—*Prefect of Police for the Duchy of Normandy;* Master Bonpierre—*the baker;* Virgil DuCormier—*Master Chef;* Goodman Lourdan—*innkeeper at the Gryphon d'Or;* Sir Pierre Semmelsahn—*a Master Magician;* Goodman Domreme; Mary—*the Dowager Duchess of Cumberland;* Stanislaw—*King of Courlandt, and heir to the throne of Poland;* Lady Marta de Verre; Lord Brummel—*General Lord Halifax;* Sir Felix Chaimberment; Master Sorcerer Dandro Bittman; Major von John of the New England Legion; Baron Hepplethong; Sir Moses Benander—*Royal Chirurgeon;* King John IV.

13. ***A Study in Sorcery.*** New York: Ace Books, c1989, 184 p. ISBN: 0441790925; 9780441790920.

The Anglo-French Empire (Mostly in New England), March 1989. Lord Darcy and Master Sean O Lachlainn are sent across the ocean to New England to investigate the murder of a young Prince of the Azteque Empire. He was found in the ultimate locked room—an Azteque Temple that has been locked both by physical locks and by magic for more than a century. It seems as though, in a temple that no man could enter, the Prince was sacrificed in a forbidden rite.

Associates: In England: King John IV; Lord Peter Whiss—*chief of His Majesty's Most Secret Service.*

In New England: His Grace Charles, Duke of Arc—*Imperial Governor of New England;* Julian Despaige—*his ward, whose twin brother is in England;* Father Adamsus—*an exorcist;* Lord John Quetzal—*forensic sorcerer;* the Count de Maisvin; Master Sean O Lochlainn—*the Angevin Empire's Chief Forensic Sorcerer;* Lieutenant Assawatan; Chief Vincetti—*the Plainclothes Chief Master at Arms;* Lady Irene Eagleson; Major Sir John DePemmery; Chief Chisolnadak of the Mulgawas; Mullion—*who acts as Lord Darcy's valet;* Lord Lloriquhali; Don Miguel; and Chichitoquoppi—*Prince Ixequatle's manservant.*

On their way to New England: Colonel Hesparsyn—*commands Company B of the Duke's Own New England Regiment;* Lord Chiklquetl—*the Azteque High Priest*, the Priests of the Flame carry the Eternal Flame into New England to rededicate Tsaltsaluetol's temple; Lieutenant MacPhearling—*Company B's Magic Officer;* Sergeant Travis; and Captain Flagg.

GIBBONS, Dave. Worked with Alan Moore on *Watchmen*. See MOORE, Alan: Watchmen.

GILMAN, Dorothy. (Also writes under her married name as Dorothy Gilman Butters)

The Clairvoyant Countess

Genres/Themes Crossed: Paranormal X Police Procedural.

Subjects/Character Types: Clairvoyants X Police Procedural.

Series/Stand-Alone: Series, best read in order. Detective-Lieutenant Pruden and Madame Karitska meet in *The Clairvoyant Countess.*

Detective: Countess Marina Karitska has always been psychic. When she was a child, she was beaten for it. She never used it to make money until a few months before the events recounted in *The Clairvoyant Countess.* She had been working as a milliner in Trafton when she began dreaming about a house that she had never seen before, with a sign in the window: "Madame Karitska Readings." She found the house, rented an apartment within it, and set out her sign.

Detective-Lieutenant Pruden found Madame Karitska's address in the engagement calendar of Alison Bartlett, at the scene of the young woman's murder. He is certain that Madame Karitska is a charlatan from the moment they meet. Yet her prediction about his father comes true, and the routine lines of investigation of Alison Bartlett's murder turn up nothing. He finally follows up on a suggestion from Madame Karitska, that he look into the death of Alison's mother. Once the case is closed, he goes to thank Madame Karitska. She tells him that he is more flexible in his thinking than she had expected, and so their friendship begins.

Known Associates: Detective Lieutenant Prudent's colleagues are Sergeant Swope and police photographer Charlie Ogilvy. In the course of the book, Madame Karitska befriends two psychics, Mr. John Faber Jones and Gavin Ulbright O'Connell, and a musician, John Painter.

Premise: Countess Marina Karitska's dreams told her to begin business as a psychic. She did, and finds that her gifts are needed not only by the neighborhood romantics, but also by other budding psychics, by people who are in serious trouble, and by a police officer who was originally a skeptic but who comes to rely on her talent.

Comment: *The Clairvoyant Countess* was written between *Mrs. Pollifax* novels. Originally Dorothy Gilman envisioned it as a stand-alone, but several years later she wrote a sequel, *Kaleidoscope.*

Literary Magic & Mayhem: There is something about Dorothy Gilman's heroines. They are down-to-earth, but extremely spiritual. Spending time with them is a joy. The cases related in the book owe something to Madame Karitska's psychic abilities and something to straight police work. She talks about how a tiny change in perspective can completely alter the viewer's perceptions:

> It is like a kaleidoscope . . . a small shift of focus and one sees beyond the illusion to the reality. You look at things one way, I another, but you need only shift your attention and you too will see. (*The Clairvoyent Countess* p. 79)

Explorations: What does Mr. Faber-Jones do when he needs to improve his life? How does he handle his gift?

When Detective Lieutenant Pruden protests that he didn't want Madame Karitska to intervene, all he did was to bring her a list of 14 objects and ask for her comments. Her response is "The ways of God and karma are exceeding wondrous, are they not?" (p. 54). In this book, when did Madame Karitska, seemingly accidently, arrive in a place in which she could help someone at just the right time?

THE CASES

1. ***The Clairvoyant Countess.*** New York: Fawcett Crest, c1975, 224 p. ISBN: 0449213188.

TRAFTON, 1975? Madame Karitska sets up shop as a psychic in Trafton and finds herself called on by romantics, children who have lost pets, and Detective-Lieutenant Pruden. Once he has exhausted all other avenues of investigation, he tries the path that Madame Karitska pointed out. It works. He comes back, a little less skeptical and much more interested. Over the course of the book they help each other in many different investigations.

ASSOCIATES: Sergeant Swope and police photographer Charlie Ogilvy—*Detective Lieutenant Pruden's colleagues;* Kristan Seversky—*Madam Karitska's landlord (an artist);* Mr. Faber-Jones—*a reluctant psychic;* John Patinter—*a would-be thief and a gifted singer/songwriter.*

In the case of Alison Bartlett: Carl Madison—*Alison's stepfather;* Eben Johnson—*the attorney.*

In the case of the thefts at St. Bonaventure's: Gavin Ulbright O'Connell—*who felt that he must go home.*

In the murder investigation of Arturo Mendez: Luis—*Arturo's brother;* Maria Ardizzone—*Luis' determined girlfriend;* Mrs. Malone—*Luis and Arturo's landlady;* Patrolman Bill Kane—*who knows the people on his beat;* Mr. LeCruz—*a shopowner;* Madame Souffrant—*who practices voodoo;* Mrs. Materas—*who knows the ice cream business;* R. Ramon—*proprietor of the Bazaar Curio Shop;* Carlos Torres—*his errand boy.*

At Mr. Faber-Jones's dinner party: Dr. Berkowitz, Dr. Jane Tennison, Peter Zoehfeld, and Mr. Lucas Johns—*guests who play an interesting parlor game.*

In the witch investigation: Mrs. Eva Trumbull—*who collected things;* Kathy and Birch Donlap—*the golden children;* Mrs. Dunlap—*a strict mother;* Joe Lister—*a suspicious type;* Johnny Larkin—*who carefully observed his own illness;* Mrs. Larkin—*his mother;* Mr. Lister—*auto body shop owner;* Cas Johnson—*a mechanic.*

In the investigation into a daughter's death: Ellen and Fritz Heyer—*who came to Madame Karitska for reassurance that their daughter, Jan, is at rest;* Miss Brylawski—*Jan's boss;* Harry Jones—*Jan's coworker;* Tommy

Brudenhall—*Carol's boyfriend, he left town;* Chick and Deirdre—*two of Jan's patients;* Detective-Sergeant Michelangelo—*who brought essential information;* The Chief—*a sceptic who's willing to take a chance.*

2. ***Kaleidoscope.*** New York: Ballantine Books, c2002. 256 p. ISBN: 9780345448217; 0345448219.

TRAFTON, APPROXIMATELY A YEAR AFTER MADAME KARITSKA SET UP HER SIGN. Madame Karitska becomes involved in a number of cases. There are several major events playing out in this book. A cult, run by a conman, brings in believers but won't let them leave. It's called the *Guardians of Eden.* The daughter of a friend of Madame Karitska joins, and Madame Karitska, Lieutenant Pruden, and Amos Herzog work to uncover the cult's secrets. Madame Karitska meets a CIA agent who believes that terrorists will try to bring down the nation's electrical grid. He learns about her gift and asks for her help. There are also a number of shorter cases in the book. Shining through every encounter are Madame Karitska's faith in God and karma, her determination to help others, and her belief that people must make the most of the choices that they are given.

ASSOCIATES: Sergeant Swope and Officer Margolies—*Detective-Lieutenant Pruden's colleagues;* Jan Hyer (Heyer)—*the Detective's fiancé;* Kristan—*landlord and artist;* Sreja Zabredi—*who drives a hard bargain;* Georges Verlag—*a diamond salesman who recognizes Madame Karitska;* Betsy Oliver—*who has questions regarding devotion;* Alpha—*Betsy's husband and Guardians of Eden convert;* Ginny Voorhees—*Darlene Cahn's roommate;* Professor Robert Blake—*Darlene Cahn's fiancé;* Jenny—*mute nine-year-old suspect in the murder of John Epworth;* Joanna—*John's wife;* Abby Jacoby—*Joanna's old friend;* Louise Devoe—*a child psychologist;* Everett Harbinger—*an attorney;* The Chief—*whose skepticism is warranted (this time);* Anna—*who's afraid her husband is betraying her in Denby Maine;* Mario Cialini—*who has always believed his son Luca is cursed;* Jason Hendricks—*who has been ill ever since he returned from Africa;* Dr. Idowi—*who helps Jason;* Dr. Berkowitz—*a man of courage (he chances another Faber-Jones party);* Tanya Jamison—*Pisces Record Company's business manager;* Roger Gillespie—*a CIA agent;* Joe Witkowski—*an electrician;* Brother Robin—*a.k.a. Charley Schumacher, a.k.a. Duct Tape Carley; a holy leader;* Frank Johnson—*an FBI Agent;* John Mayfield—*a robber;* Laurie Faber-Jones—*who agrees to help Daniel Henry at his charity thrift shop;* Amos Herzog—*jewel thief (retired);* Kate Margus—*who is writing a book on actress/singer Charmian Cowper;* John Painter—*who has a rare recording of Charmian Cowper;* Shana—*who tells fortunes in a carnival owned by Max Saberhagen;* Jake Bodley—*a local gangster;* Ben—*who works for Jake.*

GILMAN, Laura Anne.

STAYING DEAD

Genres/Themes Crossed: Secret Society, Blended Society X Hard-Boiled Mystery. Initially the Talent and fae comprise the Cosa Nostradamus, a secret society. In later stories, the secrecy is deteriorating: some humans realize that there is more to their world than they had imagined.

Subjects/Character Types: Spell-Casters (referred to in this series as Talent), fae (referred to in this series as Fatae). The Fatae include piskies, fairies, griffins, centaurs, gnomes, demons, angels, and others) X Private Investigators, Thieves.

Series/Stand-Alone: Relationships, characters, the protagonist's world view, and the society change over the course of the series. The novels should be read in order.

Scene of the Crime: Present day Manhattan.

Detective: Twenty-seven-year-old Genevieve "Wren" Valere calls herself a thief, but society considers her a Retriever. A Retriever recovers missing or stolen items for their rightful owners. (Since the client is always right, the rightful owner is, by definition, the person who is paying her.) Such rightful owners hire Retrievers to recover items while avoiding the fuss, bother and paperwork entailed in reporting thefts to the police or to the insurance companies. Wren can control *current;* that is, she can perform magic. The term "magic" has fallen into disfavor. "Talent" is the word used to describe people who can alter reality through the use of the current that they control. The knowledge to control current is acquired through a mentor; Wren's was John Ebenezer. He "wizzed," lost control of the current, so that he went insane before her training was complete. Wren's innate Talent is Disassociation: it makes her so unobtrusive that she is almost invisible. It is difficult for her to command attention even when she wants to do so. She can use current to force others to pay attention to her, as well as to perform a variety of other tasks, some of which are useful for locating missing objects, such as Reading Magic, which allows her to follow the trail of magic used in the past, and others that are useful for heists, such as Levitation. She also picked up a host of non-magical skills, such as picking locks, that are useful in her work.

Known Associates: Sergei Didier, art dealer and Wren's partner in the Retriever business for 10 years. When they meet at his art gallery, Wren must deal with his assistant, Lowell. P. B. (not his real name, P. B. is short for "polar bear"), who is a demon (one of the Fatae), a dealer in information, and a friend. Lee Mahoney (Talent), a sculptor, is also a friend. When Sergei was young and idealistic, he worked for The Silence. His mentor there was Andre Felhim. Andre's current associate is Poul Jorgunmunder. Wren's mother, Margot Valere, shows up sporadically.

Premise: Theoretically, every human being can do magic by manipulating the energy that imbues everything in the world. Practically, only a few people are pure conductors for that energy, so only a few achieve full mage status. Other humans are *Nulls* to a greater or lesser extent (some have a trace of the Talent needed to control energy). In the pre-industrial world, people with Talent pulled energy from nature, where, outside of lightning, it can rarely be found in high concentrations. The electronic age was a godsend to magic users: ready access to current handed the Talent the keys to the civilized world. Most of the Talent have joined the Mage's Council, a group that provides governance, safety, and health benefits. Those who refuse to join are called "lonejacks." There is a wider community called the *Cosa Nostradamus* that incorporates all magical people: Council members, lonejacks, and Fatae. It is more a label than a true community: every magical creature is sure of his or her own subspecies' superiority and looks out for his or her subspecies' interests. Many of the Fatae are ancient breeds, all except the demons who were created by magic. Back in the mists of time, a mad Talent decided to manipulate several fae, human, and animal races together to create an interesting subspecies of servants. Over millennia, the parent genes reasserted themselves and the bloodline splintered into several different types, all recognizable by their red eyes. The *Cosa* named them all "demon," lumping them together and linguistically linking them with evil. At the beginning of the series, Nulls (people with little or no Talent) are unaware of the *Cosa,* even when living side by side with the Fatae. Many Fatae pass as humans, the others keep out of sight. One plotline in the series is the Nulls' gradual discovery of the *Cosa*. One of the first organizations of Nulls to discover and find use for the *Cosa* was The Silence. It was founded in the early 1900s by a group of wealthy men who decided to put their power into an organization built to "defend and protect against the world's darkness." Sergei joined them when he was young and idealistic. Now he thinks of them rather cynically as an organization committed to do-gooding through violence.

Comment: Laura Anne Gilman has written for the *Buffy the Vampire Slayer* series (her series entries were *Visitors* and *Deep Water*) and for the *Quantum Leap* series (co-authoring the series entry *Double or Nothing* with C. J. Henderson).

The first four books in the series seem to take place within the same year. The reference to natural disasters in *Burning Bridges* indicates that the year is

2005. As in many series in which the year is not specified, it might be better to think of this series as simply set some time in the present.

Laura Anne Gilman blogs at http://cosanostradamus.blogspot.com/.

Literary Magic & Mayhem: This is a complex series that explores a number of interesting ideas. Unfortunately, the ideas being explored don't always mesh. For instance, the concept of "retrievers" fits well into a series of cynical, somewhat humorous, caper stories. The themes of racism and bigotry are so dark, so serious, that they don't really fit in with that same sort of humor, yet they are themes that are explored very well in this series. The series could easily stand on the slow discovery of the magical community by Nulls and their reaction to the Talented and the Fatae. It's fascinating when it explores the coalition of people who have, in the past, focused only on their own interests. The series would have worked as one or the other, but the sections that focus on the bigotry and violence of the society seem out of step with the lighter sections of each book that focus on retrieval jobs.

The narrative includes great stretches of exposition. Some of it is well set up, some is distracting. For instance, naming some of the Fatae demons and others of the Fatae angeli necessitates an explanation the first time the terms are used in each book. The fact that the explanation includes a little history, a little myth, and a description of the rather cruel joke that is at the bottom of the name "demon" gives the reader the information that the *Cosa* are not particularly gentle, wise, or humane; it reveals one aspect of an ugly strain of bigotry that has been passed down through the generations. On the other hand, there are Sergei's musings, for instance in *Burning Bridges*, when, right after he has been given information on treachery and murder, he focuses on lock deicing:

> The streets were cleared, for the moment. A few cars were parked on the side of the road, coated with ice on the windows, a dusting of snow on the hoods and roofs. He hoped to hell the owners had quality lock deicers, otherwise they weren't going to be getting into the cars any time soon. (p. 323)

Even if the point were to show that he is aware of all the details around him all the time, the emotional investment in "hoping to hell" at this moment, right after he's focused on monstrous acts, seems odd. The supernatural elements that should add an extra fillip to the story fall curiously flat; even the messages from Seers don't exactly hit the mark. It would be wonderful if an exploration of them after the fact brought out new and interesting facets of the plots. The messages are included in the *Explorations* section of this review, in the hope that the reader can elicit something from them.

The main characters are interesting, but not engaging. In later books, the Fatae seem warmer than the human protagonists. The author did a wonderful job with the villains, giving them noble rationales, along with intelligence and determination.

Explorations: The fortunes from Noodles (a Chinese food takeout place near Wren's apartment) are written by a Seer. How do the fortunes relate to the stories?

Staying Dead: "It's not the dying which is so bad, but the staying dead."

Curse the Dark: Wren's is "The heart is the only thing that can hurt you."; Sergei's is "If you must curse the dark, remember it is only fallen light."

Bring it On: Sergei pockets his; it said, "Bring it on."; Shig's is "You will dance on the edge of disaster, but learn many new steps."; P. B. refuses to discuss his. He also picked up Wren's and, when he breaks it open, he finds that hers says, "This fortune not for you."

Burning Bridges: Wren has begun to avoid Noodles, but the Seer tracks her down to bring her this fortune: "A hungry man might as well cook his soup off a burning bridge as a campfire."

Free Fall: Sergei avoids the Chinese restaurant and gets Thai food instead. He finds the Seer's fortune cookie in the bag: "Falling is not failure but a failure to resist."

THE CASES

1. ***Staying Dead.*** New York: Luna, 2004, 344 p. ISBN: 0373802099.

MANHATTAN, MAY **2005**? A bizarrely Talented thief has managed to steal the cornerstone, used as the basis for the protection spells on the headquarters of the Frants Enterprises building (built in 1955), without disturbing the rest of the structure. Wren's job is to retrieve it. The retrieval should be simple, not easy, but at least straightforward. What Wren doesn't know is the nature of the protection spell, and what she doesn't know could kill her.

ASSOCIATES: Sergei—*Wren's partner;* Rafe—*the guard detailed to assist her;* P. B.—*demon, a contact who brings Wren information;* Oliver Frants—*the client, a business owner;* Denise Macauley, Marco, Randolph, and suspect Chief Technical Officer George Margolin—*all employees of Frants;* Stuart Maxwell—*wizzart, known to the Talented as the Alchemist;* KimAnn Howe—*a leader in the Mage Council;* Dancy, Adam, Clara Maroony—*a few employees of The Silence;* Andre Felhim—*Sergei's original mentor in The Silence;* Poul Jorgunmunder—*Andre's associate;* Lee and Miriam Mahoney—*friends of Wren;* Officer Ben Doblosky—*human, Talent;* Beth Sanatini, Matthew Prevost, Stephen Langwon—*humans;* Sandy and Leshiy—*Fatae;* Jamie Koogler—*ghost.*

2. "Palimpsest," a short story in *Powers of Detection: Stories of Mystery and Fantasy* edited by Dana Stabenow. New York: Ace Books, 2004, p. 133–53. ISBN: 0441011977.

MANHATTAN, JULY 2005. Sergei has two jobs for Wren. The first is a piece of cake, retrieving a painting from The Meadows. The second is trickier, it's a job from the Silence. She makes the deadly mistake of trying to combine the two jobs.

ASSOCIATES: Sergei Didier—*Wren's partner;* Bob Goveiss—*pawnshop owner;* Goid—*piskie.*

3. "Overrush," a short story in *Murder by Magic: Twenty Tales of Crime and the Supernatural* edited by Rosemary Edghill. New York: Aspect, 2004, p. 155–69. ISBN: 0446679623.

MANHATTAN, 2005. They'd been hired by an insurance company to prove that some of the articles on an insurance claim were still residing with their original owners. It should have been easy, almost risk free. Then Wren encountered a dead man. Through him she discovered a plot to attack those who use current, but can she stop the plotters?

ASSOCIATES: Sergei Didier—*Wren's partner.*

4. *Curse the Dark.* New York: Luna, 2005, 346 p. ISBN: 0373802277.

MANHATTAN AND ITALY, AUGUST 2005? The Mage Council has started a whispering campaign against Wren. Nothing overt, just enough to scare off business. When The Silence gives Wren and Sergei a commission, it is welcome. The job is to retrieve a stolen manuscript, the Nascanni parchment. The parchment has an odd history: no one who has ever read it has been seen alive again. It was kept between sheets of slate, in an Italian monastery. While Wren and Sergei are hot on the trail in Italy, P. B. and Lee are trying to quell the hostility that has risen between the Talented and the Fatae. The hostility level in the city just keeps ratcheting up. Are the rising tempers simply due to the unrelenting heat?

ASSOCIATES: Sergei and Wren—*who work out some of their intimacy issues in this book.*

The Silence—*is their client;* Andre Felhim—*is the contact;* Bren—*Andre's office manager;* Duncan—*is Head of Operations;* Poul Jorgunmunder and Darcy Cross—*are others who work at The Silence.* Madame KimAnn Howe—*appears once more as Head of the East Coast Mage's Council;* Brother Teodosio, Brother Alain, Brother Frederich, and Brother Aaron—*are the Brothers of the Monaci delle Santa Parole;* Anastagio and Pietro—*who are young, Talented, and fans of Wren;* Ricard, Pietro's father, and Septus—*are also Wren's fans;* Dr. Ebick—*is suspected of the theft.*

Mister Taibshe—*is at the Friesman-Stutzner Library;* Heather—*library intern;* Saul Haven—*exhibit preparator;* Lawrence—*who is marginally Talented;*

P. B.—*demon;* Lee—*lonejack;* Eshani—*troll;* Illy—*air-walker;* Forrey—*feathered serpent;* Rorani—*a dryad, considered by some to be the First Lady of the Fatae;* Melanie—*gnome;* Baxter—*Talent, is a holistic veterinarian, and wants the lonejacks to organize against the Mage's Council;* Wren's mother—*who stops in to visit Wren at an inopportune moment.*

5. *Bring it On.* New York: Luna, c2006, 377 p. ISBN: 0373802404.

MANHATTAN, NOVEMBER 2005? Wren and Sergei begin keeping secrets from each other, taking jobs for their business without consultation, drifting apart. Wren takes a job of retrieving a necklace from her client's stepmother. Sergei is offered a job by Andre, who has realized that he is being undermined by someone within The Silence. He wants Sergei to come back to work to help him clean house, and root out who is excising needed information from current files. He hopes that Sergei will have a special interest, because the information is being withheld from the files that concern cases that include a supernatural element. People are disappearing, including both some of the Talent and their Handlers. For an organization like The Silence, an organization where information is the lifeblood, such tampering is likely to get agents killed.

ASSOCIATES: Anna Rosen—*the client;* Melanie Worth-Rosen—*Council, the target;* P. B.—*demon, Wren's friend;* Danny—*Fatae, hooved type;* Bill—*lonejack, is the best translocator in Manhattan;* Joey Tagliente, Aldo, and Charlie (lonejack)—*gather information for Wren;* Sarah—*lonejack, prognosticator;* Lawrence—*Talent, a refabricator;* Bonnie—*lonejack, has a job with Private Unaffiliated Paranormal Investigators (PUPI), a sort of CSI for the magical world, after she does some forensic work for Wren she ends up taking a downstairs apartment in Wren's building;* Morgan—*is teaching the Fatae self-defense;* Wren's mother—*has lunch with Wren.*

Employees of The Silence include Andre Felhim—*who is now engaged in a turf war within the agency;* Michael—*an old friend of Sergei's;* Clare—*who has issues about "magicals";* and Poul Jorgunmunder—*who is now searching for allies against Andre;* Bren; Darcy Cross; and Jordana.

The Metropolitan Northeastern Seaboard Mage's Council: KimAnn Howe—*who sees the Council's mission as standing between the chaos of the old (pre-current) magics and the rational use of the new;* Jacob; and Colleen. Sebastion Bailey—*Head of the San Diego Council, with whom KimAnn is working on an unprecedented (and illegal, by Council rules) alliance;* Seiichi Shigenoi—*Fatae: gecko, Talent;* Geordie—*lonejack, a loudmouth;* and Clara—*lonejack who is violent.* The Lonejacks agree to work with Wren on building a non-violent coalition. Bart, Michaela, Rich, and Stephanie—*lonejack representatives to the coalition.*

6. ***Burning Bridges.*** New York: Luna, 2007, 416 p. ISBN: 0373802749.

MANHATTAN, DECEMBER 2005? Unaffiliated Talents are disappearing. The Cosa's Truce Board is in place, but the coalition is fragile. The murder of an Angeli may be its death blow. Wren is overwhelmed with politics and is grateful when Sergei contracts for a simple retrieval job: fetching some papers out of a politician's home.

ASSOCIATES: The Truce Board includes Jordan—*Council;* Ayexi—*Council;* Beyl—*Fatae: griffin;* Einnie—*Fatae: piskie;* Reynaldi—*Fatae: trauco;* Bart—*lonejack;* Michaela—*lonejack;* and Rich—*lonejack.* Members who are patrolling include Nahir—*Talent* and Twinkletoes—*Fatae: piskie.*

Dr. Gareth Hackins—*is experimenting on a lonejack;* Bethany—*the lonejack;* Wren has a Christmas Eve party for Sergei, guests include P. B.—*Fatae: demon;* Aloise—*Fatae: hill fairy;* Gorry—*Fatae: gnome;* Bonnie—*unaffiliated Talent;* and Nick—*unaffiliated Talent, Bonnie's partner.* Wren attends a New Year's Eve party that seems to be mostly lonejacks. Guests include Rosie, John Merriam; and Menachim.

Employees of The Silence include Duncan—*head of Research and Dissemination;* Melissa—*who works for Duncan;* Andre Felhim; Bren; Darcy Cross; and Poul Jorgunmunder. Ian Stosser and Nick "Nifty" Lawrence—*are the co-founders of the Private Unaffiliated Paranormal Investigators (PUPIs);* KimAnn Howe—*was mentored by Elizabeth;* Elizabeth—*warns KimAnn against her current course of action.* The Mage's Council is led by Louise (Midwest); Bee (Tucson-region); Randolph (Quebec); Jenne (Pacific Northwest); and Lizzie (Green Kingdom): the Gulf Coast branches are still in some disarray from the natural disasters. Old Sally—*the bansidhe stuffed horse, is finally captured by Wren;* Lowell—*Sergei's assistant, is infuriated when she stores it at Sergei's gallery;* Sergei—*who is stunned when Wren sends him an invitation;* Koshschey the Damned—*acts as a messenger for Wren.* Wren asks Sergei to come to the meeting, even though she is beginning to believe that their association is a mistake.

7. ***Free Fall.*** New York: Luna, 2008, 345 p. ISBN: 9780373802678; 0373802676.

MANHATTAN, MAY 2006. It was a flaw included at the very inception of the Silence: they had created the organization to stand against supernatural threats, but some who joined believed that any supernatural creature was a threat, and felt that the best way of stemming the threat was to wipe out both Talents and the Fatae. That attitude was understood to be unacceptable, but it was not eradicated. It lurked, and in the last few years a plot to set Talent against Talent and to set humans against the Fatae has borne fruit. Many have died. Most of those Fatae who cannot pass for human have fled Manhattan.

Wren sent Sergei away after the Battle at the Burning Bridge. She's taking jobs on her own. One job is a setup, someone moving her into position so that she can be assassinated. She draws upon dark current, current she's avoided in the past; and she finds it powerful. She finally realizes that the leaders of the Silence are determined to destroy all the members of the *Cosa Nostradamus*. She rallies the *Cosa*:

> The enemy we face—the organization that has decided that we—WE—are the cause of ill in this modern world—is determined to wipe us out. Not contain us, not "tame" us. Eradicate us. Exterminate us. (p. 139)

Wren decides that it is time to retrieve the Talent that the Silence kidnapped. The Silence intended to turn them against the *Cosa* and, to that end, after they were kidnapped they were brainwashed. Wren doesn't expect to be greeted as a liberator. She hopes they don't kill her before she can rescue them.

ASSOCIATES: P. B.—*Fatae: demon, now lives with Wren;* Bonnie—*unaffiliated Talent is their downstairs neighbor;* Duncan—*is now the most powerful member of the Silence;* others in the Silence include Joanie, Christina, Andre Felhim, Reese; Karl, Goran Jay, Gareth Hackins, Marc, Adam, Jodana, and Erik.

Wren recruits Danny Henrikson—*Fatae: faun;* Sua—*Fatae: griffin;* Bamidele—*Talent;* Ayexi—*Talent;* Julia—*Talent;* Gordon—*Talent;* Sean—*Talent;* Bernie—*Talent;* and George—*Talent.*

Lowell—*is Sergei's gallery assistant;* Shawn—*Sergei's doorman;* Professor Joe Doherty; Morgan—*a martial artist;* Colleen—*who worked for the Mage Council;* Ron—*a planner;* Mike and Kale—*firefighters who were colleagues of Larry Kohmer;* Larry Kohmer—*Talent;* Dora—*Talent;* Jimmy—*Talent;* Michael—*Talent;* Sue—*Talent;* Terry Kohmer—*Talent;* Livvy—*Talent;* Jody—*Talent;* Rosalle—*Talent* and Allie—*Talent.*

In 1910, the original board of the Silence included Alan, Maxwell, Mr. Carson, Mr. Van Stann; Mr. Goddard; Mr. Donnelly, Mr. Ashton Claire, Mr. Gilbert, and Mr. Jackson.

GORDON, Alan R.

THIRTEENTH NIGHT: A MEDIEVAL MYSTERY

Genres/Themes Crossed: Literary Cross-Over, Alternate History X Hard-Boiled Mystery, Espionage.

Subjects/Character Types: Literary Characters X Agent of secret organization, Espionage.

Series/Stand-Alone: There are significant changes in relationships over the course of the series. The novels are best read in order. The short stories are fun additions, providing windows into Theophilos's life, but the initial novel provides the best introduction to the series.

Scene of the Crime: Europe and the Middle East, late 12th and early 13th centuries.

Detective: Theophilos the Fool, a member of the Fools' Guild. He takes a different alias (he refers to them as *noms de bouffon*) for each new adventure, but his Guild name is always Theophilos. While in Umbria, he is known as Balaam. In Pisa he is known as Forzo. In Illyria, he is known as Feste (you may have heard of him under this name in William Shakespeare's *Twelfth Night*); he also goes by Feste in Venice and in Constantinople. In Tyre (Lebanon), he is known as Droignon. On the road in France in 1204, he is known as Tan Pierre. In Orsino he poses as a merchant, Octavius of Augsburg. In the past, Theophilos has been a Fool of legendary skill and wit, saving countless lives as he travels the world and works behind the scenes to prevent or end wars. Theophilos is haunted by memories of those people that he could not save. At the beginning of the series of books, Theophilos has retired; or, to be more accurate, he has gone into decline. The only amazing feats he is moved to perform involve imbibing large quantities of liquor. In fact, when Theophilos decides that he must take action, he is forbidden to do so: his friends believe that he is no longer able to function well enough to survive. That adventure, recounted in *Thirteenth Night,* gives him a new lease on life.

Known Associates: The pillars of the Fool's Guild include Father Gerald, who runs the Guild, Sister Agatha the Guild's Costumer, Brother Timothy, who teaches juggling, and Brother Dennis, who cares for the Guild's horses. In the course of the adventures related in these books, Theophilos marries Claudia (also known as Viola, Aglaia, and the Duchess of Orsino) who becomes an apprentice Fool in *Thirteenth Night* and a full member of the Fools' Guild in *Jester Leaps In*. They have a daughter, Portia, on Jan. 6, 1204, at the conclusion of *A Death in the Venetian Quarter*. They gain an apprentice, named Helga, in *The Lark's Lament*.

Premise: The world of Shakespeare, in fact, the world of all playwrights who wrote of wise jesters who shame and bully the powerful into doing what is right—that world is real. These jesters are members of the Fools' Guild, a (somewhat) religious order that trains novitiates in languages, music, dancing, repertoire, disguises, juggling, tumbling, fighting, passwords, and poisoning. "The arts needed to entertain, the skills needed to accomplish our hidden goals, the wits needed to survive"(*An Antic Disposition,* p. 3). The Guild then deploys the jesters to stations high and low (courts are a favorite). The Guild's overarching purpose is to increase the chances for lasting peace. The Fools act as spies, provocateurs, and sometimes even executioners; but, as a group, they prefer using their wits to using steel, and generally they work behind the scenes to influence those in power to preserve the peace.

Theo would lay down his life to bring peace to a troubled land, but he also values the Fools' mission of creating joy. When he speaks to the novitiates in *The Widow of Jerusalem,* he tells them that the Guild will warn against letting their love of performing interfere with their missions; he warns them against letting their missions interfere with their love of performing. "To bring laughter to the world is as sacred a mission as to bring peace" (p. 207).

In *Thirteenth Night,* Alan Gordon gives his apologia for the creation of the Fools' Guild. He states that there is little historical evidence for the existence of the Fools' Guild:

> ...This is that rare secret society that actually succeeded in remaining secret. In the Age of Faith, Will Durant writes of a "*confrèrie* of minstrels and jongleurs like that which we know to have been held in Fécamp in Normandy about the year 1000c; there they learned one another's tricks and airs, and the new tales or songs of the *trouvères* and troubadours" (p. 1054). Frustratingly, this is virtually the only un-footnoted line in the entire book, and I have yet to discover its source. (p. 242)

Comment: The premise is fun, and the careful attention to historical detail saves the series from being silly. These books are mystery action novels with a little bit of humor and a lot of heart. Many of the supporting characters of the Fools' Guild are heroes, and the reader will want to save them all. The research is exceptional, and the history is depicted well, particularly in the books that cover the events leading to the Fourth Crusade. The series opens with *Thirteenth Night,* which takes place in Shakespeare's Illyria, 15 years after the events of Shakespeare's *Twelfth Night.* It is therefore peopled only with imaginary characters. Subsequent books depict historical events; central to these events are the intrigues of Europe and the Middle East in the 11th and 12th centuries. *An Antic Disposition,* is based on the work of 1204 Danish history written by a historian of questionable reliability, Saxo Grammaticus. This same Danish history was used as the basis for Shakespeare's *Hamlet;* readers should not fear this retelling of the story, it is both more and less bloody than the more familiar version.

Literary Magic & Mayhem: Most of the series is told from Theophilos's point of view. The third and sixth novels in the series alternate between his point of view and that of Claudia (his wife). This allows the reader to see the machinations of the female members of the Imperial Court first hand.

Explorations: How did the Fools instigate change?

How have the characters aged (from when they were portrayed in *Twelfth Night*)?

What roles did disguises play in the story?

In retrospect, was Sebastian a victim in *Twelfth Night?* Which of Feste's gambits would have hurt others over time?

THE CASES

1. **"The Jester and the Saint,"** in *Ellery Queen's Mystery Magazine* (December 1995): 142–56; reprinted in *Once Upon a Crime II,* edited by Janet Hutchings. New York: St. Martin's Press, 1996, p. 114–27.

UMBRIA, ASSISI, ITALY, 1198. Theophilos (under the "*nom de bouffon*" Balaam) encounters the 15-year-old Giovanni de Bernardone (who later becomes Saint Francis) and helps him solve a murder.

ASSOCIATES: Saint Francis of Assisi.

2. **"The Jester and the Mathematician,"** in *Ellery Queen's Mystery Magazine* (February 2000): 90–109.

PISA, ITALY, 1198. A Saracen spy in the city of Pisa implicates the great mathematician, Leonardo Fibonacci, in a murder. It is up to Theophilos (called Forzo in Pisa) and his fellow fool the Great Frenetto (a.k.a. Fazio) to clear Fibonacci's name and capture the spy.

ASSOCIATES: The Great Frenetto—*Guild name Fazio.* Historical figures: Leonardo Fibonacci.

3. ***Thirteenth Night: A Medieval Mystery.*** New York: St. Martin's Press, 1999, 243 p. ISBN: 0312200358, 9780312200350.

ORSINO [DALMATIA], ITALY, 1201. A few of Shakespeare's comedies provide a time of comic confusion, crowned by a marriage to provide the happy ending. Have you ever wondered about the marital joy of those couples? This book is set 15 years after the events chronicled in *Twelfth Night,* and it's not pretty. *Thirteenth Night* reveals that Feste engineered the alliances that kept the stability of Orsino intact and that thwarted the plans of Malvolio. When a message is left at the Guildhall for Feste the Fool, telling him only that Duke Orsino is dead, is it a call for help, or is it a trap?

ASSOCIATES: In the Guildhall: Father Gerald—*who leads the Guild;* Brother Timothy—*juggling;* Niccoló—*who will take Theo's part in the Guildhall play;* Brother Dennis—*in charge of the stables;* and Sister Agatha—*who costumes*

Theo for the trip. Monsieur Francesco—*who admonishes Theo's horse to carry Theo carefully;* Zeus—*Theo's horse.*

Domino—*the chief fool of Venice;* Malvolio—*who is bent on revenge against all of those who thwarted him 15 years ago (those events are recounted in Shakespeare's Twelfth Night);* Captain Perun—*who upholds the law (more or less) in Orsino;* Alexander—*the innkeeper of the Elephant;* Agatha—*Alexander's daughter;* Newt—*the stable boy;* Sir Toby—*who married Maria;* Master Isaac—*assistant to the Duke's steward;* Sir Andrew—*an alchemist;* Viola—the *Duchess of Orsino*, Mark and Celia—*her children;* Malachi—*a servant in the household;* Claudius—*the Duke's steward;* Sebastian—the Duke's brother-in-law, Countess Olivia—*who is rich, married Sebastian;* Fabian—*managers her estate;* Hector—*who saw the old Duke fall;* Bobo the fool.

4. ***Jester Leaps In: A Medieval Mystery.*** New York: St. Martin's Minotaur, 2000, 276 p. ISBN: 0312241178.

CONSTANTINOPLE, BYZANTINE EMPIRE, 1202. Constantinople is poised on the brink of chaos. The current Emperor has neglected the defense of the city, and his nephew has been spotted in Germany, mustering support to seize the throne. In the middle of all of this, all five of the Fools stationed in Constantinople have disappeared. Theophilos (as Feste) is sent to find a way to stabilize the situation and prevent a war.

ASSOCIATES: Viola—*apprentice fool, Theophilos's wife, travels under the name Claudius, adopts the name of Aglaia, and is given the guildname of Claudia when she becomes a fullfledged Fool;* Troubadour Tantalo—*who brings an assignment from Father Gerald;* Captain Perun—*who sees Theophilos and Viola out of Orsino;* Fat Basil—*a fool in Thessaloniki;* Simon—*an innkeeper in Constantinople;* Michael—*the huntsman*, Asan—*who is probably a pickpocket*, Stephanos, and some Russians—*all stay at the inn.* Cnut, Stanislaus, and Henry—*are soldiers.* Samuel—*who arranges the entertainment in the Hippodrome;* Thalia—*the Fool, used to be Theophilos's lover;* Zintziphitzes—*once a Fool, is now a preacher;* Father Essias—*rules the thieves in Constantinople;* Father Theodore and Father Melchior—*work for Father Essias;* New Fools come to Constantinople, including Rico—*the dwarf, who became the Emperor's favorite;* Plossus—*who was a great success entertaining in the Hippodrome;* and Alfonso—*the troubadour.*

Historical figures include the members of the Imperial family of Constantinople: Alexios Angelos—*the Emperor;* Euphrosyne—*the Empress;* their daughters Irene—*married to Alexios Palailogos*, Anna—*married to Theodore Laskaris*, and Evdokia. Isaakios—*Alexios's brother who he imprisoned;* Michael Stryphnos—*the Grand Duke of the Navy, is Euphrosyne's brother-in-law;* George Oinaiotes—*the Grand Chamberlain;* Constantine Philoxenites—*a eunuch, the Imperial Treasurer;* Senator Niketas Choniates—*who plays a small part in the story.*

5. "**The Jester and the Thieves,**" in *Ellery Queen's Mystery Magazine* (October 2004): 72–85.

CONSTANTINOPLE, BYZANTINE EMPIRE, 1202. This story is an interpolation into the events near the beginning of *Jester Leaps In* while Feste is Head Fool of Constantinople, with only Claudia beside him. Father Essias commissions Feste to discover which one of three of his thieves has stolen from the Thieves' Guild. Knowing that discovering the truth will condemn one man to death, but that not discovering the truth will condemn three men (two of them comparatively innocent) to death, Feste reluctantly complies.

ASSOCIATES: Father Essias—*who rules Constantinople's thieves.*

6. ***A Death in the Venetian Quarter: A Medieval Mystery.*** New York: St. Martin's Minotaur, 2002, 288 p. ISBN: 0312242670.

CONSTANTINOPLE, BYZANTINE EMPIRE, 1203. In the shadow of the Fourth Crusade Feste, the Chief Fool of Constantinople is commanded to investigate the death of an Imperial spy. This was no simple murder; Feste suspects that it is the one untidy thread of an intricate plot to deliver the city to the Crusaders.

ASSOCIATES: The book opens with the Fools celebrating the ascension of Viola (a.k.a. Aglaia, a.k.a. Claudia) from Apprentice to Jester. The Fools of Constantinople include Feste—*Viola's husband*, Rico—*the dwarf*, Plossus, and Alfonso—*the troubadour*. The Venetian Quarter of Constantinople includes Vitale's boarding house. Boarders include John Aprenos—*John the Huntsman* and Tullio—*the carpenter;* Andrea Ruzzini—*the man in charge of Camilio Bastiani's funeral;* Signor Domenico Viadro and Signor Ranieri—*two of the mourners;* Father Essias—*the leader of the Thieves;* Father Theodore and Father Melchior—*work for Father Essias;* William and Philip—*Englishmen who work for Philoxenites;* Nicolò Rosso—*the courtier;* Count Sebastion—*Viola's brother, is one of the Crusaders;* Raimbaut de Vaquiras, Tantalo, Giraut, and Gaucelm—*are troubadours;* Cnut, Stanislaus, and Henry—*are soldiers;* Demetrios Gabras—*Keeper of the Inperial Silk.*

In Thessaloniki, Claudia and Theophilos stay with Fat Basil until after Portia is born on the 12th day of Christmas.

Historical figures include the members of the Imperial family of Constantinople: Alexios Angelos—*the Emperor;* Euphrosyne—*the Empress;* their daughters Irene—*married to Alexios Palailogos*, Anna—*married to Theodore Laskaris*, and Evdokia—*who has decided that she is in love with the prisoner Alexios Doukas;* Isaakios—*the Emperor's brother, imprisoned by the Emperor;* Michael Stryphnos—*Euphrosyne's brother-in-law, he's the Grand Duke of the Navy;* George Oinaiotes—*is the Grand Chamberlain;* Constantine Philoxenites—*a eunuch, is the Imperial Treasurer;* Senator Niketas Choniates—*who plays a part in this story.*

7. **"The Jester and the Captain,"** in *Alfred Hitchcock's Mystery Magazine*, vol. 51 iss. 3 (March 2006): 72–87.

CONSTANTINOPLE, BYZANTINE EMPIRE, SPRING 1203. Plossus finds Henry, Captain of the Varangian Guard, hung over, despondent, and ready to give up his post. He's on the third day of a three-day leave, and he lost his uniform's sash last night. He will be a laughingstock, a guard who couldn't defend his badge of office, who had it stolen right off his body. Henry cannot face the humiliation. Feste is more concerned that the sash and the badge could be used by a saboteur to gain access to critical resources in Constantinople. The Fools take up the case and follow Henry's trail of debauchery in search of his sash.

ASSOCIATES: Feste—*who leads the Fools of Constantinople;* Aglaia—*Feste's wife, a fool;* Rico—*the dwarf, a fool,* Plossus—*a fool;* Henry—*Captain of the Varangian Guard;* Emeric—*the goldsmith;* Otto—*Emeric's bodygyard;* Cyril—*tapster at the Two Heads of John tavern;* Marcus—*tapster at the Poseidon's Trident tavern;* and Anna—*the veiled barmaid at the Poseidon's Trident tavern.*

8. ***Widow of Jerusalem.*** New York: St. Martin's Minotaur, 2003, 276 p. ISBN: 0312300891, 9780312300890.

ACRE, ITALY, 1204 AND TYRE, LEBANON, 1191. Rome has begun to persecute the Fools and the Guild has fled from the Guild Hall. Theophilos and Claudia rescue the sign on of the Scarlet Dwarf and follow the Guild into hiding. As they travel, Theophilos tells the story of the scarlet dwarf, Scarlet the Chief Fool of Jerusalem, and the summer of 1191: Jerusalem was captured by Saladin in 1187 and refugees fled to Tyre. The Fools Scarlet and Droignon worked to uphold the peace of the city and the outlying tent city of refugees while working covertly to strengthen Queen Isabelle's claim to the throne of Jerusalem.

ASSOCIATES: Scarlet(t) the Dwarf—*Chief Fool of Jerusalem;* Blondel—*a troubadour;* Ambroise—*a jongleur;* Balian d'Ibelin—*one of Conrad's advisors;* William, Ralph, and Hugh—*the brothers Falconberg, they also have Conrad's ear;* Clarence d'Anjou—*Richard's envoy;* Ibrahim, Magdalena, Sara, and Peter—*are Scarlet's apprentices;* Leo and Balthazar—*are refugees;* Mary—*the dancer, is Balthazar's wife;* Matthias—*the sailing master;* Droignon—*King Denis's Fool;* Father Gerald—*who leads the Fools, sends Theophilos on another mission;* Perrio—*a.k.a. Peter, a new fool, is sent with Theophilos;* Lepos—*a fool in Nicosia;* King Amaury of Lusignan—*enjoys the antics of Lepos, Theophilos, and Perrio.* Historical figures: Isabelle—*Queen of Jerusalem;* Conrad—*Marquis of Montferrat (Isabelle's husband);* Richard the Lionheart; Henry of Champagne; the Duke of Burgundy; and the Bishop of Beauvais.

9. ***An Antic Disposition.*** New York: St. Martin's Minotaur, 2004, 337 p. ISBN: 0312300964, 9780312300968.

SWABIA, GERMANY, 1204 and SOUTH JUTLAND, DENMARK, 1157. The religious order of the Fools' Guild was founded by a fool. One of their precepts has always been that they stand against power when they feel that the powerful are on the wrong path. Their founder instructed them to ignore Rome when they feel it has lost its way. Rome is not accustomed to insubordination from its religious houses. The leaders of the Guild realized that Pope Innocent III had come to the point where he felt that the Guild's mockery of church hypocrisy outweighed its usefulness to the Church, and they managed to evacuate the Guild House a few days before the Pope sent troops to destroy the Guild. Now the Fools' Guild is in hiding in the Black Forest. Every night, Father Gerald chooses one of their company to provide the afterdinner entertainment until Thomas points out that it's unfair because Father Gerald himself can never be chosen. Thus challenged, Father Gerald begins a story, a story from the time when Father Gerald was the first fool of Denmark, of a young fool named Terrence who was sent to deflate the ambitions of a man who would be King of Denmark. The mission was not a great success, but at least one good thing survived Terrence's posting to Jutland. The novel is based on the same story that inspired *Hamlet.*

ASSOCIATES: Claudia—*Theophilos's wife;* Helga—*who is conscripted by Claudia to watch the baby;* Brother Dennis—*who proved to be an incompetent nanny;* Portia—*the baby;* Father Gerald—*who has led the Fools into hiding.*

Denmark, 1157: Terence of York—*Yorick the fool;* Father Gerald—*a fool;* Larfner—*a fool;* Magnus—*a farmer;* Knud Magnusson, Valdemar (son of Knud Lavard), Sveyn Peder, and Ørvendil—*four men, each of whom believes that he should rule Denmark.* Gerutha—*Ørvendil's wife;* Amleth—*his son;* Gorm—*Ørvendil's drost;* Signe—*who marries Gorm;* Alfhild and Lother—*their children;* Fengi—*Valdemar's man;* Axel—*who becomes Bishop Absalon of Roskilde;* Carlo and Reynaldo—*itinerant brickmakers;* Michel—*who works with the students in Paris;* Horace, Rolf, and Gudmund—*are a few of the students in Paris;* La Vache and Horace—*are two of the Fools of Paris.*

10. ***The Lark's Lament.*** New York: St. Martin's Minotaur, 2007, 274 p. ISBN: 0312354266, 9780312354268.

MARSEILLE AND MONTPELLIER, 1204. Father Gerald has sent Theophilos and his family on a mission. They must convince Abbot Folc, who used to be a troubadour (under the name of Folquet, his Guild name was Marcello), to intercede with the Pope to stop the persecution of the Fools' Guild. Folc's price is for Theophilos to find the person who committed murder within his Abbey's walls.

ASSOCIATES: Theophilos—*a.k.a. Tan Pierre, travels with his family;* Claudia—*his wife who is using the nom de bouffon, Domna Gile;* Portia—*their daughter;* and Helga—*their apprentice.*

Members of the community at the Abbey Le Thoronet include Brother Antime—*the cellarer;* Brother Calvet, and Brother Pelfort. Hélène—*Folquet's wife;* Julien Guiraud—*Hélène's brother;* Pantalan—*guildname of Artal, the fool of Marseille;* Roncelin, Viscount Barel—*is on the throne of Marseille;* Eudiarde—*is his Viscountess;* Troubadour Pierre Vidal—*who knew some of the song that is the key to the past;* Pedro—*the King of Aragon, visits Marseille, leaving his wife in Montpellier;* Laurent—*Barel's servant, pays Theophilos to carry a letter from him to Léon;* Léon—*seneschal to Lady Marie, Countess of Montpellier;* Reynaud—*the Blacksmith;* Grelho—*Montpellier's fool, is living in reduced circumstances;* Lady Marie—*the Countess of Montpellier;* Guilhema—*her daughter;* Brother Guilhem—*who avoided conflict by retreating from the world;* Jacquette—*who remembers the song;* Berenguer and Rocco—*Landrieux's stewards;* Philippe Landrieux—*who did his best to protect his mother.*

11. ***The Moneylender of Toulouse.*** New York: St. Martin's Minotaur, 2008, 322 p. ISBN: 9780312371098.

SAINT CYPRIEN AND TOULOUSE, FRANCE, 1204. Now that the Guild has Folquet's help Father Gerald sends Theophilos and his family to rid Toulouse of its old Bishop and see Folquet take his place (and to prevent the inevitable war that will come when Count Raimon can no longer control the ambitious nobles of his court).

ASSOCIATES: Father Gerald—*who assigns Theophilos (a.k.a. Tan Pierre) to the position of Chief Jester of Toulouse;* Claudia—*Theophilos's wife, is using the nom de bouffon, Domina Gile;* Portia—*their daughter*, Helga—*their 12-year-old apprentice.*

The community of Toulouse includes Bishop Raimon de Rabastens; Father Mascaron; Milon Borsella—*the merchant;* Béatrix—*his wife;* Bonet—*his older brother, who inherited the family sawmill;* Brother Vitalis—*his younger brother, who took Benedictine orders;* Evrard—*the keykeeper of Milon Borsella's household;* Jordan—*a fool, guildname of Rollo, he hoped to become Chief Jester;* Pelardit—*a quiet fool;* Martine—*Jordan's wife;* Oldric—*Master of the Revels;* Count Raimon the Sixth; the Countess Éléonor—*his wife;* Bernard—*Count of Comminges;* Arnaut Guilabert—*who is wealthy;* Gentille—his *wife;* Audrica—*Arnaut's maidservant;* Armand—*the drunkard;* Egidius—*the trumpeter;* Brother Donatus; Calvet—*the baile;* Honoret—*Theo's landlord;* Peire of Castelnau—*a papal legate;* and Sancho.

GORMAN, Ed and Martin H. Greenberg. (Editors)

Once Upon a Crime

Genres/Themes Crossed: Anthropomorphic Animals, Secret Society X Hard-Boiled Mystery, Traditional Mystery.

Subjects/Character Types: Witches, Psychics, Ghosts, Dwarves X Private Investigators, Amateur Sleuths.

Series/Stand-Alone: Anthology of short stories.

Scene of the Crime: Varies.

Detective: Varies.

Known Associates: Varies.

Premise: Well-known mystery writers were challenged to use the fairy tales collected by the brothers Grimm as the basis for new stories. Some are retellings of the fairy tales, some are updates, and some simply use the fairy tale as a jumping off point for another story.

Comment: These stories were written for this anthology. Each author met the challenge in a different way. The results are exciting and strange.

Ed Gorman won the 1988 Shamus Award for Best P.I. Short Story for "Turn Away," which was published in the *Black Lizard Anthology of Crime Fiction*. In 1994, he was nominated for the Shamus Best Original P.I. Paperback for *Shadow Games*. His Jack Dwyer tales have been nominated repeatedly for the Shamus: in 1986 for Best First P.I. Novel for *New Improved Murder;* in 1988 for Best P.I. Hardcover for *The Autumn Dead;* in 1989 for Best P.I. Short Story for "The Reason Why," which was published in *Criminal Elements;* and in 1997 for Best P.I. Short Story for "Eye of the Beholder," which was published in *The Autumn Dead and A Cry of Shadows.*

In 1994, the Anthony Award for Best Critical Work and the Macavity Award for Best Critical/Biographical Work was awarded to *The Fine Art of Murder,* which was edited by Ed Gorman, Martin H. Greenberg, Larry Segriff, and Jon L. Breen. In 1999, Ed Gorman was nominated (along with co-editor Martin Greenberg) for the Macavity Award for Best Critical/Biographical Work and the Agatha for Best Non-Fiction Work for *Speaking of Murder.*

In 1992, Ed Gorman won the Spur Award for best short fiction for his story "The Face."

In 1995, Ed Gorman's collection *Cages* won the International Horror Guild Award for Best Collection and was nominated for the Bram Stoker

Award for Best Fiction Collection. In 2001, his collection *The Dark Fantastic* was nominated for a Bram Stoker award.

In 2003, the Mystery Writers of America presented Ed Gorman with the Ellery Queen Award for outstanding work in the mystery-publishing industry.

His Web site, at http://www.newimprovedgorman.com/, links to a short biography, a selective bibliography of his works, and to his blog.

Martin Greenberg has co-edited over nine hundred anthologies, earning the title "King of the Anthologists." He won the 2005 Prometheus Special Award (along with Mark Tier) for the anthologies *Give Me Liberty* and *Visions of Liberty*. With Ed Gorman, he won the 1994 Anthony Award for Best Critical Work and the Macavity Award for Best Critical/Biographical Work for *The Fine Art of Murder*, and in 1999 was nominated (along with co-editor Ed Gorman) for the Macavity Award for Best Critical/Biographical Work and the Agatha for Best NonFiction Work for *Speaking of Murder*. He won (along with Jon L. Breen) the 1991 Anthony Award for Best Critical Work for *Synod of Sleuths; Essays on Judeo-Christican Detective Fiction*.

Literary Magic & Mayhem: The old archetypes meet strange new adventures in the hands of these writers.

Explorations: How did knowledge of the original story add to the experience of reading the newer version?

THE CASES

1. ***Once Upon A Crime.*** New York: Berkley, 1998, 416 p. ISBN: 0425163016; 9780425163016.

CONTENTS: After Happily Ever *by Gillian Roberts;* Clever Hans *by Jon L. Breen;* Heptagon *by Joan Hess;* It Happened at Grandmother's House *by Bill Crider;* Now Fetch Me an Axe *by Simon Clark;* Old Sultan *by Mat Coward;* Harvest Home *by Elizabeth Engstrom;* Prince Charming *by William L. DeAndrea;* Rapunzel *by Jane Haddam;* Resurrection Joe *by Gary A. Braunbeck;* Rapunzel's Revenge *by Brendan DuBois;* Snow White and the Eleven Dwarfs *by Edward D. Hoch;* Swan Song *by John Lutz;* The Better to Eat You With *by John Helfers;* Of the Fog *by Ed Gorman;* The Brave Little Costume Designer *by Les Roberts;* The Emperor's New Clothes *by Simon Brett;* The Musician of Breman, GA *by Peter Crowther;* Anniversary Ball *by Audrey Peterson;* Invisible Time *by Janet Dawson;* Love and Justice *by Kristine Kathryn Rusch;* The Twelve Dancing Princesses Revisited *by Anne Wingate;* Thousandfurs *by Doug Allyn;* Gerda's Sense of Snow *by Sharyn McCrumb.*

GREEN, Simon R.

SOMETHING FROM THE NIGHTSIDE

Genres/Themes Crossed: Blended Society X Hard-Boiled Mystery.

Subjects/Character Types: Alternate Earth, Angels (in *Agents of Light and Darkness*), Demons, Spell-Casters (various one-spell characters, including John Taylor, along with Merlin in *Paths Not Taken*), Zombies (the Dead Boy) X Private Investigator, Noir.

Series/Stand-Alone: These should be read in order, but at intervals. The author has a few pet phrases that are repeated often enough to become annoying if the books are read in one fell swoop. There are short stories that feature other characters in the Nightside; they give background on some of the minor players and can be read at any point.

Scene of the Crime: Present day (mostly present day) Nightside (a land hidden under London, a place where it is always 3:00 am. in the morning, but the dawn never comes.)

Detective: John Taylor ran from the Nightside with a bullet in his back five years ago. He found that, on the surface in London, his special gift of "finding" didn't work so well. On the other hand, nobody was trying to kill him. It struck him as a pretty good deal, and he had sworn never to venture into the Nightside again. Then a woman comes to him offering a lot of money—of course, it wasn't enough money to lure him into the Nightside. She's beautiful, but he's too smart to expect romance in the Nightside. Her daughter is missing and in danger. John Taylor is all crust on the outside, but he has a soft heart and can't abandon a young girl to the Nightside. He takes the case.

Known Associates: The Harrowing, an almost endless army of creatures. Small groups of them have been tracking John to assassinate him for as long as he can remember. Suzie Shooter (a.k.a. Shotgun Suzie). When Joanna Barrett asks if Suzie is really as dangerous as is rumored to be, Taylor replies:

> More if anything...She built her reputation on the bodies of her enemies, and a complete willingness to take risks even Norse berserkers would have balked at. Suzie doesn't know the meaning of the word fear. Other concepts she has trouble grasping are restraint, mercy and self-preservation. (p. 63, Something *from the Nightside* within the omnibus edition *A Walk on the Nightside.*)

Walker has been empowered by the Authorities to go wherever he needs to, do whatever he has to, and command anyone, living, dead or in between, to carry out the Authorities' wishes. Alex Morrisey is the bartender at the oldest bar in existence, *Strangefellows*, which is guarded by Merlin Satanspawn (deceased, and yes, *that* Merlin); Lucy and Betty Coltrane are *Strangefellows'* bouncers; Razor Eddie, Punk God of the Straight Razor, drinks for free at *Strangefellows* (in return he never kills anyone on the premises); Father Pew regards John Taylor as Hellspawn but can't resist trying to save him; The Collector (Mark) once worked for the Authorities along with Walker and John Taylor's father; Cathy Barrett, whom John saved from certain death, decided that she wanted to stick around in the Nightside and became John's secretary; Mr. Julien Advent, the Victorian Adventurer, is gallant and daring, he was the greatest hero of his age. He disappeared in 1888, and came out of a timeslip in the Nightside in 1966. Now he is owner and editor of the *Night Times.* The Dead Boy, who was murdered at age 17, 30 years ago. He made a deal with the devil to come back so that he could exact revenge. He should have read the fine print. His soul is chained to his corpse: he's essentially a zombie.

Premise: John's gift goes beyond simply finding things. He can use it to find an enemy's weak spot, and then use it to attack. He uses his gift rarely. Whenever possible, he uses nothing more than his quick wits, his terrifying reputation, and a pocketful of condiments.

Comment: Simon R. Green has said that when he was growing up his favorite female characters were Emma Peel (from the the television show *The Avengers*) and Sarah Kingdom (a cop in the old *Dr. Who* television series). He works hard on creating strong female characters. His other cross-genre series, *Hawk and Fisher,* features a husband and wife team ("A Conversation with Simon R. Green: An Interview with Lisa DuMond" dated February 2001, posted on the SF Site at http://www.sfsite.com/02b/srg98.htm.).

His work takes a long hard look at good and evil and focuses on integrity, loyalty, and honor.

Literary Magic & Mayhem: John Taylor is a tough guy with a heart of gold and a smart mouth. He's had enemies since the minute he was born. From his first moments, there were people who were trying to kill him, and he had no idea who they were or why they wanted him dead. The frequent attacks were only part of the nightmare that was his childhood. He felt abandoned, not just by his mother (who left), but also by his father, even though his father remained physically present. In John's words,

> they've been sending agents to try and kill me ever since I was a child. It has something to do with my absent mother, who turned out not to be human. She disappeared shortly after my father discovered that, and he spent what

> little was left of his life drinking himself to death. I like to think I'm made of harder stuff. Sometimes I don't think about my missing mother for days on end. (p. 284, *Nightingale's Lament*, within the omnibus edition *A Walk on the Nightside*)

His adulthood isn't a great deal better: "For a time, I was happy. It was like waking up in a foreign country" (p. 49, *Something from the Nightside,* within the omnibus edition *A Walk on the Nightside*). John encounters one of his closest friends, Razor Eddie, in the Nightside's future, and Eddie says: "I should have killed you . . . when I had the chance. Before you . . . destroyed us all" (p. 73, *Something from the Nightside,* within the omnibus edition *A Walk on the Nightside*). When John realizes that something he will do in the future will destroy the world, he asks Eddie for advice. Eddie suggests that he kill himself (and Eddie is John's *friend . . .*).

The author has some favorite lines that show up again and again. If the books were read with a decent interval between titles, the lines would probably feel amusing and comfortable, like old friends. Suzie Shooter's introduction is one example: "This . . . is Suzie Shooter. Also known as Shotgun Suzie, also known as Oh Christ, it's her, run" (p. 163, *Agents of Light and Darkness,* within the omnibus edition *A Walk on the Nightside*).

Explorations: What interesting moves does John use to vanquish the villains?

At what point should John have asked more questions of his client?

Would John be better off in topside London?

THE CASES

1. **"Appetite for Murder,"** a short story in *Unusual Suspects* edited by Dana Stabenow. New York: Ace Books, 2008, p. 243–62. ISBN: 9780441016372.

NIGHTSIDE, 200? The story of the retirement of Sam Warren, the first detective in the Nightside.

ASSOCIATES: Mr. Pettigrew—*Chief Librarian of the H. P. Lovecraft Memorial Library;* Ms. Fate—*a Nightside superheroine;* Dr. West—*coroner;* the three witches of Shadow Deep; Charles Peace—*burglar, the Governor of Shadow Deep.*

2. ***Something From the Nightside.*** New York: Ace Books, 2003, 230 p. ISBN: 0441010652.

NIGHTSIDE, 2003? AND FUTURE. John Taylor was born in the Nightside; he left it in a hurry, leaving frustrated assassins in his wake, when he was 25 years old. That was five years ago. He's led a quiet existence in London, and he treasures the peace. He's vowed never to go back, and then a woman shows up, beautiful, rich, and with a story that would break your heart. Her runaway daughter may have been lured into the Nightside. John Taylor goes back into the dark, to save the girl. In his search for her, he finds himself in a future Nightside, one in which his world has been destroyed, and he is told that he was the engine of that destruction.

ASSOCIATES: Joanna Barrett—*a client;* Father Pew; Alex Morrisey—*owner of Strangefellow's Bar;* Lucy and Betty Coltrane—*are Strangefellows' bouncers;* Razor Eddie; Shotgun Suzie; the Collector; Walker; and Cathy.

3. ***Agents of Light and Darkness.*** New York: Ace Books, 2003, 233 p. ISBN: 0441011136.

NIGHTSIDE, 2003? **(A year after the events in *Something from the Nightside*)**. Walker offered John Taylor a profoundly dangerous job: to find a way to calm Jessica Sorrow the Unbeliever. John searched for something that could return to her some measure of belief. Then he set up a meeting in St. Jude's church to return to her a toy bear that meant something to her when she was human. The meeting goes better than he should have expected (he's alive at the end of it). He's sitting quietly, trying to recover when a man is murdered in front of his eyes by someone searching for the Grail. John's gift is finding, and he's pretty sure that he could find the Grail and sell it for a fortune. He should have realized that if a prize of such power were to be found in the Nightside, angels from both above and below would be free to go after it. He should have realized how unlikely it would be for the Holy Grail to be found in the Nightside.

ASSOCIATES: Jessica Sorrow the Unbeliever; Alex Morrisey; Jude—*a man who wishes to hire John on behalf of the Pope;* Lucy and Betty Coltrane; Shotgun Suzie; the Demon Lordz; Mr. Bone and Mr. Blood; Walker; the Speaking Gun—*the only gun that can kill angels;* the Bedlam Boys; Nasty Jack Starlight; Razor Eddie; La Belle Dame Sans Merci; Merlin Satanspawn—*deceased;* and the Collector.

4. ***Nightingale's Lament.*** New York: Ace Books, 2004, 244 p. ISBN: 0441011632.

NIGHTSIDE, 2004? AND FUTURE. John Taylor managed to put Prometheus Inc. out of business rather quickly, cutting off the power to almost half of the Nightside. Partly to stay out of Walker's sight, John Taylor takes on a new client. It's the father of the newest local star. She's estranged from her family. He just wants to know that she's safe and happy. Why would he need John Taylor for that? Because his daughter's biggest fans are committing suicide after (sometimes during) her concerts.

ASSOCIATES: Vincent Kraemer—*a client;* Melinda Dusk—*a.k.a. The Hanged Man's Beautiful Daughter, deceased;* Quinn—*a.k.a. SunSlinger, deceased;* Alex

Morrisey; Cathy Barrett; Charles Chabron—*a client;* Rossignol—*a.k.a. the Nightingale;* Mr. and Mrs. Cavendish—*who are managing Rossignol's career;* Ian Auger—*her roadie(s);* Billy Lathem—*a.k.a. Count Entropy;* Father Pew; Mr. Julien Advent; Argus of the Thousand Eyes—*gossip columnist;* Annabella Peters—*reporter;* Sylvia Sin—*the Cavendish's last great discovery;* the Dead Boy; The Primal; the divas; and The Harrowing.

Note: Ace Books re-released the first three novels in an omnibus edition in 2006 entitled A Walk on the Nightside.

5. **"The Nightside, Needless to Say,"** a short story in *Powers of Detection: Stories of Mystery and Fantasy* edited by Dana Stabenow. New York: Ace Books, 2004, p. 22–36. ISBN: 0441011977.

NIGHTSIDE, 2004?. Larry Oblivion searches for his murderer.

ASSOCIATES: Larry Oblivion—*who left his wife when he fell in love with his client;* Donna Tramen—his wife; Margaret "Maggie" Boniface—*his client, then his partner, she was once known as Mama Bones;* Big Max Maxwell—*Larry's rival.*

6. ***Hex and the City.*** New York: Berkley Pub. Group, c2005, 233 p. ISBN: 0441012612.

NIGHTSIDE, 2005? Lady Luck hires John Taylor to investigate the origins of the Nightside. He's hardly begun when he's warned off the investigation. It's not only his enemies who are trying to stop him; his friends are desperate to end the investigation as well. John is stubborn, but it's more than stubbornness that keeps him going. As he investigates, he begins to find tantalizing hints about his mother. John has wanted to know about his origins for as long as he can remember. He doesn't even know if his mother is human. How can he turn away when he's finally getting closer to the answers?

ASSOCIATES: Lucretia Grave—*auctioneer;* Deliverance Wilde—*fashion consultant to the Faerie of the Unseeli Court;* Sandra Chance—*consulting necromancer;* The Painted Ghoul; Cathy Barrett—*John's secretary;* Lady Luck; the oracle in the well in the mall; the Madman—*who sees beyond illusions to the point that reality now conforms to his belief;* Sinner—*who sold his soul for true love;* Pretty Poison—*succubus, the Sinner's love;* the Reasonable Men; Jimmy Hadleigh—*professional snob;* Henry Walker—*who works for the Authorities;* Mark Robinson—*the Collector;* Bad Penny; Alex Morrisey—*owner of Strangefellows Bar;* Lucy and Betty Coltrane—*Strangefellows' bouncers;* Merlin Satanspawn—*deceased;* the Harrowing; Jessica Sorrow, the Unbeliever; Count Video; Larry Oblivion; King of Skin; Annie Abattior; Julien Advent—*the Victorian Adventurer;* Herne the Hunter; Sister Morphine; the Lamentation; the Lord of Thorns; Lilith—*Adam's first wife;* Pew; and the future Shotgun Suzie.

7. "**Razor Eddie's Big Night Out**" (illustrated by Chris Hill), in *Cemetery Dance,* Issue #55, 2006, p. 45–50. ISSN: 1047-7675.

NIGHTSIDE, 2006? The Authorities told Walker to reorganize the Street of Gods. He's been cleaning it up by evicting the gods with few followers and adjusting the rents to favor the powerful: improving the neighborhood so that the remaining religions can turn a higher profit. The one who witnessed the events that altered Eddie's life goes to Rat's Alley and asks Eddie, Punk God of the Straight Razor, for help. (In *Hex and the City,* John Taylor mentions that Razor Eddie is not available because he's currently occupied on the Street of Gods. This is the story of Razor Eddie's activities from an eyewitness's perspective.)

ASSOCIATES: Sister Morphine; Herne the Hunter; a Grey alien; Jacqueline/Hyde; Razor Eddie—*"an extremely upsetting force for Good," p. 46;* Mad Old Alice; Bast; Walker—*the voice of the Authorities;* Jonathon, Martha and Francis—*one of Walker's Holy Trios;* Hecate—*the goddess next door to the church of the 21st century Dagon;* Dagon.

8. ***Paths not Taken.*** New York: Berkley Pub. Group, c2005, 262 p. ISBN: 0441013198.

NIGHTSIDE, 2005? AND PAST. Eamonn Mitchell stumbled into the Nightside. Now he's being haunted by younger versions of himself. They seem to be angry with him. He hires John to stop the harassment.

John knows that he must stop his mother at any cost. His enemies know it also and, since John is what gives her a link to the Nightside, they feel that the simplest way to stop her is to kill John. Unfortunately, it looks as if John's friends will eventually come to agree.

ASSOCIATES: *Present:* Cathy—*John's secretary;* Eamonn Mitchell—*a client;* Alex Morrisey—*owner of Strangefellows Bar;* Tommy Oblivion—*the existential detective;* Mr. Alexander—*president of Widow's Mite;* Count Video; the Shadow Men; Shotgun Suzie—*a.k.a. Suzie Shooter;* and Old Father Time.

In the Sixth Century: Merlin Satanspawn; Hebe—*cup bearer to the old Roman gods;* Nimue—*the witch;* Sir Kae—*Arthur's brother.*

In the Second Century: Tavius—*leader of the Watch;* Poseidonis—*god of the seas;* Marcellus and Livia—*who run the bar Dies Irae;* Herne the Hunter; Hob In Chains; Tomias Squarefoot; and the Lord of Thorns.

Pre-history: Lilith, Gabriel from Heaven, and Baphomet from Hell.

9. ***Sharper than a Serpent's Tooth.*** New York: Berkley Pub. Group, 2006, 247 p. ISBN: 0441013872.

NIGHTSIDE, 2006? AND FUTURE. John Taylor returns from the past determined to go to war with his mother. Before he can begin to gather his army, he receives a call from Walker. Walker has ordered John's secretary, Cathy, kidnapped. If John doesn't turn himself in, Cathy will be killed. All the while, John's mother, Lilith, is plotting to take back the Nightside. John's enemies from the future, those who were his friends and comrades, search desperately for a way to destroy him to save their world.

ASSOCIATES: Shotgun Suzie—*a.k.a. Suzie Shooter;* Alex Morrisey—*owner of Strangefellows Bar;* Sneaky Pete; the Doormouse; Razor Eddie—*the Punk God of the Straight Razor;* Tommy Oblivian—*the existential detective;* Sandra Chance—*the consulting necromancer;* Lilith; Walker—*the Voice of the Authorities;* the Dead Boy; Julien Advent—*the Victorian Adventurer;* the Beadle—*who runs a fairy sweatshop;* Larry Oblivion; King of Skin; Annie Abattoir; Ms. Fate; Harper of the Authorities; the Lord of Thorns; Dominc Flipside; Cold Harald; Whispering Ivy; Merlin Satanspawn—*deceased;* Sister Morphine; Madeleine; Old Father Time; and the Collector.

The Future: Larry Oblivion—*the deceased detective;* Jessica Sorrow; Count Video; King of Skin; and Annie Abattoir.

10. *Hell to Pay.* New York: Berkley Pub. Group, 2007, 264 p. ISBN: 9780441014606.

NIGHTSIDE, 2007? AND FUTURE. The immortal Jeremiah Griffin built his business empire over centuries. He all but owns the Nightside. He recently decided to change his will and leave his empire to his granddaughter, Melissa. Three days after he changed his will, his solicitor was murdered. A few days after that, Melissa disappeared. Jeremiah hires John Taylor to find his granddaughter. If she has been killed, he wants John to find the body and find out who killed her. John opens his sight to find Melissa and is forcibly shut down. It looks like he's going to have to do this the hard way.

ASSOCIATES: The immortal Griffins: Jeremiah Griffin—*the patriarch;* Mariah—*his wife;* William and Eleanor—*their children;* Gloria—*who married William;* Melissa—*their daughter;* Marcel—*married Eleanor;* Paul—*their son;* Ramon—*Eleanor's latest boytoy;* Bruin Bear and the Sea Goat—*are William's best friends;* Hobbes—*the Griffon family butler;* the Dead Boy; Alex Morrisey—*owner of Strangefellows Bar;* Betty and Lucy Coltrane—*Strangefellows' bouncers;* Harry Fabulous—*Unnatural Inquirer reporter;* Mr. Tumble—*the Caligula Club's bouncer;* Mr. Herbert Libby—*owner of Roll a Dice Casino;* Jimmy Thunder—*God for Hire;* Mistress Mayhem; Larry Oblivion—*the deceased detective;* Lady Orlando; Cobweb—*elf;* Moth—*elf;* Walker—*who still has the Voice, but no longer works for the Authorities;* Sister Josephine—*of the Salvation Army Sisterhood;* Chuck Adamson—*the god of Creationism;* and Shotgun Suzie—*a.k.a. Suzie Shooter.*

11. *The Unnatural Inquirer.* New York: Berkley Pub. Group, 2008, 246 p. ISBN: 9780441015580.

NIGHTSIDE, 2008? As John Taylor says: "Cases are a lot like buses; you wait around for ages, then three come along at once." In this book he solves two. At the beginning of the book, John has just wrapped up a case for the H. P. Lovecraft Memorial Library. He has no time to rest. Shotgun Suzie has been unable to complete an assignment that she accepted from Walker, and John steps in to help. Suzie's been searching for Max Maxwell, who used the Aquarius Key to open doors to other dimensions and enslave the voodoo gods. The gods managed to escape his control and possess some of the best bounty hunters in the Nightside. They're tracking Max Maxwell and destroying anything and anyone who gets in their way. Walker's assignment is simple: find the voodoo, god-possessed bounty hunters and free them; then send the gods back to their own dimension. (Simple is not necessarily the same as easy.) Suzie and John track Max to an abandoned carnival (the Fun Faire) and face the gods, as well as the derelict and the cursed carnival attractions, which include the I-Speak-Your-Weight machine that reveals terrible secrets, the Merry-Go-Round where the horses come alive, and the ferocious dodgem cars. John and Suzie (and others) are leaving the fairgrounds when John gets a phonecall summoning him to the offices of the *Unnatural Inquirer*, where they offer him the job of finding a DVD that the newspaper purchased from a man who claims to have somehow tuned in and recorded the Afterlife. They not only offer him a job; they offer him a million pounds, which makes it impossible to walk away, even when they saddle him with the daughter of a succubus for a partner.

ASSOCIATES: Shotgun Suzie—*a.k.a. Suzie Shooter, the love of John's life;* Walker—*who is looking for new Authorities;* Max Maxwell—*the Voodoo Apostate;* Cathy—*John's 18-year-old secretary;* Jimmy—*a copyboy;* Harry Fabulous—*a stringer;* Bettie Devine—*demon girl reporter;* Gaylord du Rois—*editor of the Unnatural Inquirer;* Scoop Malloy—*sub-editor of the Unnatural Inquirer;* Pfred—*Hawk's Wind Bar & Grille waitress;* Dagon. Stack! The Magnificent—*a slumming alien;* the Elegant Profundity; an avatar of the Church of Clapton; and the God of Lost Things.

General Condor, Uptown Taffy Lewis, and Queen Helena, ex-Monarch of the Ice Kingdoms—*vie for Walker's backing.*

The Director of the Museum of Unnatural History—*who takes great glee in informing John that he must get past a Tyrannosaurus Rex to speak to The Collector;* Bettie Divine—*reporter for the Unnatural Inquirer, is assigned to accompany John while he works on the case;* Rick Aday—*Bettie's ex, investigative reporter for the Night Times*, Lovett—*reporter from the Nightside Observer;* and Bozie—*a caricaturist;* Queen Helena—*who gathers a retinue consisting of the manky dregs of The Nightside's aristocracy;* Zog—*King of the Pixies;* His Altitude Tobermoret; Prince Xerxes—*the Murder Monarch;* and King Artur—*of Sinister Albion.*

The Cardinal—*who doesn't want to see the Afterlife Recording;* Alex Morrisey—*owner of Strangefellows Bar;* Betty and Lucy Coltrane—*Strangefellows' bouncers;* Thallassa—*the sorcerer;* Pen Donavon—*a man who betrayed his dog*, Prince—*his dog;* Ace—*a.k.a. Trevor, leader of Clan Buckaroo;* Kid Cthulhu—*who hired the Clan Buckaroo;* and The Removal Man.

12. "Lucy, at Christmastime," a short story in *Wolfsbane and Mistletoe* edited by Charlaine Harris and Toni L. P. Kelner. New York: Ace Books, 2008, p. 27–31. ISBN: 9780441016334.

NIGHTSIDE, CHRISTMAS EVE. Leo Morn (werewolf) promised Lucy that he'd love her forever and a day. He sees her at *Strangefellows Bar* every Christmas Eve.

ASSOCIATES: Lucy—*deceased;* Alex Morrisey—*who tends the bar at Strangefellows Bar;* Harry Fabulous—*a salesman;* Tommy Oblivion—*the existential private eye;* Ms. Fate—*transvestite superheroine;* Prince of Darkness; Mistress of the Dark; and St. Nicholas.

13. *Just Another Judgment Day.* New York: Ace Books, 2009, 263 p. ISBN: 9780441016747.

NIGHTSIDE, 2009? Percy D'Arcy is desolate. His friends have been admitted to the *Guaranteed New You Parlour*, and every time they emerge from treatment, they look younger. The *Guaranteed New You Parlour* won't accept him as a client. His life is falling apart: his friends look like teenagers; his friends say that he no longer fits into their crowd; and he's found a wrinkle! He hires John Taylor to investigate the *Guaranteed New You Parlour.*

Walker hires John on behalf of the New Authorities for the second case in the book. The Walking Man, the wrath of God in the world of man, sent a letter of the editor of the *Night Times* to announce that he is coming and the people of the Nightside could put their affairs in order before he kills off the guilty. (As Jessica Sorrow points out, so many people are guilty of *something*...) The New Authorities want the Walking Man stopped and they believe that John Taylor may be able to stop him.

ASSOCIATES: Percy D'Arcy—*an aging client.*

Dr. Dougan, Baron Victor von Frankenstein, Stephan Shooter, and Joan Taylor—*of the Guaranteed New You Parlour;* Henry Walker—*who asks John to come and meet the new Authorities*: Victorian Adventurer Julian Advent—*who is now editor of the Night Times;* Jessica Sorrow, the Unbeliever—*her disbelief can be fatal;* Anna Abattoir—*spy, assassin and courtesan;* Count Video—*lord of binary magics;* King of Skin—*who is more than a man and less than a god;* and Larry Oblivion—*the dead detective*: Augusta Moon—*professional troubleshooter;* Janissary Jane—*demon-killer;* Zhang—*the Mystic;* Sebastian Stargrave—*the Fractured Protagonist;* Bulldog Hammond—*a criminal;* Chandra Singh—*a monster-hunter and holy-warrior;* Penny Dreadful—*a bodyguard for Paul and Davey Hellsreich, who are drinking at the Boy's Club;* Tamsin

MacReady—*the current Rogue Vicar;* Sharon Pilkington-Smythe—*Tamsin's bodyguard;* The Lord of Thorns—*who looks after St. Jude's church;* the Walking Man—*a.k.a. Adrien Saint, his wife and children were killed by a joyriding hit and run driver, he comes to the Nightside and who attacks the Temple of the Unspeakable Abomination and then begins taking down the rest of the street;* Razor Eddie—*who shows up to defend his friend Dagon;* Mr. Usher—*the human face of The Gun Shop;* Suzie Shooter—*a.k.a. Shotgun Suzie, works with abused children and is surprised when she finds a little healing for herself.*

14. "The Difference a Day Makes," a novella in *Mean Streets.* New York: Roc, 2009, p. 71–140. ISBN: 9780451462497.

NIGHTSIDE, 2009? Liza Barclay lost all memory of the last 24 hours of her life. She hires John Taylor to find her recent past.

ASSOCIATES: The Dead Boy—*John's ally;* Liza Barclay—*the client;* Frank Barclay—*her husband;* the Brittle Sisters of the Hive; and Bary Kopek—*who speaks for Silicon Heaven.*

ASSOCIATED STORIES:

"Some of These Cons go Way Back," *Cemetary Dance* #60 (2009): 87.

NIGHTSIDE, 200? Harry Fabulous set out to work a quick con, to get a little cash. Then he got sidetracked by a spectacularly beautiful creature with a terrible story. Trying to help her is the first half-way decent thing that Harry has done in years.

ASSOCIATES: Albert—*the doorman at the Heaven's Doorway club;* The Lord of the Dance—*who is carefully ignoring his ex;* The Dancing Queen—*the ex;* the Painted Ghoul—*in his clown's makeup;* Aimee Driscoll—*who can still be conned (she's not the only one).*

GREENBERG, Martin H. Co-editor (with Ed Gorman) of *Once Upon a Crime.* See Gorman, Ed: Once Upon a Crime.

GREENBERG, Martin H. Co-editor (with Isaac Asimov and Charles G. Waugh) of *Isaac Asimov's Wonderful World of Science Fiction Anthology #5 Tin Stars.* See Asimov, Isaac: Isaac Asimov's Wonderful World of Science Fiction Anthology #5 Tin Stars.

GREENBERG, Martin H. Co-editor (with Charles G. Waugh) of *Sci-Fi Private Eye.* See Waugh, Charles G.: Sci-Fi Private Eye; *Supernatural Sleuths.* See Waugh, Charles G.: Supernatural Sleuths.

GREENBERG, Martin H. (Editor)

VAMPIRE DETECTIVES

Genres/Themes Crossed: Secret Society X Hard-Boiled Mystery, Police Procedural.

Subjects/Character Types: Vampires X Private Investigators, Police.

Series/Stand-Alone: Anthology of short stories.

Scene of the Crime: Varies.

Detective: Varies.

Known Associates: Varies.

Premise: In the introduction, Ed Gorman writes about Edgar Allan Poe's contention that humans need both the fantastic and the rational. He points to *The Murders in the Rue Morgue* as the beginning of the genre that combined the two. The stories in this anthology combine the dark myth of the vampire with the rationality of the detective story.

Comment: Martin Greenberg served on the faculty of the University of Wisconsin, Green Bay, as a professor of Regional Analysis and Political Science from 1969 until his retirement in 1996. From the beginning, he incorporated science fiction into his courses, and in January 1970, another professor (Patricia Warrick) asked him to lecture her freshman Liberal Education Seminar on the future of politics. He noticed that she was using a science fiction book as one of class's textbooks and offered to return to give a science fiction lecture. Professor Warrick asked him if he'd ever considered combining his interest in political science with his interest in science fiction. Greenberg has said that was a career-changing moment. It led to the creation of his book *Political Science Fiction*, a textbook of science fiction stories that illustrate political science concepts, which he edited with Warrick. It was the first of a number of educational anthologies that were published as the *Through Science Fiction* series. These included *Dawn of Time: Prehistory through Science Fiction, Run to Starlight: Sports through Science Fiction, Social Problems through Science Fiction, The New Awareness: Religion through Science Fiction, Introductory Psychology through Science Fiction, Criminal Justice through Science Fiction, The City, 2000 A.D.: Urban Life through Science Fiction, No Room for Man: Population and the Future through Science Fiction, School and Society through Science Fiction, Anthropology through Science Fiction, International Relations through Science Fiction, Sociology through Science Fiction,* and *American Government through Science Fiction*. His involvement in the creation of those anthologies paved the way for further work in developing science fiction anthologies.

Later in Greenberg's career, he worked on the development of a science fiction cable network. He and his partners sold the network, and it has now become the Sci-Fi Channel.

Greenberg is the only person to have swept the Milford Award for science fiction editing, the Ellery Queen Award for mystery editing, and the Bram

Stoker Award for supernatural horror editing. In his retirement, he is focused on his company, Tekno Books, which develops and packages approximately 150 books each year.

Literary Magic & Mayhem: Some of the stories written for this anthology are episodes in well-known series. Tanya Huff contributed a story in which Vicki Nelson defends Toronto without the help of Henry Fitzroy. P. N. Elrod contributed a story that begins with Jack Fleming dragging himself out of Lake Michigan once again. There are also stand-alone stories from authors who wrote few, if any, other vampire stories. Short story master Edward D. Hoch contributed a Simon Ark story, and William Sanders contributed an epistolary story of letters written to Vlad! It's a varied collection of works by excellent writers.

Explorations: Were both the strengths and the weaknesses of a vampire displayed in the story?

THE CASES

1. ***Vampire Detectives.*** New York: Daw Books, 1995, 316 p. ISBN: 0886776260; 9780886776268.

CONTENTS: Introduction *by Ed Gorman;* Vampire Dollars *by William F. Nolan;* This Town Ain't Big Enough *by Tanya Huff;* Girl's Night Out *by Kathe Koja and Barry N. Malzberg;* Home Comforts *by Peter Crowther;* Origin of a Species *by J. N. Williamson;* Fangs *by Douglas Borton;* The Night of Their Lives *by Max Allan Collins;* Night Tidings *by Gary Alan Ruse;* Godless Men *by James Kisner;* No Blood for a Vampire *by Edward D. Hoch;* The Count's Mailbox *by William Sanders;* Tom Rudolph's Last Tape *by John Maclay;* The Turning *by Jack Ketchum;* You'll Catch Your Death *by P. N. Elrod;* Shell Game *by John Lutz;* The Secret *by Barbara Paul;* Blind Pig on North Halsted *by Wayne Allen Sallee;* Phil the Vampire *by Richard Laymon;* Undercover *by Nancy Holder.*

GRUBER, Michael.

TROPIC OF NIGHT

Genres/Themes Crossed: Secret Society X Police Procedural.

Subjects/Character Types: Santeria, Shaman, the Devil X Police Procedural.

Series/Stand-Alone: These should be read in order, there are changes in the relationships between the characters.

Scene of the Crime: Florida, present day.

Detective: Iago Xavier "Jimmy" Paz is the bastard son of Margarita Paz, a detective on the Miama Police Department. He is known as a brilliant detective, a man of unshakable calm, and a snappy dresser. He always looks sharp. He's famous in the Miami Police Department for not sweating. Even after chasing a criminal for six blocks, he looks pressed, neat, and dry. It annoys other officers, and is one of the reasons that it's hard to find him a partner. Another is prejudice. From the point of view of Officer Gomez (who is also technically a Cuban-American mulatto), there are many reasons to dislike Paz,

> the first thing being his color and his features and the fact that, although possessing such a color and such features, he was yet undeniably Cuban. Paz was, technically, a mulatto, and technically, so was Gomez, but Paz was clearly on the black side of the line and Gomes was on the white, like some 98 percent of the Cubans who had fled Castro for America, and therein lay the agony of Jimmy Paz's life. (p. 24)

Known Associates: Mami (Margarita Paz), Jimmy Paz's mother; Paz's first partner in the Homicide Division was Cletis Barlow; Cletis has a wife (Edna) and a son (James); Paz's second partner was Tito Morales; his many girlfriends include the poet Willa Shaftel and the therapist Dr. Lorna Wise. Paz's immediate superior is Lieutenant Posada, head of the Homicide division that is part of the Criminal Investigation Section. In Valley of Bones, the Criminal Investigation has an ex-FBI agent as its new Head; his name is Major Douglas Oliphant.

Premise: There is more to this world than most people see. Anthropologist Marcel Vierchau, a celebrity lecturer on campus in Jane's junior year, performed some simple tricks of legerdemain and then asked the audience if they believed that he had performed real magic; half-a-dozen jokers raised their hands to say "yes." He responds,

> "I will be available for worship after the lecture," he remarked, to more chuckling. "But most of you do not, and properly so, for you are all materialist empiricists. That is your culture." (p. 82)

He goes on to talk of the beliefs in other cultures, where magic is simply a useful technology. It works for anyone, no matter what their beliefs. He likens it to a gun that can kill people whether or not those people believe in guns. He describes a little of this technology:

> Among traditional peoples where the shamanic technologies are well developed, the manipulation of the consciousness has advanced to a much

> higher degree. We have ample evidence that, for example, shamans and sorcerers can enter the dreams of sleeping people and stage-manage their dream state. Sorcerers can elicit in their subjects psychic states that are somewhere between dreaming and sleeping, so that the subject entertains elaborate illusions that seem undeniably real, a kind of induced psychosis. (p. 83)

He goes on to state that sorcerers can manipulate the body through the manipulation of the consciousness, curing (or causing) disease. Marcel immersed himself in the work of sorcery. He trained as a shaman with the Chenka in Siberia. Later, he takes Jane with him, and she learns something of the magic. If there is someone who knows the ways of power and who is willing to teach, then it is possible to learn magic. However, it is dangerous. Some people who have the power are more likely to trick apprentices than to teach them. Some are so malevolent they will twist the soul of anyone who comes within their reach. Power is not a toy.

In the second book, Paz encounters another form of power. He deals with a woman who is possessed by Satan. In the third, a shaman uses his ability to shape change to commit murders in Miami. Paz's mother's knowledge of Santería helps him protect himself and his family.

Comment: *Tropic of Night* was Gruber's first novel.

Literary Crimes & Chimes: The book depicts a society in which people are very conscious of race and a police department that is, perhaps, overly politically correct. For instance, Paz expects to get little grief over shooting a perpetrator who is black because Paz is also black:

> There was even a little shoot-out, although the mope had only been wounded and nobody got on Paz's case because he, too, was black and so, under the peculiar rules of American police practice, he had a license to shoot down citizens of whatever color with only nonhysterical investigation to follow. (p. 23)

Paz expresses his machismo through crudity in language. He obsesses about other officer's opinions of him and assumes that everyone's perception begins with the color of his face and the cast of his features. The narrative moves from third-person descriptions of actions to Paz's first person sensory perceptions, to Paz's conclusions or deeper perceptions. At times this progression bogs down the story:

> [Paz] walked into the apartment. It was hot and it stank with a stink so forty-weight-crankcase-oil heavy that it seemed to drag the lungs down into the belly. The termperature had been in the nineties, cooking the carnage in the airless apartment, which would have been bad enough, but this

was something else. The agents of decay and dissolution must have been helped by some elaborate butchery. (p. 24)

The style works better when it is used in scenes where there is a frightening transition from normal reality to something else:

"I . . . was wrong. Here. He's here." Her voice was low, strangled.

"Where?" Paz looked wildly around the restaurant. Sweat burst out on this forehead. There was something funny now about all the patrons. They weren't eating and chatting and laughing, as they usually did. They were staring at Paz and Jane, and there was something odd about their faces, they seemed peculiarly flat and brutal, the flesh sagging like candle wax. They had too many teeth. (p. 376)

Explorations: Was the style of the narrative effective or distracting?

What different types of experiences did people have with shamans of different tribes?

What roles does ethnicity play in the novel? How and when is it important to people?

THE CASES

1. ***Tropic of Night.*** New York: HarperCollins Publisher, c2003, 419 p. ISBN: 0060509546.

MIAMI, FLORIDA, 200? Jane Doe is a woman who treasures her anonymity. She knows someone is after her and she knows the police can't stop him. She was once a graduate student in anthropology. She and her husband, DeWitt Moore, an African-American poet and playwright, traveled to Nigeria. Jane was doing research on the Olo, learning about their religion and the spiritual powers they wield. Her husband fell under the influence of a malevolent witch and became a sorcerer. He returned to America, safe because so few would believe in his powers. He set about murdering pregnant women to use their unborn children in ceremonies to raise his power. Jane soon figured out that he was murdering people; but she also knew that she could not stop him; his powers make it almost impossible for him to be caught. When she realized that he would kill her because she knew what he was, she faked her own death and went into hiding. Moore continues to get away with murder. Once Paz is on his trail, Jane decides to make a stand, and together they work to bring Moore to justice.

ASSOCIATES: Margarita "Mami" Paz—*Paz's mother;* Jane Doe—*poses as Dolores Tuoey;* Luz—*the daughter Jane acquired.* In flashbacks, Jane mentions her family: DeWitt Moore—*Jane's husband;* Mary—*Jane's sister;* Josiah "Josey" Mount—*Jane's half-brother.* Miami PD officers include: Captain

Arnie Mendés—*homicide unit commander;* Romeo Posada—*Paz's homicide shift lieutenant;* Cletis Barlow—*Paz's partner;* Patrolman Bubba Singleton; and Officer Gomez. Detective Captain Jerry Heinrich—*an NYPD police officer.* In the course of the investigation, Paz speaks to: Doris Taylor—reporter for the *Miami Herald;* Professor Lydia Herrera—*ethnobotanist;* Dr. Maria Salazar—*expert on indigenous religions;* Tanzi—*a witness;* Mrs. Meagher—*Tanzi's grandmother.* Other characters include: Lisa Reilly—*a therapist;* Beth Morgensen—*a doctoral student;* Mrs. Waley, Lulu, and Cleo—*Jane's co-workers;* Lou Nearing—*who recognizes Jane.*

2. ***Valley of Bones.*** New York: HarperCollins Publisher, c2005, 436 p. ISBN: 0060577665.

MIAMI, FLORIDA, LATE SUMMER (CONTEMPORARY). Paz is plagued by nightmares, a remnant of the horrors of his last adventure. He doesn't need another encounter with evil, but it is not up to him. Emmylou Dideroff, the obvious (too obvious?) perpetrator of a murder, shows him the Devil once again. Emmylou's therapist, Lorna Wise, also gets a glimpse of the Devil and works hard to rationalize it away.

ASSOCIATES: Margarita Paz—*Paz's "Mamí" (mother);* Tito Morales—*who becomes Paz's partner in this book;* Lieutenant Posada and Major Douglas Oliphant—*others in law enforcement;* Emmylou Dideroff—*the only suspect in the murder of Jabir al-Muwalid;* Dr. Lorna Wise—*Paz's new girlfriend and Emmylou's therapist;* Rigoberto Munoz—*a paranoid schizophrenic and yet a tool of the Lord;* Sheryl Waits—*Lorna's best friend and wife of a colleague of Paz;* David Packer—*Emmylou's landlord (Emmylou lived on a boat);* Jack Wilson—*Emmylou's employer;* Mickey Lopez—*Lorna's therapist;* Dr. Howard Kasdan—*an ex-lover of Lorna;* Willa Shaftel—*a poet and at the beginning of the book she is Paz's lover;* Cletis Barlow—*Paz's ex-partner;* Edna Barlow—*Cletis's wife;* James Barlow—*their son.*

3. ***Night of the Jaguar: a novel.*** New York: HarperCollins Publisher, 2006, 372 p. ISBN: 0060577681.

MIAMI, FLORIDA, SEVEN YEARS AFTER VALLEY OF THE BONES. Developers are targeted for a strange death, so strange that Paz, retired from the force but known as a man who can get to the bottom of weird crimes, is asked to assist the police. As Paz investigates, his family is stalked in their dreams. Paz realizes that he must become an initiate in Santería and gain union with the *orisha* to protect his family. (Paz becomes Oshoshi, Lord of the Hunt and Lord of Beasts.)

ASSOCIATES: Margarita Paz—*Paz's mother "Mamí";* Dr. Lorna Wise—*Paz's wife;* Amelia Paz—*Paz and Lorna's six-year-old daughter;* Tito Morales—*Detective on the Miami PD, he was Paz's partner before Paz retired;* Major Douglas Oliphant; Bob Zwick; Beth Morgensen; Moie—*the animal spirit doctor of the Runiya in the Puxto Reserve area, was baptized Juan Bautista;*

Father Perrin; Jennifer Simpson, Scotty (Nature Boy), Luna, Kevin (Jennifer's boyfriend), Rupert Zenger, Evangelina Vargos (Geli), and Nigel Cooksey (the professor)—*are the members of the Forest Planet Alliance Foundation;* Antonio Fuentes, Yoiyo Calderón (the father who would not acknowledge Paz), Cayo Garza, and Felipe Ibanez—*are the officers of Consuela Holdings;* Gabriel Hurtado—*was hired by Calderón;* Victoria Calderón de Pinero—*Calderón's daughter.* Julia from the botánica, Pedro Ortiz, the babalawo, and Ms. Margarita—*are the members of the Santería Congregation.* Yetunde—*is Paz's name-in-religion.*

Guadiano, Stefano. Worked with Ed Brubaker, Greg Rucka, and Michael Lark on *In the Line of Duty.* See BRUBAKER, Ed: In the Line of Duty.

GUILFOILE, Kevin.

CAST OF SHADOWS

Genres/Themes Crossed: Man as Creator X Traditional Mystery (gone wrong).

Subjects/Character Types: Future Technology (clones) X Amateur Sleuth (Contemporary).

Series/Stand-Alone: Stand-alone.

Scene of the Crime: Chicago, in the future.

Detective: Dr. Davis Moore is one of the country's leading experts on cloning and cloning ethics. *Chicago* magazine has named him one of the city's "Top Docs." He is a partner in *New Tech,* a Chicago fertility clinic that offers cutting-edge cloning services as well as more traditional fertility procedures. When he feels that the police have not done enough to bring his daughter's killer to justice, he begins his own investigation.

Known Associates: Dr. Moore's wife, Jackie, and his daughter Anna Kat. His colleagues in the clinic are Gregor, Pete, and Dr. Joan Burton. His patients are Terry and Martha Finn, and their (cloned) child Justin.

Dr. Moore hires private investigator Big Rob. Big Rob's operative, Sally Barwick, interviews Mrs. Lundquist. Phil Canella is the investigator that Jackie hires. Private Investigator Scott Colleran of Gold Badge Investigations also sends some work Sally's way. Miss Hannity is AK's (Anna Kat's) coach. Libby Carlisle is AK's friend. AK has relationships with Sam Coyne and Daniel. The senior class president of A.K.'s high school is Mark Campagna. Police officer Ortega investigates AK's murder. Officer Crippen investigates Phil Canella's death. Detective Teddy Ambrose is trying to find the serial killer dubbed the Wicker Man. Ricky Weiss of Brixton, Nebraska, provides a tip on AK's killer: he believes it is quarterback Jimmy Spears. Rick's wife is Peg. Mary Ann Mankoff is principal of the Brixton High School that Jimmy Spears attended. Ms. Eberlein is Justin's teacher. Dr. Keith Morrow is the child psychologist who sees Justin. Graham Mendelsohn is Davis's attorney. Mickey Fanning "Mickey the Gerund" regards himself as a righteous man and is employed by the *Hands of God.* Harold Devereaux maintains a web hit list of doctors, clinics, and researchers involved in cloning. Byron Blakey Bonavita is the FBI 's main suspect in most of the cloning-related killings. Reverend Garner McGill is a leader in the anti-cloning movement, and he cheers on the *Hands of God.* Christopher Bel Geddes is the son of Dr. Oliver Bel Geddes. Stephen Malik is the *Chicago Tribune* Editor who hired Sally Barwick as a reporter. In *Shadow World* characters include Donna and Lindsay, Shadow Justin, Shadow Sally (reporter), and Shadow Sam.

Premise: The book is set in a future in which cloning is a proven medical process, used in order to avoid hereditary diseases and as an infertility treatment; but cloning is still politically controversial. Protestors try to close clinics and even post hit lists of doctors who perform the procedure. Cloning is governed by strict laws. Donors must give express permission before their tissue can be used to create a clone. Clones can be made from the tissue of those who have died, but only if their permission is on file. Egg, sperm, and tissue donors may give permission for their genetic material to be used for cloning, but it is unlawful to use their tissue to create a clone until after they die. Only one clone can be made from a donor's tissue. After a viable clone is created, the remainder of the tissue must be destroyed. Doctors are permitted to match hair and eye color with the prospective parents, but gender selection must by law be random. Clones are tracked by physicians for ongoing research, but the information on individuals is protected by privacy laws.

Comment: The action in the book spans two decades. During that time a new video game, *Shadow World,* becomes the most popular multiplayer game in America, being played regularly by an estimated 40 percent of the population. The game takes place in an exact (or as close to exact as programmers can make it) replica of the world. Approximately one quarter of the players are "True to Lifers"—players who recreate their own lives in the game. The similarities between this game and Linden Lab's *Second Life* game are obvious. We may be closer to this future than we know.

Kevin Guilefoile's Web site at http://www.guilfoile.net/ includes information on his books, and a page with links to his newspaper columns and other writings at http://www.guilfoile.net/kevin.php.

Literary Magic & Mayhem: Kevin Guilfoile is known as a humorist; he's written short stories in a faux-gumshoe serial featuring the atheist Madalyn Murray O'Hair solving crimes in Dante's hell. *Cast of Shadows* is his first novel. This is not a humorous novel. It shows readers a father's grief as he moves from mourning to obsession. All the characters are well developed, and the changes wrought in them by the crime and its aftermath are all too real. The book explores moral questions of vigilantism, as well as of medical issues. Kevin Guilfoile stated (in an interview for a March 6, 2005, issue of the Pittsburgh Tribune Review) that he created characters who have passionate and deeply held beliefs for cloning, and characters who have passionate and deeply held beliefs against cloning, but that he kept his own views on cloning out of the narrative. He also said that one thing that interested him about writing genre fiction was that there are more and better opportunities to surprise readers when they are familiar with the conventions of the genre.

One interesting aspect of the book is the moral questions raised by the doctor's ability to create clones. He refuses to clone his dead daughter, AK, and uses the law as an excuse. His wife wonders what it would be like to have her back, to start over and give Anna Kat a chance to live out her life. Davis is appalled, and his wife is surprised, asking if he, the champion of cloning, regarded a cloned child as not quite real. He responds,

> She's real to the new family. To people who knew the original, she wouldn't be real at all. To them, she's a doppelgänger. A smudged copy. A ghost with no memory. Would AK be AK without that scar across her knuckles? The one she got learning to ride a bike? If she had fillings in different teeth? If she were a swimmer instead of a setter? Afraid of heights instead of spiders? If she liked English better than math? (p. 57)

He says that, "to certain people," clones are not-quite-real projections of the originals, a "cast of shadows," and asks, whether another little girl walking around in a shell that looked like their daughter wouldn't just accentuate the void that her death left in their lives.

Explorations: What motivates the doctor? Is he looking for justice or vengeance or just for answers?

Where do his investigations go wrong?

Would it be horrible to clone a lost loved one?

THE CASE

1. ***Cast of Shadows.*** New York: Knopf, 2005, 372 p. ISBN: 0060577681.

CHICAGO, YEAR UNKNOWN. Fertility doctor Davis Moore is something of a celebrity. Cloning is still controversial, but he's helping hundreds of couples create their families. Davis's 17-year-old daughter is brutally raped and murdered. The case is never solved, and it eats away at Davis and his wife Jackie. Eighteen months after the crime, the police call Davis to come and collect AK's belongings. They assure him that they have not given up. The belongings have been photographed, the DNA from the sperm has been mapped. The police accidentally include the semen sample and some hairs that were part of the physical evidence on the scene in the package with AK's clothing. That vial contains the DNA of the man who raped her. Davis becomes obsessed with using it to track down AK's murderer.

ASSOCIATES: See above.

H

HAINES, Carolyn.

THEM BONES

Genres/Themes Crossed: Paranormal X Traditional Mystery.

Subjects/Character Types: Ghosts X Amateur Sleuth (Contemporary) in *Them Bones.* In *Buried Bones* Sarah begins to work as a professional private investigator.

Series/Stand-Alone: The *Sarah Booth Delaney* series (also known as the *Mississippi Delta Mystery* series) features a network of supportive relationships between the women who are the heart of these books, and those relationships develop through the course of the series. To understand and appreciate it, the series should be read in order.

Scene of the Crime: Present-day Zinnia, Mississippi (Sunflower County). (Except for *Wishbones,* which is set in California and Costa Rica.)

Detective: Sarah Booth Delaney is the last of the Delaneys. Sarah's mother and father died in a car accident when she was 12 years old; after that, she was raised by her Aunt LouLane. At the opening of the series, Sarah is 33 years old and has just given up on her dream of a career in the theater. She left New York and returned to her ancestral home, Dahlia House. She's broke, unemployed, and unwed. She believes that she is a failure; the bank is about to foreclose on her home. While Sarah is something of a rebel, she feels strong ties to the land that her family has held for generations; she would do almost anything to save Dahlia House. Since Sarah's return, she has been haunted by the ghost of her great-great-grandmother's nanny, Jitty. Jitty goads Sarah into taking action to save her home, and tries to goad her into wedding and bedding (or just bedding) various eligible men to continue the Delaney line.

Known Associates: Jitty, the ghost of Sarah Booth's great-great-grandmother's nanny. She lived through the Civil War and died of old age in 1904. She haunts Sarah at Dahlia House. Sweetie-Pie is Sarah's red tic hound. Tinkie Bellcase Richmond, an old friend from Miss Nancy's cotillion and etiquette classes, becomes Sarah's partner in the detective business. Chablis is Tinkie's dog. Cecily "Cece" Dee Falcon was born Cecil, but had her gender changed at a nice clinic in Sweden; now she's the society editor of the *Zinnia Dispatch*. Harold Erkwell works at the Bank of Zinnia. Hamilton Garrett V, of the Garretts of Knob Hill, works from Paris, finding funding for an organization that searches for missing people (kidnapping victims, refugees, etc.); but he occasionally visits Zinnia. Zinnia's Sheriff is Coleman Peters. He has been trying to get out of a bad marriage for years, but his insane wife, Connie, is determined to hold onto him. Millie Roberts owns and runs Millie's, the local diner. Tammy Odom does fortune telling as "Madame Tomeeka." She has a daughter named Claire.

Comment: The series' timeline hangs on a statement in *Ham Bone* that a Category 5 storm interfered with Mississippi bookings. If that refers to 2005's Atlantic Hurricane Season, then *Ham Bone* takes place in 2005. That same book mentions that Sarah Booth has been back in Zinnia for approximately a year, setting the dates for the rest of the series.

The author's Web site, at http://www.carolynhaines.com/, includes information on the books, and stories, the author's newsletter, and interviews with some of the characters in the series!

Literary Magic & Mayhem: Carolyn Haines's writing evokes the South in setting, in characters, and even in mood. The characters are wonderful and have unexpected depths; for instance, Tinkie the "Daddy's Girl" and Chablis, the tiny dog she carries around, both have more brains and more spine than anyone would guess. Then there's Cece, who remembers when, as 13-year-old Cecil, he looked at Hamilton Garrett V and thought that he was gorgeous, then realized that that most boys didn't regard other males as gorgeous (the sex-change operation later in life helped Cecil become a ravishing woman). Jitty was a slave (she's now a ghost) who hangs onto her existence at Dahlia House because a Delaney is still in residence. Jitty behaves as if she is Sarah Booth's elderly and opinionated aunt, taking a great interest in the continuation of the Delaney family. The books are populated with funny, sometimes outrageous, women who give each other grief but who also help each other survive through times of trouble.

The author gives us lines that are warming, as well as some that are cutting. For instance, when musing about Cece's eventual success in her hometown (other newspapers would not hire her after her sex change), Sarah's comforting thought is that "Home is where they have to accept you" (*Them Bones,* p. 32). In thinking about the changes in another woman, Kincaid, she makes this chilling observation:

> Kincaid had come home from Europe a different girl. I always thought it was marriage—that she'd given up the aspects of herself that made working in tandem with a dolt unacceptable. Self-mutilation was considered part of the price of security for women in my set. (*Them Bones,* p. 36)

In the small town of Zinnia, the past is present in many ways. One of them is that everyone remembers Sarah's parents, particularly her mother. Her mother had a social conscience: at a time when she was expected to devote herself to finding a husband and settling down, she became politically active. Her slogan was "Give a damn," and she changed her suitor, James Franklin Delaney, into an activist before they began their romance. Her family was furious: her name was no longer spoken in her family's Meridian, Mississippi, home, but she made phone calls to and received phones calls from the Kennedy administration (*Them Bones,* p. 121). In the town of Zinnia, she is remembered with admiration and love.

Explorations: What does Jitty's presence contribute to the book? What would the book be like without Jitty?

Is Tinkie the fragile empty-headed woman that she seems?

To what extent do people invent who they are in this society? To what extent are they bound by the past? Under what circumstances is the past a comfort? When is it something to overcome?

THE CASES

1. ***Them Bones.*** New York: Bantam Books, c1999, 318 p. ISBN: 0553581716; 9780553581713.

ZINNIA, MISSISSIPPI, NOVEMBER 2004. The bank is about to foreclose on Dahlia House, and Sarah would do anything to save it. She has a loan officer who's offering to help in return for some "companionship," and a ghost who recommends a career in dognapping. She has too much pride to ask her wealthy friends for help. Her best friend is frantic that a flame from her past is coming back to Zinnia. Sarah begins by looking for background information on this mysterious man, and ends up opening the Delaney Detective Agency to bring in some cash.

ASSOCIATES: Jitty—*deceased, haunts Sarah in dresses from the 1970s;* Tinkie—*Sarah's friend;* Chablis—*Tinkie's dog;* Oscar—*Tinkie's husband;* Cecily "Cece" Dee Falcon—*the society editor of the Zinnia Dispatch;* Harold Erkwell—*loan officer of the Bank of Zinnia;* Hamilton Garrett V—*who is interested in Sarah;* Sylvia Garrett—*Hampton's sister;* Veronica Hampton Garrett—*Hamilton's mother;* Sheriff Coleman Peters; Millie Roberts—*who owns the local diner;* Madame Tomeeka—*a.k.a. Tammy Odom, the fortune teller;* Claire—*her daughter;* Kincaid Maxwell—*a socialite who stayed with Hamilton in Europe;* Deputy Gordon Walters—*Pasco's son;* Fel Harper—*the incompetent coroner;* Isaac Carter—*owner of Zinnia International Export;* Delo Wiley—*who sold James Levert land when no one else would sell to an African-American.*

2. ***Buried Bones.*** New York: Bantam Books, 2000, 354 p. ISBN: 0553581724; 9780553581720.

ZINNIA, MISSISSIPPI, DECEMBER 2004. Lawrence Ambrose has led a full life, and he's planning to reveal every embarrassing detail in his tell-all memoirs. He holds a Christmas Eve dinner party at which he apologizes in advance for the light his biography is going to shine on the dark secrets of the lives of his dinner guests and others in Zinnia. Christmas morning, Sarah finds a body. One of her old teachers demands that she find the killer.

ASSOCIATES: Jitty—*deceased, haunts Sarah in 1950s dresses, promoting family values;* Tinkie—*Sarah's business partner;* Chablis—*Tinkie's dog;* Lawrence Ambrose—*was a friend of Sarah's parents;* Brianna Rathbone—*Lawrence's biographer;* Layton Rathbone—*Brianna's father;* Harold Erkwell—*who's worried that Lawrence is up to something;* Lillian Sparks—*who has given years to preserving Zinnia's history;* Dean Joseph Grace—*name-dropper extraordinaire*, Tilda Grace—*the Dean's wife;* Madame Rosalyn Bell—*dance mistress;* Willem Arquillo—*painter;* Cecily "Cece" Dee Falcon—*the society editor of the Zinnia Dispatch;* Sam Rayburn—*movie producer;* Bailey Bronson—*bookstore owner;* Sweetie-Pie—*a red tic hound, Harold's Christmas gift to Sarah;* Sheriff Coleman Peters; Doc Sawyer—*who is competent;* Millie Roberts—*owns Millie's Café, she hears and remembers all the local gossip;* Beverly McGrath—*Millie's aunt, remembers the gossip of the past;* Johnny Arbritton—*the local telephone man;* Baxter Matthews—*veterinarian;* Madame Tomeeka—*a.k.a. Tammy Odom, the fortune teller;* Claire—*her daughter;* Ramone Gilliard—*who delivers a eulogy;* Boyd "Catfish" Harkey—*the most famous lawyer in the Delta;* Senator Jebediah Archer; Deloris—*the Senator's daughter;* Edy Lavert—*who inherited Quarter Moon Lodge;* Johnny—*her son;* Ruth Ann Welsh—*who feels she owes Tinkie;* and Hamilton Garrett V—*who hasn't given up yet.*

3. *Splintered Bones.* New York: Delacorte Press, c2002, 308 p. ISBN: 0385335903; 9780385335904.

ZINNIA, MISSISSIPPI, MARCH 2005. Stable owner Eulalee "Lee" McBride was an abused wife. When her husband was killed, she confessed that she killed him during a fight. Sheriff Coleman Peters doesn't believe that she is guilty, and he has a philosophical problem with seeing an innocent woman convicted of murder.

ASSOCIATES: Jitty—*deceased, haunts Sarah in Sarah's own sweatclothes; she's on a mission to get Sarah to improve her grooming. Once she has made her point, she moves on to futuristic fashions;* Sweetie Pie—*Sarah's red tic hound;* Tinkie—*Sarah's business partner;* Oscar—*Tinkie's husband; their marriage changes in this book;* Chablis—*Tinkie's dog;* Cecily "Cece" Dee Falcon—*the society editor of the Zinnia Dispatch;* Millie Roberts—*who hears all the local gossip at Millie's Café;* Sheriff Coleman Peters—*whose wife is filing for a divorce. He asks Sarah Booth to be his date for the Chesterfield Hunt Ball;* Eulalee "Lee" McBride—*who wants Sarah to take care of her daughter Kip while Lee is in jail;* Katrina Lee "Kip" Fuquar—*Lee's daughter;* Bradford "Bud" Lynch—*the trainer at the Swift Level stables;* Roscoe—*who works at the Swift Level stables;* Harold Erkwell—*of the Zinnia National Bank;* Al Redding—*a gossipy reporter in Kerrville;* Carol Beth Farley—*who is known for doing whatever it takes to get what she wants;* Benny—*her husband;* Nathaniel Walz—*developer;* Krystal Brook—*a.k.a. Simpson Maes Fielding, a country singer;* Mike Rich—*Simpson's husband, is her manager;* Virginia Davis; Doc Sawyer—*who performed the autopsy;* Lillian Sparks—*who works to preserve Zinnia's history;* Malone Beasley—*who showed up with a tux;* John Bell "J. B." Washington—*the blues man from Greenwood;* Tony LaCoco—*who leant Lee money;* Mary Louise—*a survivor of an unhappy marriage;* Tom Smith—*known as TomcatTupelo, an Elvis impersonator;* Kinky Friedman—*who came to Zinnia to help Sarah track down a cat murderer;* Reveler—*a horse, a gift from Lee.*

4. *Crossed Bones.* New York: Delacorte Press, c2003, 335 p. ISBN: 0385336594; 9780385336598.

ZINNIA, MISSISSIPPI, SUMMER 2005. Blues Blizzard Scott Hampton was arrested for the murder of piano player Ivory Keys. They had met in prison and become fast friends. When Scott was released, Ivory hired him to play guitar at his club, Playin' the Bones. Mrs. Ida Mae Keys does not believe that Scott would lift a hand against her husband. She hires Sarah to find the real killer.

ASSOCIATES: Jitty—*deceased, haunts Sarah in clothing from the 1960s;* Sweetie Pie—*Sarah's red tic hound;* Reveler—*Sarah's horse;* Tinkie—*Sarah's business partner;* Oscar—*Tinkie's husband;* Chablis—*Tinkie's dog;* Cecily "Cece" Dee Falcon—*the society editor of the Zinnia Dispatch;* Millie Roberts—*who hears all the local gossip at Millie's Café;* John Bell "J. B." Washington—*the blues man from Greenwood;* Sheriff Coleman Peters—*who is trying to save his marriage;* Connie—*Coleman's wife, who told Coleman that she is pregnant;* Deputy Dewayne Dattilo; Deputy Gordon Walters; Cricket—*the police dispatcher who is trying to get Coleman into her bed (Sarah refers to Cricket as Bo-Peep);* Tinkie—*who sets Sarah up for a blind date with Bridge Ladnier;* Marshall Harrison—*who accosts Sarah at The Club;* Stuart Ann "Nandy" Shanahan—*who pickets for Scott's release;* Judge Clarence Hartwell; Prosecutor Lincoln Bangs; Madame Tomeeka—*a.k.a. Tammy Odom, psychic;* Spider and Ray-Ban—*bikers from the racist prison gang The Bonesmen;* Emanuel—*Ivory and Ida Mae's son;* Bernard—*the bartender at The Club;* Mollie—*Bernard's wife, she is a seamstress;* Wilbur Ward—*who lives close enough to the High School to see the kids cutting class.*

5. ***Hallowed Bones.*** New York: Delacorte Press, c2004, 338 p. ISBN: 0385337787; 9780385337786.

ZINNIA, MISSISSIPPI AND NEW ORLEANS, LOUISIANA, OCTOBER 2005. Sister Mary Magdalen hires the Delaney Detective Agency (*Delaney and Richmond, Private Investigators*) to clear healer Doreen Mallory of the charge that she murdered her own daughter. The case takes Tinkie and Sarah to New Orleans, where they tangle with a senator, a televangelist, and the daughter of a Mafioso. Sarah is skeptical of claims about supernatural healing, but Tinkie, who has found a lump in one breast, seems all too eager to believe.

ASSOCIATES: Jitty—*deceased, dresses as a flapper and harangues Sarah about women's liberation;* Sweetie Pie—*Sarah's red tic hound;* Reveler—*Sarah's horse;* Tinkie—*Sarah's partner, Tinkie has found a lump in her breast;* Oscar—*Tinkie's husband, he is terrified that he will lose her;* Chablis—*Tinkie's dog;* Sheriff Coleman Peters—*who is trying to save his marriage for the sake of his unborn child;* Connie—*his wife, the pregnancy seems to be damaging her health;* Rinda Stonecypher—*Connie's best friend,is the new police dispatcher;* Hamilton Garrett V.—*who tries one last time to win Sarah;* Harold Erkwell; Millie Roberts; Madame Tomeeka; Deputy Dewayne Dattilo; Doc Sawyer; Doreen Mallory—*daughter of crazy Lillith Lucas, is now a faith healer;* Sister Mary Magdalen—*who believes in Doreen;* Penny McAdams—*a nurse at the Zinnia Health Department, she's a sadist who keeps files on people, railing at Sarah because Sarah kicked her in the shin and ran away from her during Sarah's first grade vaccinations;* Attorney Arlin McLain—*who is known for his calm and reason;* Rebekah—*Doreen's daughter, her father is probably one of three men;* Senator Thaddeus Clay—*may be Rebekah's father;* Oren Weaver—*a televangelist, may be Rebekah's father;* Michael Anderson—*Doreen's financial manager, may be Rebekah's father;* Mrs. Ellisea Clay—*the Senator's wife, used to be a cover girl (before that she was a man);* Cecily "Cece" Dee Falcon—*the Zinnia society editor; makes no secret of the fact that she used to be a man;* Detective LeMont—*who is in charge of the investigation, protects Ellisea;* Mr. Boudet—*Ellisea's father, is a Mafioso;* the Crenshaws—*are religious fanatics who adopted Doreen's bother;* Adam—*the name the Crenshaws gave him;* Kiley Crenshaw—*is Adam Crenshaw's widow;* Mollie Jacks—*the best seamstress in Zinnia, was forced into retirement by arthritis, until she was cured by Doreen;* Pearline Brewer—*Rebekah's nanny, was paid by the Senator;* Trina Zebrowski—*mounted policewoman, is dating Michael and renting an apartment in Doreen's building;* Jake O'Banyon—*is the high-powered New Orleans lawyer hired for Doreen;* Deputy Coot Henderson—*Lillith's lover, took to drink after she died in a fire.*

6. ***Bones to Pick.*** New York: Kensington Books, c2006, 300 p. ISBN: 0758210906; 9780758210906.

ZINNIA, MISSISSIPPI, NOVEMBER 2005. Zinnia's high society is in an uproar. Quentin McGee has returned, and she has written a book, *King Cotton Bleeds,* that airs all their dirty laundry. She rakes up scandals and questions bloodlines, even pointing out who does not have a legitimate claim to membership in the United Daughters of the Confederacy! She is found dead, horribly murdered. Her lover, Allison Tatum, is charged with the murder. Allison's brother, Humphrey Tatum, hires Sarah to clear Alison's name.

ASSOCIATES: Jitty—*deceased, haunts Sarah in clothing from 18th-century France;* Sweetie Pie—*is Sarah's red tic hound;* Reveler—*is Sarah's horse;* Tinkie—*Sarah's partner, is grieving for the daughter she lost long ago;* Oscar—*Tinkie's husband;* Humphrey Tatum—*who is known countywide for his kinky romantic escapades, hires Sarah;* Harold Erkwell—*president of the Bank of Zinnia, threatened to kill Quentin;* Gertrude Stromm—*is owner of The Gardens Bed and Breakfast, where Allison and Quentin were staying;* Millie Roberts—*owner of Millie's Café, remembers all the local gossip;* Cecily "Cece" Dee Falcon—*is the society editor of the Zinnia Dispatch;* Acting Sheriff [Deputy] Gordon Walters and Deputy Dwayne Dattilo—*are the law in Zinnia while Coleman Peters is away trying to resolve his marital difficulties with his wife;* Connie—*Coleman's wife, was never pregnant, she invented the baby to hold on to Coleman;* Jasmine Paul—*Booking It's storeowner, did not order enough copies of King Cotton Bleeds;* Umbria—*Quentin's sister, bought and burned her entire stock;* Virgie Carrington—*who ran a school for girls;* Quentin and Allison—*were both students;* Sixty-four-year-old Doc Sawyer—*who won the position of County Coroner in the last election;* Franklin and Caledonia McGee—*Quentin and Umbria's parents;* Peggy Greene—*the librarian at the Greenwood Public Library;* Rutherford Clark—*Umbria's husband;* Roger Dendinger—*is the Funeral Director;* Lorilee Brewer and Marilyn Jenkins—*are graduates of the Carrington School who attend the funeral;* Genevieve Reynolds—*who vows to write her own, more positive, book;* Bernard—*the barkeep at The Club;* Jocko

Hallett—*an attorney;* Jolene Loper—*a beautician;* Madame Tomeeka—*a.k.a. Tammy Odom.* At the end of the book, Coleman tells Connie that they're getting a divorce.

7. **"Miracle Bones,"** in *A Kudzu Christmas: Twelve Mysterious Tales,* edited by Jim Gilbert and Gale Waller. Montgomery, Alabama: River City Publishing, 2005, p. 139–50. ISBN: 1579660649; 9781579660642.

ZINNIA, MISSISSIPPI, DECEMBER 2005. Cece isn't used to caring for infants, but she is willing to babysit. She places the baby in the cradle in the outdoor crèche to get a great photograph, and then she gets distracted and goes off to work. She races back as soon as she remembers the baby. He is gone. Cece calls for help and Tinkie and Sarah (along with hound Sweetie-Pie) race to find the child before the snow begins falling.

This story is not an amazing mystery, but it does provide an interesting chapter in the relationship of Tinkie and Oscar.

ASSOCIATES: Jitty—*deceased, is dressed bizarrely (even more bizarrely than she is usually dressed) to celebrate the season as she haunts Sarah;* Cecily "Cece" Dee Falcon—*society editor of the Zinnia Dispatch;* Tinkie—*Sarah's partner;* Sweetie Pie—*Sarah's red tic hound;* Chablis—*Tinkie's tiny Yorkie;* Christoph Becker—*an infant;* Sheriff Coleman Peters; Oscar—*Tinkie's husband.*

8. ***Ham Bones.*** New York: Kensington Books, c2007, 275 p. ISBN: 0758210922; 9780758270920.

ZINNIA, MISSISSIPPI, JANUARY 2006. Sarah Booth left New York a year ago, giving up on her dream of becoming a star. When part of the show schedule for a production of *Cat on a Hot Tin Roof* is derailed by hurricane damage, the New York traveling company changes the venue from the Beau Rivage Casino to Zinnia, and Sarah is asked to understudy the role of Maggie. When the leading lady dies and when Sarah takes her place, she becomes the chief suspect. Sarah's heart breaks when Sheriff Coleman Peters arrests her.

ASSOCIATES: Jitty—*deceased, haunts Sarah in clothing from the antebellum South;* Sweetie Pie—*Sarah's red tic hound;* Reveler—*her horse;* Tinkie—*Sarah's partner, the lump in Tinkie's breast has vanished;* Coleman Peters—*who should be a free man by spring;* Connie Peters—*whose insane behavior may have been caused by her recently diagnosed brain tumor.*

Keith Watley—*will direct the Zinnia production of Cat on a Hot Tin Roof;* Graf Milieu—*who used to live with Sarah, will play Brick;* Renata Trovaioli—*has the part of Maggie;* Sir Alfred Bascombe—*will play Big Daddy;* Bobbe Renshaw—*is the make-up artist;* Kristine Rolofson—*pickets the theater;* Cecily "Cece" Dee Falcon—*is the society editor of the Zinnia Dispatch;* Harry DeLa Bencher—*is Sarah's attorney;* Deputy Gordon Walters and Deputy Dwayne Dattilo—*are Sheriff Coleman's deputies;* Gabriel Trovaioli—*is Renata's brother;* Betsy "Booter" Gwen—*was hired by Gabriel to follow Sarah and find evidence of Sarah's guilt;* Millie Roberts—*owner of Millie's Café, is a steadfast friend;* Laura La Burnisco—*owns the La Burnisco Salon in Memphis;* Neil Sheffield—*owns Zinnia's feed store;* Nancy—*who works at the feed store;* Tammy Odom—*who tracks down Sarah to tell her of a vision of Sarah in danger;* Doc Sawyer—*is Zinnia's coroner and an old friend of Sarah's family;* Robert Morgan—*was a fan and a friend of Roberta;* talent agent Lester Lee and director Federico Marquez—*come to the last performance to see Sarah Booth;* Harold Erkwell—*who holds the strike party to celebrate the production's triumph after the run of the play.*

9. ***Wishbones.*** New York: Kensington Books, c2007, 275 p. ISBN: 0758210922; 9780758270920.

ZINNIA, MISSISSIPPI, HOLLYWOOD, CALIFORNIA AND PETALUMA, COSTA RICA, SPRING 2006. Sarah Booth gets her big break, a chance at a Hollywood screen test for a part in director Federico Marquez's remake of *Body Heat.* She leaves her beloved Zinnia to travel with Graf Milieu to Hollywood. A bizarre series of events mars Sarah Booth's time in Hollywood. She overhears actress Suzy Dutton's furious complaint that Federico had promised her the part of the female lead in *Body Heat.* Someone breaks into the home where Sarah is staying to write a threat across a mirror. The house is threatened by a blaze, and they learn the next day that the fire was the work of an arsonist. Then Sarah finds a body, gets the role in *Body Heat,* and is grateful to escape Hollywood. The movie cast and crew go to Petaluma, Costa Rica to shoot the movie, but the danger seems to follow them. The house in which they're staying is said to be haunted; and as one accident after another slows production, rumors begin to circulate that the movie is cursed.

ASSOCIATES: Jitty—*deceased, haunts Sarah in the guise of one leading lady after another;* Federico—*the director;* Sweetie Pie—*Sarah's dog;* Ron O'Gorman—*the screenwriter who is told to write the dog into the movie;* Sheriff Grady King—*who seems to regard Sarah as his chief suspect;* Jovan—*a Victoria's Secret model who is Federico's girlfriend;* Suzy Dutton—*an actress who was once promised the role that will be played by Sarah Booth;* Graf Milieu, Ashton Kutchner, and Mickey Rourke—*are others in the cast;* Dallas Brown—*the costume designer;* Sally—*who does make-up;* Joey—*the prop-man;* Ricardo—*Federico's son;* Estelle—*Federico's daughter;* Regena Lombardi—*Estelle's roommate;* Daniel Martinez—*the head of Promise Security Agency, he loves Estelle;* Senor Lopez—*who gives Tinkie and Sarah modified blueprints of the house;* Estoban Gonzalez—*Federico's father-in-law;* Cecily "Cece" Dee Falcon, Millie Roberts, and Tinkie Richmond (and Chablis)—*come to visit Sarah Booth who is filming on location in Petaluma;* Dr. Milazo—*is the veterinarian who treats Chablis;* Carlita Gonzalez Marquez—*deceased, Federico's wife;* Sergeant Calla—*of Petaluma's police department;* and Patsy Kringel—*Petaluma research librarian.*

10. ***Greedy Bones.*** New York: Minotaur Books, 2009, 310 p. ISBN: 031237710X; 9780312377106.

ZINNIA, MISSISSIPPI, SPRING 2006. When Tinkie heard that her husband Oscar was deathly ill she flew home. Sarah Booth came with her. They found Oscar in a coma, stricken down by a disease that no-one recognizes. Soon he is joined by others with the same symptoms, but no-one knows the cause. All of them spent time at the old Carlisle farm hours before they became ill. Personnel from the Centers for Disease Control come and quarantine the site. They find genetically modified corn that grows so quickly that it would be possible to grow two crops in one season. They find odd mutated green boll weevils, that are destroying the cotton. Neither seems to be the cause of the illness.

Tinkie watches over Oscar, trying to hold death at bay while Sarah Booth searches for the answers that will lead to a cure.

In this book Sarah and Coleman work to re-establish their friendship. Coleman becomes interested in a lady from the CDC. Graf proposes to Sarah.

ASSOCIATES: Jitty—*deceased, haunts Sarah while dressed in rags, and sings to her while dressed as a 1930s chanteuse;* Sweetie Pie—*Sarah's red tic hound;* Chablis—*Tinkie's dog;* Reveler and Miss Scrapiron—*Sarah's horses;* Tinkie—*Sarah's best friend, stands outside a hospital room, willing her husband to stay alive, Tinkie's faith works against her as she tries to find a spiritual reason for the "plague";* Oscar Richmond—*Tinkie's husband, is in a coma, stricken down by an unknown illness;* Regina Campbell and Luann Bigley—*real estate agents who are suffering from the same malady;* Deputy Gordon Walters—*falls victim to the illness after he visits the Carlisle land;* Doc Sawyer—*is working around the clock trying to keep his patients alive;* Mr. Avery Bellcase—*Tinkie's father;* Harold Erkwell—*president of the Bank of Zinnia, Sarah slips and mentions Jitty to him and now he is curious;* Sheriff Coleman Peters—*who works at being a friend to Sarah;* Gertrude Stromm—*the owner of The Gardens Bed and Breakfast, she loathes Sarah Booth;* Millie Roberts—*owner of Millie's Café;* Cecily "Cece" Dee Falcon—*joins the investigation, in this book she is attracted to one of the chief suspects;* Luther Carlisle—*who has been talking to a land developer;* Erin Carlisle—*Luther's sister who will prevent the sale of the Carlisle land;* Jimmy Janks—*a developer;* Mrs. Kepler—*the town librarian;* Peyton Fidellas—*of the Epidemic Intelligence Services of the Centers for Disease Control, his specialty is airborne diseases and chemical reactions;* Bonnie "Beaucoup" Louise McRae—*whose specialty is parasitic life-cycle development;* Joe Downs—*of Mississippi Agri-Team, they lease the Carlisle property;* Chancery Clerk Attila Lambert—*who helps Sarah go through the public records of the Carlisle family;* Sonja Kessler—*the illegitimate daughter of Gregory Carlisle, half-sister to Luther and Erin;* the McBanes—*who purchased the Janks home;* Toke Lambert—*who found that someone with a great deal of money is bankrolling*

Jimmy Janks' business; Deputy Dewayne—*who doesn't trust Bonnie McRae;* Madame Tomeeka—*a.k.a. Tammy Odom, who dreamed of fresh dirt in the Delaney family cemetery;* Sarah Booth's mother—*deceased, who breaks some rules to be there when Sarah Booth needs her;* Graf Milieu—*who sends Sarah an engagement ring.*

HALE, Michael.

A Fold in the Tent of the Sky

Genres/Themes Crossed: Paranormal, Time Travel X Traditional Mystery.

Subjects/Character Types: Time Travel, Telepathy, Clairvoyance X Amateur Detective (Contemporary).

Series/Stand-Alone: Stand-alone.

Scene of the Crime: Present-day St. Martin, France/Netherlands Antilles, Vancouver, Canada, and St. Paul, Minnesota. 1942 Batavia, New York; 1919 (séance with clairvoyant Sarah Pope); 1969 Los Angeles, California (Barker Ranch); 1843 Hamburg, Germany; and other times from Earth's past.

Detective: Peter Abbott never knew the date of his birth. He was abandoned by his mother, and he developed a strange awareness of other people. When he touches people, or even touches objects that they have touched, he hears their thoughts and sometimes sees flashes of their futures. When he was in college, he participated in an experiment to earn a little money. The experiment was designed to measure extrasensory perception. The researcher drew a card from a shuffled "Zener" card deck, and the subject tried to guess the symbol on the card. Peter's first-time results were stunningly accurate. The researcher brought him back for two more sessions, and in those, his results were normal. Years later, another researcher, reviewing the results, realized that Peter displayed mindreading abilities in the first session and precognitive abilities in the last two sessions. Peter's guesses in the last two sessions had reliably predicted the next card that the researcher was going to draw from the deck, rather than reading the researcher's thoughts about the card that the researcher was viewing. A consortium created to find a way to make a profit by developing and utilizing psychic ability is given this information, and Peter is recruited to join their *Calliope Project.*

Known Associates: *Calliope Associates* employs Elijah "Eli" Thornton, Jane Franklin, and lab supervisor Mike Blenheim. They recruit Pamela

Gilford, who can sense people's thoughts and sometimes sees glimpses of their futures through touch. She once broke through time to the extent of disrupting a séance held in 1919, almost half a century before she was born. Other recruits include Larry McEwan, who can project images onto film; Anita Spalding, ghost hunter; Gordon Quarendon, dowser; Simon Hayward, who has huge potential in many fields; Ron Koch, who used precognition to handicap horse races and who obsesses over the chances he lost by not following his instincts. In other timelines, researchers include Jeff Sanderson, and recruits include Jenny, a psychic.

Premise: *Calliope Associates* was envisioned as a type of private investigation agency that would employ various types of psychics, work with them to develop their abilities, and then deploy them to gather information. Eli Thornton explains (p. 65) that they are not trying to understand the paranormal; they will leave that to the scientists and statisticians. They just want to *use* the paranormal. Reliability is important, and they believe that it can be developed, but repeatable experiments are not the issue. The issue is to build a good enough track record to be able to charge enormous sums for fetching information that no one else can access. They will specialize in hidden information, secret information, and even in information that was lost in the past.

Comment: Canadian Michael Hale has had a rich and varied career in the arts. He worked in theater, collaborating with theater director Peter Melnick on music and sound effects for the Theatre Passe Muraille's Seed Program. He wrote his first novel, *The Other Child,* while working as a graphic designer. (It was retitled *Wakings* and short-listed in the 1984 Seal Books First Novel Contest.) He wrote his second novel, *A Fold in the Tent of the Sky,* while traveling throughout the United States and Canada with a production of *Show Boat,* in which his wife was a cast-member.

Literary Magic & Mayhem: *A Fold in the Tent of the Sky* starts out slowly, exploring the world as experienced by the psychics who will become *Calliope* recruits. *Calliope* personnel begin to contemplate the possibility that some of the psychics will be able to remote-view places that are removed from them temporally as well as spatially. There are passages that speculate on what would happen if someone changed the past. When disaster strikes, few people remember anything about the original timeline. It takes an effort to convince the company that the original timeline was different. Once they are convinced, they develop rules to protect both the psychics and the world, but one of the recruits has never believed that any rules should apply to him.

Hale's depiction of the confusion and fear brought on each time history changes is excellent. The far-reaching effects of small changes are fascinating.

The idea that the universe would have an interest in maintaining the original timeline is intriguing. Several of the characters are very well drawn. *Calliope* recruits a disparate group of psychics, most of whom had spent their lives hiding their skills. The frictions and petty irritations that are manifest in this group ring true, and are elements that keep the story at an engagingly human level. The book does not fit our preferred definition of mystery. because the action of the plot is not driven by the search for the truth about a suspected crime. This book fits the second definition, in that the Library of Congress gives it the genre subject heading "Detective and Mystery Stories." The first part of the book focuses on the psychics; most of the rest of the book follows one of the psychics as he realizes that one of their group must be changing history and tries to find ways to hold on to the true timeline and stop the sociopath who is changing the world.

Explorations: Would murder be a greater or lesser crime than traveling to the past to prevent a specific person's conception?

If lost information could be retrieved from the past, what information would be most interesting or most useful?

Eli Thornton shows the recruits the May 28, 1843 Hamburg photograph (p. 67). What does its existence in the original timeline imply?

THE CASE

1. ***A Fold in the Tent of the Sky.*** New York: William Morrow and Co., 1998, 355 p. ISBN: 0688157572.

EARTH'S PRESENT AND PAST. The Calliope Project was created to develop and harness paranormal ability. Project researchers combed through years of the results of myriad psychology projects, news articles, and sources of rumor to find a handful of promising subjects. The project is half experimental lab and half profit-making business. The backers are certain that paranormal talent exists, but know that it is unstable. Their view is that it doesn't have to be 100 percent reliable to be useful.

The test subjects are a varied lot. They have different gifts and different personalities, but all are fascinated by the ways that their abilities develop once their talents are measured and nurtured. Some develop more quickly than others do. Some are fascinated by the possibilities, others by the power, and at least one of the recruits is willing to commit murder. When one of the recruits begins meddling with history, Peter Abbott finds that he is the only person who remembers the original timeline. No one else believes that there has been any change. He alone remembers enough to try to restore the history that was.

ASSOCIATES: See above.

HAMBLY, Barbara (Joan).

THOSE WHO HUNT THE NIGHT

Genres/Themes Crossed: Secret Society X Traditional Mystery (Historical).

Subjects/Character Types: Vampires X Amateur Sleuth (Historical).

Series/Stand-Alone: The first book introduces the characters and the society. These should be read in order.

Scene of the Crime: Edwardian London, in a world in which vampires walk the night.

Detective: Dr. James Claudius Asher, author of *Language and Concepts in Eastern and Central Europe,* an Oxford don who teaches philology at New College, and who, for 17 years, traveled Europe ostensibly gathering information on languages and the folklore, while also collecting information for Queen (and, later, King) and country. He acted as an espionage agent up until eight years before the events related in *Traveling with the Dead.* That career ended when he had to kill an innocent boy. He had been staying in South Africa with a Boer family named van der Platz. They trusted him and their 16-year-old son, Jan, befriended him and became his loyal shadow. When Jan overheard enough to realize that James was a spy, James had to kill him to protect his contacts. Heartsick and disillusioned, James Asher retired from the "Great Game." Dr. Asher is carefully nondescript, quiet, bookish, and extremely observant.

Known Associates: Lydia Asher (James's wife) is an unconventional woman, a doctor who is fascinated by the new germ theory. She works treating the destitute and performing research at the Radclyffe Infirmary. Don Simon Xavier Christian Morado de la Cadena-Ysidro was made a vampire in the year 1558, in England, having accompanied his Majesty King Philip II of Spain when King Philip came to marry the Henry VIII's first surviving daughter (Bloody Mary).

Premise: The world's vampires have formed small, enclosed societies, each group separate from the others and each led by a "Master" vampire. The Master sets the rules of the society and usually reserves to him or herself the right to create new vampires. Vampires must kill regularly: without the kill they become slow, stupid, careless, weary; without the kill they will soon die. Vampires have two chief defenses: the first is that the living do not believe in the walking dead; the vampires' second defense is time—they survive for centuries. If suspicions are raised, the vampires can afford to lie low for years, until suspicions fade away. These two factors have kept them relatively safe for centuries, but in the past few months, four of the vampires of London have been killed, killed in ways that show that someone knows their nature, and therefore, their vulnerabilities. Don Ysidro decided that they needed a man who was able to walk in the sunlight, who was skilled in research, who held a knowledge of the old legends, and who had a talent for spying and killing. He knew of only one such man. Some time ago, Don Ysidro's solicitor (an obliging young man who is happy to meet with him outside of normal business hours) gossiped to him that one of the Oxford Dons had done some "good work" for the Foreign Office. Don Ysidro, with a vampire's love of secrets, had examined the dates of publications of Oxford Dons and compared them with places and times of political unrest. He finds James Asher, and James Asher sounds exactly like the man that the vampires need.

Comment: *Those Who Hunt the Night* won the Locus Award for Best Horror Novel in 1989. *Traveling With the Dead* was a Locus Award nominee in 1996 and won the Lord Ruthven Award in 1996. These have been the only two books in the series for over a decade, In 2006, Barbara Hambly stated that there will be another novel or two in this series. She had written an outline for the third book in the series, and it was with an editor. At the time, the news was posted on Ms. Hambly's Web site (http://www.barbarahambly.com/index.htm), she had not yet heard from the editor. The Web site includes biographical information, information on her books, and a section entitled "Oft-asked Questions," which includes a question on the status of her different series. That page can be checked to see if there has been progress on selling another James and Lydia Asher book.

Literary Magic & Mayhem: Beautiful, evocative writing coupled with characters that are pragmatic, intelligent, and honorable—this is a wonderful series. The combination of pragmatism and honor leads James and Lydia Asher to evaluate the ethical issues involved in helping vampires. This is one of the few vampire series in which the main characters begin by trying to calculate the number of humans murdered over the course of centuries by a single vampire. They do not romanticize the vampires; they clearly see them as killers. If James Asher thought he could protect his family, he would side with the vampires' enemy in a heartbeat. The vampires themselves have obviously discussed the moral implications of their continued lives. More than one of them compares the taking of lives to sustain his or her existence with the taking of lives to safeguard a country's existence. In *Those Who Hunt the Night,* Don Ysidro compares the work he is asking Asher to perform with the work Asher did as a spy.

> Don't pretend you did not know that you were hired to kill by other killers in the days when you took the Queen's Coin. Wherein lays the difference between the Empire, which holds its immortality in many men's consciousness, and the vampire, who holds it in one? (p. 24)

Those Who Hunt the Night explores questions of morality and belief. This series is set in Edwardian times, and people are just coming to grips with the idea that germs, which they cannot see, can kill them. At one point, James asks Lydia if she could believe in vampires, and she answers:

> Probably as much as you do. That is, there's a lot of me that says, "This is silly, there is no such thing." But, up until a year or so ago, nobody believed there was such a thing as viruses, you know. We still don't know what they are, but we do know now they exist, and more and more are being discovered. (p. 49)

Her straightforward exploration of the subject is one of the joys of the novels. The reader can picture Don Ysidro's face as, in *Traveling with the Dead,* she rattles off ways in which to discover a vampire nest in a city. He has been dealing with a rather mystical hypnosis, and she speaks of shell corporations set up to pay household bills over long periods of time, houses that have extensive cellars, payments made in gold or credit, but never in silver, and so forth. In comparison to his powers, the list seems remarkably mundane, one of the many humorous aspects of the books.

Traveling with the Dead explores questions such as what makes life valuable and what one would do with time if one lived for centuries. It also spends some time exploring Lydia's life and her memories in a way that provides insights into the constraints placed on women at this time.

Explorations: Which vampires arouse your sympathies? What makes them interesting or likable? What makes them frightening?

How is Lydia treated by others? Does James treat her differently?

What did you think of the ending? Is it happily ever after?

THE CASES

1. ***Those Who Hunt the Night*** (published in England as ***Immortal Blood***). New York: Ballantine Books, 1988, 296 p. ISBN: 0345343808.

ENGLAND, 1907. When Don Ysidro demands James Asher's help in discovering who is murdering the vampires of London, Asher does not dare refuse. He knows that the knowledge that is being shared with him, to make him the weapon the vampires need, is also a death sentence. Once he knows their ways and their weaknesses, he will not be allowed to live. He goes through the investigation trying to solve the mystery while finding a way to protect himself and those he loves.

ASSOCIATES: James Asher—*who takes the lead in this investigation;* Lydia Asher—*his wife.* The vampires of London: Don Simon Xavier Christian Morado de la Cadena-Ysidro—*who was made a vampire in the year 1555 by Rhys the White;* Bully Joe Davies—*made a vampire in 1907 by Valentin Calvaire;* Lord and Lady Ernchester—*whose given names are Charles and Anthea, became vampires in 1682, made by Grippen;* Lionel Grippen—*the Master vampire of London, made in the mid 16th century by the then Master of London, Rhys the White;* Chloé Winterdon—*made within the last two decades, by Grippen.*

Elysée de Montadour—*the MasterVampire of Paris made in the early 1870s;* Serge—*a vampire;* Hyacinthe—*a vampire from Charleston;* Brother Anthony—*of the order of the Friars Minor, a very old vampire;* The Honorable Evelyn Westmoreland; Horace Blaydon—*a pathologist;* Dennis Blaydon—*his son, Denis was a friend of Westmoreland.*

2. ***Traveling with the Dead.*** New York: Ballantine Books, 1995, 343 p. ISBN: 0345381025.

ENGLAND, 1908. The world is on the brink of war, and James Asher, who was once a spy, has no illusions to comfort him. He knows how dangerous the world is, and when he sees the vampire Charels Farren with Ignace Karolyi, an agent of the Austrians, he is one of the few people who can appreciate how very much more dangerous it could become. He follows them, and sends a message to his wife Lydia, telling her that he will hand the case off and return by nightfall. His second telegram, which tells Lydia enough that she fears he will fall into a trap, comes a short time later. Lydia would turn to the devil himself to try to bring Asher home safely. The closest devil she knows is Don Ysidro.

ASSOCIATES: James Asher—*who saw an unholy alliance;* Lydia Asher—*his wife, who is determined to save him;* Ignace Karolyi—*an agent of the Austrian secret service;* Charles Farren—*vampire, The Third Earl of Ernchester;* Anthea—*vampire, his wife;* Streatham—*Head of the Paris branch of the Department (England's secret service);* Edmund Cramer—*an information agent;* Miss Margaret Potton—*who will act as duenna to Lydia;* Dr. Bedford Fairport—*a man interested in immortality;* Artemus Halliwell—*Head of the Vienna branch of the Department.*

The vampires of Vienna: Count Batthyany Nikolai Alessandro August—*the vampire Master of Vienna;* and Grete—*vampire, his wife.*

The vampires of Constantinople: Olumsiz Bey—*the vampire Master of Constantinople, a.k.a. The Malik of Stamboul, Wafat Sahib, and The Deathless Lord.* Zardalu, Jamila Baykus, Haralpos, Habib, and Pelageya—*are the vampire fledglings living with him*: Sayyed—*Bey's servant, lives with them as well.*

Lady Clapham, Sir Burnwell, Ambassador Lowther, Prince Andrei Illyich Razumovsky, Herr Franz Hindl, and Monsieur Demerci—*are members of the diplomatic community of Constaninople*: Helm Musefir—*the storyteller;* Jacob Zeittelstein; Zenaida—*vampire, Bey made her long ago and she has gone insane, she lives in the harem;* Gölge Kurt—*vampire, a.k.a. The Shadow Wolf.*

HAMILTON, Laurell K.

Guilty Pleasures

Genres/Themes Crossed: Blended Society X Traditional Mystery.

Subjects/Character Types: Vampires, Zombies, Shape Changers X Traditional Mystery.

Series/Stand-Alone: Many people who enjoy the earlier novels feel that the series deteriorated when it began to emphasize the erotic encounters rather than the mystery plots. (It has been described as moving from "whodunnit" to "who's doing whom.") It is a steady progression, the emphasis does not move back to mystery further in the series (at least not so far). Readers should begin with the first novel and read the series in order, moving to other series if they get to a point where they would prefer more of an emphasis on mystery elements.

Scene of the Crime: Primarily Saint Louis, modern day.

Detectives: Anita Blake begins the series as an animator working for *Animators Inc.* As an animator, she raises the recently dead, primarily to settle legal issues such as inconsistencies in wills or to help solve crimes involving the deceased. Anita is also sometimes employed by the local police to hunt down and kill vampires and other supernatural creatures that are actively posing a threat to the general public. Because of her efficiency and ruthlessness in carrying out these slayings, she is called "The Executioner" by the local denizens of the night. As the series goes on, Anita is empowered by the local vampire master, granting her increased strength and endurance as well as forging a psychic connection between herself, the vampire master, and a werewolf. Anita becomes a carrier for several strains of lycanthropy, but does not undergo any transformations herself, instead calling upon the innate powers of the beasts that infected her. Late in the series, Anita gains a portion of the vampiric curse of her master vampire. This particular curse, called the Ardeur, is an unquenchable sexual desire from which a vampire can gain strength rather than through traditional feeding.

Known Associates: Jean Claude, a powerful, centuries-old vampire who, following the events of the first book, becomes the master vampire of Saint Louis.

Richard Zeeman is a prominent local werewolf whom Anita dates during the series. A triumvirate is formed between Richard, Anita, and Jean Claude. Later in the series, Richard's relationship with Anita becomes strained. Micah Callahan is a wereleopard with whom Anita begins a relationship late in the series. Nathaniel Graison is another wereleopard, a former drug addict, and prostitute with whom Anita shares a romantic relationship. Damian is a thousand-year-old vampire who becomes Anita's vampire servant after she uses her abilities as an animator to raise him from true death. This is a reversal of the role that a human normally plays for a vampire. Anita forms a triumvirate with Damian and Nathaniel. Edward is a borderline psychotic, and professional mercenary and assassin, who occasionally hunts vampires with Anita. He is so brutal in his killings that the vampire community refers to him as "Death." Bert Vaughn is the founder of *Animators Inc.* Bert is portrayed as being more fond of money than he is of his coworkers.

Premise: The series follows Anita Blake as she transitions from being a hunter of the supernatural to being a prominent member of the local supernatural society.

Comments: The series initially deals with crimes related to the supernatural. Anita is called in by the local authorities or blackmailed by local supernatural creatures to solve crimes and stop the perpetrators. As the series goes on, Anita shifts from being a more or less normal human into an increasingly powerful being who gains status in the society she used to terrorize. Later entries deal less and less with crimes, and increasingly focus on the romantic life of Anita and her ever-growing harem of supernatural creatures. This has led to criticism from a number of longtime fans of the series who are displeased with the shift from mystery fiction to erotica. The descriptions of sex are generally graphic and frequently violent. The first book in the series, *Guilty Pleasures,* has been adapted into a comic book by Marvel comics and the comic book issues have been collected into the graphic novels *The First Death* and *Guilty Pleasures* (volumes 1 and 2). The subsequent books are also being serialized as comics.

Laurell K. Hamilton's official Web site is http://www.laurellkhamilton.org. It includes links to her blog (http://blog.laurellkhamilton.org/) and her MySpace page (http://www.myspace,com/laurellkhamilton), as well as links to interviews and podcasts, and provides information on her books.

Literary Magic and Mayhem: The undead and shape-shifters are real and this fact is known to the general public. These supernatural creatures are all given equal rights as citizens of the United States. This has resulted in a great deal of political divisiveness among voters, with the formation of groups like the *League of Human Voters,* a group dedicated to preserving and protecting the rights of normal humans, and the *Church of Eternal Life*, a religion that guarantees eternal life to its members by arranging for them to become vampires.

Explorations: What effect would legally recognizing and conferring citizenship upon the undead have on politics and the economy?

At what point does an individual cease to be human?

THE CASES

1. ***Anita Blake, Vampire Hunter. The First Death.*** New York: Marvel, 2008, unpaged. ISBN: 9780785129417.

St. Louis, Missouri, present day. Sergeant Storr asks Anita for help in an investigation into vampire attacks on children. For the first time, Anita actively hunts the killers. She and Manny work together to try to find the vampire who is guilty of the murders. Anita meets Hean-Claude and develops a working relationship with Edward. The first half of the book is the graphic novel. The second half is an encyclopedia of character and setting descriptions for the series. The material was originally published in comic book form as *Laurell K. Hamilton's Anita Blake, Vampire Hunter. The First Death #1–2, and the Anita Blake. Guilty Pleasures Handbook.*

Associates: Sergeant Storr; Zerbrowski; Dave—*vampire, an ex-police officer who now is a bartender;* Jean-Claude—*vampire, owner of the Guilty Pleasures strip club;* Sean—*vampire, one of the dancers at the club;* Manny—*Anita's mentor;* Bert—*Anita's boss;* Edward—*an assassin.*

2. ***Guilty Pleasures.*** New York: Jove, 2002, 272 p. ISBN: 051513449X.

St. Louis, Missouri, present day. Anita is forced to look into a series of murders being committed against vampires after the vampire master of the city, Nikolaos, arranges for a vampire to gain sway over one of Anita's friends.

Associates: Jean-Claude, Edward, Willie McCoy, Dead Dave, Luther, Ronnie, Jamison, Dolph, Zerbrowski, Malcolm, Catherine, Monica, and Phillip, Rafael.

3. ***The Laughing Corpse.*** New York: Jove, 2002, 304 p. ISBN: 0515134449.

St. Louis, Missouri, present day. Anita is called out to investigate the grisly murder of a family. While investigating, Anita is threatened by both a wealthy man seeking to get Anita to animate one of his long dead ancestors and another powerful necromancer. Anita also attempts to sort out her role as Jean-Claude's human servant.

Associates: Jean-Claude, Bert, Ronnie, Charles, Jamison, Dolph, Zerbrowski, Willie McCoy, Antonio, Dead Dave, Wheelchair Wanda, Irving, Luther, John Burke, and Maroni.

4. ***Circus of the Damned.*** New York: Jove, 2002, 336 p. ISBN: 0515134483.

St. Louis, Missouri, present day. A pack of vampires is committing a series of murders and Anita is called in to find and stop them. While Anita is investigating the crimes, she must fend off a slew of people attempting to get her to reveal the daytime resting place and identity of the new master vampire of the city.

Associates: Jean-Claude, Richard Zeeman, Bert, Ronnie, Dolph, Zerbrowski, John Burke, Larry Kirkland, Stephen, Jeremy Reubens, and Edward.

5. ***The Lunatic Café.*** New York: Jove, 2002, 384 p. ISBN: 051513452X.

St. Louis, Missouri, present day. Shapeshifters are disappearing, and Anita decides to investigate while also exploring her new relationship with Richard, a werewolf.

Associates: Jean-Claude, Richard Zeeman, Bert, Ronnie, Dolph, Zerbrowski, Clive Perry, Irving, Robert, Stephen, Lillian, Gretchen, Jason Schuyler, Wallis, Gabriel, Elizabeth, Christine, Chief Garroway, Rafael, and Edward.

6. ***Bloody Bones.*** New York: Jove, 2002, 384 p. ISBN: 0515134469.

St. Louis and Branson, Missouri, present day. Bert sends Anita to Branson on a job to raise an entire 200-year-old cemetery. While in Branson Anita and Jean-Claude are drawn into investigating a series of murders involving vampires.

Associates: Jean-Claude, Richard Zeeman, Bert, Larry Kirkland, Dolph, Jason Schuyler, Raymond Stirling, Ms. Harrison, Lionel Bayard, Mr. Quinlan, Mrs. Quinlan, Ellie Quinlan, Jeff Quinlan, Sergeant Freemont, Officer Wallace, Agent Elwood, and Agent Bradford.

7. ***The Killing Dance.*** New York: Jove, 2002, 400 p. ISBN: 0515134511.

St. Louis, Missouri, present day. A contract is put out on Anita's life. While attempting to determine who wants her dead, Anita becomes embroiled in the politics of Richard's werewolf pack. Anita also spends time sorting out her romantic life.

Associates: Jean-Claude, Richard Zeeman, Edward, Rafael, Catherine, Monica, Robert, Dolph, Zerbrowski, Willie McCoy, Lillian, Christine, Jason Schuyler, Stephen, Jamil, Gregory, Sylvie, Mrs. Pringle, Damien, Liv, Harely, Cassandra, Sabin, and Dumare.

8. ***Burnt Offerings.*** New York: Jove, 2002, 400 p. ISBN: 0515134473.

St. Louis, Missouri, present day. Anita is asked to investigate a series of arsons that may be the work of a pyrokinetic. Representatives from the vampire council in Europe arrive to attempt to overthrow Jean Claude, causing chaos in the vampire and shifter communities.

Associates: Jean-Claude, Richard Zeeman, Larry, Ronnie, Dolph, Zerbrowski, Clive Perry, Tammy Reynolds, Damian, Asher, Liv, Willie McCoy, Irving, Jason Schuyler, Jamil, Stephen, Sylvie, Teddy, Kevin, Lorraine, Cherry,

Elizabeth, Nathanial, Vivian, Zane, Lillian, Rafael, Ernie, Gwen, Hannah, and Captain McKinnon.

9. *Blue Moon.* New York: Jove, 2002, 432 p. ISBN: 0515134457.

St. Louis, Missouri and Myerton, Tennessee, present day. Richard is falsely accused of rape while working on his masters degree in Myerton, Tennessee. Anita is called by Richard's brother to attempt to clear Richard's name, and she becomes involved in a conflict with Myerton's vampire master.

Associates: Jean-Claude, Richard Zeeman, Nathaniel, Dolph, Damian, Asher, Jason, Cherry, Jamil, Daniel Zeeman, Charlotte Zeeman, Verne, and Marianne.

10. *Obsidian Butterfly.* New York: Jove, 2002, 608 p. ISBN: 0515134503.

St. Louis, Missouri and Santa Fe and Albuquerque, New Mexico, present day. Richard calls in a favor that Anita owes him and asks her to help him investigate a series of possibly supernatural killings in New Mexico.

Associates: Edward, Jean-Claude, Richard, Donna, Peter, Becca, Bernando, Olaf, Cesar, Seth, Lieutenant Marks, Detective Hernando Ramirez, Doctor Evans, Lenora Evans, and Agent Bradford.

11. *Narcissus in Chains.* New York: Jove, 2002, 656 p. ISBN: 0515133876.

St. Louis, Missouri, present day. While Anita tries to reconnect with her friends after alienating herself from them, local shape-shifters begin disappearing. Anita investigates the disappearances, but things are complicated when she develops the *Ardeur*, a supernatural ability and need to feed on power through lust.

Associates: Jean-Claude, Richard Zeeman, Nathaniel, Micah, Ronnie, Belle Morte, Gregory, Damian, Narcissus, Sylvie, Cherry, Zeke, Gina, Asher, Dolph, Zerbrowski, and Jason Schuyler.

12. *Cerulean Sins.* New York: Jove, 2004, 560 p. ISBN: 0515136816.

St. Louis, Missouri, present day. Jean-Claude's master makes a play for power in the city while Anita tries to sort out her own love life and investigate a series of murders involving a mysterious shape-shifter.

Associates: Jean-Claude, Richard Zeeman, Micah, Nathaniel, Damian, Asher, Dolph, Zerbrowski, and Jason Schuyler.

13. *Incubus Dreams.* New York: Jove, 2005, 752 p. ISBN: 0515139750.

St. Louis, Missouri, present day. Anita's romantic life shifts as she gains a better understanding of the Ardeur. A series of vampire serial murders is investigated.

Associates: Jean-Claude, Richard Zeeman, Micah, Nathaniel, Damian, Asher, Malcolm, Requiem, Byron, Primo, Wicked, and Truth.

14. *Micah.* New York: Jove, 2006, 288 p. ISBN: 0515140872.

St. Louis, Missouri and Philadelphia, Pennsylvania, present day. Anita is called away to Philadelphia on business and uses this as an opportunity to connect with Micah, one-on-one.

ASSOCIATES: Micah, Nathaniel, Larry Kirkland, Tammy Kirkland, Agent Franklin, and Special Agent Fox.

15. ***Danse Macabre.*** New York: Jove, 2007, 576 p. ISBN: 0515142816.

ST. LOUIS, MISSOURI, PRESENT DAY. Anita is concerned over a possible pregnancy, as vampire masters from other cities arrive in Saint Louis, at Jean-Claude's invitation, to see a performance by a vampiric ballet troupe.

ASSOCIATES: Jean-Claude, Richard Zeeman, Micah, Asher, Damian, Nathaniel, Ronnie, Belle Morte, Augustine, Haven, Samuel, Leocothea, Sampson, Thomas, Cristof, Jason Schuyler, Requiem, Graham, Claudia, Fredo, Joseph, Valentina, Wicked, Truth, London, and Elinore.

16. ***The Harlequin.*** New York: Berkley Hardcover, 2007, 432 p. ISBN: 0425217248.

ST. LOUIS, MISSOURI, PRESENT DAY. The Harlequin, a secretive group of vampires in the service of the Mother of Darkness, choose Anita as their target.

ASSOCIATES: Jean-Claude, Richard Zeeman, Micah, Nathaniel, Asher, Damian, Malcolm, Belle Morte, Edward, London, Cisco, Remus, Rafael, Donovon, Joseph, Haven, and Perdy.

17. ***Blood Noir.*** New York: Berkley Harcover, 2008, 340 p. ISBN: 9780425222195.

ST. LOUIS, MISSOURI AND CHARLESTON, NORTH CAROLINA, PRESENT DAY. Anita agrees to accompany Jason to his hometown to visit his dying father and assist in reconciling the father and son's relationship. While there, she must contend with Marmee Noir's machinations and a case of mistaken identities involving Jason and the son of a presidential candidate.

ASSOCIATES: Jason Schuyler, Jean-Claude, Richard Zeeman, Nathaniel, Irving, Jamil, Shang-Da, and Micah, Perdy.

HARRIS, Charlaine.

DEAD UNTIL DARK

Genres/Themes Crossed: Blended Society (Vampires have "come out" at the onset of the series. Shape-shifters reveal their existence to the world in *Dead and Gone*), Secret Society (other "supes" remain hidden) X Traditional Mystery.

Subjects/Character Types: Vampires, Telepathy, Werewolves, Fairies X Amateur Sleuth (Contemporary).

Series/Stand-Alone: Sookie grows and changes during the books. Relationships among the characters also change. Some key events are related in the short stories. The series should be read in order.

Scene of the Crime: Present-day Louisiana.

Detective: Sookie Stackhouse has been a telepath since childhood. People desperately cling to the normal; telepaths don't fit in their worldview. The fact that Sookie occasionally slips and responds to a question not yet asked, or to a comment not yet voiced, causes the people around her to fear her. People avoid Sookie, dismiss her as simple or insane (or both), or regard her as a freak. Her own family punished her for making up stories when she repeated what she had heard telepathically. Teachers, even teachers who puzzled out the truth about Sookie, repeatedly had her tested for disabilities, because she seemed inattentive in school. (The constant chatter of other minds made it difficult for Sookie to concentrate.) Sookie regards her telepathy as a disability and knows that knowledge of it would cause others to shun her. She works hard to keep her reactions to others' emotions and her responses to their thoughts under tight control. Whenever she is around people, she focuses most of her attention on trying to block their thoughts and maintaining a calm demeanor. The day she met her first vampire, she learned that she could not hear vampires' thoughts. Time spent in their company is blissfully quiet. This is Sookie's chance for a (relatively) normal relationship. As the series continues, she finds that her disability is considered a gift in the supernatural community. Among supernaturals, her telepathy is valued, while humans continue to treat her as "crazy Sookie."

Known Associates: Sookie's mother and father died when she was seven. Her grandmother, Adele Hale Stackhouse, took in Sookie and her brother, Jason. At the outset of the series, Sookie lives with her grandmother, while Jason lives in town. As far as Sookie knows, her only other relatives are her grandmother's brother (Sookie and Jason's Uncle Bartlett Hale) and an estranged cousin, Hadley.

Sookie works for Sam Merlotte at Merlotte's bar. Sam usually tends bar. When Sam needs a night off, Vietnam veteran Terry Bellefleur fills in for him. Most of the staff at the bar come and go, but Sookie's friend Arlene works as a waitress there throughout the series. Four times married (and four times divorced), Arlene is always on the lookout for her next true love, and she dates different men in different books. The Bon Temps police force includes officers Kenya Jones and Kevin Prior, Detective Andy Bellefleur, and Sheriff Bud Dearborn. When the series begins, vampires have recently revealed themselves, and the first one that Sookie meets is her neighbor, Bill Compton. He takes her to the Shreveport vampire bar, *Fangtasia*, and introduces her to its co-owners, Eric Northman and Pam. People Sookie sees often include her friends, JB du Rone, Tara Thornton, and her brother's best friend, Hoyt Fortenberry.

Premise: The creatures of myth are real, and have been in hiding for millennia. The development of a synthetic blood adequate to sustain vampires made it possible for vampires to reveal their existence to the public. The vampires broadcast information about themselves: that they are people who have a severe allergic reaction to sunlight, silver, and garlic; who have abnormally long lifespans; and who happily subsist on synthetic blood. (Obviously the public-relations objective of presenting themselves as nonthreatening was more important than revealing the truth.) Different countries responded in different ways. The authorities in some countries immediately denounced vampires and began hunting them down. In the United States, vampires were viewed as a disadvantaged minority population suffering from a misunderstood illness, a population that must be protected against discrimination. American authorities worked to establish vampires' legal rights, thrill-seekers sought vampire companionship, and criminals created a black market for vampire blood. Other supernatural populations (such as werewolves and fairies) maintain secrecy. Over the course of the series, public sentiment against the vampires increases, led by a hate group that operates under the guise of a church (*The Fellowship of the Sun*).

Comment: At the 2006 WorldCon Science Fiction Convention, Charlaine Harris described *Dead Until Dark*'s rocky road to publication. The novel was repeatedly rejected, and editors' comments were contemptuous. They were brutal, so much so that Ms. Harris's agent refused to let her see some of the rejection letters. After two years, and many rejections, John Morgan of Ace accepted it. Soon after publication, the book was short-listed for the Agatha, the Dilys, and the Compton Crook Awards. It won the Anthony Award for best paperback novel for 2002. The HBO television show *True Blood* is based on the series.

The events in *Definitely Dead* occur before Hurricane Katrina. The events in *All Together Dead* follow the disaster. With that benchmark, dates for the series are extrapolated, usually based on Sookie's age. Sometimes, when characters are thinking about ages, they may misplace a year or two, so the chronology may not be entirely correct. There are some questions about where the short stories fit into the chronology. Colonel Flood's presence in *Fangtasia,* in "Dracula Night," was one element that was used to place that short story in the sequence. Unless otherwise indicated in the "Associates" section, characters listed are human.

Charlaine Harris's Web site at http://www.charlaineharris.com/ includes biographical information and interviews, information on the books and short stories, a link to her blog (on which she discusses books), and a page of Frequently Asked Questions.

Literary Magic & Mayhem: Sookie is naïve and has been taught her entire life that there is something wrong with her (her telepathy). She is embarrassed by her "disability." She does her best to think well of others, a sweet-natured resolution that breaks down when she can hear their thoughts. She works so hard to get along in this world that readers quickly come to feel protective of her. One theme that runs through the book is how people treat those who are "other." Sookie has been in that category all of her life. Now that the vampires have gone public, they have become the focus for people who are looking for a target for hatred and abuse. Even the relatively decent townspeople are quick to lump all vampires together, to think the worst of all vampires based on the bad behavior of a few, and to act as if the lives of those who are different are worth little.

Explorations: One theme running through these books is how people treat those who are different. How does Sookie see herself? Who taught her that her gift was a disability? How do different people treat Sookie? What does she expect?

How does Sookie treat those who are different from "regular" humans?

How are characters changed by their relationships? Is Sookie's sense of self strong enough that she remains true to her values? Is Arlene's? How strong are the core values of others?

To what extent do different humans differentiate between vampires? How many people see the vampires as individuals?

As the series develops, one value Sookie wrestles with is loyalty. Should her first loyalty be to the humans who shunned her, or to the supernatural community that has valued and protected her?

THE CASES

1. ***Dead Until Dark.*** New York: Ace Books: Berkley Pub. Group, 2001, 260 p. ISBN: 0441008534.

BON TEMPS (A SMALL TOWN IN NORTHERN LOUISIANA), SPRING 2004. Sookie has wanted to meet a vampire ever since they revealed their existence to the world. Within hours of meeting Bill Compton, a vampire, she saves his life. Within days, she sees that life at risk once more, as single women in Bon Temps are found not just murdered, but also bitten. Sookie is sure that "Vampire Bill," as he is called, is innocent (at least of those murders), and she sets out to investigate, in an effort to protect him.

ASSOCIATES: Adele Hale Stackhouse—*Sookie's grandmother;* Bartlett Hale—*Adele's brother, Sookie's great-uncle;* Jason Stackhouse—*Sookie's brother;* Sam Merlotte—*shape-shifter: usually changes into a dog, owner of Merlotte's bar,*

Sookie's boss; Terry Bellefleur—*bartender;* Layfayette Reynold—*cook;* Dawn Green, Charlsie Tooten, and Arlene—*waitresses;* Rene Lenier—*Arlene's ex-husband, they are dating once again;* Lisa—*Arlene's five-year-old daughter;* Coby—*Arlene's eight-year-old son.*

Detective Andy Bellefleur and Sheriff Bud Dearborn—*head the murder investigation;* Officers Kenya Jones and Kevin Prior—*work the case;* Mike Spencer—*the Parrish Coroner;* Bill Compton—*vampire, he accedes to Sookie's grandmothers request that he speak of his time in the War Between the States to her historical group, the Descendents of the Glorious Dead;* Diane—*vampire;* Liam—*vampire, his companion is Janella Lennox;* Malcolm—*vampire, whose companion is Jerry;* Eric Northman—*vampire, who is co-owner of the Shreveport vampire bar, Fangtasia;* Pam—*vampire, Eric's business partner;* Long Shadow—*vampire, Fangtasia's bartender;* Bubba—*vampire, his existence explains all the strange sightings over the years;* young Harlen Ives—*vampire from Minneapolis.*

Liz Barrett—*is dating Jason;* Mack and Denise Rattray—*vampire drainers;* Portia Bellefleur—*attorney;* Mr. Sterling Norris; Hoyt—*Jason's best friend;* Maxine Fortenberry—*Hoyt's mother;* JB du Rone—*who is beautiful and somewhat simple;* Sid Matt Lancaster—*a lawyer;* Desiree—*who is sent to Bill as a gift from Eric;* Dr. Sonntag—*who introduces herself to J.B.;* Tina—*Sookie's cat,* and Dean—*the collie.*

2. ***Living Dead in Dallas.*** **New York: Ace Books: Berkley Pub. Group, 2002, 262 p. ISBN: 0441009239.**

BON TEMPS, LOUISIANA AND DALLAS, TEXAS, FALL 2004. Sookie has already learned that there are things that science cannot explain; she thinks of herself as straddling the boundary between the world of normal people and the world of supernaturals. The funny thing is that while she gives her loyalty to the normal people, the society that values her is the vampires'. Sookie is faced with two mysteries in this volume. One is close to home: the murder of a friend. The other is in Dallas. Sookie made a deal with Eric, that if she used her telepathy to identify the criminal humans preying on the vampires, those humans, and others who are implicated, would not be killed. Eric has now gone a step further, and offered her services (at a substantial fee) to the vampires of Dallas. One of their nestmates has gone missing, and they fear he has been kidnapped, perhaps killed. In the course of the investigation, Sookie's life is threatened by humans! People belonging to a church called *The Fellowship of the Sun* target her as someone who aids and abets vampires. Sookie must rely on other supernaturals to save her.

ASSOCIATES: Jason Stackhouse—*Sookie's brother;* Bill Compton—*vampire, is dating Sookie;* Sam Merlotte—*shape-shifter: usually changes into a collie, owner of Merlotte's bar, seems interested in dating Sookie;* Terry Bellefleur—*bartender;* Layfayette Reynold—*cook;* and Anthony Bolivar—*vampire, cook;*

Arlene, Charlsie Tooten, Danielle Gray, and Holly Cleary—*waitresses;* Micah—*Charlsie's husband.*

Liz Barrett—*is dating Jason;* Hoyt Fortenberry—*Jason's best friend;* Officer Kevin Prior, Alcee Beck, and Sheriff Bud Dearborn—*investigate the murder;* Detective Andy Bellefleur—*who is not (officially) investigating this case;* Attorney Portia Bellefleur—*Andy's sister, is also not officially involved in the case.*

Tara Thornton—*Sookie's friend;* Benedict "Eggs" Tallie—*Tara's boyfriend;* JB du Rone—*Benedict's friend;* Mike Spencer—*Bon Temps' funeral home director and coroner;* Jan Fowler—*partied with Lafayette;* Cleo and Tom Hardaway—*were at that same party;* Dean—*the collie;* Eric Northman—*vampire, who dresses in spandex to help Sookie find the truth;* Pam—*vampire, one of Eric's oldest friends;* Chow—*vampire, Fangtasia's bartender;* Stan Davis—*who leads the vampires of Dallas;* Isabel—*vampire, she has a human lover;* Hugo Ayres—*Isabel's lover;* Farrell—*vampire;* Rachel—*vampire;* Joseph Velasquez—*vampire;* Trudi Pfeiffer—*Joseph's human girlfriend;* Dr. Ludwig—*species unknown, works for Eric;* Bethany Rogers—*waitress at the Dallas vampire bar called "The Bat's Wing";* Re-Bar—*bouncer at The Bat's Wing;* Godfrey—*vampire, a renouncer;* Steve Newlin—*who runs The Fellowship of the Sun;* Sarah Newlin—*Steve's wife;* Polly Blythe—*the Fellowship ceremonies officer;* Gabe—*who works for The Fellowship;* Barry the bellboy—*telepath;* Luna Garza—*were-bat;* Dr. Josephus—*probably a shape-shifter;* Callisto—*maenad.*

3. *Club Dead.* New York: Ace Books, 2003, 258 p. ISBN: 0441010512.

Bon Temps, Louisiana and Jackson, Mississippi, December 2004. Bill has been kidnapped, and the vampires of Louisiana need him found. At least, they need the knowledge that he put into his database, and, since they can't find the database, they need to rescue Bill. (Vampires are nothing if not practical.) They come to Sookie for help. Even though she knows that Bill has betrayed her, Sookie pretends to know nothing of the database. She's playing a dangerous game, but she wants Bill rescued and she can't rescue him by herself. She heads for Mississippi, with a werewolf as a guide, and begins searching for Bill.

Associates: Sookie's co-workers at Merlotte's bar include Sam Merlotte—*shape-shifter: usually changes into a dog, bar owner;* Arlene—*waitress, her latest flame is Buck Foley;* Charlsie Tooten—*waitress;* and Sue Jennings—*waitress.*

Jason—*Sookie's brother;* Bill Compton—*vampire, he was Sookie's lover, now he has left Sookie;* Lorena—*the vampire who turned Bill into a vampire, she was his lover for years and now she has called him back to her;* Alcide Herveaux—*werewolf, helps Sookie in Jackson Mississippi;* Janice Herveaux Phillips—*Alcide's sister;* Dell Phillips—*Janice's husband;* Terence—*werewolf, Alcide's packmaster;* Jerry Falcon—*werewolf;* Debbie Pelt—*were-lynx, Alcide's ex-fiancé;* Charles Clausen—*were-owl, Debbie's new fiancé;* Bubba—*vampire who can sometimes be coaxed into singing;* Eric Northman—*vampire, Sheriff of Area 5 of Louisiana;* Pam and Chow—*vampires who answer to Eric;* Russell Edgington—*vampire, the King of Mississippi;* Betty Jo Pickard, Ray Don, Bernard, Lorena, and Franklin Mott—*a few of the vampires of Mississippi;* Tara Thornton—*Sookie's friend, Tara is dating Franklin Mott (vampire);* Talbot—*Russell's lover;* and Steve Newlin—*who is recognized by Sookie.*

4. ***Dead to the World.*** New York: Ace Books, 2004, 291 p. ISBN: 0441011675.

BON TEMPS, LOUISIANA, DECEMBER 2004–JANUARY 2005. On the last night of the year, Sookie finds a man running naked down the road. He's a vampire. He's not precisely a friend, but she can't just leave him out in the cold. Her generosity drags her into the middle of a war between different parts of the supernatural communities of Shreveport. Within a day of her taking the vampire into her home, Sookie's brother Jason disappears. Sookie hopes that she will find her brother when they find the villains who are trying to take over Northern Louisiana. Unfortunately, the help so freely offered by the humans of Bon Temps cannot be effective if they don't know the whole story; Sookie cannot reveal it because lives depend on her secrecy.

ASSOCIATES: Jason—*Sookie's brother is dating Crystal Norris;* Crystal Norris—*were-panther;* Carla Rodriguez—*Jason's ex-girlfriend;* Shirley "Catfish" Hennessey—*Jason's boss;* Hoyt Fortenberry—*Jason's best friend;* Sookie's coworkers at Merlotte's bar are: Sam Merlotte—*shape-shifter who prefers to change into a collie*, Alphonse "Tack" Petacki—*the cook;* Arlene—*a waitress who is dating Tack*, Holly Cleary—*Wiccan and waitress*, Danielle Gray—*Wiccan and waitress*, Charlsie Tooten—*waitress;* Chuck Beecham, Terrell, attorney Sid Matt Lancaster, Officer Kevin Prior, Officer Kenya Jones, Detective Andy Bellefleurs, and Andy's sister, Portia—*are bar patrons.*

Packmaster Colonel John "James" Flood, Alcide Herveaux, Maria-Star Cooper, Verena Rose Yancy, Emilio, Sid, Portugal, Culpepper, Amanda, and Parnell—*are the Shreveport werewolves;* Debbie Pelt—*were-lynx, Alcide's girlfriend;* Marnie "Hallow" Stonebrook—*leader of the witches, she attacked Eric when he indicated that he was not interested in her;* Mark—Hallow's brother; Parton, Chelsea, and Jane—*are witches who Sookie tries to save;* the vampires of Shreveport include Eric Northman—*Sheriff of Louisiana Area Five;* Pam—*Eric's business partner and friend;* Chow—*Fangtasia's bartender;* Gerald and Clancy—*Pam's nestmates;* Bubba—*who is disappointed that Sookie and Bill are no longer together;* Belinda and Ginger—*are humans who work at Fangtasia;* Bill Compton—*vampire, he is in Peru for the majority of the story;* Calvin Norris—*packmaster of the were-panthers of HotShot;* Crystal—*were-panther, Calvin's niece;* Dawn—*werepanther, Crysta's sister;*

Felton Norris—*werepanther, their neighbor;* Tara Thornton—*one of Sookie's best friends;* Claudine Crane—*a fairy who helps Sookie;* and Shreveport Police Officer Detective Dan Coughlin.

5. "Dracula Night," in *Many Bloody Returns.* New York: Ace Books, 2007, p. 1–20. ISBN: 9780441015221.

SHREVEPORT, LOUISIANA, FEBRUARY 2005. Halloween and Dracula's birthday (February 8) are the only two holidays that vampires observe. Eric Northman is particularly excited about Dracula's birthday. Legend has it that Dracula himself chooses to attend one birthday celebration each year, surprising the hosts. Eric is certain that his celebration at *Fangtasia* will be the one so honored this year. He invites Sookie and she buys a new dress (on sale) to come to the party.

ASSOCIATES: Eric Northman—*vampire, one of Fangtasia's owners;* Pam—*vampire, who co-owns the bar;* Others at the party include Bill Compton—*vampire;* Colonel Flood—*werewolf;* Calvin Norris—*werepanther;* Lyle—*vampire;* Clancy—*vampire, Fangtasia's manager;* Milos Griesniki—*vampire, Fangtasia's new bartender;* Sam Merlotte—*shape-shifter: usually changes into a dog, owner of Merlotte's;* Arlene—*waitress at Merlotte's;* Hoyt Fortenberry—*Merlotte's customer.*

6. "Fairy Dust," in *Powers of Detection: Stories of Mystery and Fantasy.* New York: Ace Books, 2004, p. 69–88. ISBN: 0441011977.

BON TEMPS, LOUISIANA, SPRING 2005. Claudine's sister and brother, Claudia and Claude, worked at a strip club called "*Hooligans.*" Then Claudia disappeared. Claudine knew Claudia had been murdered when Claudine's spirit visited Claudine to say goodbye. Fairies leave no earthly remains; Claude and Claudine cannot even prove that their sister was murdered. But they know, and they know that only three people had the opportunity to kill her. All three have motives. Claudia was not a particularly nice fairy; she made plenty of enemies. Claude and Claudine need Sookie's help to identify which of the three suspects is a murderer.

ASSOCIATES: Claudine—*fairy;* Claude—*fairy, Claudine's brother;* Rita Child—*who owns Hooligans;* Jeff Pucket—*a bouncer at Hooligans;* Barry Barber—*a.k.a. Ben Simpson,who dances at Hooligans.*

7. "Dancers in the Dark," in *Night's Edge.* Don Mills, Ontario: HQN Books, c2004, p. 251–377. ISBN: 0373770103.

RHODES, ILLINOIS, 2005. Rue May is running from her past, running from the woman who she used to be, Layla LaRue LeMay, and running from the man who almost killed her. When he catches up with her, it's up to her friends to save her.

ASSOCIATES: Sylvia Dayton—*owner of Blue Moon and Black Moon Enterprises;* dancers include Thompson—*vampire;* Sean O'Rourke—*vampire;*

Julie; Megan; Hallie; Rick—*vampire;* Phil—*vampire;* Karl—*vampire;* David—*vampire;* Abilene—*vampire;* and Mustafa.

Denny James—*the driver;* Haskell—*vampire, provides protection to the dancers;* Carver Hutton IV—*a guest at Connie and John Jaslow's party;* Charles Brody—*a boor;* Kinshasa—*Rue's neighbor;* Sergeant Will Kryder—*retired;* Judith—*Sergeant Kryder's wife.*

8. *Dead as a Doornail.* New York: Ace Books, 2005, 295 p. ISBN: 0441012795.

Bon Temps, Louisiana, 2005. The shifters are being victimized. It's particularly frightening because no one except other supernaturals knows of their existence. It seems unlikely that the police will ever solve the crimes, since they appear to be random killings of humans who have nothing in common. The shifter community must undertake their own investigation. Some may leap to judgment; many believe that the most likely suspect is Sookie's brother Jason, and, to a few in the shifter community, summary execution seems like a sensible way to lower the risks.

One of the shifters who was attacked was Sookie's boss Sam. Sam sends a request for a stand-in bartender to Eric, and Eric sends the charming vampire Charles Twining. Sookie's house is set afire by an arsonist. It's suspected that the attack was planned by a member of the hate group, *The Fellowship of the Sun.*

Colonel John Flood's death leads to competition for the leadership of the *Long Tooth Werewolf Pack.* Alcide Herveaux (werewolf) asks Sookie to attend the competition and to use her gift to detect any cheating. At the competition Sookie meets the were-tiger Quinn.

Associates: Jason—*were-panther, Sookie's brother;* Crystal Norris—*were-panther, who is dating Jason;* Sookie's coworkers at Merlotte's bar include bar owner Sam Merlotte—*shape-changer: usually a dog;* Terry Bellefleur—*bartender;* Charles Twining—*vampire, bartender;* Sweetie Des Arts—*cook;* Anthony Bolivar—*vampire, cook;* Arlene—*waitress, who meets and dates arson investigator Dennis Pettibone in this book;* Holly Cleary—*Wiccan, waitress;* Danielle Gray—*Wiccan, waitress;* Charlsie Tooten—*waitress*, and Jada—*waitress.* Vampires at the vampire bar Fangtasia include Eric Northman and Pam—*Fangtasia's co-owners;* Charles Twining—*bartender*, Thalia, Indira, and Maxwell Lee.

Calvin Norris—*werepanther, HotShot packmaster;* Terry—*werepanther, his daughter;* Maryelizabeth Norris—*werepanther, Terry's mother;* Dawson—*werewolf, he acts as Calvin's guard when Calvin is hospitalized;* Patrick Furnan—*werewolf, contender for the position of packmaster of the Long-Tooth Pack;* Jackson Herveaux—*werewolf, is the other contender for packmaster;* Alcide Herveaux—*werewolf, Jackson's son;* Christine Larrabee—*werewolf, widow of packmater Colonel Flood;* Libby Furnan—*werewolf, Patrick's wife;* Cal Myers—*werewolf, Furnan's second;* Amanda—*werewolf;* Maria-Star Cooper—*werewolf;* Claudine Crane—*fairy who wants to protect Sookie;* Claude Crane—*fairy, Claudine's brother;* Quinn—*were-tiger, who is at the packmaster contest to keep the candidates honest;* and Dr. Ludwig—*who is there to keep them alive (if possible).*

Private investigators Jack Leeds and Lily Bard Leeds—*are searching for information on the missing Debbie Pelt;* Franklin Mott—*vampire, has given Sookie's friend to another vampire;* Tara Thornton—*Sookie's friend;* Mickey—*vampire who is dating Tara;* Justine—*Jeff Marriot's mother;* Jay—*Jeff Marriot's brother, they are certain that Jeff was not a bigot.*

Bill Compton—*vampire, who is dating Selah Pumphrey;* Selah Pumphrey—*real-estate agent;* Portia Bellefleur—*attorney;* Jeff LaBeff—*garbageman;* Mark Duffy—*college student;* Detective Andy Bellefleur—*who is dating Halleigh Robinson and wants to know if she is completely human;* Halleigh Robinson—*schoolteacher, who was impressed by Claude;* Shirley "Catfish" Hunter, Hoyt Fortenberry, and Ralph Tooten—*serve in the volunteer fire department;* Greg Aubert—*witch, Sookie's insurance agent;* Randall Shurtliff—*building contractor;* Delia—*his wife;* Sheriff Bud Dearborn; Dago Guglielmi; Liz Baldwin; and Jane Bodehouse.

9. "One Word Answer," in *Bite.* New York.: Berkeley, 2005, p. 33–58. ISBN: 051513970X.

Bon Temps, Louisiana, 2005. Mr. Cataliades, a half-demon lawyer, comes to bring sad news to Sookie. Hadley, her cousin, had "an unfortunate incident" and is dead. She had been out of touch for so long that Sookie hadn't even known that she had become a vampire, and certainly hadn't known that Hadley had been a favorite of the vampire Queen of Louisiana. Sookie is told that Waldo (another of the Queen's favorites) and Hadley had gone to a "City of the Dead," an aboveground cemetery in New Orleans, to try to raise the ghost of voodoo queen Marie Laveau. There Hadley had been set upon and killed. Sookie learns enough about Hadley's death to choose her own method of revenge, but her plans are different from those of the Queen.

Associates: Mr. Cataliades—*a half-demon who works for the vampire Queen of Louisiana;* Bubba, Waldo, Bill Compton, and the Queen of Louisiana—*are all vampires.*

10. *Definitely Dead.* New York: Ace Books, 2006, 324 p. ISBN: 0441014003.

Bon Temps, Louisiana, March 2005. It's spring, and love is in the air. A lot of wedding planning is going on in the shifter and human worlds (much to the profit of Tara Thornton of *Tara's Togs*). Things are more complex in the vampire world. The big marriage and tactical alliance have already taken place. The Queen of Louisiana, Sophie-Anne LeClerq, married the King of

Arkansas, Peter Threadgill. News of the marriage plan was a blow to Sookie's cousin Hadley, who had been made vampire by Sophie-Anne and who had become Sophie-Anne's favorite. In a fit of jealousy, she stole one of the wedding gifts; its loss could cause Sophie-Anne to lose her kingdom. With Hadley dead (definitely and finally dead), there is no one who knows the location of the missing bracelet. Sophie-Anne needs to find it. Sookie doesn't mind helping, but she's really more concerned about the death of the messenger that the Queen sent to her and about the corpse she found in her cousin's closet.

When Sookie is in the hospital, she is (maybe unfortunately) visited by both Eric Northman (vampire) and Bill Compton (vampire). This is the book in which Sookie's feelings for Bill are finally "definitely dead."

Sookie has always tried to keep a low profile, but when Holly's son Cody goes missing, Sookie quietly steps in to help the police.

ASSOCIATES: Jason—*were-panther, Sookie's brother;* Crystal Norris—*were-panther, she is dating Jason;* Dr. Amy Ludwig—*a supernatural who provides Crystal with medical help;* Detective Andy Bellefleur—*who proposes to Halleigh;* Halleigh Robinson—*who says "yes" to Andy;* Portia Bellefleur—*Andy's sister;* Glen Vicks—*Portia's fiancé;* Calvin Norris—*werepanther, is ready to post the banns for Crystal and Jason;* Bill Compton—*vampire, is still dating a human real-estate agent;* Selah Pumphrey—*the real estate agent;* Quinn—*were-tiger, is dating Sookie.*

Barbara and Gordon Pelt—*werewolves, Debbie's parents, are still searching for answers about Debbie's disappearance;* Sandra—*werewolf, their daughter, will do whatever it takes to get those answers.*

Cody—*waitress Holly's son;* Halleigh Robinson—*Cody's teacher;* Mrs. Garfield—*the school Principal;* Madelyn Pepper—*custodian;* Detective Andy Bellefleur and patrolmen Kevin Prior and Kenya Jones—*search for Cody;* Sheriff Bud Dearborn—*was on the spot, but doesn't know what happened.*

Detective Dan Coughlin—*investigates the attack on Sookie and Quinn;* Detective Cal Myers—*werewolf;* Alcide Herveaux—*werewolf;* Maria-Star Cooper—*werewolf;* and Amada—*werewolf, owner of the werewolf bar, The Hair of the Dog;* George and Clete—*werewolves involved in the second attack.*

Sam Merlotte—*shape-changer: usually a dog, the owner of Merlotte's bar;* Callie Collins—*the cook;* Rafe Prudhomme—*who is involved in the hate-group, the Fellowship of the Sun, and is dating Arlene;* Arlene—*waitress, she is attending Fellowship meetings with her new man;* Holly Cleary—*Wiccan, waitress;* Danielle Gray—*Wiccan, waitress;* Tanya Grissom—*the new waitress.*

Mr. Cataliades—*the Queen of Louisiana's lawyer;* Amelia Broadway—*witch, Hadley's landlord;* Bob Jessup, Patsy Sellers, and Terencia Rodriquez—*are Amelia's co-practitioners;* Jake Purifoy—*werewolf who is deceased and rising;*

Sophie-Anne Leclerq—*the Queen of Louisiana;* Rasul, Melanie, Chester, Bubba, Sigebert, Wybert and Andre—*are the queen's guards;* Peter Threadgill—*vampire, the King of Arkansas, Sophie-Anne Leclerq's husband;* Jade Flower—*one of Peter's guards;* Everett O'Dell Smith—*who is sent by the Queen to help Sookie pack Hadley's belongings;* Lieutenant Governor David Thrash—*werewolf;* Genevieve—*werewolf, his wife.*

11. "Tacky," in *My Big Fat Supernatural Wedding.* New York.: St. Martin's Griffin, 2006, p. 201–29. ISBN: 0312343604; 9780312343606.

RHODES, ILLINOIS, JUNE 2005. Generally, vampires and werewolves do not socialize. A vampire–werewolf wedding is unheard of, and, with vampires having made themselves known to humans, and with werewolves still passing as humans, it's dangerous. There are many humans who are not only willing, but also anxious, to stop a wedding between a vampire and a person that they believe is human. Dhalia, who is to be a bridesmaid at her friend Taffy's wedding, is worried.

ASSOCIATES: Dhalia Lynley-Chivers—*vampire;* Glenda Shore—*vampire;* Taffy—*vampire, the bride;* Don Swiftfoot—*werewolf, the groom;* Todd—*werewolf;* Amber—*werewolf and Don's ex-wife;* Cedric—*vampire, the area sheriff;* Fortunata—*vampire.*

12. "Lucky" short story in *Unusual Suspects* edited by Dana Stabenow. New York.: Ace Books, 2008, p. 1–28. ISBN: 9780441016372.

BON TEMPS, LOUISIANA, SEPTEMBER 2005. Greg Aubert believes that someone is sabotaging his insurance agency and asks Sookie to investigate. (He's afraid that if he asks the police they will find out that he's a witch.)

ASSOCIATES: Greg Aubert—*witch, Sookie's insurance agent, admires the warding spells around Sookie's house;* Amelia Broadway—*witch, Sookie's housemate, she put up the wards;* Marge Barker—*Greg Aubert's secretary;* Christie—*his wife;* "Little Greg"—*his 19-year-old son;* Lindsay—*his daughter;* Dustin—*Lindsay's new boyfriend, he is secretive about how he spends his days;* Terry Bellefleur—*who had bad luck with his dogs until he took his insurance business to Greg;* Bob the cat—*a mistake that Amelia is trying to rectify;* Bill Compton—*vampire;* Dustin—*vampire;* Diane Porchia—*the insurance agent of Liberty South;* Alma Dean—*her secretary;* Bailey Smith—*insurance agent;* John Robert Briscoe—*insurance agent;* Sally Lundy—*his secretary.*

13. *All Together Dead.* New York: Ace Books, 2007, 323 p. ISBN: 9780441014941.

RHODES, ILLINOIS, SEPTEMBER 2005. Feelings are running high against the vampires. *The Fellowship of the Sun* finds new converts every day. Sookie's long time friend, Arlene, is one of them. Sookie knows that she herself is different, maybe not a vampire, but not altogether human either. She also knows many "supes" (supernatural beings) who are wonderful people. The

Queen of Louisiana, Sophie Ann Leclerq, has offered Sookie a temporary job: to be part of the Queen's entourage at the vampire convention. Sookie is excited, not frightened. It hasn't occurred to her that she is the only credible witness to the King of Arkansas's death. It has occurred to her to wonder about her own loyalties when she reads human minds to gain information for a vampire queen, but Sookie knows that the Queen is innocent (at least relatively innocent, at least of the crime of murdering the King of Arkansas). Many people warn Sookie against attending the convention, all for different reasons. Sookie refuses to heed their warnings. She hasn't been there long before she discovers murdered vampires and a bomb planted near the Queen's room. By the end of the book, she will know the identity of the murderer(s) and the bomber.

ASSOCIATES: Amelia Broadway—*witch, Sookie's housemate;* Bob—*who is currently Bob the cat;* Jason Stackhouse—*were-panther, Sookie's brother, in this book Jason marries Crystal;* Crystal Norris—*were-panther, she admires other men while she marries Jason;* Quinn—*were-tiger, he and Sookie are dating;* Calvin Norris—*were-panther, Crystal's uncle;* Hoyt Fortenberry—*Jason's best friend;* Frannie—*Quinn's sister;* Tara Thornton and JB du Rone—*are Sookie's closest friends;* Sam Merlotte—*shape-changer: usually a dog, owner of the bar where Sookie works;* Arlene—*a waitress, she is still attending Fellowship of the Sun meetings with Rafe Prudhomme;* Holly Cleary—*Wiccan, a waitress;* Danielle Gray—*Wiccan, a waitress;* Halleigh Robinson—*who has a wedding shower;* Lynette Robinson, Portia Bellefleurs, Elmer Claire Vaudry, Marcia Albanese, Selah Pumphrey, Tara Thornton, and Maxine Fortenberry—*are wedding shower guests;* Eric Northman and Pam—*vampires, co-own the bar Fangtasia;* Clancy—*vampire, he manages the bar;* Felicia—*vampire, bartender;* Indira, Maxwell Lee, and Thalia—*are the vampires who take shifts serving as tourist attractions at the bar;* Bobby Burnham—*human, he is Eric's business manager.*

Convention attendees include 16 vampire Kings and Queens of the southern and midwestern states. They include Isaiah—*The King of Kansas;* Russell Edgington—*The King of Mississippi who marries Bartlett Crowe at the convention;* Bartlett Crowe—*the King of Indiana;* Stan Davis—*the King of Texas;* and Sophie-Anne Leclerq—*The Queen of Louisiana.*

Each of the Kings and Queens have their own retinue. The King of Kansas has Batanya and Clovache—*Britlingens, bodyguards.* The King of Texas has Joseph Valasquez—*his sergeant at arms;* Rachel—*vampire;* and *Barry Horowitz—telepath, who is now known as Barry Bellboy.* The dead King of Arkansas has a delegation, including Jennifer Cater—*vampire, who is bringing a wrongful death suit against the Queen of Louisiana;* Simon Maimonides—*part-demon, a lawyer;* and Henrik Feith—*vampire.* The

Ancient Pythoness—*vampire, is the judge for the trial.* The Louisiana delegation includes Andre, Sigebert, Rasul, and Carla—*Sophie-Anne's guards;* Eric Northman—*Sheriff of Area Five;* Gervaise—*Sheriff of Area Four;* Cleo Babbitt—*Sheriff of Area Three;* Pam—*a vampire;* Bill Compton—*a vampire;* Jake Purifoy—*a werewolf who was turned into a vampire;* Mr. Cataliades—*part-demon;* Diantha—*part-demon and niece of Mr. Cataliades;* Johan Glassport—*human, a specialist in vampire law;* and Sookie.

Carla Danvers—*human, Sookie's roommate;* Todd Donati—*Chief of Hotel Security;* Christian Baruch—*vampire, the hotel manager-architect who fancies himself as the next King of Louisiana;* Julian Trout—*a weather witch;* Olive—*Julian's wife;* Sean and Layla—*vampires, dancers of Blue Moon Productions;* Claudine—*fairy;* Tara Thornton—*Sookie's friend;* and Arlene—*who tells Sookie to stay away from the vampires.*

14. ***From Dead to Worse.*** New York: Ace Books, 2008, 350 p. ISBN: 9780441015891.

BON TEMPS, LOUISIANA, OCTOBER 2005. Hurricane Katrina killed both humans and supernaturals. The hurricane also destroyed homes and other property, leaving some of the survivors impoverished.

The hurricane demolished many of the vampire Queen of Louisiana's holdings. Suspicion that she murdered her husband damaged her politically, and an attack by *The Fellowship of the Sun* left her gravely injured. She's weak. The power struggle for the leadership of the Shreveport Werewolf Pack left the pack divided. The pack is weak. Nature abhors a vacuum. The absence of effective leadership is a strong pull for the ambitious. Sookie is neither vampire nor werewolf, but she is affiliated with both of those communities.

Sookie's lover, the were-tiger Quinn, has been missing for weeks, so she is on her own. Sookie is no match, physically, for even the weakest vampire or werewolf, but she is valiant and will do her best to help her friends. One ally of Sookie is her roommate Amelia. Amelia has great power, but insists on experimenting with spells that are beyond her skill. She had to leave New Orleans in some haste. She had turned her lover, Bob, into a cat, and then she found that she could not turn him back. Amelia regards this as a simple mistake. Her coven would consider her lapse in judgment to be a criminal act. Amelia decided to hide out in Bon Temps, avoiding her mentor, Octavia, until she can rectify matters by turning Bob back into a human. She hasn't made much progress.

Unfortunately, the greatest constant in Sookie's supernatural relationships seems to be the enmity of Debbie Pelt. Debbie has been dead for months. Debbie's sister Sandra is bent on revenge and hires an agent to make Sookie miserable.

A powerful fairy demands that Eric bring Sookie to him. Eric refuses until he understands why the fairy wants to meet her. Through the fairy, Sookie learns more about her family and learns the whereabouts of Hadley's son.

Vampire Bill pledges his undying love and offers to die for Sookie. (It's difficult to see how his death would improve the situation, but it's a grand gesture. On the other hand, Eric hints that any harm to Sookie will lead to unimaginable misery from an unnamed source . . . less romantic, but possibly more effective.)

There are many mysteries in the book. Who killed Maria Star? What happened to Quinn? Why has Tanya Grissom befriended Crystal Stackhouse? Where is Hadley's child? Sookie actively searches for answers to all of them but is not successful on her own. Many of the mysteries are answered through the efforts of others, or are simply resolved by events as they unfold.

ASSOCIATES: Halleigh Robinson—*a bride who asks Sookie to stand in as one of her bridesmaids;* Andy Bellefleur—*Halleigh's groom;* Portia Bellefleur—*another bride, it's a double wedding;* Glen Vick—*Portia's groom;* Al Cumberland—*werewolf, the wedding photographer;* Maria-Star Cooper—*werewolf, his assistant;* Sam—*a shape-shifter, is Sookie's boss, and tends bar at the wedding;* Bill Compton—*vampire, who seeks Sookie out to tell her his feelings;* Selah Pumphrey—*Bill's date, who overhears the exchange;* Calvin Norris—*were-panther;* Tanya Grissom—*were-fox, Calvin's date;* Terry Bellefleur—*who helps out with the bar at the wedding;* Jonathan—*a vampire;* Amelia Broadway—*witch, Sookie's housemate;* Bob Jessup—*who is currently Bob the cat;* Copley Carmichael—*Amelia's father;* Octavia Fant—*Amelia's mentor;* Tyrese Marley—*Copley Carmichael's chauffeur, Tyrese earns Sookie's gratitude by splitting some wood;* Holly Cleary—*Sookie's coworker;* Hoyt Fortenberry—*is dating Holly;* Maxine and Ed—*are Hoyt's parents;* Jason—*a were-panther, is Sookie's brother;* Crystal—*a were-panther, Jason's wife, is pregnant;* Eric Northman—*vampire,he regains his memory of the time he spent with Sookie in this book;* Pam—*vampire, dates Amelia;* Bill Compton—*Sookie's neighbor;* Pam—*Eric's business partner;* Sigebert—*an ancient vampire.* The vampires of Louisians all owe fealty to the vampire Queen of Louisiana, Sophie-Anne Leclerq. Victor Madden, Sandy Sechrest, and Jonathan—*are vampires who owe fealty to the King of Nevada, Felipe de Castro.* Barbara Beck—*librarian, the wife of police officer Alcee Beck;* Dove Beck—*is Alcee's cousin.*

Patrick Furnan—*werewolf, packmaster;* Alcide Herveaux—*werewolf, he will challenge Patrick Furnan;* Tray Dawson and Amanda—*are werewolves who have aligned themselves with Alcide Herveaux;* Cal Myers—*is a werewolf who Patrick believes is loyal;* Priscilla Hebert—*werewolf, who is related to Cal;* Quinn and his mother—*are both were-tigers;* Frannie—*Quinn's sister;* Claudine—*a fairy who does her best to protect Sookie;* Claude—*a fairy who is insultingly indifferent to Sookie's ex-friend Arlene's charms;* Niall Brigant—*a fairy, Claude and Claudine's grandfather;* Remy Savoy—*who was once married to Sookie's cousin Hadley;* Hunter—*telepath, their 4-year-old son;* Kristen Duchesne—*Remy's girlfriend.*

15. "An Evening with Al Gore," a short story in *Blood Lite,* edited By Kevin J. Anderson. New York: Pocket Books, 2008, p. 167–90. ISBN: 1416567836; 9781416567837.

BRACEFIELD, MASSACHUSETTS, 200? Toddy Makepeace was inspired by a speech made by Al Gore. She and her husband agree to hold a benefit for the environment, hoping to raise both money and consciousness. They invite people whose companies are major polluters. If they don't agree to change their ways it's all right. Toddy has a Plan B.

ASSOCIATES: [some information has been omitted to avoid spoilers] Toddy—*an environmentalist;* Mark—*her husband;* Purcell and Deena Collville—*their friends;* Marchesa, Paula, Anna Clausen, and others.

16. "Gift Wrap," a short story in *Wolfsbane and Mistletoe* edited by Charlaine Harris and Toni L. P. Kelner. New York.: Ace Books, 2008, p. 1–18. ISBN: 9780441016334.

BON TEMPS, LOUISIANA, CHRISTMAS EVE 2005. Sookie is all alone on Christmas Eve. She decides to go for a walk in the woods and finds someone who needs her help. In this story Sookie takes some actions that are exactly what any reader would expect of her, but she takes one action that seems out of character. It is possible that she was influenced in ways that she could not anticipate, given what she knew.

ASSOCIATES: Preston Pardloe—*supernatural;* Ralph—*werewolf;* Curt—*werewolf;* Niall Brigant—*fairy, Sookie's great-grandfather.*

17. *Dead and Gone.* New York: Ace Books, 2009, 312 p. ISBN: 9780441017157.

BON TEMPS, LOUISIANA, JANUARY 2006. The shape-shifters reveal their existence to society and, for the most part, seem to be accepted. Within families acceptance is not always so easy. Some people feel that those they love deceived them. There are problems between Sam's mother and his stepfather and he goes back to Texas, leaving Sookie in charge of the bar.

Running the bar is a great deal of work. Sookie is happy to help Sam but, when someone they know is found murdered and crucified behind the bar, Sookie feels overwhelmed. Sookie's brother Jason is a suspect once more. Sookie is still angry with him because Jason tricked her into witnessing his wife Crystal's infidelity, but she wants her brother cleared of murder. She's willing to use her gift to try to find the murderer.

In this book there is a war on Earth between different factions of the fairies. Niall's enemies have realized that Niall loves Sookie and they look for a way to hurt him through harming or killing her. Remy Savoy calls to ask Sookie for help with his son Hunter. Sookie promises to come to help but not for a few weeks. (She doesn't want to tell Remy about the attempts on her life, but those attempts have alerted her to the danger of being known to the fae. Sookie won't go to see Hunter until the danger is past, because she is afraid that a visit from her would lead the fae to him.)

ASSOCIATES: Amelia Broadway—*a witch, Sookie's roommate;* Octavia Fant—*a witch who has closer friends than Sookie realized;* Sam—*a shape-shifter, Sookie's boss;* Holly—*wiccan, Sookie's co-worker and Hoyt's girlfriend;* Arlene—*who used to be Sookie's friend, but is now involved with the hate group Fellowship of the Sun;* Whit Spradlin—*Arlene's boyfriend and a Fellowship of the Sun official;* Jason—*a were-panther, Sookie's brother;* Mel Hart—*a were-panther, Jason's new sidekick;* Bill Compton—*a vampire, Sookie's first love;* Clancy—*a vampire, works for Eric;* Tray Dawson—*a werewolf, he is dating Amelia Broadway;* Terry Bellefleur—*a bartender, a Vietnam veteran who suffers from PTSD;* Antoine Lebrun—*Merlotte's short order cook;* D'Eriq—*who helps out in at the bar and is happy and excited about shape-shifters;* Tanya Grisson—*a were-fox who is seriously involved with Calvin Norris;* Sarah Jen—*a mail carrier who decides that Sam is a good man;* Bobby Burnham—*who works for Eric and is not a fan of Sookie;* Eric Northman—*a vampire who protects Sookie from the new King of Louisiana by tricking her into participating in a vampire marriage ceremony. In this book Eric tells Sookie about his past and how Appius Livius Ocella turned him into a vampire.* Pam—*a vampire who is Eric's business partner and Sookie's friend;* Thalia—*a vampire who works at Eric's bar;* Victor Madden—*a vampire who acts as the representative for Louisiana's new vampire king, Felipe de Castro;* Quinn—*a were-tiger who wants a private meeting with Sookie;* Special Agent Sara Weiss—*is from the New Orleans office of the FBI;* Special Agent Tom Lattesta—*is from the Rhodes office of the FBI;* Crystal Norris Stackhouse—*a were-panther who is Jason's pregnant (and cheating) wife;* Calvin Norris—*a were-panther, Crystal's uncle and the leader of the Hotshot pack;* Dawn—*a were-panther, Crystal's sister;* Jackie—*a were-panther who is Crystal's cousin;* Police Detective Andy Bellefleur, Police Detective Alcee Beck, and Sheriff Bud Dearborn—*law officers in Bon Temps;* Tara du Rone—*the pregnant owner of Tara's Togs and one of Sookie's oldest friends;* Louis Chambers—*a man from Octavia's past;* Diantha—*the part-demon niece of Mr. Cataliades;* Helen Ellis—*who provides babysitting for Arlene's children Coby and Lisa when Arlene needs them to get out of the house for a little while;* Donny Boling—*Whit's friend;* Jane Bodehouse—*an alcoholic who is trying to stay sober;* Bubba—*who is sent by Eric to protect Sookie;* Dr. Ludwig—*a surgeon to supernaturals.*

Niall—*the fairy prince is Sookie's great-grandfather;* Dermot—*a half-fairy who is one of Niall's three sons, he looks like Jason (Dermot's twin brother Fintan was Jason and Sookie's grandfather);* Dillon—*a fairy, one of Niall's sons;* Claude and Claudine—*fairies who are Dillon's children. Claudine is knitting baby clothing with very sharp needles.* Breandan—*the other fairy prince, Niall's nephew, rival, and enemy;* Lochlan and Neave—*fairies who are in league with Breandan.*

GRAVE SIGHT

Genres/Themes Crossed: Paranormal X Hard-Boiled Mystery.

Subjects/Character Types: Psychics (seeing the moment of someone's death) X Amateur detective (Contemporary).

Series/Stand-Alone: Relationships change and Harper makes a little progress in her personal quest during the course of the series. This series should be read in order.

Scene of the Crime: Present-day United States (the city varies, depending on the case).

Detective: Harper Connelly was struck by lightning when she was 15 years old; since then, she has been able to feel the presence of the dead when she is in the vicinity of their remains. She and her brother Tolliver started *Connelly Lang Recoveries*, a business that offers services that employ Harper's gifts, about four years before the events depicted in *Grave Sight.*

Known Associates: Family is important to Harper. She comes from a dysfunctional blended family. Harper's first family dissolved after her father went to prison; by that time her mother was probably a drug addict. When Mrs. Connelly (Harper's mother) remarried, she married another addict, Matt Lang (Tolliver's father); he came to the marriage with two sons, Tolliver and Mark. Mrs. Connelly already had two daughters, Cameron and Harper. It was not an idyllic second marriage for either, but it did produce two more children, Mariella and Gracie. Mariella and Gracie were neglected by their parents, who were too involved with their addictions to spare time for their children. Cameron, Harper and Tolliver basically raised Mariella and Gracie while trying to keep up appearances so that no one would guess at the disaster that was their home life. Mark, Tolliver's older brother, was living on his own. He would come by to make sure the family had food. When Harper was 17, Cameron was abducted as she was walking home from school. The investigation exposed the conditions at the Lang household, and Harper was put into foster care. Tolliver, at age 20, was placed with his brother, Mark. Three-year-old Mariella and five-year-old Gracie were placed with Harper's Aunt Iona and Uncle Will.

Premise: The world is filled with dead people. Harper can sense the presence of them all. As she describes it to Hollis:

> It's like a buzzing. A humming. In my bones, in my brain. It almost hurts. The closer I get, the more intense it gets. And when I'm close, when I'm in the body's presence, I see the death. (*Grave Sight,* p. 106)

She can find the remains, and when she does, she has some idea of who they were and she feels a little of what they felt in the last few seconds of their lives (which can be extremely disturbing). Unfortunately, she cannot see the other people who were with them when they died. She cannot see the face of a murderer. While she can't identify a murderer, the amount of information she can give about the death, when coupled with evidence from the body itself once she has found it, can revitalize the police investigation. In general, the police are often skeptical, suspicious, and even hostile to Harper—not trusting her gifts, or, for that matter, her. Harper and Tolliver feel that they have to stay and help the investigations in whatever way they can. The only advertising they have is by word of mouth. They can't afford to be known as the suspicious people who were only released because no one could find the proof that they were involved in the murder. So they stay, embroiled in an investigation in which they are not wanted.

Comment: Charlaine Harris spoke to a number of people who have survived being struck by lightning before writing these books. Symptoms such as frequent headaches, shaky hands, and weakness in limbs are common; as is, unfortunately, her portrayal of the attitude of medical personnel towards people who have survived a lightning strike (the belief that if people survived, they must be fine, that there are no lingering effects is common).

Literary Magic & Mayhem: Harper is an interesting mixture of kindness and cynicism. She simply has no illusions: her early life forced her to deal with a very grim reality, and her worldview does not include an expectation that people will behave with decency. It's disconcerting, but also interesting and strangely touching. Her kindness comes out in unexpected ways, such as helping someone avoid confronting something that that person does not want to face, or worrying about a virtual stranger. She feels very strongly about family, paying close attention to relationships in other families and trying very hard to maintain the relationships in her own. In *Grave Surprise,* many of her longstanding relationships begin to change in fundamental ways.

Explorations: Sookie is naïve and sweet, but Harper is certainly not naïve. How does the protagonist's outlook change the narrative?

Many mysteries use a female-in-jeopardy strategy to heighten narrative tension, expose the depths of the villain's character, or to bring the story to a resolution. In some ways, these books follow that convention; in others, they turn it on its head. In what ways did the author play with that convention in the book?

THE CASES

1. ***Grave Sight.*** New York: Berkley Prime Crime, 2005, 263 p. ISBN: 0425205681.

SARNE, ARKANSAS, AUTUMN 2004. Six months ago, Dell Teague and Monteen (Teenie) Hopkins went out into the woods. A hunter found Dell's body: he had been shot, but no one ever found Teenie. Now there are murmurings in the town of Sarne that maybe Dell murdered Teenie and then shot himself. Dell's mother is desperate to clear his name. So desperate that she wants Teenie found, dead or alive.

ASSOCIATES: Tolliver—*Harper's brother, age 27;* Sheriff Harvey Branscom; Paul Edwards—*lawyer;* Sybil Teague—*a rich widow who is worried about her son's reputation;* Terence Vale—*Mayor;* Deputy Hollis Boxleitner—*Teenie Hopkins brother-in-law;* Helen Hopkins—*Teenie's mother;* Geneva Roller—*a client;* Patsy Bolton—*Geneva's lawyer;* Mary Nell Teague (Nell)—*Sybil Teague's daughter;* Scotty; Justin; Cody; Elijah Gleason—*the funeral home director;* Annie Gibson—*a friend of Helen;* Vernon McCluskey—*the owner of the hotel where Harper and Tolliver are staying in Sarne;* Jay Hopkins—*who was married to Helen;* Deputy Bledsoe; Art Barfield—*Harper and Tolliver's lawyer;* Phyllis Foliette—*the lawyer Art sends to help them.*

2. ***Grave Surprise.*** New York: Berkley Prime Crime, 2006, 295 p. ISBN: 9780425212035.

MEMPHIS, TENNESSEE. NOVEMBER, 2005. When professor Nunley asked Harper to come and demonstrate her gift for his class, he was expecting her to be an obvious and somewhat incompetent con artist. He was planning on demonstrating his brilliance while debunking a fraud. Instead he got Harper. In an unfamiliar graveyard that had been untouched for almost 200 years, Harper moved from grave to grave without examining the headstones, successfully identifying the dead and telling his class the causes of their deaths. Then she found a puzzle. One grave had two bodies, and one of the bodies was recent.

ASSOCIATES: Tolliver—*Harper's brother, age 28;* Dr. Clyde Nunley—*a professor at Bingham College;* Anne—*his wife;* Joel and Diane Morgenstern—*who asked Harper for help in locating their daughter Tabitha 18 months ago;* Whitney—*Joel's first wife, she died of cancer;* Victor—*Joel and Whitney's son;*

Felicia Hart—*is Whitney's sister;* Fred Hart—*Whitney's father;* Ben and Judy Morgenstern—*Joel's parents;* David Morgenstern—*Joel's brother;* Detective Corbett Lacey; Detective Brittany Young; Shellie Quail—*from Channel 13;* Art Barfield—*Harper and Tolliver's lawyer;* Blythe Benson—*the Morgenstern family's lawyer;* Agent Seth Koenig; Private Detective Rick Goldman; Xylda Bernardo—*a psychic;* Manfred—*Xylda's grandson, also a psychic;* Josiah Poundstone—*deceased;* Mariella—*Harper and Tolliver's 9-year-old sister;* Gracie—*Harper and Tolliver's 11-year-old sister;* Dr. Hatton.

3. ***An Ice Cold Grave.*** New York: Berkley Prime Crime, 2007, 280 p. ISBN: 9780425217290.

DORAVILLE, NORTH CAROLINA, JANUARY, 2006. Sandra Rockwell ran for Sheriff when she felt that more attention needed to be paid to the disappearances of some local boys. She knew of several who had vanished, but she couldn't stop the disappearances. In the year since she has been Sheriff, boys have continued to go missing. She's afraid that she has a serial killer on her hands, and she doesn't know how to find out. Then she hears of Harper and mentions her gift to a local woman whose grandson is missing. The grandmother raises money from the townspeople and they hire Harper. It's the first time she's worked on a case involving a serial killer. She always wants to find the body, to give the family and, perhaps, the victim closure. Now she has another concern: she needs to find out enough information to help investigators stop a killer before he strikes again.

ASSOCIATES: Tolliver—*Harper's brother;* Sheriff Sandra Rockwell; Deputy Rob Tidmarsh; Twyla Cotton—*who raised money in the hope that Harper could help her grandson Jeff;* Parker McGraw—*her son;* Carson McGraw—*Parker's son;* Dr. Thomason; Agents Max Stuart and Pell Klavin; Manfred Bernardo—*psychic;* Rain—*his mother;* Xylda—*his grandmother;* Barney Simpson—*hospital administrator;* Heather Sutcliff—*his assistant;* Pastor Doak Garland of Mount Ida Baptist Church; Tom Almand—*psychologist;* Chuck Almand—*his sociopathic 13-year-old son;* Ted Hamilton; Abe Madden—*ex-Sheriff;* Cleda Humphrey—*funeral director.*

HARRIS, Charlaine and Toni L. P. Kelner.

MANY BLOODY RETURNS

Genres/Themes Crossed: Secret Society, Blended Society, Paranormal X Traditional Mystery, Hard-Boiled Mystery.

Subjects/Character Types: Spell-Casters, Vampires, Werewolves, Ghosts X Amateur Sleuths, Santa Claus, Private Investigators.

Series/Stand-Alone: A series of anthologies of short stories. The anthologies can be read in any order.

Scene of the Crime: Varies.

Detective: Varies.

Known Associates: Varies.

Premise: When the editors were first asked to put together an anthology, they decided to challenge authors to write stories that combined vampires (the dead) with birthdays (celebrations of life). The results were varied in theme, but uniformly excellent in quality. The anthology was very successful: different authors took the two elements and combined them in very different ways. When the editors were asked for another anthology, they stuck to their successful method of combining a monster with a celebration. In the second case, it was werewolves and Christmas. Once again, the combination proves fascinating.

Comment: Charlaine Harris is the author of the *Southern Vampire*, the *Harper Connelly*, the *Aurora Teagarden* and the *Lily Bard, (the Shakespeare's Landlord)* series. The first Aurora Teagarden mystery, *Real Murders,* was nominated for the 1990 Agatha Award for Best Novel. The first Southern Vampire mystery, *Dead Until Dark,* won the 2002 Anthony Award for Best Paperback Original, and was nominated for both the 2001 Agatha Best Novel Award and the 2002 Dilys Award. The second in the series, *Living Dead in Dallas,* was nominated for the 2002 Sapphire Award for Best Science Fiction Romance Novel.

Toni P. Kelner is the author of the *Laura Fleming* series and the *Where are They Now?* series. She also writes short stories. "Skull and Cross-Examinations," published in Ellery Queen's Mystery Magazine, has been nominated for the 2008 Best Short Story Agatha Award. "How Stella Got her Grave Back," published in *Many Bloody Returns,* was nominated for the 2008 Anthony Award for Best Short Story. "Sleeping with the Plush" won the 2007 Agatha Award for Best Short Story, and was nominated for the 2007 Anthony Award for Best Short Story. "Bible Belt" was nominated for the 2003 Macavity Award for Best Short Story. "The Death of Erik the Redneck" was nominated for the 1996 Agatha Award for Best Short Story. She also writes essays, articles, and limericks (a few of which can be found at http://www.tonilpkelner.com/limericks.php). Information on her works, her biography, and a link to her blog can be found at http://www.tonilpkelner.com/.

Literary Magic & Mayhem: Well-known authors wrote new stories for these anthologies. Some of the stories involve series characters, others are stand-alones.

Explorations: Were all the monsters in the story villains?

THE CASES

1. ***Many BloodyReturns: Tales of Birthdays with Bite.*** New York: Ace Books, 2007, 355 p. ISBN: 9780441015221.

CONTENTS: A Few Words *by Charlaine Harris and Toni L. P. Kelner;* Dracula Night *by Charlaine Harris;* The Mournful Cry of Owls *by Christopher Golden;* I was a Teenage Vampire *by Bill Crider;* Twilight *by Kelley Armstrong;* It's My Birthday, Too *by Jim Butcher;* Grave-robbed *by P. N. Elrod;* The First Day of the Rest of Your Life *by Rachel Caine;* The Witch and the Wicked *by Jeanne C. Stein;* Blood Wrapped *by Tanya Huff;* The Wish *by Carolyn Haines;* Fire and Ice and Linguini for Two *by Tate Hallaway;* Vampire Hours *by Elaine Viets;* How Stella Got Her Grave Back *by Toni L. P. Kelner.*

2. ***Wolfsbane and Mistletoe.*** New York: Ace Books, 2008, 340 p. ISBN: 9780441016334.

CONTENTS: Gift Wrap *by Charlaine Harris;* The Haire of the Beast *by Donna Andrews;* Lucy, at Christmastime *by Simon R. Green;* The Night Things Changed *by Dana Cameron;* The Werewolf before Christmas *by Kat Richardson;* Fresh Meat *by Alan Gordon;* Il est Ne *by Carrie Vaughn;* The Perfect Gift *by Dana Stabenow;* Christmas Past *by Keri Arthur;* SA *by J. A. Konrath;* The Star of David *by Patricia Briggs;* You'd Better Not Pyout *by Nancy Pickard;* Rogue Elements *by Karen Chance;* Milk and Cookies *by Rob Thurman;* Keeping Watch Over His Flock *by Toni L. P. Kelner.*

HARRIS, Robert.

FATHERLAND

Genres/Themes Crossed: Alternate Earth (Alternate History: Germany won WWII) Dystopia X Police Procedural.

Subjects/Character Types: Alternate Earth (Alternate History: Germany won WWII) X Police Procedural.

Series/Stand-Alone: Stand-alone.

Scene of the Crime: Berlin, Germany, which won WWII, 1964. (The week leading up to the celebration of the Führer's 75th birthday.)

Detective: Forty-two-year-old Detective Xavier March, an officer in the "Kripo" (Kriminalpolizei) has become disillusioned. He fought for the Fatherland, spending months in a U-boat during WWII. He became a detective after the war, and now he's on a treadmill: he hasn't been promoted in a decade, even though he has given his life to his work. Some consider him an "asocial." He hasn't joined any of the endless National Socialist Associations; he doesn't contribute to Winter Relief. In some quarters, those that matter, March is regarded with suspicion. He's being watched by the Gestapo.

Known Associates: Pili, March's son, lives with March's ex-wife, Klara. In the course of the book, March forms a new relationship with American Charlotte "Charlie" Maguire. March shares an office with Max Jaeger. Rudolf "Rudi" Halder is an old friend; he and March went through the war together. Now he's an historian in the Central Archives.

Premise: On the Russian Front, after the German army was turned back from Moscow in 1941, the Germans took the Caucasus and cut off the flow of oil to Russia. The Soviet Union surrendered in 1943. Germany defeated the British Empire after they realized that Britain's code experts had broken the Enigma code. Germany then sent disinformation to trap and destroy the British Fleet. Britain was forced to sign an armistice in 1944. Churchill and others who led the war effort were forced to flee into exile in Canada. Germany put Edward VIII on the throne. The United States defeated Japan with an atomic weapon in 1945; in 1946, Germany forced the United States to broker a peace agreement by exploding an atomic *v-3* missile over New York City. Germany annexed Eastern Europe and most of the Soviet Union. As the controlling member of the European Union, it had preferential trading status with Western Europe and Scandinavia. The world now has two superpowers: Germany and the United States; they are engaged in a Cold War. At the opening of this book, Germany is preparing for an historic meeting between President Joseph P. Kennedy and the Führer, Hitler. The Greater German Reich has carefully buried most of the evidence of the Holocaust. Officials have spent years claiming that most of the Jewish population that seemed to have disappeared was simply relocated to sparsely populated areas in the East. Their silence is attributed to the inadequate communication infrastructure and the difficulties of travel in those areas.

Comment: The book was the basis of the 1994 HBO movie *Fatherland*. The movie ends somewhat differently from the novel. In the novel the final statement is one expressing Xavier's hope; the movie ends with a voiceover epilog in which Pili, now an adult, explains how the truth was accepted by the world.

Literary Magic & Mayhem: March doesn't keep his cynicism to himself, a dangerous trait in the National Socialist State, as in this exchange, in which duty-officer Krause is trying to absolve March of the responsibility of following through on the case by pointing out that he works harder than any other detective in the place, yet gets no reward for his efforts:

> March had rolled the list of missing persons into a tube. He leaned forward and tapped Krause lightly on the chest with it. "You forget yourself, comrade," he said, "Arbeit macht frei." The slogan of the labor camps: Work makes you free.
>
> He turned and made his way back through the ranks of telephonists. Behind him he could hear Drause appealing to Helga. "See what I mean? What the hell kind of a joke is that?" (p. 18)

The appalling, but logical, extrapolation of the Nazi society is very well done. The 1935 Race Defilement Act; the slavery of the Poles, Czechs and Ukrainians; and the treatment of political dissidents are unfortunately believable, combining the worst of the history of many countries. The characters are entirely believable, even—perhaps especially—when their actions are disappointing.

The student war protests (this time in Germany, with the Beatles being pop icons speaking against the ongoing, low-level war in the Urals) are encouraging. The population's exhaustion with the constant high-level (red) terrorist alerts and the continuing war provide an interesting perspective, particularly in view of the fact that the novel was written in 1992.

Explorations: What character's actions were most disappointing?

What did Charlie and March have in common?

How are March's feelings about his apartment related to his feelings about the uses of concentration camp prisoners' hair?

At what point in the book was there the most hope for a better tomorrow?

THE CASE

1. ***Fatherland.*** New York: Random House, 1992, 338 p. ISBN: 0679412735.

Berlin, Germany, and Zurich, Switzerland, April 1964. An act of kindness, taking a routine assignment that should have fallen to officemate Max Jaeger, causes Detective Xavier March to become lead investigator for a case that looks, at first, like a simple drowning. The case automatically has prominence because the body was found within 300 yards of an area that houses the party elite, including Goebbels. The victim is a man whom no one seems to have missed; he is not on any of the missing-persons lists. March persists, and finds the victim's identity through fingerprints. The victim's prints are on file because he was arrested once, in the company of the Führer, in 1923, before the Nazi regime came to power. The victim is Josef Bühler, one of the glorious pioneers of the National Socialist Revolution. March's investigation uncovers a conspiracy, directed from the highest reaches of the Gestapo. It's all linked to a massive cover-up; the truth threatens the powerful. The truth is not welcome, but Xavier is too wrapped up in his investigation to stop.

ASSOCIATES: Charlotte "Charlie" Maguire—*New York Times reporter;* Frederick Jost—*an SS cadet from the Sepp-Dietrich training academy who was out running when he discovered the victim;* Spiedel—*police photographer;* SS Surgeon August Eisler—*pathologist;* Krause—*the duty officer;* Paul "Pili" March—*March's 10-year-old son who is excited to finally be old enough to be a member of the Pimpfen (when he's 14, he will automatically move to full membership in the Hitler Youth);* Max Jaeger—*a good Nazi, he shares an office with March, sometimes they work together on a case.* Otto Koth—*Head of the Fingerprint Section;* Walther Fiebes—*a Kripo Officer in the Sexual Crimes Division;* Rudolf "Rudi" Halder—*a war comrade of March, now an Historian in the Central Archives;* Karl Krebs—*a civilized SS officer, hated by his boss;* Odilo Globocnik—*Krebs' boss.*

Historical Figures: Odilio "Globus" Globocnik—*a brutish SS officer who hates the more able men whom he supervises;* Artur Nebe—*who seems to be a good Nazi, Chief of the German Police Force;* Reinhard Heydrich—*the Chief of the Reich Main Security Office, he was given orders for the Final Solution by Goering, (in the book, he has survived the 1942 attempt on his life and has been promoted to Reichsführer-SS, Head of the Reich Security Office, second only to Hitler.* Note: Historically, Heydrich helped organize the Wannsee Conference, where the Final Solution (Hitler's planned extermination of the Jews) was accepted as Reich policy. Martin Luther—*Foreign Ministry liaison to the SS;* Dr. Josef Bühler—*Secretary for the General Government;* Dr. Roland Freisler—*of the Reich Ministry of Justice;* Otto Hofmann—*of the Race and Resettlement Main Office;* Dr. Gerhard Klopfer—*from the NSDAP Chancellery;* Friedrich Wilhelm Kritzinger—*from the Reich Chancellery;* Dr. Rudolf Lange—*the Commander of the SD for Latvia;* Georg Leibbrandt and Dr. Alfred Meyer—*of the Reich Ministry for the Occupied Eastern territories;* Heinrich Müller—*of the Gestapo;* Erich Neumann—*from the Office of the Four Year Plan;* Dr. Karl Eberhard Schöngarth—*of the Gestapo;* Dr. Wilhelm Stuckart—*from the Reich Ministry for the Interior;* Adolf Eichmann—*who took the minutes at the Wannsee Conference;* Führer Adolf Hitler—*who is almost 75 years old;* Hermann Goering—*who was thought to have died in 1951;* Heinrich Himmler—*who was thought to have died in 1962;* Joseph Goebbels—*the man in charge of the Nazi Propaganda Ministry;* Winston Churchill and Princess Elizabeth—*who live in exile in Canada;* Edward VIII and his consort Wallis—*the Emperor and Empress of the British Empire;* Joseph P. Kennedy, Sr.—*(JFK's father), President of the United States;* Karl Donitz—*the Grand*

Admiral of the Kriegsmarine; Charles Lindbergh—*the United States Ambassador to Germany.*

HARRISON, Harry. (Legalized from Henry Maxwell Dempsey)

The Stainless Steel Rat Is Born

Genres/Themes Crossed: Science Fiction, Time Travel X Caper, Police Procedural.

Subjects/Character Types: Future Universe, Space Travel, Time Travel X Caper, Police Procedural.

Series/Stand-Alone: James DiGriz's situation and his alliances change over the course of the series, so it's best to read these in order.

Scene of the Crime: Approximately 34000 A.D., the Universe.

Detective: James Bolivar DiGriz wanted more out of life than the boring existence that was laid out for him, so he set out to learn how to be a crook. He went as far as he could on his own, then decided that he needed a mentor. To that end, he plotted his arrest so that he could enter prison to meet criminals. He found them lacking. He broke out and tracked down a criminal genius called "The Bishop," who had never been caught. Their relationship was unfortunately brief. Jimmy lied, conned, and stole his way through the next few years. He lived, as much as possible, outside of normal society, which gave him an unusual perspective and access to some sensitive information. He occasionally came across heinous crimes perpetrated by governments, and would turn them in to the Galactic League Navy. In return, Captain Varod of the League Navy repeatedly warned Jim to give up his life of crime and to steer clear of the Galactic Navy. Jim did his best to steer clear of all official agencies. He was doing his best to mind his own (larcenous) business when he was cornered by the government and conscripted to work in the Special Corps, an elite law-enforcement and spy agency staffed by ex-criminals like himself.

Known Associates: The Bishop was James's mentor and friend. James is eventually recruited by Harold Peters Inskipp "Inskipp the Uncatchable," commander of an elite police force called the Special Corps. Inskipp was a criminal himself, as were all of his agents. One of James's first assignments for the Special Corps is to trace down a homicidal criminal mastermind. In the course of that investigation, he met his wife, Angelina. In later books, their twin sons James and Bolivar take a part in the action. Professor Coypu developed the Time Helix for the Special Corps. Continuing villains include The Kekkonshiki, a.k.a. "The Gray Men," who are capable of manipulating others' minds.

Premise: In the far future, the galaxy has become so civilized as to be boring, at least on most planets. A combined treatment with genetic control and mechanized personality adjustments for those who struggle against society has created planets of meek, mild, "socially adjusted" people who are content to fulfill their duties as cogs in the wheels of the Galactic League. Those whose criminal tendencies are discovered early are "adjusted"; late-blooming criminals are incarcerated until their personalities can be replaced. Jimmy diGriz's ambition was to be a great criminal, and so asked The Bishop to teach him all he knew. The Bishop rejected the term "criminal." He taught James that their role was not criminal, but rather that they were benefactors, risking life and limb for all humanity, the last people who would stand against the suffocating social order:

> We are Citizens of the Outside. We have rejected the simplistic, boring, regimented, bureaucratic, moral, and ethical scriptures by which they live. In their place we have substituted our own far superior ones. We may physically move among them—but we are not of them. Where they are lazy, we are industrious. Where they are immoral, we are moral. Where they are liars, we are the Truth. We are probably the greatest power for good to the society that we have discarded. (*The Stainless Steel Rat is Born*, Ch. 14)

He goes on to paint them as the saviors of society. They keep the police busy, give them a reason to buy fancy new equipment, and entertain the masses with their criminal exploits.

Comment: The series began with a short story entitled "The Stainless Steel Rat," which was published in a 1957 issue of *Analog*. It generated enough interest for a second story with the same character. Harrison then expanded those into a novel, which became *The Stainless Steel Rat,* the first book written in the series. Later Harrison went back and wrote the prequels: *The Stainless Steel Rat is Born, The Stainless Steel Rat is Drafted,* and *The Stainless Steel Rat Sings the Blues.* The series inspired a board game that was published by SPI in the magazine Ares in the late 1970s. *The Stainless Steel Rat, The Stainless Steel Rat Saves the World,* and *The Stainless Steel Rat for President* were adapted into comic strip form for early issues of *2000 AD.* The comic was written by Kelvin Gosnell and drawn by Carlos Ezquerra.

In the books, the common galactic language is Esperanto, a language created on Earth to be a facilitator between cultures, meant to be a truly international language. Some of the later books end with a note from the author promoting the language and providing a source for further information.

The author's Web site, http://www.harryharrison.com/, includes biographical information, information on his books, and links to his blog at http://harryharrison.wordpress.com/, where he has posted some of his short stories.

Literary Magic & Mayhem: This is a lighthearted series, and maybe it should not be searched for deep social content. There are characters, however, who waltz through difficulties, who sneer at regulations, who laugh at red tape; and they're fun to watch. They include The Saint (from the series written by Charteris), Phryne Fisher (from the series written by Greenwood) and The Stainless Steel Rat.

Explorations: Jim frequently talks to himself. Why? How does it help him? What purpose does it serve in the narrative?

Are intelligence and imagination assets or handicaps in the societies depicted in the books?

What rules comprise the personal moral codes of different characters?

THE CASES

1. ***The Stainless Steel Rat Is Born.*** New York: Bantam Books, 1985, 219 p. ISBN: 0553247085; 9780553247084.

THE PLANET BIT O'HEAVEN AND THE PLANET SPIOVENTE, CIRCA 33948 A.D. Seventeen-year-old James DiGriz, having exhausted all the legitimate resources that could set him up on a successful life of crime, decides to find a criminal mentor. Since they keep criminals in jail, he goes to jail. He finds the inhabitants disappointing, so he leaves. He has one lead, the name "The Bishop."

ASSOCIATES: The Bishop—*is 17-year-old James's friend and mentor;* Captain Garth—*who is willing to take a bribe;* Bibs—*one of Garth's crew;* Capo Doccia—*who sees no value in change;* Tars Tukas—*Doccia's slave master;* Dreng—*a farm boy;* Capo Dimonte—*the enemy of Capo Doccia;* Captain Varod—*of the League Navy.*

2. ***The Stainless Steel Rat Gets Drafted.*** New York: Bantam Books, c1987, 256 p. ISBN: 0553052209.

THE PLANETS NEVENKEBLA AND CHOJECKI, CIRCA 33949 A.D. Eighteen-year-old James sees an opportunity to avenge a friend's death, and jumps at the chance. He's in the wrong place at the wrong time (with the wrong I.D.) and gets himself conscripted into an army with orders to invade a peaceful planet. The foundation of this stainless steel rat's moral code is that he will not kill.

This is not a philosophy shared by his commanders, but the people who wage the war will be the ground troops. The question is, who will they follow?

ASSOCIATES: Bibs—*one of Captain Garth's crew;* Captain Varod—*of the League Navy;* Captain Grbonja—*who is about to retire;* Jak—*who felt Jim needed new papers;* Drill-sergeant Klutz; Morton—*a.k.a. Lieutenant Hesk, a recruit;* Corporal Gow; Corporal Gamin; General Zennor; Acting First Sergeant Blogh; General Lowender; Major Kewsel; Corporal Aspya. The inhabitants of Chojecki include Stirner—*Bellegarrique Generating Plant #1 engineer;* Sharla; Librarian Grene; Doctor Lum; old Czolgoscz—*the perfect host;* Neebe—*the president of the cycling club;* Mark Forer—*robot and philosopher.*

3. ***The Stainless Steel Rat Sings the Blues.*** New York: Bantam Books, c1994, 229 p. ISBN: 0553096125.

THE PLANETS PASKÖNJAK AND PRISON PLANET LIOKUKAE. CIRCA 33951 A.D. The military found an ancient alien artifact, then lost it when the ship carrying it crashed into a prison planet. Admiral Benbow hatched a plan to force a criminal to recover it for them. He decided to use the Stainless Steel Rat, and to that end he baited a trap and caught him, then poisoned him. The poison works slowly. Jim has about a month to retrieve the artifact and get the antidote. The first trick is to get to the planet in a disguise that will allow him entry into every part of the society. He decides to go as a musician, and the military helps him form a band named *The Stainless Steel Rats* for this mission.

ASSOCIATES: Colonel Neuredan; Pederasis Narcoses—*attorney;* Professor Van Diver; Admiral Benbow—*Head of League Navy Security.* Zach—*who is recruited by Jim to help set up the band, The Stainless Steel Rats;* Madonette—*the lead singer of The Stainless Steel Rats;* the bearded Ffloyd—*on winds, principally the bagpipes;* the gray-haired Steengo—*on strings, principally the fiddelino;* Jim—*is faking percussion, pretending to play to tracks that Zach set down;* Barry Moyd Shlepper—*who composed their music.*

On Liokukie, the society of criminals has been left to fester for generations, occasionally augmented by new groups of prisoners. The society is now a relatively stable collection of gangs, many of them are religious gangs. King Svinjar—*leader of the Machomen;* Arroz conPollo—*the leader of one of the nomadic Fundamentaloid gangs;* Iron John—*leads the Paradisians;* Hingst and Afatt—*are the Paradisian's official greeters for males;* Ljotur—*Sergeant of the Guard;* Sjonvarp—*is the top trader in the marketplace;* Heimskur—*the man who was given the artifact;* Madonette—*who is relegated to the female half of the city;* Mata—*who meets Madonette;* Bethuel—*the guard;* Dreadnought—*one of the Survivalists;* Indefatigable—*the Survivalists' field commander;* Commander/Alphamega—*is involved in both sides of the (long past)*

Breakdown Wars; Vesta and Othred Timetinker—*are searching through time for the artifact;* Captain Tremearne—*is the only officer on the planet who has been told of the band's mission; he is not only competent, he is also compassionate and trustworthy.*

4. **"The Fourth Law of Robotics,"** in *Foundations Friends: Stories in Honour of Isaac Asimov,* edited by Martin H. Greenberg. New York: Grafton, 1991, p. 389–406. ISBN: 0812567706, 9780812567700.

PLACE UNKNOWN, CIRCA **2295**? Dr. Susan Calvin (great-niece of the famous Susan Calvin) is presented with proof that a robot committed armed bank robbery. If word gets out, it could mean ruin for her company, U.S. Robots and Mechanical Men, Inc. James diGriz passed the bank soon after the theft; with his senses honed by decades of criminal activities, he immediately spots the clues that it was a robot crime. The robot got to the bank first, but that doesn't mean that there can be no profit for others. Jim immediately realizes the toll this could take on the robot industry and heads for U.S. Robots to offer his services (for a fee) to quietly track down the guilty robot. (This story is not exactly in the spirit of Asimov's *Robot* series, at least in the behavior and attitude of the robots, and is not exactly in the spirit in Harrison's *Stainless Steel Rat* series, at least in the callousness shown by Slippery Jim; but it is a Harrison *Stainless Steel Rat* story, published in an anthology honoring Asimov.)

ASSOCIATES: Dr. Susan Calvin; Dr. Mike Donovan; Dirty Dan McGrew.

5. ***The Stainless Steel Rat.*** New York: Berkley, 1971, c1961, 160 p. ISBN: 425020150

SEVERAL PLANETS, INCLUDING CITTANUVO AND FREIBUR, CIRCA 33966 A.D. Jim diGriz has been rolling along, skipping from planet to planet, trying (and succeeding) at a new scheme on each. He never repeats himself and he never gets caught until the Special Corps takes an interest. Instead of arresting him, they offer him a job. They believe that one should set a thief to catch a thief. Jim is sent to training and is horribly bored; he has the knowledge and the wits to be a full agent, but he's planet-bound as a trainee. When Inskipp finds Jim hard to deal with, he sticks Jim in the library to teach him discipline. Giving Jim the tools to do research may not have been the smartest move. Within days, Jim is on a clandestine hunt of his own, more fascinated than appalled at what he discovers:

> Bit by bit a pattern started to emerge. A delicate webwork of forgery, bribery, chicanery and falsehood. It could only have been conceived by a mind as brilliantly crooked as my own, I chewed my lip with jealousy. (Chapter 5.)

Jim adopts the *noms de cop* Grav Bent Diebstall and throws himself into the action, at times using the name Hans Schmidt, as well.

Associates: Harold Peters Inskipp—*the criminal who looted the Pharsydion II in mid-flight, now the Head of the Special Corps;* President Ferraro—*who's either a patsy or a madman;* Captain Steng—*who is not happy at having his ship used for bait;* Pepe Nero—*a criminal mastermind;* Angelina—*a.k.a. Englea, his assistant;* Full Agent Ove Nielson; Zug of Freibur—*who is starved for conversation;* Dr. Mcvbklz; Dr. Vulff Sifternitz—*who lost his license years ago;* Freiber's King Villelm and his Queen; the Royal Attorney; and the Count of Rdenrundt.

6. ***The Stainless Steel Rat's Revenge.*** New York, Walker, 1970, 185 p. ISBN: 0802755259.

Various planets, including Lamata, Cliaand, and Burada, circa 33968. The unthinkable has happened. A successful planetary invasion has taken place. In fact, more than one. The League would like it stopped, now. As the Cliaand military prepares for intersteller conquest, the League looks for someone who can throw a wrench into the invasion.

Associates: Angelina and Jim marry at the outset of the book; Harold Peters Inskipp—*Jim's boss;* Pacov—*Ratunkowy's bodyguard;* Flight-Major Vaska Hulja; Kraj; Otrov; Pire; Sergeant Taze of the Buradian Guard; Dr. Mutfak; Hamal—*who has a difficult time taking on a woman's role.* The book includes the first appearance of the Gray Men. Jim uses the alias Pas Ratunkowy for this mission.

7. ***The Stainless Steel Rat Saves the World.*** New York, Putnam [1972], 191 p. ISBN: 039911047X.

Special Corps Main Station (circa 33975), New York City (1975), London (1807), Earth (circa 53975). Someone, somewhere, somewhen, is tampering with time. The Special Corps was their first target. Inskipp is gone. Other top people have also disappeared. They must send someone back in time to destroy the forces deployed against them before it is too late. There's no way that Jim is patsy enough to take on this assignment, until his family disappears.

Associates: Professor Coypu of The Corps—*who has lectured on the impossibility of time travel (it was a smokescreen—the Corps has had time travel for years);* Angelina—*Jim's wife;* their six-year-old twins. 1976: Slasher and Secretary Miss Kipper. 1807: Brewster, Luke, Guy, Count d'Hesion, Major Rene' Dupont, Napoleon, and He. Circa 53975: Diyan—*a Martian on earth*, and He.

8. ***The Stainless Steel Rat Wants You.*** New York: Bantam, ©1979, 155 p. ISBN: 533126253.

Planets Blodgett, Kekkonshiki, and Special Corps Main Station, circa 33987 a.d. With lawful employment comes lawful taxes, most of the time. James and Angelina have been industriously dodging them for years. When the Intersteller Internal and External Revenue kidnap Angelina, James gets the twins out of boarding school to help him rescue her. Inskipp steps in with an assignment for Jim. The satellite base on Kakalak-two was the site for a meeting of all planetary Chiefs of Staff of the League Navy. The Chiefs of Staff, the base, and the satellite have all disappeared.

ASSOCIATES: Angelina—*Jim's wife;* James and Bolivar—*their 18-year-old twins;* Colonel Dorsky; Inskipp; Professor Coypu; Admiral Schimsah; Garbaj—*an alien, First Official of War Council;* and Commander Sess-Pula—*an alien.*

The grey men: Commander Kome; Hanasu—*Headmaster of the Yurusareta School;* Yoru—*a student;* Bukai and Ahiru—*searchers;* Kaeru—*the cook.*

Jay Hovah—*Morality Corps top executive;* Incuba—*an agent;* Kangg—*from a parallel universe;* Ga Binetto—*a temporal constable.* Jim deGriz uses the aliases Sleepery Jeem of Geshtunken and Sleepery Bolivar, who has Ann-Geel as his Chief of Staff.

9. ***The Stainless Steel Rat for President.*** New York: Bantam, ©1982, 185 p. ISBN: 0553227599; 9780553227598.

PLANETS BLODGETT AND PARAISO-AQUI, CIRCA 33992 A.D. It has been 113 years since there was a murder on Blodgett. Faced with the crime, the police of Blodgett ask Jim deGriz for help. Faced with the opportunity to be a good citizen and assist the officers, Jim, of course, declines. Later that day, faced with the same opportunity in the form of an assignment from Inskipp, Jim begins his investigation.

ASSOCIATES: Angelina—*Jim's wife;* James and Bolivar—*their 18-year-old twins;* Captain Kretin—*of the Blodgett Police.* Special Corps Agent Charley—*who delivers orders from Inskipp;* Inskipp—*Head of the Special Corps.*

On Paraiso-Aqui: Jorge—*their tourist guide;* Flavia—*his co-conspirator;* Police Captain Oliveira; Viladelmas Pujol—*an officer;* Ricard Gonzales de Torres y Alvarez—*the Marquis de la Rosa;* General-President Julio Zapilote; Adolfo, Santos, and Renata—*who are card sharps;* Duke Penoso; Joyella—*a tourist from Phigerinadon II;* Edwin Rodriguez—*presidential bodyguard;* Captain Ciego de Avila.

Jim diGriz uses a variety of aliases: Jamie; Sir Hector Harapo, Kinght of the Beeday; Wurble from Blodgett; and General James diGriz of POOPI (the Paramilitary Organization of Political Investigation).

10. ***The Stainless Steel Rat Goes to Hell.*** New York: TOR, c1996, 253 p. ISBN: 0312860633.

PLANETS LUSSUOSO AND VULKANN, CIRCA 33997 A.D. The Temple of Eternal Truth offers worshippers a sneak peak at Heaven, for a price. Angelina wants a better look at the con, but things go wrong and the Temple is blown to bits, with no sign left of Angelina. DiGriz calls in the troops—first his sons, and then the Corps—to find her.

ASSOCIATES: On Lussuoso, the characters include Rowena Vinicultura—*the most beautiful and the most boring woman on Lussuoso;* Bolivar and James—*the twins;* Captain Collin; Vivilia VonBrun—*who is gorgeous and rich.*

On Vulkann, the characters include Deveena "Dee" De Zoftig; Slakey/Fanyimadu/Father Marablis/Baron Krümmung; and Maudi Lesplances. In Hell, Special Agent Sybil—*who is sent by Inskipp;* Cuthbert Podpisy—*Professor of Comparative Anatomy;* Stakey—*Professor of Physics;* Professor Coypu—*who invented the Time Helix;* Captain Grissle—*of the Space Marines;* Dr. Mastigophora—*the Corps' leading psychosemanticist;* Grusher—*of the Paradise construction crew;* Buboe and Berkk—*in Purgatory;* The book ends with the twins planning their marriages. Jim diGriz uses the aliases Admiral Sir James DiGriz and Sire Diplodocus.

11. ***The Stainless Steel Rat Joins the Circus.*** New York: TOR, 1999, 269 p. ISBN: 0312869347.

PLANETS USTI NAD LABAM, ELYSIUM, AND FETORR, CIRCA 33999 A.D. The richest man in the galaxy offers Jim and Angelina four million credits a day to find out who is systematically robbing him. Young James finds that traveling circuses are the common link among all the places involved in the thefts. Slippery Jim decides to join up as a magician.

ASSOCIATES: The client, 40,000-year-old Imperetrix Von Kaiser-Czarski—*"Kaizi" to his friends, he developed the first longevity drug;* Angelina—*Jim's wife;* James—*Jim and Angelina's son;* Sybil—*James's new wife;* Bolivar—*Jim and Angelina's son;* Sybill—*Bolivar's wife;* Hedy Lastarr and The Great Grissini—*are at the Happy Hectares retirement home;* Igor—*of Fetorr, he has a truck;* Ringmaster Harley Davidson, Strongman Puissanto, the four-armed Gar Goyle, the Snailman, and the Bird Girl—*are members of Bolshoi's Big Top;* Captain Kidonda—*of The Serious Crime Squad;* Inspector Mwavuli—*of the National Security Police;* Hafifu—*of the Computer Crime Corps;* Captain Wezekana—*of the Alien Interrogation Police;* Baridi Baraka—*roboreporter;* Paka—*who knows something of Kaizi's business;* Puissanto and Iba—*who work with Paka.* Jim diGriz's stage name is The Mighty Marvell. At the end of this book he is planning to retire and write his memoirs.

12. ***Stainless Steel Visions.*** Illustrated by Bryn Barnard. New York: T. Doherty Associates, 1994, c1993, 254 p. ISBN: 0812535294.

This is a selection of Harry Harrison's short stories: The Streets of Ashkelon. Toy Shop. Not Me, Not Amos Cabot! The Mothballed Spaceship. Commando Raid. The Repairman. Brave Newer World. The Secret of Stonehenge. Rescue Operation. Portrait of the Artist. Survival Planet. Roommates. The Golden Years of the Stainless Steel Rat.

Most of these are not Stainless Steel Rat stories, except for the last one:

"The Golden Years of the Stainless Steel Rat," a short story in *Stainless Steel Visions,* edited by Bryn Barnard. New York.: T, Doherty Associates, 1994, c1993, p. 235–54. ISBN: 0812535294.

TERMINAL PENITENTIARY "HELL'S WAITING ROOM," DATE UNKNOWN. Slippery Jim once again gets himself arrested. He's turning sentimental in his old age and there's a job that can only be pulled from inside the prison.

ASSOCIATES: Warden Sukks; Bogger—*a guard;* Burin Bache—*the best forger in the galaxy;* Angelina; Pepe Nero.

ASSOCIATED WORKS

13. ***You Can Be the Stainless Steel Rat.*** New York: Ace Books, 1988, 156 p. ISBN: 0441949789.

PLANET SKRALDESPAND, YEAR UNKNOWN. The reader is sent on a mission to kidnap a scientist who has developed the most deadly weapon ever conceived. From the forward:

> Welcome to the Special Corps, O new recruit. You hold in your hand your first assignment as a Trainee Field Agent, this assignment being cunningly disguised as a paperback, role-playing, book.

Fun, but some of the numbering is off, and readers who are anxious to lose may be disappointed. Note: *Geisteskrank* is German for "insane," and *Skraldespand* is Danish for "trashcan."

ASSOCIATES: Professor Geisteskrank; Betsy; Hairy Harry—*the Killer Cannibal;* Sadie the Sadistic; Sluj; Robbing Good; Betsy Booster.

HARRISON, Kim.

TWO GHOSTS FOR SISTER RACHEL

Genres/Themes Crossed: Blended Society X Hard-Boiled Mystery.

Subjects/Character Types: Alternate Earth (Magical), Spell-Casters (Witches), Werewolves, Vampires X Bounty Hunter (Inderland Security runner), Private Investigator.

Series/Stand-Alone: This series includes changes in characters and relationships, and should be read in order. In fact, the short story "Two Ghosts for Sister Rachel" is immeasurably helpful in understanding the protagonist. Any reader who begins with the first novel and finds the protagonist too abrasive should go back and read this short story.

Scene of the Crime: Alternate Earth, present day.

Detective: Rachel Mariana Morgan was born with a rare genetic blood disease, a disease that had a 100 percent fatality rate. Mr. Kalamack, a friend of her father, was working on genetic research, ostensibly to find cures for rare diseases, in reality trying to find information that would help his people, the elves. He stumbled across an extremely expensive, difficult, and protracted course of treatment that could save Rachel's life. He used it twice, on Rachel and on one other witch. Both survived. She stayed at his "Make a Wish" camp for children with fatal diseases, undergoing treatment until she was 12 years old. Even after she was released, she was still frail, she tired easily, and she had watched the friends she had made in the camp die. People expected her, in fact they all but demanded, that she keep herself safe and protected, that she rest frequently, as she was so easily exhausted, and that she creep carefully through her life. Rachel developed into an abrasive, headstrong, adrenaline junkie. She not only copes with danger, she actively seeks it. She drove herself to become stronger and trained in the martial arts. She became determined to join Inderland Security; a police force that keeps the peace among the magical people who came out of hiding in the 1960s. Against all odds she makes it, and then finds that the work is more routine and restrictive than she expected.

In *Dead Witch Walking,* Rachel collars a leprechaun for tax evasion and negotiates for three wishes in return for "losing the paperwork." It's her chance to get out of Inderland Security, but being a "runner" (bounty hunter/police officer) is all that she knows, so she sets up shop as a sort of private investigator.

No one knew that Rachel's birth defect also enabled her to perform demon magic. It had been thought that no one who could live on Earth and walk in sunlight could perform demon magic. Now, thanks to Mr. Kalamack's genetic manipulations, there are two witches who can.

Known Associates: In *Dead Witch Walking,* two beings were in the cab with Rachel and the leprechaun when Rachel made her decision. Each of them decided to ask for a wish in return for working with Rachel in her new private investigation agency. Jenks, a pixie, started out as Rachel's backup. He offered to leave Inderland Security for one of the leprechaun's three wishes (he wants sterility because his wife feels that she has had enough children). Ivy Tamwood, born a vampire, was once assigned as Rachel's partner in Inderland Security. In return for one of the wishes, she leaves Inderland Security to join Rachel in business.

Premise: In 1966, a bio-engineered virus escaped the lab and attached itself to genetically modified tomatoes, and touched off a worldwide pandemic. By 1969, a quarter of all humans were dead. Elves had died out (almost) completely, and the other Inderlanders: witches, the undead, trolls, pixies, leprechauns, and so forth were virtually untouched. The Inderlanders kept the world running while the humans coped with illness. When the pandemic was over, the Inderlanders came out of hiding and took up their lives beside the remaining humans. The humans, suddenly realizing that the existing law-enforcement agencies included many Inderlanders, dismantled the existing agencies and created the human-run Federal Inderland Bureau (FIB) to monitor Inderlander activities. The out-of-the-closet, out-of-work Inderlanders who had been police officers created their own law-enforcment agency, called Inderland Security (I.S.). The I.S. handles the supernatural crimes that are out of the FIB's league.

Comment: Kim Harrison envisioned the original story arc as being told through a series of six books. Elements cropped up in the middle of the series (book four or five) that would lead to a second story arc. Rachel faces issues that get progressively darker as the series moves forward. Not every book has a happy ending. The story arc spans six books, so the darkest-before-the-dawn scene may appear at the end of one of the works; the reader must hope that things will improve as the story continues (in the next book). Actions have consequences, and more than one character makes bad choices.

Kim Harrison's Web site includes links to interviews and some essays on the world of the books: http://www.kimharrison.net/index.html.

Literary Magic & Mayhem: This is a fun series with a well-realized world; including artistic touches such as inderlander non-PC slang terms for humans (day-tripper, domestic, squish, off-the-rack, and snack) and a complex and coherent magical system. It plays with the question of whether or not anyone can out-bargain a demon (and shows the pitfalls of hubris). The main character, Rachel Morgan, has many flaws, sometimes contradictory flaws. She's extremely loyal to Ivy, but is willing to let her boyfriend, Nick, take risks with a demon, risks that Rachel is better equipped to handle. She is rarely careful of others' feelings, lashing out unfairly at her friends whenever she gets angry, but she knowingly walks into dangerous, even potentially deadly situations to support Ivy. She often shows more temper than sense; it's almost as dangerous to be her ally as her enemy. Other characters are both interesting and admirable; for instance, Jenks the pixie is irritating, loyal, brave, and a good father; Ivy the abstaining-from-drinking-blood vampire is the picture of noble suffering.

Explorations: How do the characters' backgrounds shape who they are?

In this series, what does it take to beat evil? Can evil be beaten? What role does friendship play in the fight?

What kinds of risks did the author take? How likable are the characters?

THE CASES

1. **"Two Ghosts for Sister Rachel,"** in *Holidays are Hell.* New York: Avon Books, 2007, p. 1–105. ISBN: 9780061239090.

THE HALLOWS (ACROSS THE RIVER FROM CINCINNATI), WINTER SOLSTICE 1999. Rachel was expected to die young and, even after she beat the disease, she was frail and tired easily. She has spent her life trying to toughen up, taking every challenge, even earning a black belt in martial arts. Now she's determined to follow in her father's footsteps and become a runner for Inderlander Security. Her brother Robbie wants her to be protected, to continue her studies and give up any idea of a job that would be physically demanding. They compromise, agreeing that if Rachel can perform an 800-level summoning spell and summon the ghost of her father, they will ask him and abide by his decision. The summoning works, but not in the way they expected. Rachel and Robbie find themselves trying to help track down a rogue vampire before he can strike again.

ASSOCIATES: Robbie—*witch, Rachel's 26-year-old brother, who left Cincinnati four years ago right after their father's death;* Pierce—*who was executed for witchcraft in 1842;* Rachel's mother.

2. **"Undead in the Garden of Good and Evil,"** in *Dates from Hell.* New York: Avon Books, 2006, p. 1–105. ISBN: 006085409X; 9780060854096.

THE HALLOWS (ACROSS THE RIVER FROM CINCINNATI). This story gives a taste of the mind-games used to warp Ivy Tamwood. Ivy is working Homicide, and she's up for her six-month evaluation, but her boss is more interested in crushing her than supporting her, and she's having some control issues....

ASSOCIATES: Art—*vampire, Ivy's boss;* Kisten—*vampire, Ivy's lover;* Officer Rat—*vampire;* Mia Harbor—*banshee.*

3. ***Dead Witch Walking.*** (Reprint edition.) New York: HarperTorch, 2004, p. ISBN: 0060572965.

THE HALLOWS (ACROSS THE RIVER FROM CINCINNATI), JUNE 2006. Rachel's been getting lousy assignments since she brought the Mayor's son in for Wereing outside of the full moon. Her boss hates her, her life and her skills are deteriorating. She has decided that she wants out of her contract. The last person who quit Inderland Security died of a small case of spontaneous combustion. Rachel has to figure out how to get out, how to stay alive, and how to start her own business as a private investigator.

ASSOCIATES: Jenks—*a pixie;* Matalina—*a pixie, Jenks's wife;* Jax—*a pixie, their oldest son;* Jacey, Jhem, Jinni, and Josie—*pixies, their other children;* Keasley—*a witch, is Rachel's new across-the-street neighbor.*

At Rachel's office: Denon—*a turned vampire and Rachel's boss;* Ivy Tamwood—*a born vampire, she used to be Rachel's partner;* Francis

Percy—*a warlock (not good enough to be a witch), the office snitch;* Megan—*the receptionist.*

Councilman Trenton Kalamack—*no one knows if he's human or Inderlander.* The people who work for him include Quen—*elf, the Councilman's Head of Security;* Jonathan—*the Councilman's publicity advisor;* Sara Jane Gradenko—*the Councilman's new secretary;* Mr. Faris—*a bioengineer.*

Jim and Randolph Mirick—*are at the rat fights;* The Bloody Baron—*Nicholas Sparagmos,was bespelled into rat form;* Captain Edden—*who offers Rachel a job as an FIB consultant;* Rose—*who works for Edden;* Cliff—*the Bouncer at The Blood and Brew Pub;* Piscary—*who is the oldest known vampire in Cincinnati;* Kisten Felps—*vampire scion of Piscary;* and Clayton—*an honest cop.*

4. ***The Good, the Bad, and the Undead.*** New York: HarperTorch, 2005, p. ISBN: 0060572973.

Cincinnati and The Hallows, September 2006. Sara Jane was kind to Morgan when Morgan was trapped as a mink by Councilman Kalamack. Now Sara Jane is asking the FIB for help. There is a serial killer targeting witches and warlocks and her boyfriend, Dan Smather, has been missing for over 24 hours. The FIB wants Morgan to look into the disappearance, hoping that it will give them a lead on the serial killer. Morgan wants to help Sara Jane because she remembers the girl's kindness and pities her for being caught in the employment trap of Councilman Kalamack.

Associates: The detective agency named Vampiric Charms has three partners: Jenks—*the pixie,* Ivy Tamwood—*the vampire,* and Rachel Morgan—*the witch.* Keasley—*a witch, lives across the street;* Matalina—*a pixie, is Jenks's wife;* Jax, Jhem, Jinni, Josie, and little Jacey—*pixies, are their children*: Captain Edden; Detective Glenn (Edden's son); Rose; Officer Dunlop; and Lewis—*all work for the FIB.* Sara Jane Gradenko—*is Vampiric Charms's "client" (via the FIB);* Councilman Trenton Kalamack—*elf, is Sara Jane's employer;* Quen—*elf, is Kalamack's Head of Security;* Jonathan—*Kalamack's publicity advisor;* Dan Smather—*Sara Jane's boyfriend, is missing;* Dr. Anders—*teaches a class at the University of Cincinnati;* Janine and Paula—*are two of her students;* Denon—*a bitten vampire from I.S., used to be Rachel's boss, now he seems to have come down in the world;* Piscary—*the most powerful vampire in the city;* Kisten Felps—*Piscary's scion;* Nicholas "Nick" Sparagmos—*is dating Rachel;* Alice—*Rachel's mother;* Algaliarept—*the summoning name of a demon;* Sharps—*the troll under Twin Lakes Bridge in Eden Park;* Mrs. Sarong—*owner of a Cincinnati werewolf baseball team, The Howlers;* Matt Ingle—*whose job is baseball park ley-line security.*

5. ***Every Which Way but Dead.*** (Reprint edition.) New York: HarperTorch, 2005, p. ISBN: 006057299X.

CINCINNATI AND THE HALLOWS, DECEMBER 2006. Rachel brought down Piscary, an ancient vampire, and that set off a world of trouble. To survive her last battle with him she made a deal with the demon Algaliarept. He agreed to testify against Piscary, and to let Rachel keep her soul in return for her accepting the position of familiar. She accepted, and managed (for a while) to get the better of her bargain with the demon. Piscary's murder convictions will keep him locked away for several centuries. That should be good news, but it has left a power vacuum in Cincinnati and a new vampire, Saladan, intends to take over.

Saladan demands protection money from Takata's band, to ensure a trouble-free Winter Solstice charity concert. He threatens to create sufficient trouble to get the band's MPL (Mixed Population License) revoked if they don't pay. Another of Saladan's new business ventures involves the drug, brimstone. Rachel applauds anyone ruining the profits of Councilman Kalamack's illegal brimstone operation, until it becomes evident that the strategy for taking over the business involves cutting the drug with something deadly. Saladan can find a profit in death; at least Piscary and Kalamack wanted the humans alive so that they could be profited from again. Everyone wants Rachel to step in against this new vampire threat.

ASSOCIATES: Vampiric Charms is a detective agency owned by Jenks—*the pixie*, Ivy Tamwood—*the vampire*, and Rachel Morgan—*the witch*. Ceridwen "Ceri" Merriam Dulciate—*is the elf who was Algaliarept's last familiar;* Keasley—*a witch, Rachel, Ivy, and Jenks's across-the-street neighbor, takes in Ceri;* Jax—*pixie, Jenks's oldest son;* Jih—*pixie, Jenks's oldest daughter;* Jessie—*pixie, another of Jenks's daughters;* Nicholas "Nick" Sparagmos—*Rachel's boyfriend and, unfortunately, her familiar;* Takata—*the warlock lead singer in the world's first openly Inderland Band, which became world-famous in the 1960s and still going strong;* Arron—*a vampire, works with Takata;* Ripley—*the werewolf drummer;* Kisten Felps—*a vampire who wants to date Rachel, is working hard to hold Piscary's criminal empire together while his boss is in prison;* Steve—*the bouncer at Piscary's Pizza;* Mike the DJ—*at Piscary's;* Lee—*a.k.a Stanley Salaman, a witch;* Candice—*a vampire, Salaman's partner;* Councilman Trenton Kalamack—*elf;* Quen—*elf, Kalamack's Head of Security;* Jonathan—*Kalamack's publicity advisor;* Maggie—*Kalamack's cook;* Ellasbeth Withon—*Kalamack's fiancé;* Mr. Randal—*is a living vampire, Ivy's father;* Erica Randal—*is a living vampire, Ivy's little sister;* Dorothy "Skimmer" Claymor—*a living vampire, Ivy's friend, is visiting town while she works to get Piscary out of prison;* Algaliarept—*a demon;* Randy—*who works on Rachel's hair;* Newt—*who has a demon for a familiar, helps Rachel (for a price);* David Hue—*werewolf, insurance adjuster, offers to make Rachel part of his pack so that she can get on the company plan for insurance purposes;* Mrs. Avers—*is an associate from the insurance office;* Howard—*used to be David's partner.*

6. ***A Fistful of Charms.*** New York: HarperTorch, 2006, 544 p. ISBN: 0060788194.

CINCINNATI, THE HALLOWS, AND MICHIGAN, MAY 2007. Nick skipped town without saying goodbye, and he took Jenks's oldest son, Jax, with him. When something happens to Nick, Jax calls home. He knows that he's somewhere in Michigan, but not where. Jenks, still estranged from Rachel, plans to go to rescue Jax on his own. Matalina is afraid that he will be killed; the cold is dangerous to Pixies, many slow down and hibernate through the winter, often not awakening in the spring. She asks Rachel to help, and Rachel and Jenks build a temporary truce to go on the rescue mission.

ASSOCIATES: Jenks—*a pixie, who Rachel re-sizes through demon magic to a six foot four inch gorgeous man;* Matalina—*pixie, Jenk's wife;* Jax—*pixie, their son;* Ivy Tamwood—*a vampire, Jenks and Rachel's partner in the Vampiric Charms detective agency;* David Hue—*werewolf insurance adjuster;* Mr. Finley—*werewolf, David's boss;* Karen—*is the first wolf that Rachel bests in a fight for alpha female;* Ceri—*elf;* Jih—*a pixie, Jenks's oldest daughter, has moved and now claims Ceri's garden as her territory;* Rex—*the kitten whose warmth kept Jax alive;* Captain Marshal—*a witch, teaches scuba, and helps Rachel and Jenks get to Bois Blanc island;* Debbie—*is Captain Marshal's jealous assistant;* Walter Vincent—*werewolf, the alpha trying to take over three packs;* Pam—*werewolf, is Walter's female;* Aretha—*is a wolf from the island;* Brett and Randy—*are other weres on the island;* Nick—*who traded information about Rachel to demons, even when he knew Rachel was alive (he traded more information after he thought that she was dead).*

7. ***For a Few Demons More.*** New York: HarperCollins, c2007, 456 p. ISBN: 0060788380; 9780060788384.

CINCINNATI AND THE HALLOWS, JULY 2007. Rachel is possessed by the demon Newt, who came to The Hollows determined to retrieve something that she believes is in Rachel's possession. Rachel manages (barely) to fight her off and ends up with Newt's keeper, the demon Minias, owing her a favor. She's not at all sure that that's a good thing: few benefit through any bargain with a demon. Trent Kalamack is getting married, and he has the audacity to ask Rachel to pose as a bridesmaid to work security at the wedding. (He is willing to pay well.) Unfortunately, the wedding party includes Lee Saladan, who should be trapped as Algaliarept's familiar in the ever-after. Rachel is shocked when she sees him walking up the basilica steps, and even more shocked when she realizes that Algaliarept has possessed him. Algaliarept is bound by his oath and cannot attack Rachel, but Saladan also wants her dead. Algaliarept is not bound from making sure that she is vulnerable and then leaving Saladan to let him finish the job. On top of all of this, unregistered female werewolves are being murdered, and Rachel's alpha male, David Hue, is a prime suspect.

ASSOCIATES: The partners in Vampiric Charms detective agency are Jenks—*the pixie*, Ivy Tamwood—*the vampire*, and Rachel Morgan—*the witch.* Keasley—*a witch whose house is across the street from Vampiric Charms;* Ceridwen "Ceri" Merriam Dulciate—*the elf who was Algaliarept's last familiar, is living with Keasley;* Trent and Quen—*elves, are stunned to meet Ceri, an elf who is generations older than any other living elf (a fact of particular interest when one considers that demons and elves fought by tampering with genetics);* Matalina—*a pixie, Jenks's wife, is ill;* Jenks and Matalina's children include Jhan—*a pixie, who is learning the ropes from Jenks*, Jih—*a pixie, who is being courted by three Pixies in Ceri's garden*, Jocelyn—*a pixie, their youngest daughter, who made it safely through the Winter;* David Hue—*a werewolf, who invited Rachel into his pack;* Brett Markson—*werewolf, is trying to find a way to join Rachel and David Hue's pack;* Detective Glenn—*human, works out an arrangement for Rachel to see the bodies of the unregistered weres;* "The Iceman,"—*the human at the morgue who helps Rachel;* Denon—*a turned vampire, was Rachel's boss in the I.S.; her leaving (or, more accurately, Ivy's leaving) cost him in terms of status both at work and in the vampire society;* Skimmer—*a living vampire, is interested in rekindling her romance with Ivy;* Councilman Trenton Kalamack—*elf, is planning to marry an elf of good family;* Ellasbeth Withon—*elf, Trenton's fiancé;* Quen—*elf, is Kalamack's Head of Security;* Tom Bransen—*is a witch who works for I.S.; he knows that Rachel is performing demon magics, and he is not appalled;* Simon Ray and Mrs. Sarong—*are werewolf alphas who want to hire Rachel;* Patricia—*is Mrs. Sarong's daughter;* Kisten—*vampire, is developing a relationship with Rachel, and he has been almost single-handedly holding Piscary's empire together while Piscary is in jail;* Steve—*who works at Piscary's for Kisten;* Lee Saladan—*witch, becomes possessed by the demon Algaliarept;* Dr. Ford Miller—*a human, works for the FIB, but he is also an empath, which helps him in his work as a counselor;* Newt—*the only female demon, can cross into the world without being called;* Minias—*demon, is her keeper;* Dr. Williams—*who can't resanctify the church.*

8. "Dirty Magic" short story in *Hotter than Hell*, edited by Kim Harrison. New York: Harper, 2008, p. 469–91. ISBN: 9780061161292.

THE HOLLOWS, PRESENT DAY. Banshee Mia Harbor managed to use the psychotic rages of her husband Remus to create their beautiful daughter Holly. Innocent little Holly made a breakthrough. She demonstrated that it is possible to force emotional energy back into a human. When they don't feel as drained after an encounter, humans feel safer, and they leave themselves progressively more vulnerable. Holly taps Remus's emotions so often that he no longer experiences the emotional highs and lows, the terrific rages that sustained Mia's hunger for emotion. Mia finds herself walking down the street of an old lover, Tom. There is such anger in Tom. There is such hunger in Mia.

ASSOCIATES: Tom—*Mia's old lover.*

9. ***The Outlaw Demon Wails.*** New York: HarperCollins, c2008, 455 p. ISBN: 9780060788704.

CINCINNATI AND THE HALLOWS, OCTOBER 2007. Rachel thought that the demon Algaliarept was safely locked up in the ever-after; it never occurred to her that a demon can be summoned from anywhere in the ever-after, even from the confines of a cell. Someone is summoning "Al" specifically for the fun of loosing him into the world. The demon-summoner isn't breaking the law; it's not illegal to summon demons. He's not using the demon as a murder weapon, he's not commanding Al to go forth and kill Rachel. He doesn't have to. Al decided to kill Rachel all by himself. Rachel must find out who hates her enough to call forth Al and to free him into reality. Then she has to figure out how to stop him. On top of all of that, she has a deadline: demons can only be summoned after sunset, so Rachel has until then to prevent Al from being summoned into the world.

Rachel actually meets and survives this deadline for several days in this book. Each day requires a new tactic. She's as heedless of her own safety as ever, but in this book she's doing all she can to mend relationships and protect those who love her. She's a little more thoughtful and shows more empathy. In this book, she also learns to use ley-line magic to kindle light. This is a spell that no other witch can perform. Rachel finds out how different she is from other witches. She learns some of the secrets of the ancient history of the ever-after, and she can see how that history and her own life may change the future.

ASSOCIATES: Gargoyles are to witches as pixies are to elves (they like to be near them and help them in small ways). Bis—*the gargoyle, has taken up residence in the belfry of the church where Ivy (vampire), Rachel (witch), and Jenks's family (pixies) live;* Ryan Cormel—*vampire, was brought in to take over Piscary's camarilla;* Keasley—*a.k.a.* Leon Bairn, *a witch, he has watched out for Rachel, Jenks, and Ivy since they moved into the neighborhood;* Alice—*Rachel's mother, who has been making a good living selling charms that she's not licensed to craft;* Takata—*witch, the world-famous singer;* Captain Marshal—*the witch who helped Jenks and Rachel get to Bois Blanc Island in A Fistful of Charms, he was forced out of business and he has come to Cincinnati to build a new life;* Tom Bansen—*the witch who recruits for a fanatical black-arts cult, (works for Inlander Security);* Matalina—*pixie, Jenks's wife, is frail;* Jih—*a pixie, keeps Keasley's garden;* Rex—*a kitten, kept Jenks's son Jax alive last winter;* Ceridwen "Ceri" Merriam Dulciate—*the elf who was the demon Algaliarept's last familiar;* Quen—*elf, who works for the millionaire Trent;* Trent—*pureblood elf, whose father saved Rachel and Lee from a rare genetic blood disease;* Jon—*Trent's bodyguard;* Gerald—*Trent's security officer;* Dr. Anders—*witch, she taught a course in ley line magic at a local college and she flunked Rachel;* David Hue—*werewolf, Rachel's pack alpha, an insurance investigator;* Howard—*David's old business partner;* Betty—*who is interviewed by David and Rachel as they search for demon-related damage;* Sampson—*Betty's dog;* Algaliarept—*a demon who would like to get his hands on Rachel;* Minias—*demon, Algaliarept's jailer;* Newt—*the only female demon;* Dallkarackint—*a.k.a. Dali, demon, a civil servant;* FIB Detective Glenn Rose—*he helps Rachel by calling the animal protection agency.*

10. ***White Witch, Black Curse.*** New York: HarperCollins, c2009, 504 p. ISBN: 9780061138010.

The Hallows, December 2007. Glenn's friend Tom was killed and Glenn finds and confronts the murderers. They attack him and flee, leaving him for dead. Glenn's father, Edden, receives no assistance from Inderlander Security, and asks Rachel and Ivy to come and take a look at the crime scene. They become embroiled in the effort to find the murderers.

Rachel continues to struggle to remember the events of the night of Kisten's death. She and Ivy visit Skimmer in prison, hoping to find some answers. (The guards let Rachel and Ivy in simultaneously, even though it's against the rules. It's too dangerous for Rachel, but the guards wouldn't mind at all if Rachel were attacked and murdered during the visit.)

Ivy, Rachel, and Jenks realize that their home is haunted. Rachel is excited to learn that the ghost is someone she knew long ago. Jenks is terrified; the ghost has been in the church for months; he knows all their secrets. Jenks believes he may be a spy or, even worse than that, someone Rachel will decide she loves.

Al comes to Rachel while she's having a discussion with someone and, seeing an opportunity, he snatches Rachel's companion. Rachel is furious and frightened. His actions make it clear that he feels he has a right to kidnap those who are close to her whenever he crosses into her reality at her invitation. She agreed not to summon him into a circle that would prevent him from harming those around her or from snatching beings from this world and selling them into slavery in the ever-after. Now she realizes that she must force him to give his word that he won't harm or kidnap others when he gains entry into the world through her invitation.

After Rachel is shunned; her mother can no longer make a living selling charms. Rachel's mother moves to California to live near Rachel's brother Robbie and her children's birth father, Takata.

ASSOCIATES: Ford—*empathy wants to help Rachel recover her memories;* FIB (Federal Inderland Bureau) Detective Glenn—*loves tomatoes;* Edden—*Glenn's adoptive father, is Captain of the FIB's Cincinnati division;* Mia Harbor—*banshee, adopted the identities of the dead Tilson family for herself, her husband, and her daughter;* Remus—*Mia's husband;* Holly—*banshee, Mia's daughter;* Tom Bansen—*a shunned witch;* Marshal—*witch, Rachel takes him to dinner at her mother's home;* Alice—*witch, Rachel's mother;* Robbie—*Rachel's visiting brother;* Pierce—*ghost, witch, Rachel once worked a spell that gave Pierce a temporary body, Rachel intends to use it again;* Bis—*gargoyle, guards the church where Ivy, Rachel, and Jenks's family live;* Jenks—*pixie, his family is wintering in Rachel's desk so that they don't have to hibernate;* Matalina—*pixie, Jenks's wife, tries to come up with winter clothing that will keep him warm when he ventures outside;* Rex—*the cat, may have been frightened of the ghost;* Dr. Mape—*who meets with Rachel and Ms. Walker;* Ms. Walker—*a.k.a. The Walker, banshee, wants to know how Rachel survived a banshee attack;* Ivy—*living vampire, sneaks Rachel out of the hospital through the children's wing;* Daryl—*one of the children at the hospital;* Erica—*living vampire, Ivy's sister;* Ryan Cormel—*vampire;* Guard Miltast—*witch, seems disappointed when Rachel survives her prison visit;* Skimmer—*living vampire;* Algaliarept—*a.k.a. "Al", demon, warns Rachel that Pierce will try to kill her;* Marshal—*witch, is able to use his blood to invoke charms that would not invoke with Rachel's blood;* Quen—*elf, works for the millionaire Trent;* Trent—*pureblood elf, whose father saved Rachel from a rare genetic blood disease.*

HART, Carolyn G.

GHOST AT WORK

Genres/Themes Crossed: Paranormal X Traditional Mystery.

Subjects/Subgenres: Ghosts X Contemporary Amateur Sleuth.

Series/Stand-Alone: This novel is the first in a new series, the *Bailey Ruth Raeburn Mystery Series.* The second will be released October 27, 2009 and the title will be *Merry, Merry Ghost.*

Scene of the Crime: Present-day Adelaide, Oklahoma.

Detective: Bailey Ruth Raeburn led a charmed life from the time she was seven years old (and a sailor saw her tumble overboard, dived after her, and kept her afloat until a passing sailboat picked them up) until the day she died. She drowned many years later when her boat, the *Serendipity,* capsized while she and Bobbie Mac were on a fishing trip. Now, years after her death, she has decided that it's time to give back by volunteering to help people in need.

Known Associates: Bailey Ruth's handler is Wiggins. (He runs The Department of Good Intentions.)

Premise: Bailey Ruth Raeburn volunteered in her community while she was alive. (She was President of the Alter Guild.) She has been dead for over 20 years. Heaven is very nice (Bailey's husband Bobbie Mac loves the fishing), but the afterlife is somewhat dull. Bailey decides that it's time to help those who are in dire straits, and she applies at The Department of Good Intentions to get assigned to help someone on Earth. There, she's told that she must memorize and commit to the Precepts.

Precepts for Earthly Visitation

1. Avoid public notice.
2. No consorting with other departed spirits.
3. Work behind the scenes without making your presence known.
4. Become visible only when absolutely essential.
5. Do not succumb to the temptation to confound those who appear to oppose you.
6. Make every effort not to alarm earthly creatures.
7. Information about Heaven is not yours to impart. Simply smile and say, "Time will tell."
8. Remember always that you are on the earth, not of the earth.

She is accepted (on probation) as an emissary from the hereafter.

Comment: In a November 18, 2007, in a *Washington Post* column entitled "A Writer of Murder Mysteries Looks Back at the Body Count and Asks What Made Her Do It" Ms. Hart discussed the path she took to become a mystery novelist. She had been a journalist, but gave up her job when she had children. She missed writing, so she entered a contest to write a young adult mystery novel. Her *The Secret of the Cellars* won the contest and was published in 1964. Ms. Hart has written two children's mysteries, three young adult suspense novels, and 36 adult mystery or suspense novels. About *Ghost at Work,* Ms. Hart said that she had never had more fun writing a book. In a *Read Street* interview (http://weblogs.baltimoresun.com/entertainment/books/blog/2008/10/carolyn_hart_on_good_vs_evil.html), Carolyn Hart said that her editor described this book as "whimsy with a mystery." In that interview Ms. Hart talks about good and evil. The murder victim in *Ghost at Work* engaged in evil. He used his wealth and political power to bully others, even resorting to blackmail. He destroyed the lives he touched. His victims and the people who loved his victims are the suspects in his murder. Even those who are innocent of murder have taken actions that they knew were wrong. They violated professional oaths, personal honor, and sacred vows. They can be blackmailed; if their actions came to light their reputations would be destroyed. None of them are angels, but as Ms. Hart has said:

> Within mysteries and within ourselves, the desire to be good and the struggle to avoid evil is forever waged... The reader sees what happens when characters succumb to evil... Yet the mystery in its resolution always celebrates goodness, and the light overcomes the dark (quoted from "Carolyn Hart on Good vs. Evil" on the *Baltimore Sun*'s Read Street blog from the Bouchercon October 7, 2008, http://weblogs.baltimoresun.com/entertainment/books/blog/bouchercon/).

Literary Magic & Mayhem: Bailey is goodhearted, protective, and impulsive. She punctures the self-importance of the pompous mayor, confounds the Police Chief, and conspires with her great-granddaughter Bayroo. Her good qualities, such as her empathy, combined with her bad qualities, such as her scapegrace attitude towards authority, make her a likable protagonist.

Bailey's daughter Dillon is "on the sassy side of 45" in 2007. Dillon was old enough to be furious when Bailey accompanied Bobby Mac on the fatal fishing trip. Bailey's mother was a flapper when she was young. Today, Bailey looks as if she is in her twenties, but she died when she was much older. She knows nothing of computers or cell phones. Altogether it seems likely that Bailey grew up in the 1930s and 1940s. It's interesting to see the methods that she uses to assert her will. They include a fair amount of game-playing, including coy statements, lying, and strategic tears.

Explorations: What actions left people open to blackmail? How would matters have been resolved if there had been no blackmailer involved?

Bailey violates the Precepts often. When are the violations justified? When are they not justified?

How does Bailey react to people with authority who have no power over her? How does Bailey react to people with authority who do have power over her? How does Bailey work to get what she wants? How would Bailey be different if she'd grown up in a different era?

What actions of Bailey's changed people's lives? How were they changed?

THE CASE

1. ***Ghost at Work.*** New York: HarperCollins Publishers, 2008, 290 p. ISBN: 9780060874360.

ADELAIDE, OKLAHOMA, OCTOBER 2007. Bailey Rae Raeburn died decades ago. She has enjoyed herself in Heaven, and she wants to give back, to help others. She volunteers at The Department of Good Intentions. She pictures her first assignment, maybe in Paris. Bailey always wanted to go to Paris. It's never too late! Unfortunately, she doesn't speak French. In Heaven everyone can communicate, no matter what language they speak. Bailey thought that if she were on a mission for Heaven, people in Paris would have no trouble understanding her. Wiggins breaks the news that things work differently on Earth than they do in Heaven, telling her that the crux of the situation is that "There is not here." Bailey thinks:

> I suspected this was more profound than I could manage. I'm bright enough, but I have my limits. Deep thoughts remain precisely that, deep thoughts, and I don't have a shovel. (p. 9)

Wiggins decides to assign her to her home town, Adelaide, Oklahoma, and is just beginning her orientation to being an "emissary" (he objects to the word "ghost") when there is an emergency. Bailey is thrown into the situation before she has even read through the precepts. She finds herself at the rectory, where the rector's wife has just discovered a body. Ever helpful, Bailey reveals herself and helps move the body. Having begun by tampering with a crime scene, she continues by robbing the body, moving the weapon, and abetting another in destroying evidence. Then, knowing that she has made it more difficult for the authorities to solve the crime, Bailey takes on the task of discovering the murderer.

ASSOCIATES: Kathleen Abbott—*great-grandniece of Bailey Ruth;* Father Bill Abbott—*Kathleen's husband;* Bayroo—*their 11-year-old daughter;* Lucinda Wilkie—*Bayroo's best friend;* Travis Calhoun—*a 15-year-old celebrity who has never had a homemade birthday cake;* Sexton Isaac Franklin, his wife Evelyn, Elise, Rose, Irene Chatham, and Jeff Jameson—*are members of St. Mildred's Episcopal Church;* Law enforcement officers include Police Chief Sam Cobb; Detective Sergeant Hal Price—*who finds Bailey Ruth attractive;* Officer Anita Leland—*who enjoyed giving Daryl Murdoch speeding tickets;* Sergeant Lewis; and Officer Jake Harmon. Dillon—*Bailey Ruth's daughter;* Robert MacNeill Raeburn III—*Bailey Ruth's son;* Mayor Neva Lumpkin; Bob Shelton—*Georgia*

Hamilton's lawyer; Walter Carey—*Daryl Murdoch's ex-partner;* Judith—*Daryl Murdoch's wife;* Kirby—*his son;* Lily Mendoza—*Kirby's girlfriend;* Mrs. Talley—*who Daryl forced to fire Lily;* Patricia Haskins—*Daryl's secretary, is trying to get everything in order before closing the office;* Cynthia Brown—*was Daryl's current girlfriend.*

HIGHTOWER, Lynn.

DETECTIVE DAVID SILVER SERIES

Genres/Themes Crossed: Blended Society X Police Procedural.

Subjects/Character Types: Aliens X Police Procedural.

Series/Stand-Alone: Series. Major changes take place in the characters and the relationships, so the series entries should be read in order.

Scene of the Crime: Earth, 2040s.

Detective(s): When David Silver was a child, his father went out for doughnuts and never came back. David and his mother Lavinia moved into the underground slums of Little Saigo. They put themselves under the protection of Maid Marion. David's mother wouldn't let him get branded with a *toogim* symbol because she believed that it would be more difficult for him to escape the slums if he bore the mark.

Known Associates: David's wife Rose used to work for the Drug Enforcement Agency (which, at this time, is part of the military). She left the agency after her partner was tortured and murdered; now she works for a militant animal rights organization doing whatever it take to close down bad labs. Rose and David's daughters are Kendra, Lisa, and Mattie. The family acquires a variety of animals that Rose rescues and brings home. In *Alien Blues* they have a dog who answers only to the name "Dead Meat" (that had been the name on the cage where Rose found him). Rose's partner is Haas. David's partner Mel Burnett is Rose's brother. Other cops on the Homicide Task Force include Captain Halliday, Della Martinas, and Pete Ridel.

Premise: The Elaki, a race of aliens with superior technology, have colonized Earth. Their presence is mostly benevolent. They have developed a cure for schizophrenia and are working on cures for addictions and eating disorders; but they have taken the best jobs, they make the most money, and many of them seem to regard humans as an interesting but primitive species. Humans have become second-class citizens on their own planet. It's not just that the Elaki are more powerful. The worst problem is that humans, even self-possessed and competent humans, have become convinced of their own inferiority. For instance, when David meets a bigoted Elaki, he feels self-conscious:

> David was aware of her cool lime scent. He wondered if she was bothered by his human cheese smell...
>
> David did not like the feel of the Ambassador, or the waves of contempt that emanated from Cook and Slyde. More so than the usual reaction? Could he blame them for not wanting cheesy people in their restaurant? (p. 46)

Comment: After earning her bachelor's degree in journalism, Lynn Hightower spent a little time writing television commercials, then returned to college to get a master's degree in business administration. Before she finished the program, she realized that business administration was not her passion, and she changed her life to focus on her writing.

Lynn Hightower won the 1984 Shamus Award for Best First PI Novel for *Satan's Lambs*. Her book *The Debt Collector* was a nominee for the 2001 Mary Higgins Clark Award. She teaches in the U.C.L.A. Extension Writers' Program. Her Web site, http://www.lynnhightower.com/index.html, includes biographical information, and information on her books.

Literary Magic & Mayhem: The series includes a sensitive depiction of the loneliness of a marriage, in which the husband and wife are not able to share their lives. There are too many heartbreaking details to count. For instance, David has learned to take comfort in talking to Rose while she sleeps. He started telling her about his day, his concerns, and his joys while she slept when their children were young, and Rose was so exhausted that she would fall asleep the moment that they got into bed. Now, this speaking in the dark to someone who will neither respond nor remember anything he says has become his way of sharing his life.

David's mother, Lavinia Hicks Silver (1986–2040), was a depressive, and David is painfully aware of Rose's depressive episodes. Every day he checks to see how she spent the day. Did she find the energy to move from the porch swing? He tries to help her, but feels powerless. David is a very decent person. His father disappeared when David was young, and seven years later, when his father was declared dead, David said the Kaddish for him every day for 11 months. Even while he wondered whether his father died or abandoned the family, David missed him and said the Kaddish, feeling that someone should say it because it would have meant so much to his father.

Explorations: If a technologically advanced species traveled to Earth, what is the best that humans could expect?

How would humans be likely to treat the aliens?

Many of the characters live in some degree of mental anguish. How do different people cope? How do others help them? There is a saying: "Be kind to the people you meet for everyone is fighting his own battle."

THE CASES

1. *Alien Blues.* New York: Ace Books, 1992, 251 p. ISBN: 0441644600.

SAIGO CITY, CALIFORNIA, SUMMER 2040. Captain Halliday assigns an Elaki named String to work with David and Mel on their cases. Mel is furious, but soon finds ways to amuse himself at the Elaki's expense, and gradually comes to enjoy String's company.

David and Mel finally get a break in the Machete Man case. The murderer's latest victim escaped before he could touch her, but even after David learns what she saw, he can't discern the serial killer's pattern for choosing victims. The list of victims continues to grow and soon includes cops and aliens (Elaki). It is perplexing. There is no record (at least none that humans can access) of Elaki committing serious crimes. There is such a social distance between humans and Elaki that it is difficult to imagine a human murdering an Elaki. Yet Elaki are dying. Their deaths are clearly premeditated murders. Who would kill an Elaki?

In the course of the investigation, David runs into other crimes. There have been midnight abductions of tunnel dwellers from the underground slums of Little Saigo. Rose and Haas discover a terrifying illegal lab set up for drug testing on animals. Through a transfer of memories from one Elaki, David learns that another Elaki is a killer.

ASSOCIATES: Millicent Darnell—*who escaped the Machete Man;* Dennis Winston—*Millicent's son;* Alex—*is Dennis Winston's cat;* Tester—*is an Elaki who works with Dennis Winston;* Captain Roger Halliday—*heads the Homicide Task Force;* David Silver, Mel Burnett, Della Martinas, and Pete Ridel—*are homicide cops;* Dawn Weiler—*is an FBI profiler assigned to the Machete Man case;* Mr. Puzzle Solver—*a.k.a. Sheesha, an Elaki assigned to the Homicide Task Force as an advisor;* Mr. String—*an Elakii, an Izicho Representative, assigned to the Task Force as an advisor;* Lieutenant Coltrane—*the head of the Vice Task Force;* Vern Dyer, Harry Myer, and Ian Shavstik—*are cops assigned to vice;* Judith Rawley—*Dyer's girlfriend;* Miriam and Bradston—*who work in the morgue;* Rose—*David's wife and Mel's sister;* Kendra, Lisa, and Mattie—*David and Rose's three daughters*: "Dead Meat"—*a dog Rose brought home, he was rescued during her raid on an illegal lab and only answers to Dead Meat;* Haas—*Rose's business partner, who tries to rename the dog Hilde;* Ms. Cook (Elaki), Mr. Slyde (Elaki), and Claude (Human)—*are staff at The Ambassador Restaurant (which does not cater to humans);* Maid Marion—*who helps the people in Little Saigo;* Naomi Chessfield—*a tunnel-rat in Little Saigo;* Bertie, Santana, and Quintero—*are others who David encounters in Little Saigo.*

2. *Alien Eyes.* New York: Ace Books, c1993, 245 p. ISBN: 044101688X.

SAIGO CITY, CALIFORNIA, SUMMER 2042. Something strange is happening in the Elaki communities of Earth. An old political feud has re-ignited. Many years ago, the Guardians spoke out against the Izicho (Elaki secret police). Rogue Izicho captured and tortured some of the Guardians; they engaged in home-invasion *cho* killings. Eventually the Izicho policed themselves and threw out the rogue officers. The memories live on. It is difficult for Guardians to accept Izicho. For the last 19 months, there have been cho killings on Earth. Elaki from the Guardians have begun to speak out on Earth, and the Izicho are under suspicion. Once more, the Izicho decide that they must police their own ranks. They send for new Izicho from the home planet to come to Earth and conduct the investigation. Some Izicho make arrangements to come, but they never meet with the Izicho on Earth.

David and Mel have been working on the cho killings for 19 months. Their partner, String, has been acting in a strange and secretive fashion, and that has put a strain on their team. They spend part of their time suspecting String, and part of their time covering for him. Recently the Saigo Police Department has been put under the command of F. Angelo Ogden. He assigns three new Elaki to the Homicide Task Force. They are regarded as spies throughout the department, and the squad bands together to impede their investigations. At the completion of the investigation, it strikes David that he would have treated them differently if they'd been human, but since they were Elaki, he never thought of them as rookies.

ASSOCIATES: Mel Burnett and the Elaki, String—*are David's partners;* Captain Roger Halliday—*head of the Homicide Task Force, is David's boss;* Della Martinas and Pete Ridel—*are homicide detectives in Saigo City PD;* Miriam Kellog—*coroner's technician;* Officer Janet Kellog—*Miriam's sister;* Officer Daley, Officer Vanelli, and the incompetent Officers Gaskin and Bertelli—*also work for the Saigo City PD;* Commander F. Angelo Ogden—*the new leader of the department, he will go to any lengths to get good press;* Walker, Thinker, and Ash—*are three new Elaki who have been added to the Homicide Task Force;* Rose—*David's wife;* Kendra, Lisa, and Mattie—*are their daughters;* Alex (cat), Hilde (dog), a calf, a llama, and an ostrich that Rose rescued from a poorly-run petting zoo—*are the family's pets;* Packer—*a.k.a. Dahmi, an Elaki who from all accounts was an ideal Mother-One;* Painter—*an Elaki, Dahmi's neighbor;* Doctor Aslanti; Wendy and Lawrence McCallum—*the parents of Mark McCallum;* George and Mickey—*Wendy and Lawrence's grandchildren;* Stephen Arnold—*Charlotte McCallum's father;* Ben Smed—*a campus cop;* Dreamer (Elaki) and Tate Donovan—*are students;* Angel Eyes—*an Elaki, the founder of the Guardian party, now a guest lecturer at the School of Diplomacy;* Weid—*an Elaki, Angel's companion/bodyguard;* Pierre—*who runs the Café Pierre;* Yahray—*an Elaki, an elderly Mother-One who has been standing outside of the police station;* Calii—*an Elaki, Yahray's grown-up pouchling, he left for Earth eight years ago;* Biachi—*an Elaki, a relative of String, Biachi will be guarded by Rose;* Haas—*Rose's partner, now has two prosthetic legs.*

3. *Alien Heat.* New York: Ace Books, 1994, 230 p. ISBN: 044100072X.

Saigo City, California, July 2043. Bomb threats tie up the grid, slowing fire engines as a fire rages through a bar and the houses near it. In the end, over 200 humans and Elaki are killed. It's the most recent in a string of fires, and arson investigators suspect insurance fraud.

Theresa Jenks left her family three months ago. For years she'd been despondent over the death of her first son. Eventually she found comfort in the Mind Institute's teachings. Her husband, Dr. Jenks, and her son, Arthur, bring psychic Teddy Blake to Saigo to find her.

One of the themes of this entry in the series is the new closeness of Elaki–human interactions. The societies are becoming more integrated. The Saigo Police Department is considered a pioneer in adding Elaki officers to police units. Now, most units include Elaki. There are clubs, bars, and restaurants where Elakis and humans interact. There are a few Elaki-human couples. Some members of both societies are enraged. The Kahaners are an Elaki group that hates humans; the SCAE (Skinhead Christians Against Elaki) are a human group that hates Elaki; both groups hate the mingling of the two species. The Elaki Benevolent Association works to promote the peaceful coexistence of the races with its Racial Harmony Award.

In this book a psychic finds David's father and he finally knows the truth. This book includes other major changes in the personal lives of the detectives. David realizes that his marriage may be ending. Both David and Rose know that something has gone very wrong with their marriage, and neither knows what to do about it. They share a love for their children, but everything else in their marriage has ended. As David's family unravels String begins a family. String, Warden, and Doctor Aslanti form a family (chemaki) to care for Calib.

Associates: Mel Burnett and String (Elaki)—*are David's partners;* Walker (Elaki) and Della Martinas—*other members of the Homicide Task Force;* Captain Roger Halliday—*leads the Homicide Task Force;* "Wart" Warden (Elaki) and Yolanda Free "Yo Free" Clements—*are Arson Squad detectives with the Saigo City PD;* Calib—*is Yolanda's son;* Miriam Kellog—*a coroner's technician, is dating Mel;* Dawn Weiler—*an FBI agent who warns David that the FBI is investigating him;* John Brevitt and Grey Peterson—*are other FBI agents;* Smokar (Elaki)—*an ATF officer;* Penny—*a.k.a. LaFarge, a four-year-old;*

Mr. Tatewood—*a real estate broker who is receiving hate mail from the SCAE (Skinhead Christians Against Elaki);* Mr. Cromwell—*a bar owner;* Ms. Ellis Clay—*a retriever (garbage worker);* Barclay—*her dog;* Jordiki—*a psychic of the Mind Institute;* Alford Crumbo—*who works for the Institute;* Candy Andy—*a psychic;* Psychic Teddy Blake—*a psychic who came to Saigo to help Arthur;* Arthur—*Dr. Jenks and Theresa Jenks's son;* Rose—*David's wife;* Mattie, Lisa, and Kendra—*their daughters;* Elliot—*the kids missing pet iguana.*

4. *Alien Rites.* New York: Ace Books, 1995, 221 p. ISBN: 0441002196.

Saigo City, California, 2044? Three-week-old infant Hank Trey died of a mysterious ailment. The police investigation is not complete, but the public is convinced that his mother, Annie Trey, poisoned him. Now the baby's father, Luke Cochran, is missing, and she is in the spotlight once again. When Cochran's bloody car is found near Elaki-Town, homicide is called in to investigate. David meets Annie Trey at the scene. He is soon convinced that she is a good mother; but he has known good mothers who have done terrible things.

Miriam Kellog worked on the autopsy of little Hank Trey. She had not completed her work when she disappeared. She's Mel's girlfriend. They had a fight, and at first he thought that she was avoiding him, but when the investigation of Luke Cochran begins, Mel realizes that she disappeared the same night as Luke. No one will admit to having seen Miriam in the last five days. Mel is almost in despair, believing that both she and Luke have been killed.

David comes down with a rare disease. There is a treatment, but the prognosis is not good. He wishes that he'd seen Teddy again, that he had more time with his children, that he'd spent the time to repair his motorcycle. He realizes that what he wants most is to complete the investigation and find Miriam, so, with his family's support, he returns to work.

Associates: Captain Roger Halliday—*who runs the Homicide Task Force;* Mel Burnett and String (Elaki)—*are David's partners;* Della Martinas and Walker (Elaki)—*are also on the Homicide Task Force;* Miriam Kellog—*a coroner's technician, has been dating Mel;* Detective Vincent Thurman—*an officer on the Saigo PD's Missing Persons Task Force;* Patrolman Alec Arnold; Samuel Caper—*a new Crime Scene Unit technician;* Vanessa—*a forensic mechanic;* Sergeant Courtney; Luke Cochran—*who is missing;* Tina—*Luke's mother;* Sifter Chuck (Elaki)—*an antiques store owner;* Professor Elizabeth Dunkirk—*a researcher;* Angie Nassif—*a social worker;* Crystal—*who lives with Angie;* Annie Trey—*a 19-year-old who David believes to be a good mother;* Jenny—*Annie's 18-month-old daughter;* Eddie Eyebrows, Mr. Dandy, the singer Valentine, Valentine's daughter Cassidy, and Cassidy's kitten, Baby Blue—*live in Annie's apartment house in Cracker Village, and are Annie's friends;* Officer Janet Kellog—*Miriam Kellog's sister;* Dr. Aslanti—*who diagnoses David as having a rare (and usually fatal) disease;* Rose—*David's wife;* Pid—*a very sick pig that Rose rescued;* Mattie, Lisa, and Kendra—*are David's daughters, they are focused on nursing Pid back to health.*

HOOD, Robert. Co-editor (with Stuart Coupe and Julie Ogden) of *Crosstown Traffic: Romance, Horror, Fantasy, SF, Western Invade Crime Fiction.* See Coupe, Stuart: Crosstown Traffic: Romance, Horror, Fantasy, SF, Western Invade Crime Fiction.

HUFF, Tanya.

BLOOD PRICE

Genres/Themes Crossed: Secret Society X Police Procedural.

Subjects/Character Types: Vampires, Werewolves, Zombies, Ghosts, Demons, Spell-Casters (Sorcery) X Amateur Sleuth (Contemporary), Police Procedural.

Series/Stand-Alone: The characters change over the course of the series, so these are best read in series order.

Scene of the Crime: Toronto, Vancouver, and London, Canada.

Detectives: Tanya Huff has created two interlocking series of mysteries with different protagonists.

Henry Fitzroy is the protagonist of the *Smoke* novels. He is a 450-year-old vampire. The bastard son of Henry VIII, Fitzroy makes his living writing historical romance novels based on his own life under the pseudonym of his half sister, Elizabeth Fitzroy.

Vicki "Victory" Nelson is the protagonist of the *Blood* novels. She was a police officer who suffered from a deteriorating eye condition that gradually robbed her of her night vision. Rather than taking a desk job, Vicki retired from the force and became a private investigator. Vicki's nickname is derived from her extraordinary success rate with cases, but this is probably due to the fact that she is stubborn to the point of refusing to ever give in or be beaten by anything, accepting only total victory. Towards the end of the *Blood Books*, Henry is forced to turn Vicki into a vampire in order to save her life.

Tony Foster was a troubled teen in Toronto who began a relationship with Henry Fitzroy and managed to pull his act together. At the end of the *Blood Books*, Henry and Tony move to Vancouver, and while there, Tony begins working on a television series about a vampire detective. In the *Smoke Books,* Tony discovers that he is a sorcerer and begins training to use his newfound magical powers.

Known Associates: Mike Celluci was Vicki's partner on the police force. Mike is a rival with Henry, competing for Vicki's affection.

Premise: Vampires are real and live by a code of conduct that requires that they do not slaughter the innocent, do avoid detection, and do not invade another vampire's territory. Other supernatural creatures exist and magic is real. Henry Fitzroy and the individuals associated with him attempt to solve mysteries involving supernatural entities preying on the innocent citizens of their home towns.

Comments: This series is composed of two interconnected series, the *Blood Books* and the *Smoke and Shadows* Books. The *Blood Books* focus on Vicki Nelson and are set primarily in Toronto. The *Smoke and Shadows Books* focus on Tony Foster and are set primarily in Vancouver. Henry Fitzroy is the only character to appear throughout the two interrelated series, and although he is not the central character of either series, he is the strongest link between the two. For this reason, the two series are sometimes collectively referred to as the *Henry Fitzroy Mysteries.* Each series can be read independently, although the books within each series should be read in order. The *Blood Books* have been adapted as a television series for the Lifetime network under the title "Blood Ties." It premiered in the United States on March 11, 2007. At this time the show is not in production. Two seasons exist on DVD and can be viewed on the Lifetime Network website (http://www.mylifetime.com/on-tv/shows/blood-ties/full-episodes-season-1/video). The *Blood Books* series has been collected in three omnibus books, with two of the original novels in each book. The third omnibus includes the fifth book and all of the short stories related to the series, collected under the title *Blood Bank.* This is the most efficient way available to collect these short stories, the majority of which had previously been published across multiple anthologies published over the course of nearly a decade. Anyone who wishes to ensure that they do not miss out on any of the stories involving these characters would be wise to collect the third omnibus rather than purchasing the fifth book as a single volume.

Tanya Huff blogs at her Live Journal page at http://andpuff.livejournal.com/.

Literary Magic and Mayhem: The dialog and the temperaments of the main characters provide some of the humor of the series. Vicki's temper is legendary. The triangle, when she is caught between two very different men, both of whom she loves, is intriguing.

Henry Fitzroy is the bridge between the two series. When he and Vicki need to live in different cities, he leaves Toronto and moves to Vancouver. Tony accompanies him.

Explorations: How does territoriality relate to love? To success?

How does a willingness to compromise, or a lack thereof, relate to love? To success?

THE CASES

1. ***Blood Price.*** New York: DAW, 2007, 272 p. ISBN: 0756405017 (with *Blood Trail* as *The Blood Books, Vol. 1,* ISBN: 0756403871).

TORONTO, CANADA, MODERN DAY. A series of violent murders in Toronto seems to point towards the impossible—a vampire. Vicki Nelson is drawn into the investigation, along with her former partner Mike Celluci, and she meets Henry Fitzroy.

ASSOCIATES: Mike Celluci, Dave Graham, PC West, Caroline, Greg, Mrs. Hughes, Mrs. Kopolous, Dr. Singh, Dr. Anderson, Thomas, Alex, Isabella, Coreen, Tony Foster.

2. ***Blood Trail.*** New York: DAW, 2007, 304 p. ISBN: 0756405025.

TORONTO AND LONDON, CANADA MODERN DAY. The werewolves of London, Ontario have been targeted by a hunter who has discovered their true nature. The werewolves ask Henry Fitzroy for help, and Henry asks Vicki to come with him to help with the investigation and keep him safe while he is vulnerable during the day.

ASSOCIATES: Marjory Nelson, Mike Celluci, Greg, Rose Heerkens, Peter Heerkens, Stuart Heerkens-Wells, Nadine Heerkens-Wells, Donald Heerkens, Colin Heerkens, Daniel Heerkens-Wells, Jennifer Heerkens-Wells, Marie Heerkens-Wells, Frederick Kleinbein, Tony Foster, Dr. Dixon, Arthur Fortrin, Barry Wu.

3. ***Blood Lines.*** New York: DAW, 2007, 272 p. ISBN: 0756405033 (with *Blood Pact* as *The Blood Books, Vol. 2,* ISBN: 075640388X).

TORONTO, CANADA MODERN DAY. Henry Fitzroy is haunted by dreams involving the sun and turns to Vicki for help. Mike Celluci is investigating a series of murders at a museum hosting a special Egyptology exhibition, and is convinced that the culprit is a mummy brought back to life.

ASSOCIATES: Mike Celluci, Marjory Nelson, Dave Graham, Constable Trembley, Constable Harper, Kevin, Raymond Thompson, Dr. Shane, Tony Foster, Inspector Cantree, Staff Sergeant Gowan.

4. ***Blood Pact.*** New York: DAW, 2007, 336 p. ISBN: 0756405041.

TORONTO AND KINGSTON, CANADA MODERN DAY. When Vicki's mother, Marjory Nelson, dies, Vicki travels to Kingston to make the funeral arrangements, only to find that her mother's body has disappeared. Vicki is drawn into an investigation to uncover the grisly experiment that led to her mother's death.

ASSOCIATES: Mike Celluci, Mrs. Shaw, Mr. Hutchinson, Mr. Delgado, Tony Foster, Reverend Crosbie, Detective Fergusson.

5. ***Blood Debt.*** New York: DAW, 2007, 336 p. ISBN: 075640505X (with a collection of short stories titled *Blood Bank* as *The Blood Books, Vol. 3,* ISBN: 0756403928).

TORONTO AND VANCOUVER, CANADA MODERN DAY. Henry is being haunted by ghosts who seem to be seeking a means towards justice and vengeance against their murderers. In an attempt to solve the cases, Henry calls on Vicki Nelson for help, and must see if two vampires can manage to get along long enough to solve the cases.

ASSOCIATES: Mike Celluci, Tony Foster, Corporal Roberts, Lisa Evans, Mrs. Munro, Mr. Swanson, Richard Sullivan, Inspector Cantree, John, Gerry, Ms. Chou, Sebastian Carl, Jenna Carl, Haiden, Bynowski, Gabriel Constantine, Lori Constantine.

6. ***Blood Bank.*** (This is a collection of short stories originally published elsewhere, bound with *Blood Debt* as *The Blood Books, Vol. 3,* ISBN: 0756403928).

SHORT STORIES: This Town Ain't Big Enough. What Manner of Man. The Cards Also Say. The Vengeful Spirit of Lake Nepeakea. Someone to Share the Night. Another Fine Nest. Scleratus. Critical Analysis. So This Is Christmas. Writing "Stone Cold." "Stone Cold" screenplay.

7. ***Smoke and Shadows.*** New York: DAW, 2005, 416 p. ISBN: 0756402638.

VANCOUVER, CANADA, PRESENT DAY. Tony's show is the scene of a murder by a mysterious figure, more shadow than substance. Tony and Henry join forces with Arra Pelindrake, a special-effects wizard as well as genuine spell-casting wizard, in order to repel the otherworldly beings responsible for the murder.

ASSOCIATES: Mason Reed, Peter Hudson, Lee Nicholas, Chester Bane, Everett, Rachel Chou, Rajeet Singh, Jennifer, Zev Cero, Amy, Barb Dixon, Arra Pelindrake, Daniel, Veronica, Nikki Waugh, Adam Paelous, Constable Danvers, Constable Elson.

8. ***Smoke and Mirrors.*** New York: DAW, 2006, 416 p. ISBN: 0756403480.

VANCOUVER, CANADA, PRESENT DAY. An episode of *Darkest Night* is being filmed on location in a mansion being used by the show as a haunted house, but things turn ugly when it is discovered that the house is actually haunted.

ASSOCIATES: Mason Reed, Peter Hudson, Lee Nicholas, Adam Paelous, Everett, Brenda, Tina, Karen, Mr. Brummel, Zev Cero, Cassie, Stephen, Graham, Wanda, Sorge, Sharyl, Ruth, Amy, Ashley, Brianna, Constable Danvers, Constable Elson, Chris, Tom, Karl, Pavin, Ujjal, Chester Bane.

9. *Smoke and Ashes.* New York: DAW, 2007, 407 p. ISBN: 0756404150.

VANCOUVER, CANADA, PRESENT DAY. Tony must improve his skills as a wizard and protect Leah Burnett, a stuntwoman and millenia-old priestess, or face a massive invasion of demons.

ASSOCIATES: Mason Reed, Peter Hudson, Lee Nicholas, Adam Paelous, Everett, Zev Sero, Leah Burnett, Angela, Karen, Keisha, Walter Davis, Constable Elson, Ujjal, Sorge, Kevin Groves, Padma Sathaye, Chester Bane, Alison Larkin, Amy, Rachel Chou, Brianna, Pam, Daniel.

HUSTON, Charlie.

ALREADY DEAD

Genres/Themes Crossed: Secret Society X Hard-Boiled Mystery.

Subjects/Subgenres: Vampires, Zombies X Private Investigator.

Series/Stand-Alone: The relationships and alliances change over time. Joe changes too, partly in his understanding of the reality behind the masks worn by different people, and partly in his understanding of himself and his own priorities.

Scene of the Crime: Present-day Manhattan.

Detective: "Joe Pitt" is Joe's *nom de guerre;* his original name was Simon. He was born in the Bronx in 1960, and was on the streets and doing drugs by the time he was 15 years old. When he was 17, he was bitten by a *Vampyre* (vampire) who was slumming; he left Joe for dead. Terry Bird found him bleeding to death, picked him up and took him home. For a while, Joe worked for Terry Bird, who runs The Society, then he went his own way. He tries to stay independent of all of the Vampyre gangs by being useful to many of them. He works, for the gangs and for individuals as a private investigator.

Although he died when he was 17, at the beginning of the series he looks as if he's about 28. If he drank more blood and didn't suffer any physical traumas he would look younger.

Known Associates: Joe's girlfriend Evie is HIV-positive and avoids intimacy because she is afraid of passing on the disease. This works well for Joe. He feels that no one is sure that the *Vyrus* (vampire virus) that turns humans into Vampyres cannot be transmitted by sex, and he's determined that he will never pass the Vyrus on to anyone. She thinks that Joe is being noble, which makes him feel guilty, but he can't tell her the truth without telling her about Vampyres. He could cure her HIV by giving her the Vyrus. It's a temptation.

Premise: There are Vampyres in New York. Most are part of one clan or another. In Manhattan there are many clans: The Bulls and Bears have the territory at the tip of Manhattan, near the territory of The Wall, and The Dusters. Those clans have peripheral roles in the series. The main players are members of The Society, which is run by Terry Bird; The Coalition, with Dexter Predo as the Head of the Coalition's Secret Police; and The Enclave, with Daniel as their leader. There is a map of the territories at the beginning of each book. (Later in the series The Hood with territory up above The Coalition plays a major role.)

Vampyres stay hidden. If necessary, they will kill to keep their existence a secret. The Society's reputation is that it is relatively benevolent. The Coalition's reputation is that it is businesslike and ruthless. The Enclave's reputation is that the Vampyres who belong to it are crazy. The members of The Enclave believe that one day one Vampyre will find a way to use his will to overcome the Vyrus, and that he will evolve into a higher being—his example will show others the way.

The series traces the disillusionment of a character who regarded himself as tough and cynical from the pages of the first book. It's not just that the world is evil; it's that it's so much more evil than he thought.

Comment: The series is very dark, very adult. It's only one of Charlie Huston's series. He has also authored the *Henry Thompson* trilogy: *Caught Stealing, Six Bad Things,* and *A Dangerous Man*. Mr. Huston has also written stand-alone novels (the most recent is *The Mystic Arts of Erasing All Signs of Death,*) and comic books, including *Moon Knight* for Marvel Comics. Charlie Huston's Web site is located at: http://www.pulpnoir.com/.

Literary Magic & Mayhem: The combination of complex characters, fast pacing, and a cynical narrator make these interesting reads. Over the course of the series, the good guys are revealed as self-interested, deadly, lying politicians; and the bad guys, who originally looked simply vicious and amoral, are revealed as profoundly evil. It's astonishing to find that Joe Pitt, who initially comes across as a cynical hard-case, was actually naïve.

Mordant humor in the narration and in the dialog provides comic relief. For instance, at one point (*Already Dead,* p. 41) Joe uses the word "zombies" in front of Terry Bird, Tom Nolan, and Lydia Miles. Tom is furious:

> That's what I'm talking about, that right there. We rejected that term, man. We voted. They're not zombies. That belittles their status as victims, man.

Terry, of course, agrees.

> The term zombie does put the onus for their actions on them and implies blame.

(It turns out that they had agreed on the term "VOZ," or "Victims of Zombification.") Then Lydia objects,

> I'm still opposed to the use of the word victim. It suggests weakness, helplessness.

And on it goes. All of this as part of a discussion over whether or not they should interrogate Joe before they kill him. The combination of their distraction over politically correct terms while they cold-bloodedly discuss Joe's path to his final death is both hysterical and chilling.

Joe Pitt is a character who's just trying to get along. He's hoping to be left alone. It's not going to happen. Joe is an asset, and every powerful player in Joe's world works to find ways to force Joe into his or her service.

Explorations: Did the Enclave's philosophies seem realistic when first encountered? Why or why not? Did the perception of their philosophy and capabilities change during the course of the book?

Were sections of the book funny? Did any of the conversations between Vampyres seem strangely familiar?

How did different members of The Society use political correctness?

Did Terry Bird's actions match the image he works to project? In what ways did they match? In what ways were his actions at odds with his image?

THE CASES

1. ***Already Dead.*** New York: Ballantine Books, 2005, 268 p. ISBN: 034547824X; 9780345478245.

MANHATTAN, SUMMER 2005. Joe came across the zombies by chance. He tracked and destroyed the kids who were infected, but he didn't find the carrier, and he left one uninfected young witness alive. The Coalition is displeased. They order him to find the carrier, but his investigation goes awry. An admission of failure could be fatal, so he lies. (If he's discovered in a lie? That could also be fatal.) Joe's trying to find the carrier quickly (and quietly) when Head of Coalition Security, Dexter Predo, sends him another case. It seems simple, if urgent. Find Amanda, the missing daughter of the wealthy Marilee Ann Horde. Find her fast, there are monsters out there.

ASSOCIATES: Evie—*is Joe's girlfriend;* Terry Bird (Vampyre)—*runs The Society, Joe used to work for him;* Hurley (Vampyre)—*Terry's enforcer;* Tom Nolan (Vampyre) and Lydia Miles (Vampyre)—*are part of inner circle of The Society;* Philip Sax—*is a toady who wants to be made a Vampyre;* Dexter Predo (Vampyre)—*is the head of the Coalition's Secret Police;* Marilee Ann Horde—*a client sent to Joe by Dexter Predo;* Daniel (Vampyre)—*head of the Enclave;*

Christian (Vampyre)—*head of the Dusters;* Billy—*the bartender at the Niagra;* Dr. Dale Edward Horde—*Marilee's husband, he has his own plans;* Leprosy—*is a homeless man who lives in the park;* Gristle—*is his dog;* Whitney Vale—*Amanda's friend and an actress in porn films;* Chubby Freeze—*pornographer;* Missy and Dallas—*who work for Chubby;* Chester Dobbs—*the private investigator who found Amanda the last time she ran away;* Sela (Vampyre)—*Lydia's friend.*

2. *No Dominion.* New York: Ballantine Books, c2006, 251 p. ISBN: 9780345478252.

MANHATTAN, WINTER 2006/2007. Joe's trying to spend a pleasant night at a bar with Evie when a man goes wild. The bouncer thinks that the man is on PCP, but Joe can smell that he's a Vampyre. Joe thinks that he's simply a Vampyre that went insane—loudly, violently, spectacularly insane. His actions endanger all Vampyres. If the police are called in and no bullet can stop this guy... He's a security risk. Joe takes care of the immediate problem by moving the Vampyre out of The Society's territory and putting him down.

Joe thought the Vampyre was crazy because Vampyres don't get high, they can't. The Vyrus is too efficient; it cleans all poisons out of the blood almost before the effects can be felt. Junkies who get infected with the Vyrus have tried everything and have not been able to find any way to get high. Joe was wrong, such a drug exists.

It's been a year since Joe took a stand against The Coalition and times are lean. Joe finally swallows his pride and goes to The Society to ask for work. The job that Terry gives him is to find the source of the drug that's taking hold in the Vampyre community.

There is only one part of Joe's life that he cares about with all his heart. That is Evie. In the course of this book, she receives bad news about the course of the HIV virus that has infected her. She relies on Joe, and his absences cause her to demand to know the truth about his life.

ASSOCIATES: Evie—*Joe's girlfriend, she has HIV and the viral load has increased;* Gears—*is the bouncer at Doc's;* "The Spaz" (Vampyre)—*who went on a rampage in public;* Terry Bird (Vampyre)—*who runs The Society, Joe used to believe in Terry and The Society and at that time he worked for them;* Hurley (Vampyre)—*Terry's enforcer;* Tom Nolan (Vampyre)—*is now in charge of The Society's security;* Lydia Miles (Vampyre)—*is also part of the inner circle of The Society;* Philip Sax—*who has always been a small-time drug dealer;* Dominick—*the doorman at Blackie's bar;* The Count (Vampyre)—*who invites Joe to his home;* Poncho (Vampyre), Pigtails (Vampyre), and PJs (Vampyre)—*are the nicknames Joe gives The Count's roommates;* Sela (Vampyre)—*renounced The Society and joined The Coalition;* Amanda Horde—*who needed to live in Coalition territory;* Daniel (Vampyre)—*heads the Enclave;* D.J. Grave Digga

(Vampyre)—*who runs The Hood's territory;* Percy the barber (Vampyre)—*who trims hair in The Hood;* Papa Doc (Vampyre); Timberlands (Vampyre) and Shades (Vampyre)—*are the nicknames Joe gives to two thugs who work for D.J.;* Mrs. Vandewater (Vampyre)—*of the Morningside Settlement, she gives Joe surprising information. Since she gave it to him under duress, he makes the mistake of believing her.*

3. *Half the Blood of Brooklyn.* New York: Ballantine Books, c2007, 223 p. ISBN: 9780345495877.

MANHATTAN AND BROOKLYN, SUMMER 2007. Evie has been hospitalized with the AIDS virus. She's dying. Joe is desperate. He would infect her if she were willing and if he knew that she would survive the process. (Many people die a swift and brutal death as soon as they are infected with the Vyrus, only a few survive to become Vampyres.)

Joe now works for Terry Bird of The Society. Terry isn't interested in Evie's health. He has a job for Joe, and it needs to be done now. The power struggle between The Society and The Coalition is escalating. Terry is working on alliances for The Society, and he orders Joe to act as chauffer/bodyguard for an exchange that will support the negotiations.

Another problem is plaguing the Vampyre clans of New York. There's evidence that there has been a murder by a "Van Helsing," a human with the knowledge to murder Vampyres. What's odd is that he murdered Solomon, the "Candy Man." Solomon wasn't a Vampyre. He just sold blood to Vampyres in the basement of his candy store. The way in which he was killed makes it clear that the killer knows that Vampyres exist and how to kill them. The murder took place in The Dusters' territory, but The Society and The Coalition are concerned as well. All the Vampyres have an interest in seeing the murderer stopped.

Amanda Horde and The Count (Vampyre) are both searching for a cure for the Vyrus. The Enclave, as always, is searching for a way to use the Vyrus to transcend the boundaries of this world.

ASSOCIATES: Evie—*Joe's girlfriend, is dying;* Terry Bird (Vampyre)—*of The Society is trying to recruit other clans;* the Docks clan boss (Vampyre); Gooch (Vampyre)—*his goon;* Christian (Vampyre)—*of the Dusters clan thinks that there is a Van Helsing in New York;* Dexter Predo (Vampyre)—*head of the Coalition's Secret Police;* Sela (Vampyre)—*who works to bring Joe to Amanda;* Amada Horde—*a rich 17-year-old who trusts Joe;* Philip Sax—*who calls Joe to get help with The Count (Vampyre);* The Count (Vampyre)—*who is falling apart;* Lydia Miles (Vampyre)—*who has helped Joe to escape The Society in the past;* Daniel (Vampyre)—*of the Enclave is preparing to walk into the dawn;* Stretch (Vampyre)—*a.k.a. Abe, leader of The Freaks clan*, Vendetta (Vampyre)—*a.k.a. Hannah*, Harm (Vampyre)—*a.k.a. Sarah*, Hatter

(Vampyre), Glasseater (Vampyre), and Strongman (Vampyre)—*are all related to the Vampyres led by the Rabbi Moishe.* Rabbi Moishe (Vampyre)—*leader of a vampyre clan that is keeping kosher;* Axler (Vampyre)—*Moishe's son*, Selig (Vampyre), Matthew (Vampyre), David (Vampyre), Hesch (Vampyre), Rachel, and Leah—*are all part of Moise's clan;* Joseph (Vampyre)—*lives under the Enclave.* Hurley (Vampyre)—*Terry's enforcer;* Chester—*the beggar;* Tenderhooks (Vampyre)—*a Duster clan member;* and Deveroix (Vampyre)—*a Coalition enforcer.*

4. *Every Last Drop.* New York: Ballantine Books, c2008, 252 p. ISBN: 9780345495884.

South Bronx and Manhattan, Summer 2008. Joe can't return to Manhattan, and even though his boyhood home was in the Bronx, it doesn't feel like home now because Evie's in Manhattan. Joe is captured, maimed, and offered a job that will take him back to the island. How can he refuse?

Word has spread that Amanda Horde is working on a cure for the Vyrus. Vampyres are flocking to her side. Hundreds of Vampyres: rogues, refugees from off the island, and even some who have deserted from their clans, have come to the tenements where she's set up her headquarters. That many Vampyres in one place is not a stable situation. The Society is worried. The Coalition is worried. Sela, Amanda's lover and self-appointed bodyguard, is worried. Joe has never been one to calm the waters. The question is, will he provide the information that makes the situation explode?

Associates: Evie—*Joe's girlfriend, he left her with The Enclave;* Esperanza Lucretia Benjamin (Vampyre)—*is the closest thing the Concourse has to a boss;* Gum Snapper (Vampyre)—*a.k.a. Meager*, Moustache (Vampyre)—*a.k.a. Low*, Do-rag (Vampyre), and Police Cap (Vampyre)—*are cutting a swath through the South Bronx;* Mr. Alistair Lament (Vampyre) and Mrs. Maureen Vandewater (Vampyre)—*differ in their opinions on the way to mold young Vampyres;* Skag Baron Menace (Vampyre)—*is head of the Mungiki;* Dexter Predo (Vampyre)—*head of the Coalition's Secret Police, wants Joe to spy on Amanda Horde;* Terry Bird (Vampyre)—*head of The Society, just wants money;* Terry and Hurley—*have recovered from Sela's (Vampyre) attack;* Sela (Vampyre)—*protects Amanda Horde;* Gladstone (Vampyre)—*works for Amanda Horde;* The Count (Vampyre)—*has a new dream, he is working to be head of the Enclave;* Philip Sax—*is still trying to find a way to profit.*

I

IRVINE, Alex.

BATMAN: INFERNO

Genres/Themes Crossed: Science Fiction, Blended Society X Hard-Boiled Mystery.

Subjects/Character Types: Super Heroes, Super Villains X Amateur Sleuth (Contemporary).

Series/Stand-Alone: Stand-alone.

Scene of the Crime: Gotham City in the second year of Batman's career.

Detective: Bruce Wayne witnessed the murder of his parents as a small boy and vowed to dedicate his life to fighting crime. After years of training around the world, he returns to his home city of Gotham and takes on the role of the masked detective, Batman.

Known Associates: Lucius Fox, the head of research and development for Wayne Enterprises is a friend to Bruce Wayne. Alfred Pennyworth, Bruce Wayne's butler and confidant, serves as the voice of reason and a sounding board for Bruce's ideas. Captain James Gordon, originally tasked with bringing in the Batman, has instead forged an alliance with the Batman in order to restore order to Gotham and weed out corruption in the GCPD.

Premise: Gotham City is the home of Batman. The city has long been a magnet for bizarre criminals, many of whom are insane. Bruce Wayne's parents were felled by such a criminal, and capturing that criminal and others became his life's purpose. He intentionally developed his skills so that he would become a master crime-fighter. He studied science so that he could design technology that would give him an edge, and studied martial arts so that he could defeat criminals in combat.

Comments: Alex Irvine is a young writer who has written a few noteworthy novels, primarily in the science fiction and fantasy genres. Of particular interest to the work set out in this book may be "Have Robot, Will Travel," a story set in the world of Isaac Asimov's *Robot* series. *Batman: Inferno* is the first comic-related book by Irvine, since writing this he has written a book centering on Marvel Comics' *Ultimates, The Ultimates: Against All Enemies. Batman: Inferno* is set in the early years of Batman's career, but uses prevalent modern technology such as the Internet. This is probably due in part to the popularity of the recent Batman movie *Batman Begins.*

Literary Magic and Mayhem: The action of the novel is interspersed with news columns and articles depicting the mixed perception and ambivalence of the Gotham public towards their masked defender. The newsprint style may borrow from Irvine's experience working as a reporter for the Portland Phoenix.

Explorations: How can individuals who hide their identity ever be fully trusted?

THE CASE

1. ***Batman: Inferno.*** New York: Del Rey, 2006, 339 p. ISBN: 0345479459

GOTHAM CITY, THE SECOND YEAR OF BATMAN'S CAREER. Enfer, a serial arsonist, is terrorizing Gotham. After one of his blazes is set in Arkham, the Joker finds his way into the Bat Cave and begins impersonating Batman. Batman must stop Enfer and reclaim his identity from the Joker.

ASSOCIATES: Lucius Fox—*a scientist and inventor;* Alfred Pennyworth—*Batman's butler and confidant;* Rafael del Toro—*Gazette columnist;* Duane Trask—*Globe columnist;* Tiffany Haskell—*real estate scion;* Enfer—*Gotham City's newest criminal menace;* Dr. Jonathon Crane—*the asylum's director;* Gavin O'Connor—*Gotham Globe Reporter;* Gillian O'Connor—*Gotham Globe Reporter;* the Joker—*who had been locked-up;* Vicki Vale—*reporter;* James Gordon—*Police Captain;* Two Face—*who should be locked-up;* Commissioner Piskura—*who has his own agenda;* Ruben Cuellar—*a detective;* and Ed Coover—*Fire Chief.*

IVAN, Brandon. Worked with Michael Avon Oeming on *The Cross Bronx.* See: OEMING, Michael Avon: The Cross Bronx.

J

JAKUBOWSKI, Maxim and M. Christian. (Editors)

THE MAMMOTH BOOK OF FUTURE COPS

Genres/Themes Crossed: Science Fiction, Man as Creator, Dystopia X Police Procedural.

Subjects/Character Types: Science Fiction, Sentient Computers X Police Procedural.

Series/Stand-Alone: Anthology of short stories.

Scene of the Crime: Varies.

Detective: Varies.

Known Associates: Varies.

Premise: Maxim Jakubowski and Muncy Christian brought together a collection of noir stories set in the future, and featuring police officers.

Comment: Maxim Jakubowski has written novels and short stories, edited anthologies, published the imprints Black Box Thrillers, Blue Murder, and Eros Plus. He opened the first specialist crime and mystery bookstore in the United Kingdom (Murder One), and has been a crime columnist and the *Guardian's* reviewer of mystery and crime books. He has been the literary director of London's Crime Scene Festival and a consultant to Italy's International Mystery Film Festival, *Noir in Fest.* He won the 1992 Anthony Award for Best Critical Work for *100 Great Detectives or the Detective Directory.*

Muncy Christian has worked on over fourteen anthologies. His erotic short fiction has proved extremely popular. In 2007, his novel *The Very Bloody Marys* was published. The protagonist is a gay vampire that is a San Francisco cop named Valentino.

Literary Magic & Mayhem: Previously published stories from some of the giants of the science fiction field as well as from newcomers to the genre.

Explorations: How would you define noir? Did the story fit your definition of noir?

What was the most interesting aspect of the future world? Is it something that would necessarily lead to a dystopian future?

THE CASES

1. ***The Mammoth Book of Future Cops.*** New York: Carroll & Graf Publishers, 2003, 498 p. ISBN: 078671204X; 9780786712045.

CONTENTS: Celebrate the Bullet *by Richard Paul Russo;* Glass Earth, Inc. *by Stephen Baxter;* Footprint on Nowhere Beach *by Conrad Williams;* The Shape of Murder *by Ian Watson;* The Incorporated *by John Shirley;* Seiza *by Steven Schwartz;* Axl against the Immortals *by Jon Courtenay-Grimwood;* Offenders *by Mat Coward;* Violation *by William F. Nolan;* Needle Taste *by M. Christian;* An End to Hunger *by China Miéville;* A Scanner Darkly *by Philip K. Dick;* The Mojave Two-Step *by Norman Partridge;* Blood Sisters *by Joe Haldeman;* Heartache *by Stuart Young;* Mindstalker *by Martin Edwards;* Thighs *by Melanie Fogel;* The Uncertainty Principle *by John Moralee;* Prison Dreams *by Paul J. McAuley;* Three Bananas *by Larry Tritten.* You Never Know *by Carol Anne Davis;* Play Nice *by J.E. Ashley;* Me and My Shadow *by Mike Resnick;* Gone Bush *by Chris Amies;* Digital Honey *by Liz Evans;* Blankie *by Paul DiFilippo;* No Better Than Anyone Else *by Molly Brown;* So Napoleon Almost Slept Here, Right? *by O'Neil De Noux;* Professionals *by Keith Brooke;* Fishing *by Jay Caselberg;* In Silver A *by Cecilia Tan;* Sleep That Burns *by Jerry Sykes;* Ravens *by Stephen Dedman.*

K

KELNER, Toni L. P. Co-editor (with Charlaine Harris) of *Many Bloody Returns* and *Wolfsbane and Mistletoe*. See Harris, Charlaine: Many Bloody Returns.

KERR, Philip.

A PHILOSOPHICAL INVESTIGATIONS

Genres/Themes Crossed: Science Fiction, Dystopia X Police Procedural, Inverted Mystery.

Subjects/Character Types: Science Fiction, Dystopia X Police Women, Police Procedural.

Series/Stand-Alone: Stand-alone.

Scene of the Crime: England, 2013.

Detective: Chief Inspector Isadora "Jake" Jakowicz was an abused child. At times she wishes that the abuse had been something as easily understood as molestation. Instead she was subjected to constant verbal and emotional abuse by her father. What may be worse was that she witnessed him subjecting her mother to the same treatment. Today she believes that her father hated her mother.

Known Associates: Jake forms her own team of experts for the investigation: Cambridge Forensic Psychiatry Professor Waring; Lombroso Program Head of Psychiatry Doctor Carrie Cleobury; Detective Inspector Stanley;

and Detective Sergeants Yat Chung and Jones. Jake does not seem particularly close to anyone. Her relationship with the killer seems as intimate as her relationship with her psychotherapist, Doctor Blackwell.

Law enforcement personnel include: Assistant Police Commissioner Gilmour; Detective Superintendent Colin Bowles of the Birmingham City Police; Commander of the Murder Squad Keith Challis (Jake thinks of him as Poison Challis); Detective Inspector Ed Crawshaw; Chief Inspector Cormack; Scenes-of-crime officer Sergeant Bruce; Scenes-of-crime officer Dalglish; and Police technician Maurice. Lester French is the firearms expert in the Forensic Pathologist's Office at the Yard.

Mark Woodford is the private secretary of Junior Home Office Minister Grace Miles MP.

People who work on the Lombroso Program include Professor of Neuroendocrinology David Gleitmann; Doctor Stephen St. Pierre who was formerly the head of computer security for the British Army; and Doctor Tony Chen who counseled a VMN-negative codenamed Wittgenstein.

Doorman Phil's wife has her own theories on the murder. Trinity College Master Sir Jameson Lang teaches philosophy at Cambridge and writes detective novels. Oliver John Mayhew probably hadn't expected to be the *victim* of a crime. The killer's analyst is Doctor Wrathall. Mr. Grubb owns the club where Clare the stripper works. Mr. Kyriakos Parmenides is a witness. Mrs. Porter works at the Ministry of Health. Paul Esterhazy works at the hospital pharmacy.

Premise: Scientists have discovered the chemical mechanisms that predispose individuals to violent behavior. They can test for VMN (Ventro Medial Nucleus) which inhibits SDN (Sexually Dimorphic Nucleus), an area of the brain in men that acts as a repository for the male aggressive response. Men who are VMN-negative are considered potentially violent. In 2010, Britain began a campaign to test all males for VMN levels. The testing is coordinated through a computer named L.O.M.B.R.O.S.O. (Localization of Medullar Brain Resonations Obliging Social Orthopraxy). L.O.M.B.R.O.S.O. keeps files on all men identified as VMN-negative. Files are assigned code names to ensure privacy. L.O.M.B.R.O.S.O. is linked to the central police computer and monitors the names of men listed as suspects for violent crimes. If anyone listed as a suspect is VMN-negative, then L.O.M.B.R.O.S.O. sends the file to the detective in charge of the investigation.

Comment: Philip Kerr's Web site at http://www.pbkerr.com/flash/index.html includes biographical information, a link to his blog, information on his books, and an intriguing study kit for readers who have been given a school assignment focusing on his juvenile series, *The Children of the Lamp*, which is written under the name P. B. Kerr.

Literary Magic & Mayhem: The book begins with a chapter on the police investigation, written in the third person. The next chapter is written in the first person, and is told from the point of view of the murderer. The story proceeds with the two voices taking turns, intertwining the stories of the killer and the police who are tracking him.

There is an odd subtext to the novel, one of enmity between the sexes. A large part of it is the protagonist's worldview. It goes far beyond Jake having a chip on her shoulder. She loathes the men with whom she interacts, and her perceptions of them are distorted by hate. At the same time, many of these men treat her with complete disrespect. Some are decent human beings, but a bizarre number of them are, at best, insensitive boors. For instance, she finds photographs of herself naked that were created by the criminal. She feels violated, but she takes them to a police technician so that they can be tested for physical evidence. The technician takes great pleasure in leering over and commenting on the photographs. In another example, her boss overrides her concerns and orders up a tactical squad, refusing to hear out her concerns, dismissing them with a comment about "bloody female intuition." Many of the characters display a variety of casual prejudices.

Explorations: At one point, the murderer sees another VMN-negative man on the street and thinks that the man looks as if he's heading away from some dastardly act. Then he thinks:

> More likely hurrying to commit one... It's only a matter of time before neuronal connectivity makes itself apparent, for him just as for me. Freedom consists of the impossibility of knowing actions that still lie in the future. (p. 11)

This is a man who clearly believes that biology is destiny, that the VMN-negative diagnosis predicts behavior. Does he believe in free will? Does the society he lives in believe in free will?

Characters make many sweeping statements about people of different ethnicities. What were some of them? Characters (even characters other than Jake) make such statements about gender as well. What were some of those? How does the culture they live in inculcate such attitudes?

When people go to see their psychotherapists, does the therapy seem to help them?

Society's fears about the VMN-negative population seem to be borne out by the statistics. How would the process of creating L.O.M.B.R.O.S.O. reports on suspects affect investigations? To what extent should the reader believe the statistics?

THE CASE

1. ***A Philosophical Investigation.*** New York: Farrar, Straus, and Giroux, c1992, 329 p. ISBN: 0374231761; 9780374231767.

ENGLAND, FEBRUARY 2013. Chief Inspector Isadora "Jake" Jakowicz heads a team that is working to identify and stop a serial killer.

The murderer was recently diagnosed as VMN-negative. He was stunned. In his words, he went "from good citizen to social pariah in the space of a single afternoon" (p. 50). He fears that the information on his diagnosis might become public, and hacks into the L.O.M.B.R.O.S.O. computer to remove it. Once there, he finds the names of other VMN-negative individuals, and he begins removing them from society.

ASSOCIATES: See above.

KIMBERLY, Alice. (Pseudonym for husband and wife team Alice Alfonsi and Marc Cerasini.)

THE GHOST AND MRS. MCCLURE

Genres/Themes Crossed: Paranormal X Traditional Mystery.

Subjects/Character Types: Ghosts X Amateur Detective (Contemporary).

Series/Stand-Alone: Characters change in the course of the series, so it is best to read it in order.

Scene of the Crime: Present day Quindicott, Rhode Island.

Detective: Jack Shepard, a private investigator who died in 1949, and Mrs. Penelope Thornton-McClure, a woman who is rebuilding her life after her husband's suicide. Penelope is a quiet, gentle woman with a steel spine and an unholy curiosity. She meekly worked around her self-centered husband, Calvin, and after his death, she quietly acquiesced to the demands of his wealthy and dictatorial family. At least, she put up with them until they demanded that Penelope and Calvin's son, Spencer, be sent to a boarding school in England. She refused to allow Spencer to be sent away, upon which the McClures threatened to cut her off without a penny. Her response was to take the insurance money from Calvin's death and move herself and Spencer to her hometown in Rhode Island.

Known Associates: Penelope co-owns the bookstore with her 72-year-old Aunt Sadie. Penelope's son, Spencer, is seven years old at the beginning of the series. Her *bête noir* is her sister-in-law Ashley McClure-Sutherland, who is certain that Spencer would be better off at a boarding school in England rather than living in Rhode Island with his mother.

As owners of a small business in Quindicott Penelope and her aunt belong to the The Quindicott Business Owners Association. This group includes the owners from the neighborhood businesses. The Association President (and owner of Cranberry Street Hardware) is Bud Napp. Penelope's friend Professor J. Brainert Parker belongs to the association because he is a part owner of the Movie Town Theater and he acts as the Association's secretary. Other members of the Association include Linda Cooper-Logan and her husband Milner, who run the Cooper Family Bakery; Fiona Finch and her husband Barney who own Finch Inn. Mailman Seymour Tarnish, who has been a small business owner since he purchased an ice cream truck which he runs on weekends. Mr. Koh is the owner of Koh's Grocery. Joe Franzetti owns Franzetti's Pizza Place. The garden store owner is Chick Pattelli. Glenn Hastings owns Hastings Pharmacy. Gerry Kovacks owns Cellular Planet. This group meets frequently in the course of the series. They support each other in many ways.

Premise: Private investigator Jack Shepard followed a lead into a little bookstore in 1949, and was murdered. His spirit was trapped in the store, unable to communicate with anyone until Penelope Thornton-McClure walked into the place. Until they met, she didn't know that she could see and hear ghosts. When crimes take place in the store, she asks Jack for help. With Jack's mentoring, she becomes a fair investigator.

Comment: Husband-and-wife team Alice Alfonsi and Marc Cerasini write *The Haunted Bookshop Mysteries* under the pseudonym of Alice Kimberly. (They co-author *The Coffeehouse Mysteries* under the pseudonym of Cleo Coyle.) Between them, the couple has authored more than sixty books and scripts, including biographies, science fiction novels, mystery novels, and novels based on movies, television series, and comic books. Their Web site at www.CoffeehouseMystery.com includes coffee lore, recipes, links to interviews, and information on the books.

Literary Magic & Mayhem: Each novel starts with a quotation from *The Ghost and Mrs. Muir*, written by Josephine Aimée Campbell Leslie under the pseudonym R. A. Dick, and first published in 1945. Each chapter begins with a quotation, many taken from classic mystery short stories, novels, and films. The relationship between the ghost and Mrs. McClure is reminiscent of the relationship between the title characters in *The Ghost and Mrs. Muir*, but the relationship in *The Ghost and Mrs. Muir* had more power and pathos, more intensity. Jack's amused flirting with Penelope keeps the repartee light. The attraction seems to be one more of convenience (here is the first woman who has been able to see him in over 40 years) than of passion. It seems pale in comparison to that between Captain Gregg and Lucy Muir (in the movie) or to that between Captain Gregg and Carolyn Muir (in the television series), especially in the beginning of the series. It may develop more passion as the series continues. The depiction of the petty politics of a small town, the friendships between Penelope and many members of the community, and the determination of Penelope to support her son combine to make this an engaging series.

Explorations: How do the quotations enhance the story?

What did Jack think of Timothy Brennan? Was he right?

What are Penelope's experiences with death? Is she grieving when she meets Jack? Why or why not? Does Jack help?

What are Penelope's chief concerns?

How does Spencer change during the book?

How does Penelope change in the course of the book?

THE CASES

1. ***The Ghost and Mrs. McClure.*** New York: Berkley Prime Crime, 2004, 261 p. ISBN: 0425194612.

The book is prefaced by this quote from R. A. Dick's *The Ghost and Mrs. Muir:*

> "You mean there is a hell?" asked Lucy.
> "Some people might call it so," said the captain.
> "There's a dimension that some spirits have to wait in till they realize and admit the truth about themselves."

QUINDICOTT, RHODE ISLAND, 1949 AND SEPTEMBER 2004. When Aunt Sadie wrote Penelope that she was going to close down the bookstore that had been in the Thornton family for generations, Penelope offered to sink all her money into the shop and become a co-owner. Determined to revive the business, they re-name and re-model the store, and organize author signings to bring in new customers.

Their first signing is for best-selling author Timothy Brennan. He immortalized Private Investigator Jack Shepard in the *Jack Shield* series. Brennan was a young reporter when Jack was a successful private investigator. They weren't close, but somehow Brennan managed to grab Jack's case files after Jack's death.

Tragedy strikes at Brennan's signing. He dies. It's bad enough that the bookstore was the site of a murder. It's worse when the police discover that Penelope was the last person (other than the Timothy Brennan) to handle the weapon.

At first, Penelope was terrified that the voice she heard in her head was a sign that she was going insane. After a while, she trusted Jack to teach her the basics of investigation, and she began to enjoy his company.

Associates: Spencer—*Penelope's seven-year-old son;* Sadie Thornton—*Penelope's aunt;* Private Investigator Jack Shepard—*deceased, but no longer unheard;* Timothy Brennan—*author of the Jack Shield series;* Shelby Cabot—*a representative of Brennan's publisher;* Josh Bernstein—*Shelby's assistant;* Deirdre Brennan-Franken—*Brennan's daughter;* Kenneth—*Deidre's husband.*

The Quindicott Business Owners Association includes: Linda Cooper-Logan and her husband Milner—*who run the Cooper Family Bakery;* Fiona Finch and her husband Barney—*who own Finch Inn;* Seymour Tarnish—*the mailman, he operates the town's ice cream truck on weekends;* Mr. Koh—*owner of Koh's Grocery;* Joe Franzetti—*who owns Franzetti's Pizza Place;* Professor J. Brainert Parker—*part owner of Movie Town Theater;* and Association President Bud Napp—*owner of Cranberry Street Hardware.*

Chief Ciders—*leads the Quindicott Police Force;* Eddie Franzetti and Welsh Tibbet—*officers on the force;* Detective-Lieutenant Roger Marsh—*of the Crime Investigation Unit of the State Police';* Councilwoman Marjorie Binder-Smith—*a.k.a. the Municipal Zoning Witch;* Reverend Waterman—*whose concerns focus on the town's parking;* Vinny Nardini—*of the Dependable Delivery Service;* Howie Westwood—*who claims to be editor of Independent Bookseller Magazine;* Ashley McClure-Sutherland— *Penelope's sister-in-law;* Anna Worth—*Newport cereal-heiress;* Dr. Stuart Nablaum—*Anna's therapist;* and Mina Griffith—*new bookstore employee.*

2. ***The Ghost and the Dead Deb.*** New York: Berkley Prime Crime, 2005, 262 p. ISBN: 0425199444.

The book is prefaced by this quote from R. A. Dick's *The Ghost and Mrs. Muir:*

> I did not lead a very wise life myself, but it was a full one, and a grown up one. You come of age very often through shipwreck and disaster, and at the heart of the whirlpool some men find God.

New York City, July 1946 and Quindicott, Rhode Island, July 2005. Author Angel Stark has written tell-all books in the past, tracing her path from depression to substance abuse to therapy. She was a debutante from a family with old money, and her gossipy books have alienated old friends. Her latest explores an unsolved crime, the murder of Bethany Banks; and in the process it damages the reputation of everyone who was at the debutante's ball the night of the murder. The book is slated to be a bestseller. Penelope invites Angel to the Buy the Book bookstore for an author signing, and is pleased when she accepts. The questions-and-answers session at the signing includes a shouting match; that same evening someone attacks Ms. Stark outside the bookstore; and that night she disappears. Penelope tries to uncover the truth while avoiding her husband's relatives, one of whom attended the last ball of Bethany Banks.

In the course of this book, Penelope finds an old buffalo nickel that belonged to Jack. She discovers that, as long as she's carrying it, he can accompany her away from the bookstore.

ASSOCIATES: Spencer—*Penelope's son, now nine years old*, Aunt Sadie Thornton—*now 73;* Private Investigator Jack Shepard—*deceased, but no longer confined to the bookstore.*

1946: Emily Stendall—*who was Jack's client;* Joey "Lucky Joe" Lubrano—*an elevator operator.*

2005: Those attending Angel Stark's signing at Buy the Book include Dana Wu—*Angel Stark's publicist;* J. Brainert Parker—*English professor and literary critic;* Fiona Finch; Johnny Napoli—*nephew of hardware store owner Bud Napp;* Seymour Tarnish—*outspoken mailman;* Kiki Langdon—*a friend of Bethany;* Victoria Banks—*who was Bethany's younger sister;* Courtney Peyton Taylor and Stephanie Usher—*friends of Victoria;* and Mina Griffith—*bookstore clerk.*

Those at the dance the night of Bethany's murder include: Donald Easterbrook—*Bethany's fiancé;* Henry "Call Me Hal" McConnell—*who had a crush on Bethany;* Angel Stark—*who was taking notes;* Johnny Napoli—*a waiter;* and Katherine "Kiki" McClure Langdon—*one of the McClures.* The Quindicott Business Owners Association meets, including: Linda Cooper-Logan, Milner Logan, Seymour Tarnish, Fiona Finch, Mr. Koh and his 18-year-old niece Joyce, and J. Brainert Parker. Other characters include Officer Edward Franzetti; Chief Ciders; and "La Princessa" Ashley McClure-Sutherland—*Penelope's sister-in-law.*

3. ***The Ghost and the Dead Man's Library.*** New York: Berkley Prime Crime, 2006, 258 p. ISBN: 0425212653; 9780425212653.

The book is prefaced by this quote from R. A. Dick's *The Ghost and Mrs. Muir*:

> What you need young woman, is a trip around the Horn with a southeaster tearing the guts out of you and all hands on deck, with the sea coming over green for three nights and three days—then you'd sleep in sacking and be thankful.

NEW YORK CITY, OCTOBER 1946 AND QUINDICOTT, RHODE ISLAND, OCTOBER 2006. A man from Aunt Sadie's past, Peter Chesley, offers Sadie and Penelope the opportunity to sell off some of his rarest books for a generous commission. He dies before they've had a chance to unload the books from Penelope's car. It's uncanny. He seems to have foreseen his death. He had told Aunt Sadie that if he died, she should keep the proceeds from the sales. A customer hears them speaking about the books and offers an outrageous sum for a single volume from the Phelps printing of the collected works of Edgar Allan Poe. Within a day, the customer is dead and the book is missing.

The bookstore is beset by offers for other volumes in the collection. It seems that printer Eugene Phelps sent out a letter to prospective customers stating that he'd hidden clues to the location of a literary treasure in his edition of Poe's complete works. They sell another of the books from Peter Chesley's library and the customer who purchased that book meets with a fatal apparent accident. Coincidence? Penelope is afraid that someone is willing to kill to get his hands on the volumes. The police dismiss her concerns. If she wants to see the crimes investigated, she will have to investigate them herself (with help from Jack, Brainert, and Seymour).

In 1946, Baxter Kerns III hired Jack to investigate the background of Vincent Tattershawe, his sister Dorothy's fiancé. Jack found a conman, but it wasn't Tattershawe.

ASSOCIATES: Spencer—*Penelope's 10-year-old son;* Sadie Thornton—*Penelope's 74-year-old aunt;* Private Investigator Jack Shepard—*who takes Penelope back to 1946.*

1946: Baxter Kerns III—*one of Jack's clients;* Dorothy Kerns—*Baxter's sister;* Miss Mindy Corbett—*Vincent Tattershawe's secretary.*

2006: Boyce Lyell—*a schoolyard bully who torments Spencer;* Claymore Chesley—*the Acting Principal at Spenser's school;* Officer Durst and Detective Douglas Kroll—*of the Newport Police Department;* Detective-Lieutenant Roger Marsh—*of the Rhode Island State Police;* Officer Eddie Franzetti—*who is a friend of Penelope;* Quindicott Police Chief Cider—*who is not;* Officer Bull McCoy—*the Police Chief's nephew;* and Officer Womack—*who is not impressed by books;* Associate Professor Nelson Spinner—*a Poe expert.* Mina Griffith and Garfield Platt—*Buy the Book's part-time clerks;* Rene Montour—*who purchases one of the Poe volumes;* Susan Keenan—*a Buy the Book customer;* Dr. Conte—*professor of comparative literature;* Dr. Rhajdiq—*a physician;* Raymond—*Peter Chesley's son;* and Dr. Fortino—*a physician at the Benevolent Heart Hospital.*

Members of the Quindicott Business Owners Association include: Penelope and her Aunt Sadie; Bud Napp; Mr. Koh; Fiona Finch; Linda Cooper-Logan and Milner Logan; Professor J. Brainert Parker; Seymour Tarnish; Chick Pattelli; Glenn Hastings; and Gerry Kovacks.

4. ***The Ghost and the Femme Fatale.*** New York: Berkley Prime Crime, 2008, 235 p. ISBN: 9780425218389.

The book is prefaced by this quote from R. A. Dick's *The Ghost and Mrs. Muir*:

> But that was life...light and shade...a coming in of the tide and a going out.

NEW YORK CITY, APRIL 1948 AND QUINDICOTT, RHODE ISLAND, MAY 2007. A group of investors led by literature professor J. Brainert Parker purchased and renovated the single screen *Movie Town Theater* in Quindicott. Their grand-opening weekend features B-movie actress Hedda Geist and her leading man Pierce Armstrong. Ghost Jack Shepard takes Penelope back to 1948, where he never had a chance to finish gathering the evidence against philanderer Nathan Burwell. Penelope notices that the dress worn by the "chippy" with District Attorney Burwell is the same as the one worn by Hedda Geist in *Wrong Turn*. That connection to Irving Vreen's movie studio Gotham Features proves to be the key to a crime that was never truly solved. In the present day, the consequences of that crime continue. An accident almost kills the keynote speaker on the opening night of the *Movie Town Theater's* film noir festival. Another accident causes her death the next day. Her papers are stolen before they can be examined, and the carnage continues. Police Chief Ciders dismisses Penelope's theories, and medical examiner Dr. Rubins offers her a prescription for her nerves. No one wants to believe that a murderer is at the film festival. The police will do nothing to investigate.

ASSOCIATES: Spencer—*Penelope's 11-year-old son;* Sadie Thornton—*her 75-year-old aunt;* Private Investigator Jack Shepard—*who resolves a cold case from 1948 in this book.*

1948: District Attorney Nathan Burwell's wife—*who hired Jack to follow her cheating spouse;* Wilma Brody—*a bit-part actress;* Benny Seelig—*the studio manager and property master;* Hedda Geist—*a stunning starlet;* Egbert "Bert" P. King—*a private investigator.*

2007: J. Brainert Parker, Dean Wendell Pepper, and 85-year-old Hedda Geist-Middleton—*Movie Town Theater investors.* People at the Grand Opening include: Harmony Middleton—*Hedda's granddaughter;* Dixon Gallagher—*who is working part-time at Bud Napp's hardware store;* Maggie Kline—*screenwriter;* Dr. Irene Lilly—*film noir researcher;* Barry Yello—*owner of FylmGeek.com;* Amy Reichel—*FylmGeek's Webmistress;* and Pierce Armstrong—*an actor.* The Quindicott Police Department includes: Chief Ciders; Officer Bull McCoy—*the chief's nephew;* and Officer Eddie Franzetti—*who was a friend of Penelope's brother.*

There is unrest in Quindicott! It involves: Councilwoman Marjorie Binder-Smith—*who unfairly targets Quindicott's business owners with outrageous tickets and fines* and hardware-store owner Budd Napp—*who vows to run against Marjorie for Town Council.* Members of the Quindicott Business Owners Association rally to Budd's side. They include: Penelope and her Aunt Sadie; Gerry Kovacks; Mr. Koh; Cooper-Logan and Milner Logan; Glenn Hastings; Fiona Finch; J. Brainert Parker; and Danny Boggs. As ice-cream truck owner (and mailman) Seymour Tarnish says about the council-woman's actions: "This is facism—and I know governmental persecution when I see it! I'm a federal employee!" (p. 187).

Other characters include Vinny Nardini—*Dependable Delivery Service man;* Mina Griffith and Bonnie Franzetti—*bookstore clerks;* Dr. Randall Rubins—*Quindicott's new medical examiner;* and Virginia—*Dean Pepper's ex-wife.*

5. ***The Ghost and the Haunted Mansion.*** New York: Berkley Prime Crime, 2009, 281 p. ISBN: 9780425224601.

The book is prefaced by this quote from R. A. Dick's *The Ghost and Mrs. Muir*:

> Don't you see . . . if everyone rushes off at the slightest sound, of course the house gets a bad name. It's too ridiculous, really, in the twentieth century to believe in apparitions.

New York City, September 1947 and Quindicott, Rhode Island, June 2007. Mailman Seymour Tarnish may have been the reclusive Miss Timothea Todd's best friend. He sometimes brought her lunch along with her mail, and they often spent a little time talking about books. Penelope saw him leaving the area when she took Miss Todd her monthly order of mysteries. Then she found Miss Todd, dead, a look of terror upon her face. Penelope called the police, and Chief Ciders and his oafish nephew decided that Seymour was a likely murder suspect, until the doctor on the scene stated that Miss Todd had died of natural causes.

Miss Todd's solicitor, Emory Stoddard, tells Penelope, her aunt, and Seymour that Miss Todd left her books to Penelope and her aunt; the rest of her estate (including the mansion and its outbuildings) she left to Seymour. They are all stunned. Then he delivers the news that the mansion is haunted. Seymour is undaunted. He decides to call in the *Ghost Zappers* to exorcise any spirits. He generously offers to send them to exorcise Quindicott when they finish with the mansion. Penelope is in a panic. She doesn't want to lose Jack now.

A few of *Buy the Book's* customers are offended by the cardboard cutout of Zara Underwood, porn queen turned author. When Penelope wonders if they should take it down, her Aunt Sadie's response is that the cut-out "standee" is appropriate advertising for the book, and that if it angers some customers, they can buy a different book. She says, (in part):

> I'm not saying Zara Underwood and her ghostwriter are geniuses, or even that this year's roster of bestselling authors will stand the test of time. But, you know, the novel itself was once considered a "disreputable" genre; and

some of the greatest books ever written—in my humble opinion—would be dismissed today as "popular" fiction, given the literary theories of the moment. (p. 97)

Her complete diatribe on literary snobbishness and censorship is magnificent. It's worth the price of the book!

ASSOCIATES: Spencer—*Penelope's 11-year-old son*, Sadie Thornton—*Penelope's 75-year-old aunt*, and Private Investigator Jack Shepard—*deceased.*

1947: Timothy Brennan—*reporter;* Birdie—*waitress;* Mac Dougherty—*newsstand owner;* John James "J. J." Conway—*Jack's 12-year-old client;* Mrs. Dellarusso—*who lost her only son in the war;* and Curly the Bookie.

2007: Bud Napp—*who is running for councilwoman Marjorie Binder-Smith's seat on the Town Council;* Marjorie Binder-Smith—*who has instructed Jim Wolfe's construction crew to block Bud's shop entrance;* Miss Ophelia Tuttle—*Attorney Emory Philip Stoddard's receptionist, she can see Jack Shepard;* Seymour Tarnish—*who used to take the time to visit with Miss Timothea Todd when delivered her mail.*

Guests at Timothea Todd's wake include Fiona Finch—*innkeeper;* J. Brainert Parker—*literature professor;* Dean Wendell Pepper—*Dean of St. Francis's;* Leo Rollins—*electronics store owner;* Harlan Gilman—*Seymour's ex-housemate;* Mrs. Arthur Fromsette—*April Briggs's mother;* Charlene Lindsey-Fabian—*who is involved in opening a chain of bed-and-breakfasts;* and Hardy Miles—*who tends bar;* and Kenny Vorzon of Spirit Zappers—*who shows up at the wake after midnight to interview Seymour.*

Rachel Delve—*the medium at an RIPS* (*Rhode Island Paranormal Society*) *séance;* Bonnie Franzetti and Dilbert Randall—*Buy the Book clerks;* Binky Stuckey—*who believes that cardboard cutouts should be decently clothed;* Chief Ciders, Deputy Chief Eddie Franzetti, and officer Bull McCoy—*the Quindicott Police;* Dr. Randall Rubino—*who acts as a medical officer for the QPD.*

The Quindicott Business Owners Association includes Bud Napp, Linda Cooper-Logan and her husband Milner, Mr. Koh and his daughter Joyce, Chick Pattelli, J. Brainert Parker, and Fiona Finch.

KOONTZ, Dean, Kevin J. Anderson, and Ed Gorman.

FRANKENSTEIN

Genres/Themes Crossed: Secret Society, Man as Creator X Police Procedural.

Subjects/Character Types: Literary Figures X Police Procedural.

Series/Stand-Alone: Characters, relationships and the setting develop over time. The series should be read in order.

Scene of the Crime: New Orleans.

Detectives: Carson O'Connor and Michael Maddison are the youngest and second-youngest people to ever become detectives in New Orleans. Carson is driven by a desire to prove herself and clear her father's record while taking care of her autistic younger brother. Michael plays the role of foil to her straight man, supporting his partner in her ambition to succeed and her confidence that Carson's father was not a dirty cop.

Known Associates: Jonathon Harker and Dwight Frye, a rival team of detectives. Arnie O'Connor, Carson's autistic younger brother. Vicky Chou, Arnie's live in care taker, who feels she owes Carson for O'Connor's past assistance. Jack Rogers, the police coroner. Luke, one of Jack's assistants. Kathleen Burke, police psychiatrist, and close friend to Carson. Deucalion, Victor's first creation, a 200-year-old self proclaimed monster.

Premise: A series of bizarre murders have mutilated bodies turning up in New Orleans, with limbs or organs removed from the bodies. This series of murders sets detectives Maddison and O'Connor on a path that leads them to the realization that the creature responsible for the murders is inhuman, and that his creator may be even more terrifying.

Comment: This story was initially conceived as television miniseries, but Koontz disliked the direction it was taking in the studio's hands. He withdrew from the deal, and set about turning the story into a trilogy of novels.

Dean Koontz co-authored the first book in the series, *Prodigal Son*, with Kevin J. Anderson. He co-authored the second book in the series, *City of Night*, with Ed Gorman. The third book *Dead and Alive* is a solo effort, due out July 28, 2009.

Literary Magic & Mayhem: In this world, Shelley's classic novel was based on a local ghost story about events which actually happened. Frankenstein's monster lives to the modern day, but thinks that his creator is long-since dead. The public has no knowledge of the existence of the monster or of his maker. Many of the movies based on Shelley's *Frankenstein*, and even the Munsters television show, are referenced in the series. There are also some paranormal phenomena explored: psychic powers allowing communication between distant bodies, and uncanny intuitions.

Explorations: What should science pursue?

What does it mean to be human?

What is the nature of the soul?

THE CASES

1. ***Dean Koontz's Frankenstein, Book One, Prodigal Son.*** New York: Bantam, 2005, 512 p. ISBN: 0553587889. (Co-authored by Dean Koontz and Keven J. Anderson.)

NEW ORLEANS, PRESENT DAY. Carson and Michael investigate a series of bizarre murders. Over the course of their investigation, they discover that there are non-human entities in the world, and are assisted by one as they try to stop another.

ASSOCIATES: Deucalion, Jonathan Harker, Dwight Frye, Jelly Biggs, Arnie O'Connor, Vicky Chou, Nancy Whistler, Jack Rogers, Luke, Kathleen Burke, Taylor Fullbright.

2. ***Dean Koontz's Frankenstein, Book Two, City of Night.*** New York: Bantam, 2005, 496 p. ISBN: 0553587897. (Co-authored by Dean Koontz and Ed Gorman.)

NEW ORLEANS, PRESENT DAY. Carson and Michael attempt to track down Victor Helios while being pursued by members of the New Race sent to destroy them. More members of the New Race begin to undergo bizarre and dangerous changes, and Victor's hold on them begins to crumble.

ASSOCIATES: Deucalion, Jelly Biggs, Arnie O'Connor, Vicky Chou, Jack Rogers, Luke, Winona, Aubrey Picou, Lulana St. John, Evangeline Antoine, Pastor Kenny Laffite, Nebo, Liane Chou.

KOONTZ, Dean.

IN ODD WE TRUST

Genres/Themes Crossed: Paranormal X Traditional Mystery.

Subjects/Character Types: Psychic (sees ghosts), Ghosts X Amateur Sleuth (Contemporary).

Series/Stand-Alone: There are major changes in Odd's life over the course of the series. These should be read in order.

Scene of the Crime: Pico Mundo, a fictional town in fictional Maravilla County in Southern California, present day.

Detective: Twenty-year-old Odd Thomas left home when he was 16. He couldn't escape the ghosts whom he could see, but he could escape his mother, a woman who should have been certified long ago. (His father, terrified of her, abandoned her and Odd when Odd was an infant.)

The love of Odd's life is a young woman named Bronwen (Stormy) Llewellyn. Odd believes that they are fated to be together forever. His proof of this is that they have matching birthmarks, and that, many years ago, at a carnival, they received a card from a fortune-telling machine "The Gypsy Mummy" that read, "You are destined to be together forever." Stormy keeps this card in a frame on the wall of her apartment.

Odd works as a frycook for Terri Stambaugh, the woman who gave him a job when he left home. Odd's psychic gifts are almost enough on their own to overwhelm him. He leads the simplest life he can manage. He does his best to help everyone, including the dead. In his own words, "I see dead people. But then, by God, I do something about it" (*Odd Thomas*, p. 29).

Known Associates: Among the few who know of Odd's gifts are his girlfriend (and later, fiancé) Bronwen (Stormy) Llewellyn. When Stormy and Odd were 16, they decided that they were soulmates, and they have been together ever since. Others who know include a young man who has been Odd's friend from the time they were six years old, Danny Jessup; Odd's boss, friend, and mentor Terri Stambaugh; Odd's friend P. Oswald Boone (the man who encouraged him to begin writing); Odd's friends the Chief of Police Wyatt Porter and Wyatt's wife, Karla Porter. One of Odd's frequent companions from the spirit world is Elvis Presley.

Premise: Odd Thomas has been able to see spirits since he was young. They do not speak to him, but sometimes they lead him to things that they need someone to discover. Odd also possesses a gift that he calls "psychic magnetism." If Odd is thinking about a person and allows himself to wander or drive aimlessly, he will usually come across that person in short order. Odd also sees other things, among them beings that he refers to as "bodachs." Bodachs seem to congregate around people or at a site that will soon be involved in great, almost epic, misfortune, terror and grief. This talent allows Odd to know that some catastrophe that will ruin many lives is going to occur in the near future. His job, when he sees the bodachs, is to detect the nature of the catastrophe and to divert it.

Comment: Dean Koontz won an *Atlantic Monthly* fiction competition when he was a senior in college. He has been writing ever since. When he started out, he had a day job, and wrote in the evenings and on weekends. His wife offered to support him for five years while he worked to establish himself as an author, and the rest is literary history. Mr. Koontz has written 10 titles that rose to the number one spot on *The New York Times*' hardcover bestseller list: *One Door Away From Heaven*, *From the Corner of His Eye*, *Midnight*, *Cold Fire*, *The Bad Place*, *Hideaway*, *Dragon Tears*, *Intensity*, *Sole Survivor*, and *The Husband*. Mr. Koontz states (on his Web site: http://www.deankoontz.com) that the character of Odd Thomas came to him fully-formed, whispering in his ear while he was working furiously to meet his deadline for *The Face*. He believes that there will be six books in the *Odd Thomas* series. There is also an Odd Thomas Web site at http://oddthomas.deankoontz.com/, which includes an Odd Thomas webisode entitled "Odd Passenger."

Literary Magic & Mayhem. Mr. Koontz blends humor with suspense and gives readers unforgettable and lovable characters. His main characters are not just creatures of action, they also search for meaning in their lives, giving a philosophical, sometimes even a theological, aspect to these works. Odd Thomas is wonderful narrator. It is a pleasure to spend time with him, his worldview is loving, spiritual, and courageous. Odd Thomas is, in some ways, an unreliable narrator, but only in the interest of telling his story in such a way that the reader lives in the moment with him.

Explorations: (These explorations focus on the novels rather than on the graphic novel, simply because the narrator, who is not present in the same way in the comic format, is so interesting.) Mr. Koontz's narrators have humor, but are also philosophical; their observations are often insightful, amusing, and touching. For instance, in *Odd Thomas*, Odd often offers a profound insight, then undercuts the moment with humor. Did these observations enhance or interrupt the narrative? How did they affect the reader's perception of the character? What were the best observations? Did any just not work? Does how well these work vary with different books in the series?

Odd Thomas is written as a story told by Odd after the events in the book took place. So it is after those events that he begins the narrative by telling the reader that he is a complete nonentity, of absolutely no interest to any of the news media. Is this true? Is Odd likely to seek the world's acclaim, or to feel deserving of it? What are the hints that many people hold Odd in much higher esteem than he realizes? What are some examples of his humility?

Writer Hannah Arendt, observing the trial of Adolf Eichmann, spoke of "the banality of evil." In *Forever Odd*, there is evil of epic proportions, but there are also minor characters who demonstrate a level of self-absorption and short-sightedness that many would consider unforgivable. Is this more banal type of evil unusual? How does Odd cope with it? Did it contribute in any way to who he is today?

THE CASES

1. ***In Odd We Trust.*** (Created by Dean Koontz, written by Queenie Chan and Dean Koontz, illustrations by Queenie Chan.) New York: Ballantine Books, 2008, 190 p. ISBN: 9780345499660.

Pico Mundo, some time prior to August 2004. Sherry Sheldon, the Gordon's housekeeper, has been getting strange, threatening letters. They weren't explicit enough for the police to take any action. Then one afternoon, a miscommunication causes her to be out grocery shopping when young Joey Gordon gets home early from school. Sherry walks in 15 minutes after Joey and finds him stabbed, murdered. Odd can see Joey, but Joey seems frightened of him, and Odd isn't sure how to help.

ASSOCIATES: Seven-year-old Joey Gordon—*deceased;* President Lyndon B. Johnson—*deceased;* Elvis Presley—*deceased;* Terri Stambaugh—*Odd's boss;* Police Chief Porter—*Odd's friend;* Sherry Sheldon—*the Gordon's housekeeper;* Stormy Lewellyn—*Odd's girlfriend and Sherry's friend;* seven-year-old Angelica Smithburn; and Kyle Bernshaw.

2. *Odd Thomas.* New York: Bantam Books, 2003, 399 p. ISBN: 0553802496.

PICO MUNDO, AUGUST 2004. Something strange is happening in Pico Mundo. Bodachs are gathering, presaging some terrible tragedy. Odd is the only one in town who can see them; and, although the Chief of Police believes Odd and is anxious to avert whatever disaster is about to happen, there just isn't enough information to mount an effective defense. Odd begins his own investigation, following a man who seems to attract the bodachs, doing everything in his power to save those people whose deaths he witnessed in his dreams, and searching for answers to stop a massacre before it takes place.

ASSOCIATES: Stormy Lewellyn—*Odd's fiancé;* P. Oswald Boone—*Odd's writing mentor;* Wyatt and Karla Porter—*Odd's friends* (*Wyatt is the Chief of Police*); Terri Stambaugh—*Odd's boss;* and Elvis—*Odd's frequent companion.*

Co-workers at the Pico Mundo Grille include Helen Arches—*waitress,* Bertie Orbic—*waitress,* Viola Peabody—*waitress;* and Poke Barnet—*the short order cook for the other shift.*

Simon Varner, Bern Eckles, Sonny Wexler, Jesus Bustamante, Billy Munday, Alice Norrie, and Rafus Carter—*officers on the Pico Mundo Police force;* Izzy Maldanado—*the Sheriff's crime scene technician.*

Other residents of Pico Mundo include Odd's mother—*who is still beautiful;* Odd's father—*who is still weak;* Britney—*Odd's father's new girlfriend;* 5-year-old Nicolina and 7-year-old Levanna—*Viola's daughters;* Harry Beamis—*who produces the radio show All Night with Shamus Cocobolo;* Shamus Cocobolo—*the show's host;* and Stan "Spanky" Lufmunder—*the engineer for the show.*

Others include 12-year-old Penny Kallisto, Harlow Landerson, and Bob Robertson. Eileen Newfield—*the Chief of Police's sister;* and Jake Hulquist—*the Chief's best friend.*

3. *Forever Odd.* New York: Bantam Books, 2005, 334 p. ISBN: 9780553804164.

Pico Mundo, February 2005. Odd is awakened by a murdered man. He races to the man's home to try to stop another killing, and instead, he finds that one of his closest friends has been kidnapped. He must not only find him, but also rescue him from an insane killer who has decided to add Odd's soul to her collection.

Associates: Danny Jessup—*who lives with osteogenesis imprefecta* (*brittle bones*): Dr. Wilbur Jessup—*deceased, Danny's father;* P. Oswald Boone—*whose cat, Terrible Chester, likes to pee on Odd's shoes;* Wyatt and Karla Porter—*the police chief and his wife are friends of Odd;* Terri Stambaugh—*Odd's friend;* and Elvis—*deceased;* Datura—*a madwoman with power;* Andre and Robert—*her chevals;* Father Sean Lewellyn—*Stormy's uncle.*

4. *Brother Odd.* New York: Bantam Books, 2006, 364 p. ISBN: 9780553804805.

St. Bartholemew's Abbey, December 2005. Odd was just about at the end of his rope after the events related in the last two books. His friend, Chief Wyatt helped him request time in the quiet sanctuary of St. Bartholemew's Abbey. St. Bartholemew's has a school, a place for children who have been injured to the point that they also need a retreat. Odd becomes a member of the abbey community, he is so trusted in the community that the abbot, knowing of Odd's gift, gives him a universal key so that he can try to encourage the resident ghost, Brother Constantine, to move on to the next world. After months of healing, Odd is sitting by the window at night, waiting to watch the snow fall, when he spots a bodach. He knows his time of rest is over. He can only hope that this time he is able to save everyone from the coming catastrophe.

Associates: P. Oswald Boone—*Odd's friend;* Boo—*deceased, the Abbey's dog;* Sister Angela—*the Mother Superior;* Father Bernard— *the Abbot;* Brother Knuckles (née Salvatore)—*the Cellarer;* Brother Constantine—*the poltergeist;* Sister Regina Marie—*a cook;* Sister Miriam—*who was a social worker before taking the veil;* Sister Clare Marie—*a sweet and gentle person;* Brother Matthias—*who loves Gilbert and Sullivan;* Brother Leopold—*who may be retaining ties to his old life;* Brother Quentin—*who used to be a police officer;* Brother Fletcher—*a musician;* Brother John—*who was the famous physicist.* Others at the abbey include: Brother Alfonse; Brother Augustine; Brother Kevin; Brother Rupert; Brother Rafael; Brother Maxwell; Jacob Calvino—*an artist;* Flossie (Christmas) Bodenblatt—*who wants to work with dogs;* Rodon Romanovich—*a baker, a Hoosier, and maybe a poisoner;* The Reaper—*also called the Neverwas.*

5. *Odd Hours.* New York: Bantam Books, 2008, 352 p. ISBN: 9780553807059.

Magic Beach, January 2006. Odd's nightmares are of a red tide, a tide of death. He knows they have meaning, he knows he must act, he just doesn't know what to do. Everything is set in motion when he is accosted on the beach. A man grabs his arm, and suddenly the nightmare vision rises up: they both see it. It turns out that the man is a conspirator in a plot to import weapons and that the vision convinces him that Odd is moving against the conspiracy. Suddenly, Odd is being hunted, and he knows that he must elude the hunters and resolve the mystery before the nightmare of the red tide comes true.

ASSOCIATES: Boo—*deceased, Odd's dog;* Lawrence "Hutch" Hutchinson—*Odd's employer;* Annamaria—*the Lady of the Bell;* Frank Sinatra—*deceased, but he still has a temper;* Blossom Rosedale—*who was burned by her father;* Sam Whittle—*deceased;* Raphael—*the dog;* the Reverend Charles Moran—*who has merry eyes;* Melanie—*the Reverend's wife;* Hoss Shackett—*Magic Beach Chief of Police;* Utgard Rolf—*a walking mountain with a little beard;* Birdena "Birdie" Hopkins—*who offers Odd a lift;* Joey—*who sees no reason for extraneous personnel;* Buddy—*who shares Joey's view;* Valonia Fontenelle—*who admires ruthlessness.*

L

LACKEY, Mercedes.

CHILDREN OF THE NIGHT

Genres/Themes Crossed: Secret Society X Traditional Mystery.

Subjects/Character Types: Guardians, Vampires, Spell-Casters (Witches), Clairvoyents X Amateur Sleuth (Contemporary).

Series/Stand-Alone: The changes in the characters over the course of the series make this a series that should be read in order.

Scene of the Crime: Dallas, Texas, 1987.

Detective: Diana Tregarde earns her bread by writing sentimental, blatantly melodramatic romance novels. Her non-paying work is standing between the world and the forces of darkness.

Known Associates: Morrie is Diana's agent. He talked her into fulfilling a contract on a romance novel, and she found that she was good at writing them. Lenny Preston is Diana's upstairs neighbor; after *Children of the Night,* Keith is his partner and André is Diana's lover. He was made a vampire during the French Revolution (he was suspected of being a royalist sympathizer and a young woman offered him an alternative to the guillotine). He came over to America with the Lowara gypsies. In the late 1960s and early 1970s, while she was a college student, Diana rescued a number of people with psi ability. Some of them became members on what they came to call the "Spook Squad." They faced many dangers together, and became lifelong friends. Diana saved Mark Valdez when, drunk, he tried to summon a ghost that almost took over his body. Diana saved Larry Kestrel by stopping him from suicide; he hadn't known he was clairvoyant, and had spent a couple days being hounded by the ghost of someone he had known. He had thought he was going insane. Diana was able to lay the ghost, and Larry's fears, to rest.

Premise: There are people who are born with strong magical powers; they are the "Guardians." They are not organized, at least not by regular human means. There are frequently "coincidences" that put them where they need to be. Most big cities have at least one, because predators come to big cities to hunt. "Teachers" are also born; they recognize Guardians and make sure that they get the education they need to preserve and protect. They also reassure Guardians that the fact that they sense things invisible to the people around them is natural, even valuable, not crazy. Diana's grandmother was a Teacher. Guardians are compelled to help; they cannot turn down a request for aid:

> Guardians become Guardians because they have no choice. Because you either use what you have, or—or the things the Guardians Guard against come hunting you. Even if you want to be left alone, they'll come hunting you, and come for you when they are most ready. So you deal with them before that can happen. (*Children of the Night*, p. 39)

The mythos of the world changes in its details (but not in its general outlines) in the different books. The first book written was *Burning Water*. In it, the person who helped Diana was her great-grandmother, and Diana's involvement in protecting others is described as a personal decision:

> I do this probably for the same reason that you became a cop, Mark—there are things out there that people need to be shielded from. Since I have the talent and the knowledge—it's almost a duty for me to stand in the line of fire. And unfortunately I don't know of anyone better equipped than I am who isn't already out fighting fires of his own. (*Burning Water*, p. 131)

Comment: The premises on which this world is based are defined most clearly in *Children of the Night*. It might be best to read them in chronological order, which puts that first, rather than in published order which puts *Burning Water* first.

In *Burning Water*, the reader is likely to recognize the trappings of the Aztec ritual (for instance the removal of the still-beating heart) very quickly, and may wonder how the sleuths could be so obtuse. The explanation in the narrative is that the villains are able to block even the thoughts of the people who are investigating the crimes.

Mercedes Lackey has stated that this series was discontinued for two reasons: (1) poor sales (she is, after all, a professional writer- this is not a hobby), and (2) some insane and frightening people decided that the mythos of the stories was real and, when Mercedes Lackey tried to convince them that fiction is, well, fiction, they turned ugly. So, unfortunately, the series will not continue beyond the three novels and the short stories. (For more information, see her essay "The Last Straw" at http://www.mercedeslackey.com/features_laststraw.html.)

Literary Magic & Mayhem: The secondary characters are not only well-drawn, they are compelling. Flashbacks introduce members of the Spook Squad in *Burning Water* and *Jinx High*, the internal struggle and personal growth of Diana's old boyfriend, Dave, in *Children of the Night*. Her gifts include empathy and as her insights are described the readers come to know the characters as well, as in this passage, in which she first empathically reads André:

> There was guilt there, and mourning, and a deeply felt depression that seemed a great deal like her own. His eyes held shadows within shadows; shadows of pain, and a loneliness that had endured longer than anything she'd ever known. (*Children of the Night*, p. 143)

All the stories reveal characters who have encountered pain, all give readers people to care about. Diana is also interesting. She is strong and compassionate, brave and giving, she also has some refreshing ideas about religion (she's Wiccan). One interesting element of the books is how power is depicted as nothing more than power; it requires sacrifice, but is not intrinsically good or evil. The theology of the world is well-thought-out, and is discussed by Diana and Mark in *Burning Water*.

One interesting aspect of the series as a whole is that Diana's solutions aren't any better than the research on which she based them. If she never knew the nature of the evil she faced, she would not be completely successful against it.

Explorations: What did each person who had power sacrifice to get that power? Did that person sacrifice something of his or her own, or something that belonged to someone else?

How did what was sacrificed define who was good and who was evil?

What are Diana's limitations?

What would have had to change for the ending to be entirely happy? How would the story have played out with that change?

THE CASES

1. ***Children of the Night.*** New York: TOR, 2005, c1990, 317 p. ISBN: 0765313189.

New York, 197?. Diana's friend Annie is well into her ninth month of pregnancy. To help out, Diana agreed to mind Annie's occult shop. In some ways, doing so has given her custody of the insanity that is Annie's business life. Witch wannabees, serious practitioners, tourists looking for thrills, reporters looking for sensational stories, those who are powerful and evil, who try to use the shop as a hunting ground, and the terrified people they hunt: from behind the cash register Diana can see the occult world. Diana offers protection to a young gypsy, Janfri, and finds herself taking a stand against vampires. Things only get worse when a friend who is gifted with the sight asks Diana to come to the morgue, and she finds a corpse that has had its soul torn from it.

ASSOCIATES: Morrie—*Diana's agent;* Annie Sandstrom—*owner of the shop Bell, Book and Candle;* Lenny Preston—*Diana's friend and upstairs neighbor;* Keith—*Lenny's friend.*

Members of the band, The Children of the Night: Jason Trevor—*lead singer;* Dave Kendall—*on guitar, (Dave used to date Diana; they split up when he told her that she had to choose, it was either Ouija boards or him...);* Jack Prescott—*drummer;* and Doug—*who plays bass.*

André LeBrel—*vampire, Diana invites him into the shop, then into her home;* Jim—*the bartender at Logres;* Master Jeffries and Hidoro—*the world became a more dangerous place when these monsters made a deal...*

2. **"Nightside"** first published in *Marion Zimmer Bradley's Fantasy Magazine* #6, 1989; now distributed online through FictionWise.com.

NEW YORK, SPRING 198? There's a "Ripper" loose in New York, and Diana needs André's help. It hunts beneath the dark moon and rips the souls from its victims. Neither Diana nor André has ever seen anything like it.

NOTE: In this one Diana knows André: they are not living together, and neither has ever encountered anything dead with the soul ripped from it. It's an interesting story, and it is listed as a Diana Tregarde story, but it seems more like a story that may have been a false start to the series than a story written as an episode in the series.

ASSOCIATES: André LeBrel—*vampire;* Dr. Crane.

3. ***Burning Water.*** New York: TOR, 2005, c1989, 332 p. ISBN: 0765313170.

MEXICO CITY, MEXICO, 1985–1986 AND DALLAS, TEXAS, 1987. In the last year, there have been signs of something wrong in Dallas. It's as if something has set off those who are sensitive to psychic manifestations. Violence (particularly at mental institutions) has increased; odd religious cults have become prominent; hospitals have had increased psychiatric admissions; and the Gypsies have fled the city. When cattle mutilations began, Mark had suspicions about paranormal activity, suspicions he couldn't share with the rest of the police force. The problem was particularly bad on the ranch of a friend of Mark's, his herd was targeted over and over again. Somewhat embarrassed, Mark snuck out during the full moon and warded the ranch. The depredations against that ranch stopped, but the cattle mutilations continued on other ranches. For Mark, that confirmed that the problem was arcane in nature, but he could not find a way to stop it on his own. Now the killers have expanded their activities and are starting to kill humans. Mark wanted to bring Diana in on the investigation. He convinced his Chief that she's an expert on modern cults, and that she should be brought in as a consultant. Diana quickly learns that the group behind the killings is extremely powerful, so powerful that they are able to block her and other practitioners. Diana wants to run, but she can't. She knows that she and Mark are the only ones standing between a city of innocents and something powerful, hateful, and hungry for blood.

NOTE: The sources used to research the cultures of Mesoamerican Indians are listed in the Afterword.

ASSOCIATES: Lupe—*who was a 17-year-old maid in Mexico before the earthquake; after the earthquake, she became Chimalman: handmaiden to a god;* Robert Fernandez—*the photographer who believes that Lupe will help him make his fortune;* Sherry Bryce Fernandez—*his wife;* Bobby—*their son.*

Detective Mark Valdez—*who calls Diana when he needs a consultant on the occult;* Chief of Detectives Samuel Clemens Grimes—*Mark's boss;* Homicide Detective Dr. Alonso Frederico Ramirez—*a sensitive on the police force;* Charlie Mountainhawk—*a beat cop who is a sensitive;* and Lydia—*the dispatcher, also a sensitive;* Doreen Mountainhawk—*Charlie's wife;* Johnnie Mountainhawk—*Charlie's brother;* Juanita Valdez—*Mark's Aunt Nita, who knows enough to feel and recognize power;* Pablo—*the leader of the Jaguar gang;* Noble Williams—*a voudoun;* Theresa Montenegro—*a bruja;* Yanfri and Dobra—*Lowara Romany (gypsies);* Marion—*a clairvoyant with 13 cats;* and Athena—*a healer, she accepts a job as Diana's friend Len's hospice caregiver.*

4. ***Jinx High.*** New York: TOR, 2006, c1991, 335 p. ISBN: 0765313197; 9780765313195.

JENKS, OKLAHOMA, 1988. There is something powerful, old, and evil hunting the kids at Jenks's High School. Larry Kestrel is a sensitive. He used to be one of the members of Diana's "Spook Squad" when they were students at Yale. After he is called to the hospital to pick up his son, Derek, from an accident that could have been fatal, Larry faces the fact that something arcane is going on and that it's beyond his skills to protect his son. By apparent coincidence, Derek's Honors English teacher, Ann Greeley, is looking for a professional writer to engage her students and bring them out of the depression brought on by the death of another student. Derek mentions this to his father, who immediately calls Diana, and she volunteers. Unfortunately, the evil that is out to get Derek is both older and trickier than Diana.

ASSOCIATES: Larry Kestrel and Mark Valdez—*two of Diana's friends and members of her Spook Squad from college.*

Most of the other characters in the book are from the High School: Ann Greeley—*Honors English teacher;* Fay Harper—*the most popular girl in school;* Buffie Gentry—*a girl who dared to challenge Fay;* Jillian McIver—*Fay's best friend;* Derek "Deke" Kestrel—*who is going steady with Fay;* Sandy Foster—*Jillian's boyfriend, he is a football player;* Bob William—*Captain of the football team;* Alan—*Derek's best friend;* George Louvis—*another friend of Derek's, George plays a Gibson guitar in the band The Persuaders (other band members are Steve and Paul);* Monica Carlin—*who has some psi talent and just moved to the city;* Rhonda—*Monica's mother;* Joy Harris—*a friend of Monica's;* Tannim—*makes a guest appearance (he is from Mercedes Lackey's Serrated Edge series).*

5. "Satanic, Versus" first published in *Marion Zimmer Bradley's Fantasy Magazine* #10, 1990; now distributed online through FictionWise.com.

New York, 199? Diana and André attend the Romance Writers of the World Halloween party as John Steed and Mrs. Peel. One of the guests attempts to summon Mr. Tall, Dark, and Handsome and comes within a hair's breadth of turning the party into a massacre.

Note: One of the most entertaining aspects of this story is the banter between Diana and Robert Harrison regarding "whoopee witches." That concept and the character, Robert Harrison, are based on the game *Stalking the Night Fantastic* by Richard Tucholka.

Associates: André LeBrel—*vampire;* Robert Harrison—*a client of Diana's agent Morrie;* and Valentine Vervain—*who was originally named Edith Bowman,and is another of Morrie's clients.*

6. "Killer Byte" first published in *Marion Zimmer Bradley's Fantasy Magazine* #23, 1994; now distributed online through FictionWise.com.

Hartford, Connecticut. 199? André comes across a predator while he is cruising bulletin boards on the web. He and Diana decide to attend a meeting that has been set up with a 15-year-old girl.

Associates: André LeBrel—*vampire;* Shadow-walker—*a.k.a. "John Smith";* Nightshade—*a.k.a. Brenda Doyle, age 15.*

Lark, Michael. Worked with Ed Brubaker, Greg Rucka and Stefano Guadiano on *In the Line of Duty.* See BRUBAKER, Ed: In the Line of Duty.

LOEB, Jeph and Tim Sale.

Batman: The Long Halloween

Genres/Themes Crossed: Science Fiction X Hard-Boiled Mystery.

Subjects/Character Types: Superheroes X Amateur Sleuth (Contemporary).

Series/Stand-Alone: The two graphic novels in this series should be read in order. They are set in the era of *Batman: Year One* by Frank Miller, but fall into the mystery genre in a way that Year One does not. Year One may be viewed as the first book in this series, despite being by a different writer and artist, but is not necessary for these stories to be fully enjoyed.

Scene of the Crime: Gotham City, the first or second year of the Batman's career.

Detective: Bruce Wayne witnessed the murder of his parents as a small boy and vowed to dedicate his life to fighting crime. After years of training around the world, he returns to his home city of Gotham and takes on the roll of the masked detective, Batman.

Known Associates: Alfred Pennyworth, Bruce Wayne's butler and confidant, serves as the voice of reason and a sounding board for Bruce's ideas. Commissioner James Gordon, originally tasked with catching the masked vigilante patrolling Gotham's streets, has since become one of the Batman's allies in his war on crime by secretly giving him information on what the police know with regard to prominent crimes. The district attorney, Harvey Dent, forms the third member of their secret alliance, whose purpose is to bring justice back to the streets of Gotham. Dick Grayson is a young boy who grew up as a circus acrobat, and is adopted by Bruce Wayne after Dick's parents are murdered while performing on the trapeze.

Premise: In the early years of the Batman's career, Gotham is still in the grip of organized crime. The mob is more entrenched in Gotham at this point, rather than the more colorful villains that will become the stable of antagonists through most of Batman's career.

Comment: Jeph Loeb worked for several years as a producer on the television series *Heroes*. Tim Sale's artwork is featured prominently in the series. Loeb has also worked as a producer on *Lost* for NBC and *Smallville* for the CW. Tim Sale's official Web site is http://www.timsale1.com/.

Literary Magic & Mayhem: The emphasis in these books is on the struggle that the organized crime families are going through as their city is taken over by a masked detective and costumed villains. As much time is spent looking at how the crime families of Gotham feel about changes as is spent watching the Batman attempting to solve crimes.

Explorations: How different are the activities of organized crime families and the costumed criminals that are supplanting them?

Which group poses a more genuine threat to citizens?

THE CASES

1. ***Batman: The Long Halloween.*** New York: DC Comics, 1999, 369 p. ISBN: 1563894696.

GOTHAM CITY, THE FIRST OR SECOND YEAR OF BATMAN'S CAREER. In Gotham City in the not so distant past, the organized crime families, led by "The Roman," are struggling to hold onto their power. People associated with the Roman start turning up dead, shot with the same gun, on national holidays. Police Commissioner James Gordon and DA Harvey Dent turn to their friend, the Batman, to help sort out the crimes.

ASSOCIATES: James Gordon—*Gotham's police commissioner;* Harvey Dent—*Gotham's District Attorney;* Alfred Pennyworth—*Bruce Wayne's butler.*

2. ***Batman: Dark Victory.*** New York: DC Comics, 2002, 392 p. ISBN: 1563898683.

GOTHAM CITY, A YEAR AFTER THE EVENTS OF THE LONG HALLOWEEN. The remnants of the Roman's crime family are again targeted by a serial killer, along with corrupt members of the police force. The method of murder this time involves hanging the victim in public places with partially solved games of hangman found on the victim's body. With the Holiday killer behind bars, Commission Gordon again turns to the Batman for assistance.

ASSOCIATES: James Gordon—*Gotham's police commissioner;* Alfred Pennyworth—*Bruce Wayne's butler;* Dick Grayson—*Bruce Wayne's ward.*

M

MACAVOY, R. A.

Tea with the Black Dragon

Genres/Themes Crossed: Lone Supernatural X Traditional Mystery.

Subjects/Character Types: Slightly Supernatural Human X Amateur Sleuth (Contemporary).

Series/Stand-Alone: The first in the series, *Tea with the Black Dragon*, should be read first. It is the best introduction to the characters.

Scene of the Crime: California (San Francisco, San Mateo, Stanford), 1983.

Detective(s): Martha Macnamara, who rushed to San Francisco when her daughter called and asked for her help. Mayland Long who was introduced to Martha by bartender Jerry Trough. After the meeting (in which she mentions that she will be sitting Zazen at 5:00 am the next morning) Mayland thinks:

> Zen . . . to have come so far, to this stone city where the ocean was on the wrong side of the sun, to wait and watch himself age with cruel speed, foreign in form, in speech, in feeling . . . Here to find again the trace of his own interminable, floundering search. And in such an unlikely shape as that of Martha Macnamara. (p. 14)

Mayland begins to work with Martha, to help her and to learn from her.

Known Associates: Martha's 24-year-old daughter, Elizabeth "Liz" Macnamara, loves her mother, but is somewhat exasperated by her mother's approach to life. Jerry Trough, a bartender, introduces Martha and Mayland. Liz went to college at Stanford University; Fred Frisch met her there. They were both students in the computer science degree program.

Premise: Dragons are (or, at least, were) real. Black dragons were scholars, and one, while searching for enlightenment, was turned into a man.

Comment: *Tea with the Black Dragon* was nominated for the Nebula Award for Best Novel in 1983 and for the Hugo Award for Best Novel in 1984. R. A. (Roberta Ann) MacAvoy won the John W. Campbell Award for Best New Writer in 1984.

Literary Magic & Mayhem: Martha Macnamara is an extraordinarily appealing character. She combines a philosophical outlook with a quiet and abiding joy; she shows enormous courage and determination. In their initial meeting, she and Mayland discuss music, Yeats, and Thomas Rhymer's story (including the most interesting part, which is what happens after the events recounted in Scott's ballad). Mayland tells it so beautifully that Martha says that she believes he must have been told it by Thomas himself. Mayland responds:

> "From the Rhymer?" He leaned forward and lifted his eyebrows in mock wonderment. "How could that be? He was unconscious during the crux of the story. I have the story from the boy, of course. The Rhymer's son.
> "Beautiful boy," he added, after a moment. "Resembled his mother."
> Martha blinked twice. The hour and the moment combined to overwhelm her. Cradling her head in her arms she laughed until she hiccupped. (p. 9)

The second in the series has less philosophy and fewer conversations between Mayland and Martha.

Explorations: Some of Martha's statements strike Mayland with particular force. What are they? What does she teach him?

When and how does Mayland gain strength?

What was Liz looking for in life? What did she want to achieve? Did she get it? How did that work out?

What impresses Fred about Mayland? What impresses Mayland about Fred?

At the tea shop, Martha tells Mayland that he should stop helping her; at Fred's apartment Mayland tells Fred that he should stop helping him. How are the situations different? How are they the same?

THE CASES

1. ***Tea with the Black Dragon.*** New York: Bantam Books, 1983, 166 p. ISBN: 0553232053.

SILICON VALLEY IN CALIFORNIA, 1981. Martha Macnamara flew to San Francisco when her daughter, Liz, called her for help. Now she can't find Liz. Mayland Long offers his help in the search for her daughter. Within a day of beginning the search, they both know that something has gone terribly wrong.

ASSOCIATES: Elizabeth "Liz" Macnamara—*Martha's 24-year-old daughter;* Jerry Trough—*a bartender;* Fred Frisch—*owner of a shop called Friendly Computers;* Professor Carlo Peccolo—*mentored Liz;* Liz's boss—*Floyd Rasmussen;* and Doug Threve—*who is one of Liz's business associate at RasTech.*

2. ***Twisting the Rope.*** United States: e-reads, c1986, 1999, 179 p. ISBN: 158586059X.

SANTA CRUZ, 1986. Martha put her musical education to a different use, fiddling with Celtic bands. Now she's formed her own, for a limited tour. They're eight weeks into the tour and things are going sour. St. Ives does his best to make everyone's lives a misery, and Mayland is ill. Martha's three-year-old granddaughter has taken to wandering off, 500 dollars from the gate receipts have gone missing, and the sleazy agent who was to pay the band for their gig in Santa Cruz never appeared. Then there is murder, and Mayland is the chief suspect. Martha vows to learn the truth about the death.

ASSOCIATES: The members of Macnamara's band: Theodore "Ted" Poznan—*the laid back California guitarist;* Elen Evans—*the harpist;* Pádraig O Súilleábhain—*an accordion player from Ireland;* and George St. Ives—*an unpleasant man who plays the pipes.*

Other characters include: Martha "Marty" Rachel Frisch-Macnamara—*Martha's three-year-old granddaughter;* Mayland Long—*who is acting as the band's road manager;* Donald Stoughie—*booking agent for Landaman Hall;* Sandy Frager—*a friend of Elen's, Marty's babysitter;* Officer Dan Sherer—*who found the body;* Detective-Sergeant Anderson—*who is investigating. Matha's daughter, Elizabeth Macnamara;* David Alexander—*Long's attorney;* Jerry Carver—*a thief of silk.*

MCGRAW, ROYAL. Worked with Paul Dini on Batman Detective. See DINI, Paul: Batman Detective.

MEAN STREETS.

MEAN STREETS

Genres/Themes Crossed: Paranormal, Secret Society, Blended Society X Hard-Boiled Mystery

Subjects/Character Types: Spell Casters, Ghosts, Psychics X Private Investigators.

Series/Stand-Alone: Anthology of short stories.

Scene of the Crime: Varies.

Detective: Varies.

Known Associates: Varies.

Premise: New stories about well-known paranormal private investigators: Harry Dresden, John Taylor, Harper Blaine, and Remy Chandler.

Comment: This volume provides a smorgasbord of "tastes" of the four series. Readers new to the genre can sample all four, gain general knowledge of the genre, and decide which series they would like to pursue.

Literary Magic & Mayhem: The stories cover recent cases in the careers of characters from well-established series. The novellas are designed to incorporate enough backstory so that new readers can enjoy them without having read the previous series entries.

Explorations: How different was the world of the stories from the world in which we live?

THE CASES

Mean Streets. New York: Roc, 2009, 342 p. ISBN: 978041462497.
CONTENTS: The Warrior *by Jim Butcher;* The Difference a Day Makes *by Simon R. Green;* The Third Death of the Little Clay Dog *by Kat Richardson;* Noah's Orphans *by Thomas E. Sniegoski.*

MELTZER, Brad and Rags Morales.

IDENTITY CRISIS

Genres/Themes Crossed: Science Fiction, Blended Society X Hard-boiled Mystery.

Subjects/Character Types: Super Heroes, Super Villains X Amateur Sleuth (Contemporary).

Series/Stand-Alone: Stand-alone.

Scene of the Crime: The story takes place predominantly in Gotham City and Metropolis, but covers nearly every corner of the Earth portrayed in the DC Comics universe.

Detectives: The story follows several detectives and members of the Justice League of America and the Justice Society of America as they attempt to solve the murder of a loved one. Bruce Wayne witnessed the murder of his parents as a small boy, and vowed to dedicate his life to fighting crime as the Batman. Oliver Queen was stranded on a deserted island as a young man, and had to hone his archery skills to survive. When Queen returned to civilization, he dedicated himself to fighting crime and standing up for the common man, as the Green Arrow. Ralph Dibny was a detective who gained the ability to stretch his body in fantastic ways, and became the hero known as the Elongated Man.

Known Associates: The Justice League of America, especially Superman, who fights for truth, justice, and the American way; Wonder Woman, the exiled Princess Diana of the Amazons; Zatana, a powerful practitioner of magic; Wally West, the most recent hero to wear the mantle of the Flash; Kyle Rayner, the newest Green Lantern of Earth; Hawkman, a powerful flying warrior; the Black Canary, a detective and martial artist; Ray Palmer, who can shrink in size as the hero called the Atom. The Justice Society of America, a group of heroes dedicated to instructing the younger generation of heroes. Of special note in the JSA is Doctor Midnight, a scientist able to see into the EM spectrum, and Mr. Terrific, a technological genius. Tim Drake, who recently revealed to his father that he has been serving as Batman's partner, the newest Robin. Lois Lane, reporter for the Daily Planet and wife of Clark Kent, Superman.

Premise: There are beings in the universe who use super powers, some of these beings are from other planets, some are from Earth's superhuman races, some have been granted powers through mystical means, some simply mimic having superpowers through the use of technology; all are living undercover in Earth's human society.

Comment: Meltzer has said that one of his intentions with this graphic novel was to defend the Silver Age of comics, when costumed heroes battled villains in larger-than-life scenarios. Because of the way in which he went about this defense, his miniseries tends to be either loved or hated by fans. Some view it as a harmful alteration of the history of their beloved characters, while others see it as a fascinating look at the moral issues involved in maintaining the safety of the people one loves.

Brad Meltzer's Web site at http://www.bradmeltzer.com/ includes information on his books, his music, and his comics, as well as biographical information, his blog, and message boards. Rags Morales sometimes posts information on current projects on Comic Space at http://www.comicspace.com/rags_morales/ and has a page that displays (and sells) some of his artwork at http://www.theartistschoice.com/ragsmorales.htm.

Literary Magic and Mayhem: There are several detectives throughout the series, each trying to solve the same crime. Meltzer hops back and forth between several different characters and groups of characters, following each one's progress in solving the case.

Exploration: To what lengths are you justified in going when attempting to protect the people you love?

What sort of accountability do masked vigilantes have? What sort of accountability should they have?

THE CASE

1. ***Identity Crisis.*** New York: DC Comics, (reprint edition) 2006, 296 p. ISBN: 1401204589.

GOTHAM CITY, METROPOLIS, NEW YORK CITY, SAN FRANCISCO, LOS ANGELES, CENTRAL CITY, PRESENT DAY. One of the most important rules for most costumed heroes is to protect their secret identities. Ralph Dibny had always operated openly as the Elongated Man, believing it was necessary for the public to know who their protectors were. After several years of retirement from super-heroics, Ralph's wife is murdered in their home. This murder starts to unravel hidden secrets of the Justice League, and is further complicated when threatening notes start arriving addressed to the family members of other prominent heroes who had gone to great lengths to conceal their identities. The best detectives of the Justice League start trying to solve the crime without revealing to each other the secrets that they'd hidden for years.

ASSOCIATES: See above.

MICHAELS, Kasey.

MAGGIE NEEDS AN ALIBI

Genres/Themes Crossed: Literary Cross-Over, Secret Society X Traditional Mystery.

Subjects/Character Types: Literary Cross-over (characters from books stepping out into the world) X Amateur Sleuth (Contemporary).

Series/Stand-Alone: There is a surprising amount of character development (in the literary characters) and there is a great deal of change in relationships. These should be read in order.

Scene of the Crime: Present day New York.

Detective: Maggie Kelly, writer of historical mysteries. When her fictional detective enters the real world and begins detecting, Maggie joins in.

Known Associates: Alexandre Blake, Viscount Saint-Just, a character out of Maggie's fantasies (well, out of her books), a nicely built six-foot-two figment or, rather, hunk, of Maggie's imagination. He was designed by combining the best features from many eras: Beau Brummel's casually rumpled hair, Paul Newman's blue eyes, Val Kilmer's lips... "A composite for her readers to fantasize about as their husbands or boyfriends watched television in their boxer shorts and scratched their butts" (p. 14, *Maggie Needs an Alibi*).

Siant-Just was a fictional Regency gentleman who solved crimes; now he's a living, breathing man in Maggie's apartment, having arrived with his sidekick, Sterling Balder. Maggie is the only person who knows of their origins. Other characters include Bernice Toland-James, Maggie's brilliant, insightful editor and friend; Tabby Leighton, Maggie's agent; and Tabby's cheating husband, David; Argyle Jackson (also known as Socks), the doorman in Maggie's building and an aspiring actor; Dr. Bob Chalfont, Maggie's therapist, whom she began seeing two years ago to get help to quit smoking. Dr. Bob has helped Maggie plumb the depths of her problems, but, so far, there hasn't been a lot of progress in solving any of them. Felicity (Faith) Booth-Simmons was a close friend of Maggie's when they were both struggling writers, but as soon as she gained some success, she saw Maggie more as a rival than as a friend. In the first in the series, *Maggie Needs an Alibi,* Maggie meets Lieutenant Steve Wendell, who is alarmingly interested in Saint-Just, but even more interested in Maggie. When Saint-Just realizes that he must have legal identification (such as a passport) if he intends to stay in this world, he seeks out criminals: Snake (Vernon), Killer (Georgie), and Mare (Mary Louise). Maggie's terrifying mother is Alicia, and Maggie's very subdued father is Evan.

Premise: Maggie wrote characters so well, they came alive. Not in the way that writers normally talk about their characters coming alive. Maggie's came alive and decided to share her apartment. They sleep in the guest room. As Sterling puts it:

> It all began innocently enough. A desire to explore a larger world, that's what he said. A chance to step out, expand our horizons, spread our wings, and all of that. (Prologue, *Maggie Needs as Alibi*)

Comment: Kasey Michaels has written over 80 books and has won numerous awards, including a Career Achievement award for her Regency era historical romances. Her Web site: http://www.kaseymichaels.com/

describes her commitment to writing. She'd written her first book as a lark, then her oldest son became seriously ill. Ms. Michaels spent months going back and forth to the hospital, and there she noticed that the nurses and the other mothers waiting in the hospital read Romance novels. Ms. Michaels describes them as books where there is a chance of happiness; not a promise, but a chance, and states, "I know, have learned, that one of the best ways to keep your sanity is to escape reality every once in a while." One obviously-treasured reviewer comment is mentioned, from a reviewer who said *The Tenacious Miss Tamerlane* (the book that Ms. Michaels worked on during the nine months her son had to have dialysis treatments) was the reviewer's rainy day book, because if she felt down, reading the book would make her laugh. Ms. Michael's books are very successful at making readers laugh, and at providing sanity-saving escapes.

Literary Magic & Mayhem: The chronology described below is provided to inform readers of the general timeline of the books. In *Maggie Without a Clue,* the characters calculate the number of years since a man died, and his death date is given; that was used as the lynchpin for the chronology. Some of the chronological details shift a little from book to book, so the dates should be used as relative guidelines.

The books should be read in order. In the first book, the set-up is very carefully (and amusingly) laid out before the crimes begin. *Maggie Needs an Alibi* and *Maggie By the Book* are engaging romps. *Maggie Without a Clue* begins as a romp, but becomes more serious as it progresses. Sometimes authors say that their characters take on lives of their own and change the narrative. That may have happened here. In any case, the book is set up so that the characters can see justice done, but keep their own hands clean, by setting one murderer on the trail of another. After painstakingly developing and explaining that strategy, the plan changes, irrevocably changing our (and Maggie's) perceptions of the characters. This is the book where Saint-Just and Sterling become conscious that they are evolving, that they are now more than the people Maggie created. Kasey Michaels's Web site states that *Bowled Over* is the last of the *Maggie Kelly* series.

Explorations: If you could meet face-to-face with any character from literature, whom would you choose?

If you could design a hero (or heroine), what characteristics would you borrow?

Think of different sidekicks in literature (Watson, Goodwin, etc.): what purpose(s) do they serve, what do they add to a book?

What are your rainy-day books?

THE CASES

1. ***Maggie Needs an Alibi.*** New York: Kensington, c2002, 310 p. ISBN: 1575668793.

NEW YORK, JUNE 2004. Maggie Kelly, a writer of best-selling historical mysteries, is stunned when two of her fictional characters show up in her apartment. One of them is her main character, a gentleman from 1816. He's the Viscount Saint Just, Alexandre Blake, gentleman detective, and he is accompanied by his sidekick (in the novels for comic relief) Sterling Balder. Maggie is still trying to figure out what to do about this invasion when an ex-lover is poisoned in her apartment. Maggie becomes the chief suspect, Saint-Just naturally participates in the investigation. He's hampered by the necessity of maintaining a low profile. He is a hero, and keeping a low profile does not come naturally, but he has no legal documents that would explain his presence in the United States; there are no legal documents that would even explain his existence!

ASSOCIATES: Kirk Toland—*Maggie's publisher and ex-lover;* Bernice Toland-James—*Kirk's ex-wife;* Argyle Jackson (Socks)—*who almost gets his Broadway debut;* Alexandre Blake, Viscount Saint Just—*who is currently using the name Alex Blakely;* Sterling Balder—*Alex's sidekick;* Tabby—*Maggie's agent;* David Leighton—*Tabby's husband;* Nelson Trigg—*(otherwise known as The Trigger), a bean counter who cut Maggie's last series of books when he cut all the mid-list authors;* Clarice Simon—*Trigg's personal assistant;* Lieutenant Steve Wendell—*who is suspicious of St. Just;* Evan and Alicia Kelly—*Maggie's parents;* Snake—*a.k.a. Vernon;* Killer—*a.k.a. Georgie;* and Mare—*a.k.a. Mary Louise;* Miss Holly Spivak—*reporter.*

2. ***Maggie By the Book.*** New York: Kensington, c2003, 274 p. ISBN: 1575668815.

NEW YORK, SEPTEMBER 2004. Living with Saint Just is proving difficult on a number of levels. (Writing sex scenes has become embarrassing.) Saint-Just helps Maggie escape her manuscript when he decrees that they should all attend the WAR (We Are Romance) conference. He's particularly interested in entering himself and Mary Louise in a romance book cover model contest. Amidst the bizarreness of the conference, the first attacks are viewed as pranks, but they get progressively more serious. Once someone is murdered, all but the sturdiest souls leave the conference; the most committed fans, writers, models, and reporters (and the murderer) are the only people who remain.

ASSOCIATES: Saint Just—*who is looking for a means to make money;* Sterling Balder—*Saint Just's sidekick;* Mary Louise—*who cleaned up beautifully;* Bernice Toland-James—*Maggie's editor;* Dr. Bob Chalfont—*Maggie's therapist;*

Tabitha Leighton—*Maggie's agent;* Virginia Neuendorf—*an old friend of Maggie's hoping to break out of the Regency sub-genre by selling one of her three Regency Historical manuscripts before she gives birth again (which doesn't give her much time);* Bunny Wilkinson—*WAR Conference Chairperson;* Martha Kolowsky—*who does most of the convention grunt work;* Felicity (Faith) Boothe Simmons—*who sees Maggie as a rival;* Reggie "Regina" Hall—*a.k.a. Lady Twitters;* Giancarlo—*a.k.a. cover model Mel Harper;* Damien—*who hopes to be next year's hottest cover model;* Rose Sherwood—*publisher of Rose Knows Romance;* Liza Lang—*Rose's assistant;* Sergeant Willard "Willie" Decker—*whose most obvious employable quality is that he is the assistant police chief's wife's nephew;* Argyle "Socks" Jackson—*who is more than a doorman;* Jay "Jayne"—*Argyle's friend;* Lieutenant Steve Wendell—*who has his doubts about the talents of the officers of Manhattan South;* John James Neuendorf—*who arrives early;* Holly Spivak—*a reporter from Fox News.*

3. ***Maggie Without a Clue.*** New York: Kensington, c2004, 294 p. ISBN: 1575668831.

NEW YORK., SEPTEMBER 2004. Bernie's drinking has increased in the last two months since Kirk's death. She's begun having blackouts. She awakens from one, and calls Maggie, hysterically sobbing about the dead man lying next to her. At first Maggie is afraid that Bernice is hallucinating, but the truth is much worse. Maggie and Saint-Just are on the case when mobsters begin threatening the gentle Sterling. In the course of this book, all the main characters grow. Sterling shows more courage than would have been expected of his character; Saint Just knows self-doubt that his character would never have imagined; Maggie finds that a hero's actions may be less palatable in real life. Saint Just describes his and Sterling's changes to Maggie:

> Yes, you created me. I am a figment of your imagination, or at least I was. Until I took charge, took control of my own destiny, which, as it happens, brought me here. You made me, Maggie, and now I am making me...more. (p. 177)

ASSOCIATES: Sterling Balder—*who has grown beyond his position as the comic relief;* Henry—*Sterling's mouse;* Viscount Saint Just—*a.k.a. Alex Blakely, who moves out of Maggie's apartment, but ends up sleeping over;* Bernice Toland-James—*who was once married to Willard "Buddy" James;* J. P. Boxer—*attorney;* Lieutenant Steve Wendell—*who is a danger to Saint Just;* Argyle Jackson—*a.k.a. Socks, who has an audition next week;* Holly Spivak—*reporter;* Felicity Boothe Simmons—*Maggie's friend or rival, depending on what Felicity needs;* Lureen O'Boyle—*realtor;* Tabitha "Tabby" Leighton—*Maggie's agent.*

Alicia and Evan Kelly—*Maggie's parents;* George (Killer) and Vernon (Snake)—*who are now middle-management;* and Mary Louise—*who gets a contract;* Dr. Bob Chalfont—*Maggie's therapist;* Rob Bottoms—*a reporter;* Chadwick Dettmer—*the District Attorney;* Bruno and Nick—*who work for mobster Enrico Totila;* and Mrs. Irene Goldblum—*a widowed neighbor who loaned her condo to Saint-Just.*

4. ***High Heels and Homicide.*** New York: Kensington Books, c2005, 277 p. ISBN: 0758208804.

New York and England, November 2004. When Tabby sold Maggie's first three Saint Just books to a movie studio, Maggie was ecstatic. First she had to survive a three-day Thanksgiving visit with her family (and Saint Just and Sterling), then a flight to England, and then she would be feted as the author on the set of the Saint Just production. Things don't go exactly as Maggie had hoped. The family visit in New Jersey is actually slightly better than she expects, and Alex's Atlantic City gambling winnings come in handy. The jaunt to England is not idyllic. Writers are not held in high esteem. The weather is awful, with rain causing a flood that cuts off the estate where the production is filming. Within 24 hours, a man is murdered; soon it is obvious to the cast and crew that one of their number is a killer. The police cannot traverse the flood plain until morning. Those stranded at the house just have to stay alive until the law arrives.

Associates: Sterling Balder and Saint Just—*who come to Thanksgiving at Maggie's parent's home;* Mrs. Halliday—*a bank-teller;* Holy Spivak—*a reporter for Fox news;* Bernice Toland-James—*who is on the wagon;* Alicia and Evan—*Maggie's parents;* Tate—*Maggie's brother;* and Maureen—*Maggies youngest sister.*

The people on site for the production of the first Saint Just movie include: Sir Rudy Medwine—*who offered the company the free reign of his house in the hope that he'd develop a close relationship with a pretty American actress;* Byrd Stockwell—*his handsome nephew;* Arnaud Peppin—*the director;* Joanne Pertuccelli—*who is in charge of production;* Sam Undercuffler—*the screenwriter;* Troy Barlow—*a clumsy blond soap-opera star who has been cast (or miscast) to play Saint Just;* Perry Posko—*cast as Sterling Balder;* Dennis Lloyd—*cast as Saint Just's valet, Clarence;* Evan Pottinger—*cast as the villainous Lord Hervey;* Nikki Campion—*the love interest;* Marylou Keppel—*the gofer.*

5. ***High Heels and Holidays.*** New York: Kensington Books, 2006, 328 p. ISBN: 0758208820; 9780758208828.

New York, December 2004. A package arrived for Maggie while she was in England, an odd, smelly package. Socks the doorman held it for her but, concerned about the smell, he called for instructions. Saint-Just told him to open it and, learning that it contained a dead rat, asked Socks to "keep the evidence" and say nothing to Maggie. At first, Saint-Just believes that it is nothing more than an ugly prank. He keeps it from Maggie to spare her feelings. When he learns that another New York author has met an unexpected end, he wonders whether he has protected Maggie from unpleasantness, or kept information from her that would warn her of danger. The doggerel that accompanied the rat begins to look less like hate mail and more like a threat. Saint-Just decides to investigate on his own, partly to avoid frightening Maggie, partly to score in his undeclared contest against Lieutenant Wendell, and partly to put off admitting to Maggie that he had been keeping information from her. One of his difficulties is in figuring out how to protect Maggie without warning her of the danger. His plan to protect her day and night has unexpected (O.K., maybe not so unexpected) consequences.

ASSOCIATES: Saint-Just—*who decides that he needs a professional opinion on the potential danger posed by a poison-pen who sends dead rats;* Dr. Bob (Dr. Robert Lewis Chalfont)—*who is consulted by Saint Just;* Argyle "Socks" Jackson—*doorman and aspiring actor;* Paul—*the doorman on the nightshift;* Sterling Balder—*who begins work as a volunteer for the Santas for Silver;* Mr. Joshua Goodfellow—*who runs Santas for Silver;* Ms. Marjorie McDermont—*Goodfellow's secretary;* George "Killer" and Vernon "Snake"—*who were once petty criminals, then sidewalk orators, and now are acting as Santa's elves (i.e. bodyguards);* Lieutenant Steve Wendell—*who has decided that he needs to find a woman whose life is less crazy than Maggie's;* Christine Munch—*the woman.*

Alicia Kelly—*Maggie's mother, who confessed;* Evan Kelly—*Maggie's father, who got even and left;* Attorney J. P. Boxer—*who has given a manuscript of her first novel to a publisher;* Bernice Toland-James—*the publisher;* Bruce McCrae—*a gorgeous writer;* Faith "Felicity" Boothe Simmons—*an author who owns Brock, the little dog with the enormous bladder;* Jonathan West—*an author;* Valentino Gates—*a fan;* George Bryon—*a bookstore owner;* and Francis Oakes—*author;* Jeremy Bickel—*Francis's lover, who recently left Francis.*

Salvatore Campion—*a crime lord who owes Saint-Just a favor;* Tony Three Cases—*a well-known enforcer.*

6. ***Bowled Over.*** New York: Kensington Books, 2007, 288 p. ISBN: 0758208847, 9780758208842.

NEW JERSEY, DECEMBER 2004. Maggie manages to break her foot right before she, Saint-Just, and Sterling leave for a happy family Christmas. The Kelly family's celebrations have always been a trial. Maggie's mother puts considerable effort into belittling Maggie's accomplishments and criticizing her every move. Maggie's father gives Maggie quiet support. This year promises to be even worse than usual. Maggie's parents are estranged, and Maggie's father is not invited for Christmas. Maggie's favored brother, Tate, is bringing guests. Maggie's mother has given them Maggie's room and suggested that Maggie stay with her father, Evan, and come over for Christmas Day and Christmas dinner. Accordingly Maggie, Sterling and Saint-Just head for Evan Kelly's apartment. Evan is not home, but he's thoughtfully left a note and a key for them. They decide to spend some time in nearby Atlantic City and come back in the evening. They return just in time to see Evan arrested. A friend of Maggie's mother has been found dead, struck down by a bowling ball that is branded with her father's initials. Her father is arrested for murder and Maggie and Saint-Just are on the case again.

ASSOCIATES: Henry Novack—*a man who feels territorial about one slot machine;* Sterling—*who helps Maggie play the slots;* Saint-Just—*who bankrolls Maggie's gambling;* Evan—*Maggie's father;* Alicia—*Maggie's mother;* Erin—*Maggie's infallible oldest sister;* Tate—*Maggie's brother, he is the apple of his mother's eye;* Maureen—*the baby of the family;* John—*Maureen's husband;* Cynthia Spade-Whitaker—*attorney and houseguest;* Sean Whitaker—*Cynthia's husband, a realtor.*

Joe Panelli and Sam—*members of The Majestics (Evan's bowling team);* Kiki Rodgers—*realtor;* Argyle "Socks" Jackson—*an aspiring actor whose "day job" is working as the doorman at Maggie's building;* Holly Spivak—*a reporter for Fox Live at Four;* Officer Steve Wendell—*a friend;* Carol Heinie—*Evan's new girlfriend;* J. P. Boxer—*an attorney;* Lisa—*who was a high school cheerleader;* Barry Butts—*Lisa's husband, he was the high school football captain;* Mrs. McGert—*who works at the food counter at the bowling alley.*

MILLIGAN, Peter.

THE HUMAN TARGET

Genres/Themes Crossed: Science Fiction, Lone Supernatural X Hard-Boiled Mystery.

Subjects/Character Types: Slightly Supernatural Human, Advanced Technology X Private Investigator.

Series/Stand-Alone: It is essentially one story arc, so the episodes (the individual books) should be read in series order.

Scene of the Crime: Modern-day America.

Detectives: Christopher Chance is a master of disguise and impersonation. He is hired by individuals that are being targeted for assassination or murder, taking their place while he tries to stop their killer. Chance is so good at his job that he occasionally loses himself in his roles, having trouble determining if his motivations are his own or those of the person who's life he has assumed.

Known Associates: Tom McFadden is Chance's personal assistant. Chance has been training McFadden in the art of impersonation. Bruno is a restaurateur and one of Chance's closest friends and confidants, as well as serving as the middle man for Chance's business as the human target.

Premise: Christopher Chance is a detective and bodyguard, taking on the identity of the person he is protecting in order to make himself a human target. When a threat surfaces, Chance handles the problem and then moves on to his next job.

Comments: The character of Christopher Chance was originally created by Len Wein and Carmine Infantino, and starred in a series of backup stories in Action Comics, a series more popularly focusing on Superman. In 1992, the series was briefly adapted into a live action television show starring Rick Springfield.

Literary Magic and Mayhem: Chance is the greatest impersonator in the world, being able to mimic his subjects so well that even their families can not tell the difference. The ability to mimic such a diverse group of people with such precision is impossible in the real world, and the philosophical issues raised by Chance's growing inability to hold on to his own identity is an interesting element of the stories. Chance is replicating his "primaries" so well that he can't tell the difference himself.

Explorations: What is the nature of identity?

How much of ourselves do we invent?

Are we more than the sum of our habits?

THE CASES

1. ***The Human Target.*** New York: DC Comics, 2000, 104 p. ISBN: 1563896931.

HOLLYWOOD AND LOS ANGELES, PRESENT DAY. Chance begins by impersonating a preacher who is fighting drug dealers in his neighborhood, but is soon drawn into a murder plot that is targeting him. The only problem is, there seem to be two Christopher Chances.

ASSOCIATES: Earl James Junior, Bethany James, Bruno, Emerald, Becky McFadden, Sam McFadden.

2. ***Human Target: Final Cut.*** New York: DC Comics, 2003, 96 p. ISBN: 1563899043.

HOLLYWOOD AND LOS ANGELES, PRESENT DAY. After Chance takes out a serial killer who was targeting Hollywood figures, he must assume the killer's identity in order to solve a kidnapping.

ASSOCIATES: Detective Rodrigues, Dai Thomas, Bruno, R. E. Lacy, Frank White, Ronan White, Mary White, Conchita Peraza.

3. ***Human Target: Strike Zones*** New York: DC Comics, 2004, 128 p. ISBN: 1401202098.

HOLLYWOOD, LOS ANGELES AND NEW YORK CITY, PRESENT DAY. Three stories of the Human Target. A movie mogul attempts to deal with his psychological issues after the death of his son, and is targeted by an irate movie fan. Chance takes on the role of a man supposedly killed in the 9/11 terrorist attack as he attempts to outwit his corrupt corporate boss. A baseball player commits suicide, and the team's owner employs Chance to find out why.

ASSOCIATES: Frank White, Mary White, Tyrone, Bruno, John Matthews, Joe, Larry McGee.

4. ***HumanTarget: Living in Amerika.*** New York: DC Comics, 2004, 128 p. ISBN: 1401204198.

BOSTON, MIDDLE ROCK (IN MIDDLE AMERICA), LOS ANGELES, AND LAS VEGAS, PRESENT DAY. Chance takes on the role of a priest supposedly being targeted for his good public works. In the second story, Chance is mistaken for a member of a radical militant communist movement presumed dead for three decades. Chance takes the role of an old friend who has escaped from prison to spend a week on a second honeymoon.

ASSOCIATES: Carlo, Father Mike, Bruno, Nat Clarke, Charlie Rivers, Sandra Applebaum, Mary Turner, Katie Charles, Agent Williamson, Rick Rivers, Jim Grace, Maria Grace, Jennifer Gleason, Holly.

MOORE, Alan and Dave Gibbons.

WATCHMEN

Genres/Themes Crossed: Alternate History, Lone Supernatural, Dystopia X Hard-Boiled Mystery.

Subjects/Character Types: Super Heroes X Amateur Sleuth (Historical).

Series/Stand-Alone: Stand-alone.

Scene of the Crime: An alternate earth history, primarily set in the United States in the grip of the cold war during the late 1980s. The most prominently used city in the story is New York City.

Detectives: Walter Kovacs no longer uses his given name, preferring instead to use his persona as the masked detective called Rorschach. Costumed adventurers and vigilantes were outlawed in the late 1970s, but Rorschach chooses to ignore the law and continue in his masked persona. Rorschach is prone to conspiracy theories and cynicism, and can easily become focused on seemingly insignificant details. Part of the cause of Rorschach's detachment is his deeply disturbing childhood.

Known Associates: Doctor Manhattan is the only super-powered individual in the series, and is nearly omnipotent. Manhattan is completely unbound by time. He is able to recall every moment in his own life, including moments that have not yet happened; he doesn't think in terms of present, past and future, but simply in terms of what events follow other events. He will not alter events. When asked why he didn't stop a disaster from happening, he will say, "Because that's not what I did." Laurie Juspeczyk is the second woman to fight crime and seek adventure as the Silk Spectre, and is the daughter of the original Silk Spectre, Sally Jupiter. The original Nite Owl, Hollis J. Mason, was an adventurer in the 1930s, and retired in the 1960s, passing his mantle on to the second Nite Owl, inventor Dan Dreiberg. Ozymandias, Adrian Veidt, is in peak human physical condition and possesses a genius-level intellect.

Premise: Costumed vigilantes were outlawed in the late 70s, but a few individuals stayed on as government agents, notably Doctor Manhattan and the Comedian.

Comments: Alan Moore set out to create a work that would demonstrate what graphic novels as a medium were capable of, elevating them above the general conception of comic books as a low-brow form of entertainment. The artist, Dave Gibbons, added details to the work that Moore himself says he didn't originally notice. *Watchmen* received a number of awards after its initial publication over 20 years ago, including several Kirby Awards, Eisner Awards, and a Hugo Award. In 2005, *Time* magazine named *Watchmen* as one of the 100 best English language novels from 1923 to the present. The influence *Watchmen* has had within the genre is immeasurable. Anyone looking to examine the modern state of the medium or the portrayal of super-powered characters in a mature context would do well to start with *Watchmen*.

There is a list of interviews with Alan Moore at http://www.alanmooreinterview.co.uk/. *The Quietus* published an interview with Dave Gibbons on the origin of *The Watchmen* at http://thequietus.com/articles/00949-dave-gibbons-watches-the-watchmen-2.

Literary Magic and Mayhem: In *Watchmen*, there is only one super-powered character, but he is god-like in his power. Doctor Manhattan is serving as the greatest deterrent against a Soviet nuclear attack on the United States, a human weapon of mass destruction employed by the U.S. Government.

Costumed adventurers use technology and their own skills and training to fight crime, with the Nite Owl exemplifying the use of technology and Ozymandias serving as an example of the peak human condition. The government has outlawed costumed adventurers, and the general feel of the government in the series is oppressive, as is the case in many of Alan Moore's works.

Explorations: What should the role of government be in our lives?

How would it feel if you did not perceive time as linear, if you could see the future and the past just as you see this moment in time, yet you were not able to take actions that would lead to a different future?

Do the ends ever truly justify the means?

THE CASE

1. ***Watchmen (Absolute Edition).*** New York: DC Comics, 2005, 464 p. ISBN: 1401207138.

New York City, Antarctica, Mars, Viet Nam, 1940s (in flash backs) through the 1980s. The Comedian is murdered, and Rorschach sets out to solve the murder. Rorschach initially believes that all current and former costumed adventurers are being targeted, but finds the murder is tied to a much larger and more sinister plan.

Associates: Doctor Manhattan, Ozymandias, Silk Spectre I and II, Nite Owl I and II, the Comedian.

MORALES, Rags. Worked with Brad Meltzer on Identity Crisis. See MELTZER, Brad: Identity Crisis.

MORGAN, Richard K.

Altered Carbon

Genres/Themes Crossed: Science Fiction X Hard-Boiled Mystery.

Subjects/Character Types: Future Universe, Future Technology (Clones) X Private Investigator, Noir.

Series/Stand-Alone: There is the first book in a trilogy; the second and the third are not mysteries.

Scene of the Crime: 25th Century Earth, Bay City (long ago it was San Francisco).

Detective: Takeshi Lev Kovacs died recently; actually, he's died a number of times: the last time was particularly painful. He was a Lieutenant in the Envoy Corps of the U.N. Protectorate, trained as a warrior and spy, his body neurochemically enhanced. It's rare for Envoys to slow down once their tour of duty is over; they can't give up the adrenaline, and their training was designed to turn them into sociopaths, no one trusts them. About 20 percent of all serious crime is committed by ex-Envoys. Kovacs was no exception. He and his lover, Sarah, were captured and convicted after committing a brutal robbery. He was imprisoned (i.e., his cortical stack was put into storage). He awakens, "resleeved" in a new body, with an offer of six weeks' work investigating the death of Laurens Bancroft. If Kovacs is successful, the remaining 117 years of his sentence will be waived. Laurens Bancroft (in a sleeve that he had cloned from his original body, with a cortical stack that had recorded his life up until two days before his death) is Kovacs's client. Bancroft needs to believe that his death was a murder; the police are sure that it was suicide.

Known Associates: Virginia Vidaura trained Kovacs. Sarah Sachilowska, Kovacs's lover, was convicted along with him. Jimmy de Sotoa, a comrade in the Envoy Corps, died in Kovacs's arms at Innenin. Jimmy's stack was infected with a virus. He died permanently.

Premise: Humans are implanted at birth with a cortical stack that records every thought, every sensation, every experience of their lives. When they die, the stack can be retrieved and implanted into a new body; this is called "sleeving." The body is just a convenience, usually the best he or she can purchase after the original sleeve dies; the consciousness defines the person. A criminal's stack is placed in storage for the duration of the prisoner's sentence; the prisoner's body (sleeve) is sold after the cortical stack has been removed. Once the prisoner has served his or her sentence, he or she will be resleeved in a different body. The prisoner and any family who waited for him or her will have to get used to a new face, new body, even, possibly, a new gender. If a person wants to travel to another planet, the body stays behind. The information in the traveler's cortical stack is needlecast through space and put into a new sleeve at the traveler's destination. Some people are able to pay for very expensive insurance that covers their own resleeving in case of an accident that destroys their body; sometimes loved ones raise the money to pay for a resleeving. The very rich can clone themselves and be resleeved as necessary in their own bodies. Some people have religious objections to resleeving; they believe that the soul cannot be digitized. When those people die, they are permanently dead.

Comment: This is the first book of the *Takeshi Kovacs Trilogy*. It won the 2003 Philip K. Dick Award. The second book, *Broken Angels,* takes place 30 years after the events in *Altered Carbon*. It is not a mystery, it is a science-fiction action novel. In it, Kovacs, now a mercenary in a new sleeve, decides to take a chance at securing a future that won't include the repetitive deaths of his work as an Envoy for the Protectorate. He gathers together a team of people, hoping to make a fortune by grabbing an archeological treasure, a Martian spaceship. In the third book, *Woken Furies* (a thriller, but not a mystery), Kovacs must battle a younger version of himself who is trying to protect a woman who may be the key to saving his home world.

Richard K. Morgan's Web site at http://www.richardkmorgan.com/ includes information on his books, his biography, essays, and book reviews.

Literary Magic & Mayhem: This book does include graphic sex and many violent scenes; for all of that, it is fascinating, disturbing, and thought-provoking. The protagonist is a tough guy who is also an idealist, haunted by his memories. This society is rotten at its core. Money can buy immortality. Many of the rich are "meths" (short for "Methuselahs"), who have lived for centuries. They hold the most powerful position in government(s), but they have little in common, and almost no feeling for the people whom they govern. It is possible to create synthetic people: bodies can be created and invested with artificial intelligence, but real life is cheaper than artificial life. It's possible to experience anything virtually. On one occasion, Kovacs thinks about a memory that is "so real it is almost virtual." While this means that he can almost experience it again as he thinks of it, it's still a bizarre reflection on the nature of reality. At one point, in a discussion regarding a person who committed a murder, he questions whether or not the difference between reality and virtual experience is meaningful, even in the context of morality:

> Psychopath's not a narrow term anymore... I've heard it applied to whole cultures on occasion. It's even been applied to me once or twice. Reality is so flexible these days, it's hard to tell who's disconnected from it and who isn't. You might even say it's a pointless distinction. (p. 278)

Direct access to other's minds is simply part of the society. Vendors broadcast ads for, and samples of, their wares into the minds of passers-by. Irene Elliot dipped into the datastreams of travelers as they were being transported to different worlds. She and her husband sold these "mindbites." Fans of the rich and famous could sample their lives from inside their minds. Their memories, their thoughts—even their personalities—are commodities. The flip side of this terrifying intimacy/invasion is that people's bodies are also a commodity.

Recording any part of travelers' transmissions is illegal; Irene was caught and convicted: her stack is serving 30 years. Six months after she was incarcerated, Irene's husband saw her walking around. It was not Irene: her body had been purchased by some rich woman who liked variety; she would wear the body every other month. Irene's husband was distraught, and he made the mistake of telling his daughter, Elizabeth. She said, "Don't worry, Daddy, when I'm rich we'll buy Mummy back." Elizabeth then went on to work in a whorehouse to try to earn the money.

Bodies and minds can be incarcerated, purchased, and altered. The ability to alter people is also taken to depressing and frightening extremes. Kovacs talks about how Envoy training alters the mind, and so alters the personality:

> They burn out every evolved violence limitation instinct in the human psyche. Submission signal recognition, pecking-order dynamics, pack loyalties. It all goes, tuned out a neuron at a time; and they replace it with a conscious will to harm... Do you understand me? It would have been easier to kill you just then. It would have been easier. I had to stop myself. That's what an Envoy is, Curtis. A reassembled human. An artifice. (p. 265)

... and that's our hero.

Explorations: If immortality were available but limited, so that it could only be given to a few people, how would those people be chosen? How should they be chosen? Is there a reasonable way to choose?

What purpose do bad memories serve? If it were possible to excise the memory of a day that went badly, would you do it?

How is the culture of Earth different from the culture of Harlan's World? Which seems more civilized?

What would be the difference between being stored, knowing that there was no money for resleeving, and being erased?

THE CASES

1. ***Altered Carbon.*** New York: Del Rey Books, 2006, c2002, 526 p. ISBN: 0345457692.

Bay City, Earth, 25th Century. Laurens J. Bancroft made Kovacs an offer he couldn't refuse. It was not a great deal, it was just the only deal available; Kovacs's view of the situation is unflinching:

> One hundred and eighty light-years from home, wearing another man's body on a six-week rental agreement. Freighted in to do a job that the local police wouldn't touch with a riot prod. Fail and go back into storage. (p. 19)

The job is to find out the truth about the client's death. Bancroft's body was found with its cortical stack destroyed. His mind had been backed up within the last few days, and he was reloaded into another body, the most recent of a line of clones created from his original. The police ruled the death a suicide. Bancroft cannot believe that; he knows himself, and he is absolutely certain that he would not kill himself, and, somewhat inconsistently, he's absolutely positive that if he did kill himself, he would do a good enough job of it that it would be a permanent death. Bancroft is torn between self-examination, trying to understand what in his life could have driven him to self-destruction, and hurt pride; he refuses to believe that he would make such a botched job of his own suicide. The only other person who had access to his body at the time of the crime was his wife of over 200 years. It seems improbable that she would have killed him. Bancroft is so determined to get the truth that he buys Kovacs a temporary parole from prison, has him needlecast from Harlan's World to Earth, and purchases the body of an Earth prisoner for Kovacs to wear during the investigation.

ASSOCIATES: Kovacs—*a recidivist;* Warden Sullivan—*who tells Kovacs that he sees no reason "for wasting good flesh and blood on people like you" (p. 17);* Kristin Ortega—*officer in the Organic Damage Division of the Bay City Police Force, agrees;* Officer Mercer, Officer Davidson, and Detective Sergeant Rodrigo Bautista—*other officers on the force;* Laurens J. Bancroft—*Kovac's three-hundred-and-fifty-seven-year-old client;* Miriam Bancroft—*Bancroft's wife of 250 years;* Naomi—*their youngest daughter;* Oumou Prescott—*Bancroft's lawyer;* Curtis—*the Bancrofts' chauffeur.*

Kovacs stays at the *Hendrix,* a hotel with synthetic intelligence. Dimitri Kadmin—*(Dimitri the twins), assassin;* Keith Rutherford—*Dimitri's associate;* Leila Begin—*who was pregnant when Miriam Bancroft attacked her;* Dennis Nyman—*the director of Secure Holding and Clone Resleeving at PsychaSec Alcatraz;* Victor Elliot—*who owns pf Elliot's Data Linkage Brokerage;* Irene Elliot—*Victor's wife;* Elizabeth Elliot—*their daughter.*

Jerry Sedaka—*who owns Jerry's Biocabins whorehouse;* Louise—*who calls herself Anemone;* Chloe and Mac—*who were friends of Elizabeth;* Milo and Deek—*thugs;* and Oktai—*the Mongol.*

Trepp—*the torture expert at the Wei Clinic;* Director Chung—*Trepp's employers* Dr. Felipe Miller and Medic Courault—*who are associates;* Clive and Sheila—*who work at Larkin and Greene Armorers;* Elias Ryker—*who used to own Kovacs's sleeve.*

Miriam Bancroft's tennis partners include Nalen Ertekin—*the chief justice of the UN Supreme Court;* Joseph Phiri—*of the Commission on Human Rights;* and Marco Kawahara—*Reileen's son.*

Graft Nicholson—*a drunk truck-driver, who is used as a decoy;* Reileen "Ray" Kawahara—*who has so many enemies that she keeps her clones in bullet-proof wombs, Kovacs refuses to work for her, at least at first;* Emcee Carnage—*a synthetic who runs the fights;* Pernilla Grip—*works for Combat Broadcast Distributors;* Miles Mech—*who will record the fight for broadcast;* Sheryl Bostock—*who works at PsychaSec;* Daryl—*her son.*

2. ***Broken Angels.*** New York: Del Rey Books, 2004, 384 p. ISBN: 0345457714; 9780345457721.

(Note: This book is not a mystery.) Takeshi Kovacs tries to break out of the path that his envoy training determined. He works to find and acquire an artifact of immense value so that he can make his fortune.)

3. ***Woken Furies.*** New York: Del Rey Books, 2007, c2005, 544 p. ISBN: 0345499778; 9780345499776.

(Note: This book is not a mystery.) Takeshi Kovacs returns to his home planet, Harlan's world. Not only is the world primed for a second rebellion, it's primed for a second Quellist revolution. Someone is working to bring Quellcrist Falconer back from the dead. In this book, the reader learns about the forces that shaped Takeshi Kovacs.)

N

NIVEN, Larry and Steven Barnes.

DREAM PARK

Genres/Themes Crossed: Science Fiction X Whodunit.

Subjects/Character Types: Future Technology X Private Company Security Employee

Series/Stand-Alone: Series. Many of the characters gain an understanding and a respect for gaming in the course of the series. It's a different sort of character growth, but it is growth, and the series should be read in order.

Scene of the Crime: 21st-Century Earth.

Detective(s): Alex "Griff" Griffin, Head of Dream Park Security, had always regarded Dream Park gamers with condescending amusement. In fact, all of Security regarded Dream Park gamers as harmless nuts. So, security systems were not carefully designed in gaming areas. The very nature of those areas, the collaborative temporary installations by Game Masters coupled with the obsessive creative focus on the gaming experience, makes gaming areas prone to lapses in security.

Known Associates: Griff is a loner. His secretary is Millicent Summers (after the first book she transfers into Financial Operations); Alex's boss is Thaddeus Harmony, Dream Park Director of Operations. Tony McWhirter, a gamer in *Dream Park,* gathers information for Griff in *The Barsoom Project,* and is a Game Master in *The California Voodoo Game.*

Premise: Dream Park is a virtual reality Disneyland with truly mind-bending short rides and two large areas set aside for complex multi-day games. The large games are designed by Game Masters and are set in fantasy worlds, many of them based on the myths of different cultures. Games by respected Game Masters are usually tricky but internally consistent, physically demanding but winnable. They are often built around a quest filled with danger. Winning usually involves the gamers defeating villainous hordes to gain possession of an artifact that will allow them to save the world. Gamers pay high prices to participate in these games; and the games are recorded with book, movie, and electronic gaming rights, bringing in royalties for Game Masters, for Dream Park, and for the players.

Gamers build their characters over time. The basic character types are warrior, thief, cleric, magic-user, engineer, and explorer/scout. Games are judged by the International Fantasy Gaming Society, which awards points that promote characters to higher levels (with commensurate improvement in their skills, so that they are more likely to succeed in future games). Gamers who reach a high-enough level can become Lore Masters and play as the leader of a team. Lore Masters get a higher percentage of the royalties than do the other gamers.

There are three types of death in games. The first type of death is the simple death of the character. The player sees a hologram of the character (the character's ghost) and has to leave that game. (The Game Masters may have the character return to the game as a non-player character, usually a ghost or a zombie of the character played by the original player.) Characters who are simply dead may be used in future games. The second type of death is when the characters permanently die (usually as a penalty to the player for doing something that goes too far in bending or breaking the rules). The gamers call this "dead-dead": the character can never be played in a future game. The player, if he or she wishes to play future games, must develop a new character who will start from the beginning in terms of experience and skills. The third type of death is the death of the Player himself or herself. The games are designed to be reasonably safe, but they simulate dangerous situations, and injuries are common. Deaths are less common, but they happen. Dream Park has gamers sign waivers before they enter a game.

Comment: Larry Niven won a Hugo and a Nebula Award for *Ringworld* (1971), and Hugos for the Best Short Story: for "Neutron Star" (1967), "Inconstant Moon," (1972), and "The Hole Man" (1975). In 1976, he won the Hugo Award for Best Novelette for "The Borderland of Sol." He won a Prometheus Award for "Fallen Angels" in 1991. There is a fan Web site, officially sanctioned by Larry Niven: http://www.larryniven.org/. It includes information on his books, short stories, other works, and current projects.

In 2007, Niven was tapped, along with other science fiction writers, to advise the U.S. Department of Homeland Security.

The International Fantasy Gaming Society really exists, and is acknowledged in the afterword of *The California Voodoo Game*. That afterword also mentions that Stephen Barnes played in a two-day Live-Action-Role-Playing game called *Ancient Enemy* in 1990. The game was played on and near the Snake River in Colorado; it combined fantasy elements with whitewater rafting.

Dream Park itself has been a powerful idea for companies involved in the business of creating virtual reality devices. On August 24, 2005, Bob Ladrach, President of 3001 A.D., LLC, spoke of the company's Dream Park campaign to create their Trimersion headset to give gamers a 360-degree environment for gaming. Ladrach stated that the goal was to create the "Dream Park" experience in real life: gamers would be amazed and would want more. (The headset has been quite successful.)

Literary Magic & Mayhem: The books are prefaced with character lists and with a glossary of some of the terms developed for the books. The writing, particularly in *Dream Park,* shows the split in the gamers' attention: the moments when they're so absorbed in the reality of the Game Master's world that they live in that world; the moments when their suspension of disbelief fails and they're plodding through what they know is a game; and the strange disorientation when their perceptions waver between the real world and the world of the fantasy game.

Explorations: The technology has a profound effect on the people engaged in the game. Could virtual reality games be used to improve people's real lives? How?

How is this like a fantasy role-playing game from the days of gamers playing *Dungeons and Dragons*™ around a dining room table? How is it like video games or online video games? How is it like present day Live-Action-Role-Playing games? What would be added and what would be lost by playing them in the game environment of Dream Park?

How does morality change within the game? What factors affect it? How do players know what actions "the gods" will favor? How do players protect their own scores at the expense of other players, or at the expense of the game? How are any of these forms of morality shared by the people in the real world?

THE CASES

1. *Dream Park.* New York: Ace Books, 1981, 434 p. ISBN: 0932096093.

DREAM PARK (CALIFORNIA), MARCH 2051. *The South Seas Treasure Game* brings together feuding Game Master Richard Lopez and Lore Master Chester Henderson. Henderson is certain that Lopez will go to any lengths to make the gamers fail, while Lopez is determined to be so transparently fair that, when the gamers fail, it will be clear that the game was fair and that competent gamers would have won. The game is set in New Guinea in 1955. The story is that native tribes used magic to divert World War II cargo, and so increased their magical powers. One tribe stole the most powerful artifact from the others, and they are on the path to gaining incalculable power with which they mean to rule the world. The gamers' quest is to recover the cargo and break the power of the evil tribe.

In the real world, Dream Park scientists are working on an experimental drug with which they can trigger certain responses in players. It's inhaled, but there is no smell. So far, they have been able to induce tears, laughter, reflex vomiting, sleep, and brotherly love. They're testing a variant that may act as a general emotional intensifier. On the first night of the South Seas Treasure Game, one of the gamers left the others during the night, broke into Dream Park laboratories, stole the drug, and returned to the game. In the course of the theft, he was surprised by a security guard and the guard was killed. Too late, Security personnel realize that the major flaw in Dream Park's security comes from the gaming areas. As Griffin explains to Thaddeus Harmony:

> The Gamers are so out of touch with reality that they were never considered a serious threat. (p. 140)

Dream Park has sunk one-point-five million dollars into the *South Seas Treasure Game* and is expecting the game to generate revenue in excess of $22 million through film, book, programming, and holotape leasing. If they close down the game, they not only lose all that money; but they have no way to detain the gamers during the course of the investigation. Thaddeus Harmony asks Alex to join the game to conduct his investigation while the game continues.

All the novice gamers experience a sort of schizophrenic view of the world while they experience game events as if they are real, then process the information trying to see how the fake effects were achieved. It distances them from the game and makes it more difficult for their companions to maintain the suspension of disbelief necessary to become immersed in the game's world. For instance, after their first intense fight, S. J. Waters feels the need to deconstruct what he saw (the giant serpents of the lake):

> "Best damn holograms in the world. Most expensive too. The sword sensor knows whether it intersects part of the projection, and signals the computer. The snake's a computer animated projection, so—" He looked down at Acacia's sword tip waving an inch from his nose.
>
> She said, "Listen S. J., maybe you get your kicks from analyzing dreams, but I want to play and I want Tony to have the chance to play with me, okay?" (p. 86)

Alex's condescending attitude towards gamers changes as he experiences the physical and emotional rigors of the game. Several times during the course of play, he is startled by the intensity of his commitment to the team and to winning their quest.

ASSOCIATES: Richard and Mitsuko Lopez—*the game masters who created the South Seas Treasure Game*. Chester Henderson—*the Lore Master who leads the gamers*. Nine players preregistered and their characters are: Acacia "Cas" Garcia—*who plays as the warrior Panthesilia;* Tony McWhirter—*who plays as the thief Fortunato;* Gina Perkins—*who plays as the cleric Semiramis;* Adolf "Ollie" Norliss—*who plays as the warrior Frankish Oliver;* and Gwen Ryder—*Adolf's fiancé who plays as the cleric Guinevere;* George Eames—*who plays as a warrior;* Alan Leigh—*who plays as a magic-user;* Larry Garret—*who plays as a cleric;* and Rudy Dreager—*who plays as an engineer.* Chester Henderson fills the rest of his team with: S. J. Waters—*who plays as an engineer (he is a novice, Chester chooses him as canon fodder);* Mary-Martha Corbett—*who is a veteran gamer, she plays as the warrior Mary-em;* Felicia Maddox—*who plays as the thief Dark Star and is rumored to have cheated in previous games;* Bowen the Black—*Felicia's partner, he plays as a magic-user.* Chester chooses alternates: Owen Braddon—*who plays as a cleric;* Margie Braddon—*Owen's wife, who plays as an engineer;* and Holly Frost—*who plays as a warrior.*

The Game Masters create non-player characters (hired actors) who include Harvey Wayland—*who plays the guide Kasan Maibang;* Nigorai, Kagoiano, Kibugonai—*who play native bearers;* Pigibidi—*Native Chieftan of the Daribi;* Lady Janet—*a damsel in distress;* Yali—*who plays a riddle game in Heaven;* Alex Griffin—*a.k.a. Gary Tegner, who plays the thief Griffin.*

Dream Park personnel include: Thaddeus Harmony—*Alex's boss;* Millicent Summers—*Alex's secretary;* Marty Bobbick—*Alex's assistant;* and Skip and Melinda O'Brien—*Alex's friends.* Dwight Welles and Larry Chicon—*are Dream Park computer technicians;* Ms. Gail Metesky—*is Dream Park's liaison to the International Fantasy Gaming Society;* and Arlan Myers—*is the Society's official who is assigned to oversee the South Seas Treasure Game.*

2. *The Barsoom Project.* New York: Ace Books, c1989, 340 p. ISBN: 0441167128.

DREAM PARK (CALIFORNIA), 2056. Eight years ago, someone smuggled a live rifle into the *Fimbulwinter Game.* Gamer Michelle Sturgeon, immersed in her character and certain that the rifle was a prop and the blood a special effect, killed another player. The realization that she had truly killed someone unhinged her mind. The murdered player, Calvin Izumi, had no enemies. Investigators concluded that the target was not Calvin, but was Dream Park itself. The park was on shaky financial ground, and someone was mounting a takeover. The negative publicity could have brought down the entire company. Calvin's relatives helped with a cover-up to thwart the plans of whoever killed him to gain a negotiating advantage.

Michelle Sturgeon has come to the park once more and has joined the current *Fimbulwinter Game* under the name Michelle Rivers. The game had begun before this is discovered. Dr. Vail's opinion is that pulling her out might damage her further, and that there is a chance that playing the game through to the finish could help her save her sanity.

The game is of interest to the psychologist for other reasons as well. It is one of the "fat burner" games, designed to help gamers overcome eating disorders. In the game, the sun is dimming and the Earth is cooling. The gamers go on a quest to defeat the villains, who are consuming the sun's energy with their magic. They free a goddess who has become weighed down with parasites; they gain avian allies by attempting to save the birds' young from predators; they are put in the uncomfortable position of being treated as food themselves... and all this is set in a universe where meals are frequently interrupted by life-threatening events.

The entire Dream Park has been closed to the public so that it can host over thirteen-thousand dignitaries from across Earth, even including representatives from the Falling Angels (a technological nation that orbits Luna). They have been gathered by Cowles Industries and IntelCorp to show them the proposal for *Project Barsoom,* which the leaders of Cowles Industries believe to be the last best hope for humankind. They intend to terraform Mars, to start a new community that will leave the old battles of Earth behind, and they need investors. Alex Griffin is busy trying to prevent acts of sabotage that would scare the investors and kill the project. While Alex works to foil saboteurs in the real world, those involved in the game match wits against a murderer who will do anything to stop Michelle Sturgeon—before she remembers enough to identify him as the man who had arranged for a blameless man to meet his death in the first *Fimbulwinter Game.*

Marty Bobbick is assigned to bodyguard Charlene Dula, who is with the Falling Angels' delegation. She wants to play the *Fimbulwinter Game,* so Marty must play it as well. Alex Griffin has promised him a raise if he can lose 20 of the 70 pounds of extra weight that he has been carrying for the last year.

ASSOCIATES: Dream Park personnel include: Thaddeus Harmony—*Alex's boss;* Millicent Summers—*who used to be Alex's secretary and is now an executive in the Department of Financial Affairs;* Marty Bobbick—*Alex's assistant;* and Doctor Vail—*Dream Park psychologist.*

Tony McWhirter—*who Alex asks for help.* Dwight Welles—*the Game Master.* Dream Park non-player character roles are taken by a variety of actors and park employees who are trying to shed weight. These include: Robin Bowles—*professional actor who is given the caribou ear (for hearing) talisman;* Ollie Norliss—*professional actor who plays as Frankish Oliver;* Gwen Ryder—*Ollie's wife and professional actress who plays the role of Kanguq (Snow Goose);* Martin Qaterliaraq—*(Martin the Arctic Fox) professional actor who plays an Inuit sorcerer;* Marty Bobbick—*Griffin's assistant, plays as Hippogryph.*

Gamers include Charlene Dula—*of Falling Angel, whose talisman is a swatch of arctic seal fur that gives her invisibility;* Eviane—*a.k.a. Michelle Sturgeon, a.k.a. Michelle Rivers, whose talisman is a semi-automatic rifle;* Francis Herbert—*Marine;* Avram and Mazie Henderson—*husband and wife;* Max—*who wrestles professionally under the name Mr. Mountain, Max's talisman is an owl claw for strength;* Orson Sands—*Max's brother;* Kevin Titus—*whose talisman is a crumpled soot-stained skin for strength;* Trianna Stith-Wood—*a professional chef with a troubled past;* and Johnny Welsh—*a professional comedian.* Those involved in the Barsoom Project include Andrew Chala—*Pan-African Ambassador and uncle of Charlene Dula;* Kareem Fekesh—*industrialist;* and Razul—*Libyan Ambassador.*

3. ***California Voodoo Game.*** New York: Del Rey/Ballantine Books, c1992, 355 p. ISBN: 0345365984.

DREAM PARK AND MEACHAM INCORPORATED MOJAVE INDUSTRIAL COMMUNITY "M.I.M.I.C." (CALIFORNIA), 2059. The great earthquake of 1995 partially destroyed the gigantic Meacham Incorporated Mojave Industrial Community. The building complex stood empty for over 50 years, then it was purchased to be used in the creation of the *Barsoom Project.* The building must be partially gutted, and it seemed a shame not to get some use out of the spaces created as it was rehabilitated. Dream Park management decided to incorporate some of the necessary building demolition into an epic game. It's the *California Voodoo Game,* and it will be run in the building. The Game Master will be able to use real (controlled) explosions as part of the special effects. Dream Park is closed for a week and about 400 of its employees stayed in town to act as non-player characters in the *California Voodoo Game.*

One of the players is playing games within games. He sets his plans in action before the game begins. He only intends to do a little robbery, a little cheating, and a little industrial espionage for a major pay-off and the satisfaction of knowing that he beat Dream Park and Cowles Industries. He manipulates both players and non-players, moving them around in his own game. Everything goes well until one of his non-players makes a move that would endanger him. So he kills her. The murder haunts him, but he's certain that he will succeed. He knows his own abilities and does not feel at all threatened by the efforts of others.

ASSOCIATES: Dream Park and Cowles Industries employees include: Alex Griffin—*Chief of Security;* Millicent Summers—*who used to be Alex's secretary and is now a Financial Operations Officer;* Thaddeus Harmony—*Dream Park Chief of Operations;* Tony McWhirter—*Dream Park Security, data operations, International Fantasy Gaming Society Liaison, and Game Master;* Sharon Crayne—*Cowles Industries Security;* Mitch Hasegawa—*Dream Park Security;* and Dr. Norman Vail—*Dream Park Psychologist.*

The International Fantasy Gaming Society includes: Elmo and Doris Whitman—*Game Masters;* Richard and Mitsuko "Chi Chi" Lopez—*Game Masters;* and Arlan Meyers—*IFGS arbiter.*

Four teams of gamers have been accepted as players in the *California Voodoo Game*. The University of California "Manhunters" team is headed by Acadia Garcia—*who plays warrior Panthesilea;* and includes Corby Cauldwell—*who plays magic user Captain Cipher;* Mati Cohen—*who plays the cleric Top Nun;* Steffie Wilde—*who plays the engineer/scout Aces;* Terrance Coolidge—*who plays the warrior Prez;* and Corrinda Harding—*who plays a thief.*

The Texas Instruments–Mitsubishi "Cyberjocks" team is led by Alphonse Nakagawa—*who plays a warrior* and includes Crystal Cofax—*who plays an engineer/scout;* Mary-Martha Corbett—*who plays the warrior Mary-em;* Peggy Hookham—*who plays the engineer Hook;* Friar Duck—*who plays a cleric/magic-user;* and Oswald Murphy—*who plays warrior Ozzie the Pike.*

Apple Computer "Troglodykes" team's co-leaders are Twan Tsing and Tammy Romati—*who both play magic-users;* and includes "Mouser" Romati—*who plays a thief;* Appelion—*who plays a warrior/magic-user;* Gordon Reese—*who plays a scout;* and George Howards—*who plays the warrior Indiana.*

The Army team is led by Major Terry Clavell—*who plays a magic-user,* and includes Corporal S. J. Waters—*who plays a scout/ thief;* Lieutenant Madonna Phillips—*who plays a warrior;* Lawrence Black Elk—*who plays a cleric/magic-user;* General Harry Poule—*who plays the warrior/scout Evil;* and Chaim Cohen—*who plays a cleric.*

The General Dynamics team is headed by Nigel Bishop—*who plays a magic-user,* and includes Holly Frost—*who plays a warrior/thief;* Trevor Stone—*who plays a magic-user;* Tamasan—*who plays a cleric;* Ilsa Radichev—*who plays a warrior;* and Mikhail Radichev—*who plays a warrior.*

OEMING, Michael Avon and Brandon Ivan.

THE CROSS BRONX

Genres/Themes Crossed: Secret Society X Police Procedural.

Subjects/Character Types: Santeria X Police Procedural.

Series/Stand-Alone: Stand-alone.

Scene of the Crime: Present-day New York City.

Detectives: Rafael Aponte is a detective with the NYPD, formerly a devout Catholic who has fallen from his faith. Aponte had believed wholeheartedly in his faith, and later in the justice meted out by the police, but no longer seems to believe in anything. Tico Velez is Aponte's partner, a not-quite-clean cop, sarcastic funnyman to his straight-man partner.

Known Associates: Aponte is married, though his wife, "Mami" Aponte, is troubled by his faltering faith. She asks Aponte to come back to church, and suggests that he take a job with his brother's taxi company. Aponte uses the employees of his brother's company as eyes on the street, getting tips from them on people he is looking for in connection with his cases. Mrs. Ortez is a disturbing elderly widow who may practice dark arts relating to Santeria.

Premise: The religion of Santeria allows a woman in this world to create a spirit of vengeance.

Comments: Michael Avon Oeming is known for his cartoon-like art style, which sharply contrasts with the brutal stories he tells. His stories don't shy away from graphic violence or nudity when they contribute to a great story, and *Cross Bronx* is no exception.

Michael Avon Oeming's site at http://www.hiddenrobot.com/MIKE-OEMING/ includes information on current projects. There is an interview about the origins of *The Cross Bronx* on *Newsarama* at http://forum.newsarama.com/showthread.php?t=75474.

Literary Magic and Mayhem: Issues of divine justice and retribution are explored, as an image of a nearly dead girl is used when murdering those who harmed her.

Explorations: What is the difference between the justice system and divine justice?

How does faith contribute to serving the greater good?

THE CASE

The Cross Bronx. New York: Image Comics, 2007, 128 p. ISBN: 1582406901.

New York City, Modern Day. The gun of a deceased police officer turns up at mass killing of petty criminals and drug dealers. The gun leads Aponte and Velez to a widow whose daughter is in a coma after having been raped and thrown from a moving car. It seems that the widow may practice dark arts, and that the killings may be divine retribution against those who harmed a young woman.

Associates: Mrs. Aponte—*who worries about the detective;* Mrs. Ortiz—*an elderly widow;* Jerald.

OGDEN, Julie. Co-editor (with Stuart Coupe and Robert Hood) of *Crosstown Traffic: Romance, Horror, Fantasy, SF, Western invade Crime Fiction.* See COUPE, Stuart. Crosstown Traffic: Romance, Horror, Fantasy, SF, Western Invade Crime Fiction.

OWENS, Louis Dean.

Nightland

Genres/Themes Crossed: Paranormal X Traditional Mystery.

Subjects/Character Types: Shaman, Ghosts X Amateur Sleuth (Contemporary).

Series/Stand-Alone: Stand-alone.

Scene of the Crime: National forest and a couple of impoverished ranches in present-day New Mexico.

Detective: Grampa Siquani, a shaman who accompanied Billy's and Will's families when they moved from Oklahoma to New Mexico, decades before the events in this book. Grampa Siquani senses that something is wrong almost as soon as Will and Billy head into danger. He learns the specifics of the crime from a dead man, and then uses his skills to cure the ills that beset the ranches.

Known Associates: Grampa Siquani has long been accepted as some sort of ancestor of Billy Keene. He lives on Billy's land, and is Billy's only surviving family. Will Striker visits the ranch frequently; he has always been Billy's best friend. Will lives on the ranch that adjoins Billy's property. Will's household consists of himself, his wife's dog Maggie; his wife's potbellied pig, Molly; his memories of his children and his wife, Jace.

Premise: People normally aren't aware of some of the most important aspects of the world. Grampa Siquani, a shaman, is aware of the spiritual plane and can see what needs to be done.

Comment: This book does not fit our first definition of a mystery (that the action of the book is driven by someone attempting to solve a crime), but it does fit the second definition: the Library of Congress has assigned it a Form/Genre heading of Detective and mystery stories.

A recurring issue in all of Louis Owens's books is how hereditary identity can or cannot make a person a Native American. Through his characters, Owens explores the question of ethnic identity: is it formed by blood, by law, or by being brought up in the cultural community? At one point in *Nightland*, Billy makes a joke about not being part-Indian any more, because the papers proving his heritage were lost in the fire that killed his parents. Many of the characters seem ambivalent or uneasy about questions of their ethnicity. The characters in the book who are most passionate about racial identity use it to define the world in terms of "them" and "us." Paco Ortega, thinking of the massacre of Indians by Whites, says:

> Back east there was a British general named Amherst who came up with a plan to pass out smallpox-infested blankets to Indians. Those blankets killed thousands and thousands of people, especially the children and babies and old ones, and in gratitude the white people named a town and university after him.(p. 163)

He continues bitterly:

> They killed ninety percent of the Indian people who once lived on this continent. They called that genocide when the Nazis did it, but the Nazis weren't nearly as good at it as the Americans. (p. 163)

He later harkens back to the story:

> Remember those smallpox blankets they passed out to the Indians? It's very simple. I'm giving those blankets back, Duane. Drugs will destroy this country. I'm returning the gift. (p. 171)

Other characters seem to see race as an aspect of family and obligation, but not as the foundation of hatred. Grampa Siquani sees being Cherokee as a way of living that he is obligated to pass on to the next generation. He mourns:

> Cherokee people like that boy don't remember where they came from or how to talk right. The stories tell them of those sacred places, but they only see those places in the stories. And they stop listening. (p. 92)

Both Will and Odessa believe that part of the difference between white and Indian culture is the importance and malleability of stories in the two cultures. Will has always loved books:

> He came very early in his life to believe that the Cherokee world was made of spoken words, told into being with living breath, while the white world had been formed and imagined on pages that then waited patiently to be spoken into life. To his young mind, it was as if the Indian world was always new, made again and again when his father or Billy's grampa told the stories, but that the white world had been formed long ago and lay there in books ready to assume the same form each and every time the pages were opened. Like the Bible. (p. 24)

Odessa also feels that the stories of the Indians, because they are constantly retold, are alive in a way that doesn't fit with the white man's vision of the world:

> Lost tongues and lost times were things she'd given up on long before. All the real stories happened right now, were happening right now. The past was a white man's illusion, the future a white man's dream. Stories were what Indians had, and the story was born anew with every telling. What mattered was the telling, and every story could be changed, had to be. It depended upon who did the telling. (p. 144)

Mr. Owens won the Columbus Foundations American Book Award in 1997 for *Nightland*.

Literary Magic & Mayhem: The difference between the two main characters—careful Will and scattered Billy—makes an interesting contrast. Both are likeable, but they handle the situation very differently. Grampa Siquani is fascinating: his ability to know what is happening and what will happen is tempered by his inability to get his grandson to understand the seriousness of the situation. Grampa Siquani's relationship to the ghost is funny and touching. One of the themes of the book is not just loss, but absence. So much is missing, and the things that are missing were central to Will and Billy's lives. It's as if there is a negative space where their families, their prosperity, their happiness should be. Nature itself has become twisted, the water is gone, buzzards have begun to hunt chickens, a man has been impaled on a juniper tree.

Explorations: What are some of the things in the book that are absent? How has this absence affected history, families, and the land?

At the beginning of the book, the land seems to be dying. How does the land's malaise manifest itself in Will's and Billy's lives?

What are some of the pieces of evidence that Grampa Siquani possesses great wisdom? Why doesn't Billy alter his course in response to what Grampa Siquani tells him? Do any people change their plans in response to information from Grampa Siquani?

THE CASE

Nightland. New York: Dutton, c1996, 217 p. ISBN: 0525940731.

NEW MEXICO (NEAR MAGDALENA), 1996?. While hunting in Cibola National Forest, Billy sees a man drop from the sky, to be impaled upon a dead Juniper tree. The man had been holding a suitcase, which lands a short distance from the tree. Inside the suitcase is a great deal of money. Billy and Will figure out that it must be drug money, and decide that it might as well benefit them rather than the criminals who lost it. They're spotted by the criminals as they drive away with the suitcase. Soon they are being hunted by people on both sides of the law.

ASSOCIATES: Will Striker and Billy Keene—*old friends who have a stroke of luck;* Billy's Grampa Siquani—*Kaneequayokee, an old Cherokee with one foot in the mystical world and the other foot in the physical world;* Arturo Cruz—*deceased;* Carla—*Billy's ex-girlfriend;* Mouse Meléndez—*Carla's new man;* Odessa Whitehawk—*Billy's new girlfriend;* Joe—*the bartender at the Tecolote Bar;* Paco Ortega—*Arturo's uncle;* Duane Scales—*Ortega's associate.*

THE SHARPEST SIGHT

Genres/Themes Crossed: Paranormal X Traditional Mystery.

Subjects/Character Types: Shaman, Ghosts X Amateur Sleuth (Contemporary).

Series/Stand-Alone: Cole's life changes in the books, so they should be read in order.

Scene of the Crime: Present-day California and Mississippi.

Detective: Uncle Luther and Onatima (Old Lady Blue Wood) live in the swamp in Mississippi. Each of them has a great deal of power, so that their homes have become havens of safety. When Luther's family is in trouble, Luther and Onatima know it and work to aid them.

Known Associates: Uncle Luther's nephew is Hoey McCurtain, Hoey's sons are Attis (deceased) and Cole. Among Cole's friends are Lawman Mundo Morales, his wife Gloria and their daughter, Maria.

Premise: Most people see only a fraction of the world around them. Uncle Luther and Onatima have power that puts them in touch with the spirit world.

Comment: Louis Owens was Cherokee, Choctaw, Irish, and Cajun. In an interview published in *Louis Owens: Literary Reflections on His Life and Work,* he spoke about how he'd always had an extreme consciousness of his own "hybridity." He identified himself as an Indian, but he'd never been in contact with an Indian culture. He felt that he wasn't a real Indian. Many of his characters struggle with questions of where they, as people of mixed blood, fit into the world. Hoey McCurtain is of mixed blood, and he's trying to figure it all out:

> You know it says on my birth certificate? White. I never knew it until I went in the army. I asked Uncle Luther about it and he said that because my dad was white, he figured he had a choice of what to have them put down, so he told them 'white.' It's funny, ain't it, to think a man can just choose like that? . . . I figure I got the same right to choose as my dad, so I chose Indian. (*Sharpest Sight,* p. 57)

Having made a decision, he's not exactly sure how to change his life to reflect his choice:

> I thought a while back that there must be some way to live that was better than I was doing. I remembered Uncle Luther. So I been trying to remember more things, and read things, things that are Indian. I guess if I grew up over in Ireland and knew more about being Irish, I might choose that. I'm not pretending I'm not a half-breed. The damned trouble is I don't know very much. I didn't listen well enough back then. (*Sharpest Sight,* p. 59)

In that same interview, Mr. Owens said that a number of readers of mixed ancestry had told him that they struggled with some of the same questions as his characters. He expressed wonder at this, he had thought his struggle with ethnic identity was an unusual thing, but he came to believe that as America becomes more and more ethnically diverse, there will be more people struggling with these questions.

Also in that interview, Mr. Owens spoke about his time in Paris. He felt somewhat confused about his ethnicity, but the Parisians knew exactly what he should be like, they had such a complete image of the habits and character, thoughts and feelings, of a "red Indian." In *Bone Game,* there are many white characters who explain Native Americanism to Cole. It is all written with the same wry humor found throughout these works.

Bone Game is closer to the classic mystery form than the other works covered herein, but all were given a Form/Genre heading of Detective and mystery stories by the Library of Congress.

Mr. Owens won the French Roman Noir award for *The Sharpest Sight* in 1995.

Literary Magic & Mayhem: These two books are written almost as puzzles that must be fit together. Points of view change, and changes from reality to dreams or to waking dreams form a complex narrative, with layers of reality showing layers of meaning.

The ways in which white people have altered the world are depicted as either attempts to restrain nature that will ultimately fail, or as favoring death over life. For instance, there are many passages in *Sharpest Sight* that talk about the river being dammed. In one passage, Uncle Luther talks about them "building the wall" across the river so that it floods its banks, and then, when the water drains off, and the fish that were swimming in it are stranded:

> Fish swim up from the ocean like they been doing forever, but because the river's broken, the water all goes back in the ground and the fish die. I've dreamed it. The fish laying all over that white sand, drying out and dying every year. It's part of a circle, you see, and they broke the circle when they broke that river. And they're doing that all over the world, breaking all the circles. (*Sharpest Sight,* p. 97)

In *Bone Game,* Robert Jim talks about what has happened to Indian country: Navajo, Pueblo, and Hopi land. The tribes had sacred peaks and stories about the land. The white people mapped it out and then used the sacred geography as a place to create death:

> They got that Los Alamos up there in the north where they took Cochiti Indian land to plan that A-bomb. They got that Sandia laboratory over in Albuquerque in the east where they make nucular bombs. They got White Sands to the south where they fire them bombs and nucular missiles off to

see if they work...And they got that uranium mine at Laguna where they made the water poison; that's the west. (*Bone Game,* p. 88)

He speaks ironically about the white people having created death in each of the four directions, contrasting it with the tribes, which created sacred lands in the four directions.

Explorations: What kind of power do names seem to have?

What evidence is there that Uncle Luther's and Onatima's powers are not unique?

Many of Uncle Luther's stories are funny, yet have a point. This one (from page 96 of *The Sharpest Sight*) points out that the man who was challenged always had his choice of weapons, and talks about a determinedly peaceful way of life:

> One time a French man challenged a Choctaw man to a duel...When the French man showed up, the Choctaw was sitting on a keg of black powder holding a match. "Where's your keg?" He says. Ha! (*Sharpest Sight,* p. 96)

What was your favorite Uncle Luther story?

THE CASES

1. ***The Sharpest Sight.*** Norman: University of Oklahoma Press, c1992, 263 p. ISBN: 0806124040.

AMARGA (CALIFORNIA) AND MISSISSIPPI, 1992? The inside shadow is the *shilup;* the outside shadow that hangs around the body and that people see and call a ghost is the *shilombish.* When Attis is murdered, Uncle Luther realizes that Attis's shilombish is alone by the body, and he brings it to his cabin in the Mississippi swamp. Then he sends Cole on a hunt for Attis's bones so that the spirit may be laid to rest. Mundo Morales works on finding the killer, while Uncle Luther works on bringing his grandson peace.

ASSOCIATES: Attis MuCurtain—*deceased;* Mundo (Raymond) Morales—*who was Attis's friend;* Gloria—*Mundo's wife;* and Maria—*their daughter;* Cole McCurtain—*Attis's brother;* Hoey McCurtain—*Attis and Cole's father;* Onatima—*Old Lady Blue Wood;* Uncle Luther—*a wise man;* the Mondragon sisters—*who are distant relatives of Mundo Morales;* Angel Turkus—*a deputy sheriff;* Sheriff Carl Carlton—*Mundo's boss;* Bobby Bart—*who walks around town at night;* Donald Wagstaff—*head psychiatrist at the hospital where Attis lived;* FBI Agent Lee Scott—*who was a Special Forces advisor in Vietnam;* Dan Nemi—*took over the Morales land;* Helen—*Dan's wife;* Diana—*Dan's and Helen's daughter;* Jessard Deal—*owner of Amarga's toughest bar;* lawmen Hicks and Harwood—*who try to apprehend Cole on Luther's land.*

2. ***The Bone Game.*** Norman: University of Oklahoma Press, c1994, 243 p. ISBN: 0806126647.

SANTA CRUZ (CALIFORNIA), 1994? When Cole's marriage disintegrated, he took a year's leave of absence from his job at the University of New Mexico for a teaching job at University of California, Santa Cruz. His dreams grow troubled, showing him cruelties against the Indian people in the past. They seem tied to serial killings taking place near the campus. Off in the Mississippi swamp, Uncle Luther and Onatima sense Cole's dreams and realize that he is in trouble. They travel across the country to help him battle ghosts and human killers.

ASSOCIATES: Doctor Cole McCurtain—*who is now a professor;* Venancio Asisara—*deceased;* Paul Kantner—*a student of Cole's;* Robert Malin—*Cole's teaching assistant;* Alex Yazzie—a *cross-dressing Navajo who's also teaching at University of California, Santa Cruz, but who is not yet tenured;* Mundo and Gloria Morales—*old friends of Cole;* Abby McCurtain—*Cole's daughter;* Father Quintana—*a priest from the past, who is now in Cole's dreams;* Hoey—*Cole's father;* Uncle Luther—*Luther Cole, who is still wise;* Onatima Blue Wood—*who lives near Uncle Luther;* Robert Jim—*a wise man who Hoey and Luther meet on the journey;* Alex's Uncle Emmet—*who holds peyote ceremonies;* Custer—*the dog;* Emil Redbull—*who holds a sweatlodge ceremony on Cole's property;* Katherine Begay—*who was saved by Uncle Luther and Hoey.*

P

PARKER, T. Jefferson.

<u>The Fallen</u>

Genres/Themes Crossed: Paranormal X Police Procedural.

Subjects/Character Types: Human with synesthesia X Police.

Series/Stand-Alone: Stand-alone.

Scene of the Crime: San Diego, present day.

Detective: Twenty-six year old San Diego police officer Robbie Brownlaw raced into the burning Las Palmas Hotel to save the tenants. Vic Malic threw him out a window on the sixth floor. News cameras captured his fall, which would have been fatal if it hadn't been broken by a canvas awning. Robbie survived, albeit with massive head trauma. Robbie's embarrassed when people recognize him as the "falling policeman." He's been promoted twice in rapid succession, mostly so that his superiors could capitalize on the public's fascination with Robbie. Now, three years after the fall, he works Homicide.

When Robbie came out of his coma he could "see" conversation. The emotions that people feel as they speak create colored shapes that accompany their words. The net result is that Robbie can see what people feel as they speak. He's developed a reputation as someone who has good hunches—many based on knowing that the person being interviewed was feeling guilt or attempting deception as he or she spoke.

Known Associates: Robbie's wife Gina is a hairdresser. Rachel is Gina's best friend. Vince and Dawn Brancini are Gina's parents. Vic Malic, after serving time for arson and throwing Robbie out a window, has turned his life around.

Robbie's partner is Detective McKenzie Cortez. Other San Diego law enforcement personnel include: Glenn Wasserman, crime scene investigator; Eddie Waimrin who translates Egyptian, Arabic, Lebanese, and French for the department; Patrol Captain Evers; Patrol Officer Ron Mincher; Robbie's captain Jim Villas; Captain Chester "Chet" Fellowes of Vice; Professional Standards officer Roger Sutherland; Assistant Chief Bryan Bogle; and sketch artist Kathy Iles.

Garrett Asplundh worked for the Ethics Authority, its director is Erik Kaven. John Van Flyke runs the enforcement unit of the Ethics Authority, he was Garrett's immediate supervisor. The department's administrative assistant is Arliss Buntz. Garrett's wife was Stella. Their three-year-old daughter, Samantha, drowned eight months ago and their grief tore their marriage apart. Samuel Asplundh is Garrett's brother. Garrett rents a room in the Seabreeze Apartments from Al Bantour for April Holly. Those at the apartment house know Garrett as Jimmy.

Garrett's investigations included appointments with Hollis Harris whose company *Hidden Threat Assessment (HTA)* is doing business with the city; Carrie Ann Martier, an informant; and Jordan Sheehan, the Squeaky Clean madam. (Chupa Junior is her enforcer.)

Trey Vinson is evaluating San Diego's credit rating for Jance Purdew Investments. Mike, the bartender at *McGinty's Pub* offers Robbie some of their promotional marbles (they have little shamrocks and Irish lasses inside). Convict Ed Placer lives with his mother. Dale Payne, Assistant Chief of the New Orleans Police Department, searches the New Orleans Property Annex for a missing gun. Ninth District City Councilman Anthony Rood is a man who blushes easily. Abel Sarvonola the Budget Oversight Committee chairman, believes that the city should not make its problems public. Sanji Moussaraf was detained after 9/11 for insufficient reason and is now wary of the police. Cynthia and Owen James are the people who purchased the Asplundh home; Jeremiah is a neighbor boy. Reuben is the Dream Wheels manager; Cass works for him at Dream Wheels.

At the Synesthesia Society meeting Robbie meets: chapter president Moira Handler; singer Lillian Smith (who is visiting the society for the first time); author Darlene Sable; and Bart, who believes he's an expert on every type of synesthesia.

Miranda is an artist who works at Higher Grounds, she has a good eye for faces, even when people are disguised.

Premise: Synesthesia gives a detective an edge when he's investigating a homicide. (Shapes tumble or float out of people's mouths with their words and allow him to tell what emotion the person is feeling.)

Comment: T. Jefferson Parker wrote his first novel, *Laguna Heat,* on evenings and weekends while he worked as a reporter. As a reporter he won three Orange County Press Club Awards. *Laguna Heat* received excellent reviews, was made into an HBO movie, and the paperback made *The New York Times* bestseller list. Since then he was written fifteen more novels and numerous short stories. His work has won three Edgar Awards: 2000 Best Novel for *Silent Joe,* 2004 Best Novel for *California Girl;* and 2008 Best Short Story for "'Skinhead Central'—The Blue Religion." The author's Web site at http://www.tjeffersonparker.com/ provides information on his books, his biography and offers fans an opportunity to sign up for his mailing list.

Literary Magic & Mayhem: Robbie, the protagonist, is a supremely decent man. Readers will want him to succeed, prosper, and be overwhelmingly happy. The victim was also a decent man and it is interesting to see how different characters respond to information about his rescue of a young woman. There are those who smirk, those who don't believe, and those who are completely unsurprised. Different people live in very different realities, even though they are all in the same world.

There is surprisingly little reliance on the "gimmick" of synesthesia. It's part of Robbie's life, for better or worse, and there are times when it is "worse." Robbie would be a good detective without it. He's logical and has a good ear for the truth. Synesthesia is treated as part of his life, the reader learns about it, but it does not drive the investigation.

Explorations: At what point did Robbie make a decision based on his synesthesia? How big a part did it play in determining the course of the investigation?

Robbie's mother told him that a person needs three things in life to be happy: Someone to love. Something to do. And something to look forward to. (p. 83) Was that true of Robbie's life? Is it true of others?

How does Robbie's perception of "letting go" change in the course of the story? Is there a point when it changed for Garrett?

THE CASE

The Fallen. New York: St. Martin's Press, 1994, c1992, 188 p. ISBN: 0312105118.

San Diego, March 200? Garrett Asplundh had been an Internal Affairs officer in the San Diego Police Department until three months ago, when he took a job as an investigator for the San Diego Ethics Authority Enforcement Unit. (An agency designed to watch city administrators in the same way that Internal Affairs is designed to watch cops.)

He has found evidence of far-reaching corruption. It involves city officials, Vice Officers, even an outside credit rating agency. Before he can make his findings public he is murdered. Detectives Robbie Brownlaw and McKenzie Cortez are assigned the case.

ASSOCIATES: See above.

PRATCHETT, Terry.

GUARDS! GUARDS!

Genres/Themes Crossed: Blended Society X Humorous Mystery, Police Procedural.

Subjects/Character Types: Alternate Universe X Police Procedural.

Series/Stand-Alone: Sam Vimes changes, his relationships change, his opinions change, and his society changes. These should be read in order.

Scene of the Crime: Most of the books are set in Ankh-Morpork, a walled city about eight miles wide, situated on the coast of the Circle Sea. It's a port city on the River Ankh, the most polluted waterway in Discworld. The people of Ankh-Morpork are a cynical group, governed by a cynical leader, the Patrician. "Ankh-Morpork! Brawling city of a hundred thousand souls! And, as the Patrician privately observed, ten times that number of actual people" (*Guards! Guards!*, p. 77).

Detective: Samuel Vimes, at the outset of the book, is one of the three remaining members of the despised and ridiculed Night Watch. He's despondent and drunk; both conditions are chronic. However, he finds purpose during the course of *Guards! Guards!*, and turns the Night Watch around, becoming a respected (and somewhat feared) force in the city.

Known Associates: Ankh-Morpork is ruled by the Patrician, Lord Havelock Vetinari, a man with a fine sense of humor, a great deal of patience, and a phenomenal skill for manipulating others. When *Guards! Guards!* opens, the officers of the Night Watch are Captain Samuel Vimes, Sergeant Fred Colon, and Corporal "Nobby" Nobbs, all of whom are human (probably human, no one is completely sure about Nobby). In the course of that book, another man joins, Lance Corporal Carrot Ironfoundersson, who considers himself a dwarf because he was adopted and raised by dwarves. Genetically he is human. Through the course of the series, the Night Watch grows.

Lord Vetinari commands the Night Watch to hire beings of all the races that make up the city. Prominent members of the Night Watch that join after the events in *Guards! Guards!* include Lance Corporal Angua, a werewolf; Lance Corporal Detritus, a troll; and Lance Corporal Cheery Littlebottom, a dwarf. In *Guards! Guards!*, Captain Vimes develops a relationship with Lady Sybil Ramkin, who later becomes his wife.

Premise: One of the Patrician's plots for Ankh-Morpork was to have the thieves police themselves. It is cheaper and more efficient than hiring watchmen. He made a deal with the ancient Thieves' Guild: they would steal only a reasonable amount (or offer anti-theft insurance at a reasonable price) and would maintain a monopoly on theft by any means necessary. The result is order (of a type), and a City Watch that is superfluous.

Carrot Ironfoundersson (a very tall dwarf) came from the countryside (actually from a mine run by his adoptive father). It had become clear that, ultimately, he would not fit in with dwarf society (he's six feet tall and the mine ceilings are five feet high). His father, anxious to find a place where Carrot could be useful and happy, hears of the Ankh-Morpork Watch of old and writes to ask that Carrot be considered for employment in the Watch. They accept Carrot (they're actually stunned that anyone would want to join the Watch), and Carrot heads off to Ankh-Morpork. A friend of his father gives Carrot an out-of-date book on the laws of Ankh-Morpork. He studies it assiduously, earnestly determined to be an excellent Watchman and anxious to sally forth to capture evildoers.

One of Acting Lance-Corporal Carrot's first acts is to arrest the President of the Guild of Thieves, Burglars, and Allied Trades. The Thieves' Guild President is a prominent citizen. He organizes crime (as The Patrician says, if the city has to have crime, it might as well be organized). Captain Vimes smoothes things over, and tries to teach Carrot the Watch's peculiar blend of avoidance, resignation, and drunkenness. An innocent has no place in the Guards; the politics of Ankh-Morpork are likely to kill him (especially if he attempts to arrest the chief of the Assassins' Guild). An odd thing happens on the road to training Carrot: his idealism proves to be more compelling than anyone expected. Vimes pulls himself together and begins to really command the Night Watch.

Comment: Different Discworld novels focus on different groups of characters; but they're all about the same world, so some characters from the *Night Watch* series show up in non-Night Watch books as secondary characters. *The Truth* (which follows *The Fifth Elephant*) chronicles William de Worde's efforts to begin the first newspaper in Ankh-Morpork. It happens that one of the sensational stories that he is covering is a murder, in which Lord Vetinari is the chief suspect. The case is being investigated by the Watch; as the reporter follows the story, readers see the officers from the reporter's point of view. In *The Last Hero* (which follows *The Thief of Time,* which followed *The Truth*), Lord Vetinari sends Captain Carrot Ironfoundersson on a mission. In *Monstrous Regiment* (which follows *Night Watch*), readers see a few of the officers of the Watch from the point of view of Private Oliver Perks (Polly). *Going Postal* (which follows *Monstrous Regiment*), focuses on Moist, a petty con man who is given a job in the postal service. Lord Vetinari speaks to and of Commander Vimes and the Watch, but the story does not follow them. *Making Money* (which follows *Thud!*) chronicles the further adventures of Moist, as Vetinari puts him in charge of the Mint. Again, the Watch is involved in crime-solving (and peacekeeping), but the book does not focus on the activities of the Watch. Pratchett has also written the children's book that Sam reads to young Sam every night at 6:00 P.M. (in *Thud*): *Where's My Cow?* In 1998, Pratchett wrote (and Stephen Briggs, and Paul Kidby illustrated) the *Ankh-Morpork City Watch Diary 1999,* a date book that includes such things as traditions of the Watch, a sample Watch report, holidays, and famous dates.

Terry Pratchett was the United Kingdom's best selling author in the 1990s. He was the British Book Awards Fantasy and Science Fiction Author of the Year for 1994. In 1998, he was named an Officer of the Order of the British Empire for "services to literature." Every entry in his *Tiffany Aching* series has received a Locus Award for Best Young Adult Book.

His Web site at http://www.terrypratchettbooks.com/ confirms the sad news that Mr. Pratchett has been diagnosed with early-onset Alzheimer's Disease. There are links on his site that provide further information. There's a newsgroup for Pratchett fans at: alt.fan.pratchett. He has several Web sites at different publishers. This is from a message from Terry Pratchett that is on the HarperCollins page:

> Welcome to the Discworld. It started out as a parody of all the fantasy that was around in the big boom of the early 80s, then turned into a satire on just about everything, and even I don't know what it is now. I do know that in that time there's been at least four people promoted as "new Terry Pratchetts," so for all I know, I may not even still be me.

Literary Crimes & Chimes: One source of humor in these books is the footnotes. They read as if they are asides; if this were theater, many of them would be "breaking the fourth wall" to speak directly to the audience. For instance, on page 72 there is the ringing assertion that the Patrician would tolerate anything, except for anything that threatened his city. The statement is followed by an asterisk, which leads to this footnote:

> *And mime artists. It was a strange aversion, but there you are. Anyone in baggy trousers and a white face who tried to ply their art anywhere within Ankh's crumbing wall would very quickly find themselves in a scorpion pit, on one wall of which was printed the advice: Learn The Words. (*Guards! Guards!*, p. 72)

Death is a character in most of the books set in *Discworld*. He's a surprisingly reasonable and sweet-natured being. His dialogue is always written in capital letters, as in this conversation with Mr. Hopkinson, curator of the Dwarf Bread Museum, who was recently murdered and is aggravated at the ingrates who killed him. He argues with Death, telling him that he has no time for "that nonsense":

> Death was nonplussed. Most people were, after the initial confusion, somewhat relieved when they died. A subconscious weight had been removed. The other cosmic shoe had dropped. The worst had happened and they could, metaphorically, get on with their lives. Few people treated it as a simple annoyance that might go away if they complained enough.
>
> Mr. Hopkinson's hand went through a tabletop. "Oh."
>
> YOU SEE?
>
> "This is most uncalled for. Couldn't you have arranged a less awkward time?"
>
> ONLY BY CONSULTATION WITH YOUR MURDERER.
>
> (*Feet of Clay*, p. 12)

When Mr. Hopkinson announces that it is very badly organized and he will make a complaint, ending with "I pay my taxes after all," Death points out: "I AM DEATH, NOT TAXES. *I* TURN UP ONLY ONCE."

Different characters are colorful in different ways. Captain Carrot Ironfoundersson (a human who was adopted by dwarves) is one example. It's hard to know what is going on in Captain Carrot Ironfoundersson's mind. For instance on page 7 of *The Fifth Elephant,* Carrot and Commander Vimes are watching as the Fools' Guild burns. (When the people fighting the fire are clowns, their instincts take over around buckets, water, and ladders; which leads to more pratfalls than fire fighting.)

> The fire had taken hold in a first-floor room.
>
> "If we let it burn it'd be a blow for entertainment in this city," said Carrot earnestly.
>
> Vimes looked sideways at him. That was a true Carrot comment. It sounded as innocent as hell, but you could take it a different way.
>
> "It certainly would," he said. "Nevertheless, I suppose we'd better do something."

People are never sure if Carrot is a halfwit, a wise man, or just putting them on. He's amazingly effective.

Explorations: What was the best footnote?

THE CASES

1. ***Guards! Guards!: A Novel of Discworld.*** London: Victor Gollancz, 1989, 288 p. ISBN: 1568651937.

DISCWORLD (ANKH-MORPORK), CENTURY OF THE FRUIT BAT. It was a dark and stormy night when the Unique and Supreme Lodge of the Elucidated Brethren of the Ebon Night met and agreed to overthrow the government of Lord Vetinari. They use a spell from a stolen library book to summon a dragon (a huge dragon, the dragon of myth, Draco Nobilis); hoping that the dragon-created carnage would invoke fear and cause the citizens to riot (and demand better leadership). With the city in chaos and the citizens clamoring for better leadership, The Brethren will seize the moment, depose Vetinari, and install a puppet king. The dragon is duly summoned, but controlling it is more difficult than they expected. Captain Vimes is faced with a number of inexplicable disappearances (and ashes) and sets out to investigate. His suspicion that the deaths are the work of a real dragon, a dragon as large as the dragons portrayed in ancient myths, is met with derision. The people come to believe Captain Vimes when they see the dragon firing their city.

ASSOCIATES: Sergeant Fred Colon—*human;* Corporal "Nobby" Nobbs—*probably human;* Lance Corporal Carrot Ironfoundersson—*a very tall dwarf who petitioned to join the Ankh-Morpork City Watch;* Lady Sybil Ramkin—*who gives the Watch a swamp-dragonas a mascot;* Errol—*the swamp-dragon;* Lord Vetinari—*the Patrician;* Lupine Wonse—*the Patrician's secretary;* the Librarian of Unseen University—*who was turned into an orangutan long ago and wants a stolen library book returned, he is deputized;* Mr. Cut-Me-Own-Throat Dibbler—*who sells cuddly stuffed dragons and sausages;* DEATH—*Death.*

2. ***Men at Arms: a Novel of Discworld.*** New York: HarperPrism, 1996, 341 p. ISBN: 0061092185.

DISCWORLD (ANKH-MORPORK), CENTURY OF THE FRUIT BAT. On the eve of the anniversary of the Battle of Koom Valley, a dwarf is killed. The dwarves suspect the trolls (of course). Other odd crimes are happening in the city. There's a theft, which is not unusual in itself, but this theft is singular; few people are insane enough to steal from the Assassin's Guild. A second crime, the murder of a swamp dragon named Chubby, is just odd. Vimes's investigation includes questioning Assassins, and the head of the Assassins' Guild complains to Lord Vetinari. Vetinari orders Vimes to cease investigations involving the theft at the Assassins' Guild; he hopes that his orders will have the "intended effect." Vimes continues to investigate. Vimes has a deadline; he intends to retire from the Watch when he marries Lady Sybil. On the eve of Vimes's retirement Vetinari orders the Night Watch to stand down and has them disarmed by the Day Watch. The quarrel between the trolls and the dwarves escalates; and under the incompetent Day Watch, civil unrest claims Ankh-Morpork.

ASSOCIATES: Captain Vimes—*who is leaving the Watch to marry Lady Sybil Ramkin (her crazy uncle Lofthouse is giving her away)*. Members of the Night Watch include: Sergeant Fred Colon—*human;* Corporal "Nobby" Nobbs—*probably human;* Lance-Constable Angua—*werewolf;* Lance-Constable Detritus—*troll;* Lance-Constable Cuddy—*dwarf;* and Captain Carrot Ironfoundersson—*a human who was brought up as a dwarf.*

Carrot organizes the members of the disbanded Night Watch into a citizen militia. Beings who are conscripted into the Citizen Militia include: Lance-Constable Bluejohn—*troll;* Lance-Constable Bauxite—*troll;* Lance-Constable Hrolf Pyjama—*dwarf;* Lance-Constable Silas Cumberbatch—*human.*

Captain Quirke and Skully Muldoon—*members of the Day Watch;* Gaspode—*is a dog with chronic intelligence.* Big Fido; Black Roger; and Butch—*other dogs.* The leaders of the city include: Lord Vetinari—*the Patrician;* Dr. Cruces—*Master of the Assassins;* Queen Molly—*of the Beggars;* Lettice Knibbs—*Queen Molly's lady's maid;* Dr. Whiteface—*of the Fools' Guild.* Lord Rust; Viscount Skater; Lady Selachii and Lady Sara Omnius—*are others who have power in the city.* DEATH—*has power everywhere.*

The faculty of the Unseen University includes: the Librarian—*an ensorcelled orangutan;* Archchancellor Minstrum Ridcully; the Bursar; the Dean. The anniversary of the Battle of Koom increases the tension between the dwarf and troll communities, which include Mr. Abba Stronginthearm—*dwarf* and Coalface—*troll.* Beano and Boffo—*are members of the Fool's Guild.* Others characters include Willikins—*Sybil Ramkin's butler;* Edward, Lord d'Eath—*of the Assassin's Guild;* Mr. Bjorn Hammerhock—*dwarf ironmonger;* Leonard da Quirm—*inventor;* Mrs. Cake—*the psychic landlady;* Zorgo—*the retrophrenologist;* Sham Harga—*who sells coffee;* Mr. Cut-Me-Own-Throat Dibbler—*who sells other things, some of them edible.*

3. ***Feet of Clay: a Novel of Discworld.*** New York: HarperPrism, 1996, 249 p. ISBN: 0061052507.

DISCWORLD (ANKH-MORPORK), CENTURY OF THE FRUIT BAT. Commander Samuel Vimes is not comfortable with his new lot in life. He has come up in the world, his shoes are too comfortable, and there are people cooking his food, setting out his clothing and generally being helpful in a horribly subservient way. His wife even expects that someone else will shave him, but there Vimes draws the line:

> Vimes had protested that he'd spent too many years trudging the night-time streets to be happy about anyone else wielding a blade anywhere near his neck, but the real reason, the unspoken reason, was that he hated the very idea of the world being divided into the shaved and the shavers. Of those who wore shiny boots and those who cleaned the mud off them. (p. 4)

(He concludes his somewhat serious meditation with the fact that every time he sees the butler folding Vimes clothing, he must suppress "a terrible urge to kick the butler's shiny backside as an affront to the dignity of man." Ending a passage of noble thought with a moment of slapstick is pure Pratchett.)

While Vimes tries to work out the ramifications of his new place in the world, a serial murderer kills two harmless old men: a priest and a museum curator. Vimes is beginning his investigation when Lord Vetinari is struck down (almost struck down: clearly poisoned, but not dead yet). Vimes doesn't know whom to trust. Almost anyone might want to kill the Patrician.

ASSOCIATES: Commander Sam Vimes—*Duke of Ankh-Morpork;* Lady Sybil Ramkin—*his wife (a.k.a. Sybil Vimes);* Sergeant Fred Colon—*a human who is looking forward to retirement at the end of the month;* Corporal the Right Honorable the Earl of Ankh Nobby Nobbs—*probably human, and the only surviving heir of the last Earl of Ankh;* Captain Carrot Ironfoundersson—*who was once a foundling and was fostered by dwarves:* Lance-Constable Angua—*a werewolf and Carrot's girlfriend;* Constable Visit-The-Infidel-With-Explanatory-Pamphlets—*human;* Constable Downspout—*gargoyle;* Sergeant Detritus—*troll;* Wee Mad Arthur—*gnome;* Corporal Cheery Littlebottom—*a dwarf alchemist who joins the Watch and is told by Commander Vimes to stay out of trouble:*

> If troll officers call you a gritsucker they're out, and if you call them rocks, you're out. We're just one big family and, when you've been to a few domestic disputes, Littlebottom, I can assure you that you'll see the resemblance. (p. 15)

In this book, Cheery explores her femininity and changes her name to Cheri. Lord Vetinari—*the Patrician, is poisoned,* and Vimes calls in the most reliable healer he knows, Dr. James Folsom—*a.k.a. Doughnut Jimmy, a large-animal veterinarian.* Others who appear include Father Tubelcek—*human;* Mr. Hopkinson—*of the Dwarf Bread Museum;* DEATH—*Death;* Mr. Cheese—*owner and barkeep at The Bucket;* Duck Man—*human;* Coffin Henry—*human;* Foul Ole Ron—*human;* Arnold Sideways—*human;* Mr. Drumknott—*Vetinari's personal clerk;* Mr. Ironcrust—*dwarf;* Igneous—*a troll potter;* Igor—*a barkeep;* Shlitzen—*the bogeyman;* Mr. Gerhardt

Sock—*the butcher:* Dorfl—*Gerhardt Sock's golem;* Thomas "Stronginthearm" Smith—*the blacksmith;* Dibbuk—*the foundry's golem;* Mr. Preble Skink—*who owns the timber yard;* Mr. Oresmiter—*dwarf;* Mr. Gimlet—*of Gimlet's Hole Food Delicatessen;* Wee Mad Arthur—*a gnome who sells rats to Mr. Gimlet;* Death of Rats—*who appears to rats when they die;* Mr. Catterail—*who runs a sewing sweat shop;* and Mrs. Easy—*who was a neighbor of Vimes when he was growing up on Cockbill Street.*

High society includes Mrs. Rosemary Palm—*head of the Guild of Seamstresses;* Mr. Potts—*of the Bakers' Guild;* Mr. Boggis—*head of the Thieves' Guild;* and Dr. Downey—*head of the Assassins' Guild;* Mr. Slant—*zombie President of the Guild of Lawyers;* Doc Pseudopolis—*of the Guild of Gamblers;* Queen Molly—*of the Beggars' Guild;* Mr. Carry—*the candle maker;* Lady Selachii—*who invites Nobby to her soirée;* Croissant Rouge Pursuivant—*who is a herald;* the Dragon King of Arms—*vampire, Croissant Rouge Pursuivant's boss,*

4. *Jingo: a Novel of Discworld.* New York: HarperPrism, 1996, 249 p.

DISCWORLD (ANKH-MORPORK, LESHP, AND KLATCH), CENTURY OF THE FRUITBAT. Ankh-Morpork has been at peace, or at least a state of non-war with Klatch for almost a century. Now, when the continent of Leshp rises back out of the sea (as it does periodically), two fishermen almost come to blows: Solid Jackson claims Leshp for Ankh-Morpork, and Greasy Arif claims Leshp for the Seriph of Al-Khali of Klatch. Soon both countries are Leshp mad. War Councils in each strategize to defend "their" territory. Leaders in Klatch and Ankh-Morpork decide to try diplomacy before going to war. The Seriph sends his brother, Prince Khufurah, for talks in Ankh-Morpork. Things go badly when someone tries to assassinate the Prince. Vimes tries to solve the case to avert a war.

ASSOCIATES: Solid Jackson and his son—*fishermen of Ankh-Morpork;* Greasy Arif and his son, Akhan—*fishermen of Klatch.* Members of the Watch include: Commander Sam Vimes—*Duke of Ankh-Morpork;* Captain Carrot—*a natural leader;* Sergeant Angua—*werewolf;* Sergeant Fred Colon—*human;* Corporal "Nobby" Nobbs—*human until proven otherwise;* Sergeant Detritus—*troll;* Constable Cheery Littlebottom—*dwarf;* Constable Reg Shoe—*zombie;* probationary Constable Buggy Swires—*gnome;* Constable Dorfl—*golem;* and Constable Downspout—*gargoyle.*

The Patrician's War Council includes: Lord Downey—*of the Assassins' Guild;* Mr. Burleigh—*president of the Guild of Armorers;* Mr. Boggis—*of the Thieves' Guild;* Mr. Slant—*zombie president of the Guild of Lawyers;* Lord Selachii—*who wants to teach Johnny Klatchian a lesson;* Lord Rust—*a military man;* Lieutenant Hornett—*his aide;* and Mr. Frostrip—*of the Guild of Accountants.*

Mrs. Spent—*Ossie Brunt's landlady.* Daceyville "Snowy" Slopes—*who is a hired killer who lacks the education to be an assassin.* Mr. Goriff—*a Klatchian immigrant who owns the restaurant Mundane Meals on Scandal Alley;* Janil—*Goriff's son.* Mr. Wazir—*a bookseller who is determined to take a stand on Klatchian rights.* Prince Khufurah—*the brother of the Seriph;* Prince Cadram—*the Seriph;* 71-hour Ahmed—*who guards the Prince Khufurah in Ankh-Morpork;* Archchancellor Ridcully—*who expects to give Prince Khufurah an honorary degree.* Prince Kalif—*Klatch's deputy ambassador to Ankh-Morpork.* Others encountered include Lady Sybil—*Vimes's wife;* Mrs. Cake—*who runs a small house of ill-repute;* Leonard of Quirm—*inventor;* Mr. Jenkins—*Captain of the Milka;* Jabbar—*of the D'regs;* Willikins—*Vimes's butler, a man who bites the noses off his enemies.*

5. *The Fifth Elephant: a Novel of Discworld.* New York: HarperCollins, c2000, 321 p. ISBN: 0061051578.

DISCWORLD (ANKH-MORPORK), CENTURY OF THE FRUITBAT. The Patrician sends Vimes on a diplomatic mission. The mission is to the frightening land of Uberwald which has variously been described as "a mystery inside a riddle wrapped in an enigma" (p. 14) or as a "misery wrapped in a enema" (p. 68). What's left of the Night Watch investigates the murder of prophylactic maker Mister Sonky and the theft of a copy of a ceremonial Scone of Stone from the Dwarf Bread Museum. Vimes had been concerned because the diplomatic mission requires his presence at the ceremony to crown the Low King of the dwarves. That ceremony involves the scone; a new king cannot be put on the throne without it. It seems an odd time for the copy to go missing. It turns out that his mission calls for as much detecting as it does diplomacy. (Which is fortunate: Vimes' long suit has never been diplomacy. Still, his heart is in the right place, and he doesn't allow himself to be pushed around, which might be more effective than diplomatic speeches.)

ASSOCIATES: His Grace the Duke of Ankh-Morpork, Sir Samuel Vimes—*Commander of the Ankh-Morpork Night Watch and head of a diplomatic mission to Uberwald.* The diplomatic party was intended to include Lady Sybil—*his wife;* Willikins—*his butler;* Sergeant Angua—*werewolf;* Sergeant Detritus—*troll;* Corporal Cheery Littlebottom—*dwarf;* and Inigo Skimmer—*diplomat.*

Watch Officers left in the city include Captain Carrot—*a human raised by dwarves, he has a serious relationship with Sergeant Angua and in this book he resigns from the Watch;* Acting Captain Fred Colon—*human;* Corporal "Nobby" Nobbs—*newly elected president of the Guild of Watchmen;* Constable Ping—*the human officer who was first on the scene of the dwarf museum robbery;* Sergeant Stronginthearm—*dwarf;* Lance-Constable Bluejohn—*troll;* Constable Chert—*troll;* Constable Reg Shoe—*zombie;* Constable Buggy Swires—*gnome, Reg's partner;* Constable Visit-The-Infidel-With-Explanatory-Pamphlets—*human;* Constable Downspout—*gargoyle;* and Constable Dorfl—*golem.*

Other citizens of Ankh-Morpork include Patrician Havelock Vetinari—*who usually has good reasons for his actions;* Drumknott—*Vetinari's head clerk;* Leonard of Quirm—*inventor;* Mr. All Jolson—*restaurateur;* and Gaspode—*dog.*

Characters living in the Uberwald include Lady Margolotta—*vampire;* Igor—*her servant;* Baron von Uberwald and the Lady Serafina von Uberwald—*Agua's parents;* Wolfgang von Uberwald—*her brother;* Captain Tantony—*who guards Vimes;* Dee, and Albrecht Albrechtson—*are two of the Uberwald dwarves of Shmaltzberg;* and Gavin—*a wolf who is a friend of Angua's.*

Sybil tries to give Sam news all through the book, but it's never the right time. She finally corners him and tells him that she is pregnant.

6. ***Night Watch: a Novel of Discworld.*** New York: HarperPrism, 1996, 249 p.

Ankh-Morpork, May 25 present day and 30 years ago, in the year of the Dancing Dog (Century of the Fruit Bat). Thirty years ago (in the Year of the Dancing Dog), the paranoid Patrician, Lord Winder, oppressed the people of Ankh-Morpork. He developed a branch of the Watch to act as secret police (they are popularly called "the Unmentionables") and set up many laws (including a curfew) to trap conspirators. There weren't many conspirators before Winder started taking draconian measures; people disappearing into the lair of the Unmentionables did wonders to increase popular dissent. Commander Samuel Vimes remembers those days. He'd just joined the Treacle Mine Road Night Watch House and was being trained by Sergeant John Keems when the city rioted and the Treacle Mine Road Night Watch House took the side of the citizens. Keems was killed, but he'd given Vimes the foundation for making decisions (primarily about which orders you follow, and which orders you don't follow). Those who stood with Keems remember him on the anniversary of his death.

On that anniversary, 30 years after those riots, Sam is trying to wrap up his duties and pay his respects quickly; Lady Sybil is in labor to give birth to their child. Then Sam gets word that the Watch has finally trapped a serial killer named Carcer. Vimes orders them all to keep Carcer from escaping and moves forward to apprehend the killer himself. In the ensuing events, during a thunderstorm, on top of the Unseen University Library, Vimes and Carcer are hurled back 30 years in time. Carcer comes to and joins in the mugging of the nearest man, who happens to be John Keems. Keems is on his way to report for duty at his new post at the Treacle Mine Road Night Watch House. Keems is killed. Vimes is found by a seamstress and given medical aid, but is soon apprehended by the Watch. He has several problems: he must see that young Lance-Constable Samuel Vimes gets pointed in the right direction;

he must apprehend Carcer, whose brand of homicidal insanity is likely to be attractive to the current Patrician; and he must find a way back to his family.

ASSOCIATES: In the present: Commander Sam Vimes—*Duke of Ankh-Morpork;* Lady Sibyl—*his wife, she is in labor;* Willikins—*the butler;* Jocasta Wiggs—*assassin;* Lord Vetinari—*The Patrician;* Drumknott—*Vetinari's chief clerk;* Carcer—*a schizophrenic killer;* Legitimate First—*a gravedigger;* Cut-Me-Own-Throat Dibbler—*a salesman.* Sergeant Colon; Corporal "Nobby" Nobbs; Captain Carrot; Corporal Cheery Littlebottom (dwarf); Sergeant Detritus (troll); Constable Igor (Igor); Corporal Ping; Constable Reg Shoe (zombie); Corporal Buggy Swires (gnome)—*the officers of the Night Watch.* Dr. Mossy Lawn—*who treats the poor.*

Thirty years ago: Commander Sam Vimes—*Duke of Ankh-Morpork in a time when no-one knew him;* Rosie Palm—*a seamstress;* Miss Sandra Battye—*really a seamstress;* Dr. Mossy Lawn—*who treats the poor;* Dotsie and Sadie—*the Agony Aunts;* Sweeper, Lu-Tze, and Soon Shine Sun—*of the order of the History Monks;* Qu—*the order's Master of Devices.* Captain Tilden; Sergeant Winsborough Knock; Corporal Quirke; Lance-Corporal Ned Coates; Lance-Constable Samuel Vimes; Constable Wiglet; Scutts; Corporal Fred Colon; Constable Waddy; Snouty; Captain Ron Rust; and Sergeant Dickens—*are the officers of the Watch.* Captain Findthee Swing; Henry the Hamster; Sergeant Carcer; Gerald Leastways; and the clerk, Trebilcock—*are the officers of the Cable Street "Watch" (the secret police, the "Unmentionables").* Guild Master Doctor Follett—*leads the Assassins' Guild;* "Ludo" Ludorum—*a student;* Downey—*a student,* and Havelock Vetinari—*a student with unorthodox theories on camouflage.* Others who play a part include: Madam Roberta Meserole—*Vetinari's Aunt;* Nobby Nobbs—*a street urchin;* Joss Gappy—*apprentice shoemaker;* Major Clive Mountjoy-Standfast—*who is not a fool;* Captain Tom Wrangle—*of Lord Selachii's Light Infantry;* Trooper Gabitass—*who gathered information;* Lord Albert Selachii and Lord Charles Venturi—*whose families are feuding;* Sub-lieutenant Harrap—*who brings word that Snapcase is now Patrician;* Mr. Slant—*zombie head of the Guild of Lawyers and advisor to Lord Snapcase.*

7. ***Thud!: a Novel of Discworld.*** New York: HarperPrism, 1996, 249 p.

DISCWORLD (ANKH-MORPORK), YEAR OF THE PRAWN. Commander Vimes believes that the Night Watch must keep the peace. On the eve of the anniversary of the dwarf-*versus*-troll Battle of Koom Valley, there is precious little peace to keep. Any dwarf or troll can recount the story of the battle: years ago at Koom Valley: an evil army of dwarves ambushed a gentle group of wandering trolls *or,* an evil army of trolls ambushed a gentle group of wandering dwarves, depending, of course, on the point of view (short or tall) of the speaker. Feelings in Ankh-Morpork are running high, and it's

Vimes's job to make sure that they don't, so to speak, run riot. A Grag (dwarf holy leader) is inciting the city dwarves to mayhem. Then the Grag is found murdered, with a troll's club near the body. If Vimes is to prevent an Ankh-Morpork re-enactment of the Battle of Koom Valley, he needs to bring the murderer to justice—fast!

Associates: Commander Sam Vimes—*Duke of Ankh-Morpork;* Lady Sybil Ramkin—*his wife;* Young Sam—*their son;* Purity—*Young Sam's nursemaid;* Willikins—*the Vimes's ancient butler;* Lord Vetinari—*the Patrician;* Drumknott—*his head clerk;* Sergeant Fred Colon—*human;* Corporal (Nobby) Nobbs—*probably human;* Captain Carrot Ironfoundersson—*human who was brought up as a dwarf;* Sergeant Angua—*werewolf;* Sergeant Detritus—*troll;* Sergeant Cheery Littlebottom—*dwarf;* Sergeant Dorfl—*golem;* Constable Visit-The-Ungodly-With-Explanatory-Pamphlets—*human;* and Lance Constable Salacia. Deloresista Amanita Trigestatra Zeldana Malifee "Call me Sally" von Humpeding—*a vampire, who joins the Watch in this book.* Mr. Chrysophrase—*troll, crime lord;* Mr. A. E. Pessimal—*human, city inspector, who was inducted as an Acting Lance Constable;* Brick—*a troll who was attacked by Acting Lance Constable Pessimal;* Betty "Tawnee,"—*who is Nobby's new girlfriend and a dancer at the Pink PussyCat Club;* Otto Chriek—*vampire, the Times iconographer;* Mr. John Smith—*vampire President of the Ankh-Morpork Mission of the Uberwald League of Temperance;* Mrs. Doreen Winkings—*treasurer of the Ankh-Morpork Mission of the Uberwald League of Temperance;* Igor—*an Igor;* Grag Hamcrusker—*a deep-downer dwarf;* Constable Mica—*troll;* Constable Bluejohn—*troll;* Constable Schist—*troll;* Constable Brakenshield—*dwarf;* Constable Haddock—*human;* Sir Reginald Stiched—*curator of Fine Art at the Royal Art Museum;* Constable Ironbender—*dwarf;* Constable Ringfounder—*dwarf;* Helmclever—*dwarf;* Ardent—*dwarf;* Constable Fittly—*human;* Special Constable Andy Hancock—*human;* Special Constable Mr. Boggis—*head of the Guild of Thieves;* Special Constable Vinnie "no ears" Ludd—*human;* Special Constable Harry "Can't Remember His Nickname" Jones—*human;* Special Constable the University Librarian—*orangutan;* Mr. Shine—*the unacknowledged king of the trolls;* Miss Pickles/Miss Pointer—*who keeps secrets from herself;* Phyllite—*troll;* Nils Mousehamer—*dwarf;* Gabbro—*troll;* Grag Bashfull Bashfullsson—*dwarf;* Setha Ironcrust—*dwarf;* Grabpot Thundergust—*dwarf;* Gimlet Gimlet—*dwarf owner of a string of delicatessens;* Helmclever—*dwarf;* Wiggleigh—*of Unseen University;* the Summoning Dark—*which comes when a dying dwarf draws a certain symbol with his blood;* Archchancellor Mustrum Ridcully—*who believes it may be quasidemonic;* Berenice Waynesbury—*née Mousefather, a.k.a. Bunty;* DEATH—*Death;* Captain Gud—*dwarf;* Rhys Rhysson—*dwarf, the Low King of the dwarves;* and Mr. Pony—*of the Artificers' Guild.*

R

RAIMONDI, Pablo. Worked with Peter David on *Madrox: Multiple Choice*. See DAVID, Peter: Madrox: Multiple Choice.

RESNICK, Michael D. (Editor)

WHATDUNITS

Genres/Themes Crossed: Science Fiction, Man as Creator, Secret Society X Hard-Boiled Mystery, Traditional Mystery, Police Procedural.

Subjects/Character Types: Aliens, Robots, Clones X Amateur Sleuths, Private Investigators, Police.

Series/Stand-Alone: Anthologies of short stories.

Scene of the Crime: Varies.

Detective: Varies.

Known Associates: Varies.

Premise: When Mike Resnick was offered the opportunity to create an anthology of short stories that combined science fiction and mystery, he sat down and wrote out synopses for possible stories. He then offered the scenarios to the authors selected for the book, and they chose from among those possibilities and wrote the stories for *WhatDunIts*. He followed the same procedure for *More WhatDunIts,* except that all the authors who were asked to contribute had also worked as editors.

Comment: Mike Resnick's Web site at http://www.fortunecity.com/tattooine/farmer/2/ includes news, links to a selection of his articles, and stories, and a bibliography of his work.

In *WhatDunIts*'s introduction, he describes Isaac Asimov's *The Caves of Steel* as the first book-length science fiction mystery.

Mike Resnick is a prolific writer. His fiction has won numerous awards:

1983—*Birthright: the Book of Man* (novel) was nominated for a Locus Award.

1987—*Santiago* (novel) was nominated for a Locus Award.

1988/89—*Ivory: A Legend of Past and Future* (novel) was nominated for a Nebula and a Locus award.

"Kinnyaga" (short story/novelette) won a Hugo and was nominated for a Nebula and a Locus.

1989/1990—"For I Have Touched the Sky" (novelette) won Japan's Hayakawa; Poland's "Sfinks" and was nominated for a Hugo, a Nebula, and for a Locus award.

1990/91—"The Manamouki" (novelette) won the Hugo and was nominated for Nebula award.

"Bully!" (novella) nominated for a Hugo, a Nebula, and a Locus award.

"Bwana" (novella) nominated for a Locus award.

1991/92—"Winter Solstice" (short story) nominated for a Hugo and a Locus award.

"One Perfect Morning with Jackals" (short story) nominated for a Hugo and a Locus award.

"Over There" (novelette) nominated for a Locus award.

1992/93—"The Lotus and the Spear" (short story) nominated for a Hugo, and a Locus award.

Alternate Kennedys (anthology) nominated for a Locus award.

Alternate Presidents (anthology) nominated for a Locus award.

Mike Resnick was nominated for a Locus for Best Editor award.

1993/94—"Mwalimu in the Squared Circle" (short story) was nominated for a Hugo and a Locus award.

Alternate Warriors (anthology) nominated for a Locus award.

Mike Resnick was nominated for a Locus for Best Editor award.

1994/95—Awarded the Skylark (the "Edward E. Smith Memorial Award for Imaginative Fiction") for lifetime achievement in Science Fiction.

"Seven Views of Olduvai Gorge" (novella) won a Hugo, a Nebula, and was nominated for a Locus award.

"A Little Knowledge" (novelette) nominated for a Hugo, and a Locus award.

"Barnaby in Exile" (short story) nominated for a Hugo, and a Locus award.

The Passage of the Light: The Recursive Science Fiction of Barry N. Malzberg (collection authored by Barry N. Malzberg, and co-edited by Mike Resnick and Anthony R. Lewis) nominated for a Locus award.

1995/96—"Bibi" (novella coauthored with Susan Shwartz) was nominated for a Hugo, a Nebula, and a Locus award.

"When the Old Gods Die" (novelette) won a Locus, and Poland's Sfinks and was nominated for a Hugo and a Nebula award.

1997/98—"The 43 Antarean Dynasties" (short story) won a Hugo and was nominated for a Locus award.

"The Land of Nod" (novelette) was nominated for a Hugo, and a Locus award.

1998/99—"Kirinyaga: A Fable of Utopia" (novelette and collection) won Japan's Seuin-sho and Poland's Nowa Fantastyka Poll; the collection was nominated for a Locus award.

1999/2000—"Hunting the Snark" (novella) was nominated for a Hugo, a Nebula, and a Locus award.

"Hothouse Flowers" (short story) was nominated for a Hugo award.

"The Elephants on Neptune" (short story) was nominated for a Hugo and a Nebula award.

"Redchapel" (novelette) was nominated for a Hugo award.

"Putting it Together" was nominated for a Hugo award.

2001/02—"Old MacDonald Had a Farm" (short story) nominated for a Hugo award.

"I Have This Nifty Idea..." nominated for a Hugo award.

2003/04—"Robots Don't Cry" (short story) nominated for a Hugo award.

New Voices in Science Fiction (anthology) was nominated for a Locus award.

Stars: Original Stories Based on the Songs of Janis Ian (anthology edited by Janis Ian and Mike Resnick) was nominated for a Locus award.

Mike Resnick was nominated for a Hugo Award for Best Editor.

2004/05—"Travels with My Cats" (short story) won a Hugo and was nominated for a Nebula award.

"A Princess of Earth" (short story) was nominated for a Hugo award.

Mike Resnick was nominated for a Hugo Award for Best Editor.

2005/06—"Down Memory Lane" (short story) nominated for a Hugo award.

2006/07—"All the Things You Are" (novelette) nominated for a Hugo award.

Worldcon Guest of Honor Speeches (nonfiction collection edited by Mike Resnick and Joe Siclari) nominated for a Locus award.

2007/08—"Distant Replay" (short story) nominated for a Hugo award.

2008/09—"Alastair Baffle's Emporium of Wonders" (novelette) won a Hugo award.

"Articles of Faith" (short story) nominated for a Hugo award.

Mike Resnick was the Worldcon Guest of Honor in 2007. He recently became BenBella Books' science fiction editor.

Literary Magic & Mayhem: It's interesting to compare the scenario to the finished story. It allows the reader to enjoy the puzzle of how the story was worked out by the writer as well as enjoying the puzzle of the mystery story.

Explorations: How did the writer embroider upon the chosen scenario?

How did the story work as a puzzle?

What was interesting about the world described in the story?

THE CASES

1. ***Whatdunits.*** New York: Daw Books, 1992, 335 p. ISBN: 0886775337.
CONTENTS: Introduction *by Mike Resnick;* True Faces *by Pat Cadigan;* Gut Reaction *by Jack C. Haldeman II;* Loss of Phase *by Anthony R. Lewis;* Its Own Reward *by Katharine Kerr;* Monkey See *by Roger MacBride Allen;* Heaven's Only Daughter *by Laura Resnick;* Heaven Scent *by Virginia Booth;* Lost Lamb *by Barbara Delaplace;* Cain's Curse *by Jack Nimersheim;* Murder On-line *by John DeChancie;* Color Me Dead *by Sandra Rector and P.M.F. Johnson;* Signs and Stones *by Judith Tarr;* Murder Under Glass *by Bob*

Liddil; It's the Thought That Counts *by Michael A. Stackpole;* The Colonel and the Alien *by Ralph Roberts;* Obscurocious *by Ray Aldridge;* An Incident at the Circus *by Rick Katze;* Dead Ringer *by Esther Friesner and Walter J. Stutzman.*

2. *More Whatdunits.* New York: Daw Books, 1993, 332 p. ISBN: 0886775574, 9780886775575.

CONTENTS: Introduction *by Mike Resnick;* Worthsayer *by Stanley Schmidt;* For Love of Juoun *by Jane Yolen;* DragNeuroNet *by John Gregory Betancourt;* Bauble *by David Gerrold;* Ashes to Ashes *by Beth Meacham;* The lady Louisiana Toy *by Barry N. Malzberg;* Alien Influences *by Kristine Kathryn Rusch;* The Pragmatists Take a Bow *by Thomas A. Easton;* Sincerity *by Patrick Nielsen Hayden;* Dark Odds *by Josepha Sherman;* Things Not Seen *by Martha Soukup;* Windows of the Soul *by Susan Casper;* The Whole Truth *by Susan Shwartz;* Way Out *by Jody Lynn Nye and Bill Fawcett;* The Killer Wore Spandex *by Brian M. Thomsen;* Catachresis *by Ginjer Buchanan;* Flight of Reason *by Tappan King;* She Was Blonde, She Was Dead—and Only Jimmilich Opstromommo Could Find Out Why!!! *by Janet Kagan;* The Ugly Earthling Murder Case *by George Alec Effinger.*

Rhine Research Center. (Editor)

Mystery in Mind Anthology

Genres/Themes Crossed: Paranormal, Secret Society X Traditional Mystery.

Subjects/Character Types: Spell-Casters, Shape-Shifters X Private Investigators.

Series/Stand-Alone: Anthology of short stories.

Scene of the Crime: Varies.

Detective: Varies.

Known Associates: Varies.

Premise: Stories of mysteries with paranormal elements.

Comment: The Rhine Research Center began as the Duke University parapsychology laboratory founded by Dr. J. B. Rhine in the 1930s. The laboratory now functions as an independent non-profit in Durham, North Carolina, and is devoted to research and education on parapsychology. They sent out a call for submissions for the anthology and received over 150 submissions. Research Center staff chose the works to be included in the anthology.

Literary Magic & Mayhem: Well-known and new authors wrote stories of ghosts, psychic phenomena, and death for this anthology. Most of the stories are stand-alones, except for "Burden of Guilt" by Rosemary Edghill, which features her series character Bast.

Explorations: Why would a serious parapsychological research team choose the story for publication?

THE CASES

Mystery in Mind: a Collection of Stories of the Paranormal. Durham, NC.: Rhine Research Center, 2002, 206 p. ISBN: 0972749403, 9780972749404.

CONTENTS: A Little Light on the Subject *by Martha C. Lawrence;* Cold Case *by L. L. Bartlett;* Hidden in Plain Sight by *Skye Alexander;* The Bag Lady Caper *by Margaret DiCanio;* Sara Morningsky *by Lee Driver;* The Storm *by Jon Fabris;* The File on Virginia Fairchild *by J.M.M. Holloway;* The Worst Thing *by Helen Rhine;* After the War *by David Terrenoire;* Future Imperfect *by Nicholas Knight;* Chance *by Elorise Holstad;* A Lover's Understanding *by Patricia Harrington;* Animism *by George M. Scott;* The Thirteenth Hole *by Lee Driver;* Art Eternal *by Nicole Burris;* Guilt *by Sarah E. Glenn;* Switching Chairs *by Amanda Marie;* Special *by Jordan Carpenter;* Emily Sees Red *by J.M.M. Holloway;* Haunted *by Scott Nicholson;* The Believers *by Didier Que'mener;* Unique Tours, Ltd. *by Michele Lassig;* Burden of Guilt *by Rosemary Edghill.*

RICHARDSON, Kat.

GREYWALKER

Genres/Themes Crossed: Secret Society X Hard-Boiled Mystery.

Subjects/Character Types: Ghosts, Vampires, Spell-Casters (Witches) X Private Investigator.

Series/Stand-Alone: Harper learns more about her gift and builds interesting relationships during the course of the series. These should be read in order.

Scene of the Crime: Present-day Seattle.

Detective: Harper Blaine makes her living as a private investigator.

Known Associates: Dr. Skelleher, who accepts that there are more things in heaven and earth than are dreamt of in medical textbooks and refers Harper to Ben and Mara Danziger. They're professors with an interest in the paranormal. Their infant son is Brian, and their household ghost is Albert. Other allies that she meets along the way include Quinton, a man of extraordinary talent with machinery and computer software, and William Novac, an antiques auctioneer.

Premise: In the course of a case, Harper was so badly injured that she died. She was brought back to life within a few minutes, but something had changed. She now lives with a foot in both worlds, the normal world and a world that exists in between this world and the next. The Danzigers refer to this in-between world as the "Grey." The Grey is inhabited by ghosts and by various types of magical beings. The Danzigers knowledge of the Grey is mostly theoretical, so they're not the most reliable of guides; but they're the only guides that Harper has. The Grey is not a place that Harper can access at will. Instead, there are moments when it sucks Harper in, and she can't find a way out to the everyday world. She knows it is dangerous, but there is no way to avoid it.

Comment: In a *Paranormality* interview on October 11, 2006 (http://paranormalityuniverse.blogspot.com/2006/10/first-sale-stories-kat-richardson.html) Kat Richardson revealed that an inspiration for the series was the television show *My Partner the Ghost*. She played with the premise of a private investigator who works *with* the ghost of his deceased partner and came up with the concept of a private investigator who works *for* ghosts. The series is set in Seattle and has a strong sense of place and of Seattle history. Kat Richardson's home page is at http://www.katrichardson.com/.

Literary Magic & Mayhem: Harper is tough but goodhearted. She's learning, and the reader gains understanding of Harper's powers and of the worlds she sees as she learns. The steps that she must take, the careful progress, coupled with sudden and sometimes frightening breakthroughs, are interesting, and make it clear that the power available is not a toy. She knows first hand how dangerous it is, but she has no choice: if she does not learn how to work with it, she will be swallowed up. Harper is not outrageously noble, but she tries to do what's right. The moments when she must choose between competing evils are both chilling and thought provoking. The romantic aspects do not dominate the book; instead, they reveal the characters in moments of particular vulnerability. One theme that runs through the series is that of people trying to connect, to support, and to understand each other. The romances, the friends, the mentors, even some of the villains, all serve to illuminate that theme in different ways. The interconnectedness of people of magic and of things is one of the most interesting aspects of the series.

Explorations: For Greywalker: What did you think of the ending?

How would the series be different if Mara were the protagonist? How would it change the mood of the series? What did the choice of Harper as protagonist give to the series?

In the series, different people are introduced not only to powers, but also to an entire world that they never imagined. Is there a moral responsibility to support those who are new? How do the different characters handle this question? Is it a moral or a practical question for those who choose whether or not to help?

THE CASES

1. ***Greywalker.*** New York: Roc, c2006, 341 p. ISBN: 045146107X.

SEATTLE, 2006. Harper is just trying to get by as an investigator, and to hold on to her sanity as a human being. It's not easy. She's having increasingly strong episodes of contact with the paranormal world. They're preceded by nausea and vertigo, she feels the threat of attack while she's immersed in the paranormal world, and she has an increasingly difficult time fighting her way back out. Mara Danziger gives her valuable information and even some training, but she doesn't know enough to appreciate the reality of the dangers that Harper is facing. Mara just knows that something is terribly wrong. There is a drain and a corruption of the power that is available in the world, and Mara suspects that Harper is somehow involved in the problem. Harper slowly comes to the conclusion that Mara is right. Harper may have to disappoint a client and incur the wrath of a vampire to avert a catastrophe.

ASSOCIATES: Dr. Skelleher—*who sends Harper to friends of his after warning her that their ideas sound like they're straight out of "Twilight Zone";* Ben and Mara Danziger—*who know a little about the "Grey";* Grigori Sergeyev—*one of Harper's clients, he hires Harper to find a parlor organ;* William Novak—*an interesting man;* Michael—*his brother;* Mrs. Ingstrom—*who must sell the goods from the Ingstrom Shipwrights warehouse;* Brandon—*who owns the auction business;* Colleen Shadley—*one of Harper's clients, she hires Harper to find her son;* Cameron—*Colleen's son;* Sarah—*Cameron's sister;* Chaos—*Harper's pet ferret.*

Harper also meets many of the vampire community of Seattle, including: Edward Kammerling—*their leader;* Alice Liddell—*who would like to see Edward toppled;* Carlos—*a necromancer as well as a vampire;* Gwen—*who tries to be negligible;* and Wygan—*the most frightening of them all.* Quinton—*helps Harper set up a burglar alarm in her office.*

2. ***Poltergeist.*** New York: Roc, 2007, 341 p. ISBN: 9780451461506.

SEATTLE, OCTOBER 2006. Pacific Northwest University Professor Tuckman, a psychologist, worked to replicate the "Philips" experiments. These showed that a group of people can, through the combined power of their minds, create all the phenomena that would normally be ascribed to a poltergeist. The group is given a target ghost. It seems that, if the manifestations can be attributed to an outside entity, the ghost, then the members of the group, become less self-conscious, and the power of the manifestations increases. It also seems that tension between the members of the group increases the power of the manifestations. Dr. Tuckman is actually running two experiments. The first, the one that the group of volunteer subjects knows about, is the replication of the Philips experiments. The personality they're trying to use as a focus for the group energies is Celia Falwell, who died in 1943. They've been successful in using this focus to create PK (poltergeist-like) activity. The second experiment, the one that is hidden from the volunteers, involves Dr. Tuckman's observations of the volunteer group. This second experiment is being run with the help of a confederate that the professor planted in the group of "volunteers." The confederate's name is Mark Lupoldi. Mark's job is to help create PK effects far beyond what the group can actually accomplish so that Professor Tuckman can observe the group dynamics as they seem to tap into extraordinary power. Dr. Tuckman expected the group to create some minor audio and telekinetic effects, and he intended to escalate matters using Mark. In the beginning, all went as planned. Mark created some fake PK effects, the group's enthusiasm and confidence increased, and the group began to create some real effects on their own. Then matters began to spin out of Dr. Tuckman's control. He'd planned to have Mark create some more exciting fake effects, but before he did so, the group created more powerful phenomena on their own. In fact, the PK effects were so far beyond Dr. Tuckman's expectations that he suspects a hoax. He cannot figure out how these new effects are being faked, and he hires private investigator Harper Blaine to find out who is sabotaging his experiment. Unlike Dr. Tuckman, Harper does believe in poltergeists. If she finds out that the phenomena are the work of a poltergeist, she will have a hard time convincing her client of the truth.

ASSOCIATES: Mara Danziger—*a witch who is helping Harper learn to cope with the Grey;* Ben Danziger—*Mara's husband who is an expert on the theoretical aspects of the Grey;* Brian—*Mara and Ben's two-year-old son;* Albert—*the ghost in the Danziger household;* Quinton—*an electronics genius;* Rey Solis—*Seattle Police Detective;* Phoebe Mason—*owner of bookstore Old Possum's Books 'n' Beans;* Hugh—*Phoebe's brother;* Germaine—*Phoebe's cousin;* "Poppy,"—*Phoebe's father;* and Amanda Leaman—*who works for Phoebe;* William Novak—*who's dating Harper;* Cameron Shadley—*a new vampire;* Carlos—*vampire, Cameron's mentor.*

Professor Gartner Tuckman—*Harper's client;* his research subjects are: Teril "Terry" Dornier—*a graduate student;* Denise "Frankie" Francisco—*who works in the Psychology Department;* Ken George—*a young Indian artist who had one encounter with a ghost in his childhood;* Dale Stahlqvist—*whose chief interest is money;* Carolyn "Caro" Knight-Stahlqvist—*his wife, who claims that the first lady mayor of Seattle, Bertha Knight Landes (deceased), was her great aunt;* Patricia Railsback—*housewife and mother;* Hannah, Dylan, and Ethan—*her children;* Wayne Hopke—*who was in the military;* and Ian Markine—*who is dating Ana Choi.*

3. ***Underground.*** New York: Roc, 2008, 344 p. ISBN: 9780451462121.

SEATTLE, JANUARY 2007. Harper's friend Quinton takes her to the Great Northern Tunnel to see a corpse. It wasn't hit by a train. It looks as if it was... chewed. It's not the first. Soon Harper is encountering zombies everywhere in Seattle. She and Quinton search among the homeless of Seattle trying to learn about the missing (probable victims) and trying to find the killer.

ASSOCIATES: Will Novak—*who is in a faltering relationship with Harper;* Quinton—*who comes to Harper for help in bringing the police into the case;* Law Enforcement personnel include: Detective Rey Solis—*who is both smart and tenacious;* and Reuben "Fish" Fishkiller—*coroner.* Chaos—*Harper's pet ferret;* Quinton—*an electrical genius;* Lassiter "Lass"—*a homeless man who was given an electrical device for protection;* Zip—*homeless;* Rosaria Cabrera—*homeless;* Taker and his dog Bella—*at the Bread of Life Mission;* Sandy and Blue Jay—*at the Union Gospel Mission;* Tall Grass—*a.k.a. Thomas Newman, homeless;* Jenny Nin—*homeless;* and Grandpa Dan—*homeless.* Edward Kammeling—*vampire;* and Lady Gwendolyn of Anorexia—*vampire;* Carlos—*vampire and necromancer;* Cameron—*vampire, Carlos's protégé;* Phoebe—*of Old Possum's Books 'n' Beans bookstore;* Rick—*the Underground Tour's historian;* Mara Danziger—*witch;* Ben Danziger—*Mara's husband, a scholar;* Albert—*the Danziger's ghost;* Brian—*the Danziger's two-year-old son.* Fern Laguire—*an NSA agent;* James Jason Purlis—*who is a wanted man.* Grandma Ella Graham—*who knows about Sisiutl Zeqwa, the guardian of Qamaits's pool. She names Harper Pheasant Woman.*

4. **"The Third Death of the Little Clay Dog,"** a novella in *Mean Streets.* New York: Roc, 2009, p. 145–243. ISBN: 9780451462497.

SEATTLE, OCTOBER 2007. Maria-Luz Arbildo died a week ago. She left a job for Harper. She directed that Harper would be given a bequest if Harper hand-carried a clay statue of a little dog to the grave of Hector Purecete in Oaxaca City, Mexico on the night of All Saints Day (November 1), and stayed there until daybreak on November 2.

ASSOCIATES: Attorney Nanette Grover—*acting for Maria-Luz Arbildo;* Reuben "Fish" Fishkiller—*coroner;* Chaos—*Harper's pet ferret;* Quinton—*who ferret-sits;* Mr. Will Banda—*who was Miss Arbildo's attorney;* Miguel "Mickey" and Señora Acoa—*who help Harper search for the correct grave;* Miguel can see Ernesto—*deceased* and Iko the dog—*deceased;* Mercedes Villaflores—*Miguel's aunt.* Carmen, Lucia, Maria-Luz Carmen Arbildo, her father, and Jimenez—*are all seen by Harper in the graveyard.*

ROBB, J. D.

Naked in Death

Genres/Themes Crossed: Science Fiction X Police Procedural.

Subjects/Character Types: Future Earth X Police Procedural.

Series/Stand-Alone: There are significant changes in the relationships over time. This series is best read in order.

Scene of the Crime: New York, mid-21st century.

Detective: NYPSD (New York Police and Security Department) Eve Dallas. She was an abused child who, at the age of eight, finally killed her tormentor and then ran out to the street where she was found by the Dallas Police. She grew up in a series of foster homes and threw everything she had into becoming a police officer. She regards her role as a homicide detective as standing up for those who can no longer defend themselves; she is driven to get justice for the dead. At the outset of the series, she is barely 30 years old.

Known Associates: In the first book, Eve meets Roarke, a self-made billionaire. Eve's first partner, Captain Ryan Feeney, was her mentor; now he runs the Electronics Detection Division of the NYPSD (the New York Police and Security Department). Years ago, Eve arrested Mavis Freestone; Mavis went straight, but she never became ordinary. Mavis became a singer and, somehow, through all of this, she and Eve became good friends. Dr. Charlotte Mira is an NYPSD psychiatrist: she is one of the top criminal profilers in the country, and as the psychiatric specialist attached to the NYPSD, she administers testing for fitness for duty. She is also a counselor.

Premise: In this future, there have been some technological innovations, mostly of the sort that offer convenience or save time. Cars can soar above ground traffic. An AutoChef can create hot food, usually some sort of soy product processed to resemble something else. (They can be stocked with real food, including real coffee beans to make real coffee, but that's prohibitively expensive.) In fact, most of the food available is derived from soy products. There are droids who do menial work. Commercial spaceflight exists: most flights go to resorts that have been built on other planets.

Extensive civil unrest in the first two decades of the 21st century paved the way for many societal changes. The Social Reform Army overthrew the French government (and were, themselves, deposed after only six months). In the United States, riots were put down by the Army in what came to be known as the Urban Wars. The conflict destroyed whole cities; over 30 years later, some areas have not yet been rebuilt. In the aftermath of the Urban Wars, there was massive social reform. Firearms were banned; now only licensed collectors can purchase guns. Prostitution was legalized: at the age of 18 people can apply to become "licensed companions." Licensed companions must pay licensing fees, undergo mandatory health exams (both physical and psychological screening), and pay the "sin tax." Cancer has been cured (but the common cold has not). Body enhancement has gone far beyond plastic surgery. People pay to have everything from eye color to body contours altered. New illegal designer drugs have been invented; one of the most common is "Zeus," which makes a man feel like a god.

Comment: There are people who sneer at these books because they sneer at romance authors. It's their loss; this is a fantastic series. Different books in the series explore different types of questions. Some explore humanity's responses to social changes, others explore ethical and practical questions created by new technologies.

Nora Roberts has written more than 150 romance novels. She was the first author inducted into the Romance Writers of America Hall of Fame. She writes the *In Death* series under the pseudonym J. D. Robb and also writes as Sarah Hardesty and Jill March. As of 2006, Roberts's novels had spent over 660 weeks on the New York Times Bestseller List.

Nora Roberts's Web site at http://www.noraroberts.com/ provides biographical information, information on her books, several free short stories, and a spreadsheet listing her works.

Literary Magic & Mayhem: The characters are valiant, smart, and funny. They work at jobs that mean something to them. This is a short description of Eve:

> The dead were her business. She lived with them, worked with them, studied them. She dreamed of them. And because that didn't seem to be enough, in some deep, secret chamber of her heart, she mourned for them. (Glory in Death, p. 1)

Eve's partner is Peabody. Peabody is no less driven than Eve, but she is less haunted. She cares deeply for the people she serves and protects, but is willing to explore interesting distractions which sometimes irritates Eve, as in this section where Eve chides Peabody (*Holiday in Death,* p. 94) after Peabody flirts with a suspect who's cute (and good to his mom):

> "We've got two more interviews to conduct, Peabody. Try to control your hormones."
>
> "I do, Dallas, I do." She sighed as she climbed back into the car. "But it's so nice when they control me."

One of the appealing aspects of the series is that Eve builds a family out of the people in her life. Feeney is the father figure, Mira is the mother, and Peabody is the little sister. These dynamics play out in many scenes. For instance, when Peabody has her first undercover assignment, there are many people rooting for her, supporting her, and watching over her, but they all have to stay away from the action because the suspect would run if he spotted a group of police officers. The assignment takes place at a bar that is owned by Roarke. He owns many city properties and is willing to work with the police, so police actions frequently take place at his businesses. He has helped set up the surveillance and has claimed the right to be on scene. Feeney and Eve monitor the action electronically, from a van parked on the street. When Holloway (the suspect) meets and then molests Peabody, the entire team is enraged and protective; but Peabody can take care of herself: she punches Halloway in the nose (to general approval). Eve is so angry at Holloway that she's incoherent. Feeney is just as furious, but neither can break cover. Roarke steps in as the bar owner to throw Holloway out of the bar. Holloway makes the mistake of referring to Peabody as a bitch and saying that she asked for it, and Roarke loses his temper:

> "The bitch asked for it."
>
> "Oh, now then, that was the wrong thing to say. Entirely."
>
> "His Irish comes out when he's pissed. Listen to the music of it," Feeney said sentimentally as Eve only continued to make violent sounds in her throat.
>
> On what might have been a sigh, Roarke hammered a fist into Holloway's stomach, kneed him handily in the balls, and let him drop. (*Holiday in Death,* p. 160)

One lovely aspect of the stories is that damsels in distress (particularly police officers) are always depicted as capable, including being able to handle most physical threats. Note that, in this case, Peabody took care of herself, before Roarke stepped in. It's one of the themes of the books: women are competent; if they need to be rescued, it's from a situation that would be equally difficult for a man to handle.

Readers come to know all the characters. None of the relationships are static, and one of the joys of reading the series is to see the growth in the relationships and the characters.

Nora Roberts broke one of the unwritten rules of writing early in her career when she shifted the point of view in her romance novels back and forth between the female and male leads. She made the point that there were two people involved in the romance, and that both were going through something interesting. She takes that a step further in these books, also dipping into the point of view of the murderer.

Explorations: How much have people changed in a half-century?

Roarke and Eve are both survivors who remade themselves. What was important to each? What became the core of the person Eve created? What is essential to her?

THE CASES

1. ***Naked in Death.*** New York: Berkley Books, c1995, 313 p. ISBN: 0425148297.

New York, February 2058. Eve is holding on to the ragged edge of her composure; it's taking everything she has got. She's overwhelmed by grief and by memories because she was unable to save the life of a three-year-old girl. Eve got the call when she was just blocks away from where the child was being threatened. She raced to the site, threw both caution and procedure out the window, and moved as fast as anyone could have moved. She was too late. The girl's father had killed and dismembered her. Eve finally breaks down and tells Roarke:

> "There should have been something I could have done to stop it."
> "To stop a murder before it happens, you'd have to be inside the head of a killer," he said quietly. "Who could live with that?"
> "I can live with that." She hurled it back at him. And it was pure truth. She could live with anything but failure. "Serve and protect—it's not just a phrase, it's a promise. If I can't keep my word, I'm nothing..." (p. 105)

Eve can't bear that she wasn't in time to save the child. She shot the little girl's murderer in combat as he attempted to add Eve to the list of those he'd killed; procedure dictates that she must undergo psychological testing before resuming her duties, but testing was held in abeyance by Police Chief Simpson so he could put her on another case. That case is of a murdered licensed companion (a prostitute) a girl from a wealthy and powerful family. Even worse than the fact of her murder is the note under her, a note that promises that she's just "one of six," that there will be more murders. Eve fights with her inner demons while trying to stop a serial killer.

Associates: Personnel at the New York Police and Security Department include: Chief of Police Edward T. Simpson; Commander Jack Whitney—*Eve's boss;* Captain Ryan Feeney—*who was Eve's first partner (and is now Head of the Electronic Detection Division);* and Dr. Charlotte Mira—*the department psychiatrist who tries to help Eve.*

Mavis Freestone—*Eve's best friend;* Galahad—*who was the cat of murder victim Georgie Castle;* Nadine Furst—*the Channel 75 crime reporter who receives some interesting information and goes to Eve for confirmation;*

Roarke—*a wealthy suspect, the computer calculates the probability of his guilt at 82.6 percent;* Summerset—*Roarke's butler, he informs Eve that Roarke could do better than to end up with her;* Caro—*Roarke's secretary;* Sharon DeBlass—*the first victim;* Senator Gerald DeBlass—*Sharon's grandfather;* Anna—*his wife;* Derrick Rockman—*the Senator's adjutant;* Richard DeBlass and Elizabeth Barrister—*Sharon's parents;* Congresswoman Catherine DeBlass—*Sharon's aunt;* Justin Summit—*Sharon's uncle;* Franklin—*Sharon's cousin;* Charles Monroe—*licensed companion and neighbor of the first victim;* Francois—*deli owner;* Hetta Finestein—*Eve's downstairs neighbor;* Sebastion—*a beauty consultant.*

In the course of this book, Eve and Roarke become lovers and reveal parts of their pasts to each other. Roarke feels betrayed by being the target of Eve's investigation until Feeney sets him straight. Feeney and Roarke show up to stop the killer just in time to pull Eve off him.

2. ***Glory in Death.*** New York: Berkley Books, c1995, 313 p. ISBN: 0425150984; 9780425150986.

NEW YORK, MAY 2058. Eve knew Prosecuting Attorney Cicely Towers in life. She was strong, smart, and successful. Eve did not know her as well as Eve's boss, Commander Whitney, knew her. Cicely Towers was a close friend of his family. From the moment Eve asks to interview him and his wife regarding Cicely Towers's life, Whitney is defensive. When reporter C. J. Morse begins talking about a cover-up, Eve goes on the offensive. The press is a pain; Eve and Roarke are having relationship problems; Eve's boss strikes out at her in fury, telling her that she lacks compassion. Nightmares are robbing Eve of sleep... everything is coming apart. Eve digs in and sets herself up as bait for the killer. She knows that her plans could also focus the killer on reporter Nadine Furst; Nadine was warned and knows the risks. The killer's next strike leaves Eve mired in guilt, and more determined than ever to bring him down.

ASSOCIATES: Personnel at the New York Police and Security Department include Chief of Police Harrison Tibble—*who turns out to have compassion and brains;* Commander Jack Whitney—*Eve's boss, who asks Eve to take on the investigation and then lashes out at Eve and undermines her as she's trying to do the job he gave her;* Captain Ryan Feeney—*Head of the Electronic Detection Division;* Officer Delia Peabody—*first on the scene of one of the murders, she impresses Eve;* Dr. Charlotte Mira—*department psychiatrist, demands Eve's trust and tells Eve that she, too, was a victim of abuse;* Galahad—*Eve's cat;* Mavis Freestone—*Eve's best friend, is singing at the Blue Squirrel;* C. J. Morse and Nadine Furst—*are reporters for Channel 75;* Louise Kirski—*is one of their editors;* David and Mirina Angelini—*are the children of victim Cicely Towers;* Marco Angelini—*their father;* Randall Slade—*Mirina's fiancé;* Crack—*the bouncer at the Down and Dirty club;* George Hammett—*Cicely Tower's lover;* Anna—*Commander Whitney's wife;* attorney Linda Whitney—*Anna and Jack*

Whitney's daughter; Suzanna Kimball—*the widow of a cop;* Roarke—*a suspect once more, wants Eve to commit to their relationship and move in with him.*

In this book Eve and Dr. Mira develop a relationship based on understanding and trust and Eve admits that she's having flashbacks of the abuse of her childhood.

Roarke reorganizes his business to get rid of any taint of illegal practices. Summerset, Roarke's butler is unhappy at the way Eve and Roarke's relationship is progressing, but ends up admiring Eve's best friend, Mavis. Roarke and Eve move in together and, at the end of the book, he proposes.

3. ***Immortal in Death.*** New York: Berkley Books, 1996, 312 p. ISBN: 0425153789; 9780425153789.

New York, June 2058. When Carter "Boomer" Johannsen is pulled out of the river, it is apparent that he was badly beaten before he died. Officer Peabody recognizes his name and identifies him as one of Eve's informants. Eve feels an obligation: he was one of hers. She has to fight to get assigned the case; her superiors are unwilling to have her, one of their top detectives, spend time investigating the death of a man who lived so close to the edge. Eve asks that Peabody be assigned to work with her. Together they search Boomer's apartment and find that he probably did his best to hide there in the last few weeks of his life: something had him very frightened. They also find a disk with a chemical formula. It seems to be for a new illegal drug, called Immortality, that combines the properties of uppers and aphrodisiacs with the fountain of youth. There are many who would kill for such a prize. Eve's life gets more complicated when her best friend, Mavis, is framed for murder.

Associates: Roarke—*is planning a wedding with Eve;* Leonardo—*Mavis's new boyfriend, a fashion designer working on Eve's wedding gown;* the model Pandora—*is Leonardo's bitter ex-girlfriend,* Personnel at the New York Police and Security Department include Chief of Police Harrison Tibble—*who is more of a cop than a politician;* Commander Jack Whitney—*Eve's boss, he knows that he lost her trust and friendship over the last case;* Captain Ryan Feeney—*Head of the Electronic Detection Division;* Officer Delia Peabody—*is assigned to help Eve investigate Boomer's death;* Boomer—*an informant;* Lieutenant Jake T. Castro—*of Illegal Substances (drugs);* Chief Lab Tech Dickie Berenski—*who is susceptible to bribes;* Galahad—*Eve's cat;* Nadine Furst—*the reporter on the crime beat for channel 75;* Justin Young—*actor,* Jerry Fitzgerald—*model;* Paul Redford—*producer;* Dr. Engrave—*an expert in pharmaceuticals;* Crack—*the bouncer at the Down and Dirty club;* Dennis—*who runs the ZigZag club;* Summerset—*Roarke's butler, he champions Mavis;* Biff—*a fabric expert;* Trina—*a stylist;* Dr. Ambrose—*is Head of Chemical Rehab at the Midtown Rehabilitation Center for Substance Addiction;* and Mark—*is the florist for the wedding.*

In the course of this book Eve is able to tell Dr. Charlotte Mira, department psychiatrist, that more of her memories of her father are coming back. Then she has something more than a nightmare—she has a flashback, and she knows that she killed her father.

4. ***Rapture in Death.*** New York: Berkley Books, 1996, 310 p. ISBN: 0425155188; 9780425155189.

New York, August 2058. It's a busman's honeymoon for Eve when there's a death at Roarke's half-constructed Olympus Resort. At first Eve believed that autotronic tech Drew Mathias committed suicide. After two more odd "suicides", Eve begins to wonder if he had some help.

Associates: As the book starts, Roarke and Eve are on their honeymoon at the Olympus Resort. Jack Carter—*Olympus resort tech;* Dr. Wang—*who stands in as Medical Examiner;* Reeanna Ott and William Shaffer—*who work for Roarke and were on the team that designed the Olympus Resort.*

Officer Delia Peabody—*assigned as Eve's assistant.* Others working at the NYPSD include: Dr. Morris—*Lower Manhattan City Morgue Medical Examiner;* Dr. Mira—*police profiler and counselor;* Captain Feeney—*Eve's mentor, thinks Eve's making a big deal out of a self-termination;* Commander Whitney—*who works to give her a week to complete her investigation.* Chief Dudley—*in Washington;* Vito Salvatori—*murderer;* S. T. Fitzhugh—*Salvatori's attorney;* Leanore Bastwick—*one of Fitzhugh's partners;* Arthur Foxx—*Fitzhugh's companion, he believes that Leanore is trying to steal Fitzhugh away from him;* Mavis Freestone—*who is cohabiting with Leonardo, working at the Down and Dirty club and making an album with musician Jess Barrow;* Big Mary—*who is at the recording session;* Cerise Devane—*CEO of Tattler Enterprises, she commits suicide, almost taking Eve with her;* Frank Rabbit—*Cerise's assistant;* Nadine Furst—*of Channel 75, recorded the entire episode on tape;* Summerset—*who watches Roarke for Eve;* Caro—*Roarke's secretary;* Galahad—*Eve and Roarke's cat;* Clevis—*an elderly exhibitionist.*

5. ***Ceremony in Death.*** New York: Berkley Books, 1997, 329 p. ISBN: 0425157628; 9780425157626.

New York, October 2058. It begins with a funeral, the funeral of a good cop, Frank Wojinski. At the funeral, Frank's granddaughter, Alice, slips a note to Eve, asking for a meeting. When they meet, Alice tells Eve that Frank was murdered, that he'd been investigating a dark coven. Alice had been part of that coven until she witnessed them sacrificing a child. She'd run to a white witch, but was afraid that the dark coven would find a way to get to her. She was right. Eve is soon on the trail of a multiple murderer. This book ends up walking a fine line: some of the witches are charlatans, some are simply followers of a lovely religion, some have power.

Associates: Roarke—*Eve's husband,* and Officer Peabody—*Eve's aide,* both find that they believe (at least a little) in magic. As Roarke says to Eve:

> Your world is relatively small, Eve. You couldn't call it sheltered, but it's limited. You haven't seen a giant's dance, or felt the power of the ancient stones. You haven't run your hand over the Ogham carving in the trunk of a tree petrified by time or heard the sounds that whisper through the mist that coats sacred ground. (p. 93)

Dr. Mira—*who has a Wiccan daughter;* Commander Whitney—*who orders Eve to keep all information about the investigation away from Captain Feeney;* Captain Feeney—*who was trained by Wojinski;* Sally—*Wojinski's wife;* Brenda—*their daughter;* Alice—*Brenda's daughter, her desire to compare white and black magic sets this story in motion;* and James—*Brenda's son, an electronics genius who wants to be a cop.* Mavis—*who gets a record deal and suspects that Eve set it up.* Those involved in black magic include Selina Cross—*owner of the Athame club;* Alban—*her companion;* Louis Trivane—*her attorney;* Lobar—*whose real name was Robert Allen Mathias;* and Thomas Wineburg—*of Wineburg Financial.* Those involved in white magic include Isis Paige—*who owns the Wiccan shop and consultation center;* Charles Forte—*Isis's partner;* Mirium Hopkins; Cassandra; and Leila.

6. ***Vengeance in Death.*** New York: Berkley Books, 1997, 372 p. ISBN: 0425160394; 9780425160398.

New York, November 2058. A murderer calls Eve with riddles, telling her that he's the wrath of God. His first victim was an old friend of Roarke. When Roarke learns about the murder, he realizes that it might tie in to his and Summerset's past, into crimes long since buried. He's right. In the course of the book, he must reveal part of his bloody past to Eve, and she has to decide what she's going to do about it. As the murders continue, all clues point to Summerset as the prime suspect. He's pretty sure that Eve would throw him to the wolves in a heartbeat, so he doesn't see much reason to cooperate in the investigation. Eve's sure that someone has set him up, but can she prove it?

Associates: John Henry Bonning—*who threw his partner out a window.* The NYPSD includes Chief Tibble; Commander Whitney; Officer Delia Peabody—*Eve's aide;* Ian McNab—*new to the EDD;* Detective Baxter; and Dr. Morris—*Medical Examiner.* Inspector Katherine Farrell—*is an officer in Dublin.* Summerset—*Marlena's father, he raised Roarke and now acts as Roarke majordomo;* Jennie O'Leary, Brian Kelly, Patrick Murray, and Thomas Brennan—*helped Roarke when he was tracking Marlena's killers;* Eileen—*Thomas's wife;* Shawn Conroy, Maureen Mulligan, and Sinead Duggin—*work at the "Green Shamrock";* Audrey Morrell—*is involved with Summerset;* Kevin—*a seven-year-old street urchin;* Dopey—*Kevin's kitten;*

Richard DeBlass and Elizabeth Barrister—*who lost their daughter Sharon* (see *Naked in Death*).

7. ***Holiday in Death.*** New York: Berkley Books, 1998, 326 p. ISBN: 0425163717; 9780425163719.

NEW YORK, DECEMBER 2058. The Christmas spirit seems to have taken over New York. Mayhem seems to increase with the rise of the holiday spirit. Eve revels in some of it; but then her investigation turns up a murderer dressed as Santa Claus. Even worse than that, he leaves a broach of a partridge in a pear tree with the body of the *first* victim. Eve understands that it's the first of 12 planned murders when Peabody sings her *The Twelve Days of Christmas.* Eve does everything in her power to find the killer before "Santa" strikes again.

ASSOCIATES: Roarke—*Eve's husband;* Summerset—*who's avoiding Eve;* Mavis Freestone—*Eve's best friend;* Leonardo—*lives with Mavis;* Trina—*a beautician.*

The New York law enforcement community includes: NYPSD Chief Tibble; Commander Whitney—*Eve's boss;* Captain Ryan Feeney—*who now heads EDD;* Officer Peabody—*who is not happy about working with an EDD Detective;* Ian McNab—*the EDD Detective with whom Peabody must work;* Dickie—*Lab Tech;* and Carla Rollins—*Assistant Prosecuting Attorney.* Rudy and Piper Hoffman—*are the owners/managers of the Personally Yours Dating service (Peabody refers to them as Ken and Barbie);* Clients of the dating service include Jeremy Vandoren—*who was going to propose to Marianna Hawley;* Sarabeth Greenbalm—stripper *at the "Sweet Spot";* Dorian Marcell—*who is looking for a soulmate;* Donnie Ray Michael—*who is good to his mother;* Charles Monroe—*licensed companion, he still calls Eve "Lieutenant Sugar";* Cissy—*who is now with Jacko Gonzales;* Brent Holloway—*commercial model;* Rodney—*his droid.* People who work at the All Things Beautiful Salon include Yvette—*who does not recognize "Roarke's wife";* and Simon—*who does;* Anton; and Stevie. Other characters include Nadine Furst—*reporter on the crime beat for Channel 75;* and Ms. Kates—*jeweler.*

8. **"Midnight in Death,"** in the anthology *Silent Night.* New York: Jove Books, 1998, p. 247–340. ISBN: 0515123854; 9780515123852.

NEW YORK, DECEMBER 2058 (BEGINNING CHRISTMAS DAY). Three years ago, Eve's work helped put away serial killer David Palmer. He received a sentence of eight consecutive life terms off-planet for the torture–murders he perpetrated. Now he has escaped. Eve realizes that he's in New York when the body of the judge who sentenced him is found. There's a list of six names on the body. The judge's name is at the top; Eve's name is at the bottom. What makes Eve's blood run cold is that Dr. Mira's name is one of the names in the middle.

ASSOCIATES: Roarke—*Eve's husband;* Peabody—*who comes back to work, still a little shaky from the events on Christmas Eve;* Ian McNab—*who goes off planet with Peabody to investigate computer access at the prison;* Nadine Furst—*of Channel 75 receives a disk of the first two killings;* Detective Feeney—*Head of EDD;* Dickie—*Chief Lab Tech;* Morse—*Medical Examiner;* Summerset—*Roarke's butler;* Tom and Helen Palmer—*the murderer's parents;* Lana—*a car salesman;* and Jimmy Ripsky—*who was in the wrong place at the wrong time.*

Roarke and Eve have to work out how they feel about letting each other function, even when there is danger.

9. ***Conspiracy in Death.*** New York: Berkley Books, c1999, 386 p. ISBN: 0425168131; 9780425168134.

NEW YORK, JANUARY 2059. Someone (and this someone apparently has political connections) is carefully, surgically, removing organs from the homeless and the impoverished and leaving the corpses behind. The case is a puzzle. The organs taken are too diseased and worn out to be worth anything. (At least until the killer makes an error and takes a liver from a woman, Jilessa Brown, who would have become a cancer survivor: her liver had started regenerating before she was killed.) Eve finds that some officers have taken less trouble, less time, and less effort because the victims are at the lowest strata of society. One of those officers, Ellen Bowers, is furious when Eve reprimands her. Bowers is unbalanced; she never should have been able to get on the force, and now she does her best to destroy Eve's career. Bowers is helped (and paid) by conspirators who want Eve off her current case. Eve's reputation is that she will go to the mat to protect and defend, including defending the "sidewalk sleepers"—the homeless. The killer wants her off the case; he begins with threats, but he won't stop there. This book begins with the criminal's point of view, a device that is used frequently in subsequent books.

ASSOCIATES: Roarke—*who supports, protects, and bullies Eve through her suspension;* Summerset—*Roarke's butler, who knows something is horribly wrong when Eve is civil to him;* Officer Peabody, Captain Feeney, and Detective Ian McNab—*who stand by Eve;* Commander Whitney—*who also stands by Eve, although he follows procedure;* Chief Tibble—*who does the same;* Officer Ellen Bowers—*who is bitterly jealous of Eve;* Officer Troy Trueheart—*who knows the "sidewalk sleepers" by name;* Gimp—*a homeless man;* Detective Rosswell—*who has a gambling problem;* Detective Baxter—*who gets decked by Roarke when he comes to interrogate Eve about a murder;* IAB (Internal Affairs) Detective Webster—*who must investigate the charges;* Paris Detective Marie DuBois—*who would have found out more about the Paris victim, but cats had been at the body;* Detective Kimiki—*Chicago P.D.;* Wilson McRae—*who was an officer in the Chicago Police Department, but gave up his badge and retired when his family was threatened;* Karen—*McRae's pregnant wife;* Will—*their five-year-old son;* Dr. Mira—*who counsels Roarke on how to help Eve;* Medical Examiner Morris—*who is impressed by the killer's work;* surgeon Colin Cagney—*Chief of*

Staff at the Drake Center of Medicine; Dr. Tia Wo—*one of the Drake Center's general surgeons, with a specialty in organ transplant and repair;* Dr. Bradley Young—*Chief Research Technician;* Michael Waverly—*current President of the AMA;* Hans Vanderhaven—*surgeon;* Louise Dimatto—*Cagney's niece, she runs the Canal Street Clinic;* Ledo—*who gives Eve information;* Leonardo—*who is one of the designers contributing to the Drake charity fashion show;* Mavis Freestone—*who attends the fashion show to support Leonardo;* and Nadine Furst—*Channel 75's crime reporter who uses information leaked by Eve to light a fire under the suspects.*

10. *Loyalty in Death.* New York: Berkley Books, c1999, 358 p. ISBN: 042517140X; 9780425171400.

New York, February 2059. It started simply enough, with a crime of passion. J. C. Branson's lover drove a Branson 8000 drill through his heart and then called the police to come pick her up. Eve struggles to make sure that justice is done for Branson while she tries to out-think a terrorist group that calls itself Cassandra. When Cassandra's demands aren't met, the carnage begins. Cassandra is threatening another "Arlington." On September 25, 2023, the Urban Wars were about over. The terrorist group Apollo blew up the Pentagon in Arlington, Virginia. They not only blew it up, they used an explosive that vaporized the building. It killed eight thousand people. Cassandra is following the pattern of escalating destruction that was set by Apollo. Eve's team is in a race to try to locate and evacuate Cassandra's targets before more people die.

Associates: Roarke—*whose properties are targeted by Cassandra;* Zeke—*Peabody's 23-year-old brother who comes to New York for a carpentry job;* Officer Peabody and Detective Ian McNab—*who act on their attraction to each other;* Commander Whitney and Chief Tibble—*who fight the FBI to keep the case in the hands of Eve's team;* Lieutenant Anne Malloy—*from the NYPSD Explosives and Bombs unit, she handles the team that defuses the bombs.*

Many years ago, the FBI killed the head of Apollo, James Rowan, but some of his associates are still at large: Monica Rowan—*James Rowan's wife;* Charlotte—*their daughter;* William Henson—*who was James Rowan's right hand man;* Lisbeth Cooke—*who was J. C. Branson's lover;* B. Donald Branson—*J. C.'s brother;* Clarissa Branson—*B. Donald's wife;* Chris Tipple—*who was J. C.'s executive assistant;* Suzanna Day—*the attorney who drew up J. C.'s will;* Lucas Mantz—*who is Lisbeth's criminal defense attorney;* Ratso—*who is troubled by The Fixer's (Howard Bassi's) death: he tells Eve that The Fixer had been designing explosives for someone;* Captain Ryan Feeney—*of the Electronic Detective Division, admired The Fixer's work;* Mr. Paul Lamont—*who works for Roarke;* Nadine Furst—*a crime reporter who offers to help in any way she can;* Mavis—*who returns from her successful tour and helps out with Zeke.*

11. ***Witness in Death.*** New York: Berkley Books, c2000, 357 p. ISBN: 0425173631; 9780425173633.

NEW YORK, MARCH 2059. Roarke takes Eve to opening night in his newly constructed New Globe Theater. The play is Agatha Christie's *Witness for the Prosecution,* and Eve is transported. She can exercise her deductive talents on a pretend-crime; she can solve it as if it were a game. She finds it fascinating, and she's one of the first in the theater to realize when something goes horribly wrong. The leading man is murdered before thousands of witnesses. Eve soon learns that everyone on the crew had the means and the opportunity and that everyone in the cast had a motive.

ASSOCIATES: The case has Eve thinking about true love, and she plans a romantic dinner for Roarke. EDD Detective Ian McNab—*who asks Roarke for romantic advice;* Officer Delia Peabody—*who is mortified when licensed companion Charles Monroe reveals to Eve that he and Peabody have not slept together;* Charles Monroe—*who is a romantic;* Eve—*who prefers not to know about her coworker's sex lives;* Officer Troy Trueheart—*who gets a chance to be part of the murder investigation;* Pauline Trueheart—*Troy's mother.*

The cast of *Witness for the Prosecution* includes: Areena Mansfield—*the leading lady;* Carly Landsdowne—*this play is her big break;* Michael Proctor—*understudy for the male lead;* Kenneth Stiles—*who knew the victim many years ago;* Eliza Rothchild—*who is glad to be back in the theater;* Linus Quim—*stagehand;* and Ralph Biden—*who is on the cleaning crew.*

In the course of the investigation, Eve also encounters: Marylou Jorgensen—*bookie;* Herbert Finestein—*who was assigned the autopsies by Chief Medical Examiner Morse;* Tomjohn Lewis—*who replaces Eve's computer;* Commander Whitney; EDD Captain Feeney; Dr. Mira; Nadine Furst—*crime reporter, confesses to Eve about Nadine's past relationship with the victim.*

12. ***Judgment in Death.*** New York: Berkley Books, c2000, 356 p. ISBN: 0425176304; 9780425176306.

NEW YORK, EARLY SPRING 2059. Detective Taj Kohli was killed in a club named Purgatory. Taj was moonlighting. At first glance, he was just in the wrong place at the wrong time. However, his badge was placed under the body and 30 coins were scattered around his corpse. The badge left under him convinces Eve that somebody killed him because he was a cop. Her investigation uncovers corruption within the police force; questions center on the botched arrest of drug lord Max Ricker. The Illegals' squad of the 128th planned and executed the operation. They bungled it and Max Ricker walked. The death of a second cop who was part of the operation confirms Eve's theory. She tries to save other officers, officers who resent the investigation of their squad.

ASSOCIATES: Roarke—*who punches Internal Affairs Bureau (IAB) Detective Don Webster;* IAB Detective Don Webster—*who had (or maybe has) a personal interest in Eve;* Mavis—*who gives Eve romantic advice;* Dr. Mira—*who gives*

Eve relationship advice; Max Ricker—*a vicious, possibly insane, crime lord;* Alan Mills, Detective Juliana Martinez, and Detective Taj Kohli—*who worked together to bring Max Ricker down;* Squad Captain Roth—*leads the Illegals Unit of the 128th;* Sergeant Art Clooney—*grief counselor for the 128th;* Detective Jeremy Vernon—*the oinking detective of the 128th;* Chief Tibble—*from whom the IAB is keeping secrets;* IAB Captain Bayliss, Commander Whitney, Captain Ryan Feeney, Officer Peabody, Detective Ian McNab, Chief Lab Technician Dickie Berenski, and Medical Examiner Morse—*are others who work for the NYPSD;* Attorney Canarde—*who works for drug lord Max Ricker;* Lewis and Elmore Riggs—*who also work for Ricker;* Rue MacLean—*who manages Purgatory;* Nester Vine—*who was head of Purgatory security the night Taj was killed;* Mitzi Treacher and Nancie Gaynor—*strippers at Purgatory;* Patsy—*Detective Taj Kohli's wife;* Chad—*their son;* Carla—*who is Patsy's sister.*

13. *Betrayal in Death.* New York: Berkley Books, 2001, 355 p. ISBN: 0425178579; 9780425178577.

New York, May 2059. A chambermaid in one of Roarke's hotels is brutally murdered. The hit was done by a professional, a professional whose fee is two million dollars. The maid, Darlene French, seems an unlikely target. Darlene's family and friends are clean: there's no hint of anything in any of their lives that would trigger such an attack. Once the investigation uncovers the fact that the killer did not specify a room or even a floor, it seems certain that Darlene's death was just the means to an end. The only other person who seems affected by the death is Roarke. As far as he is concerned, those who work for him are family, and he takes the death hard. Once Eve realizes that Roarke's grief is a predictable outcome, she has to wonder if that was the goal of the murder; and, if someone would so casually take a life to trouble Roarke, what is that person likely to do next?

Associates: Personnel at the Palace Hotel include: John Brigham—*Security Chief;* Ms. Natalie Hilo—*Darlene's boss;* Barry Collins—*Darlene's boyfriend;* Sheila Walker—*Darlene's coworker (and friend).*

Roarke hosts a dinner party whose guests include: Mick Connelly—*an old friend of Roarke's;* Magda Lane—*actress;* Vince Lane—*Magda's son;* Liza Trent—*actress escorted by Vince Lane;* Carlton Mince—*Magda's financial manager,* and Minne Mince—*Carlton's wife.*

Officer Peabody and EDD Detective McNab—*who quarrel over Peabody's relationship with Charles Monroe;* Charles Monroe—*who has taken Peabody to the opera;* NYPSD Commander Whitney—*Eve's boss;* Captain Ryan Feeney—*Head of EDD;* FBI Special Agents James Jacoby and Karen Stowe—*the FBI has been after Sylvester Yost for some time;* Deborah—*Mira's daughter-in-law, gives birth to Matthew James Mira;* Denise—*the receptionist at Paradise;* Martin, Letta, and Nina—*are other staff at Paradise;* Jonah Talbot—*Starline Deputy Publisher;* Dana—*Jonah's girlfriend;* Crack—*who runs the Down and Dirty club;*

Nadine Furst—*a crime reporter for Channel 75;* Mavis—*who works with Trina to get Eve information on enhancements;* Summerset—*who is targeted by a killer.*

14. "Interlude in Death," in the anthology *Out of this World.* New York: Jove Books, 2001, p. 1–94. ISBN: 0515131091; 9780515131093.

OLYMPUS RESORT, 2059. Commander Whitney ordered Eve to give a seminar at the Interplanetary Law Enforcement and Security Conference. The keynote speaker is Former Commander Douglas R. Skinner, a man who became a legend for his bravery during the Urban Wars. He requests a meeting with Eve, and offers to help her gain promotion if she will give him the evidence he needs to finally arrest Roarke. She refrains from punching him in the face, in deference to his years and past service. Then people begin dying, and all the clues point to Roarke. Eve is out of her jurisdiction. At a conference swarming with police from every inhabited planet, can Eve ensure that justice is done?

ASSOCIATES: Roarke—*who accompanies Eve to the conference;* Officer Peabody, Captain Feeney, Dr. Mira, and Medical Examiner Morris—*are others from the NYPSD;* Darcia Angelo—*is the Chief of the Olympus Police;* Commander Skinner—*who devoted years of his life trying to find a way to arrest Roarke;* Belle—*is Commander Skinner's wife;* Bryson Hayes—*is Commander Skinner's personal adjutant;* Reginald Weeks—*the Commander's bodyguard and assistant;* Zita Vinter—*who works security at the Olympus Resort.*

15. *Seduction in Death.* New York: Berkley Books, c2001, 354 p. ISBN: 0425181464; 9780425181461.

NEW YORK, JUNE 2059. When a woman plummets to the ground outside of her high-rise apartment, the first thought is that she committed suicide. The on-scene examination of the body rules that out. An examination of the victim's apartment rules out accidental death; she could not have simply fallen out the window. That leaves murder. At first, it seems likely that her death was accidental. The perpetrator meant to rape her on their date, but he also meant to leave her alive. He just didn't take enough care with the dosage of the date-rape drug he used. Eve is searching for a terrified rapist when a second woman is killed. Where there are two, there will be more, and Eve desperately tries to warn the women of the city and to solve the crimes before another woman is victimized.

ASSOCIATES: Charles Monroe and Dr. Louise Dimatto—*who become involved;* Officer Peabody and Detective McNab—*who reunite.*

Dr. Theodore McNamara—*who, 25 years ago, worked on the J. Forrester and Allegany Pharmaceuticals research project to develop drugs related to human reproduction. These included drugs to treat sexual dysfunction. Now, some of these drugs are illegally sold on the street and used as date-rape drugs.* Detective Matthew Renfrew—*who works at botching the investigation of the death of Dr. Theodore McNamara;* Captain Hayes—*Renfrew's boss and a friend of Art Clooney.* Other NYPSD personnel include Medical Examiner Morris,

Chief Lab Technician Dickie Berenski, Dr. Charlotte Mira, Officer Rinksy, and Officer Trueheart. Lucias Dunwood—*McNamara's grandson;* Kevin Morano—*Lucias's best friend;* Grace Lutz—*murder victim;* Nadine Furst—*a crime reporter who broadcasts leaked information in an attempt to warn women;* Moniqua Cline, Stefanie Finch, and Melissa Kotter—*are sure that the warning doesn't apply to them;* Alicanne Hargrove—*is a neighbor of Stefanie;* Jamal—*is a waiter at the Palace;* CeeCee Plunkett—*who was Bryna Bankhead's friend;* Mavis and Trina—*who help Eve deceive a killer;* Detective Baxter, Roarke, and Captain Feeney—*who are part of the stakeout;* Commander Whitney—*who helps take the killer down.*

16. *Reunion in Death.* New York: Berkley Books, c2001, 371 p. ISBN: 0425183971; 9780425183977.

New York, Summer 2059. When Eve returns from a two-week vacation, her desk is cleared and clean. Eve had closed her open cases before she left; when she returns, the post-arrest clean-up work has been completed as well. She turns to an examination of cold cases to see if there are any possibilities of closing one of those. She finds the murder of Marsha Stibbs, which happened six years ago. Eve counsels Peabody to think of the case as being open, not cold. The initial officer ran a solid investigation, but the case was never solved. Eve suggests that Peabody take it, act as Primary Investigator, and find the murderer. Soon after Peabody gets started her parents come to visit; then she and Eve are called to the scene of a current murder. Eve realizes almost immediately that the killer is someone she has encountered in the past, Julianna Dunne, a woman who made a career out of becoming a widow. After she killed husband number three, she was arrested and imprisoned. Eve was the only woman on the team that brought Julianna down, and the only team member that Julianna respected. Julianna uses her early parole to do her best to destroy Eve.

This book further explores the theme of family. Peabody's parents, Phoebe and Sam, come to visit. Phoebe, though a nice woman, is somewhat frightening. Peabody warns Eve that Phoebe has "the power," this strange, apparently motherly, ability to "make you do things you don't want to do, or don't think you want to do. And she'll get you to say stuff you don't mean to say. And you may even babble" (p. 24). Phoebe proves this power, first on Eve, who invites Phoebe and Sam to dinner, and then on Roarke, who invites them to stay. Roarke is a little disturbed, but more amused. He tells Eve:

> I'm no easy mark. You know that. And I swear to you even now that I'm not sure how she managed it, though manage it, she did.
>
> I'm here to tell you, the woman has something. It's not that I mind. It's a big house, and I like both of them quite a lot. But, for Christ's sake, I usually know what I'm going to say before it comes spurting out of my mouth. (p. 60)

Peabody's father is more interesting. He's a sensitive and a healer. He accidentally catches a glimpse of Eve's childhood when he's healing her, and they are both shaken. In this book, Eve travels back to Dallas and confronts some of her past. She realizes that she didn't know her name because her father intentionally hadn't given her one: it was part of his campaign to control her. Eve, worried about Roarke, goes to see Dr. Mira at home and meets Dennis, Dr. Mira's sweet-natured husband. Dr. Mira makes it clear to both Eve and Roarke that she considers them part of her family and they are also unofficially made part of Peabody's family. Peabody's mother gives Eve a family heirloom and regards it as appropriate since, by giving it to Eve, she is "keeping it in (the) family."(p. 65) Eve and Roarke celebrate their second anniversary.

ASSOCIATES: EDD Detective Ian McNab and Officer Delia Peabody—*who worked on improving their relationship with a Bimini vacation, and are now ready to work.* Detective Baxter, Commander Whitney, and Captain Feeney—*who also work for the NYPSD.* Phoebe and Sam Peabody—*Peabody's parents who come to the big city to visit;* Walter C. Pettibone III—*who is killed at his sixtieth birthday party.* Bambi—*his wife, planned the surprise party;* Dr. Peter Vance—*a friend of Walter's;* Walter Pettibone IV—*Pettibone III's son;* Nadine—*the son's wife;* Sherilyn—*Pettibone III's daughter;* Noel Walker—*Sherilyn's husband;* Mr. Markie—*the caterer;* Sing-Yu, Charlie, Robert McLean, Laurie, Gwen, Julie Dockport and Don Clump—*the caterer's staff;* Shelly—*Pettibone III's ex-wife;* Marsha Stibbs—*who was killed six years ago;* Boyd—*Marsha's widower;* Maureen—*Boyd's new wife;* Supervisor Miller—*the incompetent warden of the Dockport Rehabilitation Center;* Maria Sanchez—*one of the prison's "residents" (prisoners);* Lois Loop—*who tells Eve that Julianna planned to go after the bone man, the sheep man, the cowboy, and the Dallas dude;* Parole Officer Otto Shultz—*who believes that Julianna is different;* Lieutenant Frank Boyle and Captain Robert Spindler—*who did their best to keep Julianna in prison;* Mook—*who knows something about the cyanide black market;* Jake T. Parker—*Julianna's stepfather;* Chuck Springer—*Julianna's first lover;* Mavis and Leonardo—*who take everyone to the Down and Dirty strip club for drinks.*

17. *Purity in Death.* New York: Berkley Books, 2002, 355 p. ISBN: 042518630X; 9780425186305.

NEW YORK, JULY 2059. The chronology is a little confusing here. It is clear that *Reunion in Death* takes place immediately following *Seduction in Death.* Eve and Roarke leave for a two-week vacation at the end of *Seduction In Death,* and Eve's first day of work after that vacation is in *Reunion in Death.* Still, they have their first anniversary before the close of *Reunion in Death,* and at the beginning of *Purity in Death* "their marriage was approaching its second year" (p. 6).

Eve receives a call for help from Officer Troy Trueheart. Trueheart interrupted a brutal beating, saving the victim, but the attacker ended up dead. The dead attacker, Louie K. Cogburn, was a mild-mannered pusher who sold drugs to teenagers. He'd been getting progressively crankier for several days, had complained of headaches, and then had responded to a neighbor's complaint by bludgeoning the neighbor with a baseball bat. Then Louie went after the neighbor's girlfriend. She screamed out her apartment window for help and Trueheart raced to the rescue. Louie was almost unstoppable; he turned on Trueheart and Trueheart shot him. Trueheart's weapon was on stun: Louie shouldn't have died.

Louie's computer is impounded and sent to EDD to gather information for the investigation. The EDD officer working on the computer unit becomes insanely enraged and goes on a shooting spree in EDD. It becomes clear that someone has found a way to send a neurological attack through a computer program. The victims are carefully chosen. They're people who have escaped incarceration, people whose crimes have victimized children. The NYPSD must work not only to find the perpetrators, but also to manage public opinion. They're trying to keep people from panicking, but also trying to keep them from canonizing the murderers.

ASSOCIATES: Roarke—*who has no problem with rough justice;* IAB Detective Lieutenant Don Webster—*who does Eve a favor and takes the Trueheart investigation;* Dr. Mira—*who handles Troy Trueheart's testing;* Chief Medical Examiner Morris—*who is baffled by the brain injuries of the victims;* EDD Officer Ian McNab—*who may be permanently paralyzed;* Detective Kevin Halloway—*the officer who attacked McNab;* Mayor Peachtree—*who seems more concerned with public relations than with murder;* Commander Whitney—*who agrees that the investigation needs to take priority over press conferences;* Lee Chang—*the NYPSD media liaison;* Deputy Mayor Jenna Franco—*who becomes imbedded in the investigation;* Nadine Furst—*a crime reporter for Channel 75, she receives the killers' statements;* EDD Officer Halloway—*who takes Captain Ryan Feeney hostage;* Mavis—*who is pregnant;* Peabody—*who gets some advice from Eve on supporting McNab* (p. 173); Summerset—*who helps care for McNab;* Chief Tibble, Officer Baxter, and Detective Sergeant Thomas Dwier—*are the other NYPSD personnel;* Jamie Lingstrom—*who wants to become a cop, helps with the computer investigation;* Mary Ellen George—*who runs a licensed child care center and is a child pornographer, she was a known associate of Chadwick Fitzhugh.* Mr. Hippel—*Mary Ellen's ex-boyfriend, he went to help her when she called him;* Ralph Wooster—*Louie's neighbor;* Suzanne Cohen—*Ralph's girlfriend;* Clarissa Price—*Child Services worker;* Anna Whitney—*Commander Whitney's wife;* Colleen Halloway—*Kevin Halloway's mother;* Donald and Sylvia Dukes—*who are protected by the public's sympathy;* Joseph—*their surviving son.*

18. ***Portrait in Death.*** New York: Berkley Books, c2003, 354 p. ISBN: 0425189031; 9780425189030.

New York, August 2059. A serial killer stalks the young, the beautiful, the innocent, "those with a pure light," and then kills them and photographs them. He sends the photographs to Nadine Furst, hoping that she will understand and spread his insane beliefs.

Summerset, about to leave on a vacation, trips over Galahad (the cat), breaking a leg and injuring his shoulder.

Roarke meets Moira O'Bannion, a counselor at Dochas. Moira tells him that Meg Roarke was not Roarke's mother. Patrick, Roarke's father, murdered Roarke's mother, Siobahn Brody, when Roarke was about six months old. Roarke goes to Dublin to find the truth. Eve, realizing that he is deeply wounded, goes after him. They meet Siobahn's family.

Associates: Dr. Louise Dimatto—*shows Roarke around Dochas;* Moira O'Bannion—*head crisis counselor;* Brian Kelly—*Roarke's old friend who now owns the Penny Pig Pub;* Mr. O'Leary—*who drinks at the Penny Pig;* Donal Grogin—*who was a friend of Roarke's father;* Sinead Lannigan—*Roarke's mother's twin sister.*

Nadine Furst—*crime reporter for Ch 75 is arrested;* Carter Swan—*Channel 75's attorney;* Waldo Remke—*deli owner;* Larry Poole—*New York maintenance worker;* Madinga Jones—*was a friend of Rachel Howard's;* Leeanne Browning—*was one of Rachel's professors at Columbia;* Charlene "Charlie", Randa, and Jackson Hooper—*were classmates of Rachel's;* Angela Brightstar—*is married to Leeanne Browning;* Steve Audrey—*the bartender at Make the Scene;* Shirllee—*is a waitress at Make the Scene;* Diego Feliciano—*danced with Rachel at Make the Scene;* Kenby Sulu—*Juilliard dance student;* Chang and Lily—*Kenby's parents;* Mica Constantine—*was one of Kenby's classmates;* Ernestine Macnamara—*who is thrilled to be part of a police investigation;* Billy Johnson—*who gives Ernestine a discount on garaging her van;* Wilson Buckley—*a.k.a. Crack is Alicia Dilbert's brother;* Lucia Duberry—*Portography store manager;* Dirk Hastings—*genius;* Tourmaline—*Hastings's current model;* Robert Lewis "Dingo" Wilkens and Liza Blue—*Hastings's current assistants;* Elsa Ramerez—*Hastings's ex-assistant;* Jessie Fryburn—*who is Gerald Stevenson's loyal friend and neighbor.*

Officer Peabody and Detective McNab—*are now cohabiting;* Mavis, Dr. Mira, and Captain Feeney—*all give Eve advice;* Commander Whitney, Chief Lab Tech Dickie Berenski, Medical Examiner Morris, Detective Baxter, Officer Trueheart and ident artist Yancy—*are others who work for the NYPSD;* Mavis, Trina, and Leonardo—*who stop by to cheer up Summerset;* P. A. Spence—*is Summerset's nurse.*

Summerset and Eve come to something of a meeting of the minds over P. A. Spence, and form an alliance to help Roarke. Eve deduces that Summerset is the one who killed Roarke's father.

19. ***Imitation in Death.*** New York: Berkley Books, c2003, 342 p. ISBN: 0425191583.

New York, September 2059. A madman imitates infamous serial killers, leaving notes with the bodies of his victims to taunt Eve. First he kills a licensed companion while posing as Jack the Ripper; then he kills a woman in her home, re-enacting a crime first committed by the Boston Strangler. Eve races against time, trying to find him before he strikes again, but she fails.

Eve dreams of her mother. Roarke accepts what happened to his mother.

Associates: Summerset—*who finally leaves on vacation;* Dr. Mira—*who invites Eve and Roarke over for a family barbecue;* Dennis—*Mira's husband;* Gillian—*Mira's daughter;* Mavis—*who is now four-months pregnant;* Officer Peabody and Detective McNab—*who co-sign a lease, and Peabody takes the exam for promotion to detective;* Medical Examiner Morris—*who loses his professional detachment;* Henley, Frohickie, Cullin, Trueheart, Detective Baxter, and Captain Feeney—*are all NYPSD officers;* Detective Sergeant Haggerty—*Boston Police Department;* detectives Sloan and Baker—*Los Angeles Police Department;* Piers Chan—*Jacee Wooten's landlord;* Tressa Palank—*Jacee's counselor;* Charles Monroe—*who was acquainted with Jacee;* Jeffrey Gregg—*Lois Gregg's son, is married to Leah;* Rico Vincenti—*a local grocer;* and Mrs. Elsa Parksy—*who was Lois's friend;* Peter Waterman—*Marlene Cox's uncle;* Sela Cox—*Marlene's mother;* Dr. Laurence—*Marlene's doctor;* Katie Mitchell—*who was next on the list;* Carmichael Smith—*an international recording star;* Elliot P. Hawthorne—*is more obsessive about his golf game than his young wife;* Niles Renquist—*chief of staff for Britain's UN delegate;* Pepper Franklin—*actress;* Leo Fortney—*is co-habiting with Ms. Franklin;* Thomas Breen—*an author and professional father;* Julietta Gates—*Breen's wife;* Jed—*their son;* Serena Unger—*Julietta's lover;* Pamela—*Renquist's wife;* Rose—*is their daughter;* Sophia—*is the au pair who takes care of Rose;* Roberta Janet Gable—*who was Renquist's nanny when he was a child;* Darla—*Elliot Hawthorne's third young wife;* the club tennis pro—*is Darla's lover;* Li—*Carmichael Smith's aide;* Nadine Furst—*who recommends that Eve leak information to Quinton Post;* Mrs. Moira O'Bannion—*who wishes that she had found a way to convince Siobahn to leave Patrick Roarke.*

20. ***Remember When.*** New York: G. P. Putnam's Sons, c2003, 440 p. ISBN: 0399151060; 9780399151064.

Angel's Gap, Maryland, 2003; New York, September 2059. This novel follows the aftermath of a diamond heist across a span of more than 50 years.

The heist was planned by the ruthless Alex Crew, who enlisted the aid of good-natured Big Jack O'Hara, William Young, and Jerome Myers. Crew always intended to kill off the others and scoop up all the diamonds after the job was finished. He got as far as killing Myers; then O'Hara and Young ran. Their plan was for O'Hara to act as decoy while Young left part of the loot with O'Hara's daughter; but Myers followed Young instead of O'Hara.

Elaine O'Hara (now known as Laine Tavish) didn't recognize "Uncle Willy" until he was dying in her arms. Crew recognized her and assumes that William Young passed the diamonds to her. He's determined to get them; and has no compunction about killing to retrieve what he regards as rightfully his.

Fifty-six years later, one quarter of the diamonds from the heist have never been recovered. Samantha Gannon's book about the theft, her grandparents' recovery of most of the diamonds, and their romance becomes a best-seller and re-ignites interest in the missing jewels. Samantha's housesitter is murdered, and then the maid who comes in twice a month is murdered. Eve suspects that greed, not bloodlust, is the motive for the murders.

ASSOCIATES: 2003: Laine Tavish—*a.k.a. Elaine O'Hara, owns an antiques store in Angel's Gap;* Angie and Jenny—*work in the shop (Jenny is seven months pregnant and is the wife of Chief of Police Vince Burger);* Max Gannon—*is trying to recover the stolen gems for the insurance company;* Jasper R. Peterson—*a.k.a. "Uncle" Willy Young, stops by the store right before he is killed;* Jack O'Hara—*(who for a short time poses as Peter Pinkerton) never meant to put his daughter in danger;* Alex Crew—*who poses as Miles Alexander.*

2059: Detective Third Grade Delia Peabody—*Eve's partner;* EDD Detective McNab, Captain Ryan Feeney, and Roarke—*are also on Eve'e investigative team;* Andrea Jacobs—*Samantha Gannon's housesitter;* Tina Cobb—*who works for the Maid in New York service;* Chad Dix—*Samantha's ex-boyfriend;* Cecily Newberry—*was Andrea's boss at the Work or Play travel agency;* Essie—*Tina Cobb's sister;* Officer Baxter and Officer Trueheart—*who are investigating the murder and subsequent incineration of a Jane Doe;* M. E. Foster—*the Medical Examiner on the case;* M. E. Duluc—*the Medical Examiner in charge of the unit while M. E. Morris is on vacation;* Nadine Furst—*crime reporter for Channel 75, is after a story on the diamonds;* Laura Gregory—*Alex Crew's wife, kept running even after Crew died;* Janine and Steven Whittier—*the aliases chosen by Laura Gregory for her children;* Trevor Whittier—*Steven Whittier's son.*

21. ***Divided in Death.*** New York: G. P. Putnam's Sons, c2004, 357 p. ISBN: 0399151540; 9780399151545.

NEW YORK, SEPTEMBER 2059. When the 2:00 A.M. call goes to Roarke's unit, it's expected to be about business, not homicide. It surprises both Roarke and Eve when it's both: Caro, Roarke's administrative assistant, requests help at the scene of the murder of her daughter's husband. The daughter, Reva, is also the head of Roarke's Securecomp unit. The murder is staged to look like a crime of passion, with Reva as the chief suspect. Eve immediately suspects a frame. What she doesn't expect is espionage, or an encounter with another facet of her past.

In this book Eve and Roarke find out that the Homeland Security Organization had Richard Troy (Dallas's father) under surveillance over 20 years ago. They knew that he was abusing his eight-year-old daughter, their operatives heard and recorded her screams, and then recommended that, to protect the operation, no action be taken. Eve asks Feeney to speak to Roarke, to try to prevent Roarke from murdering the operatives who did nothing to stop the abuse of an eight-year-old girl in Dallas. There is a gap in the Homeland Security Organization's data for the May night when Troy was murdered.

ASSOCIATES: Caro—*Roarke's administrative assistant;* Reva Ewing—*Caro's daughter;* Chloe McCoy—*one of Blair Bissel's conquests;* Deena Hornbock—*Chloe's friend and neighbor;* Quinn Sparrow—*Assistant Director of Data Resources for the Homeland Security Organization, he tries to get Eve to close down the investigation;* Nadine Furst—*crime reporter for Channel 75;* Detectives Peabody and McNab—*who go to Jamaica to interview a bar owner;* Diesel Moore—*a bar owner;* Mavis, Trina, Leonardo, and Dr. Mira—*are among the guests when Roarke tries out the grill again;* Reva and Tokimoto—*help recover information from some fried computer units;* IAB Detective Don Webster, Commander Whitney, and Chief Tibble—*who block Homeland Security from forcing Eve off the investigation.*

22. *Visions in Death.* New York: G. P. Putnam's Sons, c2004, 338 p. ISBN: 0399151710; 9780399151712.

NEW YORK, EARLY FALL 2059. A serial killer rapes, murders, and then steals the eyes of his victims. Celina Sanchez wasn't on the scene, but she saw the whole thing. She's a psychic.

ASSOCIATES: Peabody—*Eve's partner and close friend, in this book Eve tells Peabody about Eve's father's death;* Yvonne "Vonnie"—*Elisa Maplewood's daughter;* Mrs. Deann Vanderlea—*is Elisa's employer;* Zanna—*Deann's daughter;* Celina Sanchez—*a psychic who had a vision of the crime;* Dr. Louise Dimatto—*a friend of Eve;* Dr. Mira—*NYPSD counselor;* Lucas Grande—*who was once involved with Celina;* Annalisa Sommers—*Grande's fiancé;* Moira O'Bannion—*is a counselor at Dochas, long ago she knew Roarke's mother;* Marjie—*Royce Cabel's fiancé;* Annalou Harbor—*who provided childcare for Breen Merriweather's son Jesse;* Mrs. Carleen Steeple—*is Lily Napier's sister;* Andy—*Carleen's husband;* Jim—*of Jim's Gym;* Mr. Ling—*also a gym owner;*

Ms. Chancy—*craft-store manager;* Kurt Richards—*clothing-store manager;* Crack—*owner of the Down and Dirty club;* Commander Whitney, Captain Feeney, Detective Ian McNab, Chief Medical Examiner Morris, Lab Tech Ursa Harro, and detectives Lansing, Jones, and Polinski—*are other NYPSD personnel who work on the cases;* Essie Fort and Mike Jacobs—*are witnesses;* Yancy—*ident artist to develop a picture of the killer;* Mavis and Leonardo—*who ask Eve and Roarke to be Mavis's backup labor and delivery coaches.*

23. *Survivor in Death.* New York: G. P. Putnam's Sons, c2005, 376 p. ISBN: 0399152083; 9780399152085.

NEW YORK, OCTOBER 2059. A quiet and efficient death squad took out nine-year-old Nixie's family. She spotted the killers and called the police; Eve caught the call, but she wasn't in time to save the Swishers. She did find Nixie, hiding, alive, and wracked with guilt that she hadn't found a way to stop the killers. Eve was the one who came and found her, and now Nixie equates Eve with safety and trusts her to find the killers. It soon becomes clear that the killers will not be satisfied until they complete the mission of destroying Nixie's family by killing Nixie.

ASSOCIATES: Linnie Dyson—*Nixie's friend;* The Dysons—*Linnie's parents, who once agreed that they would be Nixie's guardian if her parents died;* Social Worker Meredith Newman—*who tries to start the paperwork on Nixie;* Eve—*who remembers her own time in the Child Protective Services system, insists on taking Nixie home;* Grant Swisher—*was Nixie's father;* Dave Rangle—*Grant Swisher's law partner;* Sade Tully—*paralegal who runs their law offices;* Jan Uger—*who was one of nutritionist Ms. Swisher's clients;* Hildy—*who saw the killers in the neighborhood;* Mrs. Grentz—*Hildy's relative, who owns the house where Hildy lives;* Minnie Cable—*who was another of Meredith Newman's cases;* Rennie Townston—*who was Newman's supervisor;* Ramon Pasquel—*is witness to a kidnapping;* Ophelia Washburn—*is the licensed companion who propositioned the kidnappers;* Lieutenant Yancy—*is the best ident artist in the NYPSD;* Summerset, Detective Baxter, and Officer Trueheart—*who babysit the eyewitness;* Dr. Mira—*who takes issue with Eve's attitude;* Commander Whitney, Captain Feeney, Medical Examiner Morris, Detective McNab, Detective Peabody, Officer Grimes, and IAB Lieutenant Don Webster—*are other NYPSD personnel involved in the operation;* Roarke—*who tries to find a guardian for Nixie;* Leesa Corday—*who is Nixie's aunt;* Roger Kirkendall—*Dian's abusive husband;* Roxanne Turnbill—*Dian's sister;* Joshua Turnbill—*Roxanne's husband;* Lu "the Dragon"—*a three time Olympic gold medalist in martial arts who co-owns a martial arts studio with Roger Kirkendall;* Jilly Isenberry and Isaac Clinton—*worked with Kirkendall;* Leah Rames—*who found Meredith Newman's body;* Mavis Freestone—*singer, Nixie is a fan;* Kevin—*who is doing well with Richard DeBlass and Elizabeth Barrister.*

24. *Origin in Death.* New York: G. P. Putnam's Sons, c2005, 339 p. ISBN: 039915289X; 9780399152894.

New York, November 2059. The brilliant body sculptor (plastic surgeon) William B. Icove was regarded as a humanitarian. Why would anyone kill him? It turns out that the work he did openly was a very small part of his life. Eve has come to regard him as a monster as vile as any she has ever met.

In some ways this book is brilliant, in other ways it is a disappointment. Previous books in this series are satisfying on several levels. One is world building. The recognizable but different world of a future New York is as fascinating in its similarities to ours as it is in its differences. A second level is the mystery: the police procedurals are well done. A third level is the story of these characters' lives, usually told with verve and emotional scenes that are heart-tugging or hilarious (sometimes both heart-tugging and hilarious at the same time). In this book, the world-building science fiction aspects (along with the provocative moral questions they generate) are first rate. The police procedural is strong, and has the added fillip of Eve choosing justice over law, a time-honored tradition in mystery stories. However, the characters' emotional growth in the book just doesn't meet the high standards set by others in the series, although the framework is there. One of the disappointments is that the groundwork is laid so well that the reader can almost see the book that this should have been. For instance, there is a book-long buildup to a fantastic Thanksgiving scene. Roake invites 30 relatives from Ireland, Eve invites Mavis, Leonardo, Crack, Nadine and others; but Eve never fully engages in the worrying and the planning, and the book ends before the event takes place. The only payoff in bringing all these people together is a short scene in which Eve meets a few relatives and, later, a short conversation between Eve and Sinead, a conversation that has less emotional impact than the conversation they had in *Portrait in Death.* The reader doesn't see Eve or Roarke become closer to anyone in Roarke's family. Eve just learns a few more names.

Eve intentionally disobeys orders and works to thwart the law. The reasons are clear and the reader is certain to agree with her choices, but wouldn't Eve face more doubts on the way to doing this? Other aspects may not affect the story, but they are not consistent with other entries in the series. For instance, there's a one-sentence sex scene on page 70. While sex scenes are common in these books, those between the main characters are not as short and as oblique as "she ended the workout with a different sort of water exercise."

The narrative and dialog have been sharp, caustic, and have included profanity throughout the series, but they have not been crass. At one point in this book, Eve tells Roarke that she's expecting a "big, fat mess waiting to crap all over me," and Roarke comments that Eve has the "shittiest imagery going lately" (p. 248). His comment is accurate, and it means that her company is more off-putting, less fun. The same is true of the narrative. For instance, in previous books the "glop" Trina uses has been described in various disgusting but inoffensive ways; in this book, it is described as cum-like. There is also the attitude. Eve has joked about being mean throughout the series, but she has been portrayed as a caring person who had difficulty expressing caring feelings. In this and the next few, she is not just rude, she is inconsiderate, especially to her friends and allies, and she revels in being inconsiderate.

This is an excellent series, highly recommended, but this and a few of the subsequent books do not show the best of J. D. Robb's skills. There are scenes in the next few books that should have been heart-warming and funny, and instead were perfunctory (for instance the baby-gift shopping and baby-shower planning in *Born in Death*). In later books Ms. Robb begins a recovery, but even then the characters do not have quite the same banter, joy, and class that they had in earlier entries in this series.

ASSOCIATES: Lee-Lee Ten—*an international beauty who killed an attacker in self defense and then had reconstructive surgery at Icove's clinic;* Dr. Icove, Sr.—*who was universally admired;* Dr. Mira, Dr. Dimatto, and Summerset—*all knew and respected Dr. Icove, Sr.*; Summerset—*Roarke's majordomo, worked for Dr. Icove as a medic during the Urban Wars;* Pia—*who was Dr. Icove's administrative assistant;* Dr. Wilfred B. Icove, Jr.—*is Dr. Icove's son;* Avril Hannson Icove—*Wilfred's wife, she attended Brookhollow Academy;* Evelyn Samuels—*is president Brookhollow Academy;* Deena Flavia—*is Avril's "sister";* Diana Rodriguez, Darby, and an unnamed infant—*are Deena's "daughters";* Mavis—*is heading into the 33rd week of her pregnancy;* Trina—*who gives Mavis, Peabody, Eve, Louise Dimatto, and Nadine Furst beauty treatments.* Carla Poole—*who gives Roarke, Dr. Mira, and Dr. Dimatto a tour of Unilab;* McNab and Peabody—*who are going to visit her family for the Thanksgiving holiday;* Commander Whitney—*who understands the need for speed and the need to slow down an investigation;* Chief Tibble—*Heads the NYPSD;* Cher Reo—*serves as Assistant Prosecuting Attorney;* Captain Feeney—*Head of EDD;* Detective Baxter—*who goes in undercover for a body sculpting consultation;* Adam Quincy—*chief legal counsel for the NYPSD;* Chief Jim Hyer—*non-NYPSD;* and Deputy Gaitor. Detective Amaryllis Coltraine—*is newly recruited to NYPSD, she was originally from Savannah;* Medical Examiner Morris—*who begins a romantic relationship with Amaryllis;* Nadine Furst—*crime reporter for Channel 75, meets with Eve in a privacy room at the Down and Dirty.* Crack—*owner of the Down and Dirty;* Alise Brody—*Roarke's grandmother;* Sinead and Edward (Ned)—*are Alise's surviving children;* Eemon—*Sinead's son;* Conner—*Ned's son;* Maggie—*Conner's wife;* Devin—*Maggie and Conner's infant son;* Young Sean and the infant Cassie—*are two more members of Roarke's extended family.*

25. ***Memory in Death.*** New York: G. P. Putnam's Sons, c2006, 337 p. ISBN: 0399153284; 9780399153280.

New York, December 2059. The Christmas season is in full swing when St. Nick takes a header off the 36th floor of the Broadway View hotel. He shouted "Ho. Ho. Ho." all the way down; Eve and Peabody wonder what types of drugs he was using. Peabody is Primary on the case. She closes it on the same day that Eve is surprised by a visit from Trudy Lombard, who was foster mother to Eve for five-and-a-half months in 2036. When Trudy doesn't get what she wants from Eve, she goes to see Roarke. When he warns her off, she comes up with another plan, but she's murdered before she can see it through.

Associates: Max "Tubbs" Lawrence—*who steps out a window during a Tyro Communications office party;* Leo Jacobs—*who was under the window;* Ron Steiner—*Max's friend and coworker;* Martin "Zero" Gant—*who sold the revelers the "party pack" of illegal drugs;*. Trudy Lombard—*who was a foster mother in a variety of Texas towns;* police lieutenant Eve Dallas, teacher Carly Tween, and lawyer Maxie Grant—*are all girls that she fostered;* Bobby—*Trudy's son;* Zana—*Bobby's wife;* D. K.—*Bobby's partner;* Dr. Charlotte and Dennis Mira—*who exchange holiday gifts with Eve;* Peabody and McNab—*who visit his family in Scotland for Christmas;* Medical Examiner Morris—*who spends the night at Eve and Roarke's home after their holiday party;* Mavis and Leonardo—*who are getting more and more excited about the coming baby;* Nadine Furst—*Channel 75 crime reporter, is getting her own show;* Assistant Prosecuting Attorney Cher Reo—*who has Peabody testify against psychic Celina Sanchez;* Commander Whitney, Lab Tech Harvo, Detective Baxter, and Officer Trueheart—*are other law enforcement personnel involved in this case.*

26. **"Haunted in Death,"** in the anthology *Bump in the Night.* New York: Jove Books, 2006, p. 1–100. ISBN: 0515141178; 9780515141177.

New York, January 2060. Eve and Peabody investigate a murder in a building that is rumored to be both cursed and haunted. Misfortune has hounded all those who've owned it since the 1960s, when it was the home of legendary rock star (and junkie) Bonnie Bray. She disappeared; her husband, Hop Hopkins, eventually went mad and overdosed on illegal drugs in that same building. His descendent, Radcliff C. Hopkins III, is found dead on the premises. He died of gunshot wounds, wounds from a weapon that has not been manufactured for over half a century and that has been outlawed for decades. Eve is surprised and a little annoyed when both Peabody and Roarke seem to take the building's curse seriously. She refuses to believe in ghosts, even when she feels the inexplicable cold, even when she hears strange noises…even when she sees Bonnie Bray.

ASSOCIATES: Fanny Gill—*Richard C. Hopkins III's ex-wife;* Cliff Gill—*is their son;* Maeve Buchanan—*who is the daughter of the owner of Bygones, a collectibles shop that did business with Hopkins as he sold off his possessions to try to keep ownership of the building;* Ms. Sawyer—*Serenity Bray Massey's daughter;* John Massey—*Serenity Bray Massey's son;* Detective Yancy—*is the best ident artist in the NYPSD.*

27. *Born in Death.* New York: G. P. Putnam's Sons, c2006, 342 p. ISBN: 0399153470; 9780399153471.

NEW YORK, JANUARY 2060. Natalie Copperfield and Bick Byson were going to be married in May. Until then, they lived separately, but both were killed on the same night, in their separate apartments. It soon becomes clear that they had found evidence of something criminal in the accounts they managed. Link transmissions show that they had resolved to go to the police, but the killer got to them the night before they would have turned the evidence over to the authorities. While all of that is going on, a pregnant friend of Mavis's goes missing. Eve promises to find her; that investigation turns out to be much more than a simple missing-persons case.

ASSOCIATES: Roarke and Eve—*who attend childbirth classes with Mavis and Leonardo to prepare for coaching Mavis through delivery;* Tandy Willowby—*Mavis's friend;* Liane Brosh—*works at White Stork with Tandy;* Aaron Applebee—*the father of Tandy's baby;* Briar Rose Marrow—*Tandy's half-sister;* Randa Tillis—*Tandy's midwife;* Ms. Pason, Zeela and Max Patrone—*are Tandy's neighbors;* Missing Persons Unit detective Lieutenant Jaye Smith—*who helps Eve keep the missing persons case;* Eve and Dr. Mira—*are both amused at some of the aspects of Mavis's baby shower.*

Natalie Copperfield—*was a Senior Account Executive at accounting firm Sloan, Myers, and Kraus;* Bick Byson—*Natalie's fiancé and a V.P. in Personal Finance at Sloan, Myers, and Kraus;* Palma—*Natalie's sister;* Detective Baxter—*who briefly dated Palma;* Grace York—*who was going to be Natalie and Bick's neighbor;* Robert Kraus, Carl Myers, and Jacob Sloan—*are the current partners in the accounting firm of Sloan, Myers, and Kraus.* Randall Sloan—*Jacob's son and a vice-president in the firm;* Cara Greene—*Natalie's boss;* Sarajane Bloomdale—*Natalie's administrative assistant;* Myra Lovitz—*Bick's boss;* Sasha Zinka and Lola Warfield—*clients of the firm;* Mr. Walter Cavendish—*head of the New York office of the law firm retained by the Bullock Foundation;* Ms. Ellyn Bruberry—*his administrative assistant;* Madeline Bullock and Winfield Chase—*who run the Bullock Foundation;* and Lordes Cavendish McDermott—*wealthy widow of Miles McDermott;* Jake Sloan—*Jacob's grandson and namesake;* Rochelle DeLay—*who provides Jake's alibi;* Commander Whitney, Medical Examiner Morris, Lab Technician Harvo, Assistant Prosecuting Attorney Cher Reo; Detective Peabody; Captain Feeney; Detective

McNab; and Officer Trueheart—*are law enforcement personnel who work on the case;* Italy's Inspector Triveti—*who investigated a similar case;* Quentin Dallas Applebee and Bella Eve—*who arrive on the same day.*

28. *Innocent in Death.* New York: G. P. Putnam's Sons, c2007, 385 p. ISBN: 0399154019; 9780399154010.

New York, February 2060. Something is very wrong at the Sarah Child school. People are dying and Eve gets more obstruction than assistance from the school's principal, Arnette Mosebly. Eve is thrown off her stride by the look in Roarke's eyes when he has a supposedly chance meeting with a woman from his past.

Associates: Craig Foster—*was a history teacher at Sarah Child school;* Lissette Foster—*Craig's wife;* Elizabeth Blackburn—*Lissette's boss;* Cicely Bolviar—*Lissette's mother;* Henry Kowoski—*the cranky retired cop who is the Foster's neighbor.* Melodie and Rayleen—*the students who found the body;* Angela Miles-Branch—*Melodie's mother;* Allika and Oliver Straffo—*Rayleen's parents;* Cora—*their au pair;* Eric Dawson—*science teacher;* Reed Williams and Mirri Hallywell—*of Sarah Child's English Department;* Arnette Mosebly—*Sarah Child's principal;* Laina Sanchez—*school nutritionist;* Hallie Wentz—*whose daughter Emily is a student at Sarah Child;* Eileen Ferguson—*is another student's parent, she visited the school on the day of the killing;* Martin—*Eileen's son;* Ben Vinnemere—*is copyeditor for the New York Times;* Mirri Hallywell—*is dating Ben;* Nadine—*who begins her new show;* Mercy—*a production assistant on the show;* Trina—*does makeup for the show;* Natalie and Sam Derrick—*are friends of Roarke and Eve;* Magdelana Percell—*who interrupts their dinner;* Dr. Mira—*who is cheerfully ready to loathe Magdelana;* Mavis—*who spots the con;* Commander Whitney, Detective Peabody, Detective McNab, Captain Feeney, Medical Examiner Morris, Detective Baxter, Officer Trueheart, and Assistant Prosecuting Attorney Cher Reo—*are law enforcement personnel involved in the Sarah Child case.*

29. *Creation in Death.* New York: G. P. Putnam's Sons, 2007, 352 p. ISBN: 0399154361; 9780399154362.

New York, March 2060. Nine years ago, between February 11 and February 26, 2051, a serial killer stalked, kidnapped, tortured, and murdered four women. He left rings on their fingers and carved the amount of time they had endured the torture into their skin. Detective Second Grade Eve Dallas was on the NYPSD task force assigned to stop him. The task force leaked information on the ring to the media, who started referring to the killer as "The Groom." They never caught him, but the murders ceased. For a while, they thought that it was over; maybe he had died or been imprisoned for other crimes. Then, a couple of years later, the killings began again in a different city. That pattern, two or three weeks of killing followed by a year or two of inactivity, has been repeated for almost a decade. Between the periods of killing, he changes locations. In the nine years since he began, he has stalked, kidnapped, tortured and killed at least 19 other women in Wales, Florida, Romania, and Bolivia. Now another woman is found in New York City, recently killed, with every detail following The Groom's MO (*modus operandi*). Whitney assigns the case to Eve. Even as she stands over the first body, Eve knows that the killer is working on the second. Every day it takes to find him is, potentially, another victim's life.

In this book, the mood of the series gets back on track. There are funny moments over breakfast and a wonderful scene between Eve and one of the victims. For a while, some feared that Ms. Robb was becoming tired of this series and these characters. This book provides reassurance that the series will continue and that the characters that readers have come to know and love will be back!

ASSOCIATES: Roarke, Detective Peabody, Medical Examiner Morris, Officer Newkirk, EDD Captain Feeney, EDD Detective Ian McNab, EDD Detective Callendar, Detective Baxter, Officer Trueheart, Detective Jenkinson, Detective Powell, Officer Harris, and Officer Darnell—*are the people who Eve selected to be members of a task force to find the killer;* Detective Gil Newkirk—*is Officer Newkirk's father;* Detective Yancy—*the NYPSD's best police artist;* Chief Tibble, Commander Whitney, Dr. Charlotte Mira, and Chief Lab Tech Dick Berenski—*all also become involved in the case;* Zela Wood—*is assistant manager of the Starlight Club;* Jaycee York—*is Sarifina's sister;* Gia Rossi—*is a trainer and instructor at Body Works;* Pi—*is the manager at Body Works;* Ariel Greenfield—*is a baker at the event planning shop, Your Affair;* Erik Pastor—*is Ariel's neighbor;* Nadine Furst—*is a crime reporter for Channel 75;* and Chessie—*is the manager of Scentual;* Mr. Dobbins, Mr. Tomas Pella, and Mr. Hugh Klok—*were all questioned when the killer struck years ago;* Jessica Forman Rice Abercrombie Charles—*is the Chair of the Met Opera Board;* Kenneth Travers—*is a Funeral Director;* Summerset—*is Roarke's majordomo;* Brian—*is a friend of Roarke's, Brian lives in Ireland;* Trina—*is a make-up artist;* Mavis Freestone—*Eve's best friend, a singer;* Belle—*Mavis's infant daughter.*

30. ***Strangers in Death.*** New York: G. P. Putnam's Sons, 2008, 355 p. ISBN: 9780399154706.

NEW YORK, MARCH 2060 (3 DAYS BEFORE SPRING). Millionaire Thomas Anders was found dead in his own bedroom. It looks as if he died during an illicit tryst. As soon as Eve sees the scene, she suspects it was staged. On meeting Anders's wife, Eve is sure that she has found the person who designed the scene. Eve's instincts are usually right on target, but this time her chief suspect has an unbreakable alibi. She also has powerful friends who are determined to protect the poor widow from police harassment.

Baby Belle (Mavis and Leonardo's daughter) is happy and healthy. Mavis is joyful, besotted, and losing her grip on adult conversation, as demonstrated when she (and Baby Belle) end a phone call with Eve:

> "Wave bye-bye, my itsy-bitsy baby boo. Bye-bye to Auntie Dallas. Give her a cooey-dooey—"
>
> "Mavis, I'm saying this for your own good. You have to stop the insanity. You sound like a moron."
>
> "I know." Mavis's eyes, currently purple, rolled. "I can hear myself, but I just can't stop. (p. 93)

Other favorite characters return as well. Most are shown briefly; but Detective Baxter, Charles Monroe, and Louise DiMatto have more substantial roles. Eve and Roarke come to an understanding about money (his and hers).

Previous entries in the series have depicted the plight of those who are abused and victimized. This one examines some of those same themes, but goes further, drawing lines between victim responses that are understandable and those that should not be excused. At one point, speaking of a woman who stayed with her abusive husband for years, Eve says:

> She could've walked. Any time. Packed up, grabbed the kids and walked...You said she'd sacrifice for her kids, but what has she given them? What kind of life has she opened them to by letting them see, every day, that she's so weak she'll let their father slap her around, come and go as he pleases, spend his money on tricks instead of food...(p. 304)

When Mira points out that there's a difference between weak and evil, Eve's response is "Yeah, but there's sure a lot of overlap" (p. 304).

Associates: Ava Anders—*Thomas's widow;* Greta Horowitz—*the Anders House Manager;* Benedict Forrest—*Thomas's nephew, is his second-in-command at Anders Worldwide;* Frankie and Syl—*receptionists;* Leopold Walsh—*Benedict Forrest's Administrative Assistant;* Delly—*Walsh's assistant;* Gatch Brooks—*Benedict's girlfriend;* Edmond Luce—*Thomas's golf-buddy;* Linny—*is Edmond's wife;* Charles Monroe, Brigit Plowder, Sasha Bride-West, and Karla Blaze Tibble—*are all friends and defenders of Ava Anders;* Chief Tibble—*is the husband of Karla Blaze Tibble;* Sven—*is the personal trainer of Sasha Bride-West;* Agnes Morrelli—*is the Personal Assistant of Brigit Plowder;* Dr. Louise DiMatto—*comes to an understanding with Charles;* Ex-Detective Frank O'Malley—*is the doorman at Brigit Plowder's building;* Dirk Bronson—*was Ava's first husband;* Detective Peabody—*who has her first on-air interview with Nadine Furst;* EDD Captain Ryan Feeney—*who has the flu;* Detective Letterman—*who arranges transportation for his sick captain;* Officer Klink—*the transportation;* Dr. Charlotte Mira—*who helped Charles get a license as a sex therapist;* Assistant Prosecuting Attorney Cher Reo—*who gets Eve a warrant;*

Detective Baxter, Detective Ian McNab, Officer Trueheart, Chief Medical Examiner Morris and Commander Jack Whitney—*are recurring characters who all have cameos in the story;* Tiko—*who sold cashmere scarves in December;* Abigail Johnson—*Tiko's great-grandmother;* Bebe—*the daughter of mafioso Anthony DeSalvo who broke with her family when she married Luca Petrelli;* Cassie Gordon—*a stripper who engages in a little off the books work to purchase figure skating lessons for her daughter, Gracie;* Suzanne Custer—*the mother of Maizie and Todd;* Mr. Isaacs—*a grocer.*

Thirteen years ago, Luca Petrelli was beaten to death and Bebe Petrelli believes that the police didn't perform an adequate investigation. Eve promises to get the case reopened.

31. "Eternity in Death," in the anthology *Dead of Night.* New York: Jove Books, 2007, p. 1–108. ISBN: 0515143677; 9780515143676.

New York, April 2060. Socialite Tiara Kent had been thrilled with her new dream man; she called him her "Dark Prince." When Tiara is found dead, drained of blood and with fang marks on her neck, Eve knows that she must close the case fast, before the media gets hold of the "vampire killer" story.

Supernatural activity has been part of the series before this entry, in "Haunted in Death," but that was a tiny brush with the other world in comparison to this story, which involves a vampire. It's handled by Eve's being ruthlessly, almost blindly, "rational," and by maintaining at least a slim possibility that everything Eve sees is the product of chicanery.

Associates: Roarke and Detective Peabody and Detective Baxter—*are all a little more superstitious than Eve;* Detective McNab and Officer Trueheart—*are noncommittal;* Dr. Charlotte Mira; Medical Examiner Morris; Chief Lab Tech Dickie Berenski; Assistant Prosecuting Attorney Cher Reo; and Captain Ryan Feeney—*are other law enforcement personnel who appear in this story;* Estella Cruz—*Tiara Kent's maid;* Daffodil Wheats and Caramel Lipton—*were Tiara's best friends;* Iris Francine—*is Tiara's mother;* Georgio Francine—*is Iris's current husband;* Dorian Vadim—*who used to be a petty grifter and magician now owns the club Bloodbath;* Allesseria Carter—*a bartender at Bloodbath;* Kendra—*Dorian's current conquest;* Rick Sabo—*Allesseria's ex-husband.*

32. *Salvation in Death.* New York: G. P. Putnam's Sons, 2008, 353 p. ISBN: 9780399155222.

New York, May 2060. The Ortiz clan gathered at St. Cristóbal's Church for the funeral of their patriarch, Hector Ortiz. Father Flores performed the mass, and fell dead after he drank from the Communion chalice. The sacramental wine had been poisoned with cyanide. As Father López later said, "Someone used the blood and body of Christ to kill" (p. 7). Eve soon concludes that Father Flores was not what he seemed. Her investigation is proceeding when another holy man is poisoned. Jimmy Jay Jenkins, founder of the Church of Eternal Light, falls dead before a huge audience. Is someone targeting men of God?

In this entry in the series, Eve faces a woman who should have protected her daughters from her abusive husband, but who was oblivious to the molestation going on in her own home. She also interviews a priest whose innocent girlfriend was raped and murdered, and both Eve and Roarke grapple with the memories invoked by his story. It's an area in which readers can see progress in their relationship. They're better at sharing grief and at supporting each other than they were when they were first married.

Reporter Nadine Furst breaks the news to Eve that, if she's hosting Louise and Charles's wedding, she must also throw Louise a bridal shower. Nadine and Detective Peabody offer to do the planning. Nadine asks Eve to review the manuscript for a book Nadine wrote on the Icove case.

ASSOCIATES: Summerset—*asks Roarke's aunt call Roarke;* Detectives Peabody and McNab—*who quarrel with each other;* Detective Baxter—*who flirts with Officer Graciela Ortiz;* Chief Medical Examiner Morris—*who receives roses, probably from Detective Amaryllis Coltraine;* Roberto—*Hector Ortiz's son;* Madda—*Roberto's wife;* Graciela—*Hector's granddaughter;* Magda Laws, Marc Tuluz and Juanita Turner—*work at the Youth Center;* Kiz—*sizes people up through basketball;* Father Miguel Ernesto Flores, Father Chale López, and Father Martin Freeman—*all live at the rectory;* Rosa O'Donnell—*is their housekeeper;* Monsignor Alexander Quilby—*deceased, was Father Flores's mentor;*, Father Rodriguez—*whose mind wanders, worked with Miguel Flores;* Elena Solas and her daughters Barbara and Donita—*were rescued by Father Flores;* Father Stiles—*is assistant to the Bishop, and doesn't want to request the release of Father Flores's dental records;* Nadine Furst—*who airs an exclusive on the St. Cristóbal murder;* Detectives Stuben and Kohn—*who investigated gang violence involving the Soldados street gang in 2043;* Steve Chávez—*was a Soldado;* Joe Inez—*who is now married to Consuelo and has three sons, was a Soldado;* and Penny Soto—*was a Soldado.* Teresa—*was Lino Martinez's mother;* Tony Franco—*is Teresa's second husband;* David—*is their son.*

Jolene—*Jimmy Jay Jenkins's wife;* Josie Jenkins Carter—*their daughter, spiked Jimmy Jay's water bottles;* Jaimé and Jackie—*are Jimmy Jay's and Jolene's other daughters;* Samuel Wright—*a lawyer, is married to Jaimé;* Luke Goodwin—*is married to Jackie;* Billy Crocker—*was Jimmy Jay Jenkins's manager;* Clyde Attkins—*was Jimmy Jay's bodyguard;* Ulla Pintz—*was Jimmy Jay's mistress.*

Ariel Greenfeld and Erik Pastor—*who bring Eve a cake;* Mavis Freestone; Detective Trueheart; Commander Whitney; Dr. Charlotte Mira and Assistant Prosecuting Attorney Cher Rho; EDD Captain Feeney; Attorney Feinburg; Attorney Carlos Montoya; and Galahad the cat—*also appear in the story.*

33. "Ritual in Death," in the anthology *Suite 606*. New York: Berkley Books, 2008, p. 1–85. ISBN: 9780425224441.

NEW YORK, SPRING 2060. Roarke has promised Eve that they will soon leave the party they're attending at his Palace Hotel when an intoxicated, naked, blood-covered, knife-wielding man staggers into the room. Eve pulls her side-arm out of her evening bag and apprehends the man. Roarke acts as her back-up as she backtracks the suspect's trail, hoping to find that the victim is still alive. They discover the scene of a Satanic ritual that culminated in a murder in another of the hotel's suites. Roarke owns the hotel, and his personnel are implicated in the crime. Roarke and Eve both tackle the investigation, approaching it from different perspectives but working together in the end.

ASSOCIATES: Maxia Carlyle—*hosted the party;* Anton and Silk—*guests at the party;* Dr. Jackson Pike—*is the suspect who crashes the party;* Dr. Larry Collins, Dr. Peter Slone, Dr. Silas Pratt, receptionist Sarah Meeks, Nurse Practitioner Leah Burke, and Kiki—*who work with Jackson at the West Side Health Clinic;* Mika Nakamura—*who works security at Roarke's Palace Hotel;* Detective Delia Peabody; Electronic Detectives Division's Ian McNab; Chief Medical Examiner Morris and Dr. Mira—*are law enforcement personnel involved in the case;* Isis—*is a woman of power who is a friend to both Eve and Roarke.*

In this story, Eve has a short unexplained vision of a boy with shaggy hair (who's excited by flying cars), a man with gold hair, and a slim brunette woman with green eyes (p. 69).

34. *Promises in Death.* New York: G. P. Putnam's Sons, 2009, 342 p. ISBN: 9780399155482.

NEW YORK, MAY 2060. Detective Amaryllis Coltraine was lured to her death in the middle of the night. She was killed with her own weapon. Every officer of the NYPD is determined to bring down her killer.

Amaryllis "Ammy" was dating Chief Medical Officer Li Morris. Everyone on the force mourns her death and Morris's loss. Eve, Roarke, Peabody, and others do everything they can to support Morris while he mourns.

When Eve wants to cancel Louise DiMatto's bridal shower until after the case is closed, Morris tells her that life must go on. (It does, although both Eve and Peabody leave the party early to work the case.) Eve now finds it easy to tell Roarke she loves him. Belle is teething. Summerset, watching Eve try to help Morris through his grief, tells Eve that he's proud of her.

ASSOCIATES: Li Morris—*was dating Detective Amaryllis "Ammy" Coltraine;* Lieutenant Delong—*supervises the squad in which Detective Coltraine worked;* Members of Delong's squad include: Detective Patrick O'Brian—*the senior man in the squad;* Cleo Grady—*who was often partnered with Amaryllis Coltraine;* Josh Newman—*who is steady and easy-going;* and Dak Clifton—*who is hot-headed.*

Stu Bollimer—*Coltaine's informant, runs a pawnshop;* Mary Hon—*works at Coltraine's favorite Chinese restaurant;* Alex Ricker—*(son of mobster Max Ricker) was once Amaryllis Coltraine's lover;* Rod Sandy—*Alex Ricker's personal assistant;* Carmine—*Alex Ricker's driver;* Harry Proctor—*Alex Ricker's lawyer;* Internal Affairs Detective Webster—*meets with Eve at the Down and Dirty strip joint;* Crack—*owns the Down and Dirty;* Commander Whitney—*Eve's boss, receives a complaint about Eve's conduct of the investigation;* Max Ricker—*was once a crime lord, Eve brought him down and he's serving a prison sentence at the Omega penal colony;* EDD Captain Feeney—*who agrees that it is unlikely that Max Ricker would find a way to communicate with his lieutenants from prison;* EDD Detectives Callendar and Sisto—*who are assigned to investigate the suspicious lack of communication from Max Ricker;* Cecil Rouche and Zeban—*who are guards at the Omega penal colony;* Ty Clipper—*who Morris assigns to autopsy Detective Coltraine;* July Coltraine—*Ammy's brother;* Caro—*Roarke's Administrative Assistant;* Adrian and her partner Liv—*who own the Secrets lingerie shop;* Kip and Bop—*who found a body;* and Luanne Debois—*Rouche's ex-wife.*

People attending Dr. Louise DiMatto's bridal shower include Mavis Freestone (Summerset babysits Belle); Dr. Charlotte Mira; Peabody; reporter Nadine Furst; beautician Trina; and Assistant Prosecuting Attorney Cher Reo. (Roarke hosts a wild bachelor party in Las Vegas for EDD Captain Feeney; Detective McNab; Dennis Mira; Detectives Baxter and Trueheart; and the groom, sex therapist Charles).

RUCKA, Greg. Worked with Ed Brubaker, Michael Lark, and Stefano Guadiano on *In the Line of Duty.*

See BRUBAKER, Ed: In the Line of Duty.

S

SALE, Tim. Worked with Jeph Loeb on Batman: *The Long Halloween*. See LOEB, Jeph: Batman: The Long Halloween.

SCOTT, Martin (pseudonym for Martin Millar).

Thraxas Series

Genres/Themes Crossed: Blended Society X Hard-Boiled Mystery.

Subjects/Character Types: Spell Casters, Mythical Creatures, Fae X Private Investigators.

Series/Stand-Alone: Series. It is best to read the novels in order, there are dramatic changes in the political fortunes of the city through the series.

Scene of the Crime: Turai, a city in a Tolkienesque world.

Detective(s): Thraxas, an overweight 43-year-old minor sorcerer who hires out as the cheapest investigator in the city of Turai.

Known Associates: Thraxas lives in two rooms above *The Avenging Axe* tavern owned by his old comrade-in-arms, Gurd. Twenty-one-year-old Makri, a Human/Elf/Orc crossbreed (one-quarter Elf, one-quarter Orc, and one-half Human) barmaid acts as his assistant in his investigations.

Premise: Thraxas is aging and tired and wants nothing more than to drink away the rest of his life; but he has bills to pay, and so he must take cases as a private investigator. Thraxas had an excellent job as a Senior Investigator with Palace Security under Deputy Consul Rittius, until he got drunk at the Consul's wedding and made a pass at the bride. He was unemployed before the wedding reception ended, and his life has been downwardly mobile ever since. Now he regards himself as a broken-down has-been investigator and an incompetent sorcerer. Thraxas is pretty sure that anyone who could afford a better sorcerer or a more respected investigator would go to someone else. He feels that he's the last resort for the desperate and the impoverished. So, he begins his cases feeling a certain pity for his clients (unless they are rich, in which case he regards them with suspicion).

Thraxas could have been a major sorcerer; he had the native talent but lacked the drive. He drank his way through his stint in the military, but proved himself brave and loyal. He now earns the occasional large fee, and loses it at the races. He seems to be a man determined to throw away his chances at success. Makri is a young woman who escaped the orc slave pits (by killing everything that stood in her way). She's determined to absorb the culture and learning available in Turai, even though those who teach do not wish to teach women and believe that anyone with a trace of orc blood should be thrown out of the city. She has gotten further than anyone believed possible; she is the first woman (and the first person with any orc blood) enrolled in the Revered Federation of Guilds College. She works at the bar between and after classes, saving her tips and plotting ways to convince or coerce the administrators of the Imperial University to accept her as a student.

In this world, spells can have enormous power, but sorcerers must relearn spells for each use. (Once a spell is used, it is wiped from the mind of the sorcerer.) Competent sorcerers can memorize two spells at a time; extremely powerful sorcerers might be able to remember four. So, sorcerous power is limited. Sorcerers must prepare by calculating which spells will be most useful and then memorizing those spells. If their calculations are incorrect, then they are unprepared for the challenges they face that day. Thraxas can memorize one spell at a time. He often chooses a sleep spell, which is useful in a variety of situations since it will stop almost anything, yet is not lethal. If it's freezing cold and he wants to carry a warmth spell, then he must go out relatively unprotected.

Comment: Martin Millar was born in Glasgow Scotland and lives in London. He struggles against agoraphobia and keeps in touch with his fans through his Web site (www.martinmillar.com), which links to his blogs. He writes straight and fantasy fiction under his own name. Many of his works, even the fantasy fiction, include autobiographical elements. In a November 20, 2008 interview about *Lonely Werewolf Girl* he said, "Many of the things the unfortunate young werewolf suffers from have been taken from my real-life experiences." (http://www.chasingray.com/archives/2008/11/martin_millar_interview_many_o.html).

Books he has written as Martin Millar include *Milk, Sulphate and Alby Starvation* (1987); *Lux the Poet* (1989); *Ruby and the Stone Age Diet* (1990); *The Good Fairies of New York* (1992, the 2007 Soft Skull edition includes an introduction by Neil Gaiman); *Tank Girl* (novelization of the film, 1994); *Dreams of Sex and Stage Diving* (1995); *Lux and Alby Sign On and Save the Universe* (graphic novel, 1999); *Love and Peace with Melody Paradise* (1998); *Emma* (text of the play, 2001); *Suzy, Led Zeppelin and Me* (2002); and *Lonely Werewolf Girl* (2007).

The Thraxas Web site http://www.thraxas.com/ includes pictures and a map of Thraxas's world. A direct link to a mid-size version of the map is: http://www.martinmillar.pwp.blueyonder.co.uk/thcom/pops/thmap.html.

At the moment, the series is on hiatus. It was published in Britain by Orbit and in the United States by Baen. Orbit was not interested in publishing a ninth book; Baen was, but could not come to an agreement with Mr. Millar's agent. (The dispute centered on rights, not money.) At the moment, Mr. Millar is focusing his energies on other projects, but readers hope that an agreement will allow the Thraxas series to continue.

Literary Magic & Mayhem: The books are written in present tense, but the writing flows beautifully, drawing the reader into the story.

The stories are set in a world that is being destroyed by a powerfully addictive drug called *dwa*. It permeates every level of society, sapping the strength, the will, and the wealth of too many of the citizens of Turai. Thraxas's assessment: "Turai is rotting. The poor are despairing and the rich are decadent" (p. 21). Thraxas is a man who threw away his opportunities, squandering his talents to embrace the bottle and squandering his resources in pursuit of easy money at the racetrack. Both the city and the man have seen better days. Thraxas is still capable of rising to a challenge: some of his finest moments occur when his back is against the wall.

Thraxas's success owes something to his dogged persistence, more to his good luck, and most of all to the fact that Turai is a small city. Between news from the scandal sheet *The Renowned and Truthful Chronicle of all the World's Events,* rumors of unusual events, and clients telling Thraxas their sorrows, clues seem to find Thraxas before he has a chance to look for them.

Explorations: How does the author use the different attitudes towards Makri to define the characters?

Which character was the most sympathetic?

THE CASES

1. ***Thraxas.*** Published with *Thraxas and the Warrior Monks* in an omnibus edition entitled *Thraxas*: Riverdale, New York: Baen Publishing Enterprises, 2003, p. 1–224 (of 442 p.) ISBN: 0743471520.

TURAI, EARLY SUMMER. Princess Du-Akai, third in line to the Imperial Throne, hires Thraxas to retrieve love letters she wrote to Attilan, a young diplomat from a foreign power that is not a friend of Turai. He could be regarded as an enemy of the state. Thraxas is behind on his rent; he owes the mobster (Yubaxas) 500 gurans (which Thraxas had lost at the races); and he doesn't have money for beer. He's desperate enough to work.

Thraxas breaks into the Attilan's home, finds the box that should have held the letters, is spotted by a servant, and is arrested by the Civil Guard. The news of his capture and imprisonment travels through the city. Recently, a priceless length of Red Elvish Cloth was stolen. (Red Elvish Cloth is a total shield against magic. It can be used to avoid magical eavesdropping and to protect against magical attacks. By law it can be owned only by the King.) Now rumor has cast Attilan as either a thief or a receiver of stolen goods. Everyone is sure he had the Red Elvish Cloth. Thraxas is in danger because many people believe that he must now possess the cloth. Their reasoning? Attilan must have had it. It is not now in Attilan's home. Thraxas was in Attilan's home. Thraxas must have the Cloth! This belief draws attention, offers, and threats. Thraxas is offered employment to find the Cloth. At the same time, Thraxas is being threatened with death unless he hands it over. If he actually had the Cloth, he could pick between being rich or being safe. Without the Cloth, he is poor, in danger, and . . . motivated by both fear and greed to find the Cloth.

In this book the Half-Orc renegade sorcerer Horm the Dead unleashes the Eight-Mile Terror on Turai. The populace riots.

ASSOCIATES: Gurd—*owner of The Avenging Axe tavern where Thraxas lives;* Makri—his *Human/Elf/Orc crossbreed barmaid;* Tanrose—*the cook at the Avenging Axe;* Palax and Kaby—*traveling musicians who camp behind the tavern;* Karlox—*a Brotherhood enforcer who is looking forward to beating Thraxas when Thraxas can't pay his gambling debts;* Yubaxas—*the Brotherhood boss who loaned Thraxas money;* Princess Du-Akai—*who hires Thraxas to retrieve letters from the Niojan diplomat Attilan and then extends Thraxas's job to include clearing her of killing the dragon at the zoo;* Callis-ar-Del and Jaris-ar-Miat—*elves who hire Thraxas to recover the stolen Red Elvish Cloth;* Praetor Cicerius—*who hires Thraxas to clear his son of the charge of being a dwa dealer;* Cerius Junius—*the Praetor's son;* Jaisleti—*the handmaiden of Princess Du-Akai;* Prefect Galwinius, Captain Rallee, and Guardsman Jevox—*enforce the law in Turai;* Sorcerer Astrath Triple Moon—*who is grateful to Thraxas for Thraxas's sowing confusion when Astrath was brought up on charges;* Sorcerer Horm the Dead—*a Half-Orc renegade sorcerer;* Sorcerer Glixius Dragon Killer—*who wishes to blackmail the King;* Sorcerer Tas of the Eastern Lightning—*who was thought to be working for Palace Security;* Sorcerer Lisutaris, Mistress of the Sky—*who has devoted herself to the study of the drug thazis;* Sorcerer Gorsius Starfinder and the elderly Sorcerer Hasius the Brilliant—*who do their best to stand against an enraged and insane mob;* Bishop Gzekius and the local priest Derlex—*are officials of the True Church;* Taur the Centaur—*of the Fairy Glade;* Partulax—*a Transport Guild Official;* Minarixa—*the baker;* Hanama—*an assassin;* Kerk—*a dwa-dealer;* Sarin the Merciless—*who was once beaten by Thraxas;* and Pazaz—*an Orc who serves as dragonkeeper.*

2. ***Thraxas and the Warrior Monks.*** Published with *Thraxas* in an omnibus edition entitled *Thraxas*: Riverdale, New York: Baen Publishing Enterprises, 2003, p. 227–442. ISBN: 0743471520.

TURAI, SUMMER. The famous sculptor Drantaax was stabbed in the back as he was putting the finishing touches on a statue of Saint Quatinius. His apprentice, Grosex, discovered the body, then fled when Drantaax's wife Calia found him at the scene and screamed for the Guards. Thraxas still has money, so he had no intention of working for the rest of the summer. When Grosex stumbled into Thraxas's office, desperate for Thraxas's help, Thraxas had every intention of turning down the job until Prefect Tholius, hot on Grosex's heels, had Thraxas's door broken down and Grosex was dragged from Thraxas's office. After Thraxas shuts what's left of his door, he finishes his beer and starts the investigation.

Thraxas does his best to turn down a second job, this one offered by Dandelion on the behalf of dolphins. He does take a job from the drunken Soolanius, to investigate her father's, Thalius Green Eye's, death. The statue of Saint Quatinius, Drantaax's final work, has disappeared from the scene of the murder. The statue weighs two tons. That it could have been spirited off between the discovery of Drantaax's body and the arrival of the Civil Guard seems impossible. The statue had been commissioned by the warrior monks of the Cloud Temple. Their leader, the Venerable Tresius, hires Thraxas to recover the statue. Thraxas solves all the cases, but doesn't manage to please many of his clients.

ASSOCIATES: Gurd—*Thraxas's old war buddy, now owner of a tavern;* Tanrose—*the tavern's cook;* Makri—*the tavern's Human/Elf/Orc crossbreed barmaid;* Dandelion—*who speaks to the dolphins;* Soolanius—*who is drinking through her grief;* and Quen—*the whore;* Palax and Kaby—*are traveling musicians;* Cicerius—*has risen to Deputy Consul;* Other officials include: Tholius—*Prefect of the Twelve Seas;* Jevox—*a guardsman;* Captain Rallee—*who was also run out of the Palace by Deputy Consul Rittius;* Prefect Galwinius; and Deputy Prefect Prasius. Villains include: Casax—*who took over as the local Brotherhood boss when Yubaxas died;* Karlox—*who is still a thug working for the Brotherhood;* and Orius Fire Tamer—*the Brotherhood's new sorcerer.* The Venerable Tresius—*who hired an assassin;* Hanama—*Master Assassin;* Ixial the Seer—*who has enemies;* Sarin the Merciless—*who fires a crossbow bolt into Makri's chest;* Chiaraxi the healer—*who tries to help Makri;* Astrath Triple Moon—*who declares Makri dead;* Grosex—*sculptor Drantaax's apprentice;* Calia—*Drantaax's wife;* Kerk—*Thraxas's informer;* Tas of the Eastern Lightning and Lisutaris, Mistress of the Sky—*sorcerers.*

3. ***Thraxas at the Races.*** Published with *Thraxas and the Elvish Isles* in an omnibus edition entitled *Death and Thraxas*: Riverdale, New York: Baen Publishing Enterprises, 2004, p. 1–232. ISBN: 0743488504.

Turai, Hot Rainy Season. Senator Rittius blames Thraxas for the loss of his position as Deputy Consul. When he learns that Thraxas had assaulted a secret agent of the King (who had been undercover, so Thraxas didn't know that the man was an agent of the King), Rittius takes Thraxas to court, hoping to have Thraxas sentenced to rowing in a slave galley. The judge is more lenient: he only fines Thraxas, taking almost every guran Thraxas owns. Determined to win another fortune, Thraxas takes the little he has left and invests it with Honest Mox, the bookie. Makri thinks that he is a fool to risk the little money he has left; but he is so sure that Troll Mangler is going to win, that she bets the money she'd collected for the Association of Gentlewomen. Troll Mangler's chariot loses a wheel at the first turn. Thraxas is destitute and Makri faces social ruin. They both turn to gambling to try to win back their money.

Thraxas old commander, Senator Mursius, hires Thraxas to recover a painting that was stolen from his home. The Senator suspects that his wife stole from him to support her dwa habit. He doesn't want her apprehended, the scandal would ruin them both. He trusts Thraxas to discreetly locate, acquire, and return his possessions. Thraxas manages the discretion, but every other aspect of the case goes awry.

Before Thraxas recovers the stolen goods, Deputy Consul Cicerius demands that Thraxas take the job of protecting a group of orcs who will visit Turai to enter a horse in the Turas Memorial Race. Thraxas would prefer to battle the orcs rather than protect them; but his investigator's license is at risk, and Cicerius makes it clear that Thraxas will help the orcs or lose his license. When the prayer rug of the orc charioteer is stolen, Thraxas finds himself embroiled in yet another case.

Associates: Gurd—*owner of The Avenging Axe (a tavern);* Tanrose—*the cook;* Makri—*the Human/Elf/Orc crossbreed barmaid;* Palax and Kaby—*traveling musicians;* Deputy Consul Cicerius—*who gets Thraxas out of jail because he needs Thraxas to protect the Orc delegation;* Consul Kalius, Prefect Drinius, Guardsman Jevox, Captain Rallee, and Praetor Samilius—*are other officials.* Pontifex Derlex and Bishop Gzekius—*are Turai's religious authorities;* Casax—*Brotherhood boss;* Karlox—*Brotherhood enforcer;* Glixius Dragon Killer—*a sorcerer who threatens Thraxas;* Kemlath Orc Slayer—*a sorcerer who fought beside Thraxas during the last Orc war;* Kerk—*a dwa addict who passes information to Thraxas,in this book Kerk finds some of the stolen goods;* Senator Mursius—*one of Thraxas's clients;* Sarija—*Mursius's wife;* Carilis—*their servant;* Lord Rezaz Caseg—*a.k.a. Rezaz the Butcher,he leads the Orc delegation to Turai;* Orc Azgiz—*a member of the delegation;* Makeza the Thunderer—*an Orc sorcerer who has been hired to assassinate Lord Rezaz;* Honest Mox's son—*a bookie;* Melus the Fair—*a sorcerer with a reputation for integrity;* Hanama—*a Master Assassin;* Lisutaris, Mistress of the Sky—*a sorcerer who is in sympathy with the Association of Gentlewomen;* Harmon Half-Elf and Lord Llisith-ar-Moh—*sorcerers;* Minarixa—*the baker, is the local organizer for the Association of Gentlewomen;* Honest Mox—*the bookie;* Drasius—*a banker and race enthusiast;* Chiaraxi—*the healer;* Cospali—*the herbalist;* and Lothian—*an elf.*

4. ***Thraxas and the Elvish Isles.*** Published with *Thraxas at the Races* in an omnibus edition entitled *Death and Thraxas*: Riverdale, New York: Baen Publishing Enterprises, 2004, p. 233–472. ISBN: 0743488504.

TURAI (WINTER) AND ELVISH ISLE AVULA. The elf Vas-ar-Methet saved Thraxas's life in the Orc War. Now he needs help. Vas's daughter, Elith-ir-Methet, was found unconscious at the foot of the damaged sacred Hesuni Tree. A witness saw her hack at the tree with an axe and then try to light it on fire. She awaits trial and will probably be exiled. Thraxas does not hesitate. He would sail immediately to help his friend. There are other benefits: escape from Turai's winter and (Thraxas thinks) a chance to leave Makri, with whom Thraxas is quarrelling.

ASSOCIATES: The weekly game of Rak includes: Thraxas—*our hero;* Gurd—*the tavern-owner;* Captain Rallee—*an officer of the law;* Old Grax—*the wine merchant;* Ravenius—*who is wealthy;* and Casax—*the local Brotherhood boss.* Karlox—*holds Casax's money during the game;* Tanrose—*roots for Gurd;* Makri—*is the Human/Elf/Orc crossbreed barmaid who interrupts the game as Thraxas is on the verge of winning enough money to see him through the year;* Lord Kalith-ar-Yil—*elf, not only leads the elves of Avula, he also captains their ship.* On board are: Gorith-ar-Del—*elf, who is the brother of the dead Callis-ar-Del;* Osath—*elf, the ship's cook;* Isuas—*elf, Lord Kalith's youngest daughter;* Jir-ar-Eth—*elf, a sorcerer.* Turai's delegation to the upcoming Avulan Festival is also on board: Prince Dees-Akan, Deputy Consul Cicerius, Lanius Suncatcher, and Harmon Half-Elf. Eos-ar-Methet—*elf, dies in an accident aboard ship;* Lady Yestar—*elf, Lord Kalith's wife;* Firees-ar-Key—*elf, is the favorite to win the festival's battle competition in the under-15-years-old age group;* Chief tree priest Gulas-ar-Thetos—*elf, who was once Elith's lover;* Lasas-ar-Thetos—*elf, Gulas's brother, Chief Attendant to the tree;* Coris-ar-Mithan—*elf, Vas's cousin;* Camith—*elf, Vas's brother;* Visan—*elf, the Keeper of Lore;* Sendroo-is-Vallis—*a.k.a. Droo, elf, poet;* Lithias—*elf, Droo's boyfriend;* Caripatha—*elf, a weaver;* Turius—*the Ambassador;* Rekis-ar-Lin—*elf, Councilor;* Voluth—*elf, the shield maker;* Lord Lisith-ar-Moh—*elf;* and Yulis-ar-Key—*elf, Avula's finest swordsman.*

5. ***Thraxas and the Sorcerers.*** Riverdale, New York: Baen Publishing Enterprises, 2005, 262 p. ISBN: 0743499085.

TURAI, WINTER. Turai is preparing for the Sorcerers Assemblage. Deputy Consul Cicerius decides that Thraxas can help. This is both bad and good news for Thraxas. He failed his apprenticeship as a sorcerer and wants to stay as far away from the Assemblage as possible. On the other hand, he needs the money and, more than that, he needs to avoid making an enemy of Cicerius. King Lamachus and the Deputy Consul have embraced the insane idea that they can influence the election for Head of the Sorcerers Guild to favor the Turanian thazis-addict Lisutaris, Mistress of the Sky. Thraxas asks if he's going to be asked to do anything illegal, and he's told that if he is caught in any illegal action, Turai's government will disown him.

To get Thraxas admitted as an official Turanian observer to the Assemblage, Cicerius nominates him to the traditional (but, for the last 150 years, empty) post of Tribune of the People of Turai.

Lisutaris, Mistress of the Sky hires Thraxas to investigate a warning that the Simnian assassin Coinius has been hired to murder her. (She also hires Makri as a bodyguard.)

ASSOCIATES: Gurd—*owns the tavern The Avenging Axe;* Tanrose—*cooks and waits for Gurd to declare his intentions;* Makri—*Human/Elf/Orc crossbreed barmaid who is mooning over the elf See-ath;* Rezox—*a dragon-scale thief who tries to bribe Thraxas;* Rixad—*a timber dealer who hired Thraxas to investigate his wife;* Habal—*the wife;* Copro—*Turai's leading beautician;* Deputy Consul Cicerius—*who appoints Thraxas as a tribune so that he can hire Thraxas to ensure that no foreign sorcerer steals the Chief Sorcerer election;* Visus and Sininius—*Thraxas's fellow Tribunes;* Tilupasis—*who has been assigned to get Lisutaris elected.*

Turanian sorcerers at the Assemblage include: Old Hasius the Brilliant—*who is the Chief Investigating Officer at the Abode of Justice;* Harmon Half Elf; Melus the Fair; Gorsius Starfinder; Tirini Snake Smiter; Lanius Suncatcher; Capali Comet Rider; Orius Fire Tamer; Astrath Triple Moon; and Lisutaris, Mistress of the Sky.

Foreign sorcerers at the Assemblage include: Princess Direeva—*of the Wastelands;* Troverus and Sunstorm Ramius—*of Simnia;* Rokim the Bright—*of Samsarnia;* Darius Cloud Walker—*of Abelasi;* Irith Victorious—*who is an old friend of Thraxas, of Juval;* Jir-ar-Eth—*elf, of Avula;* Almalas—*of Nioj;* and Sareepa Lightning-Strikes-the-Mountain—*of Mattesh.*

Lasat, Axe of Gold—*Senior Sorcerer* and Charius the Wise—*the Acting Head of the Sorcerers* are in charge of the Assemblage. Officials of Turai include: Consul Kalius; Praetor Samilius—*head of the Civil Guard;* Rittius—*head of Palace Security;* and Captain Rallee. Hamana—*Turanian assassin;* Covinius—*Simnian assassin;* Casax and Karlox—*of the Brotherhood;* Senator Lodius—*who indulges in a little self-righteous blackmail;* Vadinex—*who is stopped from evicting 400 citizens by Thraxas, Tribune of the People;* Samanatius the philosopher—*one of Makri's favorite teachers;* Coralex—*a merchant;* Chiaraxi—*the healer;* and Rox—*the fish seller.*

6. ***Thraxas and the Dance of Death.*** Riverdale, New York: Baen Publishing Enterprises, 2007, 262 p. ISBN: 1416521445; 9781416521440.

TURAI, SUMMER. Lisutaris hires Thraxas to retrieve the Sorcerers' green jewel. It acts as an all-seeing eye and was entrusted to Lisutaris as the Head of the Sorcerers Guild so that she could use it to keep an eye on the Orcs and give warning if they were massing to invade Turai. It disappeared from her purse while she was at the racetrack. She doesn't need Thraxas to investigate; she used a spell to locate the jewel at the *The Spiked Mace* tavern. She can't march into a harbor tavern without attracting a great deal of attention, and she doesn't want the fact that she lost the jewel to become public. Thraxas's natural milieu includes taverns of all types; no one would remark on his presence at *The Spiked Mace*. Thraxas's presence doesn't cause comment; the dead men who recently held the jewel are another matter…

ASSOCIATES: Gurd—*who owns the tavern The Avenging Axe;* Tanrose—*Gurd's cook, she leaves her job and returns to her mother's home;* Makri—*crossbreed Human/Elf/Orc barmaid and student is in a murderous rage since she has been accused of theft;* Professor Toarius—*who has Makri expelled from college;* Rabaxos—*whose money was stolen;* Ossinax—*the glassmaker's son;* Avenaris—*Lisutaris's niece and secretary;* Barius—*the son of Professor Toarius.*

Dandelion—*who warns Thraxas that he is on a course that will lead to a bloodbath;* Moxalan—*who takes bets on the body count;* Parax—*the shoemaker;* Bexanos—*the ropemaker;* Gavarax—*owner of The Spiked Mace tavern;* Demanius—*of the Venarius Investigation Agency;* Sarin the Merciless—*whose fighting skills have improved;* Glixius Dragon Killer—*sorcerer;* and Horm the Dead—*Orcish Sorcerer, Lord of the Kingdom of Yal;* Casax and Karlox—*who escape the burning Mermaid tavern (the Brotherhood headquarters);* Orius Fire

Tamer—*the sorcerer who puts out the blaze.* Officials include: Consul Kalius, Captain Rallee, Deputy Consul Cicerius, and Hansius—*Cicerius's assistant.* Vadinex—*who levels a charge of cowardice against Thraxas;* Harmon Half Elf—*sorcerer;* and Princess Du-Akai.

7. ***Thraxas at War.*** Riverdale, New York: Baen Publishing Enterprises, 2006, 260 p. ISBN: 1416520503; 9781416520504.

TURAI, AUTUMN AND WINTER. Chief Sorcerer Lisutaris is certain that the Orcs are massing for war under Prince Amrag. Turai's officials reluctantly begin to prepare for war. As Tribune of the People, Thraxas participates in the Lesser War Council. Thraxas is assigned duties to prepare Turai for war.

Prefect Galwinius falls dead at a meeting of the Lesser War Council immediately after eating a pastry given to him by Senator Lodius. Senator Lodius wife Ivaris tricks Thraxas into taking the job of clearing her husband. (She behaves well, and Thraxas finds himself agreeing to help.)

Prince Dees-Akan, frustrated by Chief Sorcerer Lisutaris's insistence that the Orcs are on the move, fires her from the War Council.

ASSOCIATES: Gurd—*tavern owner;* Elsior—*the tavern cook;* Tanrose—*who is lured back by Thraxas who breaches state security and tells her of the upcoming war;* Makri—*crossbreed Human/Elf/Orc barmaid who begins teaching reading to some of the women of Turai between college sessions (she's a top student in her last year);* Dandelion—*who has figured out how to work the bar taps;* Morixa—*who has taken over the bakery;* Herminis—*who awaits execution for killing her abusive husband;* Viriggax—*a mercenary;* Toraggax—*his nephew (also a mercenary);* Horm the Dead—*a half Orc sorcerer who is enamored of Makri;* Palax and Kaby—*traveling musicians;* Hanama—*the assassin;* Prince Dees-Akan—*who leads the defense of Turai;* Senator Marius—*who promotes Thraxas to corporal;* Gravius—*Centurion of Phalanx seven;* Vadinex (Vedinax)—*who claims that Thraxas fled the Battle of Sanasa;* Samanatius the philosopher—*who joins the military;* Captain Rallee; Praetor Samilius—*Head of the Civil Guard;* Chiaraxi—*the healer;* Kerk—*Thraxas's dwa-addicted informer;* Domasius—*the lawyer;* and Kerinox—*the red-haired assassin.*

Officials involved in the War Council include Consul Kalius; Deputy Consul Cicerius; Lisutaris, Mistress of the Sky—*Head of the Sorcerers Guild;* Old Hasius the Brilliant—*Chief Sorcerer at the Palace;* Rittius—*Head of Palace Security;* Galwinius—*Prefect of Thamlin;* and General Pomius—*the highest ranking soldier in the state.* Hansius—*who assists Deputy Consul Cicerius in leading the Lesser War Council.* The Lesser War Council includes Senator Lodius; Senator Bevarius; Prefect Drinius; Prefect Galwinius; Prefect Resius; and Turai's Praetors, Tribunes, Palace officials, Civil Guards, and the military. Chef Erisox provides the food.

Lisutaris rallies Turai's sorcerers: Harmon Half Elf; Old Hasius the Brilliant; Melus the Fair; Lanius Suncatcher; Tirini Snake Smiter; Coranus the Grinder; Capali Comet Rider; Anumaris Thunderbolt; Gorsius Starfinder; Patalix Rainmaker; Ovinian the True; and even Astrath Triple Moon.

8. ***Thraxas Under Seige.*** Riverdale, New York: Baen Publishing Enterprises, 2008, 276 p. ISBN: 1416555730; 9781416555735.

TURAI, WINTER (ONE MONTH AFTER THE DEFEAT AT TURAI'S GATES). Orcs are at Turai's gates: the city is under siege. Tanrose hires Thraxas to find a treasure of 14,000 gurans that her mother believes her father hid in the city. Thraxas takes the case, partly to help Tanrose and partly because he needs the money. Glixius Dragon Killer invited himself to *The Avenging Axe's* weekly game of rak, and Thraxas needs 500 gurans to play.

Lisutaris asks Thraxas for advice in locating a sorcerous item that calls up storms, a shell called Ocean Storm. She's concerned that a powerful sorcerer such as Horm the Dead or Deeziz the Unseen could use it as a weapon against Turai.

ASSOCIATES: Gurd—*tavern owner, an old battle-companion of Thraxas;* Tanrose—*Gurd's cook and fiancé;* Dandelion—*barmaid;* Makri—*crossbreed Huamn/Elf/Orc, half-sister of Prince Amrag, barmaid;* Kaby—*the traveling musician who is the first to come down with the winter malady;* Palax—*her partner (the second to take ill);* Lisutaris—*the sorcerer (the third);* Hanama—*the assassin (the fourth);* Chiaraxi—*the healer (the fifth);* Tanrose—*the sixth;* Sarin the Merciless—*the seventh;* apprentice cook Elsior—*the eighth;* Gurd—*the ninth,* and Makri—*the tenth;* Viriggax—*a mercenary;* Samanatius—*the philosopher;* Prefect Drinius; Karlox—*an enforcer for the Brotherhood;* Kerk—*Thraxas's informer;* Nerinax—*the beggar;* Parax—*the shoemaker;* Partulax—*who delivers the beer;* Herminis—*the fugitive;* the singer Moolifi—*Captain Rallee's new girlfriend;* Ozax—*a soldier;* Marizaz—*the Orc who was the number two gladiator in the Orcish arena until Makri left;* Hansius—*Deputy Consul Cicerius's assistant;* Bishop Gzrkius; and Pontifex Derlex.

Lisutaris meets with sorcerers Tirini Snake Smiter, Harmon Half Elf, Coranius the Grinder, Anumaris Thunderbolt, Lanius Suncatcher, Melus the Fair, and old Hasius the Brilliant in Thraxas's rooms. Astrath Triple Moon is close to being accepted as a full member of the Sorcerers Guild once more.

Rak players include Glixius Dragon Killer—*sorcerer;* General Acarius—*who has time on his hands during the seige;* Grax—*the wine merchant;* Ravenius—*who is young and rich;* Casax—*local head of the Brotherhood;* Praetor Capatius; Horm the Dead—*Orcish Sorcerer and Lord of the Kingdom of Yal;* and Thraxas—*who is forwarded the money for the game by Lisutaris and Deputy Consul Cicerius.*

SHETTERLY, Will.

CHIMERA

Genres/Themes Crossed: Man as Creator X Hard-Boiled Mystery.

Subjects/Character Types: Genetically engineered species X Private Investigators.

Series/Stand-Alone: Stand alone.

Scene of the Crime: Far Future Los Angeles.

Detective: Chase Maxwell, "Max" to both friends and acquaintances, is a private investigator. Max was born to wealth, but his family was left destitute when his father's financial empire crumbled. His father committed suicide, but the debts did not die with him. To satisfy the creditors, his mother sold everything she had, then she sold herself, indenturing herself for a 10-year contract as a middle management executive. It paid off the debts, but couldn't cover Max's tuition at Yale and his sister Selene's tuition at a prep school. Max dropped out of Yale and joined the UN Peace Force. They trained him and outfitted him with an infinite pocket. He resigned from the Peace Force rather than face Court Martial after a successful mission, during which he had to be removed from command because he was unwilling to move forward when the team's actions would destroy an innocent "critter" (chimera) family.

Known Associates: The team members on Lieutenant Chase's final mission were Sergeant Eddie LeFevre, Sergeant Lupe Rivera, Lieutenant Anne Lassiter, and a Model XL-5 commandobot. His sister is dead, his mother has become an alcoholic.

Premise: Scientists have developed several servant classes. Geneticists spliced human and animal genes together to create chimeras (commonly called critters), they are created to be slaves. Roboticists have created various kinds of bots, each programmed to do a particular job. Scientists who have worked on artificial intelligence have created AIs; some people call them MIs, because how can intelligence be artificial? The cutting-edge question is whether or not a human's consciousness can successfully be moved to a created device such as a computer or a constructed body.

Comment: Will Shetterly shares a Web site with Emma Bull at http://shetterly.googlepages.com/. His blog site at http://shetterly.blogspot.com/ provides a link to his very interesting Live Journal (http://willshetterly.livejournal.com/), which includes thought-provoking comments on capitalism, class, and race.

Literary Magic & Mayhem: Chase Maxwell is a wise-cracking, tough-guy-with-a-heart-of-gold Private Investigator. He's a decent human being in a society that does not reward decency. He is of his world, in that he shares the prejudices of his society, but he rejects the values of that society when they would dictate actions that violate his moral code. When the chips are down, Maxwell cracks wise; for instance, when he's forced into a car with one of the sets of villains, he begins with "Are we there yet?" When discussing strategy with Zoe, he displays his somewhat mordant humor:

> [Max] shrugged. "Hiding tracking software in an earring must mean Gold knew the AI didn't want to be found."
> "There was nothing on my computer. I could try it on the net."
> "And find out it wipes out the IRS files?"
> "We'd be heroes."
> "Sure, everybody else wants to kill us. Why leave the feds out of the fun?" (p. 259)

It's a trait shared, although to a lesser extent, with many of the characters. The dialog in this book is a lot of fun; the themes are thought-proving; elements of the world he built explore some of the foundational philosophical questions such as "What makes something human?" and "What is our responsibility to life that we create?"—as well as questions about the extent to which individual freedom gives people the right to destroy themselves and an exploration of how different people weigh the value of time and money.

Explorations: One of the quotes in Shetterly's Live Journal is "Advocates of capitalism are very apt to appeal to the sacred principles of liberty, which are embodied in one maxim: The fortunate must not be restrained in the exercise of tyranny over the unfortunate" (Bertrand Russell). How does this relate to the book? How does Ms. Simone Agosto of Prosperity Indenture Services define freedom?

Could the concept of indenture and the behavior of people at the indenture camps be compared to aspects of our society? How do people in our society deal with easy credit, for instance in credit cards?

What animals would make interesting crosses with humans? What traits would make nice additions to the human genome?

What aspects of a creature make it morally imperative for society to accord that creature civil rights?

Does freedom include the legal right to destroy yourself? What about the moral right? Where are the boundaries?

What were Mycroft's reasons for not working on the project? Are the ramifications of the questions he asks explored in the book? Would they apply to such common science fiction technology as Star Trek's transporters? Where would they apply to other works? How often do the philosophical questions get asked when a technology offers survival? How often do they get asked when a technology offers convenience?

THE CASE

Chimera. New York: TOR, 2000, 285 p. ISBN: 0312866305.

LOS ANGELES, FAR FUTURE. Zoe was freed by Dr. Janna Gold, who then, against all convention, adopted her. Dr. Gold traveled to Los Angeles for business and was gunned down by rogue copbots before she could reach her hotel. Her dying gift to Zoe was an odd earring. Zoe took it and ran. Zoe hadn't gotten far before she was accosted by a Police Inspector (Doyle), who attacked her in an attempt to get the earring. After that, Zoe was terrified of the police, but she needed someone to discover the truth about he murder of her mother. The first few private investigators she contacted wouldn't work for critters, and she was desperate when Chase "Max" Maxwell was recommended to her. Max's voicemail said he would be gambling, so she tracks him down in Arthur's casino and offers him the job. He takes her cash and hocks her watch before he slows down enough to get a good look at her. Max, like the other PIs, has a policy against working for chimeras, but he had gambled away his retainer before he realized that his new client is part cat. He agrees to work for Zoe for one day, but by the time that day is over, he has seen too many innocents killed to be able to walk away.

ASSOCIATES: Zoe Domingo—*the client;* Arthur Madden—*the casino owner who loaned money to Max;* Bruno Samson (Human-Doberman cross), and Rashid (Human-Orca cross)—*are Arthur's enforcers;* Officer Manny Vallejo, Officer Dick Chumley, and the Technology Crimes Division's Kris Blake—*are officers who are trying to find "the earring";* Django Kay (Human-Wolverine cross)—*is passing as human;* Oberon Chain—*owner of Chain Logic;* Professor Amos Tauber—*the nation's foremost expert on non-human rights;* Mycroft—*a consultant specializing in sapience, xenogenetics, and chimera matters;* Dr. Willa Catherine Vaughn—*one of the inventors of chimeras;* Ms. Simone Agosto—*works for Prosperity Indenture Services;* Nate (Human-Weasel cross)—*the bartender;* Ruby (Human-Wolf cross) and Eddie LeFevre—*who do their best to help fugitives Zoe and Max.*

SKIBBINS, David.

EIGHT OF SWORDS

Genres/Themes Crossed: Paranormal X Traditional Mystery.

Subjects/Character Types: Tarot X Amateur Detective (Contemporary).

Series/Stand-Alone: Warren changes over the course of the series, overcoming (or at least learning more constructive ways to deal with) some of his inner demons. Relationships change over the course of the series as well. It is best to read this series in order.

Scene of the Crime: Present-day Berkeley.

Detective: "Warren Ritter" is one of the names used by fugitive Richard Green. He is a rapid-cycling manic-depressive who has been hiding from federal agents for more than 30 years. In those 30 years, he developed excellent survival skills, along with an advanced case of paranoia. He is acutely aware of the people around him. He is off the radar: no one knows his real identity, and the only personal history anyone knows about him is the one that he fabricated. He earns cash, the better to avoid leaving a paper trail of his activities. The profession he chose is tarot card reader, something that he regards as a gentle, even useful, con game. He finds it disturbing that he can't hide from the cards.

Known Associates: Rose Janeworth is Warren's therapist. Heather Talbridge (Heather Wellington) is Warren's friend. Warren's girlfriend is disabled veteran and computer hacker Sally McLaughlin. Max Valdez of Valdez Security Systems occasionally provides operatives to assist Warren's investigations. Tara is Warren's sister. Thirty years ago Cathy Witkowski was Warren's girlfriend, she is the mother of Warren's daughter Francine. Officer James McNally is Warren's best friend and shooting buddy. Philip Letour first read the Tarot for Warren in Mexico in 1970 he is the only guy that Warren knows who can actually read the future in the Tarot cards.

Premise: Richard was a member of the Weather Underground in the late 1960s. His group became progressively more radical, finally moving to violence to try to stop the Vietnam War. When he was 23 years old, Richard blew up a building, taking out a large part of his cell. Then he fled. He had some money, but needed a legitimate source of income to fend off police scrutiny. He turned to telling fortunes on the streets of Berkeley. He does not believe in the Tarot; he regards himself as perpetuating feel-good hoaxes for people who believe in that "superstitious nonsense." He's observant, and draws quick conclusions from people's manner and dress; he then extrapolates from that observed information to "read the cards" and tell them what they want to hear. He's pretty successful. When one of his clients is kidnapped, he can't stop worrying about the reading he did for her. When the police find his business card, he is too emotionally involved to run. After his first case, he is drawn into others by people who know him or know of him and were impressed by his first success.

Comment: While Warren protests that he does not believe in the cards: he finds them a little creepy. He sees patterns and sequences repeat, as if someone is trying to send him a message. He does not believe in the message, nor in the messenger, but he finds himself acting on the patterns in the card readings.

> The cards don't worry about whether or not I believe in them. Each year I do this work, the cards get pushier and pushier. They keep repeating themselves, resisting randomness. They fall again and again in the same patterns and sequences, no matter how often I shuffle them. (*Eight of Swords,* p. 26)

In 2004, the book won Malice Domestic/St. Martin's Press Best First Traditional Mystery. David Skibbins Web site at http://www.davidskibbins.com/ includes information on his life and his books, as well as a link for an online tarot reading.

Literary Magic & Mayhem: The passages regarding Warren's bipolar condition are very well done. In particular, the thought process that the reader sees when Warren is in a manic phase in *The High Priestess* is frightening, and it seems true to life. Tarot reading is explained pretty well to Warren's friend James in *Eight of Swords.* In *The Star,* Warren must deal with his illness as he works to help his daughter cope with her own bipolar disorder. He displays an honesty and commitment that deserve admiration. He leaves behind the histrionics and self-pity that he displayed in previous books and takes on the hard work of building a relationship. *The Star* is also the book that barely touches on the supernatural aspects of the series. Throughout the series, much of the basic investigative work is taken on by Warren's friends. Warren has a therapist Rose, who acts as a profiler, a hacker friend Sarah, who is willing to access law enforcement databases, and Sally's friends, including Max, are able to provide surveillance. Warren's contribution is to theorize and coordinate; he seems strangely distanced from most of the investigation. In *The High Priestess,* Warren finds out that some of his beliefs about his own past are wrong. In *The Star,* he finds out that his conception of his parents is flawed as well. He also takes on responsibilities, particularly in *The Star,* leaving behind his protracted adolescence as he does his best for the people whom he has come to love. In *The Hanged Man,* the narrative is split: part is from Warren's point of view, part from Heather's, and part from Sally's. In this book, the reader finds out that Sally has her own problems. The writing is Hemingway-esque, but it's not Hemingway. The writing improves from one book to the next, but as the series progresses, the supernatural elements become more literal and less interesting, finally tapering off to almost nothing in the third book, *The Star,* where the star of the title refers to a couple of place names and to a general theme, but is not central to the investigation. In the fourth book, the The Hanged Man tarot card acts as a goad, and The World card foreshadows changes in Warren's life; yet neither is central to the investigation.

THE CASES

1. ***Eight of Swords.*** New York: St. Martin's Press, 2004, 261 p. ISBN: 0312339062, 9780312339067.

Berkeley, present day. Warren saw evil coming in Heather's Tarot reading; but he did nothing. After all, he doesn't believe in superstitious nonsense like Tarot. Now something has happened to her and the police are investigating. Then the FBI joins the investigation. Then his sister Tara walks by him and, despite 30 years and plastic surgery, she recognizes him, yelling his real name out for everyone to hear. Normally he would run away and assume a new identity. He can't afford police scrutiny, but he saw evil in the cards and he didn't warn Heather. He can't force himself to leave while she is in danger.

Associates: Heather Wellington—*a client;* Louise Wellington—*Heather's mother;* Frank Wellington—*Heather's father;* Curtis Jackson—*Heather's boyfriend;* Hal Russell—*Heather's ex-boyfriend;* Tara—*Warren's sister;* Officer James McNally—*Warren's favorite cop;* Detective Robert Flemish—*who is searching for Heather;* Rose Janeworth—*Warren's therapist;* Sally McLaughlin—*Warren's girlfriend;* Max Valdez—*who owns a security company;* Special Agent David Stiles (FBI)—*who is investigating a kidnapping;* Philip Letour—*who can read the cards.*

2. ***The High Priestess.*** New York: St. Martin's Press, 2006, 280 p. ISBN: 0312352336, 9780312352332.

Berkeley, present day. Edward Hightower is a man from Warren's past...his far past, his secret past. When Edward approaches him and asks him to investigate the serial killing of members of the church that Edward and his sister lead, Warren can't say "no." Warren's life becomes more complex when he finds out that the church is the Fellowship of the Arising Night (a denomination of the Church of Satan). Again, he is tempted to run, but he has started relationships that hold him to this place and identity, both with Sally and with his newly discovered daughter.

Associates: Mr. Edward Hightower—*a.k.a. Stephon Ventnor;* Miko Tashima—*girlfriend of the late Roger Black;* Heather Talbridge—*a friend of Warren's;* Sally McLaughlin—*Warren's girlfrend;* Rose Janeworth—*Warren's therapist;* Philip Letour—*who can read the cards;* Leticia—*a regular client;* Grace Westin—*who runs a gift store called Heavenly Deliveries;* Veronique

Hightower—*who, 30 years ago, was Richard's lover;* Tara—*Warren's sister;* Cathy Witkowski—*Francine's mother;* Francine—*Warren's daughter;* Officer James McNally—*who is about to give up the police force and open a bike shop.*

3. ***The Star.*** New York: St. Martin's Press, 2007, 232 p. ISBN: 0312361939, 9780312361939.

BERKELEY, PRESENT DAY. Warren looks up from his tarot reading table on the sidewalk in front of Cody's Books to see his daughter Fran standing before him and asking for his help. Her estranged husband left with their infant son, threatening to have her judged an unfit mother if she tries to get her baby back. Warren can see her going through the same mood swings that have plagued him, and he finds her just as touchy and difficult to reach as others have found him. Before she straightens herself out, her husband's body washes up on the beach. Fran is the prime suspect. Warren knows the demons that drive Fran all too well. He can't be sure that she's innocent, but he is sure that she's closer to being suicidal than homicidal, and he's frightened that she'll give up before he can find out the truth.

ASSOCIATES: Fran Wilkins—*Warren's daughter;* Tara—*his sister;* Justin—*his grandson;* Sally McLaughlin—*his lover;* Heather Talbridge—*the young woman who Sally has befriended;* Eric Landon—*a friend of Warren's father;* Rose Janeworth—*Warren's therapist who begins to work with Fran;* Officer James McNally—*who is about to give up the police force and open a bike shop;* Max Valdez—*who owns a private investigation agency;* Julia Hightower—*Warren's stepmother;* Levar Walters—*a.k.a. Lebna Wekesa, a.k.a. Lawrence West, a man from Warren's past;* Officer Theodore Vespie—*who was Orrin Wilkins's partner;* the Reverend Larry Dalton—*Fran and Orrin's pastor;* Lorraine—*the Reverend's wife;* Dean Pak—*the Reverend's ex-lover;* FBI Special Agent David Stiles—*who once tried to pin a murder on Warren;* and Richard Phillips—*game developer.*

4. ***The Hanged Man.*** New York: St. Martin's Press, 2008, 228 p. ISBN: 0312377835, 9780312377830.

BERKELEY, PRESENT DAY. When Sally receives a call from an old friend, Thérèse, who has been accused of murder, Sally asks Warren for his help. He refuses. He's tired of dealing with murder; he wants a normal life. He leaves her working on the investigation and heads for home, only to get a call from Phillip Letour, who is in the hospital and needs Warren to safeguard an ancient deck of tarot cards. The cards won't leave Warren alone until he agrees to help in Thérèse's investigation.

Thérèse is a dominatrix and the murder victim was one of her clients. To further the investigation Warren must get involved in the world of bondage and domination. Sally, coping with (and sometimes working with) the voices in her head, investigates the computer aspects of the case while Heather poses as a reporter to interview the victim's business rivals.

ASSOCIATES: Sally McLaughlin—*Warren's lover;* her Goddess Council: the vengeful Venge, the gentle Psyche, and the wise Old Spider Woman; Ripley—*Sally's rottweiler;* Heather Talbridge—*a.k.a. Heather Wellington, an emancipated minor who lives with Sally;* Rose Janeworth—*Warren's therapist;* Phillip Letour—*Warren's mentor in the Tarot;* Tara—*Warren's sister;* Fran—*his daughter;* Justin—*his grandson;* Officer James McNally—*who is still on the police force;* Max Valdez—*who owns a private investigation agency;* the dominatrix Thérèse—*Sally's oldest friend (Sally knew her when she was called Doris);* Vera—*is Thérèse's slave;* Steele—*owns and teaches at The Academy of Correction;* Troy Baker—*who wants Phillip's tarot deck;* Judy Hollister—*Thérèse's lawyer;* Laura Hawkins—*COO of Hawkins Computer Defense Systems;* Edgar Allen—*who is in love with his boss;* and David Cabot—*of Cabot Security.*

STABENOW, Dana. (Editor)

POWERS OF DETECTION: STORIES OF MYSTERY AND FANTASY

Genres/Themes Crossed: Secret Society, Blended Society X Hard-Boiled Mystery, Traditional Mystery.

Subjects/Character Types: Spell-Casters, Vampires, Aliens X Amateur Sleuths, Private Investigators.

Series/Stand-Alone: Anthology of short stories.

Scene of the Crime: Varies.

Detective: Varies.

Known Associates: Varies.

Premise: Dana Stabenow asked the authors for murder in a fantasy or science fiction setting.

Comment: Dana Stabenow's Web site at http://www.stabenow.com/ includes haiku, photographs, and news along to links to series and book information, her newsletter, and categories of her blog.

Literary Magic & Mayhem: The stories, written for these anthologies, utilize fantasy elements, everything from ghosts to mages, Santa Claus to dragons, vigilantes to vampires, students to apprentices to interns... Mike Doogan has contributed an interesting science fiction story to *Powers of Detection.* Some of the stories are stand-alones, some are episodes in the lives of series characters. Many of the stories are chilling, many are humorous, most combine humor and horror through excellent storytelling.

Explorations: (NOTE: Choose from among these questions, they don't all work with all the stories in the anthologies.)

Were the first few (or the last few) sentences of the story particularly powerful or particularly amusing? In what way?

Were there any sections in the story that resonated with real world events, iconic movie moments, or archetypes?

Did the person who investigated the crime end up paying an emotional price?

Do the story characters fit into categories of good and evil?

THE CASES

1. ***Powers of Detection: Stories of Mystery and Fantasy.*** New York: Ace Books, 2004, 227 p. ISBN: 0441011977, 9780441011971.

CONTENTS: Cold Spell *by Donna Andrews;* The Nightside, Needless to Say *by Simon R. Green;* Lovely *by John Straley;* The Price *by Anne Bishop;* Fairy Dust *by Charlaine Harris;* The Judgement *by Anne Perry;* The Sorcerer's Assassin *by Sharon Shinn;* The Boy Who Chased Seagulls *by Michael Armstrong;* Palimpsest *by Laura Anne Gilman;* The Death of Clickclickwhistle *by Mike Doogan;* Cairene Dawn *by Jay Caselberg;* Justice Is a Two-Edged Sword *by Dana Stabenow.*

2. ***Unusual Suspects: Stories of Mystery and Fantasy.*** New York: Ace Books, 2008, 306 p. ISBN: 9780441016372.

CONTENTS: Lucky *by Charlaine Harris;* Bogieman *by Carole Nelson Douglas;* Looks Are Deceiving *by Michael A. Stackpole;* The House of Seven Spirits *by Sharon Shinn;* Glamour *by Mike Doogan;* Spellbound *by Donna Andrews;* The Duh Vice *by Michael Armstrong;* Weight of the World *by John Straley;* Illumination *by Laura Anne Gilman;* The House *by Laurie R. King;* Appetite for Murder *by Simon R. Green;* A Woman's Work *by Dana Stabenow.*

SULLIVAN, Mark T.

THE PURIFICATION CEREMONY

Genres/Themes Crossed: Paranormal X Traditional Mystery.

Subjects/Character Types: Shaman X Amateur Sleuth (Contemporary).

Series/Stand-Alone: Stand-alone.

Scene of the Crime: Present-day British Columbia and Alberta, Canada.

Detective: Diana Jackson, was taught by her father, her mother, and her great-uncle about how to interact with the world. This included hunting and tracking in a way that involves her spirit as well as her mind. Her family named her "Little Crow," and this name connects her to the person who she was as a child. When her mother died, Little Crow turned away from her family and her heritage and embraced being "Diana Jackson." After her father's, death she has a series of dreams that draw her back to the other side of her nature. She decides to take a hunting trip to reconnect with her spiritual self.

Known Associates: The other members of the hunting party include Earl and Lenore Addison, rich Texans who spend the time they're not hunting sniping at each other; an old friend of Diana's father, Michael Griffin (Griff); Steve Kurant, a journalist; three friends who grew up hunting together: Arnie Taylor (the pediatrician), Phil Nunn (the Viet Nam vet), and Sal "Butch" Daloia (the hippie). The people who are running the hunt are Mike and Sheila Cantrell, with help from Tim and Theresa Nelson, Don Patterson (Don and Tim are guides), and Grover, who helps around the Lodge. Diana thinks often of her father (Hart), her mother (Katherine), her great-uncle Mitchell, her husband, Kevin, and her children, Emily and Patrick.

Premise: Diana's great-uncle Mitchell's mother was Micmac; she married a Penobscot. She lived among the Penobscots until her death, but taught her son the ways of the Micmac people. This included a world view that encompasses six levels of existence: the World Beneath the Earth, the World Beneath the Water, Earth World, Ghost World, the World Above the Earth, and the World Above the Sky. What underlies them all is the life force, called Power. Everything in the world we know is simply a manifestation of this power, including us. Everything is connected. This world view alters Diana's reality; she is connected to everything in ways that seem foreign to us. This increases her awareness and knowledge of the world around her and makes her a superior tracker. She knows that she is being tracked before the first member of the hunting party is murdered. Unfortunately, the man who is hunting the hunters has skills similar to Diana's, but his are more highly developed.

Comment: The book was featured in many hunting magazines, most with praise, a few with criticism. Some parts of it read almost as a semi-mystical apologia for hunting. Hunting is described as an art in which the hunter becomes attuned to one of God's great creations, as a process of self-refinement. The unspoken message is that hunting is something powerful, but neutral, acting as a mirror to bring out the characters of the hunters. Some see it as a way to conquer nature, others as a way to master themselves. Whitetail bucks are described as the craftiest game animal in North America, treated as if they have almost mystical powers, elevated in a way that promotes the idea that hunting is an evenly matched contest between the hunter and the prey.

Sullivan's Web site at http://marktsullivan.com/ provides information about the books, some biographical information, and a link to his blog at http://marktsullivan.com/blog/blog.asp.

Literary Magic & Mayhem: The device of having Diana return to a shamanic understanding of the world—after a long period in which she had intentionally cut herself off from that world—allows the author to introduce the mystical elements of the story gradually. It creates a situation in which she can reach for developed skills, without taking them for granted. Her having to think about them and exercise them consciously delivers a thoughtful, step by step approach to this world for the reader. It includes a little theology:

> For my father and Mitchell, the deer hunt was a drama of Power. Not power in the political sense of hunter and prey, but Power in the Micmac sense; that is, the deer hunt was an act of creation, a reflection of the fluid, continuous state of transformation between life and death in which we lived. (p. 110)

along with descriptions of what it feels like, to be conscious of that world:

> I closed my eyes and repeated the sequence of memory and rhythmic breathing I had followed the evening before. Soon I could feel my heart beating outward, striking objects and reflecting back to me the energies within the predawn... The young crow cawed loudly as it left the tree. And, for a moment, I closed my eyes and left with it, soaring on an updraft until I looked down upon the forest. (p. 307)

Explorations: Life and untimely death is a recurring theme in the book. Where do you see it played out? What sort of responsibility do others have for those deaths?

How did Diana's perceptions of her mother's death change?

What were the most interesting aspects of the shamanic awareness shown by Diana and others? How did characters reach that state?

THE CASE

The Purification Ceremony. New York: Avon Books, c1997, 335 p. ISBN: 00380974282.

British Columbia, November 199? A 10-day hunting vacation turns into a battle for survival. A madman stalks hunters staying at the isolated Metcalf resort. He has destroyed their only means of communication with the outside world. No one will come and save them. The serial killer is determined and powerful. Diana Jackson (Little Crow) must embrace her own power to have any chance of stopping him.

Associates: See above.

SWANN, S. Andrew. (Pen name of Steven Swiniarski.)

FORESTS OF THE NIGHT

Genres/Themes Crossed: Man as Creator, Alien Interference, Blended Society, Secret Society X Hard-Boiled Mystery.

Subjects/Character Types: Genetically engineered species, Alien incursion X Private Investigators.

Series/Stand-Alone: The series consists of four very different books that feature different protagonists in different cities. Together they show the world as it changes. Readers interested in the world, the political conflicts and intrigues, and the stresses on the society will want to read the four books in chronological order (listed below). Readers interested in the protagonist of the first book (Nohar) may prefer to skip the second and third book of the series and simply read the first and the fourth, the books that focus on Nohar's story.

The "feel" of each book is, to some extent, set by the protagonist. Nohar is controlled and thoughtful. He is a deeply decent person and a mass of contradictions. He is the ultimate tough guy, but he loves his pet cat. He is an angry young man who is terrified that his rage will get the better of him, and so he keeps that part of his nature that he thinks of as "The Beast" under firm control. He was orphaned through the institutional bigotry of the country that accepted his people as refugees, yet he does not hate humans, his best friend is a human. He is complex and likable. Readers who enjoy the character might want to read *Forests of the Night* but skip both *Emperors of the Twilight* and *Specters of the Dawn* (using the information under "Premise" to fill in the political and social events of the years covered in the timespan encompassed by those novels, and then read the second Nohar story, *Fearful Symmetries*).

The other protagonists are very different from Nohar. *Emperors of the Twilight* features the carefully repressed, ruthless, and focused Evi. *Specters of the Dawn* centers on the self-centered and self-pitying Angelica. The four books, in order, show the revolution(s) that change the world.

Scene of the Crime: Cleveland, 2053.

Detective(s):

Nohar Rajasthan: The Rajasthans were created using tiger DNA to serve in the Indian Special Forces. Nohar is second generation; he never had combat training, but he has the Rajasthan sense of smell, reflexes, strength, and instincts, and they serve him well as a private investigator.

He's 260 centimeters tall, 300 kilos, and bipedal like all the moreaus. He was born in either 2027 or 2028. His mother Orai died when Nohar was five; he never knew his father.

Evi Isham was created in a Jordanian lab from the last commercial strain of General Purpose Human Embryo produced by prewar Japan. She was young when the lab was overrun by Israeli commandoes, who gathered up her and her 99 siblings and took them back to Israel. Colonel Abdel raised and trained her. In *Emperors of the Twilight,* she thinks often about Colonel Abdel. She is guided by his maxims and seems to think of him with fondness, but at one point she remembers him with fury.

> They said human experiments were atrocities. What were you going to do when you swept through that Jordanian facility? Kill us all?...No you couldn't do that What a waste it would have been. You took us and trained us to be your atrocities. (p. 376)

From the moment she was created Evi has been a tool, an intelligence asset, for one government or another: treated more as property than as a person. Even after franks were given civil rights (2054), she stayed in the intelligence business; and in this book she realizes that, even when she thought she was among comrades, she was never trusted or treated as an equal.

Evi met Nohar when she tracked assassin Hassan Sabah (moreau, canine) who was involved in Nohar's murder investigation in *Forests of the Night.* In the aftermath of the investigation, Evi began working for the Domestic Crisis Think Tank. She is the protagonist in *Emperors of the Twilight.* That novel opens on her 33rd birthday, December 31, 2058.

Angelica Lorenzo y Lopez: "Angel" is a moreau rabbit with a bad attitude and a vicious kick. She led the Stigmata gang in Cleveland until the gang was massacred by the Zipperheads. She met Nohar in the course of his investigation in *Forests of the Night.* Once that case closed, she moved to San Francisco, California. She is the protagonist in *Specters of the Dawn.*

Known Associates: Mandvi "Manny" Gujerat (moreau: mongoose) raised Nohar after his mother died. He is not family by blood, but he's the closest approximation of family left to Nohar. Manny works as a forensic expert for the police force when crimes involve moreaus. In *Forests of the Night,* Maria Limon breaks up with Nohar after he stands her up. (He forgot all about their date in the danger and excitement of the bloodbath at Nugoya's club.) Robert "Bobby" Dittrich was Nohar's first (and only) human friend. Officer Irwin Harsk, the detective in charge of Moreytown, has jurisdiction over any Cleveland investigation involving moreaus; the scope of his work has been broadened to cover the few franks that have been allowed into the country by the INS and who have migrated to Cleveland, simply because they are also genetically engineered.

Premise: Moreaus (made by splicing together human and animal genes) were designed by geneticists as combat troops. They were considered slaves or machines in Europe until the Pope took the stand that they had souls. The war ended in 2035. In 2041, the production lines stopped. There are literally thousands of moreau species. Even moreaus who look the same will likely be made from different combinations of genes. The result is that most pairings cannot produce children. The Bensheim Genetic Repository in Switzerland holds samples of genetic material from every known line. Dr. Bensheim was one of the genetic technicians who helped create the moreaus. He believed that every species should have the right to reproduce. Moreau females who wish to have children go to a Bensheim clinic for genetic testing, where their genetic variation is identified and they can be inseminated with sperm from their own species. In the United States the 29th Amendment (the limited Morey amendment) gave moreaus some of the rights of humans. All moreaus stand upright and are bipedal. In Cleveland, most of the moreau live in a ghetto called Moreytown.

Franks were created in Japan in defiance of the United Nations order that prohibited the manipulation of human genes. Their designers grafted manufactured parts onto genetically altered humans. When China bombed Tokyo many years ago much of the technology and information on creating and maintaining Franks was lost. The Immigration and Naturalization Service worked to keep human frankensteins out of the United States. Those that managed to get into the country had no rights and face even greater prejudice than do the moreaus.

"Pinks" is a slang term for human. It is used by moreaus and franks to express the idea that humans are weak, stupid, soft, and vaguely repellent.

The first moreau species that would breed true was engineered in South Korea in 2008, around the time of the beginning of the war for Korean unification. In 2015, an international debate regarding genetic engineering for military purposes resulted in United Nations bans on genetically engineered diseases and genetic engineering utilizing the human genome. A proposed ban on the genetic engineering of sapient animals failed. In 2017, one result of a United States constitutional convention to draft a 29th Amendment was the extension of the rights promulgated in the Bill of Rights to the sapient results of genetic engineering. In 2019, terrorist attacks sparked the Third Gulf War, which was followed by the 2024 Pan-Asian War. As India's defenses crumbled, Officer Datia Rajastahn's entire company of moreau tigers seized a cargo plane and escaped to claim refugee status in America. The airlift gained worldwide attention and became known as the Rajastahn airlift.

Datia Rajatahn became a symbol for those fighting for moreau freedom and moreau rights. America was seen as the land of hope, and moreaus flocked to it. The United States moved forward on a hopeful, generous, peaceful, and optimistic path. In 2029, the American space program reached its apex, designing space probes to find out about the neighbors of our galaxy.

In 2030, an Israeli commando group penetrated a secret Jordanian base where franks were engineered and trained as agents. The 100 immature franks found there were taken and trained as Israeli agents. From the years 2032 to 2044, a series of genetically engineered pandemics decimated Africa. In 2034, an earthquake measuring 9.5 on the Richter scale forever altered California. The last Arab-Israeli War was waged from 2034 to 2041. When it ended, radiation had made Israel uninhabitable. The remnants of the Israeli government-in-exile moved to Geneva. The Pan-Asian War ended in 2035 when Tokyo was nuked. Most of the Japanese technological advances related to moreaus and franks were destroyed.

By the end of 2037, the United States was home to more than 10 million moreau. Most of them were refugees from the various wars. In 2038, Pope Leo XIV decreed that, although genetic engineering is a sin, moreau have souls. This triggered a virtual civil war in Central America. Latin American moreau immigration to the United States quadrupled. In 2038, Mr. Binder spoke before the Cleveland City Club about America's moral imperative to accept all moreau refugees. In 2042, radical moreau leader Datia Rajastahn incited his followers to begin the Dark August riots. After the moreytown riots, Congressman Binder promised his constituents in the 12th District that he would work to ban moreau immigration. In 2043, the United States response to the riots was a contraction of hope. Optimism ended, NASA funding was cut, projects were mothballed. There was a moratorium placed on moreau immigration, and moreaus were ghettoized as a matter of public policy.

In 2045, a group that included franks was involved in a South African coup, and it was revealed that South Africa had been running a clandestine operation to create franks. Almost a million franks were living in South Africa. The coup gave full citizenship rights to franks (in South Africa). In the United States, franks had no rights at all. In 2053, Congressman Binder (who was running for a seat in the Senate) had a bill on the floor of the House of Representatives to outlaw moreau immigration and begin mandatory sterilization of all moreaus. (*Forests of the Night* is set in 2053.)

In 2054, a Supreme Court decision held that the 29th amendment applied to all genetically engineered beings, including franks. (*Emperors of the Twilight* is set in 2058.)

In 2059, the public learned that the government had been hiding evidence of an alien incursion on Earth. Soon after that discovery, the FBI moved against the militarized Moreau Defense League and touched off moreau riots across the country. (*Spectres of the Dawn* is set in October of 2059. *Fearful Symmetries* is set over a decade later, in 2070.)

Comment: S. Andrew Swann's Web site http://www.sandrewswann.com includes links to his Facebook page, as well as links to S. Andrew Swann on YouTube, Twitter, FriendFeed, and Scribd. His main site includes a feed from his blog (and a link to his blog). Some of the blog entries include his interesting thoughts on writing technique.

Literary Magic & Mayhem: The books contain many powerful and disturbing ideas and observations. For instance, in the course of his investigation in *Fearful Symmetries,* Nohar encounters a wild pack of engineered dogs. Many of them are sick, dying. They know that they will be hunted down if people know of the existence of the pack. Their leader, Elijah, tells Nohar that man will be dissatisfied until he can destroy what he has created (p. 181).

In *Specters of the Dawn,* Angelica reflects: "The world not only wasn't fair, it was actively hostile" (p. 595). At the time, it seemed like an errant smart-aleck thought. Later she is horrified to find out that she was right. The aliens (who call themselves "Race") have a moral code that supports the manipulation of societies to cause wholesale death and misery as long as Race don't dirty their hand with direct violence. One of the aliens tells her: "You do not understand. All Race does is rearrange assets to our advantage. Any Race who does more than this is ended. This is law" (p. 653). Angelica is staggered by the implications.

Nohar is the character who tries to find justice *and* tries to heal the society. (Readers may have legitimate doubts about the compatibility of those two goals.) In the end, he works to build bridges with the beings that he loves, telling a young man who felt that he fit nowhere that there was more to the old saying about species before country, that the complete saying was actually: "species before nationality, blood before all" (*Fearful Symmetries,* p. 172).

Explorations: Nohar seems to have a low opinion of society. To what extent is it justified? Where does he find hope?

What was Datia Rajasthan's legacy?

The title is from the poem "Tiger" by William Blake:

Tiger, Tiger, burning bright
  In the Forests of the Night
  What immortal hand or eye
  Could frame thy fearful symmetry?

What bearing does the poem have on the first and last entries in the series?

THE CASES

1. ***Forests of the Night*** published with *Emperors of the Twilight* and *Specters of the Dawn* in the *Moreau Omnibus.* New York: Daw Books, 2003, p. 17–234. ISBN: 0756401518.

JULY 2053, CLEVELAND, OHIO. Nohar Rajasthan was at Nugoya's club, trying to collect the fee owed him, when the shooting started. Most of the moreau patrons headed for the exit at the first sign of trouble. The Afghani assassin (canine Qandahar '24 attack strain) took out Nugoya and everyone else in the club. When the shooting paused, only the assassin and Nohar were standing. With no place to run and no place to hide, Nohar expected to die. Instead, the assassin told him that the assassination was a lesson, and for the lesson to work someone must survive to tell the tale. Nohar's gratitude at being left alive is blighted by the fact that no one is left to pay his fee. Nohar is left alive, but broke, and the rent is due.

The next morning brings a message of warning and a message of hope. The first, from Nohar's friend Robert Dittrich, warns Nohar that the FBI has come around asking questions. Apparently their agents found his survival suspicious. The second message is from a prospective client! When they meet, Nohar is surprised to find that the prospective client is a frank. Not only a frank, but a poorly-made, strangely designed, almost-not-viable frank. Worse that that, the frank, who says his name is John Smith, wants Nohar to investigate a human murder.

Nohar's business consists of conducting surveillance and missing persons (actually missing moreau) cases. Curiosity and stubbornness have often lead him into taking cases that are difficult and dangerous, but he doesn't take murder cases, and he doesn't take cases in which he, a moreau, would investigate humans. At first he turns the case down. It not only involves humans, it involves powerful humans. The victim was working on Congressman Binder's campaign to be elected to the United States Senate. The Congressman told the police to drop the murder investigation... and they dropped the murder investigation. The frank is desperate. The police won't investigate, and no human private investigator will work for a frank. Nohar is his only other option: Nohar is the only moreau with a private investigator's license in the city. He offers to quintuple Nohar's daily fee and pay a large retainer. Nohar counters with unreasonable prices, thinking that the frank will refuse. When the frank agrees to double the retainer and cover all expenses, Nohar wonders if he should have asked for more money. Against his better judgment, Nohar takes the case. (He begins his investigation by using the Cleveland Public Library's databases to gather background information.)

Nohar had been dating Maria Limón (moreau, jaguar). He felt that the relationship was serious and was stunned when she broke up with him via a message left on his link. He meets Stephanie Weir and they are attracted to one another.

ASSOCIATES: The protagonist is Nohar Rajasthan (moreau, tiger). Nugoya (frank)—*a client who avoids paying his bill;* "John Smith" (frank)—*a client who is an accountant with Midwest Lapidary Imports;* Congressman Binder—*who is running for a seat in the U.S. Senate on an anti-moreau platform;* Edwin Harrison—*Binder's campaign's legal counsel;* Philip Young—*the campaign finance chairman;* Desmond Thomson—*the campaign's press secretary;* Stephanie Weir—*Johnson's executive assistant;* Officer Irwin Harsk—*the detective assigned to Moreytown;* Evi Isham (frank)—*FBI Agent;* Patrick Shaunassy—*FBI Agent;* McIntyre and Conrad—*DEA officers;* "Fearless Leader" and "Bigboy"—*are Nohar's nicknames for two of the Ziphead gang rats who are harassing him;* Terin (female moreau, white rat)—*leader of the Ziphead gang;* Angel (moreau, rabbit)—*was the leader of the Stigmata gang until it was destroyed by the Zipheads;* Datia Rajasthan (moreau, tiger)—*Nohar's father;* Mandvi Gujerat (moreau, mongoose)—*who raised Nohar after Nohar's mother died;* Robert "Bobby" Dittrich—*is Nohar's best friend;* Hassan Sabah (moreau, Afghani canine)—*an assassin;* and Cat—*a.k.a. "the missing link" Nohar's pet cat.*

2. ***Emperors of the Twilight*** published with *Forests of the Night* and *Specters of the Dawn* in the *Moreau Omnibus.* New York: Daw Books, 2003, p. 241–454. ISBN: 0756401518.

DECEMBER 2058, MANHATTAN, NEW YORK. After the events in Cleveland, Evi was transferred to a desk job. (She wondered if the promotion was someone's idea of punishment for being involved in that mess.) She has led a bizarrely peaceful life working at a think tank for the last six years. In 2054, when the Supreme Court gave franks the same rights as moreaus, Evi considered quitting the agency; but she was in a comfortable peaceful rut and decided that boredom was no reason to quit.

Her boring life is shattered by a sniper, and she can't figure out why she would be a target. The attack on her is coordinated and deadly. It takes all of her skills to get out of her condominium alive. Then she must stay alive on the streets of Manhattan until she can figure out how (and who) to counterattack.

During the story, she's faced with questions of who deserves her loyalty. She's told, "When the shit hits the fan, species transcends politics" (p. 396). At one point Nohar, who has obviously thought about this, forces her to evaluate her position by asking her how she feels about humans (p. 416). This is particularly meaningful for Evi because it is evident that she identifies with humans. She is obsessive about disguising the eyes that mark her as a frank.

Seeing herself in a mirror without the contacts that disguise her as a human is shocking to her. It's disorienting; she feels that she looks odd. The idea that it is acceptable to be a frank seems alien to her. When someone who knows what she is comments on the beauty of her eyes, it is a life-changing event.

ASSOCIATES: The protagonist is Evi Isham (frank). Chuck Dwyer—*a neighbor;* Colonel Ezra Frey—*USMC retired (Evi's first controller in the field);* personnel at the Domestic Crisis Think Tank include: Erin Hofstadter—*German economist;* Scott Fitzgerald—*xenobiologist;* Leo Davidson; and David Price. Agent A. Sukiota—*a genetic sister to Evi;* Kris—*a young woman out driving her father's Jaguar on New Year's Eve;* Diana—*who befriends Evi at the bar;* Kijna (moreau, tiger)—*a bartender;* Richard Seger—*a Nyogi executive who assists Evi (albeit unwillingly) in her investigations;* Nohar Rajasthan—*who gives Evi the information she needs to go to ground;* General Wu Sein (moreau, ursine)—*has a secret base;* There Evi meets Corporal Gurgueia (moreau, jaguar) and Huaras (moreau, rabbit). Stephanie Rajasthan—*Nohar's wife;* Paul—*who works at New York Public Library;* Sharif (moreau, Afghani canine); Gabriel—*the assassin;* and Dimitri.

3. ***Specters of the Dawn*** published with *Forests of the Night* and ***Emperors** of the Twilight* in the *Moreau Omnibus.* New York: Daw Books, 2003, p. 461–696. ISBN: 0756401518.

OCTOBER 2059, SAN FRANCISCO, CALIFORNIA. Angel was minding her own business (getting drunk) in the moreau bar The Rabbit Hole when three toughs from The Knights of Humanity hate group decided that she looked like an easy target. She thought that she could take care of herself, but there are three of them and they have weapons. Angel manages to hurt one of them before the tide turns against her. Then a white knight (actually a British moreau lupine) named Byron Dorset comes to her rescue. He takes a continuing interest, and Angel lets herself dream of a future with him. By the time she realizes that the white knight was tarnished, it's too late. He was a schemer and a crook, and he left Angel holding the bag.

ASSOCIATES: The protagonist is Angelica "Angel" Lorenzo y Lopez (moreau, rabbit). Sanchez—*employs Angel at Ralph's diner;* Judy—*Angel's coworker;* Earl, Dwane Washington, and Chino "Chico" Hernandez—*are members of the hate gang, The Knights of Humanity.* Lei Nuygen (moreau, Vietnamese canine)—*Angel's roommate;* Balthazar (moreau, lion)—*an ancient (40-year-old) moreau;* Detective Morris White—*who is determined to bring down the Knights;* Detective Kobe Anaka—*who suspects a conspiracy;* Mrs. Gardner—*the District Attorney;* Mr. Igalez (moreau, ferret)—*of the Public Defender's Office;* Paul DeGarmo—*Byron's lawyer;* Dr. Pat Ellis—*who falsified an autopsy report;* Father Alvarez De Collor (moreau, Brazilian jaguar)—*who wants to use a moreau's death to promote himself and his causes;* Nohar Rajasthan (moreau, tiger)—*who gives Angel contact information for an honest computer expert;* Bobby Dittrich—*Nohar's best friend;* Kaji "Mr. K" Tetsami (frank)—*a local hacker;* detectives Quintara, Yara, and Lacy—*who protect Angel at a safe house;* Steve—*an FBI sociologist whom Angel meets on the way to interview aliens;* the Honorable Sylvia Harper—*who chairs the NonHuman Affairs Committee in the U.S. House of Representatives and aspires to higher office;* Daniel Pasquez—*a reporter,* Agent Conrad, and Ironwalker (moreau, lupine)—*thug.*

4. ***Fearful Symmetries: The Return of Nohar Rajasthan.*** New York: Daw Books, c1999, 280 p. ISBN: 0886778344.

FEBRUARY 2070, LOS ANGELES, CALIFORNIA. Seven years ago, Nohar retreated from society. He lives in a small cabin in the forest and hunts for food. One evening, the peace is broken by a visit from Attorney Charles Royd. He wants Nohar to find a missing 17-year-old moreau named Manuel (moreau, crossbreed of jaguar and tiger). Nohar is not interested. When a strike force attempts to assassinate him Nohar changes his mind. What he finds will change his life.

ASSOCIATES: The protagonist is Nohar Rajasthan (moreau, tiger). Stephie—*Nohar's ex-wife;* Sara Henderson (moreau, vulpine)—*who works for Charles Royd;* Maria Limón (moreau, jaguar)—*who dated Nohar long ago;* Sam (moreau, lepus) and Beverly (moreau, canine)—*are friends of Maria;* Elijah—*the leader of a pack of engineered dogs;* Nathan Oxford (moreau, kangaroo)—*who is stealing from the Compton Bensheim Clinic;* John Samson (frank)—*"The Necron Avenger" is the adopted son of Oswald Samson;* Manuel (moreau, jaguar and tiger)—*a crossbreed, has coped with human and moreau prejudice all of his life;* Frank Trinity—*is a man who is involved in extreme humanist activities;* Tabara Krisoijn—*a mercenary;* Gilbertez and Ortega—*are detectives;* and Dr. Brian Reynolds.

SYAF, Adrian. Worked with Jim Butcher on *Welcome to the Jungle, Jim Butcher's Dresden Files.* See BUTCHER, Jim: Storm Front.

T

TODD, Charles.

TEST OF WILLS

Genres/Themes Crossed: Paranormal X Police Procedural.

Subjects/Character Types: Ghosts X Police Procedural.

Series/Stand-Alone: There are a few changes in relationships, but not many. Readers should pick up any of the series; it is fascinating.

Scene of the Crime: Post-World War I England, beginning in 1919.

Detective: Inspector Ian Rutledge was an extraordinary policeman in 1914; his intuition, coupled with the understanding that it takes hard evidence to gain a conviction, made him a rising star at Scotland Yard. In 1914, he went to war. In 1916, an exploding shell buried him alive. He was found under the body of Corporal Hamish MacLeod and was sent back into battle, with the voice of the dead Hamish as his companion. His fear of living greater than his fear of dying, he put himself into danger again and again; and was bitterly amused to find himself hailed as a hero. After the war, in 1919, he returned to the Yard, afraid to rely on his intuition, partly because it seemed akin to the voice in his head, which has been diagnosed as a manifestation of shell shock. He is tall and thin, drawn and weary; afraid that others will consider him insane and take away his work.

Known Associates: Corporal Hamish MacLeod, killed in July 1916 in the trenches in France, but still Rutledge's constant companion. Chief Superintendent Bowles, Rutledge's superior, a man so consumed with envy that he prays and schemes for Rutledge's failure. Frances is Rutledge's advocate, his supporter,...his nagging sister. Jean, his fiancée, was so frightened of the man he had become that she broke off the engagement. He still compares other women to her.

Premise: The caustic irreverent voice of Corporal Hamish MacLeod haunts Rutledge. He has discovered that he cannot silence it through any act of will, and so he lives in an uneasy stalemate with his dead companion. As the series opens, Rutledge is trying to gather the shards of his life, no longer sure that he has the skill or the nerve to continue, afraid that his comrades will realize that he suffers from shell-shock and take his work away from him. The demands of his work, the concentration it takes to understand the crime and find the murderer, the exhaustion that follows and brings dreamless sleep—these are what keep the madness at bay.

Comment: This series explores the aftermath of the Great War in England. Throughout the books, the villains, witnesses, and bystanders are people who have been scarred, mentally and physically. The reader can see the ways in which people coped—from men like Rutledge who are unable to escape the war, to women who spent years in fear that their husbands or lovers would never return, to those who proudly claim that a badly maimed brother or cousin (in one case the man had lost both arms) is doing fine, or is too strong to be troubled by memories of the war. The damage of the war on the people who survived it pervades the series.

Their Web site at http://charlestodd.com/homepage/ includes information on the authors and the books.

Literary Crimes & Chimes: Rutledge is, at the outset, a sympathetic character, simply because he is so quietly and desperately engaged in so many private battles. One he knows nothing of: from the very beginning, the reader can see the petty envy of Bowles, Rutledge's superior on the force. Bowles takes pleasure in giving Rutledge assignments that are political minefields. Another of Rutledge's battles is with the voice, memory, or ghost of Hamish; a third is with his own self-doubt.

There are many passages that depict Rutledge's mental fragility. Rutledge feels close to death: it's as if he feels that he led men who were better than himself into doomed battles, and that he deserved to die in their stead. He remembers them clearly; Hamish points out that his memories haunt him. He lies to try to avoid questioning in *Legacy of the Dead* (p. 90):

> "I'm sorry," he said. "I try not to remember the war."
>
> And Hamish said quite clearly, "You remember it every hour of every day. You always will. It's the cost of surviving."
>
> And it was true.

Hamish reminds him again of the cost of his memories in *Watchers of Time* (p. 117):

> Sims shook his head. And with a lightness that was assumed to hide much deeper feelings, he said, "If I had your skill at listening, I'd be a very grateful man!"
>
> "It has haunted you, that skill," Hamish said. For Rutledge remembered clearly every word Hamish had spoken in the trenches, as if each was carved into the depths of the soul, out of reach and never worn away.

He carefully avoids giving any hint that he's hearing the voice of a man long dead. He is not only conscious of the fragility of life, but desperately conceals his secrets, even to the point of considering which effects would be sent to his sister if he were to die suddenly. Upon entering the bedroom of a murder victim, Rutledge feels his "usual sense of distaste" at having to violate the privacy of the dead, and reflects that the dead lose not only their lives but also the ability to protect their secrets. Thus:

> He himself was careful not to preserve any record of the voice in his head. There was no diary entry, no letter, not even a conversation with a friend that would distress his sister, Frances, after he was gone. Only the private files in Dr. Fleming's office, and Fleming could be depended upon to leave them sealed. (*Watchers of Time* p. 198)

This is a man who is haunted in so many ways that every step he takes forward is an act of courage: every day that he deals with the living while being haunted by the dead takes a valiant effort.

The authors imagine and portray the likely actions and reactions of members of small communities particularly well. Gossip is a force to be reckoned with, and the community can be closed against outsiders of any kind, at any time. A Scotland Yard detective is frequently regarded as such an outsider. There are passages in these stories that counter the idyllic vision of life in a small village, giving a vivid picture of the harsher realities.

Explorations: How would it impact the series if the reader knew for sure that the voice of Hamish is simply a figment of Rutledge's imagination? How would it impact the series if the reader knew for sure that the voice was the ghost of Hamish, speaking to Rutledge?

THE CASES

1. **"The Man Who Never Was"** in *Malice Domestic 9*, edited by Joan Hess. New York: Avon Books, Inc., 2000, p. 141–49.

NEAR THE FRONT, WORLD WAR I. Private Romney died, not of a bullet, but of a hole in his gas mask. His commanding officer, Ian Rutledge, sorts through Romney's personal possessions preparatory to sending them home, and makes a disquieting discovery. Who was Romney, and how did that hole come to be in his gas mask?

ASSOCIATES: Corporal Hamish MacLeod (alive).

2. ***Test of Wills.*** New York: St. Martin's Press, 1996, 282 p. ISBN: 0312144318.

ENGLAND (WARWICKSHIRE), JUNE 1919. Everyone (well, almost everyone) admired, liked, and respected Colonel Charles Harris; no one in the village can understand why anyone would have shot him out of the saddle at point-blank range. The case becomes a political hot potato when it is discovered that a witness saw the local war hero arguing with the Colonel slightly before the murder. The witness is a badly shell-shocked veteran; Rutledge knows that the man's reputation and, indeed, his mind would be shredded by the hero's defense counsel.

ASSOCIATES: Chief Superintendent Bowles—*Rutledge's boss;* Corporal Hamish MacLeod (deceased)—*Rutledge's companion;* Barton Redfern—*the landlord's nephew;* Inspector Forrest—*who knows a political minefield when he sees one;* Sergeant Davies—*part of Upper Streetham's local constabulary;* Johnston—*the butler;* Miss Lettice Wood—*the ward of Charles Harris;* Captain Mark Wilton—*who had won the VC, was seen quarrelling with the Colonel;* Mrs. Sally Davenant—*a widow, cousin of Captain Wilton;* Laurence Royston—*the Colonel's business agent;* Daniel Hickam—*who is a victim of shell shock;* Dr. Warren—*the local doctor;* Miss Helena Sommers—*who is new to the district;* Miss Maggie Sommers—*Helena's cousin, also new in the area;* Mavers—*a local rabble-rouser;* Miss Catherine Tarrant—*who Captain Wilton courted before the war;* Carfield—*the vicar;* Agnes Farrell—*an extremely level-headed woman;* Meg—*her daughter,* Lizzie—*Meg's daughter;* and Mary Satterthwaite—*the maid.*

3. ***Wings of Fire.*** New York: St. Martin's Press, 1998, 294 p. ISBN: 0312170645.

ENGLAND (CORNWALL), JUNE 1919. A serial killer is hunting in London, and Bowles wants Rutledge, the golden boy, out of the way. When the Home Office asks the Yard to look into three deaths (not mysterious deaths, but well-explained and well-investigated deaths) Rutledge is sent to Cornwall. Everyone expects Rutledge to certify the conclusions of the local police; instead, he finds a trail of murder, vengeance, and evil traversing decades and almost destroying one family.

ASSOCIATES: Mrs. Trepol—*the housekeeper;* The relatives of poet O. A. Manning (Olivia Alison Marlowe) include Susannah—*half-sister of Nicholas and Olivia;* Daniel Hargrove—*Susannah's husband;* Rachel Ashford—*a cousin on the Marlowe side, and a war widow (her husband, Peter, was a friend of Rutledge);* Stephen FitzHugh—*Susannah's twin brother;* Cormac FitzHugh—*who is not a Trevelyan.*

Chief Superintendent Bowles—*who wants Rutledge out of the way;* Corporal Hamish MacLeod (deceased)—*Rutledge's constant companion;* Constable Dawlish—*an officer in Borcombe;* Mrs. Dawlish—his wife; Mr. Smedley—*the rector;* Sadie—*who was a nurse;* Dr. Penrith—*the old doctor, he is retired;* Mrs. Hawkins—*Dr. Penrith's daughter, the wife of the new doctor;* Wilkins—*who was the gardener at the Hall;* Mr. Trask—*the innkeeper;* Thomas Chambers—*attorney;* Doctor Hawkins—*the local doctor;* Inspector Harvey—*who may have mismanaged the investigation;* and Mrs. Mary Otley—*the daughter of the woman who was nanny at the Hall.*

4. ***Search the Dark.*** New York: Thomas Dunne Books, 1999, 279 p. ISBN: 0312200005.

ENGLAND (DORSET), AUGUST 1919. Bert Mowbray was told that his wife and children had died in London while he was fighting the war in France. Years later, spotting them unexpectedly at a train station, he goes into a fury, believing that his wife had faked her own death so that she could take the children and leave him. When she is found dead, Rutledge feels that the most pressing problem is to discover what happened to the children who were with her at the station.

ASSOCIATES: Bert Mowbray—*who was in France in 1916 when he received word of his wife and children's deaths;* Corporal Hamish MacLeod (deceased)—*accompanies Rutledge;* Marcus Johnston—*attorney;* Inspector Hildebrand—*who believes that there may have been a mistake;* Mr. Jack Denton—*innkeeper;* Daniel Shaw—*Denton's nephew;* Constable Truit—*who hears about everything that goes on in his area;* Mr. Simon Wyatt—*who was in the war;* and Aurore—*his wife;* Elizabeth Napier—*who looks soft, but has a strong will;* Mrs. Joanna Daulton—*the cement that holds the community together;* Henry Daulton—*her son;* Peg—*the chambermaid;* Mrs. Prescott—*Constable Truit's neighbor;* Hazel Dixon *a witness who knows what she wanted to see;* Dorcas Williams—*maid;* Frances—*Rutledge's sister;* Ted Jimson—*who works on the farm;* Robert Andrews—*who loans Rutledge a photograph;* Rosie and Robert—*Robert's children;* Dr. Fairfield—*the local doctor;* and Marion Forsby—*who reports the gossip that she has heard.*

5. ***Legacy of the Dead.*** New York: Bantam Books, 2000, 308 p. ISBN: 0553801686.

GLASGOW, SCOTLAND, 1916; DUNCARRICK, BRAE, AND GLENCOE, SCOTLAND, AND LONDON, SEPTEMBER 1919. A campaign of anonymous letters turns the town against one young woman. They shun her, then they try to take her child, and then she is accused of a crime that would send her to the gallows. Constable Alistair McKinstry is certain that she is innocent, but he cannot find evidence to clear her. He circumvents the proper channels to ask Rutledge for help. Rutledge has a case of his own. He has been sent to speak to the irascible Lady Maude Gray about her daughter. The corpse of a young woman has been found in Scotland, and it is possible that it is the body of Eleanor Gray. Lady Gray refuses to believe that the body could be that of her daughter; and then she contacts Scotland Yard and demands that Rutledge take over the investigation. In the course of the investigation, Rutledge meets the woman that Hamish intended to marry, and finds himself investigating the case on behalf of both the living and the dead. This is a case in which Rutledge realizes that he is truly being haunted, that hearing Hamish is not a symptom of shell shock.

ASSOCIATES: 1916: "Mrs. Cook"; "Sarah."

1919: Fiona MacDonald—*who calls herself Fiona MacLeod;*, Hugh Oliphant—*her angry neighbor;* Tommy Braddock—*an odd-job man;* Molly—*his wife;* Alistair McKinstry—*the constable;* Mr. Elliot—*the Scottish minister;* Dorothea MacIntyre—*Mr. Elliot's housekeeper;* Miss Ann Tait—*the milliner;* Inspector Oliver—*who interviewed everyone who received a letter denouncing Fiona MacDonald;* Hamish MacLeod (deceased)—*who has a personal interest in the case;* Chief Superintendent Bowles—*who would be glad to throw a subordinate to the wolves;* Lady Maude Gray—*who was enraged by Inspector Oliver (and isn't much happier with Rutledge);* Morag Gilchrist—*housekeeper;* David Trevor—*who is the father of Rutledge's dead friend, Ross;* Constable Pringle—*who holds the fort while his superiors travel and investigate;* Penelope Davison—*who once employed Fiona;* Mrs. Kerr—*a gossip who did not have Fiona's new address;* Madelyn Holden—*who is frightened;* Alex Holden—*a.k.a. Sandy Holden, her husband;* Dr. Wilson—*who would recognize Maude Cook;* Ian Hamish MacLeod—*named after both Rutledge and Hamish;* Clarence—*the cat;* Drummond—*who takes Ian to feed Clarence;* Miss Drummond—*his sister;* Mrs. Atwood—*whose graciousness is backed with steel;* Burns—*the procurator-fiscal;* Betty Lawlor—*a young woman who found a brooch that had "MacDonald" engraved on its back;* Mr. Armstrong—*Fiona's attorney;* Mrs. Raeburn—*a nosy neighbor of Robert Burns;* Hugh Fraser—*attorney;* Mr. Burns—*attorney;* and Major Thomas S. Warren—*a solicitor and an historian.*

6. ***Watchers of Time.*** New York: Bantam Books, c2001, 339 p. ISBN: 0553801791.

OSTERLY AND LONDON, ENGLAND, OCTOBER 1919. A dying man (thought to be a good Anglican) shocks his family by demanding a priest. A few weeks later, the priest is murdered, his study ransacked, and the paltry parish funds pilfered. The local police coming in the next day don't know that the crimes happened in that order. They believe that Father James was a chance casualty of a panicked burglar, not the target of a murderer. The Bishop is concerned, and asks Scotland Yard to send someone to look into what seems an open-and-shut case.

Associates: Dr. Stephenson—*who attends the dying man;* Herbert Baker—*who worked as a coachman;* Martin, Dick, and Elly Baker—*Herbert's children, are at his deathbed when he asks them to fetch a priest;* Father James—*who comes to Herbert's bedside;* Mr. Sims—*the vicar;* Frances—*Rutledge's sister, she does not think that Rutledge should return from his convalescence so soon;* Chief Superintendent Bowles—*who is not overjoyed at Rutledge's return;* and Sergeant Wilkerson—*who follows up on a case;* Jean—*Rutledge's ex-fiancée;* Jason Webley—*Rutledge's friend, who warns Rutledge of Jean's upcoming wedding;* Monsignor Holston—*whose intuition told him that there was something profoundly wrong about the crime scene;* Bryony—*the Monsignor's housekeeper;* Mrs. Wainer—*Father James's housekeeper;* Inspector Blevins—*who is not sure he can be objective;* Matthew Walsh—*the strongman at the bazaar;* Mrs. Susan Barnett—*hotel owner;* Lord Sedgwick—*who invites Rutledge to lunch;* Arthur and Edwin—*his sons;* Sarah—*Father James's sister;* Priscilla Connaught—*whose life was shattered;* Frederick Gifford—*an attorney;* Peter Henderson—*who was a sniper during the war;* Mrs. Martha Beeling—*who comes by to see Mrs. Wainer and gossi*p; Marianna "May" Elizabeth Trent—*who was left a framed photograph and an obligation by Father James;* Sam Hadley—*a farmer;* Tom Randal—*whose yellow dog is roaming;* and Franklin, Taylor, and Tanner—*the constables.* As always, Rutledge is accompanied by Hamish MacLeod (deceased).

7. ***A Fearsome Doubt.*** New York: Bantam Books, 2002, 295 p. ISBN: 0553801805.

England (Kent), November 1919. As England nears the anniversary of the armistice, ghosts from the past plague Rutledge. He is faced with evidence that a man he once helped convict may have been innocent, and he catches a momentary glimpse of a soldier he believed dead. While he is plagued by doubt, not only of his abilities but also of his sanity, Rutledge is sent out on another case. Someone has been killing war veterans. They survived the horrors of the war, only to be murdered in their hometown, the place that had represented safety for all those years that they were away. The victims were all men who returned home from the war, maimed. They were going on with their lives, lives that would never match the dreams they'd held before the war. Almost a year after the Armistice, people throughout the country are trying to go on with their lives, trying to shape a new future. The widow of one of Rutledge's best friends is trying to let go of the past. She is ready to sell her home and is hoping to fall in love again.

Rutledge cannot turn away from the past: he still feels more kinship with the dead than with the living. He is distracted by the demands of the widow of a man he helped send to the gallows. Now, six years after her husband's execution, she brings Rutledge proof of his innocence. Rutledge is torn between his need to re-investigate a case that was closed before the war and his need to stop a murderer before the killer strikes again.

ASSOCIATES: Hamish MacLeod (deceased)—*haunts Rutledge;* Elizabeth Mayhew—*widow of Richard, Rutledge was best man at their wedding;* Lawrence Hamilton—*a barrister;* Lydia—*his wife;* Raleigh Masters—*a barrister;* Bella—*his wife;* Tom Brereton—*a war veteran who is losing his sight;* Melinda Crawford—*an elderly friend of Elizabeth's;* Inspector Dowling; Sergeant Burke; and Constable Weaver—*are on the force of the Marling police;* Dr. Pugh; Mr. Meade—*a house agent;* Gunter Manthy—*a.k.a. Gunter Hauser;* Alice—*the widow of Will Taylor;* Susan—*the widow of Kenny Webber;* Peter—*their son;* Peggy—*the widow of Harry Bartlett;*. Frances—*Rutledge's sister;* Ben Shaw—*a convicted killer;* Mrs. Nell Shaw—*his wife;* Margaret Shaw—*their daughter;* Henry Cutter—*the Shaw's neighbor;* Janet Cutter—*was his wife;* Police Officer George Peterson—*was Janet's son from her first marriage;* Mr. Bailey—*is the rector of their church;* Mary—*his wife;*. Margaret Shaw—*who may go into service in the country;* Bert Holcomb—*lives in Seelyham;* Inspector Bill Grimes—*the local man;* Mrs. Parker—*an elderly woman who does not sleep well;* and Miss Judson—*who corroborates Mrs. Parker's story;* Inspector Raeburn, Sergeant Gibson, Chief Superintendent Bowles, and Sergeant Bennett—*who work for Scotland Yard;*

8. ***A Cold Treachery.*** New York: Bantam Books, 2005, 373 p. ISBN: 0553803492.

URSKDALE, ENGLAND, DECEMBER 1919. Life was hard in the tiny farming community of Urskdale, but it was a community of sorts. There were no strangers in town when the bodies of the Elcott family were found. Every family in the area had been battened down in their own homes, braced against a blizzard. When the storm subsided, Gerald's brother Paul went to see if the family needed any help. He found them: Gerald Elcott, his wife Grace, her daughter, and their infant twins, all slaughtered. The body of the son, Josh, was not at the scene. The police hope that Josh escaped, but it seems unlikely that he could have survived the storm. Inspector Greeley, a practical man, sets up search parties of three, instead of two, men. It has struck Greeley that there is a very real possibility that one of his volunteers is the murderer, and one innocent man partnered with a killer would be too vulnerable. The search parties look for the boy, but also check on the other families in the area and make sure that they have not been killed as well. When Greeley notifies Scotland Yard, Chief Inspector Bowles sends Rutledge.

ASSOCIATES: Hamish MacLeod (deceased)—*haunts Rutledge;* Inspector Greeley, Sergeant Miller, and Sergeant Ward—*are on Urskdale's police force;* Henderson, Tom Hester, Drew Taylor, and schoolmaster Rupert

Blackwell—*are a few of the searchers;* the Haldnes—*who own the closest farm to the Elcott's;* Mr. and Mrs. Peterson—*who own South Farm;* James and Mary Follet—*who own an isolated farm;* Maggie Ingerson—*who lives alone except for her dog;* Sybil—*Maggie's dog;* Harry and Vera Cummins—*own the inn;* Elizabeth Fraser—*who helps them when Mrs. Cummins is indisposed;* Dr. Jarvis; Belfors—*the ironmonger, he knew Gerald Elcott's father;* Mr. Slater—*the rector;* Paul Elcott—*Gerald's brother;* Janet Ashton—*sister of Grace Elcott;* Hugh Robinson—*Grace's first husband;* and Inspector Mickelson—*who is sent to relieve Rutledge, and ends up staying at the Cummins' inn.*

9. ***A Long Shadow.*** New York: William Morrow, c2006, 341 p. ISBN: 006078671X; 9780060786717.

DUDLINGTON, ENGLAND, JANUARY 1920. Someone is stalking Rutledge, leaving shell casings to show how close he can get without being detected, and taking practice shots from cover at Rutledge, trying to terrorize him. Rutledge has been ready to die for over a year, but he doesn't want to be taken out by a sniper. Chief Constable Bowles knows nothing of this. He sends Rutledge out to the small village of Dudlington to investigate the shooting of the local constable. Constable Hensley was shot by an arrow as he clandestinely searched Frith's Wood, a place that's avoided by the villagers, who believe that it has been haunted for hundreds of years. It would have been a good location for a murder, and Rutledge wonders if it has been the scene of one more recent than the slaughter of the Saxons.

ASSOCIATES: Hamish MacLeod (deceased)—*haunts Rutledge;* Frances—*Rutledge's sister, she takes Rutledge to a dinner party;* Maryanne Browning—*the party's hostess;* Her guests include Simon—*Maryanne's brother;* Dr. Philip Gavin and his wife; George and Sally Talbot; Commander Farnum and his wife, Becky; and Mrs. Meredith Channing—*the medium.*

Sergeant Gibson—*who tells Rutledge some of Constable Hensley's history;* In Hertford: Inspector Smith—*who closed a case quickly;* Dr. Eustace—*gives Rutledge first aid;* and Tommy Crowell—*a simple young man who confessed;* Constable Hensley—*of Dudlington;* Grace Letteridge—*gave Emma the archery set years ago;* Barbara Melford—*who prepared food for Bart Hensley;* Dr. Middleton—*who retired and came to town, then ended up working again;* Frederick Towson—*rector of St. Luke's;* Mrs. Ellison—*whose granddaughter, Emma Mason, has been missing for three years;* Ted Baylor—*whose dog found the injured constable;* Joel—*Ted's brother;* Mr. Freebold—*the greengrocer;* Martha Simpson—*who went to school with Emma;* Mrs. Arundel—*the postmistress;* Mrs. Sarah Lawrence—*is one of the town's oldest residents;* Mr. Keating—*who owns the local inn, The Oaks;* Hillary Timmons—*who works at The Oaks;* Inspector Cain—*Hensley's superior;* Josh Morgan—*the owner of The Three Horses;* Dr. Mainwaring—*who acts as Scotland Yard's coroner.*

10. ***A False Mirror.*** New York: William Morrow, 2007, 384 p. ISBN: 0060786736.

HAMPTON REGIS, ENGLAND, FEBRUARY 1920. The war veterans who returned to England found that life had moved on without them. At the war's front, they imagined they would step back into their lives, but when they returned, many found that the world had changed, and their place in it was gone. Stephen Mallory returned to find that his sweetheart, Felicity, had married another man. He followed them to the little town of Hampton Regis, the better to obsess over his loss.

When Felicity's husband is brutally beaten and left for dead, Stephen becomes the main suspect. Instead of standing his ground and proclaiming his innocence, he flees so that he can tell her that he had nothing to do with the attack. His flight serves to confirm his guilt in the eyes of the local police. Stephen is sure that he cannot get a fair hearing and demands that Rutledge, whom he knew in the war, come to Hampton Regis to investigate the crime.

ASSOCIATES: Chief Superintendent Bowles—*who expected Rutledge to have destroyed himself by now, Bowles is frustrated by Rutledge's resilience;* Chief Inspector Phipps—*who has designed a carefully managed trap for a murderer;* Bevins—*a good constable;* Constable Waddington—*who often looks in on Mrs. Whittier; Rutledge directs him to watch Mr. Fields.*

Frances—*Rutledge's sister;* Melinda Crawford—*who has known Rutledge since he was a boy;* Hamish MacLeod (deceased)—*accompanies Rutledge;* Matthew Hamilton—*who knows he is lucky;* Felicity Hamilton—*his wife;* Lieutenant Stephen Mallory—*who left the war's front in early 1916 (his uncle, the Bishop, pulled strings to get him sent home);* Dr. Anthony Granville—*whose patient is very badly injured;* Mrs. Granville—*his wife, acts as his assistant;* Nan Weekes—*is the Hamilton's maid;* George Reston—*a man of business, his brother was a drunkard;* Henrietta Reston—*his wife, who has finally gained the upper hand in their marriage;* Miss Charlotte Trining—*who, like many people, regards shell-shock as a sign of cowardice;* Augustus Putnam—*the rector;* Miss Susan Esterley—*who uses a cane since her accident;* Jeremy—*a six-year-old who saw a monster;* Mrs. Cornelius—*his mother, who knows that Jeremy saw something, she sent her husband out for the police;* Dr. Hester; Perkins—*a man who has a boat;* William Joyner—*who is quite ill;* Robert Stratton—*Foreign Office, worked with Matthew Hamilton;* Miss Miranda Cole—*an honorable woman;* Dedham—*her maid;* Inspector Bennett; and Constable Coxe—*who is Nan Weekes cousin.*

11. ***A Pale Horse.*** New York: William Morrow, c2008, 360 p. ISBN: 9780061233562.

BERKSHIRE (UFFINGTON), LONDON, AND YORKSHIRE, ENGLAND, APRIL 1920. The War Office has lost track of one of their own. Gaylord Partridge (a.k.a.

Gerald Parkinson) used to work for them, and was important enough that even when he retired they kept an eye on him. He has wandered off before, and they usually send someone to watch for him and notify them when he returns. They were impressed with Rutledge's work last June in Warwickshire, and they ask that he go to Uffington to watch for Partridge's return. Hamish finds it ominous that, this time when Partridge went missing,the War Office requested that a policeman stand watch for his return.

ASSOCIATES: Hamish MacLeod (deceased)—*accompanies Rutledge.*

In London: Frances—*Rutledge's sister, drags him to a dinner party with Maryanne Browning, Meredith Channing, and the Farnums;* Freddy Masters and Edward Throckmorton—*old friends of Rutledge;* Inspector Bowles—*who sends Constable Burns to fetch Rutledge when the War Office calls with their request;* Sergeant Gibson—*Rutledge's ally at Scotland Yard.*

In Elthorpe/Dilby: Albert Harris Crowell—*is a schoolmaster at the Dilby School;* Hugh Tredworth (age 11); Johnnie Standing, Tad Medway and Bill (all age 10)—*are students of his;* Robbie Medway—*Tad's little brother, (age nine);* Alice—*Albert Crowell's wife, she was once involved with Inspector Harry Madsen;* Colonel Ingle—*Alice's father, he speaks to Martin Deloran of the War Office on her behalf;* Inspector Harry Madsen, Constable Pickerel and Constable Hood—*local law enforcement;* Miss Mary Norton and Mark Benson—*work at the Castle Arms hotel;* Hadley—*is the undergardener at the estate that includes the ruins of Fountains Abbey.*

In Uffington: Mrs. Betty Smith—*the wife of the Smiths' Castle Arms innkeeper.* Inspector Hill—*who always felt that the Tomlin Cottages was a peaceful little community.* Residents of the Tomlin Cottages are: Quincy—*who was paid by his family to leave England;* Andrew Slater—*the simple blacksmith;* Mr. Brady—*who was sent to watch over Partridge;* Maria Cathcart—*who lives in constant fear of her ex-husband;* Mr. Willingham—*who is known for his surliness;* Mr. Singleton—*the ex-soldier;* Miller—*who Slater regards as evil (Rutledge thinks Miller may have served time in prison);* and Allen—*who is dying of tuberculosis.* Miss Chandler—*who used to live in the cottages, came into an unexpected inheritance that allowed her to move to a posh nursing home.*

Peter Littleton—*Harry Shoreham's cousin in Addleford;* Elizabeth—*Peter's wife;* Llewellyn Williams—*who Rutledge interviews in Wales;* Rebecca and Sarah Parkinson—*sisters who are united in their hatred of their father,* Martha Ingram—*the maid,* and Dr. Anderson—*who comes in an emergency.*

12. *A Matter of Justice.* New York: HarperCollins, c2009, 330 p. ISBN: 9780061233593.

THE SCILLY ISLES, SOMERSET, CAMBURY, AND LONDON, ENGLAND, MAY 1920; SOUTH AFRICA, 1900. Harold Quarles's first investment was made with blood money. His investments prospered, as did Quarles, a fact which seemed, to the brother of the man Quarles had murdered, a bitter injustice. Twenty years later, Quarles was killed.

Inspector Rutledge's holiday (he took time off to attend the wedding of a friend) is interrupted by a call to investigate the murder of a wealthy London financier, a Mr. Quarles. The case is difficult. The sheer number of suspects presents problems. Everyone whom Rutledge quesitons denies killing Quarles, but admits to hating him. Most list several other people who hated him, and then add that they don't believe that any of those people would have gone so far as to murder the man. Even worse, Rutledge suspects that the local police inspector should head the list of suspects. The police inspector admits to hating Quarles, and his actions seem designed to shield any murderer. Hamish thinks that the investigation is difficult because even those who have no knowledge of the murder feel a certain gratitude to the killer and are not anxious to deliver him to the gallows.

ASSOCIATES: Hamish MacLeod (deceased)—*accompanies Rutledge.*

In the Scilly Isles: Ronald Evering—*who meets with Davis Penrith;* Mariah Pendennis—*Evering's housekeeper.*

In the 1900s in South Africa: Lieutenant Timothy Barton Evering—*led his company in the Boer War;* Private Quarles and Private Penrith—*were part of that company.*

In Somerset, in 1920: Edgar Maitland—*Rutledge's friend, marries Elise Caldwell;* Elise Caldwell—*who believes that the men who were in the war must get on with their lives;* Mr. and Mrs. Caldwell—*Elise's parents, are part of the wedding party;* Mary—*who is afraid of the storm;* Meredith Channing—*a medium, she makes Rutledge uncomfortable;* Neal Hammond—*who clearly finds Meredith attractive.*

In Cambury (where Harold Quarles's body was found): Inspector Padgett leads the local police force, which includes Constable Horton, Constable Jenkins, and Constable Daniels. Dr. O'Neil—*conducts the post-mortem examination;* Mrs. Maybelle Quarles—*Quarles's estranged wife;* Charles Archer—*her cousin;* Mrs. Downing—*the housekeeper;* Mrs. Blount—*the cook;* Betty Richards and Lily—*the maids;* Tom Masters—*who was Quarles's farm manager;* Mr. Hunter—*manager of The Unicorn;* Samuel Heller—*the rector of St. Martin's;* Mr. Michael Brunswick—*the organist at St. Martin's;* Mr. Hugh Jones—*who works as the baker at Clark and Sons, Millers;* Mrs. Jones—*Hugh's wife, she asked her husband if he had committed the murder;* Gwyneth Jones—*their daughter;* Miss O'Hara—*who told Mr. Quarles what she thought of him right in the middle of High Street;* Mrs. Newell—*Quarles's former cook;* Mr. Stephenson—*owner of Nemesis bookstore;* Miss Ogden—*his assistant;* Mr. Greer—*who owns a glovers firm;* Mr. Nelson—*a businessman;* Tom Little—*who's courting a girl from another village.*

In London: Sergeant Gibson—*is an ally of Rutledge's at Scotland Yard;* Chief Superintendent Bowles—*is not;* and Inspector Mickelson—*is a favorite of the Chief Inspector;*

Davis Penrith—*Quarles's former partner;* Jason and Laurence Hurley—*Quarles's solicitors;* and Anthony Godalming—*who was once an Anglican priest.* Rutledge goes to Mrs. Meredith Channing when he's in distress.

V

VAUGHN, Carrie.

Kitty and the Midnight Hour

Genres/Themes Crossed: Secret Society (Blended Society after the first novel) X Traditional Mystery.

Subjects/Character Types: Werewolves, Vampires, Fae (Fairies) X Amateur Sleuth (Contemporary).

Series/Stand-Alone: The short stories in this series are interesting and well-written, but they are not mysteries and they do not move the series forward. Major events occur in the novels which should be read in order, as characters undergo significant changes in the course of the series. The mystery element becomes less central to the series as it moves forward.

Scene of the Crime: Present-day Denver, Colorado; Washington, D.C.; San Isabel National Forest, Colorado; Las Vegas, Nevada.

Detective: Kitty Norville's job as a talk show host gives her some visibility, and that visibility lands her in hot water, first with her pack, then with the law. She turns to detecting because she keeps being pegged as the most logical suspect.

Known Associates: Kitty's best friend is another werewolf; his name is Theodore Joseph Gurney (T. J. for short). Kitty's Station Manager is Ozzie, and her sound engineer is Matt. Cormac is a werewolf killer who becomes a friend, and Ben O'Farrell is his lawyer.

Premise: Werewolves, vampires, and even fairies exist. They work at staying unnoticed, and are helped by the fact that most normal people don't believe in them. That all changes when Kitty goes public. She's a lifeline for those who have seen enough to believe and have wondered if they're mad, for those who have been changed and abandoned, for those who find hope in her having survived breaking out of the strict social order of the pack; but she is danger to those supernaturals who thrived on secrecy and a threat to those humans who believe that anyone who is different must also be evil.

Comment: Carrie Vaughn's Web site at www.carrievaughn.com/ includes a link to her journal: http://carriev.wordpress.com, to a free online short story ("Winnowing the Herd"), and to bibliographies of her novels and short stories.

Literary Magic & Mayhem: Kitty is a likeable, gutsy character. She was raped by her boyfriend Bill and then abandoned in the park. Zan came along and bit her, and the next morning the pack found her and took her in. Like all werewolves, Kitty must turn wolf at the full moon, and she can change at will during the rest of the lunar cycle. She works hard to maintain control of her wolf, fighting to stay in human form except during the full moon. There are stories of werewolves who had simply let the wolf take over and never reverted back to human form. Kitty believes that it happens to those who change too easily and too often. Kitty is a great show host, philosophical and wise, compassionate, but not a push-over. For instance, when a Catholic who was turned into a vampire asks if he still has a soul, Kitty's response is to ask him oblique questions about his faith. She asks if he has read *Paradise Lost*. She talks about Satan's perspective on his estrangement from God, how Satan imagines taking revenge on God for his exile. She continues:

> After reading this for a while, you realize that Satan's greatest sin, his greatest mistake, wasn't pride or rebelling against God. His greatest mistake was believing that God would not forgive him if he asked for forgiveness. His sin wasn't just pride—it was self-pity. I think in some ways every single person, human, vampire, whatever, has a choice to make: to be full of rage about what happens to you or to reconcile with it, to strive for the most honorable existence you can despite the odds.

She goes on to point out that the caller's belief in whether or not he still has a soul hinges on his belief in the nature of God. Is his God compassionate, forgiving, and all-knowing? She leaves him to answer. Many of the calls to her radio show are cries for help, some are from people who are curious, a few are simply ridiculous. Sometimes her responses are philosophical, sometimes they're snide. Her extremely logical questioning of some of the callers who hold bizarre worldviews provides comic relief, while many of the calls stir her (and the readers') empathy for callers who are coping with personal tragedy. The series includes action, detection, and romance; but the stories also explore questions about individual choice and responsibility, about prejudice and victimization, and about hope and steadfast friendships.

Explorations: In the long run, do you believe that Kitty's actions will help or destroy the supernatural population?

As the pack member with the lowest status, Kitty thinks of herself as vulnerable. How does this belief make her behave? What happens when she acts as if she has higher status within the pack?

What aspects of becoming a werewolf are seductive?

THE CASES

1. **"Looking after Family"** in *Realms of Fantasy.* Herndon, VA: Sovereign Media, v. 13, n. 2, Feb. 2007, p. 38–43. ISSN: 1078–1951.

BEN'S FAMILY RANCH, 198? Sixteen-year-old Cormac Bennett didn't move fast enough when the creature attacked his father. It's a mistake he's determined to avoid in the future. His cousin Ben accompanies him on his first full-moon hunt after Cormac's father's death.

ASSOCIATES: Ellen O'Farrell—*Cormac's Aunt, she took Cormac in when he needed a home;* David—*her husband;* and Ben—*their son.*

2. **"Winnowing the Herd"** in *Strange Horizons,* 16 October 2006, online at: http://www.strangehorizons.com/2006/20061016/winnowing-f.shtml.

DENVER, COLORADO, 2001? Skipping KNOB's staff appreciation party in a time of pending budget cuts would be tantamount to asking for unemployment. Kitty goes to the party, but the combination of vegetarian food and annoying coworkers makes unemployment look a lot like freedom.

ASSOCIATES: Station manager Ozzie; Cherie—*Ozzie's wife;* Frank—*who left his German Shepherd at home;* Perry—*the receptionist/bookkeeper;* Ike; Sean; Bill; Ann; and Beth—*are Kitty's coworkers at KNOB.*

3. **"Kitty's Zombie New Year"** (illustrated by Star St. Germain) in *Weird Tales,* Vol. 62, No. 3, (issue 345), June/July 2007, p. 41–47. ISSN: 0898–5073.

DENVER, COLORADO, 2001? Kitty is trying not to drown in self-pity. It's New Year's Eve, she's invited to Matt's party, and she has no date, no one to kiss at midnight. Events at the party remind her that being alone is far better than being with the wrong man.

ASSOCIATES: Matt—*Kitty's sound engineer (and friend);* Carson—*one of the guests;* Trish—*Carson's new girlfriend;* and Beth—*Carson's ex-girlfriend.*

4. **"Kitty Meets the Band,"** a short story in *Long Time Listener, First Time Werewolf,* an omnibus edition of Carrie Vaughn's work that includes *Kitty*

and the Midnight Hour, Kitty Goes to Washington, "Kitty Meets the Band," and *Kitty Takes a Holiday.* New York: SFBC (published by arrangement with Warner Books), 2007, p. 417–25. ISBN: 9780739482766.

DENVER, COLORADO, 2001? Kitty's topic for the evening is music and the supernatural. As part of the show, she interviews the band Plague of Locusts. Rumor has it that the quiet guy who plays the bass is possessed by the demon Morgantix. (Note: Since the band members regard her as cool but don't seem to know that she's a werewolf, this is placed before *Kitty and the Midnight Hour.*)

ASSOCIATES: Callers: Eddy—*who'd like to sell his soul to the devil to play like Hendrix;* Rachel—*who can't get Muskrat Love out of her mind;* and Ellen—*who wishes that music could bring back her dead husband.*

Rudy Jones—*lead singer for Plague of Locusts;* Bucky—*the drummer;* Len—*the guitarist;* and Tim Kane—*on bass.*

5. ***Kitty and the Midnight Hour.*** New York: Warner Books, 2005, 288 p. ISBN: 0446616419.

DENVER, COLORADO, 2005? When Kitty, the midnight DJ at KNOB in Denver, reads a news column about "batboy" on the air, all she is expecting is a little amusement between playing the records. When a supernatural calls asking for advice, she breaks the rules and tries to give some meaningful help. After that, the calls come thick and fast, and the *Kitty in the Midnight Hour* show is born. It's a call-in show for supernaturals with problems. One vampire asks her to investigate Elijah Smith's Church of the Pure Faith.

Plenty of people (well, vampires and werewolves) are extremely upset, murderously upset, at Kitty for opening up a forum where people can hear about the supernatural. When one of them sends an assassin after her, she blows her cover and admits to being a werewolf. After that, Detective Hardin asks for her help when crime scenes look as if a wolf might be involved. Apprehending feral werewolves before they kill is in the pack's best interest; so Kitty turns detective for the pack, for a vampire, and for herself.

ASSOCIATES: The local pack covers an area of 200 miles and includes 22 wolves. Carl (werewolf)—*is the Alpha male;* Meg (werewolf)—*is the Alpha female;* Zan (werewolf)—*is the wolf who bit Kitty;* T. J. (werewolf)—*is Kitty's best friend;* Ozzie—*is KNOB's station manager;* Matt—*the sound engineer for Kitty's show;* Rodney—*is the afternoon DJ;* Craig—*is Kitty's martial arts instructor;* Arturo (vampire)—*leads the local vampire Family;* Rick (vampire)—*is one of the vampires in the Family;* Estelle (vampire)—*who calls Kitty when she's trying to escape the Church of the Pure Faith;* Dr. Paul Flemming—*is an Assistant Director of the National Institute of Health overseeing the Center for the Study of Paranatural Biology;* Veronica Sevilla—*one of the show's guests;* Senator Joseph Duke—*who also comes on the show;* Cormac—*who is hired to kill Kitty;* Detective Jessi Hardin—*who investigates the attack;* Ben O'Farrell—*Cormac's, and later Kitty's lawyer;* Cheryl—*Kitty's older sister, who still tattles on her to their mother.*

6. **"Il Est Né,"** a short story in *Wolfsbane and Mistletoe,* edited by Charlaine Harris and Toni L. P. Kelner. New York: Ace Books, 2008, p. 111–38. ISBN: 9780441016334.

Unknown city in Colorado, Christmas 2005? David was turned about a year ago. He was terrified and never learned to control his wolf. He retreated from the world to live in the woods, hiding the monster that he has become. After a year of frequent changes, he feels more like a wolf that is sometimes trapped in the body of a man, rather than like a man who sometimes must change into a wolf. Kitty is estranged from her pack, exiled from her home. She buys David a cup of coffee, then hears a newsflash that a monster has been murdering people in the area. David has little memory of his last hunt . . . is she drinking coffee with a killer?

Associates: Kitty Norville—*who helps David by showing him that it's possible to live in human society;* David—*who had fled from everyone who knew him;* and Jane—*the waitress.*

7. **"Kitty and the Mosh Pit of the Damned"** (illustrated by Russell Morgan), in *Weird Tales* Vol. 61, No. 2, (issue 338), Jan.–Feb. 2006, p. 35–42. ISSN: 0898–5073.

Unknown city, 2006?. Kitty has heard rumors that the band Devil's Kitchen is fueled by some otherworldly power. Their music incites violence. She goes for an interview to find out the truth. (Story takes place less than one year after Kitty's program went national and after Kitty revealed on air that she is a werewolf.)

Associates: *Devil's Kitchen* band members include Danny Spense—*on bass,* Kent Hayden—*on lead guitar,* and Eliot Ray—*the lead singer.* Jax—*is the bartender at Glamour, where the band is playing.*

8. ***Kitty Goes to Washington.*** New York: Warner Books, 2006, 360 p. ISBN: 0446616427.

Washington, D.C, Autumn 2006? Kitty is subpoenaed to testify before Congress. While waiting to testify at the Hearings, she learns more than she expected about the Reverend Elijah Smith. Her efforts to investigate the Reverend are complicated by an attempted coup by some of the younger vampires of Washington.

Associates: Ben O'Farrell—*Kitty's lawyer, he attends the Hearings with her;* Cormac—*has been hired to provide extra security;* Senators Joseph Duke, Deke Henderson, and Mary Dreschler—*are on the special oversight committee that is holding the Hearings on the Center for the Study of Paranatural Biology.* Witnesses include Dr. Paul Flemming—*head of the Center for the Study of Paranatural Biology;* Jeffrey Miles—*a professional psychic and channeler;* Reverend Elijah Smith—*the founder of the Church of the Pure Faith, and one of the Unseelie Fae;* Robert Carr—*a filmmaker.* Other people observing the Hearings include Roger Stockton—*reporter for Uncharted World.*

Ozzie—*KNOBs station manager* and Matt—*the sound engineer for Kitty's show;* Wes Brady and Liz Morgan—*work at the Arlington, Virginia station;* Alette (vampire)—*the vampire Mistress of the City of Washington D.C.;* Tom and Bradley—*Alette's "men in black";* Emma—*the maid;* Leo (vampire)—*is the one vampire in Alette's immediate household;* Luis (were-jaguar), Ahmed (werewolf), Fritz (werewolf), and Ty (werewolf)—*are part of the lycanthropic community of Washington.*

9. **"Life is the Teacher,"** a short story in *Hotter Than Hell,* edited by Kim Harrison and Martin H. Greenberg. New York: Harper, 2008, p. 405–27. ISBN: 9780061161292.

WASHINGTON, D.C, WINTER 2006? Emma seeks her independence: she needs to know that she can take care of herself. Alette advises that she hunt in a place where she is not known, but Emma disregards that advice.

ASSOCIATES: Emma (vampire); Alette (vampire)—*Mistress of the Washington vampires;* Chris—*Emma's old friend.*

10. ***Kitty Takes a Holiday.*** New York: Warner Books, c2007, 318 p. ISBN: 0446618748.

SAN ISABEL NATIONAL FOREST, SOUTHERN COLORADO AND NEW MEXICO, 2006? Kitty has gone to ground in the aftermath of her televised shapechanging. With a book contract and a looming deadline, she's losing her fight against writer's block and depression; more and more often she is giving in to the wolf. When she is attacked by magical means, it is one more undeserved blow coming out of the blue. Cormac and Ben are also attacked, and once they rejoin Kitty, the odd attacks escalate. It looks as if a wolf is running wild on the cattle ranges. Kitty knows it's not her, but once again she must find the culprit in order to prove her own innocence.

ASSOCIATES: Ariel, Priestess of the Night—*talk show host whose show annoys Kitty;* Ben O'Farrell (werewolf)—*Kitty's lawyer;* Cormac—*the werewolf hunter, Ben's cousin and best friend.* The people of the town near the cabin include Alice—*the shopkeeper;* Joe—*Alice's husband;* Sheriff Marks—*who is an incompetent witness;* Deputy Ted—*who works for the sheriff;* Chad Baker—*a rancher;* Tony Rivera (shaman)—*a friend of Cormac's;* Louise Wilson (shaman); and Lawrence (skinwalker)—*Louise's grandfather.*

11. ***Kitty and the Silver Bullet.*** New York: Grand Central Publishing, 2008, 326 p. ISBN: 0446618756; 9780446618755.

CAÑON CITY, PUEBLO AND DENVER, COLORADO, 2007? This book is not a mystery. In this book a family emergency causes Kitty's father to ask Kitty to come home to Denver. She tries to keep a low profile, but ends up entangled in a battle for power in the Denver vampire and werewolf communities.

ASSOCIATES: Ben O'Farrell (werewolf)—*part of Kitty's pack;* Cormac—*the werewolf hunter, Ben's cousin and best friend, is also, oddly, part of Kitty's pack, even though he is human;* Dr. Elizabeth Shumacher—*is the new head of the Center for the Study of Paranatural Biology;* Jim and Gail Norville—*Kitty's parents;* Cheryl—*Kitty's big sister;* Mark—*Cheryl's husband;* 16-month-old Jeffy and three-and-a-half-year-old Nicky—*are Cheryl and Mark's kids:* Carl (werewolf)—*alpha of The Denver werewolf pack;* Meg—*his mate;* Becky; Jenny; Shaun; and Mick—*are other werewolves in the Denver pack.* Arturo (vampire)—*Master vampire of the Denver vampires;* Rick (vampire)—*who now wants to be referred to as Ricardo;* Stella (vampire); Dack (lycanthrope African wild dog)—*a member of Ricardo's group;* Charlie (vampire) and Violet (vampire)—*are also part of Ricardo's group.*

Ozzie—*KNOB's station manager;* Matt—*the sound engineer for Kitty's show;* Mercedes Cook (vampire)—*who Kitty interviews;* Detective Jessi Hardin—*now heads up the Denver Police Department's Paranatural Unit;* Officer Sawyer—*who is trigger-happy, is a member of the Unit;* and Officer Lopez—*is in the Unit.*

12. ***Kitty and Dead Man's Hand.*** New York: Grand Central Publishing, 2009, 282 p. ISBN: 0446199532; 9780446199537.

DENVER, COLORADO AND LAS VEGAS, NEVADA, 2008. The mystery in this book doesn't truly begin until more than halfway through the book. Up until that point, the story focuses on Kitty and Ben's wedding plans, and on the first television broadcast of Kitty's show. When the mystery takes hold, Kitty suspects that the local lycanthropes (felines) are being held against their will, Ben suspects that there is organized cheating going on in the hotel's poker tournament, and one of Kitty's pack gets kidnapped. In this entry in the series, Kitty and Ben marry.

ASSOCIATES: Ben O'Farrell (werewolf)—*is part of Kitty's pack;* Jim and Gail Norville—*are Kitty's parents;* Ozzie—*KNOB's station manager;* Matt—*the sound engineer for Kitty's show;* Shaun (werewolf)—*manages Kitty and Ben's bar and grill, New Moon;* Rick (vampire)—*the head of the Denver vampires;* Dom (vampire)—*the head of the Las Vegas vampires, he owns the Napoli Hotel and Casino;* Boris and Sylvia—*who are anxious to put down any werewolves they can find;* Evan and Brenda—*who are somewhat less psychotic, but who also hunt lycanthropes;* Erica Decker—*assistant producer for the first television episode of Kitty's Midnight Hour call-in show;* Nevada State Senator Harry Burger—*a guest;* Arty Gruberson—*a guest who is an Elvis Impersonator (or reincarnation);* Lisa (vampire)—*a guest;* Balthasar, King of the Beasts (feline lycanthrope)—*leads a group that has an animal act at The Hanging Gardens;*

Kay (leopard), Nick (feline lycanthrope–type unknown), Avi (snow-leopard), and Sanjay (feline lycanthrope-type unknown)—*are part of Balthasar's group;* Tiamat (vampire)—*is part of the act;* Odysseus Grant (magician)—*has his own act, he is someone who values order;* Allen Matthews—*director of hotel security;* and Detective Mike Gladden.

13. ***Kitty Raises Hell.*** New York: Grand Central Publishing, 2009, 3282 p. ISBN: 0446199540; 9780446199544.

DENVER, COLORADO, 2008. This novel completes the story begun in *Kitty and the Dead Man's Hand.* In that book, Kitty managed to escape the cult of Tiamat (an ancient Babylonian goddess of chaos). Once she returned to Denver, she thought that she would be safe. She was mistaken.

First Kitty's business is attacked, then her pack. She asks Rick, the Master vampire of Denver for assistance and is frustrated when he interprets the attacks as a vampire power play for his territory. Kitty decides to enlist other help. When *Paradox PI,* a television show that employs science to explore paranormal phenomena, comes to film episodes in Denver, Kitty schemes to enlist their aid. She's invited to accompany the crew to the haunted Flint House. The last paranormal investigator who went to Flint House died: many people believe that he was killed by the house.

As the attacks continue, random fires plague Denver. Innocents die. Kitty struggles to maintain control of her pack. Kitty and Rick's pact to support each other weakens when he refuses to accept another vampire on his territory in return for help against Tiamat.

ASSOCIATES: Ben O'Farrell (werewolf)—*Kitty's husband;* Shaun (werewolf)—*who manages the bar-and-grill New Moon that Kitty created as neutral ground for the supernaturals of Denver;* Mick Cabrerra, Becky, Tom, Dan, and Kris—*are other werewolves in Kitty's pack;* Rick (vampire)—*is the Master vampire of Denver;* Matt—*is the sound engineer for Kitty's radio show.* The stars of *Paradox PI* are: Gary Janson—*the leader;* Tina McCannon (psychic)—*the eye candy, she is also a closet psychic;* Jules Simpson—*the British science nerd who is the fifth generation of his family to belong to the Society for Psychical Research.* Peter Gurney—*Ted "T. J." Gurney's brother, comes to Denver searching for T. J.;* Gail Norville—*Kitty's mother, is undergoing cancer treatment;* Cheryl—*Kitty's sister;* Detective Jessi Hardin—*is the Denver PD's expert on paranormal situations;* Cormac Bennett—*who asks Kitty for help to research a young woman who was executed on the site of the prison over a hundred years ago;* "Roman" (vampire)—*a.k.a. Gaius Albinus, a.k.a. Dux Bellorum, was a centurion in the Roman army's tenth legion in Judea (First Century, Common Era);* Nick (feline lycanthrope)—*is the new alpha of the Band of Tiamat;* Farida (vampire)—*is the priestess of Tiamat;* Odysseus Grant (magician)—*teaches Kitty a protection spell.*

ASSOCIATED WORKS

1. **"Doctor Kitty Solves all Your Love Problems"** (illustrated by Russell Morgan), in *Weird Tales,* Vol. 57, No. 4 (issue 324), Summer 2001, p. 38–43. ISSN: 0898–5073.

DENVER, COLORADO, 2001. This short story is essentially the meeting between Kitty and Cormac depicted in *Kitty and the Midnight Hour.* It's a fun refresher on the meeting story, but not necessary for people who have read the novel.

ASSOCIATES: Matt—*Kitty's sound engineer;* and Cormac—*a werewolf hunter.*

2. **"Kitty Loses her Faith"** (illustrated by Russell Morgan), in *Weird Tales,* Vol. 60, No. 1 (issue 333), Sept.–Oct. 2003, p. 52–58. ISSN: 0898–5073.

DENVER, COLORADO, 2001. The Reverend Elijah Smith has been selling salvation to the supernatural community for some time. Vampires, lycanthropes, and others go into his compound and don't return. Kitty gets a call from a vampire who is trying to leave the church. Kitty must find a way to help, and all the while she's wondering if there's a chance that she herself can be cured. This story takes place a few months after the first short story ("Doctor Kitty Solves All Your Love Problems"). The events told here are recounted in *Kitty and the Midnight Hour.* In the novels, the story continues toward a more satisfying resolution.

ASSOCIATES: Matt—*Kitty's sound engineer;* Estelle (vampire)—*a caller who's trying to leave the Reverend Elijah Smith's Church of the Pure Faith;* Arturo (vampire)—*Master Vampire of Denver.*

W

WALTON, Jo.

FARTHING

Genres/Themes Crossed: Alternate History, Dystopia X Police Procedural.

Subjects/Character Types: Alternate Earth (Alternate History) X Police Procedural.

Series/Stand-Alone: Changes in the characters make these best read in order.

Scene of the Crime: Farthing, an estate in the English countryside, 1949.

Detectives: Inspector Peter Carmichael, an officer of Scotland Yard still growing accustomed to his role as a supervising officer. Carmichael is from a poor family, the first member of his family to make it out of their small town, and is slightly resentful towards the wealth and leisure of the English countryside.

Known Associates: Lucy Khan, the daughter of a wealthy and socially renowned family. Lucy was ostracized by much of her family and their friends for her decision to marry a Jewish man, David Khan, for love rather than engage in a more politically and socially favorable marriage. Sergeant Royston, a subordinate officer is sent with Inspector Carmichael.

Premise: The United Kingdom made peace with Hitler's Germany before America entered the war. The government adopted the repressive and militaristic qualities of the Third Reich. Most people live quiet lives, hoping to avoid police scrutiny. There is general discrimination against people of Jewish descent.

In *Farthing*, a murder occurs during a party at the estate of one of the most socially prominent families in England. The murder weapon is a dagger plunged through the heart of the man who negotiated peace between England and Germany, with a yellow star pinned to it. The implication is that the Jewish husband of the heiress to the estate is the culprit, but the investigating officer believes this to be a clear attempt at framing an innocent man.

Comments: This alternate history has been given a great deal of praise for its deft portrayal of the decline of the value of liberty and democracy in a nation transitioning towards fascism. The narration shifts between Lucy, who has a very disorganized stream of consciousness style, and Inspector Carmichael, who seems to possess a much more organized mind. The book was nominated for a Nebula Award, a Quill Award, the John W. Campbell Memorial Award for best science fiction novel, and the Sidewise Award for Alternate History. *Ha'penny* won the 2008 Prometheus Award and has been nominated for the Lambda Literary Award. See the Jo Walton journals at http://papersky.livejournal.com/.

Literary Magic and Mayhem: In the world of *Farthing*, Sir James Thirkie negotiated peace between England and Germany, which occupied virtually all of continental Europe, in the year 1941, prior to America entering World War II. As a result, Hitler stayed in power and now Germany extends from Russia to the English Channel. The social set that Thirkie was associated with, called the Farthing set after the war, became exceedingly powerful socially and politically, and now is seen by many to be the true power in England. Anti-Semitism is also a prominent feature of this imagined society.

Explorations: What characterizes a free society?

How did this version of England differ from our own version of England with regard to social normative ideals in the post-war era?

How valid are Lucy's statements regarding the complimentary nature of disorganized, irrational thought processes and logical, well organized thought processes?

THE CASES

1. ***Farthing.*** New York: TOR Books, 2007, 336 p. ISBN: 076535280X.

FARTHING, ENGLAND 1949. Following the murder of the man who negotiated peace between Hitler and England, Inspector Carmichael seeks the truth, and Lucy Kahn looks to clear her husband's good name.

Associates: Sergeant Royston—*Carmichael's sergeant and friend;* Lucy Kahn—*daughter of the hosts, she came hoping for a reconciliation with her parents;* David Kahn—*Lucy's husband, he is Jewish and was a flight lieutenant in the war;* Jem Jordan—*the mechanic;* Betty—*Jem's wife;* Inspector Yately—*a police inspector sent over from Winchester;* Jeffrey Pickens—*the footman;* Izzard—*the constable who is sent to man the gate;* Dr. Green—*a police doctor who did not conduct a thorough examination,* Angela Thirkie—*who is now a widow;* Mark Normanby—*who will be the next Prime Minister;* Daphne Normanby—*his wife;* Lord Eversley—*Lucy's father, a political leader;* Lady Eversley—*Lucy's mother, who insisted that Lucy and David come to Farthing this weekend;* Sergeant Stebbings—*whose politics dictates his theories;* Sir Thomas Manningham—*a self made industrialist who has recently been made a baronet;* Lady Catherine "Kitty" Manningham—*his young wife;* and Agnes Timms—*who was willing to give evidence.*

2. *Ha'penny.* New York: TOR Books, 2007, 307 p. ISBN: 0765358080, 9780765358080.

London, England June 1949. When the home of a prominent actress is partially destroyed by a bomb, the first thought is that it was unexploded ordinance from the war. The second thought is that the bomb was the work of Jewish terrorists. The press is full of reports of bombings and shootings perpetrated by the Jewish terrorists. The government is finding new ways to crack down. One idea is to create a Gestapo-like organization in England; they will call it The Watch, and they want Inspector Carmichael to head it. One of the reasons that the Prime Minister wants Carmichael to head The Watch is that he knows Carmichael is gay. That knowledge allows him to blackmail Carmichael into taking any action that the Prime Minister desires.

The fear of being targeted by the government overwhelms people. They turn their family members over to the police. People call and offer to give evidence against co-workers and neighbors. For instance, once Mr. Kinnerson realizes that his mother may have been making a bomb, he calls Inspector Carmichael to ingratiate himself with the police by giving evidence against his boss. Fearing that offering up his boss is insufficient he also offers to find ways to get the Inspector money.

Associates: Sergeant Royston—*who works the case with the Inspector;* Chief Penn-Barkis—*Carmichael's boss, he knows Carmichael's secret;* Prime Minister Mark Normanby and the Home Secretary, Lord Timothy Cheriton—*also know about Carmichael;* Daphne—*is Prime Minister Normanby's wife;* Jack—*is Carmichael's lover;* Inspector Jacobson—*is Jewish, and so is unlikely to ever get a promotion;* Ogilvie—*is a very efficient Deputy Inspector of the Home Office.*

The Larkin sisters were all named after women in Shakespeare, and they gave each other odd nicknames: Olivia (Tess)—*the scholar, died in an air-raid shelter;* Celia (Pip)—*became a fascist and married Himmler;* Viola (Fatso)—*became an actress;* Cressida (Siddy)—*became a communist;* Miranda (Dodo)—*became a painter and married a scientist;* and Rosalind (Rosie)—*focused on hunting and married a Duke.* Mr. and Mrs. Green and Mercedes Carl—*were actress Lauria Gilmore's servants;* Mr. Kinnerson—*was Lauria Gilmore's son;* Rachel Grunwald—*turns in Mr. Green, her uncle, because she's afraid that he will get the rest of the family in trouble;* Mrs. Channing—*the landlady who sends Mr. and Mrs. Green away.*

The conspirators include: Lord Scott—*Viola's Uncle Phil;* Malcolm Nesbitt—*Uncle Phil's secretary;* Siddy—*Viola's sister;* Loy (Sir Aloysius) Farrell—*Siddy's lover;* Irishman Devlin Connelly—*who knows about bombs;* and Bob Nash—*who was a good friend of Pete.*

Antony Bannon—*the director;* Jackie—*his assistant;* Bettina—*the wardrobe mistress;* Doug James—*plays Horatio;* Charlie Brandin—*plays Laertes;* Tim Curtis—*plays Polonius;* Pat McKnight—*plays Ophelia;* Mollie Gaston—*Viola's roommate, plays Gertrude;* and Mrs. Tring—*is employed as Viola and Mollie's dresser.*

3. ***Half a Crown.*** New York: Tom Doherty Associates, 2008, 3167 p. ISBN: 0765316218, 9780765316219.

LONDON, ENGLAND APRIL 1960. This novel follows the investigation of two conspiracies. A faction within the Ironsides is calling for better government control; their slogan is "British Power." They're speaking against the Prime Minister, calling him a weak cripple. They feel that England should have its own concentration camps, instead of shipping British citizens off to Germany. The Prince of Wales is involved. Scotland Yard is investigating rumors that some of the Jews captured by the Watch are escaping and being helped to leave the country.

ASSOCIATES: Lieutenant Commander Jacobson—*who is Jewish, and is part of the "Inner Watch";* Ogilvie—*is Watch Commander Carmichael's other Lieutenant Commander;* Miss Margaret Rose Duthie—*is Carmichael's secretary;* Sergeant Paul Evans and Inspector Fanshaw—*are other detectives in the Watch.*

Mrs. Abby Talbot—*runs an underground railroad to save some of England's Jews;* Jack—*is Watch Commander Carmichael's lover;* Chief Penn-Barkis—*runs Scotland Yard;* Inspector Bannister; Royston; and Sergeant Matlock—*are detectives at Scotland Yard.* Prime Minister Mark Normanby—*runs the government.*

Mr. Antony Bannon—*now has a political talk show called This Week;* Jackie Hardcastle—*is still his assistant.* Guests on one show include Carmichael; along with Home Secretary Lord Timothy "Tibs" Cheriton, the Duke of Hampshire; Japan's General Nakajima; and Edward the Eighth, Duke of Windsor (the terms of his abdication allow him to visit England).

Elvira Royston—*whose father died when she was eight, she is the ward of Watch Commander Carmichael who pays the Maynards so that she can live with their family;* Betsy Maynard—*is Elvira's best friend;* Mrs. Maynard—*who wants Betsy to marry her friend Lady Bellingham's son;* Sir Alan Bellingham—*Lady Bellingham's son;* the Berman family—*are one stop on the underground railroad, they help Elvira;* Irene—*is Elvira's mother;* Richard—*is Irene's husband;* Breda—*a pub owner, introduces Watch Commander Carmichael to Sir Aloysius Farrell;* Foreign Secretary Sir Guy Braithwaite—*who speaks to the Queen about the threats facing England.*

WAUGH, Charles G. Co-editor (with Isaac Asimov and Martin H. Greenberg) of *Isaac Asimov's Wonderful World of Science Fiction Anthology #5 Tin Stars.* See ASIMOV, Isaac: Isaac Asimov's Wonderful World of Science Fiction Anthology #5 Tin Stars.

WAUGH, Charles G. and Martin H. Greenberg. (Editors)

SCI-FI PRIVATE EYE

Genres/Themes Crossed: Science Fiction X Capers, Hard-Boiled Mystery, Police Procedural. (Sci-Fi Private Eye)

Paranormal X Hard-Boiled Mystery, Police Procedural (Supernatural Sleuths)

Subjects/Character Types: Future Technology, Aliens X Capers, Private Investigators, Police. (Sci-Fi Private Eye)

Ghosts, Psychics X Private Investigators, Police (Supernatural Sleuths)

Series/Stand-Alone: Anthologies of previously published short stories.

Scene of the Crime: Varies.

Detective: Varies.

Known Associates: Varies.

Premise: *Sci-Fi Private Eye* collects stories of private eyes working in the future. *Supernatural Sleuths* collects mystery stories with a hint of paranormal: ghosts or psychic phenomena.

Comment: The editors suggest that the reader's perplexity and consideration of otherworldly solutions while reading Edgar Allan Poe's "The

Murders in the Rue Morgue" could make that story the work that was the forerunner of speculative crime fiction.

Anthologies were a way of preserving and re-introducing the best of the stories from the science fiction pulp magazines. Charles G. Waugh worked as a professor of Psychology and Communications at the University of Maine at Augusta. He said that he especially enjoyed saving unjustly overlooked stories, and he co-edited many anthologies.

Literary Magic & Mayhem: The stories are excellent, written by some of the best and most well-known authors in the field.

Explorations: What made this story one that should be saved? Was it the introduction of a character or theme? A particularly interesting crime? A good puzzle? A good story about a character that is now (mostly) forgotten?

THE CASES

1. ***Sci-Fi Private Eye: Amazing Tales of Cosmic Crime from Bestselling Authors.*** New York: Roc, 1997, 346 p. ISBN: 0451455924.

CONTENTS: The Singing Bell *by Isaac Asimov;* The Martian Crown Jewels *by Poul Anderson;* A Scarletin *Study by Philip Jose´ Farmer;* The Winner *by Donald Westlake;* The Detweiler Boy *by Tom Reamy;* Time Exposures *by Wilson Tucker;* Getting Across *by Robert Silverberg;* War Game *by Philip K. Dick;* ARM *by Larry Niven.*

2. ***Supernatural Sleuths: 14 Mysterious Cases of Uncanny Crime.*** New York: Roc, 1996, 347 p. ISBN: 0451455797.

CONTENTS: Lonely Train A'Comin' *by William F. Nolan;* Vandy, Vandy *by Manly Wade Wellman;* Ghost Patrol *by Ron Goulart;* Adventure of the Ball of Nostradamus *by August Derleth and Mack Reynolds;* Gateway of the Monster *by William Hope Hodgson;* Good Judge of Character *by Susan Dunlap;* Angel of the Lord *by Melville Davisson Post;* Falling Boy *by Davaid Dean;* Existential Man *by Lee Killough;* Midnight El *by Robert Weinberg;* Cardula Detective Agency *by Jack Ritchie;* Chronology Protection Case *by Paul Levinson;* Children of Ubasti *by Seabury Quinn;* Death by Ecstasy *by Larry Niven.*

WILLINGHAM, Bill and Lam Buckingham.

LEGENDS IN EXILE

Genres/Themes Crossed: Literary Cross-Over X Police Procedural.

Subjects/Character Types: Literary Cross-over (children's stories) X Police Procedural.

Series/Stand-Alone: Stand-alone.

Scene of the Crime: Fabletown, New York City, the small community built by displaced fable and storybook characters, functioning like many similar communities to preserve the traditions of individuals that share a common culture due to their point of national origin.

Detectives: Bigby Wolf, formerly the Big Bad Wolf. Bigby was appointed the sheriff of Fabletown due largely to his tracking abilities and the fear he inspired in may of the residents.

Known Associates: Snow White, mayor of Fabletown following The Exile (when storyland characters were driven out of their homelands). Boy Blue, Snow White's assistant. Flycatcher, the former prince who had been transformed into a frog. Bluebeard, who is a pirate and an accomplished swordsman. Jack, giant killer and beanstalk climber.

Premise: Every storybook character is real, sustained by its presence in the consciousness of the mundane world. Following the attack of a mysterious enemy called "The Adversary," there was an exodus of fables and storybook characters from their homeland to the mundane world. They've been here for many years, and have made their home largely in New York City, in an area of the city they call Fabletown.

Comment: This series has received a great deal of critical acclaim, and enjoyed a lot of commercial success as well. The first volume of the story sets up a very well-done mystery, but subsequent volumes tend more towards political intrigue, and thus will not be covered in this book. The content is very adult, and may not be suitable for children.

Bill Willingham's official Web site is located at http://www.billwillingham.com/. It includes news, information on his works, biographical information, and a link to forums for readers, which is at http://www.clockworkstorybook.net/forum/.

Literary Magic & Mayhem: Every storybook character is real, and more or less immortal. Storybook animals can talk, magic and curses are used by these characters, and all of it must be concealed from the mundane population.

Explorations: How have the stories we tell changed with time?

What sort of characters and situations have we actually been describing to our children?

Did the author play fair with the mystery? Are all the clues there?

THE CASE

Legends in Exile. New York: Vertigo, 2003, 128 p. ISBN: 1563899426.

FABLETOWN IN NEW YORK CITY, PRESENT DAY. Jack claims that his on again off again girlfriend of the last several hundred years, Rose Red, Snow White's sister, has been murdered. Bigby Wolf must play the role of detective and determine what happened to Rose Red.

ASSOCIATES: See above.

WILLIS, Connie.

INSIDE JOB

Genres/Themes Crossed: Paranormal X Traditional Mystery.

Subjects/Subgenres: Ghosts, Spiritualists (Mediums) X Investigative Reporters.

Series/Stand-Alone: Stand-alone.

Scene of the Crime: Present-day Los Angeles California.

Detective: Rob is the founder, owner, editor, and reporter for *The Jaundiced Eye,* a monthly magazine that debunks fake paranormal phenomena.

Known Associates: Talented, brilliant, beautiful, rich, (and best of all, skeptical), Kildy Ross retired from acting to take up debunking. She walked into the offices of *The Jaundiced Eye* eight months ago and asked for a job as an investigative reporter. One of Rob's credos is that anything that seems too good to be true is too good to be true; so he has spent the last eight months expecting Kildy to walk right back out and leave him to work alone once again.

Premise: H. L. Mencken wrote scathing essays and editorials against con artists, frauds, medical quackery, and people who felt that science was an attack on religion. He died in 1956. What would he do if he found a way to speak to people today from beyond the grave?

Comment: Connie Willis's Web site is at http://www.sftv.org/cw/Connie Willis has won more science fiction awards than any other modern writer. Her works feature likeable characters, humor, great dialog, and fascinating situations.

Literary Magic & Mayhem: The great fun of this story is the voice of Mencken. He exhorts a spiritualist's audience to come to their senses:

> There you sit, with your mouths hanging open, like the rubes at an Arkansas camp meeting, listening to a snakecharming preacher, waiting for her to fix up your romances and cure your gallstones.

Most of the chapters are headed with Mencken quotes. Rob's unabashed joy in Mencken lore, the chapter heading quotations, and the channeled voice of Mencken are a wonderful combination.

Explorations: At what point is skepticism just a different brand of faith?

THE CASE

Inside Job. Burton, MI: Subterranean Press, c2005, 99 p. ISBN: 1596060247, 9781596060241.

LOS ANGELES AND BEVERLY HILLS, CALIFORNIA, PRESENT DAY. It's difficult to debunk con artists who claim to channel spirits from long ago. If a hoax involves physical manifestations (such as bending spoons), then there is something for the skeptic to measure, some evidence that can be uncovered. A spiritualist just claims that he or she hears something that others don't hear. Who can prove that the spiritualist didn't? Nothing in the performance lends itself to hard proof (or disproof). Rob gave up on discrediting spiritualists long ago.

When Kildy invites him to view spiritualist Ariaura Keller's performance, Rob is baffled. His research reveals that Ariaura Keller claims to channel the spirit entity Isus. She not only has the spelling of "Isis" wrong, she has identified Isus as a man. Why endure the frustration of viewing an incompetent fraud that they cannot unmask? What Rob sees surprises him, but one way or another he will explain it.

ASSOCIATES: Kildy Ross—*an investigative reporter;* Ariaura Keller (a.k.a. Bonnie Friehl, a.k.a. Doreen Manning)—*a con artist who is a better medium than she ever suspected;* Riata Starr—*an actress who does a little undercover work for Kildy;* and H. L. Mencken—*deceased but not departed*?

TO SAY NOTHING OF THE DOG

Genres/Themes Crossed: Time Travel X Traditional Mystery.

Subjects/Character Types: Time Travel X Amateur Sleuth (Contemporary).

Series/Stand-Alone: This novel is a stand-alone. Ms. Willis has set other works in the same universe (using the same time-machine). These include the novel *The Doomsday Book* (1992), the short story "Fire Watch" (1984), and the upcoming novel *Blackout* (2010).

Scene of the Crime: England, 2057, June 1888, November 1940, 2018, 1933, and 1395.

Detective: Ned Henry is an historian, his specialty is the 20th century. He works for the time travel project at Oxford University. The project is woefully underfunded and, when a prospective donor (Lady Schrapnell) wants help recreating Coventry Cathedral, all project personnel are assigned to fulfill her wishes. Ned's special project becomes recovering a Victorian monstrosity called the bishop's bird stump. The mystery is that the bishop's bird stump is not where and when it should be; the implications of that could change the world.

Known Associates: The Head of Time Travel is Mr. Chiswick; Mr. Dunworthy is in charge of the historians; Dunworthy's secretary is Finch. Others working on the time travel project include Carruthers, Ned's partner; Verity Kindle; Miss Warder, the scientist who calculates the coordinates for the drops and runs the net; and T. J. Lewis. T. J. is an undergraduate who was working at Time Travel when Lady Schrapnell coerced all the other personnel to travel back in time to gather information in support of the Cathedral Project. She could not drag in T. J. because he is of African descent, and the dates during which the Cathedral stood are off-limits to him because of societal dangers. He's the "Ensign John Klepperman" of the Time Travel unit. (In World War II, Ensign John Klepperman was the only one left alive on the bridge of his ship during the Battle of Midway; he had to take over as captain. He was not prepared for command, but he did well—until he died in the line of duty.) Also in 2057 is Elizabeth Bittner, widow of the last Bishop of Coventry Cathedral.

1888: Terence St. Trewes and his companion, Cyril; Jabez, who rents boats, Terence's professor, Professor Matthew Peddick; Miss Tocelyn "Tossie" Mering, her cousin Miss Verity Brown, and her cat Princess Arjumand. Tossie's parents: Colonel Mesiel Mering and Mrs. Malvinia Mering. The Mering's servants: their butler Baine and Jane (Mrs. Mering calls her Colleen), their maid. The Mering's neighbors are the Chattisbournes: Mrs. Chattisbourne and her daughters: Rose, Iris, Pansy, and Eglantine; their butler is Finch. The Reverend Mr. Arbitage attends the séance put on by Madam Iritosky and Count de Vecchio at Muchings End. The curate of Coventry Cathedral and Miss Delphinium Sharpe, who is a parishoner.

2018: Mr. Jim Dunworthy, Elizabeth Bittner, and Shoji.

1395: Goadahdahm Boetenneher, Gruwens.

Premise: In the early 2010s, Darby and Gentilla invented time travel, intending to plunder the past. They opened the net to take them through time and tried to bring back everything from the *Mona Lisa* to King Tut's tomb, and when that didn't work, they tried to bring back cash. If they tried to take any object out of its own time, the net would not open to let them return. Scientists concluded that this was a safety feature of the net. As Chiswick, the Head of Time Travel states:

> The space-time continuum is a chaotic system, in which every event is connected to every other in elaborate, nonlinear ways that make prediction impossible. Bringing an object forward through time would create a parachronistic incongruity. At best, the incongruity might result in increased slippage. At worst, it might make time travel impossible. Or alter the course of history. Or destroy the universe. Which is why such an incongruity is not possible. (p. 27)

Once it was realized that time-travelers could bring back nothing but information, the multinational corporations who'd been backing Darby and Gentilla's experiments lost interest. Time travel was handed over to scientists and historians. It's expensive, and there's not much funding. Oxford's project was on the verge of being closed down for lack of funding when Lady Schrapnell came in with her 50 billion pounds and her interest in rebuilding Coventry Cathedral. If she's satisfied with the help they give her to get every detail of the Cathedral ready in time for its consecration, they'll get the funds to keep the project going.

Comment: Connie Willis has won 10 Hugo Awards and six Nebula Awards. "A Letter from the Clearys" (Nebula Award for Best Short Story, 1982), "Fire Watch (1982 Nebula and 1983 Hugo Award for Best Novelette), *The Last of the Winnebagos* (Hugo and Nebula Awards for Best Novella 1989), "At the Rialto" (Nebula Award for Best Novelette 1989), *The Doomsday Book* (Hugo and Nebula Awards for Best Novel, 1993), "Even the Queen" (1992 Nebula and 1993 Hugo for Best Short Story), "Death on the Nile" (Hugo Award for Best Short Story, 1994), "The Soul Selects Her Own Society: Invasion and Repulsion: A Chronological Reinterpretation of Two of Emily Dickinson's Poems: A Wellsian Perspective" (Hugo Award for Best Short Story, 1997), *To Say Nothing of the Dog* (Hugo Award for Best Novel, 1999), *The Winds of Marble Arch* (Hugo Award for Best Novella, 2000), *The Inside Job* (Hugo Award for Best Novella, 2006), *All Seated on the Ground* (Hugo for Best Novella, 2008).

Literary Magic & Mayhem: The narrator, protagonist Ned Henry, is amusing, charming, smart, and kind. A great deal of the humor shines through in the conversations. For instance, in the following snippets of a conversation, Ned doesn't realize that he's affected by "time lag" (caused by moving through time too frequently), and he's worrying that Caruthers might be affected by time lag. Caruthers waxes lyrical about a star:

> "Above the spire. Above the smoky pall of war, above the wrack of destruc tion. Untouched by man's inhumanity to man, a high herald of hope and beauty, of better times to come. A sparkling symbol of a resurrection it yet kens not."
>
> "It yet kens not?" I looked at him, worried. "A high herald of hope and beauty?"
>
> One of the first symptoms of time-lag is a tendency to maudlin sentimentality, like an Irishman in his cups or a Victorian poet cold-sober. (p. 8)

Then Ned worries over the number of jumps Carruthers has taken in the last day, and the fact that Carruthers hasn't slept, all the while demonstrating that he himself is short on sleep and being distracted by irrelevancies, and that that's causing him to respond slowly to Carruthers's statement...(and having trouble seeing the star—blurred vision?)

> I frowned, trying to remember the checklist of time-lag symptoms. Maudlin sentimentality, difficulty in distinguishing sounds, fatigue—but he'd heard the bells, and everyone associated with Lady Schrapnell's reconstruction project was suffering from sleep deprivation. The only sleep I'd gotten in the past week was during the St. Crispin's Day War Effort Bazaar. I'd dozed off during the "Welcome" and slept through half the "Introductions of the Organizing Committee."
>
> What were the other symptoms? Tendency to become distracted by irrelevancies. Slowness in answering. Blurred vision.
>
> "The star," I said. "What does it look like?" (p. 8)

There are many running gags in the story. One is the disorientation coupled with "Difficulty in Distinguishing Sounds" of various time-travelers; another is Terence's comparisons of his and Tossie's love to the love of historically famous couples such as Romeo and Juliet (it never seems to occur to him that none of the romances he mentions ended happily). A third running joke is based on the signs posted on the grounds of a church. The church is an historic building (not to mention being a church); one would expect visitors to be welcome; however, the church and its grounds are plastered with rather harsh signs admonishing visitors about their behavior. These include a sign that warns that trespassers will be prosecuted! Ned's wandering mind comes up with other possible signs. For instance, later at the church, Tossie wonders if the building might be haunted. Ned surmises that no one has ever seen a ghost there, because if anyone had, then the churchwarden would have posted a sign admonishing ghosts to refrain from materializing. The sign could read "absolutely no ectoplasm."

In the book, the characters talk about the similarities of their efforts to those of Agatha Christie's Hercule Poirot, and the similarities of their situation to the romance between Lord Peter Wimsey and Harriet Vane in the novels penned by Dorothy Sayers.

However, the detective stories this most resembles are P. G. Wodehouse's novels of Jeeves and Wooster. (Lady Schrapnell stands in for one of Bertie's domineering aunts, and Ned takes to calling Finch "Jeeves" in praise of Finch's competence in underhanded manipulation.)

Explorations: Which events were historically pivotal? What changed during the course of the book?

Many of the characters ponder causality, either as an academic argument, or when feeling swamped with guilt. What were the different theories? How were the theories treated in the book?

THE CASE

To Say Nothing of the Dog, or, How We Found the Bishop's Bird Stump at Last. New York: Bantam Books, 1998, c1997, 434 p. ISBN: 0553099957.

OXFORD, 2057; MUCHING'S END, JUNE 1888; COVENTRY, NOVEMBER 1940; OXFORD, 2018; OXFORD, 1933; AND COVENTRY, 1395. Almost every member of the Time Travel unit has been combing the past for information to make the re-creation of the Coventry Cathedral perfect in every detail. One annoying loose end is a missing vase that is called the bishop's bird stump. It was definitely standing in front of the parclose screen of the Smith's chapel on that night in November 1940 when the Luftwaffe bombed the Cathedral. One of the historians saw it. It was a heavy metal monstrosity, and may have been chipped; but it wouldn't have been destroyed in the bombing unless it took a direct hit, and that area of the Cathedral was relatively undamaged. The size, weight, and sheer hideousness of the iron vase make it an unlikely object for theft. Even if a thief wanted it, the timing (it was in place that evening, but would have had to be out of the building before the bombing that night) is not believable. The Time Travel unit has checked and re-checked. The vase was not in the rubble the morning after the bombing.

Lady Schrapnell, the driving force behind the re-creation of Coventry Cathedral, is determined that the bishop's bird stump will be in place. They had someone go back to earlier times, when they could locate it, and make drawings, but efforts to re-create it were unsuccessful. Still, it wasn't destroyed, so it probably still exists. If they could find out what happened to it, they could recover it in the present and place it in the Cathedral. Lady Schrapnell is determined: she frequently remarks that "God is in the details" and exhorts the historians to "leave no stone unturned." At the opening of the book,

Ned has been awake for over a week and has made more time jumps than is safe. He becomes disoriented, and his partner takes him back to the present (2057) where he is diagnosed with an advanced case of timelag. Nurse Jenkins prescribes two weeks of rest, but the re-consecration of the Cathedral is in 17 days, and Lady Schrapnell doesn't believe in timelag (or in anything else that stands in her way). Ned's boss, Mr. Dunworthy, hits on the idea of hiding Ned in the past so that he has time enough to recuperate, and he gives Ned a little job to do back in 1888.

ASSOCIATES: See above.

WILSON, Colin. Worked with Ed Brubaker on *Point Blank*. See BRUBAKER, Ed: Point Blank.

WOLF, Gary.

WHO CENSORED ROGER RABBIT

Genres/Themes Crossed: Blended Human/Non-Human Society X Hard-Boiled Mystery.

Subjects/Character Types: Cartoon Characters X Private Investigator, Company Town.

Series/Stand-Alone: Stand-alones (plural) and series. Eddie Valiant and Roger Rabbit meet and part in the first novel, *Who Censored Roger Rabbit?* It is clear at the end of the novel that they will not meet again. The novel is excellent: funny, touching, and it has a great ending. Almost a decade after the novel's publication, it was used as the basis for a popular film, *Who Framed Roger Rabbit?* The film deviated from the novel so that there was a possibility of a continuing relationship between Private Investigator Eddie Valiant and Roger Rabbit. The novel *Who P-P-P-Plugged Roger Rabbit* is a sequel to the film, not to the first novel. The short story "Stay Tooned, Folks!" is a prequel to the first novel. It centers on a turning point in the life of Tadbitty Stifles. Roger Rabbit appears briefly, and Jessica Rabbit has a cameo in the short story. The short story is not a good place to begin the series. It is a slight work, more of a joke than a story. The best place to begin this series is with the original novel, *Who Censored Roger Rabbit?* If the reader wants to read the others, it is recommended that he or she work to forget *Who Censored Roger Rabbit?*, watch the film *Who Framed Roger Rabbit?*, and then read *Who P-P-P-Plugged Roger Rabbit.*

Scene of the Crime: Los Angeles and Toon Town, 1947.

Detective: Eddie Valiant, the toughest private investigator in Los Angeles. He doesn't like toons, but he'll take a job from one of them if he's broke and needs the money. He's an ex-Marine who took the seven-day course at the Acme School of Fine Detecting and set up his own agency.

Known Associates: He works alone, that's how he likes it.

Premise: Cartoon characters, or *'toons,* are alive, but are still cartoon characters. In other words, they talk in bubbles, are frequently goofy, and express themselves with stars, hearts, and so forth in their eyes. Humans and 'toons may work together, but there are few friendships across the dividing line between the species. There are rumors that a few humanoid 'toons have passed as humans: Mae West, Babe Ruth, the Marx Brothers, and Charles Lindbergh. Many humans are intensely prejudiced against 'toons. Mixed neighborhoods are described as ethnically enriched by real estate agents and as blighted by people who fight for urban renewal. There is a social hierarchy among 'toons as well. Humanoid 'toons are at the top, "barnyard" (animal) 'toons are at the bottom. A doppelganger is a mentally projected copy of a 'toon created by the energy of the 'toon's mind. 'Toons use them as stunt doubles.

Comment: Gary K. Wolf writes science fiction and fantasy. His 1981 book *Who Censored Roger Rabbit?* was the basis for the 1988 Academy Award-winning film *Who Framed Roger Rabbit?* His website (http://www.garywolf.com/) includes information on his life and his books. On the site there is an online short story, "Stay Tooned Folks!," that includes Roger and Jessica Rabbit.

Literary Magic & Mayhem: When Eddie confronts Roger with the knowledge that Roger held back information, Roger's response is: "Well, how come you didn't pry it out of me?...I mean you've got some responsibilities in this case too" (p. 15).

Jessica has a lower opinion of Eddie:

> You really are a louse, Valiant A genuine grade-A weasel.

Eddie doesn't exactly argue with her:

> I've been called worse. I've been called better, too, though I think the ones who call me worse have a firmer fix on the real me. (p. 134)

Eddie's voice is one of the best parts of the book. That, along with character growth, a good puzzle, and an interesting setting, combine to make this an excellent read.

Explorations: What was the most surprising thing about the book?

What were Eddie's preconceptions and how were they used against him?

Which characters played upon others' desires and prejudices to avoid the truth?

THE CASES

1. **"Stay Tooned Folks!"** Illustrated by Mike Cressy. An online short story that can be found at http://mysite.verizon.net/garykwolf/Staytooned folks/Staytoonedfolks.pdf.

HOLLYWOOD, 1946. Tadbitty Stifles changes his ways when the ratings dictate that it's change or die! (This is not a mystery, and does not act as a prequel to *Who Censored Roger Rabbit?* It's a stand-alone with a ribald slapstick tone that sets a very different mood from that invoked by the novels.)

ASSOCIATES: Big Bull Topman—*a Mega-mogul;* Tadbitty Stifles—*who is employed to act as personal secretary (i.e., keeper) for Big Bull's son;* Big Bull Topman Junior—*Big Bull's son;* Ike and Mike—*are Tadbitty's camera crew for his 24/7 reality program called Tinseltown Tells Tales;* Wonky the Wondrous Wizard ('toon), Poopdeck the Pirate ('toon), and Doctor Ignatz Cats ('toon)—*take Tinseltown Tells Tales in a new direction;* Leonard Holstein ('toon)—*leads the orchestra;* Chippy Charlene ('toon)—*is a member of the orchestra.* Roger Rabbit ('toon) and his wife Jessica ('toon) also appear in the story.

2. ***Who Censored Roger Rabbit? New York:*** St. Martin's Press, c1981, 181 p. ISBN: 0345303253.

LOS ANGELES, 1947. At first the job was simple. Roger Rabbit hired Eddie Valiant to find out what was going on with his contract to the DeGreasy brothers. They promised to give him his own show, but they have him playing second banana to Baby Herman. They won't star him, and they won't release him. He wanted to find out what their game was; he needed to find a way out of his contract, and he was desperate to win back his wife, Jessica. Eddie would prefer not to work for a 'toon, but times are hard and the money is good.

Then Jessica's new lover, Rocco DeGreasy, is found dead, and Roger is the chief suspect. As far as the police are concerned, it's an open-and-shut case, but Eddie doesn't like the way they ran their investigation. At least, that's what he tells himself; in truth, by that time Eddie feels a sneaking (and astonishing) sympathy for the rabbit, so he stays on the case.

ASSOCIATES: Roger Rabbit ('toon rabbit)—*is Eddie's client;* Rocco and Dominick DeGreasy—*hold Roger's contract;* Jessica Rabbit ('toon human woman)—*is Roger's wife, but she left him for Rocco DeGreasy;* Little Rock DeGreasy—*is Rocco's son;* 36-year-old Baby Herman (toon human infant)—*is the lead in the films and Roger is his sidekick;* Carol Masters—*photographer;*

Dr. Booker T. Beaver ('toon beaver)—*is a noted 'toon psychiatrist;* Captain "Clever" Cleaver ('toon human man)—*a police officer who investigates crimes involving 'toons;* Captain Rusty Hudson—*a police officer who investigates crimes involving humans;* Pops—*who runs the soda shop.* Eddie's poker buddies are Billy Donovan—*a construction worker;* Jess Westerminster—*who is wealthy;* and Harry Wayne—*bodyshop owner.* Bennie ('toon beetle)—*owns the junk shop;* Sid Sleaze—*a.k.a. Sid Baumgartner, is a 'Toon porn publisher.*

3. *Who P-P-P-Plugged Roger Rabbi? New York:* Villard Books, 1991, 255 p.

LOS ANGELES, 1947. The book begins with an apologia:

> A Memo to My Clients
>
> Roger Rabbit and his screwball buddies play fast and loose with historical accuracy.
>
> That's the way things happen in Toontown.
>
> Take a tip from a guy who's been there. Relax, hang on, and enjoy the ride.
>
> Eddie Valiant

And then it sails right into a new (and impossible, in view of the story told in the novel *Who Censored Roger Rabbit?*) novel featuring Roger Rabbit and Eddie Valiant.

When Roger Rabbit offered Eddie Valiant the job of making the *Toontown Telltale* stop printing stories of about Roger's wife Jessica's canoodling with Cary Grant, Eddie refused. He'd promised his secretary/girlfriend Doris that he'd stop taking muscle work. Roger pleaded. Eddie told him that his principles could not be bought. Roger named a price, and Eddie allowed that his principles could be rented.

ASSOCIATES: Roger Rabbit ('toon rabbit)—*is Eddie's client;* Jessica Rabbit ('toon human woman)—*is Roger's wife;* 36-year-old Baby Herman (toon human infant)—*is Roger's perennial nemesis;* Sleazy, Slimey, Dreck, and Profane—*are the humanoid 'toons who run the Toontown Telltale;* Delancey Duck ('toon duck)—*is the publisher;* Agnes Smoot—*is his secretary;* Louise Wrightliter—*a reporter;* Arnie Johnson—*a veterinarian;* Ring Wordhollow—*a Professor at UCLA;* Skipper—*the counter boy at Schwab's drugstore;* Charley Ferris—*Schwab's day manager;* Joe Bazooka—*the undefeated heavy-weight champ;* Knuckles Woburn ('toon human man)—*Joe's manager;* Harry the Hedgehog ('toon hedgehog): David Selznick Jr.—a *producer;* Pepper Potts ('toon, then human, then back again)—*Selnick's goon;* Jake—*the bartender at Jake's Saloon;* Kirk Enigman—*a shadow;* Lupe Chihuahua ('toon human woman)—*who was once Freddy's lover (before he became a zombie);* Tom Tom Le Tuit—*who wants to market an elixir that will turn 'toons into humans;* Freddy ('toon zombie)—*Eddie's brother;* Heddy (maybe 'toon)—*Eddie's sister;* Joellyn "Little Jo" (toon tiny human woman)—*Jessica's sister;* Carbunkle Chameleon ('toon rug); the Queen of Hearts—*what's left of Pepper Potts's murdered wife;* Harriet ('toon human woman)—*Roger's cleaning lady;* Clarence Centipede ('toon centipede); Large Mouth Bassinger ('toon fish); Ferd Flatfoot ('toon); Sargeant Bulldog Biscomb ('toon bulldog); Vivien Leigh; Dr. Wallace Ford; Clark Gable; Rita Hayworth; Betty Gable; Mae West; Larry Olivier; Officer Bunk Thunker; and Carole Lombard.

WREDE, Patricia C. and Caroline Stevermer.

Sorcery and Cecelia

Genres/Themes Crossed: Blended Society X Traditional Mystery.

Subjects/Character Types: Spell-Casters (Wizards and Sorcerers) X Amateur Sleuth(s) (Historical).

Series/Stand-Alone: There are significant changes in relationships, the series should be read in order.

Scene of the Crime: London and the neighborhood which includes Rushton Manor, 1817.

Detective(s): Cousins Kate Talgarth and Cecelia Rushton have been best friends all their lives. When they were young, they livened up their quiet country village with their mischief. Now that they're older they are outwardly docile, biddable young ladies. Below the surface they are both astute, stong-willed, and admirably (or alarmingly) fearless. They see much, because few people bother to put on a false front for the benefit of relatively impoverished and powerless young ladies.

Kate's Aunt Charlotte determines that Kate's beautiful sister, Georgiana, must have a London season, and carts Kate and Georgiana off to London. Cecelia would have loved to accompany them, but their families have vivid memories of the scrapes they got into in quiet Rushton and do not wish to tempt fate by throwing them together in London. So, Kate and Cecelia stay in touch through their letters during Kate's London season.

Known Associates: Cecelia's life is ruled by her Aunt Elizabeth; the rest of her immediate family includes her scholarly Papa and her brother Oliver. In the course of the first book Michael Wrexton begins to teach her magic. Cecelia finds herself working with Dorothea's annoying cousin, James Tarleton, to try to protect her cousin Kate and James's best friend Thomas, the Marquis of Schofield.

Kate's life is ruled by her Aunt Charlotte; the rest of her immediate family consists of her younger sister, Georgina. By chance, she runs afoul of Miranda Tanistry Griscomb and finds herself in the middle of Miranda's feud with Thomas, the Marquis of Schofield. Thomas's mother is Lady Sylvia Schofield.

Premise: Magic exists; the capacity to wield it runs in families. It can, in certain circumstances, be stolen from others. The process is, at best, debilitating; at worst, it is fatal for the person whose magic is stolen.

Comment: This series began as a "letter game." Players write letters to each other in character. (Caroline Stevermer, in the afterword, mentions that it may have been developed as an acting exercise.) Caroline Stevermer mentioned the game to Patricia Wrede and they agreed to play it. The first player sets the two main characters, the setting, and at least some of the conventions of the world in the first letter. The second player replies in character, and they continue from there. Some games fizzle out, but this one was successful and exciting. At the end of six months, it had come to a successful conclusion, and the authors realized that they had a book.

Patricia Wrede's Web site http://www.pcwrede.com/ includes news, appearances, her blog and information on her books. She has posted other interesting material on the web, including her Fantasy Worldbuilding Questions at http://www.sfwa.org/writing/worldbuilding1.htm.

Literary Magic & Mayhem: The voices of the cousins are one of the delights of the book. People treat them as the gently born ladies they are, in other words, as if they are delicate, insipid, and bird-witted. They respond with spirit, irritation, and deception; they make their own plans and are determined to carry them out. For example, Cecelia agrees to go for a drive with James Tarleton so that she can run an errand without her aunt's knowledge. She finds that Tarleton has his own clandestine plans, and she is irritated:

> "What have you planned?" I demanded. I had been so busy with my plans for returning Sir Hilary's book that it had not occurred to me that James Tarleton must have some purpose of his own for our ride, and I was most annoyed with myself.
>
> "Nothing you will object to," James replied in a soothing tone. I cannot think how he came to imagine that he would know what I might or might not object to. (p. 133)

One of Kate's greatest assets (besides her clumsiness) is her capacity for deception. She gets dragged to Vauxhall with the Grenvilles by Georgina, who also found a way to get word of the expedition to Oliver in the hope that it would make him jealous. When Oliver arrives, he blames Kate (she had gloomily expected that everyone who found out would blame her), and she lies to cover for Georgina, saying that they wagered on who could dance with more men, Georgina masked or Kate unmasked. He continues to upbraid her, and she agrees that it was foolish, but suggests that Oliver is being foolish too, telling him "at least I am not bacon-brained enough to preach a sermon in Vauxhall Gardens." The narrative continues:

> You may imagine Oliver's response. It was a masterpiece of priggish indignation that, reduced to its bare essentials, amounted to an accusation that we were having fun without him. (p. 63)

Explorations: What is added to the story by having it told in letters?

If you were to play a letter game, with whom would you play, where would you set it, what would be the conventions of the world?

THE CASES

1. ***Sorcery and Cecelia, or, The Enchanted Chocolate Pot: Being the Correspondence of Two Young Ladies of Quality Regarding Various Magical Scandals in London and the Country.*** Orlando, Fla.: Harcourt, c2003, 316 p. ISBN: 0152046151.

ESSEX AND LONDON, APRIL 1817. Kate, too short to see over the crowd at the Royal College of Magicians' Investiture ceremony, seeks other amusement by exploring the main floor of the castle. She finds a small door and opens it to find a charming tiny garden, a garden that is sunlit on an overcast day. She meets an odd woman who takes over Kate's will and tries to feed her poisoned chocolate. Kate has no idea who the woman is, nor why she would be an enemy. Most of what she says makes little sense, until Kate realizes that the woman has mistaken her for someone else. Kate escapes through her innate clumsiness and a good deal of luck. She has earned the gratitude of the intended victim, and the enmity of a would-be murderess. Altogether, it's making her introduction to society more dangerous than anyone ever expected.

ASSOCIATES: The delights of Essex society include the Reverend Fitzwilliam—*who discourses on the Vanities of Society and the Emptiness of Worldly Pleasures;* Mrs. Everslee—*Patience Everslee's annoying mother, who is thrilled that Georgina's absence will give Patience an opportunity to shine;* Dorothea Griscomb—*a newcomer to Essex, she is unusually lovely and compelling;* Lady Tarleton—*her aunt;* James Tarleton—*Dorothea's cousin, he seems to regard Dorothea with suspicion;* Oliver Rushton—*Cecelia's brother, he is in love with Georgina*, Jack Everslee, Martin De Lacey, and Robert Penwood—*are the other young men in Essex, most of them were also interested in Georgina, and now are interested in Dorothea.*

Sir Hilary Bedrick—*there is much excitement in the village over his investiture in the Royal College of Wizards;* Aunt Elizabeth—*does not approve of wizards and is hard-pressed to remain civil to Sir Hilary;* Cecelia's Papa—*seems oblivious, but continues to borrow books from Sir Hilary's library;* Mrs. Foley—*the gamekeeper's wife, knows something about charm bags;* and Mr. Wrexton—*a wizard.*

Society in London includes Lady Jersey—*who is a friend of Aunt Charlotte's;* the Grenvilles: Alice, George and Andrew; Michael Aubrey—*who become a favorite of Kate's sister, Georgina;* Thomas, the Marquis of Schofield—*who is joined by his mother;* Lady Sylvia Schofield—*his mother, she is rather pleased with Kate;* Frederick Hollydean—*who is odious, he has just been sent down from University;* Mr. Strangle—*Frederick's tutor;* Miranda Tanistry Griscomb—*who is powerful;* Dorothea—*her step-daughter, who is brought to London half-way through the Season;* and the Prince of Wales.

2. ***The Grand Tour, or, The Purloined Coronation Regalia: Being a Revelation of Matter of High Confidentiality and Greatest Importance, Including Extracts from the Intimate Diary of a Noblewoman and the Sworn Testimony of a Lady of Quality.*** Orlando, Fla.: Harcourt, 2004, 469 p. ISBN: 015204616X.

ENGLAND AND THE CONTINENT, AUGUST 1817. The first book was told in letters: the correspondence between Kate and Cecelia. In this book, they have no need to write to one another, since they're traveling together on a Grand Tour (along with their husbands). Instead, the second book is told in a series of different written documents, such as Cecelia's deposition and Kate's diary. It loses some of the confiding and amusing tone of *Sorcery and Cecelia.*

On their honeymoons, Thomas, Kate, James, and Cecelia take a Grand Tour of the Continent. They are troubled first by an attempted theft, then by a successful theft. They soon realize that these are only part of a pattern: there has been a series of thefts of ceremonial artifacts, and it is continuing. Soon the mystery of who is stealing the artifacts gives way to the mystery of why those objects are being stolen. The two couples track the thieves across Europe.

ASSOCIATES: In England: James Tarleton—*Cecelia's husband;* Thomas, Marquis of Schofield—*Kate's husband;* Oliver—*Cecelia's brother;* Aunt Charlotte—*who is determined to find fault;* and Aunt Elizabeth—*who isn't;* Lady Sylvia Schofield—*Thomas's mother;* Aubert—*her maid;* Cecelia's Papa—*who is her cousin Kate's Uncle Arthur;* Georgina—*Kate's sister;* Piers—*Thomas's valet.*

In Amiens: Mr. Beau Brummel; The Bishop of Amiens; Theodore Daventer and his tutor, Mr. Harry Strangle.

In Paris: Mr. Lennox and Mr. Reardon—*Lady Schofield's friends;* Miss Emily Reardon—*who is hired by Kate to be her maid;* Captain Reginald Winters—*who has worked with James and Thomas in the past;* Madame Walker—*who is hired by Cecelia as her maid;* and His Grace, the Duke of Wellington.

In Milan: the British Consul—*who made the newlyweds welcome in Milan;* the Conte and Contessa di Monti—*who throw a garden party to salute the generosity of the Conte di Capodoro;* the Conte and Contessa di Capodoro—*the Conte has just announced the donation of his collection of Roman and Etruscan antiquities to the city of Milan;* William Mountjoy—*Theodore Daventer's uncle;* and the Cavalier Leo Coducci—*a scholar and friend of Cecelia's Papa.*

In Rome: Signor Moltacchi—*an estate agent;* Lady Sutton—*the wife of Britain's ambassador;* and Mrs. Montgomery—*her mother.*

3. ***The Mislaid Magician, or, Ten Years After: Being the Private Correspondence Between Two Prominent Families Regarding a Scandal Touching the Highest Levels of Government and the Security of the Realm.*** Orlando, Fla.: Harcourt, c2006, 328 p. ISBN: 0152055487.

ENGLAND: TANGLEFORD HALL, SKEYNES (AN ESTATE OF THE MARQUIS OF SCHOFIELD), LONDON, LEEDS, HALIWAR TOWER (IN STOCKTON), 1828. The Prime Minister (known affectionately to Thomas and James as "Old Hookey") sends James on a mission. Six months ago a railway surveyor disappeared. He went out to check his maps in the English countryside one morning, having left his clothing and all his other belongings in his rented room, and he never returned. No one has seen him since that day. He was known as a sober, even staid, man. He was a Magician, and well able to take care of himself. After various agents ineffectually fumble the investigation, the Prime Minister turns to James, and James accepts the mission. Cecelia accompanies him. The investigation becomes more complicated when they realize that something magical is affecting the trains. One of the steam locomotives spontaneously and inexplicably explodes in Stockton, killing the engineer and injuring several others. Before embarking on their investigation, Cecelia and James send their children to Cecelia's cousin, Kate. Kate's sister Georgy joins Kate's household as well; she seems to have fled her own home in terror but will not speak sensibly about the cause. Strange happenings at Kate's house include everything from kidnapping to transformation. Perhaps the most ominous occurrence is the discovery that James's and Cecelia's twins are magically gifted.

This book is told in the correspondence between Cecelia and Kate and the correspondence between Thomas and James. The letters are amusing, but not as much fun as the letters in *Sorcery and Cecelia.* Now the cousins spend most of their time in the company of their brilliant husbands. It is less fun to read about their intelligent families than it was to read about some of the more foolish people in the societies they frequented in the first book. They do still have a spark; for instance:

> Even more between the two of us, Cecy, I simply cannot contain myself a moment longer. In his haste to leave Skeynes for London, thus neatly avoiding Georgy and all her sighs, Thomas has convinced himself that he is being clever. He . . . will drive to London and back, enjoying himself thoroughly the while. In his view, the mere matter of transporting a number of small children and their nurse adds nothing to the complexity of the endeavor. To you and you alone, Cecy, I must say ha! Ha! And again ha! (p. 28)

Kate's sharp observations on her husband's folly are rare, he is not a foolish man. It's a sad contrast to her letters in the first book, the folly of Cecelia's brother, Kate's sister, and the desperate mothers of unmarried daughters offered her wit a broader scope.

ASSOCIATES: Thomas, Marquis of Schofield—*Kate's husband;* six-year-old Edward and Baby Laurence—*are their children:* Nurse Carstairs—*the children's nurse;* Reardon—*Kate's maid;* Ripley—*their coachman and the bodyguard;* Piers—*Thomas's manservant.*

Georgy—*Kate's sister, the Duchess of Waltham;* Drina—*who was imprisoned with Edward.*

James Tarleton—*Cecelia's husband;* nine-year-old twins, Arthur and Eleanor; four-year-old Diana; and Baby Alexander—*are their children;* Nurse Langley—*is the children's nurse;* Walker—*is Cecelia's personal maid;* Mr. Hennesy—*is the Tarleton's butler.*

Aunt Elizabeth and Mr. Wrexton (Uncle Michael)—*have married, and they come out to act as reinforcements and messengers;* the Duke of Wellington is now the Prime Minister—*Thomas and James have worked for him before, and they affectionately refer to him as "Old Hookey";* Herr Magus Franz Wilhelm Schellen—*the surveyor-magician who set out last September to review the railway that runs between Stockton and Darlington, then to proceed to Manchester to assist with the surveying of a proposed line that would extend to Liverpool.* Duke of Waltham—*Daniel, Georgy's husband;* Mr. Ramsey Webb—*who invites James, Cecelia and Daniel to stay with him in Stockton;* Adella—*Ramsey's sister;* Fremantle—*who was discretion itself (fortunately discretion had a taste for cognac and he ended up giving Thomas some very interesting information).*

X

X-FILES. (Various authors.)

X-FILES SERIES

Genres/Themes Crossed: Science Fiction, Secret Society X Police (actually FBI) Procedural.

Subjects/Character Types: Aliens, Mythical Creatures, Future Technology, Shaman, Gods X Government Investigators.

Series/Stand-Alone: These are essentially stand-alones. People who enjoyed the series would enjoy any of them in any order.

Scene of the Crime: Washington, D.C. and other cities in the United States.

Detective: Fox Mulder, who, when he was a child, became aware that some of the things that go bump in the night are real. He was a witness to his sister, Samantha's, abduction by aliens. He believes that the truth is out there, and he's driven to find it.

Known Associates: Dana Scully, who regards herself as well grounded in reality and does her best to keep Mulder there with her. Assistant Director Walter Skinner: as Mulder and Scully's boss, he has his own agenda.

Premise: There is a department in the Federal Bureau of Investigation (FBI) that examines the cases that seem to have no natural explanation. Fox Mulder has a genius for seeing patterns in the evidence, and the patterns he sees are not constrained by what the rest of the world would consider possible. He gets handed the cases that seem, at least at the outset, to have some paranormal aspect. These cases make his superiors uncomfortable: they don't like the cases, they don't like Mulder's methods, they're not particularly happy even when he uncovers the truth.

Comment: There are three series of X-Files novels. One is aimed at a juvenile (middle grade) audience, the second is aimed at a young adult audience, and the third is written for adults. This entry covers the adult series. The series is uneven: some of the novels are more enjoyable than others. All the novels take place after the end of the first season (after the attempt to shut down the X-Files). Besides the novels, there is also Elizabeth Hand's adaptation of Chris Carter's screenplay for the X-Files movie. It is *The X-Files: Fight the Future,* (ISBN: 0061059323).

Literary Magic & Mayhem: The books are structured in the same way that the episodes were structured. The first chapter is a sort of teaser chapter that introduces the monster of the week: it shows the villain, and the menace that will be confronted by Mulder and Scully. The conspiracy elements, as well as the supernatural (or science that has advanced enough to be in the realm of science fiction) elements work well in the novels.

Explorations: How far would the conspiracy have to have gone for the government to continue support, funding, and protection for the villain?

At the end of the novel is the threat really over? What's likely to happen next? What would be the first indication that average U.S. citizens would have that something was wrong?

THE CASES

1. ***The X-Files: Goblins by Charles Grant.*** New York: HarperPaperbacks, 1994, [277] p. ISBN: 0061054143. [Science Fiction X Government Investigators]

MARVILLE, NEW JERSEY, FORT DIX AND WASHINGTON, D.C., MAY 199?Mulder, Scully, Andrews and Webber are sent to Marville, New Jersey to investigate two murders. Witnesses claim that the weapons that struck down Pierce and Ulman appeared out of nothing, and slashed their throats. One of the witnesses claims the murderer was a goblin. The other was so high on a combination of heroin and alcohol that she cannot be interviewed.

ASSOCIATES: Dana Scully—*Mulder's partner;* Arlen Douglas—*Mulder's supervisor;* Agent Licia Andrews and Agent Hank Webber—*are assigned by Arlen Douglas to assist in the investigation and to report on Mulder's activities;* Bette and Miss Cort—*administrative assistants at the Bureau;* Carl Barelli—*an old friend of Mulder's, he is a sports writer for New Jersey Chronicle;* Trudy—*is a waitress at Ripley's;* Aaron Noel—*Barney's Tavern's bartender;* Grady

Pierce—*retired Fort Dix Drill Sergeant;* Elly Lang—*who believes in goblins and is trying to mark them for the police;* Police Chief Todd Hawks, Sergeant Nilssen, Dispatcher Madeline "Maddy" Vincent and Officer Spike Silber—*are members of Marville's Police Department;* Dr. Sam Junis—*performed the autopsy;* Babs Radnor—*owns the Royal Baron motel.*

People at Fort Dix include Corporal Frank Ulman—*who was engaged to a young woman with influential relatives;* Major Joseph Tonero—*Air Force Special Projects;* Dr. Rosemary Elkhart and Dr. Leonard Tymons.

2. ***The X-Files: Whirlwind by Charles Grant.*** New York: HarperPaperbacks, 1995, 264 p. ISBN: 0061054151. [Shamanism/Telekinesis X Government Investigators]

Bernalillo and Sangre Viento Mesa, New Mexico and Washington, D.C., July 199? A series of grisly killings of both animals and people takes Mulder and Scully to New Mexico. The autopsy given to the investigators revealed that the victims were flayed alive; this infuriated the coroner. That public report was the second report she wrote; the first, accurate, report was buried on the orders of local officials. They were determined to keep all hints of odd, possibly paranormal, deaths from the public.

Associates: Dana Scully—*Mulder's partner;* Others who work at the Bureau include Assistant Director Walter Skinner, Stan Bournell, and Beth Neuhouse. Ann Hatch—*a ranch owner finds the first human remains;* Nando and Silvia Quintodo—*work on her Double-H ranch;* Sheriff Chuck Sparrow—*is the initial investigator;* Donna Falner—*an art dealer, tells him that she is concerned that Leon Ciola is back in town;* "Red" Garson—*is the local FBI agent;* Helen Rios—*is the medical examiner;* Dugan Velador—*tries to convince Father Paul to speak to the police;* Paul and Patty Deven—*escape their parent's fighting by going to the river;* Kurt and Mary Deven—*Paul and Patty's parents;* Mike Ostrand—*artist;* Nick Lanaya—*is on the Konochine Tribal Council, he trades with Donna Falkner to bring money into the tribe.*

3. ***The X-Files: Ground Zero by Kevin J.*** Anderson. New York: HarperPaperbacks, 1995, 292 p. ISBN: 0061056774. [Ghosts, Fall-out free nuclear weapons X Government Investigators.]

Teller Nuclear Research Facility, Pleasanton, California and Washington, D.C., 1994. A nuclear research facility has been experimenting with unusual components, components that seem to alter the known laws of physics, that open up new possibilities. They made Miriel Bremen question, first, where they came from, and then, what the government was going to do with them. She left the *Bright Anvil Project* and started a protest group, *Stop Nuclear Madness!* Much of the group's financing came from a nuclear test survivor, Ryan Kamida. Then the Director of *Project Bright Anvil,* Dr. Emil Gregory, died in the lab, killed by superheated air of the sort that had been associated in the past with nuclear detonations. Agent Craig Kreident conducted a preliminary investigation and recommended that the case be considered an X-File. While Mulder and Scully investigate, similar deaths take place across the country. All of dead people were somehow involved with America's nuclear weapons.

ASSOCIATES: Dana Scully—*Mulder's partner;* People who worked on Project Bright Anvil include Dr. Emil Gregory—*the director;* Miriel Bremen—*his assistant, she has left the project;* "Bear" Dooley—*who is now the Deputy Project Head;* Victor Ogilvy; Patty—*Gregory's secretary;* and Rosabeth Carrera—*who works for the Department of Energy.*

People affiliated with Stop Nuclear Madness! include Miriel Bremen—*the founder;* Becka Thorne—*receptionist;* and Ryan Kamida—*who funds the group.* Nancy Scheck—*who secured funding for Project Bright Anvil, and is having an affair with Brigadier General Matthew Bradoukis;* Captain Franklin Mesta and Captain Greg Louis—*are misileers at Vandenberg Air Force Base;* Comander Lee Klantze—*is the Executive Officer of the U.S.S. Dallas;* Captain Robert Ives—*is his commanding officer;* Oscar McCarron—*who lives in the Jornada del Muerto Desert;* Berlina Lu Kwok—*who runs the FBI Lab in Washington, D.C.*

4. ***The X-Files: Ruins by Kevin J.*** Anderson. New York: HarperPaperbacks, 1996, 264 p. ISBN: 0061057363. [Alien artifacts on Earth X Government Investigators]

XITACLAN RUINS IN YUCATAN, MEXICO AND WASHINGTON, D.C., 199? Assistant Director Skinner sends Mulder and Scully to investigate the disappearance of an archaeological team, and the subsequent appearance of some ancient Mayan artifacts. The investigation is complicated by murder, insurrection, Quetzalcoatl(s), an SOS beacon from an alien ship, and volcanic activity. In the end, Scully can't bring herself to report on some of Mulder's claims, but must report on the odd, winged serpents that she herself saw.

ASSOCIATES: Dana Scully—*Mulder's partner;* Cassandra Rubicon—*who leads a Univeristy of California, San Diego expedition to Xitaclan to excavate the Pyramid of Kukulkan and the surrounding area;* Kelly Rowan—*is the team's second archaeologist;* Cait Barron—*is the archaeological team's historian and photographer;* Christopher Porte—*is the team epigrapher;* and John Forbin—*is the team grad-student architect and engineer;* Fernando Victorio Aguilar—*is the local guide who led the archaeological team to the site.*

People in the nearby town include Carlos Barreio—*Chief of Quintana Roo's Police;* Pepe Candelaria—*Aguilar's assistant;* Xavier Salida—*drug lord;* and Pieter Grobe—*a rival drug lord.*

Byers, Langley, and Frohike—*are reporters for The Lone Gunman:* Major Willis Jakes—*is sent into the area by the Pentagon;* A. G. Pym—*of Narratives and Records;* Vladimir Rubicon—*father of Cassandra, accompanies Mulder and Scully to Xitaclan to search for his daughter.*

5. ***The X-Files: Antibodies by Kevin J.*** Anderson. New York: HarperPaperbacks, 1997, 268 p. ISBN: 0061056243. [Nanotechnology X Government Investigators]

DyMar Laboratory, Portland, Oregon and Washington, D.C., 1997. For years, brothers David and Darin Kennessy worked at DyMar Laboratory, researching cures for cancer. Six months ago, they had a falling out, and Darin left the lab. Ten days ago, protestors blew up DyMar Laboratory and then burned it to the ground. David Kennessy and Jeremy Dorman are presumed dead. *Liberation Now,* a protest group that no one ever heard of before this, has claimed responsibility. Guard Vernon Ruckman was infected with a plague in the course of his duties. Scully is baffled when the medical examiner notifies her that Vernon's body showed signs of life after Scully had performed an autopsy on it.

Associates: Dana Scully—*Mulder's partner;* Personnel at DyMar Laboratory Ruins include Vernon Ruckman—*guard;* Jeremy Dorman—*junior research partner;* Jody Kennessy—*a 12-year-old with lymphoblastic leukemia;* David and Patrice Kennessy—*his parents;* Vader—*the Kennessy's dog;*. Dr. Elliot Hughart—*the veterinarian who treated Vader;* Adam Lentz—*who oversaw the DyMar Laboratory's research;* Alphonse Gurik—*an animal rights activist, sent the letter claiming responsibility for the destruction of the lab;* Dr. Frank Quinton—*Portland's Medical Examiner;* Edmund—*his assistant;* Officer Jared Penwick and Maxie at the general store—*assist Scully in her search for Jody and his mom.*

6. ***The X-Files: Skin by Ben Mezrich.*** New York: HarperPaperbacks, 2000, 327 p. ISBN: 0061056448.

New York City and Alkut, Thailand, 2000. A skin graft from a John Doe seems to have set a mild-mannered professor on an enraged, homicidal rampage. When Mulder comes face to face with the man, he sees terror and misery, not rage. He comes to believe that this man was a victim, and wants to discover the phenomenon that changed him. Scully is on a parallel course: she wants to find the microbe that changed Stanton. Their search takes them to Thailand, to the research of a Dr. Emile Paladin, who, in the 1970s, was trying to create the perfect synthetic skin to save the war's napalm victims, and to research the god Gin-Korng-Pew, the Skin-Eater.

Associates: Dana Scully—*Mulder's partner;* Luke Canton and Emory Ross—*the paramedics who brought in the anonymous initial patient, they may have been infected;* Brad Alger and Dennis Crow—*are the interns who worked on him, they may have been infected;* Leif Eckleman—*the medical examiner's assistant who cataloged the corpse, may have been infected;* and Mike Lifton and Josh Kemper—*the young men who harvested some of the initial patient's skin for the New York Fire Department Skin Bank, they may have been infected;* Dr. Alec Bernstein—*who used some of that skin to patch up a burn-victim, may have been infected;* Professor Perry Stanton—*the burn victim, was infected, and the infection turned him into a monster;* Teri Nestor—*was the nurse working with Stanton;* Emily Kysdale—*is Stanton's daughter,* NYPD Detectuve Jennifer Barrett—*is in charge of hunting down Stanton;* Duke Baker—*Chief Resident;* Maria Gomez—*nurse;* Dr. Julien Kyle—*Fibrol's Director of Research;* Dr. Lianna Fielding—*of the Red Cross;* Allan Trowbridge—*who founded the clinic in Alkut, Thailand;* Rina—*Allan's wife;* Dr. Basil Georgian—*the CDC's Senior Infectious Disease Investigator hinders the investigation more than he helps;* Ganon—*priest of Gin-Korng-Pew, the Skin-Eater;* David Kuo—*Emile Paladin's lawyer* Quo Tien—*the son of Dr. Emile Paladin;* Andrew—*Emile's brother;* and Malku—*who acts as Mulder and Scully's guide in Alkut.*

Appendix: Further Reading

Listed by the books' or series' primary speculative fiction element.

Aliens/Interplanetary Voyages

Anthony, Patricia. *The Conscience of the Beagle.* Woburn, MA: First Books, 1993. ISBN: 18880448300. [Aliens (other planets), Robots, Psychics X Police Procedural]

Major Dyle Hollowy, Earth's toughest copy, takes his team (psychic Szabo, demolitions expert Arne, and android Beagle) to the planet Tennyson to investigate a series of terrorist attacks.

Bischoff, David. *Space Precinct* series. [Aliens (other planets) X Police Procedural]

Patrick Brogan, former New York City cop now works in Demeter City on the planet Altor. (Based on a 1994–1995 U.K. television series.)

1. *The Deity-Father.* New York: Harper Paperbacks, 1995. 289 p. ISBN: 9780061056123, 006105612X.
2. *Demon Wing.* New York: Harper Prism, 1995. 224 p. ISBN: 9780061056130, 0061056138.
3. *Alien Island.* New York: Harper Prism, 1996. 257 p. ISBN: 9780061056260, 006105626X.

Castle, Jayne. Ghost Hunters Series. [Alien artifacts (other planets) X Amateur Contemporary Sleuth]

On late 21st century Earth an energy curtain allowed humans to travel to other worlds. One of the planets they colonized was Harmony. After years of easy travel the curtain disappeared, stranding the colonists. These books take place 200 years later. The descendents of the first colonists are still learning about Harmony, coping with everything from local fauna to ancient artifacts. Each of the books follows a different protagonist. All of the books combine romance, paranormal elements, and mystery (in that order).

1. *After Dark.* New York: Jove Books, c2000. 332 p. ISBN: 051512902X.
2. *After Glow.* New York: Jove Books, c2004. 343 p. ISBN: 0515136948.
3. *Ghost Hunter.* New York: Berkley Pub., 2006. 340 p. ISBN: 0515141402; 9780515141405.
4. *Silver Master.* New York: Jove Books, 2007. 307 p. ISBN: 0515133553; 9780515143553.
5. *Dark Light.* New York: Jove Books, 2008. 390 p. ISBN: 051514519X; 9780515145199.

Drago, Ty. Phobos. New York: Tom Doherty Associates, c2003. 431 p. ISBN: 0765305445.

Lietenant Mike Brogue investigates a series of murders on the research station on Phobos.

Gilden, Mel and Dave Dorman. *Zoot Marlowe* series. [Aliens X Private Investigators]

Zoot Marlowe, alien private investigator, follows in the steps of Philip Marlowe.

1. *Surfing Samurai Robots.* New York: ROC, c1988. 252 p. ISBN: 0451451007, 9780451451002.
2. *Hawaiian U.F.O.* Aliens. New York: Penguin, 1991. 272 p. ISBN: 0451450752, 9780451450753.
3. *Tubular Android Superheroes.* New York: ROC, c1991. 288 p. ISBN: 0451451163, 9780451451163.

Goddard, Ken. *Detective Sergeant Colin Cellars* series. [Aliens (Human–alien encounters) X Government Investigators]

While investigating the murder of a friend senior crime-scene investigator Colin Cellars finds his life turned upside down by strange events.

1. *First Evidence.* New York: Bantam Books, c1999. 464 p. ISBN: 0553108646.
2. *Outer Perimeter.* New York: Bantam Books, 2001. 496 p. ISBN: 0553108832.

Kerr, Kathryn. *Bobbie Lacey and Jack Mulligan* series. [Aliens, Psychics X Police Procedural] Kathryn Kerr collaborated with Kate Daniel on *Polar City Nightmare.*

Police Corporal Baskin Ward investigates murder in Polar City on the desert planet Hagar.

1. *Polar City Blues.* New York: Bantam Books, 1990. 262 p. ISBN: 9780553285048, 0553285041.
2. *Polar City Nightmare.* London: Gollancz, 2000. 357 p. ISBN: 978057068605, 0575068604.

Resnick, Mike. *Second Contact.* New York: Tom Doherty Associates, 1990. 276 p. ISBN: 0312850212, 9780312850210. [Interplanetary Voyages X Government Investigator]

In 2065, Max Becker is ordered to defend spaceship captain Wilbur Jennings against the charge of murder. The captain insists that he is sane, that he did the killings, and that he is not guilty.

Ringo, John. *Princess of Wands.* Riverdale, New York: Baen, Distributed by Simon & Schuster, 2006. ISBN: 1416509232, 9781416509233. [Aliens (Human–alien encounters) X Police Procedural.]

Detective Sergeant Kelly Lockhart is struggling with case of mass murder in which there are no viable suspects. She finds an unlikely ally in soccer mom Barbara Everett.

Showalter, Gena. *Alien Huntress* series. [Aliens (Human–alien encounters) X Private Investigators X Romance]

Mia Snow is the head of the New Chicago Police Department's Alien Investigation and Removal Agency. Aliens and humans have co-existed on Earth for over 70 years, but that co-existence has not always been peaceful. The "cases" are written from different viewpoints. The first follows Mia Snow as she investigates murder. The second follows alien Eden Black, whose mission is to protect humans. The third follows the bionic undercover operative Mishka Le'Ace.

1. *Awaken Me Darkly.* New York: Downtown Press, 2006. 384 p. ISBN: 1416517170, 9781416517177.
2. *Enslave Me Sweetly.* New York: Downtown Press, 2006. 320 p. ISBN: 0743497503, 9780743497503.
3. *Savor Me Slowly.* New York: Pocket Star, 2007. 384 p. ISBN: 1416531637, 9781416531630.

Spencer, Wen. *Ukiah Oregon* series. [Aliens passing as human X Private Detectives.]

Private investigator Ukiah Oregon was raised by wolves. He knows little of his heritage, and his explorations reveal both secrets and danger.

1. *Alien Taste.* New York: Roc, 2001. 320 p. ISBN: 0451458370.
2. *Tainted Trail.* New York: Roc, 2002. 320 p. ISBN: 0451458877.
3. *Bitter Waters.* New York: Roc, 2003. 320 p. ISBN: 0451459229.
4. *Dog Warrior.* New York: Roc, 2004. 320 p. ISBN: 0451459903.

Zahn, Timothy. *The Green and the Gray.* New York: Tor, 2004. 443 p. ISBN: 0765307170. [Aliens (Human–alien encounters) X Amateur Sleuths, Police.]

NYPD Detective Thomas Fierenzo believes that he is working to stop a gang war, a human gang war. He's partly right…

Zeddies, Ann Tonsor. *Blood and Roses: a Jayne Taylor Novel.* New York: A Phobos Impact Book, 2005. 288 p. ISBN: 0972002677. [Aliens (Human–alien encounters) X Government Investigators X Espionage]

Even a woman who proved her courage and strength during WWI has a hard time getting a decent job in the United States in 1920. Jane Taylor ended up working for bootleggers, but was abducted and sent on a secret mission before she had time to get accustomed to the job.

Alternate Universe

Aylett, Steve. *Beerlight* series. [Alternate Universe X Crime Novel, Police, Private Investigator]

Surreal story of crime and investigation featuring Dante the thief, who lives a little ahead of his time, and the assassin Rosa Control.

1. *Slaughtermatic.* New York: Four Walls Eight Windows, c1998. 153 p. ISBN: 1568581033, 9781568581033.
2. *Toxicology.* London: Gollancz, 2001. 131 p. ISBN: 0575071109, 9780575071100.

3. *Atom*. New York: Four Walls Eight Windows, 2001. 137 p. ISBN: 1568581750, 9781568581750.
4. *The Crime Studio*. New York: Four Walls Eight Windows, 2001. 156 p. ISBN: 1568581483, 9781568581484.

Foy, George. *The Shift*. New York: Bantam Books, 1996. 515 p. ISBN: 055337544X.

[Alternate Universe, Future Technology (Virtual Reality) X Amateur Sleuth.] Alex Munn authored a virtual reality television show featuring a terrifying serial killer. Then the killer somehow escaped the boundaries of the show and is now attacking people in real life.

Resnick, Michael D. *John Justin Mallory Mystery* series. [Alternate Universe X John Justin Mallory]

New York private investigator John Justin Mallory's cases take him into a little known city of demons, leprechauns, gnomes, unicorns, and vampires.

1. *Stalking the Unicorn: A Fable of Tonight*. Amherst, New York: Pyr, 2008. 280 p. ISBN: 1591026482, 9781591026488.
2. *Stalking the Vampire: A Fable of Tonight: a John Justin Mallory Mystery*. Amherst, New York: Pyr, 2008. 268 p. ISBN: 1591026490, 9781591026495.
3. *Stalking the Dragon*. (forthcoming)

Smith, L. Neil. *Win Bear* series. [Alternate Universe (Multiverse) X Private Investigators.]

Denver Police Lieutenant Edward William "Win" Bear falls through a hole between the universes. He finds a libertarian utopia called the Confederacy and employs his training and skills to earn his way as a detective.

1. *The Probability Broach*. New York: Ballantine Books, c1980. 275 p. ISBN: 034528593X, 9780345285935.
2. *The American Zone*. New York: Tom Doherty Associates, 2001. 350 p. ISBN: 0312875266, 9780312875268.

Anthropomorphic Animals

Brown, Rita Mae. *Mrs. Murphy* series. [Anthropomorphic Animals X Amateur Sleuth]

Postmistress Mary Minor "Harry" Haristeen, her sleuthing cat Mrs. Murphy, and Mrs. Murphy's investigative partner, the dog Tee Tucker (a corgi) solve mysteries in their tiny village in Virginia.

1. *Wish You Were Here.* New York: Bantam Books, 1990. ISBN: 0553058819, 9780553058819.
2. *Rest in Pieces.* New York: Bantam Books, 1992. 292 p. ISBN: 0553077287, 9780553077285.
3. *Murder at Monticello, or, Old Sins.* New York: Bantam Books, 1994. 298 p. ISBN: 0553081403, 9780553081404.
4. *Pay Dirt. Or, Adventures at Ash Lawn.* New York: Bantam Books, 1995. 251 p. ISBN: 0553096036, 9780553096033.
5. *Murder, She Meowed.* New York: Bantam Books, 1996. 285 p. ISBN: 0553096044, 9780553096040.
6. *Murder on the Prowl.* New York: Bantam Books, 1998. 320 p. ISBN: 0553099701, 9780553099706.
7. *Cat on the Scent.* New York: Bantam Books, c1999. 321 p. ISBN: 055309971X, 9780553099713.
8. *Sneaky Pie's Cookbook for Mystery Lovers.* New York: Bantam Books, c1999. 71 p. ISBN: 055310635X, 9780553106350.
9. *Pawing through the Past.* New York: Bantam Books, c2000. 305 p. ISBN: 0553107380, 9780553107388.
10. *Claws and Effect.* New York: Bantam Books, 2001. 292 p. ISBN: 0553107437, 9780553107432.
11. *Catch as Cat Can.* New York: Bantam Books, 2002. 287 p. ISBN: 0553107445, 9780553107449.
12. *The Tail of the Tip-Off.* New York: Bantam Books, 2003. 309 p. ISBN: 0553801589, 9780553801583.
13. *Whisker of Evil.* New York: Bantam Books, 2004. 297 p. ISBN: 0553801619, 9780553801613.
14. *Cat's Eyewitness.* New York: Bantam Books, 2005. 287 p. ISBN: 0553801643, 9780553801644.
15. *Sour Puss.* New York: Bantam Books, 2006. 246 p. ISBN: 055380362X, 9780553803624.
16. *Puss 'n Cahoots.* New York: Bantam Books, 2007. 252 p. ISBN: 0553803646, 9780553803648.
17. *Santa Clawed.* New York: Bantam Books, 2008. 237 p. ISBN: 0553807064, 9780553807066.
18. *Purrfect Murder.* New York: Bantam Books, 2008. 247 p. ISBN: 0553803654, 9780553803655.

Douglas, Carole Nelson. *Midnight Louie Mystery* series. [Anthropomorphic Animals X Private Investigator]

Temple Barr, a freelance public relations consultant, and her cat Midnight Louie take turns (in alternating chapters) narrating the stories of their investigations.

1. *Catnap.* New York: TOR, 1992. 241 p. ISBN: 081516826, 9780812516821.
2. *Pussyfoot.* New York: TOR, 1993. 304 p. ISBN: 0312852185, 9780312852184.
3. *Cat on a Blue Monday.* New York: Forge, 1994. 381 p. ISBN: 0312856075, 9780312856076.
4. *Cat in a Crimson Haze.* New York: Forge, 1995. 384 p. ISBN: 0312859015, 9780312859015.
5. *Cat in a Diamond Dazzle.* New York: Forge, 1996. 414 p. ISBN: 0312860854, 9780312860851.
6. *Cat with an Emerald Eye.* New York: Forge, 1996. 384 p. ISBN: 0312862288, 9780312862282.
7. *Cat in a Flamingo Fedora.* New York: Forge, 1997. 351 p. ISBN: 0312863292, 9780312863296.
8. *Cat in a Golden Garland.* New York: Forge, 1997. 352 p. ISBN: 0312863861, 9780312863869.
9. *Cat on a Hyacinth Hunt.* New York: Forge, 1998. 383 p. ISBN: 0312866348, 9780312866341.
10. *Cat in an Indigo Mood.* New York: Forge, 1999. 381 p. ISBN: 0312866356, 9780312866358.
11. *Cat in a Jeweled Jumpsuit.* New York: Forge, 1999. 399 p. ISBN: 0312868170, 9780312868178.
12. *Cat in a Kiwi Con.* New York: Forge, 2000. 416 p. ISBN: 031286955X, 9780312869557.
13. *Cat in a Leopard Spot.* New York: Forge, 2001. 380 p. ISBN: 031285370X, 9780312853709.
14. *Cat in a Midnight Choir.* New York: Forge, 2002. 350 p. ISBN: 0312857977, 9780312857974.
15. *Cat in a Neon Nightmare.* New York: Forge, 2003. 365 p. ISBN: 076506808, 978076506807.
16. *Cat in an Orange Twist.* New York: Forge, 2004. 395 p. ISBN: 0765306816, 9780765306814.
17. *Cat in a Hot Pink Pursuit.* New York: Forge, 2005. 364 p. ISBN: 0765313995, 9780765313997.
18. *Cat in a Quicksilver Caper.* New York: Forge, 2006. 383 p. ISBN: 0765314002, 9780765314000.
19. *Cat in a Red Hot Rage.* New York: Forge, 2007. 382 p. ISBN: 0765314010, 9780765314017.

20. *Cat in a Sapphire Slipper.* New York: Forge, 2008. 396 p. ISBN: 076531861X, 9780765318619.

Douglas, Carole Nelson. *Midnight Louie's Pet Detectives.* [Anthropomorphic Animals]

Anthology of short stories, all but one written for this volume.

Daisy and the Silver Quaich *by Anne Perry;* Where Does a Herd of Elephants Go? *by Toni L. P. Kelner;* The Dark One *by Lilian Jackson Braun;* Dr. Couch Saves a Bird by Nancy *Pickard;* Fetch *by Dorothy Cannell;* Kittens Take Detection 101 *by Jan Grape;* El Lobo Rides Alone *by Bill Crider;* A Hamster of No Importance *by Esther M. Friesner and Walter J. Stutzman;* Mandy: Free to Good Home *by J. A. Jance;* On the Take *by Carolyn Wheat;* Harbinger *by Jean Hager;* Final Reunion *by Lisa Lepovetsky;* Go to the Devil *by Barbara Paul;* A Baker Street Irregular *by Carole Nelson Douglas;* Masked Marauders of the Mossbelt *by Bruce Holland Rogers;* Final Vows *by Elizabeth Ann Scarborough;* The Cage *by Ed Gorman.*

Murphy, Shirley Rousseu. *The Joe Grey Mysteries.* [Anthropomorphic Animals X Private Investigator]

Joe Grey and Dulcie are two cats that find themselves able to speak and think like humans after witnessing a murder. They assist human detectives with solving cases.

1. *Cat on the Edge.* New York: Harper Collins, 1996. 288 p. ISBN: 0061056006, 9780061056000.
2. *Cat Under Fire.* New York: Harper Collins, 1997. 256 p. ISBN: 0061056014, 9780061056017.
3. *Cat Raise the Dead.* New York: Harper Collins, 1997. 304 p. ISBN: 0061056022, 9780061056024.
4. *Cat in the Dark.* New York: Harper Collins, 1999. 320 p. ISBN: 0061059471, 9780061059476.
5. *Cat to the Dogs.* New York: Harper Collins, 2000. 243 p. ISBN: 0061050970.
6. *Cat Spitting Mad.* New York: Harper Collins, 2001. 228 p. ISBN: 0061050989.
7. *Cat on the Money.* (Published as a serial, initially in Cat Magazine until the magazine's cancellation. Currently available in its entirety online starting at www.sylviaengdahl.com/joegrey/money01.htm.)
8. *Cat Laughing Last.* New York: Harper Collins, 2002. 273 p. ISBN: 006620951X
9. *Cat Seeing Double.* New York: Harper Collins, 2003. 292 p. ISBN: 0066209501.

10. *Cat Fear No Evil.* New York: Harper Collins, 2004. 323 p. ISBN: 0066209498.
11. *Cat Cross Their Graves.* New York: Harper Collins, 2005. 305 p. ISBN: 0060578084.
12. *Cat Breaking Free.* New York: Harper Collins, 2005. 335 p. ISBN: 0060578092, 9780060578091.
13. *Cat Pay the Devil.* New York: Harper Collins, 2007. 295 p. ISBN: 0060578106, 9780060578107.
14. *Cat Deck the Halls.* New York: Harper Collins, 2008. 368 p. ISBN: 006112396X, 9780061123962.
15. *Cat Playing Cupid.* New York: Harper Collins, 2009. 368 p. ISBN: 0061123978, 9780061123979.

Astrology

Andrews & Austin. *Richfield and Rivers Mystery* series. [Astrology X Ex-Police Officers X Romance X Lesbians]

Astrologer Callie Rivers partners with her very grounded lover Teague Richfield to solve mysteries in Las Vegas.

1. *Combust the Sun.* New York: Bold Strokes Books, 2006. 204 p. ISBN: 193311052X.
2. *Stellium in Scorpio.* New York: Bold Strokes Books, 2007. 235 p. ISBN: 9781933110653.
3. *Venus Besieged.* New York: Bold Strokes Books, 2008. 224 p. ISBN: 9781602820043.

Foxx, Aleister. *Harm's Way.* New York: St. Martin's Press, 1992. 298 p. ISBN: 0312077726. [Astrology X Private Investigators]

Montreal P.I. Lee Harms consults his astrologer girlfriend Celeste to help unravel the case of a wealthy client's missing daughter.

Jorgensen, Christine T. *Stella the Stargazer Mystery* series. [Astrology X Amateur Sleuth]

Stella the Stargazer writes a column for the *Denver Daily Orion.* She utilizes her psychic gifts and knowledge of astrology to solve the mysteries she encounters.

1. *A Love to Die For.* New York: Walker and Co., 1994. 219 p. ISBN: 0802731880.
2. *You Bet Your Life.* New York: Walker and Co., 1995. 211 p. ISBN: 0802732658.

3. *Curl Up and Die.* New York: Walker and Co., 1997. 255 p. ISBN: 0802732887.
4. *Death of a Dustbunny.* New York: Walker and Co., 1998. 262 p. ISBN: 0802733158.
5. *Dead on Her Feet.* New York: Walker., 1999. 249 p. ISBN: 0802733344.

Kent, Lisa. *The 13th Sign.* Boca Raton, Fl.: Skyline Publications, c1997. 229 p. ISBN: 1889936057. [Astrology X Vigilantes X Romance]

Mather, Linda. *Zodiac Mystery* series. [Astrology X Female Detectives]

Investigator Jo Hughes uses her ability to draw up horoscopes to gain insights into her cases.

1. *Blood of an Aries.* New York: St. Martin's Press, 1994. 201 p. ISBN: 0312104294.
2. *Beware Taurus.* London: Macmillan, 1994. 192 p. ISBN: 9780333620700.
3. *Gemini Doublecross.* London: Macmillan, 1995. 200 p. ISBN: 9780333645727.

Perry, Anne (ed). *Death by Horoscope.* New York: Carroll & Graf Publishers, 2001. 324 p. ISBN: 078670845X. [Astrology X Police, Hitmen, Amateur Sleuths]

Anthology of new stories that combine the zodiac with mystery.

Introduction *by Anne Perry;* The Astrologer Who Predicted His Own Murder *by Peter Tremayne;* The Eye of the Beholder *by Lillian Stewart Carl;* Out Like a Lion *by Bill Crider;* Slaying the Serpent *by Jane Lindskold;* The Sea Horse *by Edward Marston;* The Aquarius Mission *by Brendan DuBois;* Reason to Believe *by Mat Coward;* To Catch a Fish *by Marcia Talley;* Sharing *by Jon L. Breen;* Not in the Stars *by Catherine Dain;* Keller's Horoscope *by Lawrence Block;* Star Struck *by Peter Lovesey;* Boss Man *by P. N. Elrod;* The Librarian *by Simon Brett;* Ghosts *by Kristine Kathryn Rusch;* The Blue Scorpion *by Anne Perry.*

Demons

Day, S. J. *Marked* Series. [Demons, Angels, Fae, Mages, Werewolves, Dragons X Bounty Hunter]

Eve has been branded with the Mark of Cain and so is the new bounty hunter for Heaven.

1. *Eve of Darkness.* New York: Tor, 2009. 368 p. ISBN: 0765360411, 9780765360410.
2. *Eve of Destruction.* New York: Tor, 2009. 432 p. ISBN: 076536042X, 9780765360427.
3. *Eve of Chaos.* New York: Tor, 2009. 384 p. ISBN: 0765360438, 9780765360434.

Williams, Liz. *Detective Inspector Chen Novels.* [Demons, Ghosts X Police Procedural]

In the 21st century Detective Inspector Wei Chen works out of Singapore Three's 13th precinct. There is traffic and commerce between Heaven, Earth, and Hell. Chen is a "snake agent" whose beat crosses the boundaries between worlds.

1. *Snake Agent.* San Francisco, CA: Night Shade Books, 2005. 258 p. ISBN: 159780018X, 978159800181.
2. *The Demon and the City.* San Francisco, CA: Night Shade Books, 2006. 242 p. ISBN: 1597800457, 978159800457.
3. *Precious Dragon.* San Francisco, CA: Night Shade Books, 2007. 256 p. ISBN: 1597800821, 978159800822.
4. *The Shadow Pavillion.* San Francisco, CA: Night Shade Books, 2008. 256 p. ISBN: 1597801224, 978159801225.

Dragons

Fabian, Karina. *DragonEye P.I.* series. [Dragon X Private Investigator]

The dragon detective Vern and his partner, the mage Sister Grace, go to Florida to keep the peace at a Mensa Conference.

Future Earth Society

Brown, Eric. *Penumbra.* London: Orion Books, c1999. 346 p. ISBN: 1857985923. [Future Earth, Space Flight, Aliens X Police Procedural]

In the 22nd Century Lieutenant Rana Rao (recently promoted to Homicide) hunts a serial killer in Calcutta. Pilot Bennett is hired by the Mackendrick Foundation to pilot a ship to the Rim world of Penumbra.

Douglas, Carole Nelson. *Probe series.* [Future Earth, Aliens X Contemporary Amateur Sleuth]

Psychoanalyst Kevin Blake works to help Jane Doe recover her memories, and then to protect her from government agents.

1. *Probe.* New York: TOR, 1986. 384 p. ISBN: 0812535871; 9780812535877.
2. *Counterprobe.* New York: TOR, 1988. 344 p. ISBN: 0312931026; 9780312931025.

Hoch, Edward (1930–2008). *Police Officers Carl Crader and Earl Jazine* series. [Future Earth X Police Procedural]

In the 21st century, the Computer Investigation Bureau investigates computer crime and opposes a luddite group called HAND.

1. *The Transvection Machine.* New York: Walker, 1971. 220 p. ISBN: 0802755399.
2. *The Fellowship of the Hand.* New York: Walker, 1973. 198 p. ISBN: 0802755534.
3. *The Frankenstein Factory.* New York: Warner Paperback Library, 1975. 190 p. [Man as creator X Police Procedural]

Killough, Lee. *Police Officers Janna Brill and "Mama" Maxwell.* [Future Earth X Police Procedural]

LEO (Law Enforcement Officer) Janna Brill is by-the-book, and "Mama" Maxwell never saw the reason for rules. The unlikely pair make excellent partners in a world where everyone must carry a universal identity card, police officers do not carry lethal weapons, and colonists are leaving Earth.

1. *The Doppelganger Gambit.* New York: Ballantine Books, 1979. 261 p. ISBN: 0345282671, 9780345282675.
2. *Spider Play.* New York: Warner Books, Popular Library/Questar, 1986. 232 p. ISBN: 0445202734, 9780445202733.
3. *Dragon's Teeth.* New York: Warner Books, Popular Library/Questar, 1990. 250 p. ISBN: 0445209062, 9780445209060.

Omnibus of all three books: *Bridling Chaos.* Decatur, GA.: Meisha Merlin, 1998. 609 p. ISBN: 0965834530.

McAuley, Paul J. *Whole Wide World.* New York: Tor, 2002. 399 p. ISBN: 07653922. [Future Earth, Artificial Intelligence, Post-Apocalyptic London X Police Procedural]

England is a police state, with the population under constant surveillance by ADESS, the Autonomous Distributed Expert Surveillance System. ADESS is run by an evolving artificial intelligence. Exhibitionist Sophie

Booth's apartment webcams broadcast her murder. Officer Dixon, an outcast within the police department, is assigned to the case.

McQuay, Mike. *Mathew Swain* series. [Future Earth X Private Investigator]
Mathew Swain is a tough private eye on a dystopian future Earth.

1. *Hot Time in Old Town*. Toronto, New York: Bantam Books, 1981. 214 p. ISBN: 0553148117.
2. *When Trouble Beckons*. Toronto, New York: Bantam Books, 1981. 216 p. ISBN: 0553200410.
3. *The Deadliest Show in Town*. Toronto, New York: Bantam Books, 1982. 182 p. ISBN: 0553201867.
4. *The Odds are Murder*. Toronto, New York: Bantam Books, 1983. 213 p. ISBN: 0553228560, 9780553228564.

Modesitt, L. E. (Jr.). *The Octagonal Raven*. [Future Earth X Amateur Sleuth]
Daryn Alwyn was genetically engineered. His talents helped him become a space pilot and media consultant. An attempt on his life causes him to run,. He must find out who wants him dead and bring them to justice before the assassin who has targeted him is successful.

Russo, Richard Paul: *Carlucci trilogy*. [Future Earth (San Francisco) X Police Procedural]
The well-to-do in 21st-century San Francisco inhabit the Financial District; the down-and-outs subsist in the Tenderloin. Carlucci is a decent man and a good cop, but this world is bleak and the book genre is noir.

1. *Destroying Angel*. New York: Ace Books, c1992. 230 p. ISBN: 0441142737, 9780441142736.
2. *Carlucci's Edge*. New York: Ace, c1995. 295 p. ISBN: 0441002056, 9780441002054.
3. *Carlucci's Heart*. New York: Ace, c1997. 390 p. ISBN: 0441004857, 9780441004850.

All three reprinted in one volume: Russo, Richard Paul. *Carlucci*. New York: Ace Books, 2003. 611 p. ISBN: 9780441010540, 0441010547.

Shatner, William (with some help from Ron Goulart). *Detective Jake Cardigan* series. [Future Earth X Private Investigator (ex-cop)]
Ex-cop Jake Cardigan was framed for dealing the drug "Tek," and sentenced to 15 years. Someone commuted his sentence to four years, and he is hired by the Cosmos Detecive Agency as soon as he is released.

4. *TekWar.* New York: Putnam, c1989. 216 p. ISBN: 0399134956.
5. *TekLords.* New York: Putnam, c1991. 223 p. ISBN: 0399136169.
6. *TekLab.* New York: Putnam, c1991. 223 p. ISBN: 039913736X.
7. *Tek Vengeance.* New York: Putnam, c1993. 224 p. ISBN: 0399137882.
8. *Tek Secret.* New York: Putnam, c1993. 223 p. ISBN: 0399138927.
9. *Tek Power.* New York: Putnam, c1994. 220 p. ISBN: 0399139974.
10. *Tek Money.* New York: Putnam, c1995. 289 p. ISBN: 039914109X.
11. *Tek Kill.* New York: Putnam, c1996. 256 p. ISBN: 0399142029.
12. *Tek Net.* New York: Putnam, c1997. 244 p. ISBN: 0399143394.

(There is also a *William Shatner's TekWorld* comic book series based on the novels. It is written by Ron Goulart and Evan Skolnick, and is illustrated by Lee Sullivan.)

Wilson, F. Paul. *Dydeetown World.* New York: Baen, 1989. 303 p. ISBN: 0671698281, 9780671698287. [Future Earth, Dystopia, Clones X Private Investigator]
A Jean Harlow clone tries to hire gumshoe Sig Dreyer.

Future Technology

Barnes, John. *Gaudeamus.* New York: Tom Doherty Associates, c2004. 320 p. ISBN: 0765303299. [Teleportation, Telepathy X Private Detective]
John Barnes's old friend Travis Bismarck asks for Barnes's help in a case of industrial espionage that blends together a teleportation device, a telepathy pill, a cartoon, and... reality.

Hamilton, Peter F. *Greg Mandel Mystery* series. [Future Technology, Telepathy X Private Investigator]
Greg Mandel was implanted with telepathy glands to increase his efficiency. In this world, people store a back-up copy of their personality on computer. Anyone wanting to commit murder must kill the person twice, first killing the body, and then infecting the computer with a virus to kill the back-up copy.

1. *Mindstar Rising.* New York: TOR, 1996. 383 p. ISBN: 0312859554, 9780312859558.
2. *A Quantum Murder.* New York: TOR, 1997. 352 p. ISBN: 0312859546, 9780312859541.

3. *The Nano Flower.* New York: TOR, 1998. 480 p. ISBN: 0312865805, 9780312865801.

Kerr, Philip. *The Grid.* New York: Time Warner, 1996 (first published in Great Britain as *Gridiron* in 1995). 451 p. ISBN: 0446520535. [Future Technology: Sentient Building X Amateur Sleuth, Police]

A sentient building in Los Angeles makes choices the architects never imagined.

Kornbluth, Cyril M. *Takeoff.* Garden City, New York: Doubleday & Co., 1952. 218 p. [Future Technology X Amateur Sleuth] (The book was written when a rocket to the moon was future technology.)

Dr. Michael Novak begins a job with the American Society for Space Flight, a group that claims that they are building a model of a rocket ship for research purposes. He soon becomes suspicious of their claims, and when the chief engineer is murdered, Dr. Novak begins to investigate.

Levinson, Paul: *The Phil D'Amato* series. [Future Technology X Coroner]

New York Police Department forensic scientist encounters both strange and fatal technologies, and must puzzle out how they were used to commit murder.

1. "The Chronology Protection Case" published in *Analog Science Fiction and Fact,* Sept. 1995, p. 100–118.
2. "The Copyright Notice Case" published in *Analog Science Fiction and Fact,* April 1996, p. 18–47.
3. "The Mendelian Lamp Case" published in *Analog Science Fiction and Fact,* April 1997, p. 118–146.
4. *The Silk Code.* New York: TOR, 1999. 319 p. ISBN: 0312868235.
5. *The Consciousness Plague.* New York: TOR, 2002. 316 p. ISBN: 0765300982.
6. *The Pixel Eye.* New York: TOR, 2003. 334 p. ISBN: 0765305569.

Parker, Nancy: *Double Helix.* [Future Technology (genetic engineering) X Journalist] Ashland, OR: Ashland Hills Press, 2000. 511 p. ISBN: 0964227215, 9780964227217.

Journalist Kate Lipton stumbles across Anthony Beecher's scheme to use genetic engineering to bestow immortality on a select few.

Ridley, John. *Soledad O'Roark* series. [Future Technology: Genetic Engineering, Super Villains X Police Procedural]

The United States decides to expel all "metanormals." Those that wouldn't leave are hunted down by MTacs like the Los Angeles Police Department's Soledad O'Roarke.

1. *Those Who Walk in Darkness.* New York: Warner Books, c2003. 310 p. ISBN: 044653093X.
2. *What Fire Cannot Burn.* New York: Warner Books, c2006. 310 p. ISBN: 0446612030, 9780446612036.

Sawyer, Robert. *The Terminal Experiment.* New York: Harper Prism, c1995. 333 p. ISBN: 0061053104. [Future Technology (December 2011): Man as creator (downloaded human consciousness in computers) X Police Procedural].

Dr. Peter Hobson studies death and the afterlife. He creates three electronic versions of himself. One of them is made to experience everything as an incorporeal being: it has no memory of physical existence. Another is to experience the world as if it is immortal: it has no knowledge of aging and death. The last one is the "control": a perfect mirror of Dr. Hobson. They escape the lab computer, and one of them is a killer.

Ghosts

Adams, Jane. *The Angel Gateway.* London: Macmillan, 2000. 343 p. ISBN: 033390169X, 9780333901693. [Ghosts X Police]

Sergeant Ray Flowers moves into his late aunt's cottage and finds that it is haunted. He is surprised at the connections he finds between himself and the ghost of a woman who was tried as a witch in 1643.

Black, Veronica. *My Name is Polly Winter.* New York: St. Martin's Press, 1993. 188 p. ISBN: 0312088582. [Ghosts X Amateur Sleuth]

Social historian Jessica Cameron moves into an old house near Liverpool and becomes interested in the house's previous owners. Her interest leads her to investigate the 1859 disappearance of the daughter of the house. The spirit of a witness from that time, a maid named Polly Winter, has lingered, and is willing to tell what she knows.

Caine, Leslie. *Manor of Death: A Domestic Bliss Mystery.* New York: Bantam Dell, 2006. 372 p. ISBN: 0440241774, 9780440241775. [Ghosts X Amateur Sleuth]

Interior designer Erin Gilbert stumbles across a mystery as she works to decorate a house that is haunted.

Callaghan, Mary Rose. *I Met a Man Who Wasn't There.* New York: Marion Boyars, 1997. 297 p. ISBN: 0714530190. [Ghosts X Amateur Sleuth]

Writer Anne O'Brien is haunted by the ghost of her grandfather. He urges her to write his biography, and Anne uncovers the wrongful execution of a man her grandfather defended in the prohibition era.

Carl, Lillian Stewart. *The Secret Portrait.* Waterville, ME: Five Star, 2005. 398 p. ISBN: 159143072, 9781594143076. [Ghosts X Amateur Sleuth, Police]

Magazine editor and writer Jean Fairburn travels to Scotland in search of an historic treasure, but finds the man who put her on the treasure's trail murdered in the ancient estate purchased by a dot-com millionaire.

Carey, Mike. *Felix Caster* series. [Ghosts, Succubi X Amateur Sleuth]

Free-lance exorcist Felix Fix Castor's day job is stage magician. He is frequently called to work as an exorcist by people being haunted by violent ghosts.

1. *The Devil You Know.* New York: Warner Books, 2007. 406 p. ISBN: 0446580309, 9780446580304.
2. *Vicious Circle.* New York: Grand Central Publishing, 2008. 437 p. ISBN: 0446580317, 9780446580311.
3. *Dead Man's Boots.* New York: Grand Central Publishing, 2009. 432 p. ISBN: 0446580325, 9780446580328.
4. *Thicker than Water.* London: Orbit, 2009. 512 p. ISBN: 1841496561, 9781841496566.

Clemens, Judy. *Embrace the Grim Reaper.* Scottsdale, AZ: Poisoned Pen Press, 2008. 250 p. ISBN: 1590585895, 9781590585894. [Death X Amateur Sleuth, Police]

Since the death of her husband and infant son Casey Maldonado's companion has been Death. The story of a young woman who committed suicide interests Casey. The town doesn't believe that the woman would suicide. Death encourages Casey to investigate.

Dickson, Carter. *The Department of Queer Complaints.* London: W. Heinemann Ltd., 1940. 241 p. [Ghosts X Police Procedural]

Colonel March is head of D-3, the Scotland Yard department that investigates "queer complaints and queerer people." This book includes seven "cases."

Galeron, Yasmine. *Chintz 'n China* series. [Ghosts X Amateur Sleuth]

Tea-shop owner Emeral O'Brien serves tea and reads tarot cards at her Chintz 'n China Tea Room. She is also a powerful medium, and finds herself unable to turn away when people need her help.

1. *Ghost of a Chance*. New York: Berkley Prime Crime, 2003. 262 p. ISBN: 0425191281, 9780425191286.
2. *Legend of the Jade Dragon*. New York: Berkley Prime Crime, c2004. 278 p. ISBN: 0425196216. 9780425196212.
3. *Murder under a Mystic Moon*. New York: Berkley Prime Crime, 2005. 275 p. ISBN: 0425200027, 9780425200025.
4. *A Harvest of Bones*. New York: Berkley Prime Crime, 2005. 277 p. ISBN: 0425207269, 9780425207260.

Grabien, Deborah. *Haunted Ballad* series. [Ghosts X Amateur Sleuth]

Ringan Laine's job of restoring old houses sometimes brings him into contact with the unquiet dead. He recognizes some of their stories from the folk songs that he loves. He and his lover Penny Wintercraft-Hawkes work to find peace for the spirits that have suffered so long.

1. *Weaver and the Factory Maid*. New York: Thomas Dunne Books, 2003. 182 p. ISBN: 0312314221.
2. *The Famous Flower of Serving Men*. New York: Thomas Dunne Books/ St. Martin's Minotaur, 2004. 215 p. ISBN: 0312333870.
3. *Matty Groves*. New York: Thomas Dunne Books, 2005. 246 p. ISBN: 0312333897.
4. *Cruel Sister*. New York: Thomas Dunne Books/St. Martin's Minotaur, 2006. 229 p. ISBN: 0312357575, 9780312357573.
5. *New-Slain Knight*. New York: Thomas Dunne Books/St. Martin's Minotaur, 2007. 228 p. ISBN: 0312374003, 9780312374006.

Greenberg, Martin H. John Lellenberg and Daniel Stashower. *Ghosts in Baker Street*. New York: Carroll & Graf, c2006. 232 p. ISBN: 078671400X, 9780786714001. [Ghosts, Vampires, Zombies X Amateur Sleuth]

The premise is that Holmes demanded that Watson repress the case notes for phenomena that had no rational explanation. Now that Holmes is dead, Watson believes that the world would benefit from viewing those cases that ultimately defied mundane explanation.

Foreword *by John H. Watson;* The Devil and Sherlock Holmes *by Loren D. Estleman;* The Adventure of the Librarian's Ghost *by Jon L. Brown;* The Adventure of the Late Orangoutang *by Gillian Linscott;* A Scandal in Drury

Lane, or The Vampire Trap *by Carolyn Wheat;* Sherlock Holmes and the Mummy's Curse *by H. Paul Jeffers;* Death in the East End *by Colin Bruce;* The Adventure of the Dog in the Nighttime *by Paula Cohen;* Selden's Tale *by Daniel Stashower;* The Adventure of the St. Marylebone Ghoul *by Bill Crider;* The Coole Park Problem *by Micheál and Clare Breathnach;* Some Analytical Genius, No Doubt *by Caleb Carr;* No Ghosts Need Apply? *by Barbara Roden;* Channeling Holmes *by Loren D. Estleman.*

Grey, Dorien. *His Name is John.* Austin, TX: Zumaya Boundless, 2008. 199 p. ISBN: 9781934841044. [Ghosts X Amateur Sleuth]

Elliott Smith finds himself drawn into solving the mysterious murder of the man who died next to him while he was in the hospital following a car accident.

Harwood, John. *The Séance.* Boston: Houghton Mifflin Harcourt, 2009. 328 p. ISBN: 0151012032, 9780151012039. See also The Ghost Writer. [Ghosts X Amateur Sleuth]

Constance Langton, Eleanor Unwin, and John Montague are drawn together through the unearthly Wraxford Hall in Victorian England.

Jackson, Joshilyn. *The Girl Who Stopped Swimming.* New York: Grand Central Pub., 2008. 311 p. ISBN: 044651963, 9780446579650. [Ghosts X Amateur Sleuth]

Laurel Gray Hawthorne did her best to control the world around her and make it a pretty, happy place. Then she's visited by the ghost of her 13-year-old neighbor and must dig below the surface of her community to help the child's spirit rest.

Koger, Gail and S. J. Smith. *The Ghost Wore Polyester.* Santa Fe: CrossTIME, c2004. 187 p. ISBN: 1890109762. [Ghosts X Journalists]

Psychic Tildy MacNamara suddenly finds herself the owner of a New Age book store in Sedona, Arizona. She helps solve the murder of the ghost that haunts the store.

Laurie, Victoria. *Ghost Hunter Mystery* series. [Psychics, Ghosts X]

M. J. Holliday is a medium who, with the technical assistance of her friend Gilley, hunts ghosts. They are assisted by Dr. Steven Sable, who hires them in the first novel in the series.

1. *What's a Ghoul to Do?* New York: New American Library, 2007. 304 p. ISBN: 0451220900, 9780451220905.

2. *Demons are a Ghoul's Best Friend*. New York: New American Library, 2008. 292 p. ISBN: 0451223411, 9780451223418.
3. *Ghouls Just Haunt to Have Fun*. New York: New American Library, 2009. 336 p. ISBN: 0451226305, 9780451226303.

Meyer, Joanne. *Heavenly Detour.* New York: Kensington Books, c2003. 262 p. ISBN: 0758202601. [Ghosts X Amateur Sleuth]

Annie Dowd is a ghost that attempts to assist the Manhattan detectives investigating her murder.

Scott, Holden. *Skeptic*. New York: St. Martin's Press, 1999. 322 p. ISBN: 0312193343. [Ghosts X Espionage, Amateur Sleuth]

Dr. Mike Ballantine is the chief of medicine at Boston Metro Hospital. A breakthrough at the hospital reveals the scientific explanation for the phenomena associated with ghosts, and Mike must assist secret agent Amber Chen in solving the murder of the governor and preventing the theft of the research on ghosts.

Simmons, Dan. *A Winter Haunting*. New York: W. Morrow, c2002. 303 p. ISBN: 0380978865. [Ghosts X Amateur Sleuth]

Dale Stewart returns to the town where he grew up, hoping to exorcise his demons. Someone or something begins to haunt him, and he finds that he must resolve the problems of the past.

Simmons, T. M. *Five Star Mystery* series. [Ghosts X Amateur Sleuths]

Alice Carpenter, her aunt and ghost hunting mentor Twila, and Alice's neighbor Granny Chisholm are mediums who assist people with hauntings in Texas.

1. *Dead Man Talking*. Waterville, Me.: Five Star, c2004. 375 p. ISBN: 1594142572.
2. *Dead Man Haunt*. Waterville, Me.: Five Star, 2006. 390 p. ISBN: 1594144435, 9781594144431.

Thrasher, L. L. *Lizbet Lange/Charlie Bilbo Mystery* series. [Ghosts X Police, Amateur Sleuth]

Lizbet Lange, former waitress and current heiress, strikes up a friendship and an investigative partnership with undercover officer Charlie Bilbo (deceased).

1. *Charlie's Bones*. Aurora, CO: Write Way Pub., 1998. 221 p. ISBN: 1885173474.
2. *Charlie's Web*. Aurora, CO: Write Way Pub., 2000. 223 p. ISBN: 1885173660.

Wilson, Derek. *Unquiet Spirit.* New York: Carroll & Graf Publishers, c2006. ISBN: 0786718544, 9780786718542. [Ghosts X Amateur Sleuth]

The Cambridge branch of the Psychic Investigation Unit (PIU) tries to research the ghost haunting the F staircase at St. Thomas's College, Cambridge. The don who insisted on observing the procedure falls dead. Parapsychologist Dr. Nathaniel Gye works to get to the bottom of the mysteries.

Psychics

Bartlett, L. L. *Jeff Resnick Mystery* series. [Psychics X Insurance Investigator]

A mugging leaves Jeff Resnick with broken bones, a fractured skull, and a new talent. He begins dreaming of the future and realizes that he can now see a murder before it happens. The police find his "visions" suspicious; the killer finds them dangerous.

1. *Murder on the Mind.* Waterville, Me.: Five Star, 2005. 272 p. ISBN: 9781594143588.
2. *Dead in Red.* Waterville, Me.: Five Star, 2008. 263 p. ISBN: 9781594146404.

Blackwood, Algernon. *The Complete John Silence Stories.* Mineola, New York: Dover Publications, 1997. 246 p. ISBN: 0486299422. [Psychics, Ghosts, Shape Shifters, Devil X Private Investigator?]

In 1908, the John Silence stories presented the first "ghostbuster." He reads minds, exorcises ghosts, performs magical rituals, and protects mortals from the powers of darkness. This is a collection of the classic John Silence stories.

Braun, Lilian Jackson. *The Cat Who Series.* [Psychics (both human and animal) X Contemporary Amateur Sleuth]

Newsman James "Qwill" Qwilleran's moustache occasionally bristles, giving him a premonition that something odd has happened. The cats (particularly KoKo) yowl or perform a "death dance" when there's been a crime. At times these paranormal elements are so slight that Qwill wonders if he's imagined that there is anything unusual in the cats' behavior.

1. *The Cat Who Could Read Backwards.* New York: Dutton, 1966, 191 p.
2. *The Cat Who Ate Danish Modern.* New York: Dutton, 1967, 192 p.

3. *The Cat Who Turned On and Off.* New York: Dutton, 1968, 186 p.
4. *The Cat Who Saw Red.* New York: Jove, c1986, 256 p. ISBN: 0515090166, 9780515090161.
5. *The Cat Who Played Brahms.* New York: Berkley Pub. Group, 1987, 185 p. ISBN: 0515090506.
6. *The Cat Who Played Post Office.* New York: Jove Books, 1987, 186 p. ISBN: 0515093203.
7. *The Cat Who Knew Shakespeare.* New York: Jove Books, 1988, 186 p. ISBN: 05150935826.
8. *The Cat Who Sniffed Glue.* New York: Putnam, c1988, 207 p. ISBN: 039913381X.
9. *The Cat Who Went Underground.* New York: Putnam, c1989, 223 p. ISBN: 039913431X.
10. *The Cat Who Talked to Ghosts.* New York: Putnam, c1990, 239 p. ISBN: 0399134778.
11. *The Cat Who Lived High.* New York: Putnam, c1990, 239 p. ISBN: 0399135545.
12. *The Cat Who Knew a Cardinal.* New York: Putnam, c1991, 240 p. ISBN: 0399136649.
13. *The Cat Who Moved a Mountain.* New York: Putnam, c1992, 239 p. ISBN: 0399136460.
14. *The Cat Who Wasn't There.* New York: Putnam, c1992, 238 p. ISBN: 0399137807.
15. *The Cat Who Went into the Closet.* New York: Putnam, c1993, 235 p. ISBN: 0399138307.
16. *The Cat Who Came to Breakfast.* New York: Putnam, c1994, 254 p. ISBN: 0399138684.
17. *The Cat Who Blew the Whistle.* New York: Putnam, c1995, 240 p. ISBN: 0399139818.
18. *The Cat Who Said Cheese.* New York: Putnam, c1996, 245 p. ISBN: 0399140751.
19. *The Cat Who Tailed a Thief.* New York: Putnam, c1997, 244 p. ISBN: 039914210X.
20. *The Cat Who Sang for the Birds.* New York: Putnam, c1998, 244 p. ISBN: 0399143335.
21. *The Cat Who Saw Stars.* New York: Putnam, c1998, 227 p. ISBN: 0399144315.
22. *The Cat Who Robbed a Bank.* New York: Putnam, c1998, 227 p. ISBN: 0399144315.
23. *The Cat Who Smelled a Rat.* New York: Putnam, c2001, 229 p. ISBN: 0399146652.

24. *The Cat Who Went up the Creek.* New York: G.P. Putnam's Sons, c2002, 226 p. ISBN: 039914675X.
25. *The Cat Who Brought Down the House.* New York: Putnam's, c2003, 228 p. ISBN: 0399149422.
26. *The Cat Who Talked Turkey.* New York: G.P. Putnam's Sons, c2004, 181 p. ISBN: 0399151079.
27. *The Cat Who Went Bananas.* New York: G.P. Putnam's Sons, c2004, 223 p. ISBN: 0399152245.
28. *The Cat Who Dropped a Bombshell.* New York: G.P. Putnam's Sons, c2006, 191 p. ISBN: 0399153071.
29. *The Cat Who Had 60 Whiskers.* New York: G.P. Putnam's Sons, c2007, 190 p. ISBN: 039915390X, 9780399153907.

Short Story Collections

1. *The Cat Who Had 14 Tales* (1998)
2. *The Private Life of the Cat Who* (2003)
3. *Short and Tall Tales* (2003)

Card, Orson Scott. *Homebody.* New York: HarperCollins, c1998. 304 p. ISBN: 0060176555. [Ghosts X Contemporary Amateur Sleuth]

Builder Don Lark purchased the old Bellamy house, intending to calm his mind by working on restoration. The house has secrets (as do the house's neighbors), and some of those secrets concern murder.

Caselberg, Jay. *Jack Stein Mystery* series. [Psychics X Private Investigators]

Psychic investigator Jack Stein makes a shabby living off of the information on criminal investigations that he receives through his dreams. In Wyrmhole, he accepts the Outreach Mining Company, an interplanetary conglomerate, as a client. He soon has questions about their motives.

1. *Wyrmhole.* New York: ROC/New American Library, 2003. 320 p. ISBN: 0451459490.
2. *Metal Sky.* New York: ROC/New American Library, 2004. 320 p. ISBN: 0451459997.
3. *Star Tablet.* New York: ROC/New American Library, 2006. 320 p. ISBN: 045146060X.
4. *Wall of Mirrors.* New York: ROC/New American Library, 2006. 320 p. ISBN: 0451461193.

Clark, Mary Higgins. *Before I Say Good-bye.* New York: Simon & Schuster, c2000. 416 p. ISBN: 0684835983. [Psychics X Amateur Sleuth]

Nell MacDermott's nascent psychic abilities begin to surface as she works with a medium to investigate her husband's death.

Crawford, L. F. *Fortune Cookie Karma.* Waterville, ME.: Five Star, 2005. 269 p. ISBN: 1594143110. [Psychics X Police]

Los Angeles Police Detective Art Murry and his partner Billy Kidman investigate a series of murders of psychics. Murry begins getting flashes of visions and knows that he must act, whether or not his superiors believe in his "intuition."

David, James F. *Fragments.* New York: Tor Books, 1998. 384 p. ISBN: 0812571479 [Psychics X Amateur Sleuth]

Dr. Martin theorizes that the savants who have extraordinary capabilities in one narrow area might be manifesting fragments of "the great mind." He finds a way to integrate their minds into one, never realizing that one of the savants is a killer.

David, James F. *Ship of the Damned.* New York: Tor Books, 2001. 448 p. ISBN: 0812576462, 9780812576467. [Psychics, Parallel Universe, Telekinesis X Government Investigators]

During WWII, scientists conducted the "Philadelphia Experiment" in an effort to render warships invisible. They were partially successful, and their actions left a trap that pulled in the Nimitz, an aircraft carrier. Special Projects leaders take action, accompanied by Ralph from *Fragments.*

Drake, Alison (pseudonym for T. J. MacGregor). *Tango Key Mysteries.* [Psychics, Time Travel (in *Black Water*) X Private Investigators]

A number of T. J. MacGregor's books are subtitled *Tango Key Mysteries,* but the author's Web site lists these as the only titles in the *Tango Key* series. The author has written other books set on Tango Key, an island of mystery where paranormal phenomena are common and scientists create new and dangerous technologies.

The *Tango Key Mysteries* feature psychic Mira Morales, whose talent allows her to see visions of the future. She tries to warn the police, but they will not listen...at least not until after some of her predictions come true.

1. *Hanged Man.* New York: Kensington Books, c1998. 314 p. ISBN: 9781575662664.

2. *Black Water.* New York: Pinnacle Books, 2003. 384 p. ISBN: 9780786015573.
3. *Total Silence.* New York: Pinnacle Books, 2004. 384 p. ISBN: 9780786015580.
4. *Category Five.* New York: Pinnacle Books, 2005. 384 p. ISBN: 9780786016808.
5. *Cold as Death.* New York: Pinnacle Books, 2006. 384 p. ISBN: 9780786016815.

Dyson, Wanda L. *Josiah Johnson and Zoe Shefford* series. [Psychics X Police, Government Investigators (FBI)]

1. *Abduction.* Uhrichsville, Ohio: Barbour Pub., c2003. 368 p. ISBN: 1586608126.
2. *Obsession.* Uhrichsville, Ohio: Barbour Pub., c2004. 352 p. ISBN: 1593102453.
3. *Intimidation.* Uhrichsville, Ohio: Barbour Pub., c2005. 352 p. ISBN: 1593102445.

Fennelly, Tony. *1–900-dead.* New York: St. Martin's Press, 1997. 214 p. ISBN: 0312142676. [Psychics X Journalist/Reporter]

Forty-year-old gossip columnist Margo Fortier was always interested in psychic phenomena. When a serial killer calling himself Pluto, Lord of the Underworld, targets psychics, Margo decides to play one so that she can catch the murderer. She had intended to be a fraud, but is shocked when she finds out that she really does have some psychic talent. (The first book featuring Margo Fortier was *The Hippie in the Wall.*)

Graves, Samantha. *Sight Unseen.* New York: Warner Books, 2007. ISBN: 9780446618380. [Psychics X Ex-Police X Romance]

Former thief Raven Callahan can read the emotions that are locked inside ancient objects. She's forced back into a life of crime just as ex-cop Dax Maddox begins to stalk a killer, and he encounters Raven at every turn.

Hill, A. W. *Stephen Raszer Investigations.* [Psychic X Private Investigator]

Stephen Raszer's clients hire him to help relatives escape from cults.

1. *Enoch's Portal.* Fox Point, WI: Champion Press, 2002. 304 p. ISBN: 9781891400599.
2. *The Last Days of Madame Rey.* New York: Carroll & Graf Publishers, 2007. 336 p. ISBN: 9780786718818.

Hooper, Kay. *The Bishop/Special Crimes Unit* series. [Psychics X Amateur Sleuth, Government Investigator (FBI)]

The Special Crimes Unit plays a greater role in these books as the series continues.

Stealing Shadows: Psychic Cassie Neill is able to hear the thoughts of serial rapists and killers. It made her valuable to the Los Angeles Police Department, but she felt the need to get away and move to Ryan's Bluff, North Carolina.

1. *Stealing Shadows.* New York: Bantam, 2000. 384 p. ISBN: 9780553575538.
2. *Hiding in the Shadows.* New York: Bantam, 2000. 368 p. ISBN: 9780553576924.
3. *Out of the Shadows.* New York: Bantam, 2000. 368 p. ISBN: 9780553576955.
4. *Touching Evil.* New York: Bantam, 2001. 384 p. ISBN: 9780553583441.
5. *Whisper of Evil.* New York: Bantam, 2002. 416 p. ISBN: 9780553583465.
6. *Sense of Evil.* New York: Bantam Books, 2003. 384 p. ISBN: 9780553583472.
7. *Hunting Fear.* New York: Bantam Books, c2004. 352 p. ISBN: 0553803166.
8. *Chill of Fear.* New York: Bantam Books, 2005. 336 p. ISBN: 0553803174.
9. *Sleeping with Fear.* New York: Bantam Books, 2006. 304 p. ISBN: 0553803182.
10. *Blood Dreams.* New York: Bantam Books, 2007. 336 p. ISBN: 9780553804843.
11. *Blood Sins.* New York: Bantam Books, 2008. 304 p. ISBN: 9780553804850.
12. *Blood Ties.* (forthcoming).

Hyman, Jackie. *The Eyes of a Stranger.* New York: St. Martin's Press, c1987. ISBN: 0312010176.

Diane Hanson believes that psychic Eduardo Ranier is a fraud. Worse than that, she suspects that he is a killer.

Koehler, Karen: *Blackburn and Scarletti* series. [Psychics, Werewolves, Zombies, X FBI Agent, Vatican Investigator]

Father Dorian Scarletti is a *dhampire,* a vampire slayer. FBI Agent January Blackburn is assigned to work with him on odd cases.

1. *Sins of the Father.* (2003).
2. *The Hyde Effect.* (2004). [Werewolves]
3. The Sign of Six. (2006).

The first three books are collected and reprinted in:

Koehler, Karen. *The Blackburn & Scarletti Mysteries, Vol. 1.* Effort, PA: Black Death Books (KHP Publisher), 2006. ISBN: 0976791471.

Krentz, Jayne Ann. *Whispering Springs Novels.* [Psychics X Private Investigators X Romance]

Zoe Luce is trying to rebuild her life, and leave behind the use of her psychic abilities, but they won't shut down. She knows when something terrible has happened, but she has no way to prove it to law enforcement. Private Detective Ethan Truax helps her investigate.

1. *Light in Shadow.* New York: G. P. Putnam's Sons, c2003. 384 p. ISBN: 0399149384.
2. *Truth or Dare.* New York: G. P. Putnam's Sons, c2003. 416 p. ISBN: 0399150730.

Laurie, Victoria. *Psychic Eye Mystery* series. [Psychics X Amateur Sleuth]

Abigail Cooper finally accepted her gift and set up shop as a psychic intuitive. The police don't know whether to treat her as an an ally or as a suspect.

1. *Abby Cooper: Psychic Eye.* New York: New American Library, c2004. 295 p. ISBN: 0451213637, 9780451213631.
2. *Better Read than Dead.* New York: Signet, c2005. 296 p. ISBN: 0451215583.
3. *A Vision of Murder.* New York: Signet, c2005. 296 p. ISBN: 0451217152, 9780451217158.
4. *Killer Insight.* New York: New American Library, 2006. 288 p. ISBN: 0451219333, 9780451219336.
5. *Crime Seen.* New York: Obsidian/New American Library, 2007. 293 p. ISBN: 0451222016, 9780451222015.
6. *Death Perception.* New York: Obsidian, c2008. 324 p. ISBN: 0451224868, 9780451224866.
7. *Doom with a View.* Forthcoming Sept. 2009.

Lawrence, Martha C. *Elizabeth Chase* series. [Psychics, Shaman (in *Pisces Rising* and *Ashes of Aries*) X Female Private Investigators]

Psychic Elizabeth Chase gives up her practice as a psychotherapist and becomes a private investigator. Eventually she acts as a consultant to law enforcement agencies in San Diego and, in *Pisces Rising,* she takes a case on the Temecu Indian Reservation.

1. *Murder in Scorpio.* New York: St. Martin's Press, 1995. 227 p. ISBN: 031213567X.
2. *Cold Heart of Capricorn.* New York: St. Martin's Press, 1997. 225 p. ISBN: 0312145691.
3. *Aquarius Descending.* New York: St. Martin's Press, 1999. 304 p. ISBN: 0312198299.
4. *Pisces Rising.* New York: St. Martin's Minotaur, 2000. 240 p. ISBN: 0312202989.
5. *Ashes of Aries.* New York: St. Martin's Minotaur, 2001. 241 p. ISBN: 0312202997.

Lucke, Margaret. *Supernatural Properties* series. [Psychics X Amateur Sleuth, Romance]

Realtor Claire Scanlan is selling a wonderful home that was once the setting of a grisly murder. She is surprised to find that she has some psychic abilities. Her talent, and the gorgeous owner of the property, haunts her until she is compelled to investigate.

1. *House of Whispers.* New York: Juno Books, 2008, 240 p. ISBN: 0809571587, 9780809571581.

MacGregor, T. J. See Drake, Alison.

Miller, Linda Lael. *Mojo Sheepshanks* series. [Psychics X Private Investigators]

Mojo Sheepshanks takes her ability to see ghosts in stride. It's sometimes a hindrance and sometimes a help as she begins to work as a private investigator.

1. *Deadly Gamble.* Don Mills, Ont.: HQN, c2006. 409 p. ISBN: 037377141X, 9780373771417.
2. *Deadly Deceptions.* Don Mills, Ont.: HQN, c2008. 379 p. ISBN: 0373772564, 9780373772568.

Robinson, Spider. *Zandor "Smelly" Zudenigo* series. [Psychics X Police]

All Russell Walker wanted was to be left alone, but his old roommate, a telepath nicknamed 'Smelly," will trust no one but Russell to take information to the police, and that information is needed to stop a serial killer.

1. *Very Bad Deaths.* Riverdale, New York: Baen Books, c2004. 288 p. ISBN: 074348861X.
2. *Very Hard Choices.* Riverdale, New York: Baen Pub. Enterprises, 2008. 212 p. ISBN: 1416555560.

Santangelo, Elena. *Pat Montella* series. [Psychics X Women Detectives]

Pat Montella can "see" into the past. Sometimes seeing people who died long ago.

1. *By Blood Possessed.* New York: St. Martin's Minotaur, 1999. 326 p. ISBN: 0312209606.
2. *Hang My Head and Cry.* New York: St. Martin's Minotaur, 2001. 322 p. ISBN: 0312269390.
3. *Poison to Purge Melancholy.* Woodbury Minn.: Midnight Ink, c2006. 419 p. ISBN: 0738708909, 9780738708904.

Sears, Richard. *First Born.* New York: Forge, 2000. 300 p. ISBN: 031287250X. [Psychics X Government Agent]

The National Security Agency's Neo Tech unit uses people with extrasensory perception as agents. It sends agent Casey Lee Armstrong to investigate a child born of a virgin. Casey's superiors at Neo Tech interpret her interest in the child as disloyalty, and they frame her for murder.

Shuman, George D. *Sherry Moore* series. [Psychics X Police Procedural]

Sherry Moore can see the last 18 seconds of a person's life, after the person has died.

1. *18 Seconds.* New York: Simon & Schuster, c2006. 308 p. ISBN: 9780743277167.
2. *Last Breath.* New York: Simon & Schuster, 2007. 275 p. ISBN: 9781416534907.
3. *Lost Girls.* New York: Simon & Schuster, 2008. 244 p. ISBN: 9781416553014.
4. *Second Sight.* New York: Simon & Schuster, 2009. ISBN: 9781416599791.

Van Horne, Hollie. *Speak of the Dead.* Columbiana, Ohio: Time Travelers, c2000. 218 p. ISBN: 0967455251.

Psychic and author Felicia McClellan tries to convince NYPD Lt. Harris to investigate the death of her friend Natalie. Lt. Harris is unwilling to regard Natalie's death as a homicide, but if she was murdered, he's willing to regard Felicia as a suspect.

Woodworth, Stephen. *With Red Hands.* New York: Bantam Dell, 2005. 307 p. ISBN: 0553586459. [Psychics, Alternate Earth X Government Investigator]

Natalie Lindstrom used to work as a government investigator, her psychic talents made it possible for her to interview dead victims of violent crimes. She decided to walk away from the job and build a happier life for herself and her daughter, but she can still spot injustice. She finds she can't turn her back and pretend that she doesn't know the truth.

Wright, T. M. (pseudonym is F. W. Armstrong). *Ryerson Biergarten* series. [Psychics, Ghosts X Private Investigators]

Psychic private investigator Ryerson Biergarten deals with werewolves, vampires, and ghosts. He's always willing to help the police, but is often regarded with suspicion.

The Changing. New York: Tom Doherty Assoc., 1985. 244 p. ISBN: 0812527542.
The Devouring. New York: TOR, 1987. ISBN: 0812527585.
Goodlow's ghosts. New York: TOR, 1993. 222 p. ISBN: 0312854668.
The Ascending. New York: TOR, 1994. 222 p. ISBN: 0312857292.

Reincarnation

Baranay, Inez. *Sheila Power: An Entertainment.* St. Leonards, New South Wales: Allen & Unwin, 1997. 356 p. ISBN: 1864485159.

Attempts to sabotage film producer Sheila Power's current project include murder. Sheila's story includes past-life therapy sessions, in which she remembers sexual liaisons from her earlier lives.

Goddard, Robert. *Caught in the Light.* New York: Henry Holt, 1999. 342 p. ISBN: 080506155X.

Photographer Ian Jarrett falls in love with Marian Esguard, then wonders if he loved a woman who died long ago.

Rose, M. J. *The Reincarnationist.* Con Mills, Ontario: Mira, c2007. 342 p. ISBN: 0778324206, 9780778324201.

After almost dying in a bomb blast, photojournalist Josh Ryder begins experiencing odd flashbacks: "memories" that cannot be his own, for they come from 1,600 years before he was born. He becomes involved in past-life research, finds a long-lost love, and ends up on the trail of a murderer.

Valtos, William M. *Theo Nikonos* series. (Reincarnation X Private Investigators)

The Institute for the Investigation of Anabiotic Phenomena sends private investigator Theophanes "Theo" Nikonos to investigate paranormal phenomena.

1. *The Authenticator.* Charlottesville, VA: Hampton Roads Pub. Co., c2000. 376 p. ISBN: 1571741496, 9781571741493.
2. *La Magdalena.* Charlottesville, VA: Hampton Roads Pub. Co., c2002. 397 p. ISBN: 1571742786, 9781571742780.

Short Story Collections

Long, Frank Belknap. *John Carstairs, Space Detective.* New York: F. Fell, 1949. 265 p. [Science Fiction X Detective]

A collection of stories first published in the pulp *Thrilling Wonder Stories* featuring detective John Carstairs's encounters with robots, "wobblies," and other unearthly creatures.

Resnick, Mike and Martin H. Greenberg (Eds.) *Sherlock Holmes in Orbit.* New York: DAW Books, v 1995. 374 p. ISBN: 0886776368, 9780886776367.

All-new stories of the great Sherlock Holmes encountering mysteries that include fantasy or science fiction elements and which are set in the past, the present, and the future.

The Biography Project *by Horace L. Gold;* A Man to My Wounding *by Poul Anderson;* The Winner *by Donald E. Westlake;* Booth 13 *by John Lutz;* The Wolfram Hunters *by Edward D. Hoch;* To See the Invisible Man *by Robert Silverberg;* The Man Who Collected 'The Shadow' *by Bill Pronzini;* Bernie the Faust *by William Tenn;* The Fire Man *by Elizabeth A. Lynn;* Non Sub Homine *by H. W. Whyte;* Murder 2090 *by C. B. Gilford;* The Generalissimo's Butterfly *by Chelsea Quinn Yarbro;* The Several Murders of Roger Ackroyd *by Barry N. Malzberg;* View, With a Difference *by Charles L. Grant;* The Executioner by *Algis Budrys.*

Asimov, Isaac. *Asimov's Mysteries.* Garden City, New York: Doubleday, 1968. 228 p.

The Singing bell; The Talking Stone; What's in a Name?—The Dying Night; Paté de Foie Gras; The Dust of Death; A Loint of Paw; I'm in Marsport without Hilda; Marooned off Vesta; Anniversary; Obituary; Star Light; The Key; The Billiard Ball.

Asimov, Isaac, Martin H. Greenberg, and Charles Waugh (Eds.) *The 13 Crimes of Science Fiction*. Garden City, New York: Doubleday, 1979. 455 p. ISBN: 0385152205, 9780385152204.

The Universe of Science Fiction *by Isaac Asimov;* The Detweiler Boy *by Tom Reamy;* The Ipswich Phial *by Randall Garrett;* Second Game *by Charles V. De Vet and Katherine MacLean;* The Ceaseless Stone *by Avram Davidson;* Coup de Grace *by Jack Vance;* The Green Car *by William F. Temple;* War Game *by Philip K. Dick;* The Singing Bell *by Isaac Asimov;* ARM *by Larry Niven;* Mouthpiece *by Edward Wellen;* Time Exposures *by Wilson Tucker;* How-2 *by Clifford D. Simak;* Time in Advance *by William Tenn.*

Spell-Casters

Alt, Madelyn. *"A Bewitching Mystery"* series. [Spell-Casters X Amateur Sleuth]

Maggie O'Neill takes a new job at an antique shop and finds, to her horror, that her new boss is wiccan. Gradually Maggie learns more about the religion and about her own powers.

1. *The Trouble with Magic.* New York: Berkley Pub., c2006. 261 p. ISBN: 0425207463.
2. *A Charmed Death.* New York: Berkley Pub., 2006. 289 p. ISBN: 042521317X; 9780425213179.
3. *Hex Marks the Spot.* New York: Berkley Prime Crime, 2007. 246 p. ISBN: 0425218708; 9780425218709.
4. *No Rest for the Wiccan.* New York: Berkley Pub., 2008. 304 p. ISBN: 0425224562; 9780425224564.
5. *Where There's a Witch.* New York: Berkley Pub., 2006. 289 p. ISBN: 0425228711, 9780425228715.

Andrews, Ilona. *Kate Daniels* Series. [Spell Casters X Private Investigators]

Kate Daniels cleans up magical problems in her work for the Mercenary Guild, in a world of vampires, knights, and spell-casters.

1. *Magic Bites.* New York: Ace Books, 2007. 272 p. ISBN: 0441014895: 9780441014897.
2. *Magic Burns.* New York: Ace Books, 2008. 260 p. ISBN: 0441015832: 9780441015832.
3. *Magic Strikes.* New York: Ace Books, 2009. 320 p. ISBN: 0441017029: 9780441017027.

Edghill, Rosemary. *Bast* Series. [Spell Casters (Wiccans) X Contemporary Amateur Sleuth]

The Bast series is a paranormal series, it could take place in the world as we know it. Bast is a Wiccan and people are people, in covens or out of them. Bast does her best to keep her community safe. Sometimes that involves investigating murder.

1. *Speak Daggers to Her.* New York: Forge, 1994. 222 p. ISBN: 0312856040.
2. *Book of Moons.* New York: Forge, 1995. 220 p. ISBN: 0312856059.
3. *The Bowl of Night.* New York: Forge, 1996. 220 p. ISBN: 0312856067.

Note: The three titles were republished in an omnibus edition: *Bell, Book, and Murder.* New York: Forge, 1998. 448 p. ISBN: 0312867689.

Green, Simon. *Hawk and Fisher Series.* [Spell Casters (Sorcerers) X Police Procedural]

Hawk and Fisher are husband and wife team of City Guards. Together they patrol the ancient city of Haven, a place of demons, thieves, and sorcerers. There is a prequel: *Blue Moon Rising.* New York: Roc, 1991. 476 p. ISBN: 0451450957; 9780451450951.

1. *Hawk & Fisher/No Haven fo the Guilty.* New York: Ace, 1990. 213 p. ISBN: 044584179; 9780441584178.
2. *Winner Takes All/Devil Take the Hindmost.* New York: Ace Books, 1991. 201 p. ISBN: 0441142915; 9780441142910.
3. *The God Killer.* New York: Ace Books, 1991. 229 p. ISBN: 044129460X, 9780441294602.
4. *Wolf in the Fold/Vengeance for a Lonely Man.* New York: Ace Books, 1991. 192 p. ISBN: 0441318355; 9780441318353.
5. *Guard Against Dishonor.* New York: Ace Books, 1991. 188 p. ISBN: 0441318363; 9780441318360.
6. *The Bones of Haven/Two Kings in Haven.* New York: Ace Books, c1992. 211 p. ISBN: 0441318371; 9780441318377.
7. *Beyond the Blue Moon.* New York: Roc, 2000. 496 p. ISBN: 0451458052, 9780451458056.

Note: The novels are collected in two omnibus editions, published under different titles in the United States and the United Kingdom: *Swords of Haven (US)/Haven of Lost Souls (UK).–omnibus published by Gollancz and Guards of Haven (US)/Fear and Loathing in Haven (UK))–omnibus published by Roc.*

4. *The God Killer.* New York: Thomas Dunne Books/St. Martin's Minotaur, 2006. 229 p. ISBN: 0312357575, 9780312357573.
5. *Vengeance for a Lonely Man.* New York: Thomas Dunne Books/St. Martin's Minotaur, 2007. 228 p. ISBN: 0312374003, 9780312374006.

Gustainis, Justin. *Morris/Investigations.* [Spell Casters (Wiitchs) X Private Investigators]

Supernatural investigator Quincey Morris partners with white witch Libby Chastain to investigate murders caused by magic or committed in the practice of magic.

1. *Black Magic Woman.* Nottingham, U.K.: Solaris, c2007. 336 p. ISBN: 1844165418; 9781844165414.
2. *Evil Ways.* Nottingham, U.K.: Solaris, c2009. 336 p. ISBN: 1844166538; 9781844166534.

Kittredge, Caitlin. *Black London* series. [Spell-Casters, Fae X Private Investigators]

When Pete Caldecott was 16, she was dazzled with mage Jack Winter. Then she saw him killed by a spirit that he summoned. Now she's an adult, working as a detective, and in the course of a case she finds Jack once again.

1. *Street Magic.* (2009).

Pratt, T.A. *Marla Mason* Series. [Spell-Casters (Mages), X Guardian]

Marla Mason is the guardian mage of the east coast metropolis of Felport. She brings sorcerous criminals to justice.

1. *Blood Engines.* New York: Spectra, 2007. 368 p. ISBN: 055389989, 9780553589986.
2. *Poison Sleep.* New York: Spectra, 2008. 336 p. ISBN: 055389997, 9780553589993.
3. *Dead Reign.* New York: Spectra, 2008. 336 p. ISBN: 0553591335, 9780553591354.
3. *Spell Games.* New York: Spectra, 2009. 352 p. ISBN: 0553591363, 9780553591361.

Sellars, M. R. *Rowan Gant Investigations.* [Spell Casters (Wiccans) X Contemporary Amateur Sleuth]

The Rown Gant series is a paranormal series, it could take place in the world as we know it. St. Louis City Homicide Detective Ben Storm consults with his friend Rowan Gant when he encounters clues at a crime scene that make him suspect that the murderer may have been wiccan.

1. *Harm None.* North Kansas City, MI: E.M.A. Mysteries, 2000. 378 p. ISBN: 0967822106.
2. *Never Burn a Witch.* North Kansas City, MI: E.M.A. Mysteries, 2001. 412 p. ISBN: 0967822114.
3. *Perfect Trust.* North Kansas City, MI: E.M.A. Mysteries, 2002. 369 p. ISBN: 096782219X.
4. *The Law of Three.* North Kansas City, MI: E.M.A. Mysteries, 2003. 327 p. ISBN: 0967822181.
5. *Crone's Moon.* North Kansas City, MI: E.M.A. Mysteries, 2004. 332 p. ISBN: 03967822149.
6. *Love is the Bond.* North Kansas City, MI: E.M.A. Mysteries, 2005. 346 p. ISBN: 03967822122; 9780967822129.
7. *All Acts of Pleasure.* North Kansas City, MI: E.M.A. Mysteries, 2006. 335 p. ISBN: 0967822130; 9780967822136.
8. *The End of Desire.* North Kansas City, MI: E.M.A. Mysteries, 2007. 340 p. ISBN: 0967822165; 9780967822167.
9. *Blood Moon.* North Kansas City, MI: E.M.A. Mysteries, 2008. 308 p. ISBN: 097945333X; 9780979453335.

Sumner, Mark. *Sheriff Jake Bird Novels.* [Spell Casters X Sheriff]

At the battle of Shiloh (during the Civil War) the carnage raised magic that swept across the land. In the aftermath a lawman was needed who was fast on the draw and a powerful magic user. Jake Bird took the job of Sheriff.

1. *Devil's Tower.* New York: Del Rey, 1996. 346 p. ISBN: 034540209X, 9780345402097.
2. *Devil's Engine.* New York: Del Rey, 1996. 294 p. ISBN: 0345402103, 9780345402103.

Tarot

Warner, Mignon. *The Tarot Murders.* New York: D. McKay Co., 1978. 192 p. ISBN: 067150835X. [Tarot X Amateur Sleuth]

Clairvoyant Mrs. Charles uses her knowledge of the tarot to investigate the "Tarot Murderer," a serial killer who leaves tarot cards beside the bodies of his victims.

Telepathy

Kagan, Dale A. *Lanterns Over Demner.* Philadelphia, PA: Xlibris, c2000. 158 p. ISBN: 9780738841717, 0738841714.

The planet Dauropa's Governor Eccles was taught how to block telepaths from reading his thoughts. Now he is hiding information that would reveal a murderer…

Time Travel

Baker, Virginia. *Jack Knife.* New York: Berkley Pub., c2007. 343 p. ISBN: 0515142522, 9780515142525. [Time Travel X Police Procedural]

Inspector Jonas Robb encounters David Elliot and Sara Grant, who've come back through time to Victorian London to stop a madman who is trying to change history.

David, James F. *Before the Cradle Falls.* New York: Forge, 2002. 336 p. ISBN: 0765303191. [Time Travel X Police Procedural]

When Detective Kyle Sommers investigates a series of murders, he finds an odd complication: there is an elderly man who seems to have foreknowledge of the crimes.

Dukthas, Ann. *Nicholas Segalla* Series. [Time Travel X Private Investigator]

Nicholas Segalla, an immortal, recounts his investigations into some of the most famous crimes in history.

1. *A Time for the Death of a King.* New York: St. Martin's Press, 1994. 226 p. ISBN: 0312114397.
2. *The Prince Lost to Time.* New York: St. Martin's Press, 1995. 229 p. ISBN: 0312135920.
3. *The Time of Murder at Mayerling.* New York: St. Martin's Press, 1996. 217 p. ISBN: 0312146760.
4. *In the Time of the Poisoned Queen.* New York: St. Martin's Press, c1998. 273 p. ISBN: 0312180306.

Dymmoch, Michael Allen. *The Cymry Ring.* Waterville, Me.: Five Star, 2006. 322 p. ISBN: 159414429X, 9781594144295. [Time Travel X Police Procedural]

Ian Carreg of Scotland Yard follows a suspect into the *Cymry Henge,* and they both find themselves trapped back in time.

Eubank, Judith. *Crossover.* New York: Carroll & Graf, 1992. 224 p. ISBN: 0881847461. [Time Travel X Amateur Sleuth]

Scholar Meredith Blake is assigned a room at Edwards Hall; in Victorian times it belonged to the Thornton family. She finds herself drawn back in time and feels that she must find a way to prevent a murder.

Finney, Jack. *Simon Morley Series.* [Time Travel X Amateur Sleuth]

Simon Morley takes part in an experiment in time travel. He's interested in solving a mystery in the past and he goes from the present (1969) back to 1882. He uncovers a blackmail plot, arson, and false testimony and becomes more involved in the past than he expected. (*From Time to Time* focuses on 1912. It is not a mystery novel.)

1. *Time and Again.* New York: Simon and Schuster, 1970. 399 p. ISBN: 0671204971.
2. *From Time to Time.* New York: St. Martin's Press, c1995. 303 p. ISBN: 0671898841.

Gardner, Willard Boyd. *Race Against Time: a Novel.* American Fork, UT: Covenant Communications, c2001. ISBN: 1577348052. [Time Travel, Alternative History X Police]

Salt Lake City S.W.A.T.-team officer Owen Richards finds himself back in 1838, close to the site of the Hauns Mill Massacre, and wonders if he can change history.

Misak, John. *Time Stand Still.* St. Petersburg, Fla.: Barclay Books, c2002. 320 p. ISBN: 1931402183, 9781931402187.

Private Investigator Darren Camponi is hired to recover a research project. He soon finds that he is not the only one on the trail of the stolen project: the government wants him to give up the investigation. They don't want him to be the one to recover the time machine.

Vampires

Christian, M. *The Very Bloody Marys.* New York: Haworth Positronic Press/ Harrington Park Press, c2007. 1560235357, 9781560235354.

Vampire Valentino, a trainee in the *Counseil Carmin,* works with his mentor, Pogue, to police the supernatural community of San Francisco. When Pogue disappears, it's up to Valentino to keep the peace.

Davidson, Mary Janice. *Undead* series. [Vampires X Amateur Sleuths X Romance]

This light-hearted series follows the adventures of Betsy, Queen of the Vampires. She seems like a somewhat ditzy blonde, but has a big heart (and a quick temper). There is a constant struggle for power in the vampire community. That, along with rampaging humans, bereft ghosts, and werewolves with social difficulties, keeps Betsy busy fending off attacks, rescuing allies, and solving attempted homicides.

1. *Undead and Unwed.* New York: Berkley, 2004. 288 p. ISBN: 042519485X.
2. *Undead and Unemployed.* New York: Berkley, 2004. 304 p. ISBN: 0425197484.
3. *Undead and Unappreciated.* New York: Berkley, 2005. 288 p. ISBN: 0425204332.
4. *Undead and Unreturnable.* New York: Berkley, 2005. 272 p. ISBN: 0425208168.
5. *Undead and Unpopular.* New York: Berkley, 2006. 320 p. ISBN: 0425210294.
6. *Undead and Uneasy.* New York: Berkley, 2007. 320 p. ISBN: 0425213765, 9780425213766.
7. *Undead and Unworthy.* New York: Berkley, 2008. 285 p. ISBN: 0425221628, 9780425221624.
8. *Undead and Unwelcome.* New York: Berkley, 2008. 285 p. ISBN: 0425221628, 9780425221624.

Estleman, Loren D. *Sherlock Holmes vs. Dracula: or, The Adventure of the Sanguinary Count.* New York: Peguin Books, 1979. 214 p. ISBN: 0140052623.

In 1890, Sherlock Holmes is called in to the scene of an inexplicable crime. It's a ship that was found adrift off the English coast. The crew is missing, the captain is dead, and the cargo is 50 boxes of earth.

Haddock, Nancy. *Oldest City Vampire* series. [Vampires X Amateur Sleuths X Romance]

In the 1800s, Francesca Marinelli was a young woman who had paranormal talents. She was captured, and turned into a vampire so that the vampire king Normand could control her and her gifts. She was imprisoned in that time, then forgotten. Construction workers found her during the renovation of a Victorian mansion. Her story caused a sensation, and she was hired by Old Coast Ghost Tours as a tour guide in St. Augustine.

While she's trying to live a normal life, she becomes a murder suspect. She must find the killer to clear her name.

1. *La Vida Vampire*. Berkley Trade, 2008. 304 p. ISBN: 9780425219959.
2. *Last Vampire Standing*. Berkley Trade, 2009. 320 p. ISBN: 9780425227541.

James, Dean. *Simon Kirby-Jones Mystery* series. [Vampires X Amateur Sleuths]
Simon Kirby-Jones controls his symptoms of vampirism—sun-sensitivity and a craving for blood—with medication. He's a newcomer to the quaint village of Snupperton Mumsley, and is amazed at the petty rivalries and intense relationships within the small village. When murder strikes, he feels compelled to find the killer.

1. *Posted to Death*. New York: Kensington Books, c2002. 242 p. ISBN: 1575668858.
2. *Faked to Death*. New York: Kensington Books, c2003. 225 p. ISBN: 1575668874.
3. *Decorated to Death*. New York: Kensington Books, c2004. 232 p. ISBN: 075820485X, 9780758204851.
4. *Baked to Death*. New York: Kensington Books, c2005. 248 p. ISBN: 0758204876, 9780758204875.

Killough, Lee. *Gareth Mikaelian* series. [Vampires X Police Procedural]
San Francisco police officer Garreth Mikaelian is turned into a vampire and works to keep his job and his humanity.

1. *Blood Hunt*. New York: Tom Doherty Associates, c1987. 319 p. ISBN: 08125059848, 97808125059848.
2. *Bloodlinks*. New York: Tom Doherty Associates, c1988. 345 p. ISBN: 0812520645, 9780812520644.

   (*Blood Hunt* and *Bloodlinks* were re printed in the omnibus *Bloodwalk*. Decatur. GA MM Pub., 1997. 453 p. ISBN: 0965834506.)

3. *Blood Games*. Decatur, GA: Meisha Merlin Publishing, 2001. 460 p. ISBN: 1892065414, 978189206541X.

Lake, Paul. *Among the Immortals*. Brownsville, OR: Story Line Press, 1994. 301 p. ISBN: 0934257736.
In the aftermath of the murder of one of his professors, scholar Derek Hill becomes convinced that Percy Bysshe Shelley became a vampire and is using his immortality to protect his literary reputation.

Reaves, Michael. *Night Hunter.* New York: TOR, 1995. 253 p. ISBN: 0312853181. [Alternate Universe X Private Investigator]

Los Angeles detective Jake Hull is on the trail of a murderer who beheads his victims and stuffs their mouths with garlic.

Saberhagen, Fred. *A Question of Time.* New York: TOR, 1992. ISBN: 0312851294. [Vampires, Time Travel X Private Investigator]

Nosferatu Mr. Strangeways assists private investigator Joe Keogh on his investigation of a mysterious disappearance.

Seitz, Stephen. *Sherlock Holmes and the Plague of Dracula.* Shaftsbury, VT.: Mountainside Press, c2006. 208 p. ISBN: 0970869355, 9780970869357. [Vampires X Private Investigator]

Holmes takes a missing-person case that pits him against the master vampire.

Spruill, Steven G. *Rulers of Darkness.* New York: St. Martin's Press, 1995. 357 p. ISBN: 0312131631. [Vampires X Police Procedural]

Dr. Katherine O'Keefe and Detective Merrick Chapman are assigned to track down a murderer who has been dubbed "the vampire killer." The man has an unusual disease that causes him to crave blood, and he's not the only person who's been infected.

Stein, Jeanne C. *Anna Strong Chronicles.* [Vampires X Bounty Hunter]

Anna Strong's first job is to track down the rogue vampire who turned her.

1. *The Becoming.* New York: Ace, 2006. 304 p. ISBN: 0441014569, 9780441014569.
2. *Blood Drive.* New York: Ace, 2007. 304 p. ISBN: 0441015093, 9780441015092.
3. *The Watcher.* New York: Ace, 2007. 304 p. ISBN: 0441015468, 9780441015467.
4. *Legacy.* New York: Ace, 2008. 304 p. ISBN: 044101626X, 9780441016266.

Thurlo, David and Aimée. *Lee Nez* series. [Vampires X Police Procedural]

Lee Nez is a nightwalker, a Navajo vampire, who works as a New Mexico state police officer.

1. *Second Sunrise.* New York: Forge, 2002. 336 p. ISBN: 0765304414.
2. *Blood Retribution.* New York: Forge, 2004. 271 p. ISBN: 0765304422.

3. *Pale Death.* New York: Forge, 2005. 254 p. ISBN: 0765313855,9780765313850.
4. *Surrogate Evil.* New York: Forge, 2006. 320 p. ISBN: 0765316153.

Werewolves

Douglas, Carole Nelson. *Delilah Street: Paranormal Investigator* series. [Werewolves, Vampires, Spell-Casters (Witches) X Investigative Reporter]

The supernatural world came out of hiding in the Millennium Revelation. Many humans are still stunned (although most of the kids think it's exciting.) Paranormal Investigative Reporter Delilah Street covers the homicide beat in Las Vegas for WTCH-TV.

1. *Dancing with Werewolves.* Rockville, MD: Juno, c2007. 394 p. ISBN: 9780809572038.
2. *Brimstone Kiss.* Rockville, MD: Juno, 2008. 400 p. ISBN: 0809573040; 9780809573042.

Driver, Lee. (pseudonym for S.D. Tooley). *Chase Dagger* Series. [Shape Shifters X Private Investigator]

Chase Dagger and his Native American shape-shifter assistant, Sara Morningsky, investigate murders.

1. *The Good Die Twice.* Schereville, IN: Full Moon Publishing, 1999. 292 p. ISBN: 0966602110; 9780966602111.
2. *Full Moon, Bloody Moon.* Schereville, IN: Full Moon Publishing, 2000. 280 p. ISBN: 0966602145; 9780966602142.
3. *The Unseen.* Schereville, IN: Full Moon Publishing, c2004. 305 p. ISBN: 096660217X.
4. *Chasing Ghosts.* Schereville, IN: Full Moon Publishing, 2000. 252 p. ISBN: 0978540298; 9780978540296.

Handeland, Lori. *Nightcreature* series. [Werewolves X Police Procedural/ Amateur Sleuths/Government Investigators X Romance]

Police officer Jessie McQuade hunts a killer through the forests of Miniwa Wisconsin. (This describes the first book. This series of books is a set of interlocking romance novels, each with a different protagonist and a different threat.)

Blue Moon. New York: St. Martin's Press, c2004. 342 p. ISBN: 0312991347.

Hunter's Moon. New York: St. Martin's Press, c2006. 352 p. ISBN: 0312949405, 9780312949402.

Dark Moon. New York: St. Martin's Press, c2005. 352 p. ISBN: 0312991363, 9780312991364.
Crescent Moon. New York: St. Martin's Press, c2005. 352 p. ISBN: 0312938489, 9780312938482.
Midnight Moon. New York: St. Martin's Press, 2006. 352 p. ISBN: 0312938497, 9780312938499.
Rising Moon. New York: St. Martin's Press, 2007. 352 p. ISBN: 0312938500, 9780312938505.
Hidden Moon. New York: St. Martin's Press, 2007. 352 p. ISBN: 0312949170, 9780312949176.
Thunder Moon. New York: St. Martin's Press, 2008. 352 p. ISBN: 0312949189, 9780312949181.

Kittredge, Caitlin. Nocturne City Series. [Werewolves, Spell-Casters (Magicians, Witches) X Police Procedural]

Laura Wilder, an Insoli werewolf who is also a homicide detective, travels without a pack but finds herself working with the compelling werewolf Dmitri Sandovsky. The series combines romance, magical elements, and mystery (in that order).

1. *Night Life*. New York: St. Martin's Paperbacks, 2008. 352 p. ISBN: 0312948298, 9780312948290.
2. *Pure Blood*. New York: St. Martin's Paperbacks, 2008. 352 p. ISBN: 0312948301; 9780312948306.
3. *Second Skin*. New York: St. Martin's Paperbacks, 2009. 352 p. ISBN: 031294831X; 9780312948313.

Wilks, Eileen. *The World of the Lupi*. [Werewolves X Police Procedural]

Different law enforcement personnel are protagonists in the books set in this world where the FBI has a Magical Crimes Unit. Many of the protagonists are attracted to men who are werewolves.

1. *Tempting Danger*. New York: Berkley, 2004. 320 p. ISBN: 0425198782; 9780425198780.
2. *Mortal Danger*. New York: Berkley, 2005. 400 p. ISBN: 0425202909; 9780425202906.
3. *Blood Lines*. New York: Berkley, 2007. 352 p. ISBN: 0425213447; 9780425213445.
4. *Night Season*. New York: Berkley, 2008. 352 p. ISBN: 042522015X; 9780425220153.
5. *Mortal Sins*. New York: Berkley, 2009. 352 p. ISBN: 0425225526; 9780425225523.

Zombies

Lee, Wendi. *Habeas Campus: an Angela Matelli Mystery.* New York: St. Martin's Minotaur, 2002. ISBN: 031226139X. [Zombies X Private Investigator]

A professor of anthropology specializing in the study of voodoo calls on Angela Matelli after he sees a dead student walking across the campus.

Waggoner, Tim. *Necropolis.* Waterville, Me.: Five Star, 2004. ISBN: 1594141401. [Zombies X Private Investigators]

Creatures out of nightmare have staked out their own ground and created a city they call Necropolis. It's the home of zombie private investigator Matthew Adrion. He is distracted by his struggle to keep himself together while he works on his latest case.

Author Index

Series and Title Index

Major Character Index

Genre and Theme Index

Mystery and Speculative Fiction Element Index

Location and Time Index

About the Authors

JILL H. VASSILAKOS began working in libraries as a student page. In the (approximately 40) years since then, she earned her degree in librarianship and worked at both public and academic libraries, providing reference, cataloging, and technical services, as well as managing government documents and special collections and archives. Her first book, co-authored with Michael Burgess, was *Murder in Retrospect* (Libraries Unlimited, 2005).

PAUL VASSILAKOS-LONG currently lives in Los Angeles, where he pursues many interests, some of which seem to conflict with each other at first glance; and he is attempting to follow in the family business of librarianship.